Baedeker's

France

THE AUTOMOBILE ASSOCIATION

Cover picture: The Eiffel Tower, Paris

188 colour photographs
60 maps, plans and sketches
1 large road map

Text:
Rosemarie Arnold (History)
Dr Gerhard Eckert (Introduction to France, Government and Society, Art and Culture, Economy and Communications, France from A to Z, Practical Information)
Werner Fauser (Literature, Music, Folk Traditions)
Gerald Sawade (Climate)

Editorial work:
Baedeker Stuttgart
English language: Alec Court

Cartography:
Ingenieurbüro für Kartographie,
Huber & Oberländer, Munich

Design and layout:
HF Ottmann,
Atelier für Buchgestaltung
und Grafik-Design, Leonberg

Conception and general direction:
Dr Peter Baumgarten,
Baedeker Stuttgart

English translation:
James Hogarth

© Baedeker Stuttgart
Original German
edition

© Jarrold and Sons Ltd
English Language edition Worldwide

© The Automobile Association 1981 67438
United Kingdom and Ireland
Reprinted, 1982

Licensed user:
Mairs Geographischer Verlag GmbH & Co.,
Ostfildern-Kemnat bei Stuttgart

Reproductions:
Gölz Repro-Service GmbH,
Ludwigsburg

The name *Baedeker* is a registered trademark

Source of illustrations:

Most of the coloured photographs were provided by the French Government Tourist Office. Others:

Allianz-Archiv (pp. 262, 266).
Baedeker-Archiv (p. 258).
Editions Bahon, Carcassonne (pp. 88–89).
Bavaria-Verlag, Gauting (p. 63).
Deutsche Presse-Agentur GmbH (dpa), Frankfurt/Main (p. 97).
Werner Fauser, Stuttgart (pp. 38; 106; 108, foot and right; 115; 217).
Hachette, Strasbourg (p. 100, top).
Peter Nahm, Ostfildern (pp. 32; 33; 35; 36; 39, top; 56; 57; 58; 59; 60; 63, foot; 71; 77; 80, top and right; 95; 100, right; 110, foot; 128; 137; 156, top; 166, top; 168, top; 170, top and foot; 218, top and foot; 221; 224, right; 230, foot; 233, top; 245; 246; 251; 255).
Friedrich Schley, Hamburg (p. 241).
Zentrale Farbbild Agentur GmbH (ZEFA), Düsseldorf (pp. 264, 265).

The panoramic view of Paris (pp. 198–199) was drawn by Werner Gölitzer, Stuttgart.

In a time of rapid change it is difficult to ensure that all the information given is entirely accurate and up to date and the possibility of error can never be entirely eliminated. Although the publishers can accept no responsibility for inaccuracies and omissions they are always grateful for corrections and suggestions for improvement.

Printed in Great Britain by Jarrold & Sons Ltd, Norwich

ISBN 0 86145 057 4

How to Use this Guide

The principal towns and areas of tourist interest are described in alphabetical order. The names of other places referred to under these general headings can be found in the very full Index.

Following the tradition established by Karl Baedeker in 1844, sights of particular interest and hotels and restaurants of particular quality are distinguished by either one or two asterisks.

In the lists of hotels r. = rooms, SP = swimming pool. See p. 273 for explanation of hotel categories. In the town plans the names of streets, buildings, etc., are mostly given in their French form: the meanings of common topographical terms and elements in place-names can be found by reference to the glossary on p. 271.

The symbol ⓘ at the beginning of an entry or on a town plan indicates the local tourist office or other organisation from which further information can be obtained. The post-horn symbol on a town plan indicates a post office.

Only a selection of hotels and restaurants can be given: no reflection is implied, therefore, on establishments not included.

This guidebook forms part of a completely new series of the world-famous Baedeker Guides to Europe.

The English editions are now published for the first time in this country. Each volume is the result of long and careful preparation and, true to the traditions of Baedeker, is designed in every respect to meet the needs and expectations of the modern traveller and holiday-maker.

The name of Baedeker has long been identified in the field of guidebooks with reliable, comprehensive and up-to-date information, prepared by expert writers who work from detailed, first-hand knowledge of the country concerned. Following a tradition that goes back over 150 years to the date when Karl Baedeker published the first of his handbooks for travellers, these guides have been planned to give the tourist all the essential information about the country and its inhabitants: where to go, how to get there and what to see. Baedeker's account of a country was always based on his personal observation and experience during his travels in that country. This tradition of writing a guidebook in the field rather than at an office desk has been maintained by Baedeker ever since.

Lavishly illustrated with superb colour photographs and numerous specially drawn maps and street plans of the major towns, the new Baedeker-AA Guides concentrate on making available to the modern traveller all the information he needs in a format that is both attractive and easy to follow. For every place that appears in the gazetteer, the principal features of architectural, artistic and historic interest are described, as are the main scenic beauty-spots in the locality. Selected hotels and restaurants are also included. Features of exceptional merit are indicated by either one or two asterisks.

A special section at the end of each book contains practical information to ensure a pleasant and safe journey, details of leisure activities and useful addresses. The separate road map will prove an invaluable aid to planning your route and your travel within the country.

Introduction to France   Page

Departments and Territories   8
Land and People   11
Climate   17
Government and Society   18
Regions   19
History.   22
Art and Culture.   29
Literature   41
Music   43
Economy and Communications . .   45

France from A to Z   52–258

Aix-en-Provence · Ajaccio · Albi · Alsace · Amiens · Andorra · Angers · Anjou · Arles · Auvergne · Avignon · Bastia · Belfort · Besançon · Biarritz · Bordeaux · Bourges · Brittany · Burgundy · Caen · Cannes · Carcassonne · Cévennes · Chamonix · Champagne · Chartres · Clermont-Ferrand · Colmar · Les Corbières · Corsica · Côte d'Argent · Côte d'Azur · Côte des Basques · Côte Vermeille · Dauphiné · Dijon · Gascony · Gorges du Tarn · Grenoble · Le Havre · Ile de France · Jura · Lille · Limoges · Limousin · Loire Valley · Lorraine · Lot Valley · Lourdes · Lyons · Le Mans · Marseilles · Metz · Monaco · Mont St-Michel · Nancy · Nantes · Nice · Nîmes · Normandy · Orange · Orléans · Paris · Périgord · Périgueux · Picardy and the North · Poitiers · Poitou-Charentes and Vendée · Provence · Le Puy · Pyrenees · Reims · Rennes · La Rochelle · Rouen · Roussillon · St-Malo · Savoy · Strasbourg · Toulon · Toulouse · Tours · Troyes · Vercors · Verdun · Versailles · Vichy · Vienne · Vosges

Practical Information   Page

Safety on the road   262
When to go, weather   262
Time   263
Travel documents   263
Customs regulations.   263
Currency   263
Postal rates   264
Travelling to France   264

Travelling in France   265
   Motoring
   Air services
   Railways
   Motorail
   Bus services
   Boat services

Language   269
   Summer language courses
   Numbers
   Vocabulary
   Glossary of topographical terms

Accommodation   273
   Hotels
   Youth hostels
   Holiday apartments and chalets
   Country holidays
   Camping and caravanning

Food and drink   274
   Restaurants
   Reading a French menu
   Regional specialties
   Drinks
   Wine
   French wines at a glance
   Types of grape

Recreation and Sport   282
   Bathing
   Walking
   Climbing and hill walking
   Shooting, fishing
   Riding
   Golf
   Water sports
   Caving
   Flying

Taking the cure.   285
   Spas
   Sea-water treatment establishments

Son et lumière   289
   Privately owned châteaux

National parks   291
   Regional nature parks

Caves open to the public   293
Winter sports   295
Folk traditions   298
Calendar of events   300
   Public holidays

Shopping and souvenirs   304
Information   304
   Radio messages for tourists
   Emergency calls

Index   307

Introduction
to France

The Dordogne valley

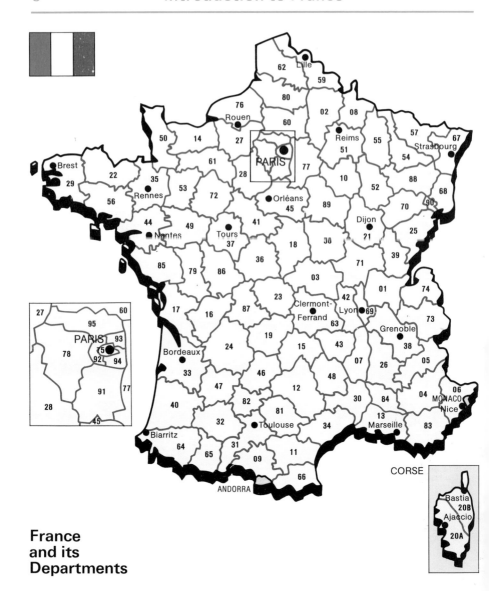

France and its Departments

France has an area of 543,990 sq. km, including Corsica but excluding its overseas departments and territories, and a population of over 53 million. It is divided into **95 departments** and **22 regions**. In addition it has six overseas departments and three overseas territories.

Since 1871 France has been a democratic republic (*République Française*) with a centralised system of administration.

The present *Fifth Republic* is based on the Constitution of 1958. Since 1962 the President of the Republic has been elected not by an electoral college but by direct popular vote. He is President of the Council of Ministers (Cabinet) and Commander-in-Chief of the Armed Forces, and in a national emergency has wide personal powers. The government is headed by the Prime Minister, who is appointed by the President.

The French Parliament consists of the National Assembly (*Assemblée Nationale:* 491 members – "deputies" – elected for a term of 5 years) and the Senate (*Sénat:* elected by the deputies and representatives of local authorities for a term of 9 years). There is also an Economic and Social Council (*Conseil Economique et Social*) with an advisory and consultative role.

France was a founder member of the European Economic Community (EEC), and the European Parliament meets in Strasbourg.

No.	Name	Area (sq. km)	Population	Chief town
01	Ain	5,756	376,500	Bourg-en-Bresse
02	Aisne	7,378	533,900	Laon
03	Allier	7,382	378,400	Moulins
04	Alpes-de-Haute-Provence	6,944	112,200	Digne
05	Hautes-Alpes	5,520	97,400	Gap
06	Alpes-Maritimes	4,294	816,700	Nice
07	Ardèche	5,523	257,100	Privas
08	Ardennes	5,219	309,300	Charleville-Mézières
09	Ariège	4,890	137,900	Foix
10	Aube	6,002	284,800	Troyes
11	Aude	6,232	272,400	Carcassonne
12	Aveyron	8,735	278,300	Rodez
13	Bouches-du-Rhône	5,112	1,632,000	Marseilles
14	Calvados	5,536	561,000	Caen
15	Cantal	5,741	166,500	Aurillac
16	Charente	5,953	337,100	Angoulême
17	Charente-Maritime	6,848	497,800	La Rochelle
18	Cher	7,228	316,300	Bourges
19	Corrèze	5,860	240,400	Tulle
20A	Corse-du-Sud	4,013	128,600	Ajaccio
20B	Haute-Corse	4,555	161,200	Bastia
21	Côte-d'Or	8,765	456,100	Dijon
22	Côtes-du-Nord	6,878	525,500	St-Brieuc
23	Creuse	5,560	146,200	Guéret
24	Dordogne	9,184	373,200	Périgueux
25	Doubs	5,228	471,100	Besançon
26	Drôme	6,525	361,800	Valence
27	Eure	6,004	422,900	Evreux
28	Eure-et-Loir	5,876	335,200	Chartres
29	Finistère	6,785	804,100	Quimper
30	Gard	5,848	494,600	Nîmes
31	Haute-Garonne	6,301	777,400	Toulouse
32	Gers	6,254	175,400	Auch
33	Gironde	10,000	1,061,500	Bordeaux
34	Hérault	6,113	648,200	Montpellier
35	Ille-et-Vilaine	6,758	702,200	Rennes
36	Indre	6,778	248,500	Châteauroux
37	Indre-et-Loire	6,124	478,600	Tours
38	Isère	7,474	860,300	Grenoble
39	Jura	5,008	238,800	Lons-le-Saunier
40	Landes	9,237	288,300	Mont-de-Marsan
41	Loir-et-Cher	6,314	283,700	Blois
42	Loire	4,774	742,400	St-Etienne
43	Haute-Loire	4,965	205,500	Le Puy
44	Loire-Atlantique	6,894	934,500	Nantes
45	Loiret	6,742	490,200	Orléans
46	Lot	5,228	150,800	Cahors
47	Lot-et-Garonne	5,358	292,600	Agen
48	Lozère	5,168	74,825	Mende
49	Maine-et-Loire	7,145	629,900	Angers
50	Manche	5,938	451,700	St-Lô
51	Marne	8,163	530,400	Châlons-sur-Marne
52	Haute-Marne	6,216	212,300	Chaumont
53	Mayenne	5,171	261,800	Laval
54	Meurthe-et-Moselle	5,235	722,600	Nancy
55	Meuse	6,220	203,900	Bar-le-Duc
56	Morbihan	6,763	563,600	Vannes
57	Moselle	6,214	1,006,400	Metz
58	Nièvre	6,837	245,200	Nevers
59	Nord	5,738	2,510,700	Lille
60	Oise	5,857	606,300	Beauvais

No.	Name	Area (sq. km)	Population	Chief town
61	Orne	6,100	293,500	Alençon
62	Pas-de-Calais	6,672	1,403,000	Arras
63	Puy-de-Dôme	7,955	590,000	Clermont-Ferrand
64	Pyrénées-Atlantiques	7,633	534,800	Pau
65	Hautes-Pyrénées	4,507	227,200	Tarbes
66	Pyrénées-Orientales	4,087	299,500	Perpignan
67	Bas-Rhin	4,787	882,100	Strasbourg
68	Haut-Rhin	3,523	635,200	Colmar
69	Rhône	3,215	1,429,700	Lyons
70	Haute-Saône	5,343	222,300	Vesoul
71	Saône-et-Loire	8,565	569,800	Mâcon
72	Sarthe	6,245	490,400	Le Mans
73	Savoie	6,036	305,100	Chambéry
74	Haute-Savoie	4,391	447,800	Annecy
75	Ville de Paris	105	2,229,900	Paris
76	Seine-Maritime	6,254	1,172,700	Rouen
77	Seine-et-Marne	5,917	755,700	Melun
78	Yvelines	2,271	1,082,300	Versailles
79	Deux-Sèvres	6,004	335,900	Niort
80	Somme	6,175	538,460	Amiens
81	Tarn	5,751	338,000	Albi
82	Tarn-et-Garonne	3,716	183,300	Montauban
83	Var	5,993	626,100	Toulon
84	Vaucluse	3,566	390,500	Avignon
85	Vendée	6,721	450,600	La Roche-sur-Yonne
86	Vienne	6,084	357,400	Poitiers
87	Haute-Vienne	5,512	352,200	Limoges
88	Vosges	5,903	397,900	Epinal
89	Yonne	7,425	299,800	Auxerre
90	Territoire-de-Belfort	610	128,100	Belfort
91	Essonne	1,804	923,100	Evry
92	Hauts-de-Seine	175	1,439,000	Nanterre
93	Seine-St-Denis	236	1,322,100	Bobigny
94	Val-de-Marne	244	1,215,700	Créteil
95	Val-d'Oise	1,249	840,900	Pontoise

Overseas Departments

No.	Name	Area	Population	Chief town
97-1	Guadeloupe	1,780	330,000	Basse-Terre
97-2	Martinique	1,106	320,000	Fort-de-France
97-3	Guyane	91,000	55,100	Cayenne
97-4	Réunion	2,511	476,700	St-Denis
97-5	St-Pierre-et-Miquelon	242	5,900	St-Pierre
98-4	Mayotte	375	43,500	Dzaoudzi

Overseas Territories

Name	Area	Population	Chief town
Nouvelle-Calédonie (New Caledonia)	19,058	145,000	Nouméa
Polynésie Française (French Polynesia)	4,000	150,000	Papéete (Tahiti)
Wallis-et-Futuna	255	8,500	Mata Utu (Ueva)

France, Britain's nearest neighbour on the continent of Europe, has long been a magnet drawing British and other English-speaking visitors across the English Channel, for many of whom it has been – and still is – their first experience of a foreign country. But whereas in the past these visitors went mainly to a few favoured areas like Paris, Touraine and the Mediterranean coast, they now travel through the length and breadth of the country and find their way into its remotest corners. They are attracted both by its enormous wealth of historical and artistic interest and by the inexhaustible variety of its scenery – from the chalk cliffs on the Channel coast and the rocky landscapes of Brittany, by way of the extraordinary volcanic hills of Auvergne and the mighty Alps, reaching their highest peaks in the Mont Blanc group, to the Mediterranean regions of Provence and the fabulous Côte d'Azur, with the rocky island of Corsica even further to the south. Perhaps there is no other country in Europe where nature and the works of man combine so harmoniously together. If there is one country to which visitors – whatever their particular interest may be – can come in the certainty that they will not be disappointed, it is surely France.

France has an area of some 544,000 sq. kilometres (including Corsica but excluding the overseas departments), bounded on the N, W and S by sea, giving it a coastline of 3100 km. Part of its southern boundary is formed by the Pyrenees, extending between the Atlantic and the Mediterranean, and its eastern frontiers with Italy and Switzerland are also formed by mountains, in particular the Alps. The frontiers with Germany, Luxembourg and Belgium to the E and NE, however, are less clearly defined and follow a fairly irregular course, with a natural frontier only towards the S, formed by the Rhine between Basle and Lauterbourg. The shape of the country has been compared to a coffee-pot; more recently it has been called the "Hexagon".

With a *population* of something over 53 million, France is much more thinly populated than Britain, with an average of 97 people to the sq. kilometre compared with Britain's 220. The difference will be borne in on the visitor as he travels through the French countryside.

The proportions of the urban and rural population are also very different in France. It has only one city with a population of more than a million – Paris, with some 2,300,000 inhabitants (or almost 10 million in the whole Région Parisienne). Apart from Paris there are 29 cities with a population over 100,000, but

Chalk cliffs near Dieppe

only two – Marseilles and Lyons – have more than 500,000 (though the conurbations round these cities both exceed the million mark). Thus in spite of the concentration of 18% of the whole population in Paris the country as a whole is much less highly urbanised than, say, Britain or Germany, and the face of France reflects this, with a landscape pattern shaped much more by small towns, villages and expanses of open country than by large cities.

The population of France includes some 4·2 million foreigners, of whom 880,000 are Portuguese, 870,000 Algerian, 560,000 Italian, 530,000 Spanish, 90,000 Polish and 50,000 Vietnamese. There are also considerable numbers of North Africans (Moroccans, Tunisians) in addition to the Algerians, particularly among unskilled workers in the towns and industrial areas. In many French towns, too, there is a relatively high proportion of coloured people, mainly from the former French colonies in Africa and the French overseas departments (Martinique, Guadeloupe, Réunion, Guyane).

The native population of France is itself very far from uniform. Although French is the language of administration and the language used in schools throughout the country, the ethnic diversity of France is reflected in the fact that 1·2 million French people in Alsace and Lorraine speak German dialects at least part of the time, at least as many (estimates varying between 1·2 and 2 million) speak Breton, 300,000 speak Catalan, 200,000 Flemish, 120,000 Italian and 100,000 Basque, while in the southern half of France a proportion of the population, whose numbers cannot be precisely established, speak the old Provençal language (Occitanian or *langue d'oc*) or one of its regional dialects. The people of Corsica have their own language, closely related to Italian. In recent years the various regional languages have been included in the school curriculum as optional subjects; and there is growing interest, particularly among young people, in the regional languages and cultures.

The *religion* professed by the majority of the population (*c.* 45 million) is Roman Catholicism. There is, however, no established church, and there is a sharp division between the spheres of the Church and the State. There are some 700,000 Jews in France, almost all living in the towns and mostly engaged in commerce and industry. There are some 900,000 Protestants, mostly in the old strongholds of Protestantism (Alsace, Lorraine, the Jura, the Massif Central, the Cévennes); two-thirds of them are Calvinists. Protestants are relatively numerous in certain professions, in banking and industry and in the officer corps.

The *topography* of France reflects the fact that the glaciers of the Ice Ages did not extend into this part of Europe. Apart from the mountains on its eastern and southern frontiers it is a country of low and medium-sized hills and plateaux cut by deep valleys. There are four main ranges of hills – the Armorican massif, the Massif Central, the Vosges and the Ardennes – with two large basins, the Paris basin and the Garonne basin, lying between them. The points of transition between these different regions are known as *seuils* (thresholds); the *seuil du Poitou* marks the boundary between the Paris basin and the Garonne basin.

The Garonne basin is covered with the masses of detritus from the Pyrenean region, which was subjected to folding under the surface at a rather earlier period than the Alps and then thrust up to its present height during the Tertiary. The large depressions between the older hills which enclose them and the younger folded hills of Alpine type are of great

Monts du Cantal, Auvergne

economic importance, providing the right conditions for the formation of valuable minerals. The depressions on the edges of the Hercynian hills and in the much folded hills of the interior contain the coal and iron worked in Normandy and Anjou. The main coalfields are now in northern France; those in the Massif Central are much smaller and more difficult to work. The coal seams on the eastern edge of the Paris basin in Lorraine – a continuation of the Saar coalfield – have no good-quality coking coal, which would have been of great value here in proximity to the local deposits of iron ore.

In the Garonne basin conditions were particularly favourable for the formation of deposits of oil and natural gas. Apart from the oilfield round Pechelbronn in Alsace, however, French oil and gas reserves began to be prospected only after the First World War, and were worked on a large scale only after the end of the Second. The great bulk of French oil and natural gas now comes from the Garonne basin, the principal fields being at Lacq (gas), St-Marcet (gas) and Parentis (oil), S of Bordeaux. Recently oil has also been worked in the Paris basin (Coulommes, Chailly, Châteaurenard, etc.).

Just as the *seuil du Poitou* marks the boundary between the Garonne and Paris basins, so a lower threshold, the *seuil du Lauragais*, lies between the Massif Central and the foothills of the Pyrenees.

Another contribution to the "open" topography of France and the ease of communications between its different parts which has so strongly influenced its

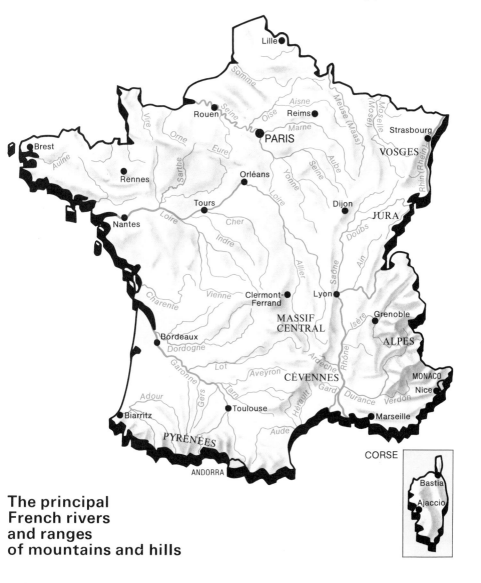

**The principal
French rivers
and ranges
of mountains and hills**

history is the long valley of the Rhône and Saône, which separates the Alps and the Jura from the Massif Central and the Paris basin and continues E to join the rift valley of the Upper Rhine. The Massif Central, although rising to heights of almost 1900 m, does not seriously hamper communications in central France, since the upward gradient from N to S is relatively gentle. Here the Loire and Allier valleys form troughs similar to that of the Rhône. Thus from Roman times at least France has presented no major obstacles to the movements of peoples, since the only high ground lies on the frontiers of the country – and even the Alps were proved by Hannibal, and later by Napoleon, to be by no means impassable.

But although France's highest mountains lie on its frontiers and are shared with other countries, they make a major contribution to the picture of France as we know it. The Alps contain not only Europe's highest peak, Mont Blanc (4810 m), but also parts of the Dauphiné and the Alpes Maritimes with their Mediterranean vegetation and sun. At the other end of the country are the Pyrenees, Europe's third highest mountains (coming after the Sierra Nevada), with passes of over 2000 m and a range of hills 450 km long rising to 2800 m in France and reaching their highest points at over 3400 m in Spain: equally attractive in both summer and winter, and thanks to their southerly situation some weeks ahead of the Alps in the return of the sun's strength after winter.

Water surrounds France on three sides, and also plays an important part in the inland regions, though only a relatively limited use is made of the rivers for navigation. The large French rivers flow radially from the centre of the country, the longest being the Loire (1020 km), followed by the Rhône, Seine and Garonne. It must be said, however, that with the exception of the Loire the "big" rivers offer fewer attractions to the tourist than the smaller ones like the Lot and the Dordogne, the Allier and the Ardèche, the Meuse and the Tarn, the Aude and the Indre, the Saône and the Aisne. The extent to which France's numerous smaller rivers give charm and character to the scenery has perhaps not always been sufficiently appreciated. They have, too, the added attraction of the many beautiful and historic old towns to be found along their banks or in their valleys. Some rivers, such as the Rhône, the Garonne and the Loire, end in deltas or estuaries of great natural beauty.

The relatively mild climate of France, which encourages tourism, also promotes the country's *agriculture*. The *primeurs* (early fruit and vegetables) which it produces supply both the domestic and the export trade; and even without the

The Col du Tourmalet in the Pyrenees

The Aiguilles de Chamonix in the Savoy Alps

crops grown in glasshouses a French vegetable market in March would still be lavishly stocked with fresh produce. The most striking evidence of the mildness of the climate, however, is provided by the vineyards which cover large areas of the country, being absent only in Brittany, Normandy and Artois, and of course in the more mountainous parts of the country.

One other feature of French agriculture which will strike any visitor to the country areas is that not all the available agricultural land is intensively cultivated: almost a third of the arable land lies fallow, degenerating into mere waste land. But though land in some parts of the country is being abandoned in this way, elsewhere it is being put to good use. This is particularly true of northern France, between the Loire and the Belgian frontier, where only 15% of the country's

agricultural land and 19% of its population produce more than 40% of its wheat and oats and over 90% of its sugar-beet, together with considerable quantities of meat and dairy produce. Western Normandy, Brittany, Vendée and the area extending S to the Massif Central are given up to stock-farming and fodder crops, producing almost half of France's butter and a third of its beef. In these areas the typical landscape pattern is the *bocage*, a patchwork of fields bounded by hedges and clumps of woodland. These are not designed – as is sometimes said – to serve as wind-breaks but to mark out property boundaries and enclose areas of pasture at less expense than walls or fences. They also provide wood in regions where it is otherwise scarce.

There is, however, timber in plenty on the plateaux of north-eastern France,

The Pont d'Arc over the River Ardèche

sidered suitable for agriculture can be used for forestry, and there has been extensive planting of new forests – mostly of conifers – since the 19th c. In the Jura and the Vosges timber and woodworking were for long the mainstay of the economy.

In the southern part of France, from the edge of the Massif Central to the Mediterranean, and also in certain Alpine valleys, the agricultural pattern is different again. Here the crops are typically Mediterranean – originally including mainly wine, grain and olives, but now also fruit and flowers, tobacco, rice and tomatoes. Mulberries were formerly grown on a large scale to provide food for silkworms, but are now of much less importance.

Here and in the mountains cattle and sheep are moved between summer and winter pastures, or are pastured on the Alpine meadows in summer and kept indoors in winter; but the traditional transhumant stock-farming is steadily declining, and the mountain grazings are increasingly being abandoned.

extending in a wide arc round the Paris basin from Touraine to the Vosges. This area alone has a quarter of France's forests, mostly deciduous. Land no longer con-

Climate

Most of France lies in the northern temperate zone, in a region of predominantly west winds where the climatic pattern over the year is governed by the alternation between depressions and areas of high pressure. Since the country is in the western part of the European continent, exposed to the sea, the continental features of its climate are moderated by oceanic influences.

The range of **temperature** between the warmest and the coldest months in the year is less than in Central Europe (Paris 3·5°C in January and 18° in July, Brest 7·5° in January and 17° in August, Nice 6·5° in January and 21·3° in July, Ajaccio 8·5° in January and 23·5° in July, compared with Munich −3° in January and 16° in July). The number of days of frost and ice declines from E to W; in the mountains it increases with increasing height. The average annual temperature is also higher than in Central Europe (Paris 11°C, Brest 12·1°, Bordeaux 12·9°, Nice 13·6°, Cannes 15·6°, Monaco 16·1°, compared with Munich 7·4°), and the growing period lasts longer. At certain points on the Channel coast, at least in a narrow coastal strip, the influence of the Gulf Stream produces a winter which is as mild as on the Mediterranean (January temperature of 6·5°C both at Cap de la Hague and at Nice). The growing period begins early in France, although by the end of the summer this advantage over Central Europe has largely been lost (July temperature of 18°C at both Paris and Stuttgart).

Precipitation (rain and snow) is distributed over the year, but whereas in Central Europe it is at its maximum in summer, France, particularly in the areas near the coast, has its highest rainfall in autumn: Paris has an annual average of 607 mm, with a minimum in February of 38 mm and a maximum in October of 60 mm, Brest an annual 842 mm (min. in May 43 mm, max. October–December 98 mm each). Except in the Mediterranean regions, however, France has sufficient rain throughout the year. In the eastern part of the country there is a more marked alternation between rainy days and dry days, and much of the total annual rainfall is contributed by heavy thundershowers. In the W much of the rain takes the form of a steady drizzle, and the number of days with some rain is high; but on the W coast, for example, it seldom rains all day. At altitudes over 1000 m in the Massif Central – in spite of the relative nearness of the sea – the snow frequently lies until May, and may hamper the movement of traffic.

The *Midi* (southern France) and Corsica fall into the Mediterranean climatic zone, with most of the rain in spring and autumn (Nice 805 mm annual average, min. July 23 mm, spring max. March 68 mm, autumn max. October 135 mm; Ajaccio 698 mm annual average, March 73 mm, October and November each 100 mm). The abundance of sunshine is one of the region's great tourist attractions, and the comparatively low moisture content of the air makes the high summer temperatures tolerable, while the nights are agreeably cool. In the absence of natural water or irrigation the vegetation is almost completely burned up. The surface temperature of the sea off the Côte

In the "Exotic Garden", Eze (Côte-d'Azur)

d'Azur and round Corsica ranges over the year between 12° and 24°C. – The pattern of rainfall is also different from the rest of France. On the Riviera the annual rainfall is sometimes higher than in Paris (Grasse 958 mm, Nice 805 mm, Paris 607 mm), but it falls on only half the number of days, mainly in autumn and spring. Frost occurs only sporadically. In certain weather conditions there may be a sudden fall in temperature, and occasionally there may even be snow; but this seldom lies longer than a few days.

In the Rhône valley and below the Cévennes cold winds may suddenly blow up at any time of year but particularly in spring and autumn. The best known of these is the *mistral*, which occurs particularly during the winter, when cold dry continental air from the high pressure area in the central plateau is drawn southward by a depression in the Golfe du Lion. The mistral may blow for between 3 and 12 days, according to atmospheric conditions, down the narrow Rhône valley into the delta, and is then usually followed by a number of fine windless days. Another wind which occurs locally from time to time is the *sirocco*, a violent S wind which may be either dry and hot or moist and warm.

The *Garonne basin* has a climate intermediate between the Atlantic and Mediterranean climates. In summer it is almost as hot and in winter as mild as the Mediterranean region (Bordeaux 20°C in July and 6·2° in January, Nice 21·2° in July and 6·5° in January). On the northern slopes of the Western Pyrenees and on the W coast, however, there may be heavy rainfall even in summer (annual average at Pau 1090 mm, July min. 63 mm, max. in April–May and November–December 100 mm); in the Mediterranean foreland of the Eastern Pyrenees the rainfall is sparse (annual average at Perpignan 598 mm, July min. 23 mm, October max. 83 mm).

Government and Society

France is a Republic – the Fifth Republic, the latest in a series reaching back to the Revolution of 1789, when the old monarchy came to an end (see below under *History*). The Fifth Republic came into being in 1958 with General de Gaulle's return to power, and a new constitution came into force on 28 September in that year. The 1958 constitution differed from earlier models in giving substantial powers to the head of state, the President of the Republic, who is the country's real political moving force. The new pattern, tailored to match the personal style of General de Gaulle, has been retained by his successors Pompidou (from 1969) and Giscard d'Estaing (since 1974).

The President of the Republic is elected by popular vote (until 1962 by an electoral college) for a seven-year term. He appoints the Prime Minister and other ministers (the latter on the recommendation of the Prime Minister), and presides over the Council of Ministers (Cabinet). He can dissolve the National Assembly but cannot himself be relieved of his position by the Assembly. He is commander-in-chief of the Armed Forces, and has extensive personal powers in a national emergency.

The French Parliament consists of two chambers, the National Assembly (*Assemblée Nationale*), which is elected for a five-year term (most recently in 1978), and the Senate (*Sénat*), which is elected for a term of nine years. All citizens over 18 have the vote. The National Assembly discusses and, together with the Senate, passes laws. In the 1978 election the largest number of seats was won by the Gaullists, with 148 seats out of the total of 482. Of the numerous other parties, some of which join to form groups, there are two with more than 100 seats in the Assembly – the Union pour la Démocratie Française, to which the Giscardists belong, with 137 seats, and the Socialist Party, which has 103. The Communist Party, the party with the largest numbers of members, has 86 seats. The government's considerable majority over the opposition (291 seats against 191) is the result of the French electoral system. The actual percentage of votes in the 1978 election was 50·74% for the government parties and 49·26% for the opposition, so that the two sides are fairly evenly balanced in the population as a whole. The government parties also have a majority in the Senate.

France is a member of the European Economic Community (EEC), but left the North Atlantic Treaty Organisation (NATO) in 1966.

The government of France is highly centralised. The country is divided into departments (*départements*), an administrative unit first introduced in 1790 of which there are at present 95 (see list on p. 9), and the departments are grouped in 22 regions (see map and table opposite). The number of the department appears in the last two figures of car registration numbers and the first two figures of post codes.

The influence of France extends beyond its European frontiers, though the days are gone when it controlled large parts of North Africa (Algeria, Tunisia, Morocco). The granting of independence to Algeria in 1962 – a step taken by General de Gaulle, to the disappointment of many of his supporters – was a development regretted by many Frenchmen; and the 1950s had already seen Indochina, Morocco and Tunisia achieving independence. Nevertheless the Communauté Française (French Commonwealth) established under the 1958 constitution as an association of former colonial territories with France still included some African countries, as well as France's overseas departments of Martinique, Guadeloupe, Réunion and Guyane, which send representatives to the French Parliament (for example Martinique has three members in the National Assembly and two in the Senate). Moreover the French language is still spoken in these overseas departments and in some of the now independent countries like Tunisia and Morocco. (And it is also an officially recognised language in large areas of Belgium, Switzerland and Canada.)

Some of the former French colonial territories have also forgotten the hostile attitudes of colonial days and established a freer and more cooperative relationship with the old colonial power, so that although France may have lost territory it has retained influence.

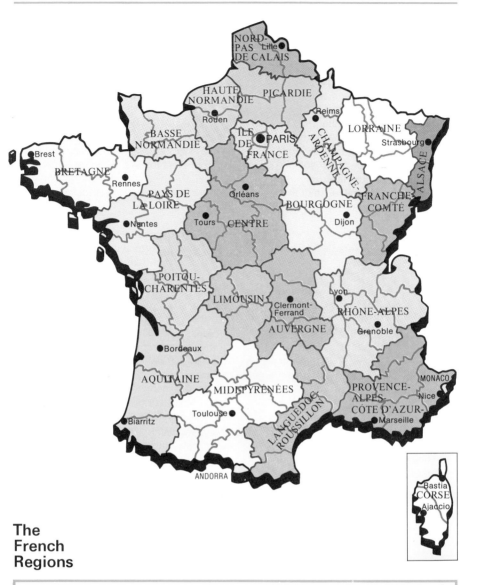

**The
French
Regions**

Name	Area (sq. km)	Population	Administrative centre
Alsace	8,310	1,517,300	Strasbourg
Aquitaine	41,407	2,550,300	Bordeaux
Auvergne	25,988	1,330,500	Clermont-Ferrand
Bourgogne (Burgundy)	31,592	1,571,200	Dijon
Bretagne (Brittany)	27,184	2,595,400	Rennes
Centre	39,061	2,152,500	Orléans
Champagne-Ardenne	25,600	1,336,800	Châlons-sur-Marne
Corse (Corsica)	8,681	289,800	Ajaccio
Franche-Comté	16,189	1,060,300	Besançon
Ile de France	12,001	9,808,500	Paris
Languedoc-Roussillon	27,448	1,789,200	Montpellier
Limousin	16,932	738,700	Limoges
Lorraine	23,540	2,330,800	Metz
Midi-Pyrénées	45,382	2,268,200	Toulouse
Nord–Pas-de-Calais	12,378	3,913,800	Lille
Basse-Normandie (Lower Normandy)	17,583	1,306,200	Caen
Haute-Normandie (Upper Normandy)	12,258	1,595,700	Rouen
Pays de la Loire	32,126	2,767,200	Nantes
Picardie (Picardy)	19,411	1,678,600	Amiens
Poitou-Charentes	25,790	1,528,100	Poitiers
Provence–Alpes–Côte-d'Azur	31,436	3,675,700	Marseilles
Rhône-Alpes	43,694	4,780,700	Lyons

The political scene in France shows that the fascination of Gaullism has gradually declined since the death of its great protagonist and that new forces are asserting themselves. There is now a rough balance between the various central parties allied with the Gaullists and the parties of the left, reflected in the narrow majorities in the election of the President in 1974 and the general election of 1978. The "Popular Front" of socialists and communists so often forecast has failed to materialise, largely because of the tactical and dogmatic attitudes of the French Communist Party.

After the death of General de Gaulle there was a major change of direction in France's foreign policy, reflected in a closer relationship to Europe and a less militantly expressed mistrust of the United States. It should not be forgotten, however, that de Gaulle himself had signed the Franco-German friendship treaty of 1963 giving official expression to a change in attitudes which had already been largely achieved in person-to-person relationships between the French and the Germans.

French society, even when expressing radical sentiments, is basically middle-of-the-road, not to say bourgeois, in its attitudes. The Frenchman's spirit of individualism, his tendency to see things in terms of black and white, is balanced by the importance which in the changed world of today is still attached to the family. Even the keen radical returns from some great demonstration against the state or the bourgeoisie into the bosom of his family, suggesting that perhaps not all the hard words spoken with such expressive power are as fierce as they sound. When all is said and done, the French recognise that the *savoir vivre* on which they pride themselves involves also an element of "live and let live", a recognition that other people are entitled to their opinions. The apparent strength of communism in France is an expression of protest against conservative rigidity and the defects of society, and of a desire to bring these feelings to the notice of those in authority; and a general election offers the opportunity to make such protests with the greatest force. It does not point to the imminence of revolutionary action inspired by class-conscious Marxist-Leninist principles. The majority of Frenchmen are no less attached to their national and individual traditions than to their freedom to express their opinions.

Although the French are fond of company and ready to enter into conversation with strangers, they are not given to inviting new acquaintances into their homes. Their domestic life tends to be kept apart from their social life, and whereas in Britain or the United States a visitor may find himself invited home for a meal or a drink the French are more likely to entertain a casual acquaintance in a café or restaurant.

The French are traditionally credited with a variety of national characteristics, some of them justified by the facts, some perhaps distortions surviving from the attitudes of the past. That they are individualists, that they attach importance to the things of the mind, that they possess great personal charm — these things do not require demonstration. They may sometimes express strong nationalist views, and it is no accident that the term chauvinism applied to extreme nationalism is of French origin. The visitor may occasionally encounter some of the less attractive aspects of French life or French attitudes, but he will also meet with much friendliness and an ever-present readiness to make human contact – particularly if he can speak at least some French.

One misleading stereotype which it seems impossible to eradicate is the legend of the sexual complaisance of French women, based no doubt on experiences in certain Paris streets – though similar experiences are equally available in every other country in the world. In fact – although in recent years the permissive society has developed in France as in other countries – the average Frenchwoman is in the first place a good cook, housewife and mother, to whom love is neither a mere casual game nor a duty but a feeling which involves her whole heart and person.

The French enjoy the same recreations and leisure pursuits as other Europeans. Half the population now take an annual holiday away from home, though most of them still spend it in France; although they are now readier to explore other countries than they were in the past, they do not cross their frontiers during the summer in such numbers as some of their neighbours.

Sport plays a great part in French life, and football is particularly popular – though France has never got higher than third place in the world championship (in 1958). Rugby is also popular in certain parts of the country. Even small towns have their own Rugby teams. In the Summer Olympics of 1976 France took sixth place; in the Winter Olympics, in spite of spectacular successes in the skiing events, it came only tenth. One of the great events of the French sporting year is the famous long-distance cycle race, the Tour de France, in which the whole population takes a passionate interest. Since the last war the Tour de France has been won fifteen times by French riders. France was the world's leading tennis nation in the 1920s, when the "Four Musketeers" (Cochet, Lacoste, Brugnon and Borotra) won the Davis Cup. A Frenchman, Petra was Wimbledon champion in 1946.

History

Prehistory and the early historical period (c. 10000 B.C. to 5th c. B.C.).

The territory of France was settled in early prehistoric times, and has yielded much evidence of the earliest human cultures.

About 10000 B.C.   *Early Palaeolithic.* Cave paintings in southern France (figures of animals, including mammoths, reindeer, etc.).

2700–1600   **Megalithic culture.** In the late *Neolithic* and early *Bronze Age* monumental graves and cult structures are built (e.g. in Brittany).

About 600   Foundation of the colony of Massalia (Marseilles) by Greek traders (Phocaeans).

After 500   The **Celts**, led by their chieftains and priests (druids), advance into France from the E. In southern France the **Iberians** (N of the Pyrenees) and **Ligurians** (on the Mediterranean coast) remain independent.

121   The **Romans** establish the province of Gallia Narbonensis (Provence) to protect the land route between Italy and Spain.

109   The Germanic **Cimbri** and **Teutons** move into Provence.

102–101   The Roman general *Marius* defeats the Teutons at Aquae Sextiae (Aix-en-Provence) and the Cimbri at Vercellae (Vercelli) in Upper Italy.

58–51   **Caesar** conquers Gaul (giving an account of his victories in "De Bello Gallico"), and the country is put under Roman civil administration. The process of linguistic and cultural *Romanisation* begins. Towns are founded (impressive remains of public buildings in Nîmes, Arles, etc.).

2nd c. A.D.   The *Christianisation* of Gaul begins.

About A.D. 300   The towns are surrounded by new walls. Lutetia (Paris) becomes for a time the residence of Roman emperors.

300–600   *Migrations of the peoples* through Gaul.

418–507   **Visigothic kingdom** in southern Gaul with its capital at Tolosa (Toulouse).

443   The **Burgundians**, after their defeat by the Huns on the Middle Rhine, establish a kingdom (Burgundy) in the Rhône valley under Roman protection. The southern part of their former territory, round Worms, is occupied by the Alemanni, the northern part, extending as far as Mainz, by the Franks.

After 449   Celts, driven out of Britain by the Jutes, Angles and Saxons, settle in Brittany, giving it its present name.

451   In the battle of the *Catalaunian Fields*, near Troyes, the **Huns**, led by *Attila*, are defeated by the Romans and their auxiliaries (Visigoths, Franks, Burgundians), and thereafter withdraw to Hungary.

The Frankish kingdom of the Merovingians and Carolingians (400–800).

The *Frankish kingdom*, the most important Germanic state of the early medieval period, provides the basis for the political, social and cultural development of Western Europe, particularly France and Germany.

After 400   **Franks** settle in Gaul as far as the Seine and Loire.

482–511   The Merovingian king *Clovis I* unites the Franks, conquers Gaul and thus becomes the founder of the Frankish kingdom.

496   The Franks defeat the Alemanni, become Catholic and thereafter receive the support of the Church.

After 511   Three new kingdoms emerge as a result of successive partitions of the Frankish kingdom – the Germanic *Austrasia*, with its capital at Reims (later Metz), *Neustria*, with Paris as its capital, and Burgundy (capital Orléans).

687   The Carolingian *Pépin of Herstal*, "mayor of the palace" in Austrasia, rules over the whole Frankish kingdom.

732   Pépin's son *Charles Martel* (the "Hammer") defeats the Arabs advancing from Spain at the *battle of Poitiers*. – Close association between Aquitaine, Burgundy and the Frankish kingdom.

751   *Pépin the Short* is proclaimed king by an assembly of dignitaries at Soissons and anointed by the Papal legate, Archbishop Boniface (Pope Zacharias having agreed to the deposition of the last Merovingian king).

754   Pope Stephen II asks Pépin for help against the Lombards and puts Rome under the protection of the Frankish king. Pépin and his sons are granted the style of "Patricius Romanorum". He cedes to the Pope the territories conquered from the Lombard king Aistulf (Pentapolis, Exarchate of Ravenna).

772–814   **Charlemagne** enlarges the Frankish empire by the addition of Upper Italy and the territory of the West Germanic peoples (Saxons and Bavarians). – The empire is divided into counties ruled by counts, and the frontiers are protected by border marches; the imperial palaces become economic and cultural centres.

800   Charlemagne's authority is confirmed by his coronation as Emperor in Rome.

From the rise of France to the age of absolutism (843–1600).

The French kingdom, supported by the Church and the towns, steadily consolidates its position, establishing itself as a *hereditary monarchy* in spite of the existence of numerous independent fiefs and territories and defending its frontiers against foreign enemies, particularly England.

843   Under the treaty of Verdun the Frankish empire is partitioned: *Charles II, the Bald*, receives the western part, whose eastern boundaries remain in all essentials the frontier between France and Germany until the late medieval period. – Carolingian kings rule France until 987.

857   The **Norsemen (Normans)** raid the western Frankish kingdom and plunder Paris.

After 888   Formation of large territorial units – Francia, Champagne, Aquitaine, Gascony, Toulouse, Gothia, Catalonia, Brittany, Normandy and Flanders.

911 *Charles III* grants the Norsemen the Duchy of Normandy.

987–1328 The **Capetians** rule France in the direct line until 1328, and in collateral lines until 1848 (with the exception of 1792–1814).

987–966 *Hugues Capet* (from "little cloak") possesses only his family territory, the Duchy of Francia (the area round Paris, extending to Orléans). Although the royal authority is still weak in face of powerful vassals, the Capetians are able to re-establish the hereditary character of the monarchy.

1066 William, Duke of Normandy, conquers England.

1096–1250 France plays a leading part in the **Crusades**. The way is prepared by the monastic orders and the Church, and the leaders are mainly French princes and nobles. The abbey of *Cluny* in Burgundy (founded 910) becomes a centre of monastic and ecclesiastical reform. – The *Carthusian* order, an eremitical order, is founded in the mountain valley of Cartusia, near Grenoble (the Grande Chartreuse). The *Cistercian* order, centred on the abbey of Cîteaux (1098), promotes scholarship and architecture and pursues the Christianisation and colonisation of the eastern German territories. A Cistercian abbot, *Bernard of Clairvaux*, is one of the leading scholars of his day.
The campaigns of conquest in the East, and the consequent contacts with the advanced culture of Islam, make possible the political, economic and cultural rise of France in the 12th c. The French nobility set the pattern of European chivalry, and the Gothic architecture and courtly literature of France exert their influence throughout Europe.

1108–37 *Louis VI* ("Louis the Stout"), subdues his rebellious vassals and founds the fortune of the Capetian dynasty.

1137–80 Under *Louis VII* begins the conflict with England. Henry II, a vassal of the French crown, possesses more than half of France.

1180–1223 Philippe Auguste recovers from 1202 onwards all the French possessions of the English king apart from Guyenne and Gascony.

1214 Philippe Auguste defeats the English and their ally Otto IV of Germany at the battle of Bouvines, strengthening the French consciousness of their national identity.

1209–29 *Albigensian wars* in southern France. The crown takes part in the repression of the Albigensian sect (named after the town of Albi) and in 1229 acquires Languedoc, bridging over the antagonism between the Frankish northern part of France and the Romance southern part.

1223–26 Under *Louis VIII* France becomes a hereditary monarchy, and Reims becomes the place of coronation of the French kings.

1253 Robert de Sorbon founds a theological college called the Sorbonne, the nucleus of the University of Paris.

1258 Under *Louis IX (St Louis)* Henry III of England loses all the English possessions in France N of the River Charente and does homage to the French king for the Duchy of Guyenne. – The French supreme court, the Parlement, obtains general recognition.

1285–1314 *Philip IV, the Handsome* (Philippe le Bel) acquires the county of Champagne and the archbishopric of Lyons.

1302 The States-General meet for the first time.

1309–77 The "Babylonian captivity" of the **Popes in Avignon**.

1328 The crown passes to the House of **Valois**, a collateral line of the Capetians (until 1498).

1333 Edward III of England claims the French crown.

1339–1453 **Hundred Years War** between France and England. Heavy defeats and grave social tensions between the nobility and the townspeople. The royal authority is shaken by peasant risings and fighting between rival groups of nobles.

1349 The heir to the French throne inherits the Dauphiné, and thereafter is known as the Dauphin.

1356 Edward III's son Edward, the *Black Prince*, defeats and captures King *John II, the Good*, at Maupertuis (SE of Poitiers).

1360 Treaty of Brétigny: Edward III gives up his claim to the French crown and receives in return Calais and SW France.

1363 John II hands over the Duchy of Burgundy to his son *Philip the Bold*.

1369 *Charles V, the Wise*, resumes the war against England and reduces English-held territory to a few main bases.

1380–1422 Under *Charles VI* (who becomes insane in 1392) the conflict between the Dukes of Burgundy and Orléans becomes increasingly bitter.

1415 Henry V of England defeats a French army at Agincourt and with the help of Burgundy occupies Paris and the whole of northern France.

1429 **Joan of Arc** compels the English army to raise the siege of Orléans, and accompanies *Charles VII* to his coronation in Reims.

1430 Joan of Arc is captured by the English and burned at the stake as a heretic in Rouen on 30 May 1431. (Canonised in 1920.)

1438 The Pragmatic Sanction secures the independence of the French church from the Papacy; establishment of the Gallican National Church.

1439 A new system of taxation, the *taille*, makes possible the formation of a standing army.

By 1453 England loses all its possessions on the Continent apart from Calais.

1461–83 *Louis XI* finally establishes the authority of the centralised monarchy over the great nobles.

1470 The first French printing press is established in Paris.

1477 On the death of Charles the Bold the Duchy of Burgundy and Picardy pass to the French crown, while his other possessions fall to the Habsburg Emperor Maximilian I: beginning of the conflict between France and the Habsburgs.

1480–91   The French crown recovers Anjou (1480), Maine, Provence (1481) and Brittany (1491).

1483–98   Reign of *Charles VIII*, who claims the kingdom of Naples as heir to the House of Anjou but is able to retain it only for a short period.

1484   Meeting of the *States-General* in Tours, with all the French provinces represented for the first time. The representatives of the towns are recognised as the "Third Estate".

1500   *Louis XII* conquers the Duchy of Milan, but is compelled to give it up after his defeat at Novara (1513).

1515   **Francis I** recovers Milan after his victory at Marignano over the Huguenots.

1519   Francis I seeks to obtain the German imperial crown, but in spite of Papal support is unsuccessful.

1521–44   Francis I fights four wars against the Habsburg Emperor Charles V. France loses Milan and is driven out of Italy.

1547–59   *Henry II*, married to *Catherine de Médicis*, persecutes the Huguenots, occupies the German bishoprics of Metz, Toul and Verdun (1522) and takes Calais (1558).

1556–59   *Franco-Spanish War*. France renounces its claims in Italy and Burgundy.

1562–98   **Wars of Religion**: Catholic party led by the Guise family, the Protestants by the Bourbons.

1572   In the St Bartholomew's Day massacre (24 August) the Huguenot leader Admiral de Coligny and thousands of his supporters are murdered on the orders of Catherine de Médicis.

1589   After the murder of *Henry III* the **Bourbons** succeed to the throne (until 1792).

1593   In order to secure peace within France *Henry IV* of Navarre becomes a Catholic ("Paris is worth a mass").

1598   The Edict of Nantes grants Huguenots conditional freedom of worship and 100 fortified places.
Henry IV restores the royal authority, severely shaken by the Wars of Religion, centralises the administration of France and bars the great nobles from maintaining their own private armies.

After 1603   Establishment of the first *French colony in Canada*.

From the age of absolutism to the end of the First Empire (1610–1815). – The age of *absolutism* brings the royal authority to its peak, but leads to economic and social changes which destroy the existing social structure. The basic ideas of the *Enlightenment*, which the *French Revolution* seeks to put into practice, do not yet establish a stable system of government but point the way towards 19th c. Europe.

1624–42   In the reign of *Louis XIII* Cardinal *Richelieu* becomes the king's chief minister and establishes the absolute authority of the crown.

1628   After the conquest of La Rochelle Richelieu puts an end to the special political position of the

Huguenots but does not interfere with their freedom of worship.

1635   Foundation of the *Académie Française* to promote art and learning.

From 1635   France becomes involved in the **Thirty Years War**.

1643–61   Cardinal *Mazarin* governs France during the minority of *Louis XIV*.

1648   Under the Peace of Westphalia France receives the Habsburg possessions in Alsace.

1648   Outbreak of the *Fronde*, a rising by the great nobles, the Parlement and the people of Paris (suppressed 1653).

1659   The Treaty of the Pyrenees ends the war with Spain. The power of Spain is broken, and France becomes a European great power.

1660   Louis XIV marries the Infanta Maria Teresa.

From 1661   **Louis XIV** reigns alone as the "Roi Soleil" (Sun King). The **absolute monarchy** reaches the height of its power in both domestic and foreign affairs, and the court at Versailles becomes the model for courtly and aristocratic life throughout Europe.
There is a flowering of *Baroque art* (Versailles, etc.), classical French *literature* (Corneille, Racine, Molière, La Fontaine), *philosophy* (Descartes, Pascal) and *painting* (Poussin, Watteau).
The financial and economic policy of *Colbert* (mercantilism) and the reorganisation of the army by *Louvois* make possible Louis XIV's wars of conquest.

1664   Foundation of the French West India Company.

1667–68   War of conquest against Spain and the Spanish Netherlands. Under the treaty of Aix-la-Chapelle France acquires Lille and other fortified towns in the Low Countries.

1672–78   War against Holland. Under the treaty of Nijmegen the Franche-Comté and certain frontier areas in the Low Countries are ceded to France.

1679–81   Annexation of Alsace (Strasbourg occupied 1681).

1685   The revocation of the Edict of Nantes causes half a million Huguenots to leave France. Persecution of the Jansenists.

1688–97   War of the Grand Alliance. The Palatinate (Heidelberg, etc.) is devastated by the French.

1701–14   *War of the Spanish Succession*. France suffers heavy defeats at the hands of the Grand Alliance (the Emperor and the German states, Spain, Britain, Sweden, Holland, Savoy).

1713   Peace of Utrecht. Philip V, Louis XIV's grandson, is recognised as king of Spain; France and Spain never to be united.

1715   Death of Louis XIV. Years of war and an extravagant court result in the economic ruin of the country, a huge national debt and the impoverishment of the peasants. France is no longer a great power.

1715–74 In the reign of *Louis XV* the Scottish-born financier *John Law* and Cardinal *Fleury* seek in vain to redress the financial situation by speculation.

1733–38 Through its participation in the *War of the Polish Succession* France acquires the right of succession to the Duchy of Lorraine, and the Duchy itself in 1766.

After 1743 The king is under the influence of his mistresses (Mme de Pompadour, Mme du Barry).

1754–63 In the Franco-British *colonial war* and the Seven Years War France loses its colonies in North America and almost all its bases in S and E India.

1768 Genoa sells *Corsica* to France.

1774–89 Attempts at reform by Louis XV's ministers (Turgot, Necker, Calonne) founder on the resistance of the privileged classes (nobility and clergy).

1789 Outbreak of the **French Revolution**. The collapse of the "Ancien Régime" results from the weakness of the absolutist system. The decline in the authority of the crown under the incapable Louis XV, failures in foreign policy and extravagant expenditure lead to criticism of the absolute monarchy, and the outdated feudal order (exemption from taxes of the nobility and clergy, etc.) produces social tensions. The well-to-do middle classes, demanding greater political rights, take up the fight against feudalism and the Church. Industrial crises resulting in high unemployment and agrarian crises caused by crop failures lead to the impoverishment of the lower middle classes and peasants. The opposition to the Ancien Régime is influenced by the ideas of the *Enlightenment* (the "Encyclopédie", Voltaire, Montesquieu, Rousseau, etc.) and by the American War of Independence.

Meeting of the *States-General* on 5 May at Versailles (the first meeting since 1614). – The *Third Estate* (the ordinary people as opposed to the nobility and clergy) declares itself a *National Assembly* (17 June) and takes the "oath of the Tennis-Court" to produce a constitution (20 June). – Storming and destruction of the state prison in Paris, the *Bastille* (14 July – now a French national holiday). The nobility begin to leave the country. – Abolition of feudal rights and liberation of the peasants (4–5 August). – *Declaration of the Rights of Man* (26 August). – The Paris mob compels Louis XVI and the National Assembly to move to Paris (5 October).

Formation of *political clubs* – the radical Jacobins (named after the monastery where they met: Robespierre, St-Just) and Cordeliers (Danton, Desmoulins, Marat), the moderate Feuillants (Bailly, Lafayette, etc.). – Nationalisation of church property (2 November).

1791 Louis XVI attempts to flee (20 June). – New constitution (3 September) establishing a **constitutional monarchy**.

1791–92 *Legislative Assembly*, with a majority of moderate Girondists but an increase in the number of radicals.

1792 With the declaration of war on Austria (April) the *Revolutionary Wars* begin. Storming of the Tuileries: the royal family are imprisoned in the Temple (10 August). "September massacres" of suspected anti-Revolutionaries. France is declared a **Republic**. – At the battle of Valmy the "cannonade of Valmy" routs the Prussian army. Revolutionary armies conquer Belgium and occupy the left bank of the Rhine.

1792–95 *National Convention*, with a radical majority (Robespierre, Danton, etc.).

1793 Execution of Louis XVI (21 January).

Mid 1793 to 1794 The Terror under **Robespierre** and the Committee of Public Safety. A Revolutionary Tribunal condemns Queen Marie-Antoinette, the Girondists and many others to death, and promulgates radical laws. Bloody repression of risings in Vendée, Brittany and the larger cities. After military defeats *Carnot* forms a people's army (the *levée en masse*) for the defence of France.

1794 Fall and execution of Robespierre (July). End of the Terror.

1794–95 Reconquest of Belgium. Holland is declared a "Batavian Republic".

1795–99 The **Directory**, a governing body of five, is too weak either to deal with the economic and financial crisis or to prevent risings of the right (royalists) and the left (an early communist movement led by Babeuf).

1796–97 *Napoleon Bonaparte* defeats the Austrians in Upper Italy and conquers Lombardy. Establishment of the "Cisalpine Republic" (Milan) and "Ligurian Republic" (Genoa).

1798–99 Switzerland becomes the Helvetian Republic, the Papal State the Roman Republic and Naples the Parthenopaean Republic. In the Egyptian Expedition Bonaparte defeats the Mamelukes in the battle of the Pyramids, but the French fleet is annihilated by a British fleet commanded by Nelson in the battle of the Nile.

1799 After an adventurous flight from Egypt Bonaparte overthrows the Directory in a coup d'état and is elected Consul by plebiscite for a ten-year term. He centralises the administration, encourages the return of many émigrés and signs a Concordat with the Pope (1801).

1801 Peace of Lunéville between France and Austria. The left bank of the Rhine remains French; recognition of the subsidiary Republics established by France.

Monument to Napoleon, Ajaccio (Corsica)

1802 Under the Peace of Amiens between France and Britain the British give up most of their overseas conquests, with the exception of Ceylon and Trinidad, while the French evacuate Egypt. – In a further plebiscite Bonaparte is made Consul for life.

1803–15 **Napoleonic Wars** with the European powers.

1803 At a meeting of the Imperial Diet in Regensburg, strongly influenced by Bonaparte, the old Holy Roman Empire is reorganised.

1804 Napoleon Bonaparte is crowned **Emperor of the French**. – French civil law is codified in the Code Civil ("Code Napoléon").

1805 Napoleon crowns himself **King of Italy** in Milan. Battle of Trafalgar: Nelson destroys the French fleet. Napoleon wins a decisive victory over the Russians and Austrians at Austerlitz (the "battle of the three Emperors").

1806 Establishment of the Confederation of the Rhine under the protection of Napoleon. – Napoleon defeats the Prussians in the double battle of Jena and Auerstedt. While in Berlin he decrees the "Continental Blockade" of Britain.

1807 Defeat of the Russians at Friedland. Establishment of the kingdom of Westphalia, with Napoleon's brother *Jérôme* as king, and the Grand Duchy of Warsaw.

From 1808 National risings in Spain against the French occupying forces.

1809 Rising in Austria. Popular rising in Tirol, led by Andreas Hofer, against the French and Bavarians.

1810 Napoleon marries the Austrian Emperor's daughter *Marie Louise*.

1812 Napoleon's *Russian campaign* turns to disaster after the burning of Moscow and the early onset of winter.

1813–15 *Wars of Liberation* by various European peoples against Napoleonic domination. Napoleon is defeated in the "*Battle of the Nations*" at Leipzig (1813).

1814 The Allies enter Paris and Napoleon abdicates; he is given Elba as a principality. The **Bourbons**, in the person of *Louis XVIII*, return to the French throne. – The first Peace of Paris (May) confines France to its 1792 frontiers.

1815 Napoleon returns to France for the "Hundred Days". He loses the decisive battle of *Waterloo* against the British and Prussians, and is exiled to the British South Atlantic island of St Helena (where he dies in 1821). In the second Peace of Paris (November) France is returned to its 1790 frontiers.

From the Restoration to the First World War (1815–1914). – The history of France during the 19th c. is mainly determined by the effects of the French Revolution and the Industrial Revolution. The *revolutions* of 1830 and 1848 give rise to movements which re-shape the political situation not only in France but in most other European countries. After 1850 France increasingly participates in the imperialist and colonialist policies of the European great powers.

1814 Louis XVIII promulgates the Charte Constitutionnelle (Constitution).

1815 Persecution of Jacobins and Bonapartists.

1825 Compensation granted to émigrés. – *Louis Braille* invents his script for the blind.

1830 The abolition of the freedom of the press and a change in electoral law lead to the **July Revolution** and the abdication of *Charles X*. The liberal-minded *Louis-Philippe*, Duc d'Orléans, is proclaimed King of the French (the "roi citoyen" or citizen king).

1830–47 Conquest of Algeria.

1843–48 *Karl Marx* living in Paris.

1848 **February Revolution** in Paris, as a result of discontent with the bourgeois monarchy and the property qualification for voting. Louis-Philippe abdicates, and France becomes a **Republic** (the *Second Republic*). First election to the National Assembly by popular vote (April).
The closing down of the uneconomic "national workshops" leads to a *workers' rising* in Paris, which is ruthlessly repressed (June). Prince Louis-Napoléon (nephew of Napoleon I) is elected President of the Republic.

1851 Louis-Napoléon's *coup d'état*. He is given a ten-year term as President in a plebiscite.

1852 After a further plebiscite Louis-Napoléon becomes **Emperor of the French** as **Napoleon III**. Supported by the Army and the Church, he pursues an economic and social policy (creation of employment by large-scale public works) and supports nationalist movements in Italy, Germany and the Balkans.

1854–56 France takes part in the *Crimean War* against Russia.

1859 France and Sardinia at *war with Austria*. Napoleon III acquires Nice and Savoy (1860), while Sardinia takes Lombardy.

1859–67 France extends its colonial possessions in South-East Asia.

1859–69 Construction of the Suez Canal by *de Lesseps*, with French support.

1861–67 The "Mexican Expedition". The Mexican Empire established by Napoleon III for Maximilian of Habsburg falls to pieces as a result of United States opposition.

1870–71 **Franco-Prussian War**. Napoleon III is taken prisoner after his defeat at Sedan, and a **Republic** is proclaimed in Paris (4 September).

1870–1940 *Third Republic. Thiers*, who had been Prime Minister in the time of Louis-Philippe, becomes President (until 1873).

1871 The *Paris Commune*, a rising by socialists and communists, is repressed by *MacMahon* (March–May).
Under the treaty of Frankfurt France cedes Alsace and Lorraine to Germany. Hostility between the two countries increases.

1879 The French Socialist Workers' Party is founded by the Marxists *Guesde* and *Lafargue*.

After 1879   Extension of France's colonial possessions – parts of Central Africa (1879–94), Tunis (1881), Indochina (1887 onwards), Madagascar (1896).

1889   Paris International Exhibition, with the Eiffel Tower. – Foundation of the Second International in Paris (1 May – now celebrated as Labour Day).

1892–93   The "Panama scandal": bankruptcy of the company founded by de Lesseps.

1892   Military alliance between France and Russia.

1894   *Lumière* invents the first cinematograph.

1895   Foundation of the Confédération Générale du Travail, a trade union organisation.

1896–1906   The *"Affaire Dreyfus"*: a Jewish officer, Captain Dreyfus, is condemned on the basis of forged documents and rehabilitated only in 1906.

1898–99   The *Fashoda incident*, when France and Britain come into conflict in the Sudan. France is compelled to abandon any idea of extending its North African colonial empire to the Upper Nile.

1902   Secret treaty with Italy over Tripoli.

1904   The **Entente Cordiale** between France and Britain: recognition of Britain's supremacy in Egypt and France's in Morocco.

1905   Law on the separation of Church and State.

1905–06   First Moroccan crisis. Germany protests against French intervention in Morocco.

1909   *Blériot* becomes the first man to fly the English Channel.

1911   Second Moroccan crisis. Germany recognises the French protectorate over Morocco in return for compensation in the Cameroons.

1912   Franco-Russian naval treaty.

From the First World War to the present day (1914–80). – France is a major theatre of war in both world wars. After the Treaty of Versailles it recovers its position as a European great power, but the desire for security prevents the development of any peaceful policy for the revision of the treaty. The Second World War alters the balance of power in Europe in favour of the USA and USSR. In consequence French policy is aimed at strengthening France's position within Europe and breaking free of United States leadership.

1914–18   **First World War.** The immediate occasion is the murder of the heir to the Austrian throne and his wife in Sarajevo (28 June 1914); the causes are conflicts between European states based on considerations of power politics (including France's desire to recover Alsace and Lorraine), competition in armaments, the difficulties of the multi-national Austro-Hungarian state, Russia's Balkan policies and over-hasty mobilisation and ultimatums. – On 3 August 1914 Germany declares war on France. In the battle of the Marne a French counter-offensive holds up the German advance (September). The war of movement develops into *trench warfare*.

1916   The battle for **Verdun** (21 February to 21 July). The French retake the Verdun defences (24 October to 16 December).

1917   German withdrawal between Arras and Soissons to the Hindenburg or Siegfried line.

1918   Beginning of the *Allied counter-offensive* under Marshal *Foch* (July). Franco-German *armistice* at Compiègne (November).

1919   France becomes a founder member of the League of Nations.
Under the Versailles treaty France recovers Alsace and Lorraine and also secures mandates over Syria and Lebanon, large parts of the Cameroons and Togoland, economic control of the Saar, the occupation of the Rhineland for a period of 15 years and the major share of German reparations. – Election victory of the National Bloc (Clemenceau, Poincaré) over the Cartel of the Left under Herriot.

1920   Military convention with Belgium and alliances with Poland (1921), Czechoslovakia (1924) and Romania (1926).

1923   Occupation of the Ruhr ordered by *Poincaré* against British resistance.

1924   Election victory of the Cartel of the Left. – France gives diplomatic recognition to the Soviet Union.

1925   *Locarno Pact*: Germany guarantees the inviolability of France's eastern frontier.

1925–26   Rising in Morocco.

1927   Repression of independence movement in Alsace.

1929   The French foreign minister, *Briand*, agrees to the evacuation of the Rhineland and the Young Plan for the reduction of German reparations. – Construction of the Maginot Line.

1931   Beginning of the *economic crisis*.

1932   Non-aggression pact with the Soviet Union.

1934   The continuing financial crisis is accompanied by a crisis of the Parliamentary system and the growth of radicalism on both the left and the right.

1935   Colonial agreement with Italy. Mutual assistance pact with the Soviet Union.

1936   The German army marches into the de-militarised Rhineland: neither France nor Britain takes any military action.
Victory of the Popular Front (communists, socialists, radical socialists) in a general election. The government led by *Blum* (1936–37) carries through progressive social legislation.

1938   *Munich agreement:* Prime Minister *Daladier* agrees to the cession of the Sudeten German areas to Germany.

1939   Franco-British guarantees to Poland (31 March), Romania and Greece (13 April).

1939–45   **Second World War.** After the German attack on Poland France declares war on Germany (3 September 1939).

1940   Beginning of the German campaign in the W (10 May), which leads to the collapse of the French army; Paris is occupied without a fight (14 June).

Armistice signed at Compiègne (22 June): France is divided into an occupied (N and E France) and an unoccupied zone. The government of Marshal *Pétain* moves to *Vichy* (1 July): end of the Third Republic.
General de Gaulle forms a government in exile in London and continues the war on the side of Britain. Within France Resistance groups are formed and carry on the fight against the German occupying forces and French collaborators.

1942   The Allies land in French N Africa (November); German troops then march into the unoccupied parts of France.

1943   De Gaulle sets up the National Liberation Committee in Algiers, which is recognised by the Allies.

1944   The *Liberation* of France begins with the **Allied landings** in Normandy (6 June) and the S of France (15 August), supported by armed French Resistance groups. De Gaulle and the Allies enter Paris (25 August). A government of national unity is formed by de Gaulle and the Resistance (August): *Fourth Republic.*

1944–45   Trials of collaborators and supporters of the Vichy régime.

1945   France obtains a seat on the Security Council of the United Nations and occupation zones in Germany and Austria.

1946   De Gaulle (head of government since November 1945) resigns. A new constitution comes into force (24 December). The French colonial empire becomes the Union Française. – Economic crises (inflation, strikes), the growing strength of the communists and the extreme right and controversy over Algerian policy lead to frequent changes of government.

1947   De Gaulle founds the *Rassemblement du Peuple Français* (RPF), a right-wing political movement.

1948   France receives aid under the Marshall Plan.

1949   France becomes a member of NATO and the Council of Europe. – The World Peace Congress meets in Paris.

1954–56   Loss of Indochina, Tunisia, Morocco, French West Africa and French Equatorial Africa.

1956   France is involved, along with Britain and Israel, in the abortive Suez war. In Algeria Gaullists and the army seize power.

1957   France becomes a member of the European Coal and Steel Community, Western European Union, the European Economic Community and Euratom.

1958   *Putsch in Algiers* (13 May). President *Coty* declares a state of national emergency and appoints de Gaulle Prime Minister with special powers. – A new presidential-type constitution is approved by national referendum: *Fifth Republic.*

1959   As President of the Republic, **de Gaulle** carries through a series of firm economic and financial measures. The Union Française becomes the *Communauté Française*: the colonies receive internal self-government or independence.

1960   First French atomic bomb exploded in the Sahara.

1962   The Evian Agreement grants Algeria independence. – De Gaulle proposes a confederation of Western European states. – Amendment of the constitution: the President of the Republic to be directly elected by popular vote.

1963   Treaty of *Franco-German cooperation.*

1964   France gives diplomatic recognition to the People's Republic of China.

1966   France withdraws from the military side of NATO.

1968   Economic and social injustices lead to *student unrest* (particularly in Paris) and a general strike (May). – The weakness of the franc leads to an international currency crisis (November).

1969   De Gaulle steps down from the Presidency and is succeeded by *Georges Pompidou.*

1971–74   Two-tier exchange rates developed in an attempt to solve the world currency crisis.

1974   *Valéry Giscard d'Estaing* elected President of the Republic.

From 1974   Steep increases in oil prices lead to a world-wide *energy crisis* and economic *recession.* Fall in imports and exports; increased unemployment, inflation. Statutory restrictions on the use of energy.

From 1975   Violence, particularly in Corsica, by pro-independence groups.

1976   France leaves the European "currency snake" and allows the franc to float. Domestic political tension (strikes and demonstrations).

1977   General strike against the government's economy programme (24 May). – Agreements on cooperation with the Soviet Union signed during a visit to Paris by the Soviet head of state, Mr Brezhnev (22 June). – Violent demonstration by opponents of nuclear power at Creys-Malville (31 July).

1978   Heavy pollution of the N coast of Brittany after the wreck of a giant oil tanker (17 March). – In a controversial military action French and Belgian troops clear rebel forces out of the copper province of Shaba (Katanga) in Zaire in order to permit the evacuation of Europeans (May). – Increasing resistance to Prime Minister *Barre*'s stringent measures designed to secure stability (June). – Bomb attack on the Palace of Versailles by Breton separatists (26 June). – Fight against inflation and unemployment. As a result of the serious state of the steel industry, the government resolves to close steel-making plants. This leads to large demonstrations in Paris (March).

1980   Hostages taken by Corsican autonomists in Ajaccio (January).

Art and Culture

In France, more perhaps than in any other country in Europe, the traveller is confronted, wherever he goes, with evidence that art and culture have from time immemorial played a central role in the life of the inhabitants. This evidence is to be found not only in Paris and the larger towns but in every part of the country, in tiny villages and the remotest corners in the countryside. We encounter it in the caves of southern France, in the Romanesque churches of Burgundy and the cathedrals of the Ile de France, in the châteaux of the Loire valley and many other regions, in a host of museums and art galleries, in the works of François Villon in the 15th c. and in modern writers like Jean-Paul Sartre, Saint-John Perse, André Gide and François Mauriac, France's four post-war Nobel Prizewinners.

It is perhaps the distinctive characteristic of France that here culture and art, which elsewhere are the preserve of a small elite, are essential elements in the life of large sections of the population. The intellectual, the "homme de lettres", does not stand apart from everyday life: he is part of it. The artist is accepted and respected, not derided as a different and eccentric species. The art and culture of our day are scarcely conceivable without the painting of the Fauves at the beginning of this century, the architecture of Le Corbusier, from French-speaking Switzerland, or the music of the Basque Maurice Ravel. Impressive as have been France's artistic achievements in the past, its contribution to the culture of the 20th c. is no less notable – the most fruitful that any nation has produced out of its own substance, with the tacit consensus of a whole people which appreciates its artists and thinkers even when it does not understand them.

Any visit to France must therefore, to a greater or lesser extent, be a cultural exploration. In France art often forms a kind of counterpoint to natural beauty; and the visitor, while enjoying one, can appreciate also something of the other.

In the course of a brief visit it is not possible to get even a fleeting impression of the whole range of French art: the best plan, therefore, is to concentrate on a particular region or a particular field. Even a visitor who confines himself to Burgundy cannot do justice to its immense variety of Romanesque architecture. A pilgrimage to the works of the modern masters of painting would involve a journey from the Pyrenees to Provence and visits to many galleries, large and small, where the work of the various modern schools is to be seen. Gothic buildings are to be found from one end of France to the other, from Amiens to Perpignan; and who shall say whether Quimper Cathedral is to be preferred to the Palace of the Popes in Avignon, or Avignon to Quimper? Those who want to cover the whole range of French art and culture and are not content with mere casual sightseeing will need to make not one but many visits to France.

Before the Romans. – The origins of art, which in its early stages is bound up with myth and religion, reach far back into the past in France. They are to be found in the *caves* where the men of the Palaeolithic period, around 15000 B.C., sought to obtain magical power over the animals who were their prey by naturalistic paintings and engravings of the different species. In Périgord, particularly in the Vézère valley and round Les Eyzies-de-Tayac, such caves are very numerous. The finest of all, the cave of Lascaux which was discovered in 1940, has unfortunately had to be closed to visitors because of the growth of algae which threaten the paintings, which can be seen only in the films shown in the adjacent information centre. But there are plenty of other caves where these earliest works of French art can still be seen *in situ* – for

Cave painting, Lascaux

example in the Grotte de Font-de-Gaume in the Vézère valley, at Niaux near Tarascon-sur-Ariège, in the Pech-Merle cave near Cabrerets (E of Cahors), at Cougnac (N of Gourdon) or in the Mas d'Azil cave, NE of St-Girons. The beginnings of sculpture can be seen in two clay figures of bison found in the Grotte du Tuc d'Audoubert, near St-Girons, and in the statues from the caves at Montespan.

The most striking evidence of Neolithic art is to be found in the megalithic cult structures – alignments of standing stones, huge individual stones (menhirs), tombs (dolmens) and stone circles (cromlechs) – which are common in Brittany, particularly round Carnac. In the Cévennes there are standing stone figures erected by the Ligurians which provide a kind of half-way house between the rough-hewn megaliths of Brittany and the stone sculpture of later periods.

Trophée des Alpes, La Turbie

Excavations at Bibracte and Vix in the Côte-d'Or have revealed a variety of works of art of the pre-Roman period – Celtic ornaments, Greek vases of clay and bronze. Those who want to see the full range of this art must go to the Museum of National Antiquities at St-Germain-en-Laye, near Paris, which has a rich collection of prehistoric, Gallic, Roman and Frankish art (either the originals or copies), housed in the 16th c. Château.

The Roman period. – The Romans lived in France and built there for some 500 years (from about 50 B.C. to A.D. 450), and the remains still to be seen can stand comparison with anything to be found in Italy itself. Most of these are in Provence, the Roman *Provincia*, but there are also important Roman remains in the foothills of the Pyrenees. The amphitheatres of Arles and Nîmes, the triumphal arches of Orange and St-Rémy, the temples of Nîmes and Vienne are universally known; but not all visitors to France realise that there are substantial remains of Roman architecture to be seen in Toulouse, Besançon, Reims, Bordeaux and other towns as well. The main tourist attractions, however, are still Arles, Nîmes, Orange and the Pont du Gard near Remoulins, and of course the various museums containing Roman material. Among the museums the Louvre in Paris must take pride of place with its magnificent collection of Roman remains, but

there are many others, at Bordeaux and Toulouse as well as Arles, Nîmes and Vienne. The new Roman museum in Lyons is notable for its sculpture and mosaics, and there are numerous regional and local museums containing a variety of material, large and small, from France's 500 years of Roman culture. And the continuity between past and present is demonstrated by the fact that in some French spas like Aix-les-Bains (between Geneva and Grenoble) and Plombières (in the Vosges) baths originally built in Roman times are still in use.

The Carolingian period is represented by comparatively few remains. In the later Roman period art and architecture began to reflect the influence of Christianity, coming in from Italy, which gave rise to the building of the first *churches* in Lyons and Vienne. Frequently pagan temples were converted into Christian shrines: a typical example is to be seen at Nîmes. The early Christian churches sometimes had a crypt, which was used to house relics of the titular saint and served a variety of other purposes, from a meeting-place for the congregation to a mausoleum. The dark crypt, reached by going down a flight of steps from the lightness of the church, had an air of mystery and sanctity. Examples of such crypts, dating from the 7th c., can be seen in the old abbey church of Jouarre, near Metz, or in the lower part of St-Laurent in Grenoble.

An important function was also performed by the baptistery in which newly admitted Christians confessed their faith, like the one at St-Jean in Poitiers (end of 7th c.).

The main innovation during this period was the development of the central space under the crossing as the religious focal point of the church. This development is seen particularly well in the church at Vignory (on the Marne), though it dates from a rather later period (consecrated 1052). It was bound up with an emphasis on the nave which led up to the altar and was made narrower by the pillars which lined it. Other characteristic examples are the churches of Tournus and Nevers.

Apart from the manuscripts to be seen in the Bibliothèque Nationale in Paris, the art of the Carolingian period (middle of 8th to end of 9th c.) is represented by the remains of its *monastic buildings.* These are sparse indeed, since the original buildings were replaced in subsequent centuries by new ones, leaving only occasional fragments of masonry built into later structures. The church at Germigny-des-Prés, near Orléans, does, however, in spite of later alteration, give some impression of the original church (consecrated 806) with its centralised cruciform layout. In the dome of the choir chapel can be seen a mosaic of angels bearing the Ark of the Covenant, a typical example of Carolingian wall decoration, which otherwise largely consisted of interlace ornament. The church of St-Pierre-aux-Nonnains, Metz, is believed to be France's oldest church, probably dating from the 7th c.; but this church, reduced to ruins and subsequently restored, was rebuilt in Gothic style to serve a convent of nuns.

Romanesque art. Buildings in Romanesque style were erected between the end of the 10th and the middle of the 12th c. The style did not appear overnight but was the result of a long process of development; it is called Romanesque because it took its main features from Roman architecture – though it was also much influenced by Byzantine and Oriental art. Nevertheless Romanesque architecture, in its organisation of space, the pattern of its façades and the structure of its doorways, is a new and original style, showing numerous regional and other variations.

Romanesque *churches* are characterised by barrel-vaulted roofs, round domes (which may form the focal point of a centralised structure) and round-headed arches, and are centred on the tower over the crossing which dominates the building. Built round this central cubic element, reaching upward in the form of a pyramid, the church is made up of a series of separate compartments of different heights. Southern France holds more closely to ancient traditions, while the north is influenced by the sturdy and primitive architecture of the Burgundians, Franks and Normans. Thus in northern France the archaic character of the Romanesque style is most evident, and the conflicts between Christianity and the intellectual ideas of late antiquity give the most subtle and compelling expression to the double allegiance of the style. In the south on the other hand, the tradition of Roman Christian art is so strong that the affinities of Romanesque are rather with the art of Roman and Byzantine antiquity.

Romanesque architecture, therefore, did not develop in a uniform way in the different parts of France. It is seen at its finest in Burgundy, where the double aspect of medieval art is expressed in its full perfection – a subtle conjunction of monkish asceticism and Christian renunciation of the world on the one hand, with the assertion of an aristocratic way of life, an established social order and physical strength on the other. It was these attitudes that gave the Cluniac order their commanding position. In Burgundy the Romanesque style is displayed in its most characteristic form, "in the strictly centralised structure of the crossing tower and the group of chapels round the choir, the regular pattern of the aisles, the uniform articulation of the walls and the barrel-vaulting which binds the whole building together" (Hamann).

The regional variations of the Romanesque style are less obvious in the larger churches, which copy features from one another and thus show a closer resemblance: St-Etienne and Ste-Trinité in Caen, St-Sernin in Toulouse, St-Gilles in Provence and Ste-Foy at Conques, for example, show common features which give them a "supra-regional" character. The little country churches, on the other hand, reveal much more of the attitudes of the local community and the men who built them.

In Normandy the walls and interiors of the churches are much more rigidly articulated – a feature which may be thought of as archaic or primitive but contains elements which point the way towards Gothic.

S and W of Burgundy, in the direction of Poitiers, there developed the *hall-church*, which shows all the characteristics of Romanesque architecture but has a nave and aisles of the same height.
In Languedoc and Périgord, round the town of Périgueux, the imitation of Byzantine models is more evident. St-Front in Périgueux is a copy, in stricter form, of St Mark's in Venice, which itself was modelled on the Church of the Apostles in Constantinople; the sequence of domes has something of a tent-like effect. Angoulême Cathedral represents a transitional stage: the centralised structure is reflected in the series of domes running from W to E, the dome in front of the choir being given greater emphasis to mark the central point of the church.
Farther S again, in Provence, the area of special sanctity under the dome gives place to a space of almost secular effect for the accommodation of the faithful: the influence here is Rome rather than Byzantium. A good example of this style is the little known chapel of St-Gabriel (12th c.) near St-Rémy, N of Fontvieille.

Similarly, differences between northern and southern France are found in the *sculpture* of the Romanesque churches. In Burgundy the figures are elongated, almost stick-like, with their robes hanging in delicate folds. In the south they are short and thickset, and their garments hang in broader folds, closer to the original form of the stone.

The sculpture of Burgundy presents an almost demoniac world which has grown out of older and more primitive conceptions – Heaven and Hell, the world above and the world below, virtues and vices, animal figures and mysterious animal forces. The mystery of the Last Judgment is a favourite theme. But the sculpture also shows delicate human feeling, a sense of fraternal community and the God who sacrificed himself for man. Here art reflects the spiritual preoccupations of the day.

In the south on the other hand, the sculpture on church façades favours

Virgin and Child, Orcival (Puy-de-Dôme)

representations of Christ and his disciples. A transitional form is found at Moissac, where Burgundian influence is more strongly evident; but here the Last Judgment shows only Christ with the Elders of the Apocalypse, as a King among kings. In Poitou and Languedoc the Ascension is the dominant theme on church façades. The archaic sculpture of the south shows closer affinities with the art of antiquity, as can be seen at Toulouse and, even more strikingly, in Provence. The façade of St-Gilles, surely the finest achievement of Romanesque art in southern France, dispenses with any element of the miraculous and is content to tell a story, in which the Apostles are brought closer to the spectator and the miracle of the Ascension is of less importance than the account of the Passion.
This seems like an anticipation of the heretical Albigensian movement which, like Calvinism in a later period, rejected the identification of bread and wine with the body and blood of Christ: the Crucifixion of St-Gilles depicts a suffering man, not the Son of God.

In France the Romanesque style is associated with the introduction and diffusion of the *Cluniac reform.* The church built at Cluny by Abbot Majolus in the second half of the 10th c., which provided the model for the church at Bernay in Normandy, shows a departure from the previous basilican type. The tower over the crossing results from the emphasis

Base of column, St-Gilles (Provence)

essential element in the language of architectural form.

The mention of Chartres – generally thought of as one of the supreme achievements of the Gothic style – in this Romanesque context is a reminder that the building of a church or cathedral with the technical resources available in the Middle Ages was not a matter of a few years' work, but might extend over several centuries. It is not surprising, therefore, to find that many buildings begun in Romanesque style incorporate later features which came into fashion while they were under construction. This is what happened at Chartres: the W doorway, built in pure Romanesque style in 1145, escaped destruction when the church was burned down in 1194 and was integrated into the Gothic cathedral begun in 1195. The figures on the doorway and in the tympana have stiff bodies but heads which are full of life and individuality. Thus a visit to Chartres affords an opportunity of seeing Romanesque sculpture and Gothic architecture in close juxtaposition.

given to the transepts, and the aisles are continued by the chapels on either side of the choir. There is no crypt, and the atrium at the W end has become a porch.

Cluny provided the model for churches at Paray-le-Monial, La Charité and Fleury (St-Benoît), and also for churches in Normandy like Jumièges. The mother church itself was destroyed after the French Revolution: had it survived it would have been the most magnificent as well as the largest of all France's Romanesque churches.

The *Cistercians*, with St Bernard of Clairvaux, were also active in Burgundy, building cruciform churches without towers and without decoration. Examples of their work are the monastic churches of Fontenay and Pontigny.

Other notable examples of Romanesque architecture are the numerous cloisters, among the finest of which is St-Trophime in Arles.

There are also very fine Romanesque wall paintings and stained glass. Perhaps the finest *paintings* are the long series on the walls and vaulting of St-Savin-sur-Gartempe (begun *c.* 1080). Beautiful Romanesque *stained glass* is to be seen in Le Mans Cathedral, St-Pierre in Poitiers, Angers Cathedral and of course Chartres: a feature which Gothic – following Romanesque and at Chartres coinciding with it – was to develop still further into an

Gothic architecture. – Although the term Gothic is now pronounced with respect, it was originally a pejorative term applied by Italian artists (probably Raphael) to a new style which made no appeal to them: Gothic was the art of the barbarous Goths, a style to be despised. It was in fact believed right down to the 17th and 18th c. that Gothic was a style invented by the Goths and later brought to France. It is now known that the pointed arch was used for the first time in the church of St-Denis in the Ile de France, and French art historians tend to refer to this style developed on the soil of France as the "style français". The Gothic style prevailed for some four centuries (from the 12th to the early 16th c.), reaching its peak in the 13th c., when most of the great Gothic *cathedrals* were built.

Whereas the Romanesque style reflected a variety of outside influences, Gothic grew up on French soil and was subject to no foreign influences. It represented a complete break with the past and an entirely new constructional system with its own internal logic. One other point – equally applicable to Romanesque architecture – should also be borne in mind: the fertility of the Middle Ages in creating fine architecture and sculpture is explicable only in the light of the profound piety of the age. It was this, too, that enabled towns and even quite small villages to find the very large sums of money involved in building the medieval cathedrals and churches. It is necessary only to compare – without prejudice – the simple and relatively inexpensive churches of undressed stone built in N Germany with the elegance and refinement of the Romanesque and Gothic churches of France to realise the fascination which Christianity must have exerted on medieval Frenchmen. It has been estimated that the building of Notre-Dame in Paris cost 120 million gold francs – an enormous sum in an age of low wages, especially when it is remembered that the whole population, from ordinary working people to the great nobles, took part in the work (as we are told was the case, for example, at Chartres).

What were the new features of Gothic? The mystical thought of the Middle Ages, in reaction against the dogmatism of the schools, strove towards the infinite, towards something beyond life on earth, something higher; and this striving heavenward found expression in the Gothic churches. The architectural means of achieving this were provided by the pointed arch, ribbed vaulting and buttresses, which together made possible a lightness of structure unknown to Romanesque architecture. The ribbed vaulting carried the vertical stresses outward, so that the line of stress and the supports which bore that stress were quite separate to the eye – a radical change as compared with ancient architecture and the styles derived from it. The vaulting in the interior of the church no longer draws the eye round the dome and down again, but attracts it ever higher (in the unfinished Beauvais Cathedral to a height of almost 50 m). In order to guide the eye upwards, into the world beyond, the churches tower high above the houses huddled round their base. It was the deliberate intention of the builders that the church should not be visible from the surrounding lanes: it was not to be seen as a mere static building but as a pointer striving vertically upwards and heavenwards. Later slum clearance may sometimes have improved the view of a cathedral, but it distorts the effect aimed at by the builders. Moreover, with the new building techniques it was no longer necessary to have solid stone walls: it was now possible to have large areas of window, with stained glass which produced new light effects in the interior. The most striking example of this is the large rose window with its delicate stone tracery which is commonly found in the W front and is one of the most characteristic features of the new style.

In the course of its four centuries of existence the Gothic style underwent changes – not necessarily always for the better. In France four main stages can be distinguished, differing from the stages recognised in English Gothic.
Early Gothic from the second half of the 12th c. (with features transitional between Romanesque and Gothic) to the first quarter of the 13th. This period saw the building of the great cathedrals of Laon, Paris, Amiens, Reims, Chartres, Bourges, Strasbourg and Beauvais – all, even in this first phase, supreme achievements of the new style.
The remainder of the 13th c. was the *High Gothic* period. There is now no trace of Romanesque influence, and a constant striving for lightness.
The 14th c. was the age of the *Rayonnant* ("radiant") style. During this period the buildings begun in the 13th c. were completed or embellished.
The 15th c. continued the development. The piers became columns which merged into the arches, and the capitals disappeared.
The 16th c. saw the beginning of the Renaissance, but during the first few decades the Gothic style continued in use in certain areas. Characteristic of this *Late Gothic* period is the *Flamboyant* ("flaming") style, with its intricate tracery weaving upward like flames. Examples of this fourth phase of French Gothic are the church at Brou (near Bourg-en-Bresse), the Palais de Justice in Rouen, the choir of Albi Cathedral and the lateral façades of Senlis, Beauvais, Sens and Limoges Cathedrals.

Apart from individual constructional features, however, the Gothic buildings achieved a quite new general effect. The cubic monumentality of the Romanesque now gave place to an active directional movement. Although a Gothic church could be seen from different points of view, the architectural treatment of the W front emphasised that this was the main entrance. There was no longer a single tower, but two towers flanking the central portion of the façade with the principal doorway. The whole of the W front, in fact, constituted a monumental entrance to the church. The central doorway and the lateral doorways leading into the aisles merged into a single unit. "These Gothic doorways are the most inviting ever created – inviting in a way that would not have been possible without their Christian inspiration. The church becomes a house of the Lord, hospitably open to all" (Hamann).

Flamboyant architecture, Brou (Bourg-en-Bresse)

Additional significance is given to the doorways by the *statues* – markedly different in both form and arrangement from those of the Romanesque period – set behind one another as if to draw worshippers into the interior. Each figure stands out by itself, free of the mass of stone. Female figures now feature more prominently than ever before – for example at Reims, Paris and Amiens. The Virgin becomes a lady of dignified mien and smiling face. Unfortunately the figures on the façade of Notre-Dame in Paris were destroyed during the Revolution (fragments in the Cluny Museum), but typical doorways with a profusion of statues can be seen at Amiens, Bourges, Auxerre, Le Mans, Rouen and Strasbourg (though Strasbourg dates from after the High Gothic period, in the 15th c.). The features of the

new style can be seen most clearly in Chartres Cathedral, if the rather stiff Romanesque figures on the W front are compared with those on the Gothic façades of the transepts, built from 1200 onwards. The later figures are graceful and expressive, with an inner life of their own.

Thanks to its complete preservation, including all its glass, Chartres Cathedral – which ranks with Strasbourg as the most visited of France's Gothic cathedrals – is the best example of French Gothic architecture at its most characteristic. This is true both of the exterior with its transepts and the statues on the W front and of the richly patterned and decorated interior; and of course it will be seen at its best by those who are fortunate enough to see it without the usual crowds of visitors.

The very name of Gothic indicates that it is a style predominantly found in northern France; but such fine Gothic cathedrals as those of Clermont-Ferrand, Albi and Narbonne should not be forgotten. In southern France the emphasis is on fortress-like structures like Carcassonne, the Palace of the Popes in Avignon and Aigues-Mortes, which show that the Gothic style could give life and vigour to *secular architecture.* Numbers of castles, town halls, law-courts, the Hôtel-Dieu in Beaune and many rich burghers' houses survive to demonstrate that Gothic architecture was not confined to churches.

Gothic *painting* is now represented mainly by the 5th c. altar-paintings to be seen, for example, in Beaune or in the Louvre and by the beautiful illuminated books of the period, most notably the Books of Hours which Dutch artists were now producing in the spirit of French Gothic. Examples can be seen in the Bibliothèque Nationale in Paris and the Condé Museum in Chantilly. Gothic art also has notable achievements to its credit in the related field of tapestry-weaving. The Louvre and Angers Cathedral ("Apocalypse", 14th c.) contain examples of this work, which disregard the rules of perspective but are nevertheless of astonishing realism.

There is a particular concentration of Gothic architecture in Normandy and the Ile de France, but Burgundy and Champagne also have fine Gothic churches (Dijon, Nevers, Auxerre, Semur-en-Auxois, Troyes).

In Anjou the Gothic style takes on a distinctive form under the influence of its ruling house, the Plantagenets. The Plantagenet style, as seen for example in Angers Cathedral, combines the Romanesque dome of Byzantine origin with ribbed vaulting; and the influence of Angers can be detected in Poitiers Cathedral and in churches in Périgord, Vendée and Limousin.

Renaissance châteaux. – If the Gothic period was the age of cathedrals, the Renaissance produced in the 16th c. the splendid châteaux which draw tourists to the Loire valley. The first impulse was given by Francis I, who not only continued work on Chaumont, Langeais and Amboise, which had been begun by Charles VIII, but went on to build Châteaudun, Chenonceaux, Blois, Chambord and Azay-le-Rideau.

Château of Azay-le-Rideau (Indre-et-Loire)

With the coming of the Renaissance the pointed arch gave place to the round-headed arch and ribbed vaulting to barrel vaulting or coffered ceilings. In earlier times castles had been built, but in these considerations of defence had been paramount; and strong defensive towers of the early medieval period can still be seen, for example, at Langeais, Montrichard, Montbazon and Beaugency. During the Gothic period the towers were round rather than square, and the buildings gradually became less severe in style. The great change, however, came in the 16th c., when the builders began to look back to Italy for models, particularly in the form of the staircases.

Most of the Renaissance châteaux are built round a square or rectangular courtyard, with towers ("pavilions") at the ends of the wings. The architects who designed them, while following Italian models, were concerned to give them a distinctive note of their own. The finest courtyard of this period is the square inner courtyard of the Louvre in Paris (though it took another two centuries to reach its present form). Building began in 1546 with the first half of the wing along the Seine and half of the adjoining W wing, and was continued by Henry II, his widow Catherine de Médicis, Henry IV and Louis XIII. Other Renaissance châteaux were built near Paris, at St-Germain-en-Laye and Fontainebleau.

From classicism to Rococo. – In Italy the Renaissance style led into Baroque, but in France a different course was followed, as is illustrated by the history of the main front of the Louvre. For this important project Louis XIV summoned the leading European architect and sculptor of the day, Bernini, who had left his mark on Rome with a series of great Baroque buildings; but Bernini's plan to rebuild and complete the Louvre in Roman Baroque style did not find favour with Louis, and the building was finished off with an imposing colonnade designed by Claude Perrault, a doctor by profession (c. 1670). The classical style had asserted its dominance.

In a sense, however, this was merely a transitional phase. Even during the reign of Louis XIV, and more markedly in the reign of his successor Louis XV, this classical style developed into a new style, to which France once again gave its distinctive stamp – Rococo. (The word comes from the French *rocaille*, meaning a heap of small stones or shells.) It can be seen as a kind of "secret" Gothic – a Gothic response to the European Baroque; but however this may be, the Rococo style, starting from France, spread out over the whole of Europe.

In the reign of Louis XIII a hesitant beginning had been made (1626) with the building of a palace at Versailles; but Louis XIV developed this modest building by the addition of transverse and lateral wings into a huge palace 580 m long. From the outside Versailles, with the Chapel and the Hall of Mirrors, still has a classical aspect, but in the other apartments in the interior Charles Le Brun could give full rein to his passion for decoration; and the effect was completed by André Le Nôtre's landscaping of the park and gardens, providing a model which was imitated all over Europe.

The Rococo style is seen at its most characteristic in the Cabinet du Conseil in the Palace of Versailles. The architecture is bound up with the wall surfaces but at the same time breaks through them. The walls are covered with intricate mouldings and hung with swags and garlands, producing a lightness of effect which seems barely solid enough to support the heavy ceiling. The Hôtel de Soubise in Paris shows Rococo at its peak in the beautiful circular saloon, which seems both enclosed and open and is further embellished with paintings which are decorative and representational at the same time.

During this period *painting* came more prominently to the fore in France, with three outstanding names: Jean-Antoine Watteau, whose pictures reflect the life of his time with a sense of movement and a delicate grace which are hallmarks of Rococo art as a whole; François Boucher, who painted Mme de Pompadour and drew the cartoons for splendid tapestries; and Nicolas Poussin, the earliest of the three, who lived in Rome from 1624 onwards and was the finest exponent of a classical style which led into Rococo art with its scenes of pastoral life.

Return to the past. – The urge to move beyond Rococo and evolve new artistic forms led to a return to the severer style of antiquity, reproduced in the *Empire* style of Napoleon's reign. Much of the townscape of Paris centres on buildings of this period, like Chalgrin's Arc de Triomphe in the Place de l'Etoile and the smaller Arc de Triomphe du Carrousel (by Percier and Fontaine) in the outer courtyard of the Louvre. The intricately swirling decoration of Rococo now gave place to massive plain rectilinear structures based on Egyptian and Italian models – buildings of a clarity and austerity which were regarded as appropriate to an age of greatness.

With this rebirth of classicism was associated a romantic mood which later found expression in an enthusiasm for Gothic, now recognised as a French creation. This had consequences which were in some respects unfortunate, in that buildings in "Gothic" style, which could not be of any real quality, were erected at the turn of the 18th and 19th c. and some genuine Gothic buildings were subjected to restoration or enlargement, losing more than they gained in the process. The past, however glorious and however authentically French it might have been, could not be brought back to life.

The most fruitful achievements of this period were in the field of *painting.* Jacques-Louis David, the founder and finest representative of the French classical school, used themes from antiquity to express the ideas of the French Revolution, but departed from the strictness of the classical style to depict Napoleon's coronation in the Louvre. He was also the outstanding portrait-painter of his day. His pupil Jean-Dominique Ingres, whose work can be seen in the Ingres Museum in his home town of Montauban, ranks higher in the opinion of posterity. He painted mythological and religious subjects, but also portraits of women which give him a place among the leading artists in this field.

There was also a *Romantic school* of French painting. Goya, after his expulsion from Spain, spent the last few years of his life in France. The leading representative of this school in the first half of the 19th c., however, was Eugène Delacroix, whose work can best be understood in the light of his declaration that the true spirit of antiquity was to be found among the Arabs. Following Ingres, he depicted great events, but also did much genre painting. He set himself up as an opponent of classicism and claimed to be a naturalistic artist, but the nature he depicted was nature in classical style, in fancy dress, not the reality of life. With him was associated another artist who achieved world fame as a caricaturist but was also a fine painter – Honoré Daumier.

The later 19th century. – For French *architecture* the 19th c. was a period of stagnation after the great achievements of the past and the imposing buildings of the Napoleonic era. The buildings of this period merely reproduced inherited architectural forms. The Paris Opéra, designed by Charles Garnier, is in the Renaissance tradition. The churches of the time show little originality, though some – like the Sacré-Cœur in Montmartre – are widely known on other grounds. Perhaps the only 19th c. building that looked forward to the future was the Eiffel Tower (1887–89, by Alexandre-Gustave Eiffel).

In the field of *sculpture* two names overshadow all the others, though their work extended into the 20th c. – Auguste Rodin and Aristide Maillol.

Rodin, the whole of whose powerful *œuvre* is brought together in the Rodin Museum in Paris, is one of the great outstanding figures of French art. It has been said that he is the only 19th c. artist who can be mentioned in the same breath as Michelangelo.

Maillol, who survived Rodin by 27 years, evolved a new classical style, particularly in his figures of women.

French *painting* exerted a decisive influence on the rest of Europe, and indeed the world, during the 19th c. The Romantic school was followed by a new realism. The landscapes and portraits of young girls by Camille Corot form a bridge between the 18th and 19th c. In the early part of the century Daumier had opened up a new field of interest in his lithographs of ordinary people. His "Washerwoman" ("La Laveuse") in particular attracted much attention. Jean-François Millet followed with his "Man with the Hoe", "Gleaners" and "Winnowers". Gustave Courbet, the leading representative of the French *realist* school, painted his "Stone-Breakers" in 1851. The pictures of this period depict the life of the day, using themes which are entirely French. Often portraying the poorest of the poor, they have a social as well as an artistic intention.

Corot, Millet and Courbet did not evolve beyond this realist approach, and it was left to the next generation to break through into new ideas. In 1837 Louis-Jacques Daguerre had invented *photography*, the development of which during the 19th c. and down to the present day has constantly confronted painters with new possibilities and new challenges. For purely representational purposes photography was now available: it must be the artist's function to provide emphasis and interpretation.

In this sense Edouard Manet marked out new directions with his use of colour. Edgar Degas went one stage farther – at first following Ingres but later associated with the Impressionists.

Impressionism was the name given to the new style, originally – like "Gothic" in an earlier age – used in a pejorative sense to refer to painters who sought to record a fleeting impression by the use of colour. It is evidence of the fruitfulness of the cultural soil of the period that a whole series of great artists almost immediately came to the fore – Toulouse-Lautrec, painter of the "vie de bohème", whose work can be seen in the Toulouse-Lautrec Museum in Albi; Auguste Renoir, who followed the line marked out by Manet and yet remained within the tradition of Rococo; Camille Pissarro and Alfred Sisley, who concentrated on landscape painting.

The technique used by Pissarro of painting with small touches of colour was developed by Georges Seurat and Paul Signac into *Pointillism*, in which the paint was applied in small dots to create the picture, an impression remote from any idea of realism.

The works of the Impressionists can now be seen in the Musée du Jeu de Paume in Paris.

Soon, however, came a new generation of painters who made a still more radical break with the past. Paul Cézanne handled his subjects with sovereign independence, using them as the occasion for creating productive formal structures. This led him to the still-life. Cézanne's work moves even farther away from nature than that of his contemporaries: his pictures create a new reality which has no existence outside the painting. Paul Gauguin, who was influenced by Cézanne, went even farther in giving colour priority over reality, and left French reality in a physical sense by setting many of his pictures in the South Seas. Vincent van Gogh was a Dutchman who as a painter belongs to France; he was associated with Gauguin, and lived and worked in Provence.

"Van Gogh's bridge" near Arles

20th century art. – Modern art starts
with the formation of a group of painters
in Paris in 1905 who deliberately called
themselves the *"Fauves"* (the "Wild
Animals"). To this group, which gave
new impulses and new directions to
European art, belonged such great modern masters as Georges Rouault, André
Derain and Raoul Dufy. Of a rather
different kind was the work of Henri
Rousseau ("Douanier Rousseau"), who
initiated the school of naïve painting
which has remained fruitful into our own
day.

Pablo Picasso, a Spaniard, came to France
as a young man and spent the rest of his
life there, exerting a powerful influence on
French art in all the various "periods"
through which he passed. He abandoned
objective representation, preferring *ab-
stract painting* in which colour and form
were more important than the subject.
Fernand Léger and Georges Braque
followed a similar approach.

Sculpture by Picasso at Vallauris (Côte d'Azur)

The Grande Motte holiday centre (Languedoc-Roussillon)

Other painters took a different course, creating a new reality under the label of *Surrealism*. This group included the Russian-born Marc Chagall, who became fully integrated into the world of French art.

Contemporary French painting shows great variety, which can be appreciated in museums and art galleries all over France, from the little Museum of Modern Art at Céret in the Pyrenees to the splendid Museum of Modern Art in Paris. Among fashionable artists of recent years the name of Bernard Buffet may be mentioned.

In the field of *architecture* new methods of construction using concrete, steel and glass came increasingly to the fore after the First World War. The industrial buildings designed by Tony Garnier marked an epoch. A Swiss working in France, Le Corbusier (real name Charles Edouard Jeanneret), achieved world fame and found many imitators with such remarkable creations as the pilgrimage church at Ronchamp (near Belfort) and the "City Radieuse", a large block of flats in Marseilles. Modern architecture, like the holiday and recreation centre of La Grande Motte (Languedoc-Roussillon) with its dramatic pyramids of flats, shows a striving towards new forms adapted to the purpose they are intended to serve and fitting into the landscape in which they are situated. Other striking creations are the futuristic Centre Beaubourg, an uncompromisingly contemporary building set down in the heart of one of Paris's historic old quarters, and the imposing complex of tower blocks at "La Défense" on the outskirts of the city.

Photography had an influence on the development of painting: it also led to the emergence of an entirely new art form, the *cinema*. This is a field in which France can claim to have led the way. The first film show was put on by Auguste and Louis-Jean Lumière in Paris in 1894, and since then many French film directors have made great names for themselves. In the first half of this century there were René Clair, Jean Cocteau, Julien Duvivier and André Cayatte; in the late 1950s the "Nouvelle Vague" (New Wave) made a great stir, with such directors as Claude Chabrol, François Truffaut, Jean-Luc Godard and Louis Malle; and since then the French cinema has continued to play a leading role in Europe.

Literature

Surely no other nation in Europe has been so productive down the centuries in every field of literature as France. Down the centuries, too, French literature has always been closely related to the intellectual trends of the day, and has occupied an important place in the public and cultural life of the country.

The history of French literature can be traced back to the Carolingian period, in the "Strasbourg Oaths" (A.D. 842), the earliest document we possess written in the vernacular and not in Latin. In the Middle Ages there was a flowering of literature, represented mainly by the *troubadours* of southern France, who wrote in the southern *langue d'oc* (as opposed to the *langue d'oïl* from which modern French developed). Epic poetry reached a peak in the 12th c. with the "Chanson de Roland" ("Song of Roland"), the author of which is unknown. The *courtly romance* of the period is seen at its finest in the work of *Chrétien de Troyes* (c. 1135–c. 1183), who wrote mainly at the courts of Champagne and Flanders. Among his works was "Perceval li Gallois", a verse tale about the hero now perhaps better known as Parsifal.

The late medieval period is notable for the work of *Guillaume de Machaut* (1300–77), who blends poetry and music into a unified whole, and **François Villon** (1431–63), a new voice in French literature. From the 14th c., too, dates the earliest French play that has come down to us, "Les Miracles de Notre-Dame". In the 16th c. **François Rabelais** (1494–1553) continues the tradition of the medieval narrative tale but blends it with humanist ideas ("Pantagruel", "Gargantua"). The masterpiece of the humanist theatre is "Les Juives" by *Robert Garnier* (1544–90). *Jean de la Taille* worked out the rules which were to be the basis of the French classical theatre.

In the 17th c. the French *theatre* rose to a peak of creative achievement, with three outstanding figures whose work has lived on into our own day – Corneille, Racine and Molière. **Pierre Corneille** (1606–48) established the French classical drama, beginning with a comedy ("Mélite", 1630) and continuing with a tragi-comedy ("Le Cid" 1636) before reaching the full measure of his powers in "Horace" (1640) and "Polyeucte" (1642). The other great classical dramatist of the period was **Jean Racine** (1639–99), with works which are still popular today – "Andromaque" (1667), "Phèdre" (1677), "Iphigénie" (1675), etc. – dealing with themes from Greek mythological history. The comic masterpieces of **Molière** (actually *Jean-Baptiste Poquelin*, 1622–73) – "Tartuffe" (1664), "Don Juan" (1665), "Le Misanthrope" (1666), "L'Avare" (1668), "Le Bourgeois Gentilhomme" (1670) and "Le Malade Imaginaire" (1673) – still hold the stage in theatres throughout the world. – Towards the end of the century **Jean de la Fontaine** (1621–95) wrote his celebrated "Fables".

In philosophy the 17th c. is notable for the work of **René Descartes** (1595–1650: "Cogito, ergo sum"), who completed the process of freeing science and learning from its theological fetters, and *Blaise Pascal* (1623–62), in whom Christian piety was combined with philosophical power and mathematical insight.

In the 18th c. literature moved from the court at Versailles into the life of the city in Paris. Salons, clubs and coffee-houses became centres of literary life. The Physiocrats were a group of political thinkers who looked to *Montesquieu* (1689–1755), author of "L'Esprit des Lois", as their leader. The reputation and influence of French literature spread throughout Europe: **Voltaire** (*François-Marie Arouet*, 1694–1778) went to Berlin at the behest of Frederick the Great, *Denis Diderot* (1713–84) was summoned to Russia by the Empress Catherine II. *Rationalism* and tolerance became the foundations of intellectual life. Belief in the future and in the goodness of man was characteristic of the period (Jean-Jacques Rousseau, "Contrat social", 1762).

The theatre was represented by a very individual dramatist, *Pierre Carlet de Chamblain de Marivaux* (1688–1763), who broached social problems even in love stories ("La Surprise de l'amour", 1722; "Les Fausses confidences", 1737). Voltaire wrote dramas in the classical tradition. *Pierre-Augustin Caron de Beaumarchais* (1732–99) wrote comedies which were gay and profound at the same time ("The Barber of Seville", 1775; "The Marriage of Figaro", 1784). During the French Revolution the stage was mainly occupied by patriotic works, now little remembered.

With *Françoise-René de Chateaubriand* (1768–1848) and *Mme de Staël* (1766–1817) *Romanticism* made its appearance in French literature. The novel, which was believed by the writers of the day to be particularly well adapted to the expression of romantic feelings and world-weariness, was the commonest literary product of the period after the French Revolution.

The novel of the Romantic period was characterised by a strong lyrical element and by autobiographical features. *Alfred de Musset, George Sand, Alphonse de Lamartine, Victor Hugo* ("Notre-Dame de Paris", 1831) and the elder *Alexandre Dumas* ("The Three Musketeers", 1844) are typical of this phase. A more personal style is shown by *Stendhal* (1783–1842), author of "Le Rouge et le Noir" (1830) and "La Chartreuse de Parme" (1839), who attached great importance to sensibility and restrained the expression of feeling. The novels of **Honoré de Balzac** (1799–1850) are already realistic in tone ("Le Père Goriot", 1835; "Les Illusions perdues", 1839). *Prosper Mérimée* (1803–70) is a master of the short story ("Carmen", 1845).

In poetry **Victor Hugo** (1802–85) dominates the whole of the 19th c. *Alfred de Musset* (1810–57) also wrote immortal poems. Both also wrote for the theatre (Hugo, "Cromwell", 1827, "Hernani", 1830, "Ruy Blas", 1838; Musset, "Lorenzaccio", 1834). The philosopher *Auguste Comte* (1796–1857) founded positivism and laid the foundations of sociology ("Cours de philosophie positive", 1830–42).

In the middle of the 19th c. the "art for art's sake" school ("L'Art pour l'art": Théophile Gautier, 1811–72) reflected a reaction against Romanticism. Under the influence of **Gustave Flaubert** (1821–80; "Madame Bovary", 1857) *realism* asserted itself. **Emile Zola** (1840–1902) at first fell in with the new trend ("Thérèse Raquin"), but then moved towards naturalism. **Charles Baudelaire** (1821–67), a sensitive poet ("Les Fleurs du mal"), also gave fresh

vigour to art criticism. In the theatre the intricately plotted comedy (Labiche) and the comedy of manners ("La Dame aux Camélias", by Alexandre Dumas the younger) were popular.

The great masters of *naturalism* were *Emile Zola* ("L'Assommoir" and other novels in the Rougon-Macquart cycle) and *Guy de Maupassant* (1850–93; "Bel-Ami", 1885, "Une Vie", 1883). *Alphonse Daudet* (1840–97) remained faithful to realism and also wrote humorous novels and short tales ("Tartarin de Tarascon", 1872). *Jules Renard* (1864–1910) was a forerunner of *Impressionism*, to which two major writers, *Anatole France* (1844–1924) and *Romain Rolland* (1866–1944) also gave their allegiance. The principal poets of the period were **Paul Verlaine** (1844–96; "Les Fêtes galantes", 1869) and *Arthur Rimbaud* (1854–91). Towards the end of the century *Stéphane Mallarmé* (1842–98) became a leader of the Symbolists, among whom was Francis Jammes (1868–1938). The stage was dominated by the boulevard theatres. *Alfred Jarry* (1873–1907) wrote a satirical farce ("Ubu Roi", 1896) which carried broad humour to the epic level. *Paul Claudel* (1868–1955) combined historical events and timeless happenings with the grotesque and the burlesque ("L'Annonce faite à Marie", 1912).

Between the two world wars there was an overwhelming profusion of different movements and trends. Poetry went in for Surrealism, while the novel developed in extravagant profusion; the theatre remained, on the whole, traditional.

The outstanding novelists of this period were **Marcel Proust** (1871–1922; "A la Recherche du temps perdu", 1913–27) and **André Gide** (1869–1951; "Les Caves du Vatican", 1914). Alongside them was a spectrum ranging from *François Mauriac* ("Thérèse Desqueyroux", 1927), a writer of Catholic inspiration, to *André Malraux* ("La Condition humaine", 1933), from *Henry de Montherlant* to *Antoine de Saint-Exupéry*, who wrote novels about his own adventures as a pilot ("Vol de nuit", 1931), from *Henri Troyat* to *André Maurois*, *Marcel Aymé* ("La Jument verte", 1933), *Albert Camus* ("La Peste", "L'Etranger") and *Pierre Benoit* ("Montsalvat" and "L'Atlantide").

In poetry *Tristan Tzara* (1896–1963) and other adepts founded *Dadaism* (1918). *André Breton* (1896–1966) was the leader of the Surrealists – *Paul Eluard* ("Guernica", 1938), *Louis Aragon, René Char*. On the fringes of Surrealism were two independent figures, *Jean Cocteau* (1889–1963) and *Blaise Cendrars* (1887–1961).

The theatre was dominated by **Jean Giraudoux** (1882–1944; "La Guerre de Troie n'aura pas lieu", 1935, "Electre", 1937), who sought to "exorcise" the tragic action by humour and wit.

The years after the Second World War were remarkably productive for the French theatre, which was given new ideas and new impulses by **Jean Anouilh** ("Antigone", 1944), *Henry de Montherlant* ("La Reine morte", 1942), *Albert Camus* ("Caligula", 1945) and above all **Jean-Paul Sartre**, the founder of existentialist philosophy ("Les Mouches", 1944; "La Putain respectueuse", 1946; "Les Mains sales", 1948). Leading exponents of the French "Nouveau Théâtre" were *Eugène Ionesco* ("Les Rhinocéros", 1960) and the Irish-born *Samuel Beckett* ("Waiting for Godot", 1953).

Music

In the field of *serious music* France has for the most part tended to be overshadowed by the music of Germany and Austria, although it has a great tradition of its own. Nevertheless, a whole range of orchestral and chamber works and a number of operas have outlived their own time and won an established place in the concert halls and opera-houses of the world.

After the emergence of *polyphony* in the 9th c. and its gradual development and refinement between the 12th and 15th c., *Josquin des Prés* (*c.*1440–*c.*1521) broke out of the old structures at the beginning of the 16th c. and developed a new musical language. He is probably the earliest French composer whose works are still regularly performed. In the 17th c. there was a great flowering of French music, with *Jean-Baptiste Lully* (1632–87), who wrote ballets and operas, *Marc-Antoine Charpentier* ("Te Deum", with the so-called "Eurovision fanfare") and *François Campra. Jean-Philippe Rameau* (1687–1764) and **François Couperin** (1626–61) dominated the decades after Lully's death. Between Rameau's death and the early works of Hector Berlioz, however, French music merely marked time, and foreign composers such as the German *Christoph Willibald Gluck*, the Italian *Luigi Cherubini* and the Belgian-born *André Grétry* (1742–1813) dominated the musical scene in Paris.

With **Hector Berlioz** (1803–69), one of the founders of "programme music", *Romanticism* came to the fore in French music. His "Symphonie Fantastique", "Harold in Italy" and "Romeo and Juliet" symphony (with choir and soloists) are still among the most popular works in the symphonic repertoire. His operas – "Damnation of Faust", "Benvenuto Cellini", "The Trojans", "Beatrice and Benedick" – are relatively seldom performed. The same fate has befallen the "grand" operas of Spontini, Auber, Halévy and Meyerbeer, but the comic operas of *Esprit Auber* ("Fra Diavolo") and *Adolphe Adam* ("Le Postillon de Longjumeau", "Si j'étais Roi") have worn better. The best known opera of the 19th c. is "Carmen" (1875), by **Georges Bizet** (1838–75), still one of the most popular operas in the repertoire. The lyrical tragic operas of *Charles Gounod* ("Faust", "Mireille"), *Jules Massenet* ("Manon", "Werther"), *Ambroise Thomas* ("Mignon"), *Léo Delibes* ("Lakmé"), *Gustave Charpentier* ("Louise") and *Edouard Lalo* ("Le Roi d'Ys") are – with a few exceptions – little known outside France.

Under the Second Empire the *operetta* developed alongside the opera. **Jaques Offenbach** (1819–80), who was born in Cologne, became the very symbol of French *esprit* and Parisian *joie de vivre* ("Orpheus in the Underworld", "La Vie parisienne", "La Périchole"). – Even before the time of Lully and Rameau the French were fond of dancing and *ballet*, and in the 19th c. imperishable contributions to the repertoire of ballet were made by Léo Delibes ("Coppélia", "Sylvia") and Adolphe Adam ("Giselle"). – In instrumental music there were the Belgian-born *César Franck* (1822–90), who had a number of followers (d'Indy, Chausson), and *Camille Saint-Saëns* (symphonies, piano, violin and cello concertos, "Carnival of Animals", "Samson and Delilah").

At the beginning of the 20th c. France's musical life was dominated by the *Impressionists* **Claude Debussy** (1862–1918), who composed orchestral works ("La Mer", "Printemps", "Jeux", "Nocturnes", "Images"), works for the piano ("Préludes", "Estampes", "Images"), chamber music and an opera ("Pelléas et Mélisande"), and **Maurice Ravel** (1875–1937), who wrote orchestral works ("Boléro", "La Valse", "Daphnis et Chloé"), piano concertos and other works for the piano, and chamber music. *Gabriel Fauré* (1845–1924) composed delicate chamber music and church music ("Requiem"). *Albert Roussel* (1869–1937) is remembered mainly for his brilliantly orchestrated ballet "Bacchus et Ariane", *Paul Dukas* (1865–1935) for a symphonic work, "The Sorcerer's Apprentice", and a ballet, "La Péri".

Around 1920 the Paris *"Groupe des Six"* turned against the Impressionist influence. The principal representatives of this group were *Erik Satie, Francis Poulenc, Darius Milhaud* and the Swiss composer *Arthur Honegger*. Among composers who remained active during the post-war years were *Olivier Messiaen* (piano and organ music, song cycles, exotic-sounding orchestral music), *Henri Dutilleux* and *André Jolivet*.

The composer and conductor **Pierre Boulez** (b. 1925) is the principal representative of *serial music* in France. He is also head of the Institut de Recherche et de Coordination acoustique/musique (IRCAM) in Paris, which is concerned with *experimental music*.

French *folk music* also merits a few words. Its traditions are still very much alive, and every part of the country has its own songs and dances, often hundreds of years old. At folk festivals and on various family and religious occasions the old tunes are still sung and played. The variety of rhythms and melodies – and of the instruments used – is remarkable, extending from the brass bands of Alsace to the Provençal *farandole*, from the Basque male voice choirs to the Celtic music of Brittany (often with bagpipes), from the Catalan *sardana* of Roussillon to the songs and dances of Auvergne.

In the field of *light music* France has developed the *chanson* into a major musical genre, which can claim an ancestry reaching back into medieval times. Singers like *Edith Piaf, Jacques Brel* (a Belgian), *Yves Montand, Gilbert Bécaud, Charles Aznavour, Léo Ferré* and *Charles Trénet* are known far beyond the bounds of France.

Economy and Communications

The two main pillars of the French economy are industry and agriculture. Although agriculture still employs almost a quarter of the population, its contribution to the national income is steadily decreasing. Some 40% of the gross national product now comes from industry and only 5% from agriculture.

Agricultural land makes up 60% of the country's total area, 53% being arable land. A further 25% is covered by forests. Most of the arable crops (wheat, barley, oats, maize and sugar-beet) are produced in the northern part of the country; the south produces wine, rice, fruit and vegetables, olives, flowers and citrus fruits. France is the world's largest wine-producing country after Italy, with an annual output of 60 million hectolitres from its 1·4 million hectares of vineyards. The main wine-growing areas are Burgundy, the south-west (round Bordeaux), the Rhône valley, the Loire valley, the Mediterranean region, Champagne and Alsace.

More than half the country's agricultural output comes from *stock-farming*, which yields meat (principally beef, poultry and mutton), milk and dairy products such as butter and cheese, together with wool, skins and hides. The main stock-farming areas are the north-west, the Massif Central and the Alps.

The scale of French *agriculture* can be indicated by a few figures. France produces 15% of the total world crop of apples (mostly the "Golden Delicious" variety) – more than either Italy or the United States. It ranks more or less equal with Italy in the production of grapes, with just under 20% of the world crop. It has 23 million cattle, including 10 million dairy cows, 10 million sheep and 200 million head of poultry. It also has 435,000 horses, more than any other country in Western or Central Europe.

Nevertheless, French agriculture still suffers to a considerable extent from insufficient mechanisation, and horses and oxen are still not uncommonly found drawing carts or ploughs. The individualism of the French peasant makes it more difficult to organise the communal use of modern equipment for which a single farm is not large enough. Frequently, too, holdings are abandoned altogether because the older generation is no longer able to run them and the younger members of the family have moved to the towns. Thus France has still to import some agricultural produce, although it has the land and the climatic conditions which would enable it to feed itself: indeed livestock and foodstuffs are among France's principal imports.

The French *fisheries* are mainly based on the Atlantic and North Sea coasts. Fish and all kinds of seafood (shellfish, oysters, crustaceans) play an important part in French cuisine. Total landings in 1977 were 916,000 tonnes.

The *minerals* of most importance to the French economy are coal, iron ore and bauxite, but France produces other minerals as well. Oil and natural gas (80,000 km of mains) make a major contribution to the country's *power supply*, 35% of which is provided by hydroelectric and some 10% by nuclear energy.

Outside Paris the principal industrial regions with their coalfields and iron mines have maintained their position. Lorraine is of more importance for its iron ore than for its coal, producing as it does

A succulent catch, Martigues (near Marseilles)

Oyster-bed, Ile de Ré (off La Rochelle)

A notable feature of the French economy is the concentration of industry and commerce in the Paris conurbation. At the beginning of the 19th c. there were, for example, 65 carpet factories in Paris, 70 cabinetmakers, 166 clockmakers, 108 perfume factories and 72 factories making artificial flowers; and Paris is still France's largest producer as well as largest consumer. Industrial firms not based in Paris like to have at least an office in the city, and the headquarters of the banks and wholesalers are in Paris as a matter of course. Paris accounts for a quarter of French industrial production and a quarter of the country's commercial turnover, and some of the country's industries are almost exclusively concentrated in and around the city – for example clothing, fashion goods, printing and publishing, perfume manufacture and leather goods. The commercial activities which promote the development of the economy are also centred in Paris; and this remains true of industries like metal-working, chemicals and clothing which are steadily expanding. Paris, with a sixth of the whole population of France, has a quarter of the population engaged in commerce (though only a fifth of those employed in industry).

more than nine-tenths of France's iron. The most important of the French coal-fields extends from Valenciennes to the Pas-de-Calais. The principal French exports are iron and steel, textiles of all kinds, motor vehicles and machinery, agricultural produce and wine, perfumes and cosmetics.

Some 40% of the population are engaged in commerce, the professions and the service trades and another 40% are employed in *industry*. The main industrial exports are machinery and motor vehicles, particularly cars. Two French car firms are among the 50 largest industrial enterprises in the world – Renault, in 27th place (ahead of Mercedes and Volkswagen), and Peugeot-Citroën in 45th place. The textile, chemical and electrical industries have also developed, in line with French economic growth generally (44% up between 1969 and 1976). This growth was achieved in spite of much loss of working time by industrial disputes: in 1976, for example, the number of working days lost by strikes in France was some nine times as much as in the German Federal Republic, and considerably higher than in Britain. Between 1971 and 1978 the French consumer price index rose from 69 to 131 (Britain 59 to 146, Germany 78 to 112). The rise in prices between 1977 and 1978 (9.2%) was lower than in Britain, Denmark and Italy but higher than in Belgium, Holland, Austria, Germany and Switzerland. The gross domestic product per head is higher than in Holland, Austria, Britain and Italy but lower than in Germany, the Scandinavian countries and Switzerland.

French *imports* and *exports* are in reasonable balance with one another, imports in 1978 being valued at 64,215 million European units of account and exports at 60,118 million. (The corresponding figures for the United Kingdom were 61,638 million and 56,090 million, for the German Federal Republic 95,405 million and 111,340 million.) French exports to the United Kingdom in 1978 were valued at 4715 million EUA, French imports from the United Kingdom at 3536 million.

Although the French economy is linked with the economies of its EEC partners there are of course significant variations between the different countries, based on differing circumstances or on the measures taken by national governments. Thus France has a higher unemployment rate (5.3% in 1978) than Germany (3.9%) but a lower rate than the United Kingdom (5.7%). The burden of taxes and social contributions is higher than in the United Kingdom but lower than in Germany – though it is notoriously difficult in this field to be sure that like is being compared with like. Compared with the United Kingdom, France has a relatively high proportion of private cars to population (315 per 1000 in 1977 compared with 254 per 1000), though a lower proportion than Germany (326 per 1000). (The production of private cars was also higher – 3·5 million in France, 1·3 million in the United Kingdom.)

France has a very extensive *road system*, with a total length of 784,000 km, compared with 347,000 km in the United Kingdom. Like the United Kingdom, it was a late starter in the development of motorways but now has a motorway network of some 4200 km (United Kingdom 2300 km). This ample provision, combined with the concentration of traffic in and around Paris, means that throughout most of the country – excluding particular areas and certain peak periods – French roads are relatively uncrowded, as the visiting motorist will discover to his pleasure.

The French *railway system*, reflecting the size of the country, is more extensive than that of the United Kingdom – 34,150 km compared with 17,980 km. In relation to area, however, it is actually lower – 62·5 km per 1000 sq. kilometres compared with 73·7. In proportion to the length of the network the French railways carry slightly fewer passengers and significantly more goods than those of the United Kingdom.

French *air services* flew 322 million km in the year 1978. International services are predominantly centred on Paris with its three airports (Roissy, Orly and Le Bourget).

France has a *merchant shipping* fleet of something over 11½ million GRT (1977), roughly the same as Italy but far short of the United Kingdom (31½ million GRT), Norway and Greece. Its tanker fleet (7½ million tons) is about half that of the United Kingdom (14·8 million tons) but more than twice that of Germany (3½ million tons). The largest French ports are Marseilles, with a turnover of 109·5 million tonnes, and Le Havre (84·1 million tonnes). France's inland shipping fleet is relatively large (5125 vessels), but its total capacity is relatively low (1·96 million tons), as is the total quantity of goods carried (86·8 million tonnes). France's inland waterways have a total length of 14,000 km (rivers 9000 km, canals 5000 km).

Château d'If, Marseilles Bay

Tourism now makes a major contribution to the French economy. In 1978 26,846,000 foreign visitors came to France, with a total of 243,348,000 bed-nights, and spent more than 24,000 million francs. This represented an increase of 3·2% in the number of visitors and 9·7% in the amount of revenue over 1977. The French government has gone to considerable lengths to promote the development of tourism. In particular it has extended the motorway network and developed a whole series of large modern holiday centres on the coast of Languedoc-Roussillon and in Aquitaine.

Charles de Gaulle Airport, Roissy

New winter sports centres, too, have mushroomed in recent years, opening up large areas in Savoy and the southern Alps. Certain places, however – Paris, the Côte d'Azur, Provence – remain the great tourist magnets, although there are always fresh discoveries to be made in the less frequented parts of the country. And no one can hope to get anything like a comprehensive view of the country in a single visit: France is so large, so varied and so full of treasures of all kinds that there are fresh delights to be discovered on every visit.

Apart from its scenery and its artistic and cultural treasures, too, France offers the attractions of its food and drink. It is the gourmet's paradise, but its appeal is to every visitor. The appreciation of a good glass of wine and a well-cooked meal is not confined to the upper stratum of society: it is found in all classes of the population and is an essential component in the French art of living.

Nor is France such an expensive country to visit as is sometimes thought. Those who want luxury hotels and five-star restaurants must expect to have to pay accordingly; but there are plenty of good and comfortable hotels at very reasonable prices, and excellent meals are to be had everywhere at prices which compare favourably with the cost of comparable meals in Britain or most other Western countries. Certainly in terms of value for money the tourist in France need have no reason to complain about the cost of his accommodation or his meals; and good drinking wine is available everywhere at prices which will undoubtedly appeal to the highly taxed foreign wine-drinker.

Finally, no visitor need be put off by the language barrier. Even the most modest attempts at speaking French will be appreciated by those you come into contact with, and some knowledge of the language will add to your enjoyment of the trip; but the French are accustomed to foreign visitors, and even total ignorance of the French language is no barrier to enjoyment of the pleasures which France and the French way of life can offer.

France
A to Z

St-Ouen, Rouen

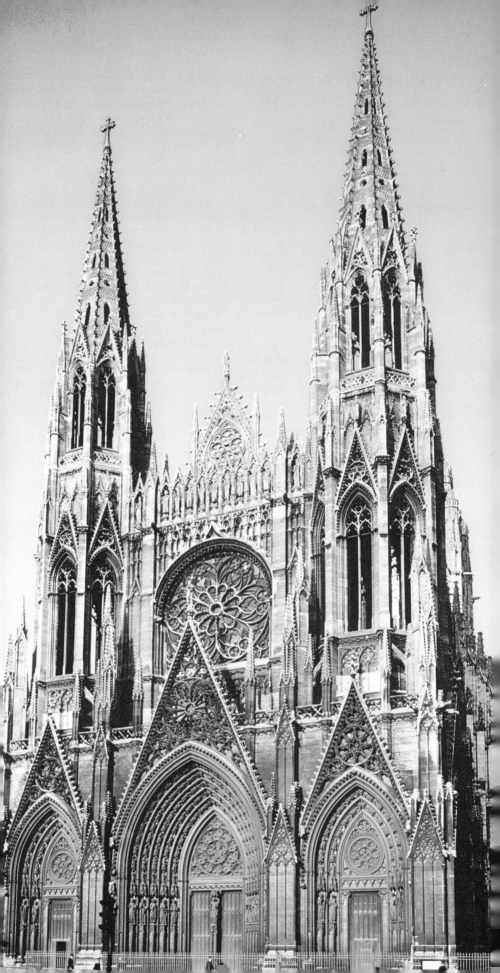

Aix-en-Provence

Region: Provence–Alpes–Côte d'Azur.
Department: Bouches-du-Rhône.
Altitude: 177 m. – Population: 144,000.
Post code: F-13100. – Dialling code: 91.

ⓘ **Office Municipal de Tourisme,**
Place de la Libération;
tel. 26 02 93.

HOTELS. – *Roy René*, I, 64 r.; *P.L.M. Le Pigonnet*, I, 50 r., on road to Marseilles; *Thermes Sextius*, II, 65 r.; *Le Manoir*, II, 52 r.; *Campra*, II, 55 r.; *Paul Cézanne*, II, 44 r.; *Novotel*, II, 80 r., Arc-de-Meyran; *Novotel*, 97 r., Beaumanoir; *Le Pasteur*, III, 20 r.; *Moderne*, III, 22 r.; *Splendid*, IV, 13 r.; *Concorde*, III, 26 r.; *Le Prieuré*, IV, 26.

EVENTS. – *International Musical Festival* (July–Aug.); *Saison d'Aix*, with open-air performances (June to beginning of Sept.).

The old capital of Provence, whose name comes from the Provençal Ais, has managed to preserve something of its typically 17th and 18th c. aspect. It lies N of the Rhône in a plain surrounded by hills, and has an attractive and imposing main street, the Cours Mirabeau, lined with plane-trees. With its university, its archbishop and its international musical festival, it is still the intellectual centre of Provence.

Apart from the thermal springs (recommended for nervous and gynaecological conditions), which have been frequented since Roman times, and its attractions as a tourist centre, Aix's economy depends on the processing of almonds for use in cakes and confectionery, in which it occupies probably the leading position in Europe.

HISTORY. – The origins of the town go back to 122 B.C., when the Roman consul Sextius established a camp near the thermal springs, calling it *Aquae Sextiae*. Twenty years later the Roman general Marius routed an army of Teutons who were advancing on Italy not far from the town. After suffering severely during the great migrations and from Saracen raids Aix enjoyed a period of prosperity during the Middle Ages as capital of the County of Provence, particularly under King René of Naples (1409–80). The town became a centre of Provençal literature, and the University was founded in 1409. In 1486 Aix passed to the French crown, and was given its distinctive architectural aspect by extensive building activity in the 17th and 18th c. The Revolutionary statesman Mirabeau (1749–91) had close associations with the town, as had the painter Paul Cézanne (1839–1906), who was born and died here. The rise of Marseilles in the 19th c. led to a temporary decline in the importance of Aix.

SIGHTS. – The town's main axis is the *Cours Mirabeau*, a shady avenue lined with plane-trees which was laid out in the 17th c. on the line of the old town walls. At intervals along the middle of the street are three fountains, including one (opposite Rue Clemenceau) with water at a temperature of 34 °C. The central point of the town is the *Place de l'Hôtel de Ville*, with the **Town Hall** (1652–68); the flower market is held in the square. Close by is the *Clock Tower* (1510). On the first floor of the Town Hall is the Méjanes Library (300,000 volumes), one of the finest in France. There are numerous aristocratic mansions of the 17th and early 18th c. in the Cours Mirabeau, Rue Espariat, Rue Gaston-de-Saporta and *Place d'Albertas*. In one of these, the Hôtel Estienne de St-Jean (17 rue Gaston-de-Saporta), is the *Musée du Vieil Aix*, with much interesting material on the history of the town.

N of the Town Hall, in *Place de l'Université* at the end of Rue Gaston-de-Saporta, is the *Cathedral* (*St-Sauveur*), with the cloister of the former monastic house. The architecture of the Cathedral shows a mingling of styles ranging over more than a thousand years, from the 5th to the 16th c.

The carved walnut doors (1505–08) of the main entrance will be opened up by the verger on request. – The INTERIOR is like a museum: the outstanding items are the *triptych of the Burning Bush (in the nave, on right), by Nicolas Froment, court painter to King René (c. 1476) and 15 Flemish *tapestries (1511) with scenes from the Passion and the life of the Virgin. The *baptistery*, to the right, is the oldest part of the church (5th c.). The little Romanesque *cloister* (12th c.) adjoining the Cathedral is notable for its elegance and lightness.

Aix's first Gothic building was the church of **St-Jean-de-Malte** (end of 13th c.), which has a spire 67 m high. The 17th c. church of **Ste-Marie-Madeleine**, with a modern façade, contains a beautiful triptych of the Annunciation (c. 1440) and, in the fourth chapel on the S side, an 18th c. marble Virgin.

The town's numerous museums include the *Granet Museum** (archaeology and art), one of the finest collections of the kind in France. It contains excavated material from the nearby Celtic settlement of Entremont, destroyed in 123 B.C. (the site can be visited) and pictures by French painters, including Granet and Cézanne. – *Cézanne's studio* is to the N of the town, in Avenue Paul-Cézanne (reached by way of Avenue Pasteur and Avenue Violette). It has been preserved as it was at the time

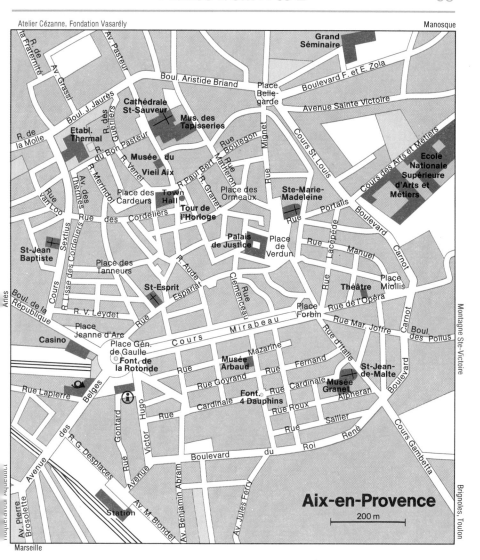

Atelier Cézanne, Fondation Vasarély   Manosque

Aix-en-Provence

200 m

of the painter's death in 1906. – The *Arbaud Museum*, in Rue du 4-Septembre, is devoted to the folk art of Provence. – The *Tapestry Museum* (Musée des Tapisseries), in the former Archbishop's Palace (Rue Gaston-de-Saporta), contains valuable tapestries, including 19 works from Beauvais. – The *Vasarély Foundation*, 2 km W of the town (near Cézanne's studio), consists of a group of buildings 87 m long. It was established by the artist himself between 1973 and 1976, and contains typical examples of his work.

SURROUNDINGS. – 14 km W is the *Roquefavour Aqueduct* (375 m long, 82 m high), built in the mid 19th c. to supply water to Marseilles.

6 km SW is *Les Milles*, with a château designed by L'Enfant (18th c.) and a park.

12 km NE is the 17th c. *Château de Vauvenargues*, which belonged to Picasso, with his grave on the terrace (not open to visitors).

Ajaccio

Region: Corsica.
Department: Corse du Sud.
Altitude: 0–18 m. – Population: 50,000.
Post code: F-20000. – Dialling code: 95.
ⓘ **Office de Tourisme**, Hotel de Ville,
     Avenue Serafini;
     tel. 21 40 87.

HOTELS. – *Castel Vecchio*, II, 100 r.; *Fesch*, II, 77 r.; *Impérial*, II, 60 r.; *Costa*, II, 53 r.; *Etrangers*, II, 46 r.; *Mouettes*, III, 18 r. – *Eden Roc*, II, 30 r., *Iles Sanguinaires*, II, 60 r., *Cala di Sole*, II, 36 r., *Dolce Vita*, II, 34 r., all on the Route de la Parata. – *Campo dell'Oro*, I, 140 r., 7 km E of the town, at the airport. – *Rallye*, II, 54 r., 6 km NE of the town in Mezzavia.

**The Corsican capital, Ajaccio (pro-
nounced Azhaksió in French, Ayácho
in Italian), lies half-way down the W
coast of the island in the gulf of the
same name, surrounded by mountains which have a covering of snow**

The harbour, Ajaccio

right into summer. The town was founded by the Genoese in 1492, and in 1811 was made capital of the island by Napoleon, replacing Bastia. As Corsica's second largest port Ajaccio carries a substantial part of the traffic to the island. In addition to its situation its attractions include a mild climate (average winter temperature 11·3 °C) and a fine sandy beach nearby.

SIGHTS. – The *Maison Bonaparte, Napoleon's birthplace (Rue St-Charles), dates from the early part of the 17th c. Napoleon was born here on 15 August 1769, but the layout of the interior dates from the end of the 18th c. There is also a *Musée Napoléonien* in the Town Hall, mainly containing material on the history of the period. Other evidence of the continuing importance of Napoleon in Ajaccio are a statue of the Emperor, a group showing Napoleon with his four brothers, a statue of the First Consul and the material displayed in the *Palais Fesch.*

The town's main street is called the Cours Napoléon. The *Cathedral*, in the Venetian Renaissance style of the second half of the 16th c., also contains mementoes of Napoleon. The *Citadel* in the old town (not open to visitors) dates from the same period as the Cathedral.

SURROUNDINGS. – 4 km W is **Monte Salario** (311 m). – 12 km W is *Cap de la Parata.

Albi

Region: Midi-Pyrénées.
Department: Tarn.
Altitude: 174 m. – Population: 50,000.
Post code: F-81000. – Dialling code: 63.
ⓘ **Office de Tourisme,**
19 Place Ste-Cécile;
tel. 54 22 30.

HOTELS. – *St-Antoine*, II, 56 r.; *Chiffre*, II, 42 r.; *Orléans*, III, 68 r.; *Cantepeau*, III, 33 r.; *Relais Gascon*, IV, 15 r.; *La Régence*, IV, 15 r.

EVENTS. – *Theatre Festival* (July); *International Amateur Film Festival* (August); *Musical Festival* (August).

This treasurehouse of art lies at a bend in the Tarn between the Garonne plain and the foothills of the Massif Central, 75 km NE of Toulouse. With its brick-built Cathedral, large squares, gardens and Renaissance façades it creates an effect of harmony and grandeur. It was the birthplace of the painter Toulouse-Lautrec.

HISTORY. – Since the 13th c. the name of Albi has been associated with the persecuted Albigensian sect. The town's name is of Celtic origin, and there was a *Civitas Albiensium* here before the Christian era. After suffering many vicissitudes under the Romans, the Visigoths and the Saracens Albi came into the hands of Charles the Bald in 843. The Albigensian wars of 1209–29 led to the almost total annihilation of the ascetic Albigensian sect. The town became the see of a bishop, and in 1679 of an archbishop, and its reputation as a centre of artistic achievement was mainly confined to the religious field until Toulouse-Lautrec added a new note in the latter part of the 19th c.

SIGHTS. – The dominant architectural feature of the town, and of the whole Tarn valley, is the **Cathedral** (*Ste-Cécile*), begun in 1282 and consecrated in 1480, a massive structure which is one of the great achievements of the brick-built Gothic of southern France. The nave is almost 100 m long, 20 m wide and 30 m high; its defensive walls tower to a height of 41 m.

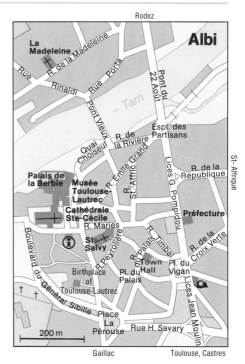

Albi Cathedral

The INTERIOR contains the largest *rood-screen* in France (*c*. 1500), a fresco of the Last Judgment and, in the choir, Old and New Testament figures dating from the same period.

To the N of the Cathedral, standing above the Tarn, is the fortified *Palais de la Berbie* (13th and 14th c.), formerly the Archbishop's Palace. It now houses the *Musée Toulouse-Lautrec*, which contains numerous paintings, drawings and lithographs by the Albi-born artist (1864–1901), together with over 200 works by his contemporaries, including Degas, Rodin, Maillol, Matisse and Rouault.

There are also magnificent *views of the Tarn valley and the bridge from the second Toulouse-Lautrec room on the right and from the terrace gardens.

The real centre of the town is the *Place du Vigan*, from which Rue Timbal runs NW, with the *Hôtel Reynès* (1530) and other old buildings. To the W of the square are the 16th c. **Town Hall** and the church of *St-Salvy* (12th–15th c.), adjoined by a 13th c. cloister. – The **Pont Vieux** (Old Bridge) over the Tarn dates from 1035.

SURROUNDINGS. – 24 km NW is **Cordes**, a walled medieval town with 13th and 14th c. Gothic houses and a market hall of 1350 with a fine timber roof. This very picturesque little town is now a settlement of artists and craftsmen.

Alsace

*Alsace, lying on the frontier between France and Germany, was for many centuries a source of dispute between the two countries. It is part of the Upper Rhine Plain, which extends from the latitude of Basle to that of Bingen. It occupies the south-western corner of the low-lying area created by the downfaulting of a rift valley and bounded on the German side by the Black Forest and on the French by the Vosges, and consists of the two departments of

Wine grapes, Alsace

Bas-Rhin and Haut-Rhin. Thanks to the shelter afforded by the bordering hills it is a region of great fertility, particularly favourable to the growing of vines, which give much of Alsace its characteristic pattern. While the Vosges rise to heights of over 1400 m, the part of Alsace whose character is determined by the Rhine is a region of flat country and lower hills extending to the edge of the Vosges, the western side of which is no longer in Alsace.

Surprisingly for a region so conveniently accessible from three countries – France, Germany and Switzerland – Alsace is a less popular tourist area than some other parts of France. Its charmingly situated little wine towns and villages frequently offer standards of cuisine well above the average, but its hotel resources are relatively limited.

The ideal way of getting to know Alsace, with its picturesque villages and towns, is to follow the *Route du Vin d'Alsace*, which pursues an attractive winding course, roughly parallel to N 83, from Strasbourg to Thann (just W of Mulhouse), and also has a northward extension into the Wissembourg area. The wine-growing region extends for a distance of 120 km and over some 100 communes, and its 12,000 hectares of vineyards produce 100 million bottles of wine annually. Within the wine-growing area are Alsace's two largest towns, both notable for their artistic treasures – **Strasbourg** and **Colmar**. The city of Strasbourg has its industrial counterpart in **Mulhouse**, so that the region has two large cities set in a landscape which is predominantly green.

HISTORY. – The Upper Rhine Plain was settled by man many thousands of years before the Christian era. Around 1000 B.C. Celtic influence began to make itself felt, but Caesar's victory over Ariovistus and his Suebi in 58 B.C. put an end to Celtic dominance and established the authority of Rome. The Roman peace, inaugurated by Augustus in 17 B.C, afforded the region 500 years of quiet and steady development. Around A.D. 300 the Romans introduced the vine into Alsace and began to produce wine. In 443 the name of Alsace (*Elisaza*, "those who live beyond the Rhine") came into use. The name was applied to the Alemanni, who had advanced from this region and were subjugated by the Franks in 496. The kingdom of the Franks fell to pieces after the death of Charlemagne, and under the treaty of Verdun in 843 Alsace, along with the central part of the kingdom, passed to Lothair. In 925 it became part of the duchy of Swabia.

In 1262 Strasbourg became an imperial city, but in 1354, along with Mulhouse, it remained outside the league formed by ten Alsatian imperial cities. In the 1520s the Reformation came to Alsace, followed soon afterwards by peasant wars and from 1568 onwards by the Catholic Counter-Reformation. – At the end of the Thirty Years War, under the Treaty of Westphalia, the Sundgau in southern Alsace and the ten allied imperial cities passed to France, and were followed 25 years later by the rest of Alsace, with the exception of Strasbourg and Mulhouse. In 1681 Louis XIV annexed Strasbourg to France, but the university (at which Goethe later studied) remained German. In 1515 Mulhouse was admitted to the Swiss Confederation.

The French Revolution, by creating the departments of Haut-Rhin and Bas-Rhin, bound Alsace more firmly to France, and in 1798 Mulhouse also became part of France. The Franco-Prussian war of 1870–71 led to the incorporation of Alsace into Prussia, and consequently into the German Empire; but the Prussian way of life did not appeal to the people of Alsace, so that after the First World War it became French again, and since then – with the exception of four years during the Second World War (1940–44) – it has remained so.

Since the Second World War, with Strasbourg as the headquarters of the Council of Europe and other European institutions, Alsace has played an important part in the move towards a united Europe: it is no longer coveted by France and Germany, but rather serves to bind the two countries together. Names like the poet Gottfried von Strassburg, the architect Erwin von Steinbach, the painters Martin Schongauer and Matthias Grünewald, and more recently, Albert Schweitzer form a link between Alsace and the culture of Germany. – Although French is the official language of administration the everyday language of a considerable proportion of the population is a dialect of German similar to that spoken in the neighbouring German province of Baden. Since 1972 German has been an optional subject in schools from the fourth year onwards, and is taken by a majority of children in both primary and secondary schools. The aim is to achieve full bilingualism in future. In 1976 Alsace became the first French region to achieve a degree of cultural autonomy.

ART. – Since the Middle Ages Alsace has played an important role in the development of art. *Romanesque architecture* is represented by a relatively small number of churches (Wissembourg, Andlau, Murbach Abbey, Lautenbach, etc.). **Strasbourg Cathedral**, recognised as a masterpiece of Gothic, was begun in Romanesque style (crypt), but from the end of the 12th c. onwards came increasingly to show Gothic features (transept), a process which reached its full expression with the building of the nave around 1250. Other important *Gothic buildings* are to be seen at Thann and Colmar. During this period the art of sculpture flourished at Strasbourg and radiated from there. – The *Renaissance* produced not only important guild houses and burghers' houses in Strasbourg and Colmar, together with the town halls of Mulhouse and Obernai, but also the greatest achievement of Alsatian art, Grünewald's **Isenheim Altar** of 1512–15. – There are few *Baroque* churches in Alsace, but important Baroque palaces in Strasbourg and Saverne. In the field of artistic achievement mention must also be made of the **medieval aspect** of many towns and villages, such as Colmar, Riquewihr, Hunspach, Kaysersberg, Turckheim, Obernai and numbers of others. These contribute, together with such masterpieces as Strasbourg Cathedral and the Isenheim Altar, to the charm which Alsace holds for so many visitors.

SIGHTS. – **Strasbourg**: see p. 240. – **Colmar**: see p. 98.

N OF STRASBOURG: **Bouxwiller**, which preserves something of the aspect of the former capital of the County of Hanau-Lichtenberg. Town Hall (1659), formerly the count's chancellery.

Haguenau (pop. 26,000), the fourth largest town in Alsace, with the nearby Forest of Haguenau. This was a favourite residence of the Emperor Barbarossa and the meeting place of important Imperial diets. Burned down in 1677; severely damaged in 1944–45. Church of St-Georges (12th c., with later additions; restored). Church of St-Nicolas (Gothic, 13th and 15th c.). Remains of fortifications, with four old gates. Municipal Museum, with much material dating from the prehistoric and early historical periods.

Soufflenheim, 14 km E of Haguenau, is an important centre of Alsace pottery manufacture.

Marmoutier, with a Romanesque *abbey church of the 12th–13th c., one of the most beautiful in Alsace, built of dark red sandstone; fine carved figures of animals on the exterior.

Niederbronn-les-Bains, on the edge of the northern Vosges, Alsace's leading spa.

Saverne, with a late 18th c. château, built in red sandstone, which belonged to the Rohan family; Unicorn Fountain. Old houses, particularly in the Grand'Rue.

Wissembourg, at the end of the Lauter valley, has a history going back to the Roman period. The town grew up round a 7th c. Benedictine abbey. In the market square is the Town Hall (1750). The beautiful church of St-Pierre-et-St-Paul, completed in the 14th c., is the largest church in Alsace after Strasbourg Cathedral. It has medieval stained glass and a crown-shaped chandelier; the W tower is Romanesque (1070). Adjoining the church are a Baroque mansion and a magnificent 14th c. cloister. Westercamp Museum, with much material dating from the prehistoric and early historical periods.

Woerth, on the Sauer, was the scene of a battle in the war of 1870–71. In front of the Town Hall is a Roman altar with figures of Mercury, Hercules, Minerva and Juno.

The *"Route des Villages Pittoresques"* offers an attractive trip from Wissembourg via Oberseebach, Hunspach, Hoffen, Leiterswiller, Oberroedern, Hatten and Rittershoffen and returning via Betschdorf, Surbourg and Soultz-sous-Forêts. The route runs through picturesque little

Fortified church and fountain, Hunawihr

villages of half-timbered houses, where traditional costumes are still sometimes worn to church.

Sessenheim NE of Strasbourg, is noted only for its associations with Goethe. It was the home of his youthful sweetheart Friederike Brion. There is a small Goethe Museum.

S OF STRASBOURG: **Altkirch**, formerly chief town of the Sundgau. Nearby is the pilgrimage chapel of *St-Morand*. In the former priory church is a Romanesque carving in high relief.

Ammerschwihr, rebuilt after destruction during the last war. Remains of two defensive towers, the Obertor (Upper Gate) and the 16th c. parish church of St-Martin.

Andlau, a wine-producing town with the remains of an abbey, the church of Ste-Richarde (11th–12th c.) and old half-timbered houses.

Barr, a little town at the foot of the Vosges in a region of vineyards. Renaissance Town Hall (1640) and charming burghers' houses of the 14th and 15th c., some of them Gothic. Important wine market in July.

Dambach-la-Ville, a little township of wine-growers and farmers, with remains of town walls, three gate towers and many half-timbered houses, particularly in the market square. Amid the vineyards is the chapel of St-Sébastien, with a Romanesque tower, a Gothic choir and a charming carved and decorated Baroque altar of the late 17th c.

Eguisheim, a wine-growing village with picturesque old streets (half-timbered houses), a fountain and tithe barns, formerly belonging to a monastic house. The octagonal moated castle (8th c., restored at the beginning of this century) was the birthplace of Pope Leo IX. On the hill behind the village are the "Drei Exen", square towers belonging to the ruined castle of Hoh-Eguisheim.

Guebwiller (pop. 12,000), at the mouth of the Lauch valley, known as Florival, the "Valley of Flowers". It is an important wine town and a good starting point for trips to the Grand Ballon and Petit Ballon in the Vosges (see p. 256). The church of St-Léger dates from the Staufen period,

and shows the transition from Romanesque to Gothic; fine sculpture on the central doorway; interior still completely Romanesque. The church of Notre-Dame is one of the few Baroque churches in Alsace; beautiful carving. The early 14th c. Dominican church contains a series of frescoes; there is a museum in the choir. Wine Fair annually in May.

Near Guebwiller is the Benedictine abbey of **Murbach**, formerly an important monastic house, with a 12th c. *church, the most important Romanesque building in Alsace, still preserving its original towers, transept and choir. – There is another Romanesque church in the nearby village of *Lautenbach*.

Kaysersberg, once an important imperial city, now a popular wine town; birthplace of Albert Schweitzer (1875–1965). The remains of the medieval fortifications, the 15th–17th c. burghers' houses and the church of Sainte-Croix make up an attractive *townscape. Early Renaissance Town Hall, begun in 1521 and extended in 1605 (council chamber with rich carved decoration). The chapel of St-Michel has well-preserved frescoes of 1464. The Albert Schweitzer House is now a museum. Above the little town loom the ruins of a former imperial castle with a keep, which was pulled down in 1632.

A picturesque corner in Kaysersberg

Kientzheim, a well-known wine town on the Route du Vin, with remains of fortifications. On the Untertor (Lower Gate), facing the "enemy" town of Sigolsheim, is a curious grotesque head. 15th c. parish church. At the Untertor is the château of Reichenbach, with an attractive wine-cellar.

Les-Trois-Epis, a pilgrimage centre since 1491, with a 17th c. chapel (pilgrimages in May and August); now also a popular tourist resort.

Molsheim (W of Strasbourg), a picturesque little town with medieval fortifications, old houses and fountains. The market square is particularly attractive, with an old guild house, the Alte Metzig, of the 16th c. and a fountain of the same period. Jesuit church (1617), one of the finest Jesuit churches in the Gothic style. – Near Molsheim is the ruined castle of *Nideck.*

In **Niederhaslach** is a church (well restored) built by the son of Erwin von Steinbach, architect of Strasbourg Cathedral.

Mulhouse (pop. 130,000, or 200,000 including suburbs), on the River Ill and the Rhône–Rhine Canal, is the second-largest town in Alsace, after Strasbourg, with a river port, an industrial zone and a university. The town suffered numerous vicissitudes before being incorporated in France in 1798. It is a good starting point for trips in the southern Vosges. The central feature of the old town is the market square, with the Town Hall (1552), a handsome Renaissance building with a council chamber containing 16th and 17th c. stained glass recalling the town's connection with Switzerland. There are numerous museums and a zoological and botanic garden. The most unusual of the museums, 2 km from the town centre in the Avenue de Colmar, is the *Schlumpf Automobile Collection (not at present open to visitors) founded by the two Swiss brothers of that name and taken over by the workers in 1977; it contains some 600 vintage and veteran cars from many different countries, including more than 100 Bugattis. Equally interesting is the *French Railway Museum in the suburb of Dornach, with locomotives and rolling stock from 1844 to the present day. Other museums are concerned with textile printing, art, his-

tory (in the Town Hall) and mineralogy. In Place de l'Europe is the 31-storey Tour de l'Europe (revolving restaurant at top).

Munster, in the Vallée de Munster, a town noted for its cheese; starting point of the "Route du Fromage" into the Vosges. Hardly anything remains of the former Benedictine abbey. Town Hall (1555); Laub (market hall) of 1503. Munster is a good centre for excursions into the Vosges.

Neuf-Brisach, on the Rhine, was designed solely for military purposes; it is now an important frontier crossing into Germany (Freiburg im Breisgau). The town, constructed for Louis XIV by Vauban, demonstrates the 18th c. fortification techniques, which are also illustrated in the Municipal Museum. There is a Vauban Museum as well. Downstream from the town are the Rhine harbour and the series of dams on the Rhine Lateral Canal.

Obernai, at the foot of *Mont Ste-Odile*, is an old imperial city of *picturesque aspect, with its walls, numerous old burghers' houses and narrow lanes. The market square, with its fountain (figure of St Odile), the 15th–16th c. Town Hall and old Gothic and Renaissance houses, has a particularly attractive old-world air. The Town Hall (decorated balcony; council

The Six-Bucket Well, Obernai

chamber of 1608) was restored in the 19th c. Another prominent landmark is the Tour de la Chapelle (lower part 13th c., upper part late 16th c.). In front of the Hôtel de la Cloche is the Puits des Six Seaux (Six-Bucket Well) of 1579, the handsomest bucket-well in the whole of Alsace. Another picturesque spot is the Place de l'Etoile, with its angular half-timbered houses and storks' nests on the roofs, set against a background of vine-covered hillsides.

Ribeauvillé is one of the most charming of the little wine towns on the Route du Vin, and is also a popular holiday resort. It is surrounded by 400 hectares of vineyards, and almost every inhabitant is engaged in wine production. It makes an attractive picture with its old half-timbered houses and the three ruined castles which dominate the town, all dating from the 11th–14th c. – Giersberg (528 m), *Ulrichsburg (530 m) and Hoh-Rappoltstein (642 m). In the Grand'Rue is the Pfeiferhaus (Musicians' House), in the Place de l'Hôtel de Ville, the Town Hall (1773–78), a Renaissance fountain and a late Gothic monastic church. There are remains of the old town walls, two gate towers known as the Tours des Cigognes (Storks' Towers), the Tour des Bouchers (Butchers' Tower) and other defensive towers. – Wine market in July; Pfeifertag (Strolling Musicians' Day) on the first Sunday in September, with a procession, folk celebrations and wine flowing from the ''Wine Fountain''.

*****Riquewihr** is one of the finest and most typical examples of a little Alsatian wine town, and one of the most popular tourist attractions, swarming with visitors in the height of the season. The favourite riesling grape is grown in the surrounding area. The main street, Rue du Général-de-Gaulle (no cars allowed in summer), is lined with fine old houses. At the upper end is the Dolder (1291), a gate tower which now houses a local museum. Beyond it is the Obertor (Upper Gate). The town is surrounded by its old walls and gate towers, and with its half-timbered houses and pretty courtyards offers a picturesque and attractive **townscape. To view the town from a distance, take a path which runs through the vineyards of Schoenenberg from the Diebsturm or Thief's Tower (1300: torture chamber). – The main event of the year in Riquewihr is the Riesling Festival on 15

Main street, Riquewihr

August and the following weekend, with the Wine Festival on two weekends in September.

Rosheim (SW of Strasbourg), on the Route du Vin, was a free imperial city. The church of *St-Pierre-et-St-Paul is one of the finest Romanesque buildings in Alsace. It is first recorded in 1051, but the present structure probably dates from about 1132. Particularly attractive features are the frieze which runs round the exterior and the unusual figures of animals and human beings on the gable. The ''Heidehuss'' (Heathens' House), of the 12th c., is the only stone-built house of the Romanesque period in Alsace. Town Hall (1775) with fountain in market square. The town has preserved its medieval walls and gate towers (13th and 15th c.) and many half-timbered houses.

Rouffach is a little town of farmers and wine-growers set between the plain and the vine-covered hillsides, with remains of the old fortifications and old burghers' houses. The church of *Notre-Dame shows the transition from Romanesque to Gothic, having been built between the 12th and 14th c.; the three towers were restored in the 19th c. Opposite the church is the Renaissance Town Hall, adjoining which is the Tour des Sorcières (Witches' Tower).

Sélestat (pop. 15,000) is a lively town which was an important intellectual and cultural centre during the Renaissance. The church of *St-Georges (12th–15th c.) is one of the most important Gothic churches in Alsace. The church of Ste-Foy is a late Romanesque building with three towers, rich *external ornament, notable capitals and a crypt. The Municipal Library, founded in 1452, recalls the town's great days as a centre of humanism (530 incunabula, 2000 16th c. printed works). The old town, between the Witches' Tower and the Clock Tower, has many attractive nooks and corners.

Thann (pop. 9000), at the S end of the Route du Vin, lies at the mouth of the Thur valley in the High Vosges, and possesses in the church of *St-Thiébaut a Gothic building which can be compared with Strasbourg Cathedral. The tower, 76 m high, is gracefully articulated. Other fine features are the double W doorway (14th–15th c.), with rich sculptural decoration, and a 15th c. doorway on the N side of the nave. The interior is also of notable beauty, with carved woodwork, stained glass and choir stalls. – Also of interest in the town are old half-timbered buildings, remains of the fortifications, the Witches' Tower (Tour des Sorcières) and the Storks' Tower. The 16th c. Cornmarket (Halle aux Blés) now houses a museum of Alsatian history.

Turckheim, at the entrance to the Munster valley, has three 16th c. gate towers, late Gothic stone and half-timbered houses, and an early 17th c. Town Hall in Renaissance style. – From Easter until autumn the night-watchman makes his rounds here every night at 10 or 11 as he did in earlier times.

Amiens

Region: Picardie.
Department: Somme.
Aititude: 27 m. – Population: 136,000.
Post code: F-80000. – Dialling code: 22.
ⓘ **Office de Tourisme**,
Rue J.-Catelas;
tel. 91 79 28.

HOTELS. – *Grand Hôtel*, II, 50 r.; *Univers*, II, 41 r.; *Carlton-Belfort*, II, 39 r.; *Nord-Sud*, II, 22 r.; *Paix*, III, 26 r.; *Francitel*, III, 20 r.; *Commerce*, III, 50 r.; *Normandie*, IV, 23 r.; *Rallye*, IV, 21 r.; *Bellevue*, IV, 30 r. – *Novotel Amiens-Est*, II, 80 r., SP, 6 km E in Boves.

Amiens, lying some 130 km N of Paris on the left bank of the Somme, here divided up into a number of branches, is the old capital of Picardy and now chief town of the department of Somme. With its magnificent Cathedral, which remained unharmed amid the destruction which the town suffered during the Second World War, it is one of France's great tourist centres. The town has long been famous for its textile industry.

HISTORY. – As *Samarobriva* ("bridge on the Somme") Amiens was the chief town of a Celtic tribe, the *Ambiani*, until their conquest by Caesar. The town's first bishop (301) was St Firmin (Firminus), who suffered martyrdom here. Raids by the Norsemen in the 9th c. caused severe devastation. At the end of the 12th c. the County of Amiens became subject to the French crown. – In 1667 an epidemic carried off 20,000 citizens of the town.

SIGHTS. – The hub of the city's life is **Place Gambetta**. From here the busy main street, *Rue des Trois-Cailloux*, runs E to the **Gare du Nord** situated on the wide boulevard which follows the line of the old town walls. Opposite the station is the *Tour Perret*, a 30-storey tower block 104 m high.

A little way NW of Place Gambetta is the *Place de l'Hôtel de Ville* (officially Place Léon Debouverie), in the centre of an area which was totally destroyed during the Second World War but has now been almost completely rebuilt. In the square is the **Town Hall** (17th–20th c.).

Some 500 m E of the Town Hall is the ****Cathedral** (*Notre-Dame*), the largest in France in terms of area (7700 sq. m), and in layout and construction the classical type of French Gothic (which also provided the model for Cologne Cathedral). Built to replace an earlier church destroyed by fire in 1218, it was begun in 1220 by Robert de Luzarches,

Amiens Cathedral

Thomas de Cormont and his son Regnault and was practically complete by 1269; the façade was added in the 15th c. Its external length is 145 m and its width 32 m (transepts 70 m). The two dissimilar towers barely rise above roof level; the S tower, 65 m high, dates from 1366, the N tower (66 m) from the beginning of the 15th c. The spire over the crossing, 112·7 m high, was built in 1529. The three doorways on the *W front, which was strongly influenced by Notre-Dame in Paris, are decorated with a profusion of statues, mostly of Old and New Testament figures, which are among the earliest great achievements of Gothic cathedral sculpture. Particularly fine is the figure of *Christ in the attitude of blessing (the "Beau Dieu d'Amiens", c. 1240) on the middle pier of the central doorway; on either side are apostles and prophets. The right-hand doorway is dedicated to the Virgin, the left-hand one to St Firmin. Above the doorways runs a gallery containing 22 statues of French kings, and above this again is a magnificent rose window, 11 m in diameter. Also very fine is the doorway in the S Transept, mainly devoted to the life of St Honoré (Honoratus), a later bishop of Amiens. On the central pier is the famous *Vierge Dorée, a much imitated masterpiece of Gothic sculpture, so called because the figure was formerly covered with gilding.

The 42·3 m high **INTERIOR, with its 126 slender pillars, is one of the world's supreme achievements in the organisation of space and shows the High Gothic architecture of northern France in its greatest perfection. In the nave are the 13th c. *tombs of Bishop Evrard de Fouilloy (d. 1222) and his successor Geoffroy d'Eu (d. 1236). – In the choir, enclosed by a magnificent wrought-iron grille (18th c.), are **choir-stalls carved by various local artists between 1508 and 1519, which are surely the richest and most beautiful in France, with no fewer than 3650 figures in some 400 scenes from the most varied fields of religious and secular life. On the altar rails (14th–15th c.) are very fine painted and gilded *carvings in high relief (scenes from the life of St Firmin, John the Baptist, etc.). Behind the high altar is the tomb of a canon named Lucas, by Blasset (1628), with a famous *weeping angel. In the left-hand transept is a much venerated relic (part of John the Baptist's head).

N of the Cathedral, beyond the church of St-Leu, is a district rather reminiscent of Venice, traversed by numerous canals. On the southern edge of this area is the city's river harbour, the Port d'Aval, from which there is an attractive view of the Cathedral.

A short distance S of Place Gambetta, in Rue de la République, is the *Musée de la Picardie, which contains ancient Greek, Gallo-Roman and Egyptian sculpture and a large collection of fine paintings (numerous French masters, mainly of the 18th c.; Flemish, Dutch, Spanish and Italian works; on the 1st floor *paintings by artists of the Amiens school, 15th and 16th c.).

SURROUNDINGS. – It is well worth while taking a trip round the "Hortillonnages", a curious market-gardening region immediately E of Amiens where fruit and vegetables are grown on land irrigated by countless little channels (rieux) carrying water from the Somme. – There are numerous British and Commonwealth military cemeteries near Amiens, particularly to the NE in the direction of Arras. – E of Amiens on N 336 is St-Quentin.

Andorra

A free state, the Principat d'Andorra, in the Pyrenees. Altitude: 939–2407 m. – Population: 25,000.
(i) Sindicat d'Iniciativa de les Valls d'Andorra, Plaça Princep Benlloch 1, Andorra la Vella; tel. 97 38 – 2 02 14.

HOTELS in Andorra la Vella. – *Andorra Park, 90 r., SP; *Andorra Palace, 140 r.; Eden Roc, 55 r.; Flora, 44 r.; President, 88 r., SP; Pyrénées, 81 r.; Mirador, 65 r.; Internacional, 50 r.; and many others.

This little principality, situated in two high valleys in the eastern Pyrenees, is one of the smallest states in Europe, with an area of 462 sq. km. It has an unusual relationship with both France and Spain, having been since 1278 under the joint protection of France and the Bishop of Urgel. Another peculiarity is that there are no taxes in Andorra, since the income from advertising on Radio Andorra and the export of electric power is sufficient to meet all the government's expenditure.

Andorra lives by agriculture, and also benefits from its strategic situation, which stood it in good stead during the Second World War. Mail is carried free of charge between the ten or so towns and villages in Andorra. The national anthem contains an appeal to Charlemagne to free Andorra from the Arabs. – The national language is Catalan, but most Andorrans also speak French and/or Spanish.

HISTORY. – During the feudal period there were bitter conflicts between the Comte de Foix and the Bishop of Urgel in Spain, which were finally settled by a compromise, the Traité de Pariage, in 1278. Thereafter Andorra ranked as a fief granted by the rulers of France and Spain. The French President now exercises the

Street scene in Andorra la Vella

functions which originally belonged to the Comte de Foix and later to the King of France; the Bishop of Urgel still retains his original position.

SIGHTS. – In the chief town, **Andorra la Vella** (1029 m), are a 12th c. church and the 15th c. **Casa de la Vall** (House of the Valley), the traditional seat of government (open to visitors). To the N, higher up, are the studios of **Radio Andorra**, a commercial radio station whose transmissions reach a European audience.

SURROUNDINGS of Andorra la Vella. – 7 km away, on the road to Spain, is the frontier post of **Sant Juliá de Loria** (939 m).

2 km NE of Andorra la Vella are the spa of **Los Escaldes** (sulphurous water) and **Encamp** (1315 m), above which is the pilgrimage church of *Notre-Dame de Méritxell*. From Encamp there is a cableway to the *Lac d'Engolasters* (1850 m). – 7 km above Encamp is **Canillo** (1560 m), an interesting village with slate-roofed houses and the 12th c. chapel of *Sant Joan de Caselles*.

20 km from Andorra la Vella is the winter sports resort of **Soldeu** (1850 m), the highest village in Andorra, with a chair-lift.

From Andorra la Vella a road runs up the *Valira del Nord* valley, passing through three tunnels, to **Ordino** (1035 m) and, 10 km farther on, the little mountain hamlet of *El Serrat* (1540 m).

Angers

Region: Pays de la Loire.
Department: Maine-et-Loire.
Altitude: 20 m. – Population: 143,000.
Post code: F-49000. – Dialling code: 41.
ⓘ **Office de Tourisme,**
71 rue Plantagenêt;
tel. 88 69 93.

HOTELS. – *Concorde*, I, 72 r.; *Anjou*, II, 53 r.; *France*, III, 62 r.; *Progrès*, III, 42 r.; *Croix-de-Guerre*, III, 27 r.;

Boule d'Or, III, 25 r.; *Champagne*, III, 24 r.; *Roi René*, 23 r.; *Royal*, III 44 r.

RESTAURANTS in the hotels; also *Le Vert d'Eau, Le Logis*.

EVENTS. – *Festival of Dramatic Art* (second half of June), in the castle.

Angers, chief town of the department of Maine-et-Loire and the see of a bishop, formerly capital of the province of Anjou, lies on both banks of the Maine, 8 km above its junction with the Loire.

In addition to its treasures of art and architecture, the chief of which is the handsome castle, Angers maintains its tradition as the "city of flowers" and an important centre of the trade in Anjou wines, and also has a steadily developing industry.

HISTORY. – Originally a Gallic settlement, Angers became the Roman *Juliomagus*. In the Middle Ages it rose to importance as the capital of Anjou and residence of the Plantagenets; in the 12th c., therefore, it belonged to England, and thereafter for a time to the kingdom of Naples. During the Second World War a provisional Polish government was established here in 1940.

SIGHTS. – The magnificent *Castle erected by Louis IX (St Louis) between 1228 and 1238 has 17 massive towers ranging in height between 40 and 50 m (originally even higher) and steeply pitched roofs. It stands on a 32 m high crag above the Maine and is entered by a drawbridge.

The INTERIOR of the castle and its chapel (15th c.) house a unique collection of tapestries of the 14th–16th c., the "Tapisseries d'Angers". The masterpiece

Castle courtyard, Angers

of the collection is an **Apocalypse of 1375–80 which originally hung in the Cathedral but was later removed and discarded; it was restored in the mid 19th c. A *glass hall* 107 m long has been built to display the tapestries, which have a length of 168 m and a height of 5 m. – The finest work in the chapel is the Flemish "Passion and Resurrection" (late 16th c.).

The *Cathedral (*St-Maurice*: 12th–13th c.) has a nave 90 m long and 17 m wide; two of the three towers are 75 m high. Well-preserved stained glass in the nave. From the Cathedral a handsome flight of steps leads down to the Maine. S of the Cathedral in *Place Sainte-Croix* is the 15th c. Logis Barrault, now housing the *Museum of Fine Arts (works by the sculptor Pierre-Jean David d'Angers, 1788–1856, and a cross-section of French painting, particularly of the 18th c.).

N of the Maine is the *Hôpital St-Jean*, in the 12th c. Plantagenet style. The main ward contains an *Archaeological Museum*, and there is a *Wine Museum* in the cellar. 500 m S is the Romanesque church of the *Trinité*, with a 16th c. bell-tower; nearby is the old abbey church of *Le Ronceray*. – The finest private mansion in the town is the *Hôtel Pincé (1530), built for a mayor of Angers, which now houses a museum of applied art.

The old CITÉ, lying between the castle and the cathedral, must be explored on foot: e.g. by going along Rue Beaurepaire (interesting glimpses of courtyards) to *Place de la Laiterie*, a square very characteristic of old Angers. – Among the city's parks and gardens two are particularly attractive – *La Garenne* to the W and the *Jardin des Plantes* in the centre of the town, with the old church of St-Samson.

SURROUNDINGS. – 5 km S is *Les Ponts-de-Cé*, with seven bridges over the arms of the Loire.

Anjou

This region, lying on both sides of the Loire with the city of Angers at its centre, bears the name of an old county (from 1360 a duchy), originally called Anjou-Plantagenêt, from which the English royal house of Plantagenet took its name. Extending round Angers for distances of up to 50 km, this sunny region offers excellent conditions for the growth of flowers and fruit, and in particular for the production of the well-known Anjou wines. Along the banks of the Loire and other rivers (the Mayenne, the Sarthe, the Loir, the Layon) and in the surrounding area are the numerous châteaux and churches which give Anjou its special charm.

The most important town after Angers is Saumur, situated on the Loire some 50 km upstream. The Route du Vin d'Anjou (speciality: rosé and sparkling wines) runs from Angers to Chalonnes, Thouarcé, Doué, Montreuil-Bellay, Saumur, Gennes, Brissac and back to Angers. The varied character of the scenery of Anjou was expressed by René Bazin in the words: "Anjou is not made all of a piece – it is composed of a hundred different landscapes." – Upper Anjou (Haut-Anjou) is the area N of Angers centred on Le Lion d'Angers.

SIGHTS. – Saumur (pop. 36,000), half-way between Angers and Tours has one of the finest of the Loire *châteaux, dominating the town with its four corner towers; it was built in the 14th c. It now contains two museums, devoted respectively to decorative art and the horse (Musée des Arts Décoratifs, Musée du Cheval). Romanesque churches of Notre-Dame-de-Nantilly and St-Pierre, both containing tapestries. In the old town described by Balzac, round the church of St-Pierre, is the 16th c. "Maison du Roi", with a charming façade. In the Quartier des Ponts between two arms of the Loire is the 16th c. Château de la Reine de Sicile. – 2 km SW in the suburb of *Bagneux* is a dolmen (megalithic tomb) 20 m high. – 11 km SE is the Château de Brézé, a moated Renaissance mansion.

Baugé, N of Saumur, a favourite resort of King René and his court, with the 15th c. château which he built there.

Gennes, between Angers and Saumur, a charming little town. Nearby is *Cunault*, with an important Romanesque *church (over 200 carved capitals).

Tiercé, N of Angers, with the moated Château de Plessis-Bourré (1467).

Fontevrault, SE of Saumur, with an 11th c. *abbey and a magnificent Romanesque abbey church (tombs of the early Planta-

Roman amphitheatre and theatre, Arles

genets); Tour d'Evrault, the abbey kitchen (12th c.).

Montsoreau, between Saumur and Fontevrault, a noted wine town with a strongly defended 15th c. castle.

Arles

Region: Provence–Alpes–Côte d'Azur.
Department: Bouches-du-Rhône.
Altitude: 10 m. – Population: 50,000.
Post code: F-13200. – Dialling code: 90.
(i) **Office de Tourisme,**
Esplanade des Lices;
tel. 96 29 35.

HOTELS. – *Jules César*, I, 60 r.; *Primotel*, II, 102 r.; *Le Mireille*, II, 29 r.; *Nord-Pinus*, III, 30 r.; *Calendal*, III, 21 r.; *St-Trophime*, III, 20 r.; *Lamartine*, IV, 30 r.; *Provence*, IV, 17 r.; *Diderot*, IV, 14 r.

RESTAURANTS in the hotels; also *Vaccarès*, *La Grappe*.

EVENTS. *Festival d'Arles* (July), with theatrical performances, dancing, music and exhibitions; *Grande Féria* (Easter), with bullfights; *bullfights*, with folk entertainments (15 July to 15 Sept.).

The city of *Arles (officially Arles-sur-Rhône to distinguish it from Arles-sur-Tech in the Pyrenees) is the gateway to the island-like region of the Camargue, but is also, in its own right, the greatest tourist centre in Provence, with imposing

Roman remains and associations with a number of artists, in particular Van Gogh. With an area of 190,000 acres, it is the largest commune in France.

Visitors are recommended to buy a combined ticket which gives admission to most of the features of interest. A special leaflet on the town's Van Gogh associations can be obtained from the Office de Tourisme.

HISTORY. – In the 6th c. B.C. Arles was settled by Greeks coming from Marseilles, and later became a Roman colony. After the destruction of Marseilles by Caesar in 49 B.C. Arles enjoyed a considerable increase in prosperity, since it then lay much nearer the sea than it does today. Christianised at an early date (the first of a series of church councils was held in the town in 314), it became in 406 the administrative capital of the whole of Gaul and occupied an area of some 300,000 sq. m. After suffering severely from attacks by Saracens and others, Arles passed to the kingdom of Burgundy in the 10th c., and in 1481 became part of France along with the rest of Provence. – Between 1888 and 1890 Van Gogh painted 300 pictures here, linking the name of the town indissolubly with his own.

SIGHTS. – The most important remains of the Roman period are the Amphitheatre, the Roman Theatre, the Baths and the Alyscamps cemetery. – The *Amphitheatre (Arènes), built soon after the foundation of the Roman colony, is one of the oldest and one of the largest in Gaul (136 m long, 107 m across, seating for 21,000 spectators). The three towers

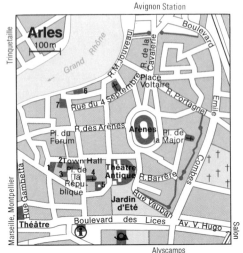

Avignon Station

Arles
100m

1 Museon Arlaten
2 Musée d'Art
  Chrétien
3 Musée d'Art Païen
4 St-Trophime
5 Cloître St-Trophime
6 Musée Réattu
7 Palais Constantin

were added in the Middle Ages when the amphitheatre was converted into a fortress. The amphitheatre is used for bullfights in summer. – A short distance away is the **Roman Theatre**, built in the reign of Augustus at the end of the 1st c. B.C. Most of the structure has been removed and re-used in later buildings, but originally the theatre had a diameter of 102 m and could accommodate 7000 spectators; it was thus comparable in size with the theatre of Orange. – The **Baths** (Palais des Thermes or Palais de la Trouille) date from the time of Constantine the Great (4th c.) and are the largest in Provence (98 by 45 m).

On the SE edge of the town is the cemetery of **Alyscamps**, which was used from Roman times until the Middle Ages. Thereafter many sarcophagi were removed; a few are to be seen in the local museums and in the former Cathedral of St-Trophime. It is difficult, however, to recapture the lost splendour of the cemetery area.

In the *Place de la République* in the centre of the town is a *granite obelisk* 15 m high. Also in the square are the **Town Hall** (16th c. clock-tower) and the former Cathedral of **St-Trophime** with its adjoining *cloister*. The church was originally built in the second half of the 12th c. as a Romanesque basilica, but the interior shows Gothic influence, for example in the choir (1430). The doorway is a masterpiece of Provençal Romanesque, comparable with that of St-Gilles (see

below under *Surroundings*). The cloister (Rue du Cloître) is unequalled in Provence for the elegance and lively imagination of its capitals. There is a marked difference between the 12th c. N and E sides and the 14th c. W and S sides, which show the hallmarks of Gothic.

The **Museon Arlaten**, founded by Mistral, is devoted to Provençal folk traditions; the *Musée d'Art Païen contains Roman material recovered by excavation; the *Musée d'Art Chrétien has the most important collection of Christian sarcophagi after the Vatican museums; and the **Musée Réattu**, in a 15th c. house which belonged to the Order of St John of Malta, contains tapestries and pictures dating from the 18th c. to modern times.

Within Arles itself the scenes of 30 pictures by Van Gogh can be identified, and there are many more in the surrounding area. A signpost points the way to the *Pont de Langlois* (restored).

Gipsy pilgrimage, Saintes-Maries-de-la-Mer

SURROUNDINGS. – Arles is a good starting point for a visit to the **Camargue** (named after a Roman senator, Camar), a flood-plain of the Rhône which has been made into a kind of island (area 560 sq. km) by the building of dykes. The chief town is **Saintes-Maries-de-la-Mer**, on the coast, which is now a popular seaside resort. It has a fortified church dating from the time of Saracen raids, to which there is an annual *gipsy pilgrimage on 24–25 May.

Roman mausoleum and triumphal arch, St-Rémy

The large herds of bulls and horses for which the Camargue was formerly famous are now much reduced in size as a a result of the development of rice-growing and vines, and have increasingly tended to become a mere tourist attraction. The numerous lagoons in the area are the haunt of great flocks of water-fowl, the most spectacular of which are the flamingoes. – The southern part of the Camargue, round the *Etang de Vaccarès*, is now a nature reserve. The animal life of the Camargue can be seen in a zoo in Saintes-Maries. Expectations based on the extravagantly enthusiastic accounts of earlier visitors to the Camargue are unlikely to be fulfilled in a brief trip through the area.

Some 15 km SW of Arles is **St-Gilles**. The *church has a remarkable triple *doorway (1180–1240, the central portion being the oldest part), comparable with that of St-Trophime in Arles. In the crypt of the Benedictine abbey church is pointed vaulting of the mid 12th c., among the oldest in France.

An interesting *round trip* of 60 km would take in **Tarascon**, the home of Daudet's famous character Tartarin, with a fine 14th–15th c. *castle on the banks of the Rhône, **St-Rémy** (handsome Roman *mausoleum and the oldest Roman *triumphal arch, dating from the time of Augustus; remains of ancient *Glanum*), Les Baux and Montmajour, and so back to Arles. – **Les Baux** (hence the name of bauxite, which was discovered here in 1822) has a ruined castle and an abandoned village occupying a commanding situation. In the Middle Ages this was the resort of troubadours. Several fine Renaissance houses and the Tour de Brau, a manor-house (museum). Les Baux is now a thriving centre of arts and crafts. The finest view is from the Tour Sarrasine. – *Montmajour Abbey: church of Notre-Dame (12th c.) and cloister with mainly Romanesque (but some Gothic) capitals; ruins of 18th c. monastic buildings; 30 m high tower of 1369 (view).

Auvergne

The volcanic landscape of *Auvergne, with its capital Clermont-Ferrand, is a part of France which

has been rather neglected by foreign visitors. It is an extensive stretch of uplands, with hills rising to 1886 m (Sancy), often rearing up unexpectedly from the plain in the form of volcanic cones like the famous Puy de Dôme (1465 m). This is the core of the high plateau land of the Massif Central, rising steeply from the Rhône valley and Provence towards the W and N. Auvergne is relatively thinly populated, with no large towns except Clermont-Ferrand.

This makes Auvergne all the more rewarding for the visitor, who in travelling about this region will find tracts of unspoiled natural beauty as well as evidence of past human occupation. In the Middle Ages many churches were built here in the distinctive Auvergnat version of the

Romanesque church, St-Nectaire

Romanesque style; but Gothic architecture is also to be found in Auvergne, though to a lesser extent. On the other hand the fortified castles and elegant châteaux found elsewhere in France are rarer in Auvergne, for the prevailing insecurity in this region at the end of the medieval period did not encourage the building of the fine country mansions of the Renaissance.

In French eyes Auvergne seems a hard and rugged land which lacks the ease and elegance of the south, and in consequence few tourist centres have grown up here in the past and their development is still slow. In northern Auvergne, on the

A volcanic landscape: the *puys*

very edge of the region, is **Vichy** (see p. 254), the only spa resort of any significance, which for a short period during the last war also played a political role. By far the most important tourist resort in the hills is **Le Mont-Dore**, lying at an altitude of 1050 m below the Puy de Sancy. Other resorts are *Châtel-Guyon* (a mineral and thermal spa), *Royat* (thermal baths), *La Bourboule* (thermal baths for children) and *St-Nectaire* (thermal baths). Thus altogether there are no more than half a dozen resorts drawing any substantial numbers of visitors – a very modest total for a region which extends for some 200 km from N to S and the same distance from E to W. And yet Auvergne can offer both a magnificiently varied landscape bearing the mark of man's hands and also the advantages of quiet and solitude.

Within this extensive area the features of most interest to visitors are likely to be the **puys**, the volcanic cones which rear up out of the landscape to the W of Clermont-Ferrand and are continued to the S by the **Mont Dore**, one of the most picturesque parts of Auvergne, a region of steeply scarped hills, deep valleys, waterfalls and lakes which also has Auvergne's highest peak, the *Puy de Sancy* (1886 m), and possesses in Le Mont-Dore a resort which is popular not only in summer as a spa but also as a winter sports resort. Still farther S are the **Monts du Cantal**, of

equally imposing aspect, with several peaks over 1700 m, including the *Plomb du Cantal* (1858 m). This is also of volcanic origin: the Cantal volcano originally had a height of 3000 m and spewed out lava over a radius of 70 km, thus in time providing the basis for fertile pastureland. After the forests were cleared they too gave place to pastureland, making possible the development of the substantial stock-farming and cheese-making activity which now exists. In the Monts du Cantal, however, the available holiday resorts are mostly small, and sometimes very small indeed; for places like *Aurillac* and *Murat* and *Vic-sur-Cère* have only a very restricted range of hotel accommodation.

SIGHTS. – One of the major attractions of a visit to Auvergne is the ****Puy de Dôme**, which towers up to a height of 1465 m, dominating the plain of Clermont-Ferrand (500 m) and its immediately surrounding uplands (1000 m). Its volcanic character was discovered for the first time in 1751. A toll road opened in 1926 runs up the hill, with a gradient of 12% (closed December–April on account of snow), replacing a narrow-gauge railway which had operated during the previous 20 years; there is also a footpath from the *Col de Ceyssat* (1078 m). The hill is associated with a memorable event in aviation history (1911), when an aircraft flew for the first time from Paris to the summit of the Puy de Dôme in 5 hours to win the Michelin Prize of 100,000 francs. From the end of the road (parking, hotel) a footpath leads up to the top, on which are the remains of a Roman temple to Mercury, a telecommunications tower and an observatory; magnificent *panoramic view.

The **Puy de Sancy**, in the Monts Dore, is reached from the Café du Pied de Sancy (9 km from Mont-Dore) by a cableway, from the upper station of which it is 20 minutes' walk to the summit; magnificent view, extending as far as the Alps. – The highest peak in the Monts du Cantal can be reached only on foot (2 hours there and back from Prat de Bouc, 4 hours from Lioran).

Château d'Alleuze (N of St-Flour), a romantically situated ruined castle.

Bort-les-Orgues, on the Dordogne, with massive phonolite columns and a large dam, the *Barrage de Bort*.

La Chaise-Dieu (between Le Puy and Thiers), a 14th c. abbey with a church and Gothic cloister; choir with carved oak stalls and fine Brussels and Arras tapestries (early 16th c.).

Conques (on the SW edge of Auvergne), a small fortified medieval town with a beautiful Romanesque church dedicated to St Foy (carving of Last Judgment above main doorway; valuable *treasury).

St-Flour

St-Flour (W of Le Puy), a little town (alt. 881 m) with a Gothic cathedral.

St-Nectaire (S of Clermont-Ferrand), a thermal resort with a fine 12th c. Romanesque church (notable capitals; treasury).

Salers (SE of the River Dordogne), a picturesque little town (alt. 951 m) with walls and old buildings, particularly in the Grande Place.

Avignon

Region: Provence–Alpes–Côte d'Azur.
Department: Vaucluse.
Altitude: 19 m. – Population : 95,000.
Post code: F-84000. – Dialling code: 90.
(i) **Office de Tourisme,**
41 Cours Jean-Jaurès;
tel. 82 65 11.

HOTELS. – *Europe*, I, 62 r.; *Regina*, II, 41 r.; *Cité des Papes*, II, 65 r.; *Bristol-Terminus*, II, 85 r.; *Palais des Papes*, III, 22 r.; *Auberge de France*, III, 22 r.; *Louvre*, III, 52 r.; *Midi*, III, 60 r.; *Constantin*, IV, 42 r.; *La Croix Blanche*, IV, 22 r.; *Angleterre*, IV, 32 r.; *Excelsior*, IV, 24 r.

RESTAURANTS in the hotels; also *Hiely*, *Helen*.

EVENTS. – Festival of Dramatic Art (July–Aug.).

Bird's-eye view of Avignon

** *Avignon, chief town of the department of Vaucluse and the see of an archbishop, is one of the most popular tourist centres in France. This city on the Rhône, enclosed in its old walls, not only offers such attractions as the Palace of the Popes and the Cathedral, perched on the 58 m high Rocher des Doms, but also radiates all the gaiety of the south, recalling the familiar song. "Sur le pont d'Avignon, on y danse".*

HISTORY. – In Gallic and Roman times Avignon (*Avenio*) was a place of little importance. In the 13th c., along with the rest of Provence, it passed into the hands of Charles of Anjou, and its rise to prominence began in 1309, when Pope Clement V was compelled to leave Rome and seek refuge in France. His successor John XXII also took up residence in Avignon, and in 1348, in the reign of Clement VI, the town became Papal property. Seven Popes succeeded one another in Avignon until Gregory XI returned to Rome in 1377. After the Great Schism in the following year, however, Avignon became the residence of the Antipopes until 1403, and thereafter it continued for almost four centuries to be ruled by Papal legates, becoming part of France only during the French Revolution (1791). But the town prospered under Papal administration: life in Avignon was pleasant, and by the 18th c. the population had risen to 80,000, not far short of the present total (though three-quarters of the population died of plague in 1721).

SIGHTS. – The visitor's first impression of Avignon, after passing through the suburban districts, is of the 14th c. *town walls (4·8 km long, with 39 towers and 8 gates). Within the walls is a town which, apart from the main traffic arteries, is a complex of narrow lanes in which the movement of traffic is difficult. In the centre of the town, at the far end of the *Cours Jean-Jaurès* and a busy shopping street, *Rue de la République*, is the *Place de l'Horloge*, with the 14th c. *clock-tower* from which it takes its name and the *Town Hall* (1845).

At the far end of the square a street leads to the ****Palais des Papes** (Palace of the Popes), with walls 4 m thick, rising in places to a height of 50 m, and massive towers which give it the aspect of a feudal castle. Four Popes were involved in the building of the Palace between 1335 and 1367. After suffering damage during the French Revolution it was used as barracks from 1810 to 1906.

The effect of the INTERIOR is considerably reduced by the lack of furnishings and decoration, but the scale of the palace, with its various halls, rooms and passages covering a total area of 15,000 sq. m, is still impressive. The various parts of the building reflect the differing characters of the Popes concerned: the older palace to the N is in soberer style, the newer one to the S more elaborate. The most important apartments are

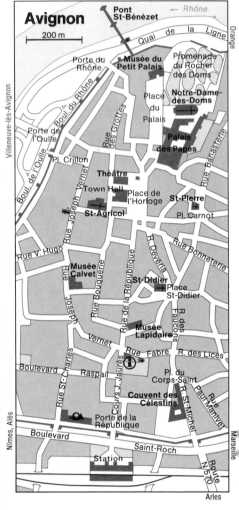

the audience hall, the consistory hall, the Pontifical Chapel and the dining room, with the adjoining kitchen and fireplace.

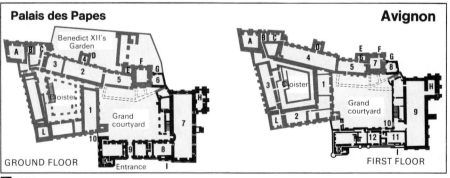

Palais des Papes   **Avignon**

GROUND FLOOR   FIRST FLOOR

Old Palace

New Palace

1 Conclave Wing
2 Consistory Hall
3 Cellar and bakery
4 Chapel of St-Jean
5 Treasury
6 Garderobe and bathroom
7 Great Audience Chamber
8 Small Audience Chamber
9 Porte des Champeaux
10 Porte Notre-Dame

A Tour de Trouillas
B Tour de la Glacière
C Tour des Cuisines
D Tour St-Jean
E Tour de l'Etude
F Tour des Anges
G Tour de la Garde-Robe
H Tour St-Laurent
I Tour de la Gache
K Tour d'Angle
L Tour de la Campane

1 Guest-Chamber
2 Household Wing (Aile des Familiers)
3 Chapel of Benedict XII
4 Banqueting Hall (Grand Tinel)
5 Chambre de Parement (Antechamber)
6 Study
7 Pope's Bedroom
8 Chamber of the Stag (above, chapel of St-Michel)
9 Pontifical Chapel
10 Window of Indulgence
11 Servants' Quarters
12 Wing of the Dignitaries

Bastia

Region: Corse.
Department: Haute-Corse.
Altitude: 15–70 m. – Population: 52,000.
Post code: F-20200. – Dialling code: 95.
(i) **Office de Tourisme**,
   35 Boulevard Paoli;
   tel. 31 02 04.

HOTELS. – *Pietracap*, I, 20 r., in Pietranera; *Ile de Beauté*, II, 57 r.; *O'Stella*, II, 30 r.; *Tyrrhénien*, III, 18 r.; *Bonaparte*, III, 23 r.; *Central*, III, 17 r.

Bastia, the largest town and principal port on the island of Corsica, grew out of a small fishing village and takes its name from a bastion (*bastida*) erected by the Genoese in 1380. As the residence of the Genoese governor and from 1570 of the bishop, Bastia became the capital of the island; but in 1811 Napoleon deprived Bastia of this status in favour of his own birthplace, Ajaccio.

This change did not, however, reduce the importance of Bastia in other respects. In many ways it still reflects its association with Genoa. Climatically the town, which lies opposite Elba and the central Italian coast, is rather cooler and therefore better suited for a summer resort than Ajaccio; and it also has the advantage of a stretch of bathing beach S of the town. It is made up of a number of different parts – the Terra Vecchia of the old fishing village, the Terra Nuova round the Citadel which stands above the harbour, the original settlement of Bastia and the modern housing area of St-Joseph.

Pont St-Bénézet, Avignon

Immediately N of the palace is the **Cathedral**, built in the 12th c. and surrounded by chapels dating from the 14th to 16th c.; notable choir. In *Place du Palais* is the *Hôtel des Monnaies* (1610), now occupied by the Academy of Music. From the gardens on the Rocher des Doms there are attractive *views, particularly of the Rhône, with the famous ***Pont d'Avignon** (properly known as *Pont St-Bénézet*), built 1177–85 and partly destroyed in 1668.

Avignon's most important museum is the ***Musée Calvet** (Rue Joseph-Vernet), one of France's leading museums, with fine wrought-iron work and a rich collection of pictures. – There are many old aristocratic and patrician houses in the streets behind the Cathedral (Rue Joseph-Vernet, Rue de la Petite-Fusterie, Rue du Roi-René).

SURROUNDINGS. – Across the river from Avignon is **Villeneuve-lès-Avignon**, originally built as a strong point facing the Papal town, later the "town of cardinals". Of its fortifications there remain the Tour de Philippe le Bel (1307) and the 13th c. *Fort St-André, with two round towers; from both of these there are fine views. Ruins of the Chartreuse du Val-de-Bénédiction, a Carthusian house built in 1356, with the tomb of Pope Innocent VI.

SIGHTS. – The building of the **Citadel**, until 1766 the palace of the Genoese governor, was begun in 1378 and completed about 1530 with the construction of the tower at the entrance. The interior courtyard is surrounded by two-storey galleries. Here too are the church of *Ste-Marie* (begun *c.* 1495, completed at the beginning of the 17th c.) and the chapel of *Sainte-Croix*, built in 1547 to house a miraculous crucifix ("Christ des Miracles") which was recovered from the sea by fishermen in 1428. Also in the Citadel are the interesting Corsican **Ethnographic Museum** and a military museum.

The OLD TOWN is a fascinating labyrinth of narrow lanes with houses up to nine storeys high. Here there are more churches and chapels, including the former cathedral (17th c.). – N of *Place*

St-Nicolas (marble statue of Napoleon), which dominates the layout of the town, is the excellent **New Harbour**.

Belfort

Region: Franche-Comté.
Department: Territoire de Belfort.
Altitude: 358 m. – Population: 60,000.
Post code: F-90000. – Dialling code: 84.

ⓘ **Office de Tourisme,**
 Place Dr-Corbis;
  tel. 28 12 23.

HOTELS. – *Lion*, II, 95 r.; *Château Servin*, III, 10 r.; *Nouvel Hôtel Américain*, III, 40 r.; *Capucins*, IV, 32 r. – In Danjoutin (3 km S): *Mercure*, II, 58 r.

EVENTS. – *Trade Fair* (May–June); "*Summer Nights*" in the Citadel (June–July).

The town of Belfort, capital of the territory of the same name, lies on the River Savoureuse, and has long been an important fortress town controlling the Trouée de Belfort, the Belfort Gap, between the Vosges and the Jura. Its defences were developed and strengthened by Vauban in 1687, and it became famous for its stubborn resistance during the Franco-Prussian War of 1870–71. – Engineering, electrical, textile and chemical industries; locomotive construction.

SIGHTS. – The central feature of the old town on the left bank of the Savoureuse is the *Place de la République*, with the large *Monument des Trois Sièges* (F. A. Bartholdi) commemorating the sieges of 1813–14, 1815 and 1870. On the N side of the square is the *Palais de Justice* (Law Courts), facing it on the S side the *Prefecture*.

To the E, in the *Place d'Armes*, are the parish church of *St-Christophe* (1725–50) and the *Town Hall* (1784). From the

Lion of Belfort

rear of the church a street runs N to the **Museum** (archaeology, history, ethnography; pictures). Then SE to the *Porte de Brisach* (1687), and beyond this along the ramparts to the imposing **Lion of Belfort* (22 m long, 11 m high: admission charge), hewn from red sandstone by F. A. Bartholdi in 1875–80 to commemorate the 1870 siege. – From the **Citadel** (historical museum) on the summit of the crag there are wide views.

Besançon

Region: Franche-Comté.
Department: Doubs.
Altitude: 246 m. – Population: 127,000.
Post code: F-25000. – Dialling code: 81.

ⓘ **Office de Tourisme,**
 Place de la Première Armée-Française;
  tel. 80 92 55.

HOTELS. – *Frantel*, II, 103 r.; *Novotel*, II, 100 r., SP; *Europe et Poste*, II, 53 r.; *Terrass'*, III, 40 r.; *Nord*, III, 40 r.

The old town of Besançon, picturesquely situated in a bend on the Doubs, on the north-western edge of the Jura, is chief town of the department of Doubs, a university town and the see of an archbishop. As an industrial town it is the headquarters of the watch and clock-making industry of the French Jura, and since the end of the 19th c. has also produced artificial silk (rayon).

HISTORY. – Besançon was the capital (*Vesontio*) of a Gallic people, the *Sequani*, who are mentioned in Caesar. In the Middle Ages it was for long the chief town of the Franche-Comté (the "free county" of Burgundy); later, under the name of *Bisanz*, it became an imperial city within the Holy Roman Empire. – Besançon was the birthplace of the poet Victor Hugo (1802–85), the sociologist Pierre-Joseph Proudhon (1809-65) and the Lumière brothers, Auguste (1862–1954) and Louis (1864–1948), inventors of the cinematograph.

SIGHTS. – The main features of interest are the *Citadel* (several museums), with fine **views* of the town and the Doubs valley; the 16th c. **Palais Granvelle**; the 12th c. **Cathedral**, with its bell-tower (rebuilt in the 18th c.) and rich treasures of art in the interior; the *Astronomical Clock* (19th c.); and a number of historic old buildings. There are also some remains of the Roman period, including the *Porte Noire*, a gateway of the 2nd c. A.D. – At No. 140 in the Grande Rue is Victor

Porte Rivotte, Besançon

Hugo's birthplace. – The most important of the town's museums is the **Musée des Beaux-Arts** (archaeological material, watches and clocks; *collection of paintings), in a building designed by a pupil of Le Corbusier. – From the *Promenade Micaud*, ½ km NE of the Museum, there is a fine view of the Citadel.

SURROUNDINGS. – The finest *view of Besançon is to be had from the *Belvédère de Montfaucon*, from which the Jura hills can also be seen in the distance. – On the far side of the Doubs is the chapel of *Notre-Dame-des-Buis* (460 m), and 400 m from this is a monumental statue of *Notre-Dame-de-la-Libération* (erected 1945), looking towards Besançon and the Vosges.

Biarritz

Region: Aquitaine.
Department: Pyrénées-Atlantiques.
Altitude: 40 m. – Population: 28,000.
Post code: F-64200. – Dialling code: 59.
(i) **Office de Tourisme,**
Cité Administrative;
tel. 24 01 08.

HOTELS. – *Palais*, I, 180 r.; *Eurotel*, I, 60 r.; *Plaza*, I, 58 r.; *P.L.M.-Hôtel Victoria-Surf*, I, 60 r., SP; *Carlina*, I, 31 r.; *Régina et Golf*, II, 45 r.; *Windsor*, II, 37

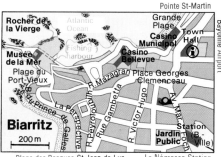

r.; *Florida*, III, 35 r.; *Fronton et Résidence*, III, 48 r.; *Palacito*, III, 26 r.; *Océan*, III, 24 r.; *Beaulieu*, III, 24 r.; *Atalaye*, III, 24 r.; *Chardons*, III, 35 r.; *Avenue*, IV, 25 r.; and many others.

RESTAURANTS in the hotels; also *Château de Brindos*, 6 km SE on the Lac de Brindos; *Café de Paris*.

Two **casinos**.

RECREATION and SPORT. – All kinds of water sports; golf, tennis, riding.

Numerous EVENTS.

Biarritz, situated on the Atlantic (Bay of Biscay) in the SW corner of France, is one of the world's most famous seaside resorts. Its magnificent *situation on a much indented, surf-beaten coast, its fine sandy beach, brine springs and mild maritime climate favoured the rise of this former fishing village, and its prosperity was ensured when the Empress Eugénie built a palace here (now the Hôtel du Palais) for herself and her court.

SIGHTS. – The principal streets of the town meet in the elongated *Place Georges-Clemenceau*, from which it is a short distance by way of *Place Bellevue* (*Casino Bellevue* on the left, *Casino Municipal* on the right) to the seafront. – The magnificent situation of Biarritz and the beauty of the coastal scenery can be appreciated from the seafront promenade. To the NE is the popular *****Grande Plage** (heavy surf), extending to the *Pointe St-Martin*, with a *lighthouse* (44 m) from which there are extensive views. Beyond this is the *Plage de la Chambre d'Amour*, with a fashionable bathing pool.

W of the Casino Bellevue the Boulevard Maréchal-Leclerc runs above the picturesque little *fishing harbour*, nestling in a rocky inlet between the *Rocher du Basta* and *Cap Atalaye*, and through a tunnel to the **Esplanade de la Vierge**. A narrow bridge leads on to the *Rocher de la Vierge*, a long narrow ridge of rock from which there are magnificent *views extending from the mouth of the Adour to the Spanish coast. – Above the Esplanade is the *****Musée de la Mer**, with an aquarium and rich natural history collections.

Farther along the coast is the rocky inlet which contains the **Vieux Port**, with a beautiful sheltered beach. From the adjoining *Esplanade du Port-Vieux* and, best

On the beach, Biarritz

of all, from the *Perspective Miramare* there are fine views of the rock-fringed Plage des Basques (bathing beach), exposed to the full force of the breakers.

To the E of the town are the *Thermes Salins* (brine springs), which are effective in the treatment of anaemia, metabolic diseases and gynaecological conditions.

Bordeaux

Region: Aquitaine.
Department: Gironde.
Altitude: 5 m. – Population: 230,000.
Post code: F-33000, – Dialling code: 56.
ⓘ **Office de Tourisme**,
12 Cours du 30-Juillet;
tel. 44 28 41.

HOTELS. – *Frantel*, 5 rue R.-Lateulade, I, 200 r.; *P.L.M.-Aquitania*, I, 200 r., *Sofitel*, I, 90 r., both 6 km N in the Quartier du Lac; *La Réserve*, 8 km NW in L'Alouette, I, 20 r.; *Bordeaux Crest*, in Gradignan, I, 150 r.; *Novotel*, Quartier du Lac, II, 175 r.; *Terminus*, Gare St-Jean, I, 100 r.; *Normandie*, 7 Cours 30-Juillet, II, 70 r.; *Majestic*, 2 rue Condé, II, 45 r.; *Royal-Médoc*, 3 rue Sèze, II, 40 r.; *Bayonne*, 4 rue Martignac, III, 33 r.; *Trianon*, 5 rue du Temple, IV, 28 r.

RESTAURANTS in most hotels; also *Dubern*, 42 Allées de Tourny.

EVENTS. – *International Festival of Music and Dancing* (spring); *International Trade Fair* (May–June).

Bordeaux, France's fifth largest city (and in terms of area the second largest), lies on the left bank of the Garonne. It is the chief town of the department of Gironde, a university town and the see of an archbishop.

This lively commercial and industrial town, a centre of the wine trade and a busy port, has nevertheless preserved much handsome and attractive 18th c. architecture in the city centre and along the Garonne.

HISTORY. – The Roman city of *Burdigala* was already famed for its wines, and it developed naturally into the capital of the province of Aquitania. In the Middle Ages it was the residence of the Dukes of Aquitaine; then after 1154 the connection with the Plantagenets led to close links with England, lasting into the mid 15th c., when Bordeaux became part of France. In the 18th c. the town enjoyed a great upsurge of prosperity, the shipping trade increased and the population was tripled to reach 120,000. This period saw the erection of the buildings which still give Bordeaux its distinctive character. In the 20th c. the town has developed into a great modern city, with a population, including the surrounding suburban districts, of well over half a million.

SIGHTS. – In the city centre three streets – Cours Georges-Clemenceau, Cours de l'Intendance and Allées de Tourny – form a triangle, within which are a number of important squares, including in particular the *Place de la Comédie*. In this square is the **Grand Théâtre**, built in 1780, which is equally imposing externally (88 m long, 47 m wide) and internally; it has a majestic façade with 12 Corinthian columns and statues.

To the N is the *Esplanade des Quinconces*, laid out 1818–28, the largest square in Europe (area 29 acres). In it

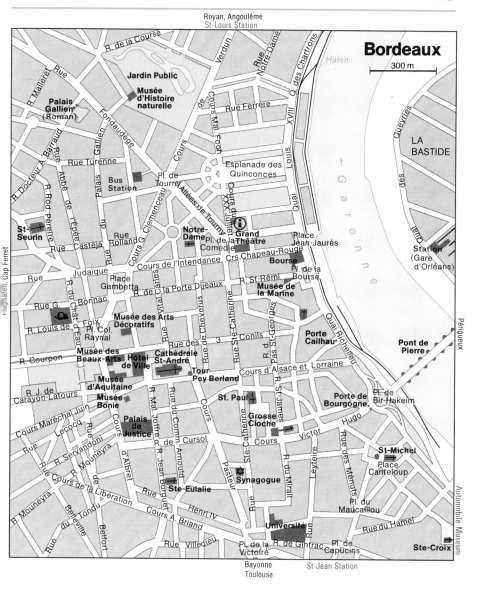

stands a *Monument to the Girondins* (see *History*, p. 25) erected in 1895. From here continue along the bank of the Garonne to see the fine façades of a row of houses in unified style erected in 1780. Here too is the *Place de la Bourse* (1730–55), with the *Fountain of the Three Graces*, the *Stock Exchange*, the *Customs House* and the *Musée de la Marine*.

In the southern part of the old town is the *Cathedral (St-André)*, the building of which extended over five centuries. The original structure, erected in the 12th c., was Romanesque, but it received considerable additions in Gothic style, among them the choir, the Royal Door and the separated bell-tower. – The church of *St-Seurin* is older, having been built in the 11th c. on the site of an earlier Merovingian basilica; the present façade was added in the 19th c.

Opposite the W front of the Cathedral is the 18th c. **Town Hall**, originally the Archbishop's Palace. In the immediate neighbourhood are two important *museums, the Museum of Fine Arts (with works by Botticelli, Rubens, Cranach and modern artists) and the Museum of Decorative Arts. In the *Jardin Public* (25 acres, with English-style lawns) is the *Museum of Natural History*. – The most imposing of Bordeaux's bridges is the 486 m long *Pont de Pierre* (1813–21), with 17 arches spanning the Garonne. It is also an excellent viewpoint from which to get a general impression of the city.

Bordeaux: Pont de Pierre and church of St-Michel

SURROUNDINGS. – To the W and NW are the vineyards which produce the famous red wines of Bordeaux, such as *Château Margaux* (28 km NW) and *St-Emilion* (beyond the River Dordogne).

To the W are **Arcachon**, the *Bassin d'Arcachon*, which offers ideal conditions for water sports, and the *Dunes of Pyla*.

To the SE is *Cadillac*, with a château built at the turn of the 16th and 17th c., notable particularly for a number of remarkable chimneypieces.

Bourges

Region: Centre.
Department: Cher.
Altitude: 130 m. – Population: 83,000.
Post code: F-18000. – Dialling code: 36.
ⓘ **Office de Tourisme,**
14 Place Etienne-Dolet;
tel. 24 75 33.
HOTELS. – *Central et Angleterre*, II, 33 r.; *Berry*, III, 54 r.; *Le d'Artagnan*, III, 53 r.; *Christiana*, III, 40 r.; *Olympia*, III, 42 r.; *Etrangers*, IV, 42 r.; *La Bécasse*, IV, 31 r.; *Idéal*, IV, 15 r.; *Cygne*, IV, 48 r.

*Bourges, one of France's leading treasurehouses of art, chief town of the department of Cher and see of a bishop, lies at the junction of the rivers Yèvre and Auron. The lofty tower of its Cathedral proclaims from afar its proud medieval past.

HISTORY. – The Gallic town of *Avaricum* was occupied and destroyed by Caesar's troops in 52 B.C.

after putting up a stubborn resistance. In the 4th c. it became the first capital of the province of Aquitania. In the early medieval period it became the chief town of a county and later of the Duchy of Berry. In 1463 Louis XI founded a university in the town, and German students from Heidelberg brought in the doctrines of Luther, which thus came to the notice of Calvin, then studying in Bourges. In 1487 two-thirds of the town was destroyed by fire, and it suffered much destruction during the Wars of Religion of the 16th c. In the 19th c. Bourges took on a new lease of life with the establishment of industry.

SIGHTS. – The **Cathedral (*St-Etienne*) is not only the dominant feature of Bourges but also one of the supreme achievements of French Gothic. It was built between 1200 and 1260, no doubt under the stimulus of the new style of architecture which had been developed in the Ile de France and with the help of craftsmen who had worked there. The W front, 55 m wide, is flanked by two towers and has a splendid rose window and five doorways, the central one being dominant; all are richly decorated with sculpture (O.T. and N.T. scenes, lives of local saints).

The outstanding features of the INTERIOR are the brilliantly coloured ****stained glass windows** in the choir, which date from around 1220; those in the lateral chapels are 15th and 16th c. – The *crypt*, known as the "underground church", is the largest in France. Built at the end of the 12th c., it is lit by 12 large windows; the roof is borne on six piers. In the crypt is the *tombstone of Jean, Duc de Berry*.

Adjoining the Cathedral is a part of the town which contains many attractive old houses. The **Town Hall**, beside the Jardins de l'Archevêché, was built in 1680 as the Archbishop's Palace. In Rue Cousalon and Rue Mirabeau are houses dating from the late 15th and early 16th c. The **Hôtel Lallemant**, a magnificent Renaissance mansion built by a 16th c. merchant, N of the Cathedral, now houses a museum of furniture and domestic equipment. The **Hôtel Cujas** (1515) is occupied by the *Musée du Berry* (archaeology, items of regional interest).

Near the Hôtel Cujas is the *****Palais Jacques Cœur**, built about 1450, one of the finest surviving town mansions in the Gothic style. Arcaded courtyard; richly decorated staircase towers leading to the upper storeys; in the Great Hall 15th c. tapestries. Even though the original furniture and furnishings are missing, this unusually luxurious house gives some impression of the high standards of accommodation enjoyed by prosperous citizens in the Middle Ages.

SURROUNDINGS. – 10 km S are the ruins of the *Château de Bois-Sir-Amé*, once occupied by Agnès Sorel, mistress of Charles VII. Farther S is the richly furnished *Château de Meillant*, completed in the late 16th c., which can stand comparison with the châteaux of the Loire valley. – 16 km NW are the ruins of a 14th c. castle which belonged to Duc Jean de Berry.

Bourges Cathedral

Brittany

The peninsula of ****Brittany (Bretagne)**, with a much indented coastline of some 1200 km and with no part of its area more than 75 km from the sea, forms a distinct geographical entity and is at the same time one of the most attractive holiday regions in western France. It contains five departments – Ille-et-Vilaine, Loire-Atlantique, Côtes-du-Nord, Morbihan and Finistère – and something like 200 holiday resorts of varying character, ranging from quiet and friendly little places in the country to smart international watering-places. Certain areas have become known by special names, such as the Emerald Coast (Côte d'Emeraude) E and W of St-Malo and the Pink Granite Coast (Côte de Granit Rose) and Jade Coast (Côte de Jade) for the resort of La Baule at the mouth of the Loire and its surroundings.

The isolated position of this projecting peninsula has left its mark on the inhabitants, who have not only given vent from time to time to their strivings for independence but have their own traditions, their own style of architecture and a language of their own. The Bretons apply the term *Armor* to the coastal regions of Brittany, *Argoet* to the interior. The inland regions are largely given up to heathland and forest, with scattered farms and villages, their fields marked out by hedges, forming a very distinctive landscape pattern. The population of some 1,200,000 is still deeply religious, and this Breton religious feeling finds expression in the characteristic churchyards with their "calvaries" (Crucifixion groups) and in the splendid religious processions (*pardons*) of Brittany. Nowadays, however, the distinctive characteristics of the country and the people, which survived in full vigour into the 20th c., are increasingly being smoothed down and assimilated to the rest of France.

Nantes, with a population of a quarter of a million, is the largest town in Brittany and, in spite of its rather outlying situation, the historical capital of the region; but **Rennes**, favoured by its more central position and its administrative functions, has become the real capital of Brittany

Belle-Ile

Calvary, St-Thégonnec

and its intellectual centre. Among the attractions of the coastal regions are the islands, mostly lying off the SW coast; the most important of these is **Belle-Ile**, which has an area of 84 sq. km.

The situation of the peninsula also influences the pattern of its economy. Although fishing (tunny, sardines, crustaceans) makes a major contribution, the leading place is taken by agriculture. This covers both meat production and dairy farming, vegetable-growing and poultry-rearing: roughly half of all the eggs eaten in France come from Brittany. Apart from the processing of local produce, industry plays a smaller part and is mainly centred on the shipyards. The tourist trade, thanks to good communications between Paris and Brittany, is now making an increasing contribution to the economy, although it is confined to the summer season between late spring and early autumn.

HISTORY. – After Caesar's troops defeated the Gallic inhabitants (who called their land *Armor*, "land of the sea") in 56 B.C. Brittany was ruled by the Romans for more than four centuries. From A.D. 460 onwards there was an influx of Celts from Britain, driven out by the invading Angles and Saxons, who called their new country Little Britain, as distinct from the "Great Britain" they had left. These new settlers remained faithful to their old religion, which indeed persisted into the 7th c. before giving place entirely to Christianity. In 799 Brittany became part of Charlemagne's Frankish kingdom, though this had little effect on its development. After suffering from a succession of raids by the Norsemen Brittany came in 1113 under the feudal overlordship of Normandy and England; and finally, after much conflict and disturbance, became part of the kingdom of France in 1532. In subsequent centuries, however, there were a number of Breton risings against the crown, which were ended by Henry IV's Edict of Nantes in 1598 and later by draconian punishments. The French Revolution of 1789 was enthusiastically welcomed in Brittany, but there were further attempted risings in the 19th c. down to 1832.

ART. – The record begins with megalithic monuments of religious significance dating from the 3rd and 4th millennia B.C. – **dolmens** and **menhirs**, standing stones set up either individually or in long **alignments**, such as are to be seen at Carnac (more than 3000 in this area alone). These monuments must reflect some kind of solar cult practised by the original inhabitants. Christian buildings in the Romanesque style are few in number and of little importance: it was only in the 15th c., under stimulus from the Ile de France and Normandy, that the first cathedrals began to be built in Brittany. Given the limited resources of the region, Brittany's nine cathedrals are relatively modest buildings, some of them not completed until the Renaissance period. Against this, however, Brittany is notable for the numbers of churches and chapels to be found scattered about the countryside, with fine interiors bearing witness to the skill of the craftsmen who built them. Typical features are the walled **churchyards** (*enclos paroissiaux*, "parish enclosures") and the **calvaries** (*calvaires*), usually with rich carved decoration.

FOLK TRADITIONS. – Like many peoples living by the sea, the Bretons have a leaning towards the supernatural and fantastic, and have developed a rich store of *legends*, including the story of Tristram and Iseult (Tristan and Isolde) which inspired Wagner's opera. The legend of the Holy Grail is also of Breton origin. This Breton belief in wonders combined with the doctrines of Christianity to produce a profound reverence for the saints. The most popular Breton saint is St Yves; and St Anne is honoured along with the Virgin as the protectress of mothers. – The famous Breton *pardons* (religious festivals with processions) mostly take place between May and September, so that summer visitors may well be fortunate enough to see one of these very characteristic Breton celebrations. The depth of religious feeling is likely to be greater in the smaller places. Entertainments of various kinds (fairs, dancing, sporting events) are associated with the processions. – Brittany has a great wealth of local *costumes*, but visitors are most likely to see them in museums, since nowadays they are usually worn only on special occasions like *pardons* or other festivals.

SIGHTS. – The *Monts d'Arrée, in western Brittany, are the highest hills in the peninsula, rising to almost 400 m. They offer a variety of good viewpoints, like the *Montagne St-Michel* (382 m).

La Baule (pop. 14,000), W of Nantes, roughly half way between that town and Belle-Ile, is a major bathing resort, with one of the finest beaches in France, many kilometres long (long seafront, with hotels and restaurants). The town is sheltered from N winds by 988 acres of pine forests. Adjoining it is the smaller resort of *La Baule-les-Pins*.

The beach, La Baule

*Belle-Ile**, S of the Quiberon peninsula, from which there are boat services (1 hour), is the largest Breton island, 17 km long and between 5 and 10 km across. In 1573 it was held briefly by England, and again in 1761 by Britain. From the chief town, *Le Palais*, an attractive road runs NW, passing a large lighthouse, to the rugged *Côte Sauvage* in the NW of the island, with the unusual *Grotte de L'Apothicairerie.* In the opposite direction, SE of Le Palais, is the *Plage des Grands Sables*, with the island's finest beach and best bathing. – Off the N coast of Brittany, in almost the same longitude as Belle-Ile, is the little **Ile de Bréhat**, $3\frac{1}{2}$ km long, which actually consists of two smaller islets, with handsome red granite rocks.

Brest (pop. 175,000), lying far to the W, is Brittany's third largest town, an important naval harbour (within France second only to Toulon), and was during the Second World War a German submarine base. It has been almost completely rebuilt after severe wartime destruction (over 90%). The best view of the extensive anchorage of Brest, one of the finest natural harbours in the world, is to be had from Cours Dayot, on the line of the old ramparts. Two bridges from which there are also fine views are the *Pont de Recouvrance (64 m high) and the Pont de l'Harteloire (634 m long, 40 m high).

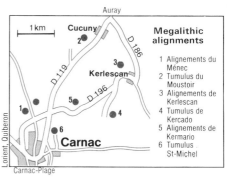

Carnac, on the S coast near the projecting peninsula of Quiberon, is famous for the thousands of *megaliths* to be seen here, including alignments of 1099 standing stones at *Le Ménec* (3 km away), and the St-Michel burial mound (from which there is a good view of the surrounding area); *Prehistoric Museum. Other megaliths of different types can be seen in the neighbourhood, at *Locmariaquer, Kermario, Kerlescan, Kercado* and *Le Moustoir*.

Standing stone, Le Ménec

Concarneau

Concarneau, France's third largest fishing port, is an important market for tunny and has numerous fish-canning plants. The *Ville Close is a picturesque little walled town, covering an area of only 350 by 100 m within its massive fortifications.

Cornouaille (Cornwall) was the name of a medieval kingdom in SW Brittany, with its capital at Quimper. Within its territory are bathing resorts like *Tréboul*, the fishing port of *Douarnenez* and the **Pointe du Raz,** a 70 m high promontory reaching far out into the sea, with the waves beating against its rocky flanks. The walk to the point is strenuous and calls for care, but it affords one of the most striking impressions of the rugged Breton coast.

The *Côte d'Emeraude (Emerald Coast) runs W from St-Malo along the N coast of Brittany. Along this coast are a number of famous bathing resorts like **Dinard, Paramé, St-Briac** and **St-Lunaire,** all linked by a coastal road. The most striking feature is *Cap Fréhel, beyond St-Cast, which rears to a height of 57 m above the sea, offering fine views of the coast. It can also be reached by boat from Dinard.

The much indented**Crozon peninsula** lies N of Cornouaille and the Pointe du Raz, with bathing resorts such as **Morgat, Camaret** and **Roscanvel.** It has a counterpart to the Pointe du Raz in the

Pointe de Penhir: from a platform 70 m above the sea there are impressive views, for example of the isolated stacks known as the *Tas de Pois* ("Piles of Peas"). To the N is the *Pointe des Espagnols*, with a view of Brest, to the S *Cap de la Chèvre*, with a view of the Pointe du Raz – also beautiful though not quite so impressive. Between the Pointe de Penhir and Cap de la Chèvre is the *Pointe de Dinan (not to be confused with the town of Dinan): fine panoramic views and the curious rock formation known as the "Château de Dinan".

A street in the old town, Dinan

*Dinan (pop. 16,500) lies at the head of a long estuary at the mouth of the River Rance, to the S of St-Malo. With its old town (15th–16th c. houses) its *castle (massive 14th c. tower) and its enclosing walls it has an attractive old-world air. Rewarding boat trip on the Rance from Dinan to Dinard or St-Malo.

*Dinard (pop. 9500) is, along with La Baule, the most elegant of the Breton

Ouessant (Ushant)

bathing resorts, and, like La Baule, attracts an international clientele. It forms a striking contrast to the nearby town of St-Malo, which can be seen from the seafront promenade on the far side of the Rance estuary. The Grande Plage, in spite of its name, is only 500 m long. Musée de la Mer, with an attractive aquarium.

Fougères (pop. 25,000), strategically situated inland NE of Rennes on the Breton border, is an old fortified town with modern industries (footwear). It has a strongly defended *castle with 13 towers set round its massive walls (13th–15th c.). The powerful impression which Fougères makes on the beholder was expressed by Victor Hugo in the words, "The question I want to ask everyone is: 'Have you seen Fougères yet?'"

Guimiliau, a small village in NW Brittany, S of Roscoff, has a particularly fine *calvary (1581–88) with more than 200 figures in scenes from the life of Christ. The *church is also of great interest.

Josselin, an inland town N of Vannes, is notable particularly for the 14th c. *Château des Rohan; the very beautiful *façade of the residential quarters is in

striking contrast with the fortified part of the castle. Church in Flamboyant style.

Nantes: see p. 159.

The **Montagnes Noires** (Black Hills), in the Monts d'Arrée, which reach heights of just over 300 m, are in process of justifying their old name as a result of reafforestation.

The island of ***Ouessant** (in English traditionally Ushant), 7 km long by 4 km across, lies off Brest and has the highest winter temperatures in France. Its main features are its rugged cliffs and the Oréac'h lighthouse, which marks the entrance to the English Channel. There is heavy shipping traffic here, with some 30,000 vessels passing the lighthouse every year. Ouessant is also of interest for its bird life, particularly in autumn.

The **Quiberon peninsula** (c. 8 km long by $1–1\frac{1}{2}$ km across), on the S coast of Brittany, was originally an island but was joined to the mainland by deposits of soil from the sea. Its varied scenery – particularly impressive along the Côte Sauvage ("Wild Coast") on the W side – attracts many visitors. Boat services from the town of Quiberon to Belle-Isle.

Quimper (pop. 61,000), in SW Brittany on the long estuary (ferry) of the Odet, on the borders of Cornouaille, has the combined attractions of its Gothic *Cathedral and its picturesque old town. It is a typically Breton town in the fullest sense of the term. The Cathedral choir dates from the 13th c., the rest of the structure from the 15th; the two spires (76 m high) were added in 1856. The interior, 93 m long and 20 m high, contains magnificent stained glass, some of it 15th c. S of the Cathedral is the Breton Departmental Museum (local archaeology, traditional costumes, etc.). Also of interest is the *Museum of Fine Arts in the Town Hall (pictures by French and foreign painters).

Rennes: see p. 228.

St-Malo: see p. 236.

Vannes (pop. 41,000), in the Gulf of Morbihan on the S coast, has a number of industrial plants but is mainly of interest for the old part of the town, particularly the Cathedral (St-Pierre), built between the 13th and the 19th c., and the old houses round it. There are also remains of the town walls, with the 14th c. Tour du Connétable. The harbour is on the southern edge of the old town.

Vitré (pop. 12,000), E of Rennes on the left bank of the Vilaine, has preserved its *old town almost intact. All of it is attractive, but the most picturesque part is the area round Rue Beaudrairie. The *castle, a massive 14th and 15th c. structure, the 15th c. church of Notre-Dame and the old town walls with their towers make up a picture to delight every visitor. – Near Vitré is the 14th c. *Château des Rochers*, famous for its association with the celebrated 17th c. letter-writer Mme de Sévigné.

Burgundy

*Burgundy (Bourgogne), lying between Dijon in the E and the Loire in the W, with Sens at its NW extremity and Mâcon in the SE, is not a clearly defined geographical region but a transitional area, extending for some 200 km in each direction. The land is flat, gently rolling or hilly, with its highest points in central Morvan (Bois du Roi, 900 m). The Monts du Beaujolais to the S, which reach heights of over 1000 m, lie outside the boundaries of Burgundy. – Burgundy, with its capital at Dijon, takes in the departments of Saône-et-Loire (chief town Mâcon) and Côte-d'Or (Dijon), together with the eastern part of Yonne (Auxerre) and the western part of Ain (Bourg).

The name of Burgundy has a variety of associations. To the historically minded it recalls the old Burgundian kingdom and the vicissitudes of its history, its establishment under the treaty of Verdun in 843 and the heroic adventures recounted in the "Nibelungenlied". For the gourmet Burgundy is a region of good wines and the numerous specialities of the *cuisine bourguignonne*, including the meat fondue which is known and appreciated far beyond the boundaries of the region. The art lover thinks of the flowering of Romanesque, and to a lesser extent, Gothic art and architecture, and will remember in particular such names as Cluny and Vézelay. In short Burgundy is a land of infinite variety which offers outstanding attractions in many different fields of human activity.

With all this, however, Burgundy has only one town of any size, **Dijon**. It has numbers of small towns and villages which reflect the generally agricultural character of the country. There is, of course, some industry in Burgundy: **Le Creusot**, in the S, is a centre of steel-working and heavy industry, and **Chalon-sur-Saône** is also very much an industrial town; but in the economy of Burgundy this is of subsidiary importance compared with stock-farming and to a lesser degree forestry (though there are some 296,000 acres of forest in Morvan), and – with occasional exceptions – will not interfere with the tourist's enjoyment of the scenery and other attractions of the region.

Visitors tend to think of Burgundy as a single unit, but to the inhabitants themselves this is by no means the case. They see it as made up of a whole range of smaller areas, like the hilly and wooded district of Morvan which has already been referred to. Many of these areas are named after particular towns, like **Senonais** (round Sens) in the NW, **Nivernais** (Nevers) and **Auxerrois** (Auxerre). The best known of them all is the **Côte d'Or**, or *Côte* for short, the wine-producing region which extends S from Dijon

Porte du Croux, Nevers

kingdom of Burgundy, which in 1032, in the reign of Emperor Conrad II, was incorporated in the German Empire (the "Holy Roman Empire"). The western part of the territory then passed to the West Frankish kingdom and developed into the independent **Duchy of Burgundy** – the region now known as Burgundy – which became a pillar of the Christian Church. Here *Bernard of Clairvaux* (1091–1153), fighting against the pomp and magnificence of Cluny, established his position as the strongest and most influential personality in the West. When Burgundy passed in 1363 from a collateral line of the Capetians to Philip the Bold of Valois, this marked the beginning of a brilliant period of expansion towards the North Sea and the Jura. With the death of Charles the Bold in 1477 the Duchy of Burgundy passed to France, of which it has now formed part for five centuries.

ART. – Although Burgundy has some remains of Roman art and architecture, as at *Autun*, and Carolingian art is represented in *Dijon*, its great period of artistic achievement began in the 11th c. with the flowering of Romanesque architecture, sculpture and painting which continued into the 12th. It is as if, around the year 1000, a new impulse came to Christian art in this region. Characteristically, Burgundy's numerous Romanesque village churches for long remained unnoticed, and it was only in the 19th c. that art historians fully recognised and appreciated their importance. There are now something like 350 churches to be seen in Burgundy, and obviously, with the best will in the world, the ordinary visitor can visit only a small selection of them; and this unfortunately means that famous churches like those of *Vézelay*, *Tournus*, *Autun* and of course *Cluny* attract swarms of tourists, while the more remote churches continue to be neglected. It is perhaps hard to believe that there is such an artistic no man's land in the very heart of Burgundy.

towards Beaune and Chagny, with villages whose names are synonymous with those of famous wines, such as *Gevrey-Chambertin*, *Nuits-St-Georges* and *Pommard*. Driving through this area is like reading a wine-list; and everywhere visitors are offered the opportunity of tasting and buying the wines at the producers' establishments. Other sub-regions of Burgundy are known for their agricultural produce – **Charollais** for its white cattle which are also reared in **Auxois**, Nivernais and **Puisaye** and are widely exported, or **Bresse** in the SE corner of Burgundy, whose succulent chickens are an indispensable element in the gourmet cuisine of half Europe. Visitors who are seeking the quintessence of Burgundy, however, should look for it in the **Dijonnais**, the area round Dijon, which contains all the characteristic features of the region, from the limestone plateau to the vine-covered slopes of the Côte.

HISTORY. – Although Burgundy is an area of passage, a transit route, it also has modest traces of prehistoric settlement. Between 60 and 50 B.C. Caesar's troops pressed forward into Burgundy, and in 52 B.C. broke the stubborn resistance of the Gallic chieftain Vercingetorix at Alise-Ste-Reine, NE of Semur-en-Auxois. In subsequent centuries Roman civilisation and the Christian faith gradually spread throughout the region. In the 5th c. the *Burgundians* migrated from the Middle Rhineland into the Saône plain and gave their name to this new home. In 534, however, the Burgundian kingdom was conquered by the Franks. When the Frankish kingdom was divided up in the treaty of Verdun (843) two independent kingdoms came into being in the eastern part of its territory. In 934 these were combined to form the

Abbey church, Cluny

The name of **Cluny**, however, is a reminder that the main features of the Burgundian Romanesque style spread from here over the rest of Europe, after the erection by the Benedictines of Cluny of what was until the 16th c. (when St Peter's in Rome was built) the largest church in Christendom. It was begun in 1088 and completed about 1130, but after the French Revolution was "demolished and destroyed in the most criminal fashion" (Raymond Oursel). What visitors see today is no more than a poor fragment – though still an impressive one – of the original church. Without the example of Cluny, however, many of the churches of Burgundy could not have been conceived. Art historians are still at a loss to explain this great creative flowering of architecture and sculpture in Burgundy over the space of a century and a half: they cannot say what impulse set this great building programme in motion or how, in terms of the material resources available, it was successfully carried through.

It is not surprising that after such an apotheosis of art and architecture devoted to the glory of God, the Gothic style which began about the middle of the 12th c. to radiate from the Ile de France made only slow progress in Burgundy and is represented by a relatively small number of buildings – small, at any rate, in comparison with the numbers of Romanesque churches. Examples of Gothic churches are Notre-Dame in Dijon and Auxerre Cathedral. The Flamboyant style of the 14th c. made even less impact in Burgundy, and Renaissance influence is also limited. Burgundy has few châteaux comparable with those of the Loire valley.

SIGHTS. – **Ancy-le-Franc** (E of Auxerre) has a Renaissance château of 1546, restored in the 19th c.

Autun (pop. 23,000), SW of Dijon, has a number of Roman structures on the E side of the town, including a theatre with a diameter of 150 m, two Roman gates, the Porte d'Arroux and Porte St-André, and remains of a tower-like temple of Janus (24 m high, 17 m in diameter). Its finest building is the 12th c. *Cathedral (St-Lazare), with a Last Judgment in the tympanum of the main doorway. N of the Cathedral, in the Hôtel Rolin, is a museum with prehistoric material and examples of medieval art.

The best general view of **Auxerre** (pop. 40,000), on the Yonne, is to be had from the right bank of the river or from one of the bridges. Charming old houses in Rue de l'Horloge (late 15th c. clock-tower), Rue de Paris, Rue Joubert, Place Robillard and Place Charles-Surugue. Of three notable churches the abbey church of St-Germain is the oldest; it has a Carolingian crypt. The Gothic *Cathedral (St-Etienne), built between the 13th and 16th c., has a W front 50 m high with three richly sculptured 13th c. doorways; fine interior.

Beaune (pop. 20,000), centre of the *Côte d'Or* wine-producing area, was from the 14th c. onwards, together with Dijon, the residence of the Dukes of Burgundy, and is still surrounded by defensive walls, now frequently occupied by wine-cellars. The chief attraction is the *Hôtel-Dieu, built in the mid 15th c. as a hospital, which is a typical example of Flemish Gothic. It has a picturesque courtyard from which there is a view of the main hospital ward (used as such until 1971), 72 m long, with gaily decorated gables. It is now an old people's home. The kitchen and pharmacy have preserved their medieval aspect. The museum contains a polyptych of the Last Judgment by Roger van der Weyden and a number of tapestries. N of the Hôtel-Dieu is the Romanesque church of Notre-Dame, in Cluniac style, with medieval frescoes and tapestries. Wine-lovers will want to visit the Wine Museum in the Hôtel des Ducs de Bourgogne. Beaune still has a number of 16th c. houses, particularly in Rue de Lorraine.

Bourg-en-Bresse (pop. 45,000), in the SE tip of Burgundy, is noted for the chickens reared in the area, well known to gourmets, but also possesses a jewel of medieval art in the *monastery of Brou*, in a SE suburb of the town. The monastery was begun in 1506 and completed in 1532 with the construction of the church.

The INTERIOR of these fine buildings, in a style transitional between Flamboyant and Renaissance, is even finer than the exterior. Notable Renaissance doorway. – In the *choir* are 74 elaborately carved oak *choir-stalls* (1530–32) and three splendid **tombs**. – The *nave*, notable for its lightness, has a fine *rood-screen* and beautiful brilliantly coloured *stained glass*. – In the chapel of Marguerite de Bourbon (on left of choir) are a *marble altar* depicting the Seven Joys of the Virgin and colourful stained glass based on a work of Dürer's. – The monastery has three cloisters – a large one, a small one (1506) and one for the kitchens, originally belonging to an earlier Benedictine priory. This part of the monastery contains a *Folk Museum*.

La Charité-sur-Loire, N of Nevers, was once an important port on the Loire. The church of Notre-Dame (in Cluniac style, consecrated 1107) is a remarkable example of Burgundian Romanesque architecture in spite of the damage it has suffered.

Charlieu, near the Loire in the extreme S of Burgundy, has remains of a Benedictine abbey, the main features being a 12th c. Romanesque doorway and a late 15th c. cloister. Some distance away is the cloister of a former Franciscan friary, also worth seeing. There are a number of old houses (13th–16th c.) around Place St-Philibert, including the Maison des Armagnacs and the Maison des Anglais.

Cluny recalls not only its medieval past but also an important and widely in-fluential phase of Romanesque archi-tecture. This little town in southern Burgundy, W of the Saône, rose to prominence in the Middle Ages through its Benedictine monastery, founded in 910, from which new impulses and intellectual stimulus went out to 2000 Cluniac houses, a profound and penetrat-ing influence which also found distinctive expression in architecture. The mona-stery's status was fully reflected only in its third church, built in 1089 – 171 m long, with four lateral aisles and five towers over the transepts. Most of this, regrettably, was destroyed after the Re-volution. The old defensive walls of the

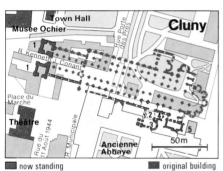

now standing   original building

1 Les Barabans
2 Clocher de l'Eau-
  Bénite
3 Chapelle St-Etienne
4 Chapelle St-Martial
5 Chapelle Bourbon

monastery are represented only by three towers and the Porte des Jardins. Of the *abbey church of St-Pierre-et-St-Paul only the S transept, with two towers, is preserved, but this is sufficient to show something of the scale of the original. Around the monastic complex are other buildings, such as the *Façade of Pope Gelasius II (13th c.) and the abbey complex, including the Palais de Jean de Bourbon and the Palais de Jacques d'Amboise, now the Town Hall. Typically, the magnificent figured *capitals from the church – masterpieces of early Roman-esque – are now to be seen in the granary (farinier). – In the town itself, some distance from the monastery, is the church of Notre-Dame, built shortly after 1100 and later altered in Gothic style.

An important part of Burgundy, famous as one of the major wine-producing areas, is

the **Côte d'Or**, known simply as the "Côte", the ridge of low hills which runs S from Beaune, with a series of villages whose names are a roll-call of the wines of Burgundy – Chenove, Brochon, Gevrey-Chambertin, Vougeot, Vosne-Romanée, Nuits-St-Georges, Aloxe-Corton, Pom-mard, Volnay, Meursault, Puligny-Montrachet, Santenay. To the wine-lover the very names are music, and a visit to the vineyards and the caves where the wines can be sampled will be a memorable experience.

The former abbey of **Fontenay**, NW of Dijon, gives a lively impression of the life of a 12th c. Cistercian house – the more so because of its excellent state of pre-servation. The church, consecrated in 1147, is one of the oldest surviving Cistercian churches in France.

Morvan (*Monts du Morvan*) is a range of hills between the Loire and the Saône, outliers of the Massif Central which rise to heights of around 900 m. With their areas of woodland, fields bounded by hedges, numerous lakes and dams they offer great attractions to nature-lovers and fisher-men.

Nevers (pop. 48,000), on the Loire, is noted for its china, and in its *Cathedral (St-Cyr-et-Ste-Juliette) possesses a church which displays the whole gamut of architectural styles from the 10th c. to the 16th. Porte du Croux, a handsome gateway which formed part of the town's defensive circuit of walls; *Palais Ducal, in Renaissance style.

Paray-le-Monial, W of Cluny, has the *Sacré-Cœur church, a miniature coun-terpart of the abbey church of Cluny (whose abbot directed the construction, begun in 1109).

The magnificently situated château of **La Rochepot**, towards the S of the Côte d'Or, dates from the 12th and 15th c.

Semur-en-Auxois, NW of Dijon, is a picturesque little town, with the church of Notre-Dame and remains of the old fortifications.

Sens (pop. 28,000), in NW Burgundy, has a fine *Cathedral, the earliest of the great French Gothic cathedrals (begun in 1140), with excellent stained glass of various dates between the 12th and 17th c. Many old houses.

Sully, W of Beaune, has a 16th c. château with an extensive park.

Tanlay, in northern Burgundy, has a château (built 1550) which is a good example of French Renaissance architecture.

Tournus, on the Saône N of Mâcon, has the former *abbey church of St-Philibert (10th and 11th c.), of fortress-like appearance.

Vézelay, S of Auxerre and NW of the Monts de Morvan, possesses one of the supreme achievements of French Romanesque architecture in the **abbey church of Ste-Madeleine, crowning the hill up which the little village straggles. Outstanding features are the Romanesque West Porch, 22 m long, the tympanum of the central doorway (which ranks with Autun as the finest achievement of Romanesque sculpture) and the capitals (particularly in the nave) with their abundance of carved figures. Here in 1146 St Bernard launched the call for the Second Crusade.

Caen

Region: Basse-Normandie.
Department: Calvados.
Altitude: 8 m. – Population: 125,000.
Post code: F-14000. – Dialling code: 31.
ⓘ **Office de Tourisme,**
Place St-Pierre;
tel. 86 27 65.

HOTELS. – *Relais des Gourmets*, 13 rue de Geôle, I, 26 r.; *Malherbe*, Place Foch, II, 100 r.; *Moderne*, 116 Boul. Gén.-Leclerc, II, 60 r.; *Univers*, 12 Quai Vendeuvre, II, 24 r.; *Dauphin*, 29 rue Gemare, II, 14 r.; *Place Royale*, Cours A.-Briand, III, 43 r.; *Métropole*, Place de la Gare, III, 36 r.; *Terminus*, Place de la Gare, III, 30 r.; *Paris*, Route de Paris, IV, 25 r.; *Rex*, Place de la Gare, IV, 25 r.

Caen, situated on the River Orne 14 km above its outflow into the Channel, is the chief town of the department of Calvados and of Lower Normandy and the seat of a university. Although two-thirds of the town was destroyed during the Allied landings in June–July 1944, it is still, after large-scale reconstruction and with its magnificent, almost completely unscathed churches, second only to Rouen as one of the great tourist centres of Normandy. The port to the E of the town is one of the most important in France.

SIGHTS. – The central point of the town is the *Place St-Pierre*, with a monument to Joan of Arc (1964). Here too is the church of *St-Pierre (13th–14th c.), with a 75 m high clock-tower (1308), whose boldly soaring spire was destroyed in 1944 and later rebuilt. The interior is notable for a magnificent *apse, with rich decoration and unusual stalactitic vaulting. – Opposite St-Pierre to the W is the *Hôtel d'Escoville*, a Renaissance mansion of 1538 (restored) with a beautiful courtyard.

Occupying an extensive area on the hill which rises immediately to the N of Place St-Pierre is the **castle** built by William the Conqueror, now laid out in gardens, which is entered through the 14th c. *Porte des Champs* on the E side. In *Rue de Geôle*, which runs along the W side of the castle, is the *Maison des Quatrans* (No. 31), a handsome half-timbered house built in 1381. – N of the castle are the imposing new buildings of the **University**. A short distance W is the unusual church of *St-Julien*, on an elliptical plan, built in 1958 on the site of a church destroyed in 1944.

Some 500 m E of Place St-Pierre, at the end of *Rue des Chanoines*, is the *Place de la Reine-Mathilde*, in which is the splendid Romanesque abbey church of *La Trinité** or of the *Abbaye-aux-Dames*, built by William the Conqueror's wife Matilda to expiate the offence of marrying her cousin. Impressive interior. In the nuns' choir (accessible only from the adjoining Hôtel-Dieu, a hospital built in the 18th c. on the site of a Benedictine abbey also founded by Matilda) is the queen's tomb, and beneath this is a crypt.

S of Place St-Pierre is the ST-JEAN district, rebuilt after wartime destruction, with the church of **St-Jean** (14th–15th c.; severely damaged in 1944 but since restored) and the wide *Avenue du 6-Juin* (D-day 1944), which runs S over the Orne to the **railway station**. – Some 1500 m S of the station is the *Château d'eau de la Guérinière* (by G. Gillet, 1957), a water-tower built in the shape of a top.

Rue St-Pierre, the main street of the old town, runs SW from Place St-Pierre. 200 m along this street, on the right, are two handsome half-timbered houses (Nos. 52

and 54). Farther along, also on the right, is the church of *St-Sauveur* (14th–15th c.), with a beautiful tower and a richly decorated apse (1546). Rue St-Pierre continues past the church through a part of the town which was not destroyed during the last war, and ends in *Place Malherbe*. A short distance S is the Jesuit church of *Notre-Dame-de-la-Gloriette* (1648).

From Place Malherbe Rue Ecuyère runs W to *Place Fontette*, with the 18th c. *Palais de Justice* (Law Courts). From here Rue Guillaume-le-Conquérant continues W to the imposing abbey church of ***St-Etienne** or of the *Abbaye-aux-Hommes*, built by William the Conqueror in 1066, along with an abbey of which little now remains, in expiation of his sin in marrying within the prohibited degrees. The choir and towers, in early Gothic style, were added in the 13th c. In the impressive *interior (115 m long, 24 m high) a stone in front of the high altar marks the position of William's tomb, destroyed by Calvinists in 1562. – Adjoining the church on the S are the *abbey buildings*, largely rebuilt in the 18th c., which were occupied for many years by the Lycée Malherbe; part of the buildings are now used as the Town Hall. Richly decorated interior (beautiful wrought-iron banisters, fine panelling, large refectory, etc.: conducted tours).

From the Romanesque *cloister* there is an attractive view of the church towers. – A number of charming old houses, includ-

ing the Hôtel d'Escoville, also survived wartime destruction.

A short distance NW of St-Etienne, on the S side of an attractive churchyard, is the disused church of **St-Nicolas** (1083–93), with a fine Romanesque West Porch and a beautiful apse facing towards the churchyard.

Cannes

Region: Provence–Alpes–Côte d'Azur.
Department: Alpes-Maritimes.
Altitude: at sea level. – Population: 71,000.
Post code: F-06400. – Dialling code: 93.
ⓘ **Office de Tourisme,**
   Gare SNCF (Railway station);
   tel. 99 19 77.
   Palais des Festivals et des Congrès, La Croisette;
   tel. 39 24 53.

HOTELS. – *Majestic*, L, 300 r.; *Carlton*, L, 330 r.; *Martinez Concorde*, L, 400 r.; *Sofitel-Méditerranée*, L, 125 r.; *Grand Hôtel*, L, 75 r.; *Cannes Palace*, I, 100 r.; *Savoy*, I, 55 r.; *Connet et de la Reine*, I, 52 r.; *Suisse*, I, 64 r.; *Acapulco*, II, 59 r.; *Beau Séjour*, II, 46 r.; *Paris*, II, 50 r.; *Orangers*, II, 40 r.; *Splendid*, II, 63 r.; *Atlas*, III, 52 r.; *Bristol*, III, 19 r.; *Corona*, III; 20 r.; *Soleil d'Azur*, III, 40 r.; *La Bessonne*, IV, 22 r.; *Bourgogne*, IV, 21 r.; *Florian*, IV, 21 r.; *Régence*, IV, 32 r.

Three **casinos**.

EVENTS. – **International Film Festival** (April–May); *International Fireworks Festival* (August); battles of flowers; Gastronomic Weeks.

*Cannes, lying in the Bay of Napoule on the Mediterranean coast of France, owes its popularity to its

La Croisette, Cannes

Carcassonne

beautiful setting in front of a range of hills, its mild climate and the elegance of its amenities and its social facilities and events. The climate, with an average winter temperature of almost 10 °C (50 °F), favours the growth of subtropical vegetation, including palm-trees. There is a magnificent long beach of fine sand.

HISTORY. – The beginnings of Cannes (originally *Canois*) go back to the 10th c. On his return from Elba Napoleon landed in Golfe-Juan on 1 March 1815 and made for Cannes, from which he set out to cross the Alps on the road (passable even in winter) which is still known as the *Route Napoléon*. Cannes owed its rise to prosperity to Lord Brougham, who built himself a house in the tiny fishing port in 1834 and thereafter spent the winter there, an example which soon began to be followed by the British aristocracy. In 1835 mimosa was brought in from San Domingo, and mimosa plantations now cover an area of some 700 hectares, making a substantial contribution to the local economy, the other major element of which is tourism.

SIGHTS. – The central feature of Cannes is the ***Boulevard de la Croisette** (''La Croisette'') which runs along the seafront,

a popular promenade with palms and flowerbeds, luxury hotels and fine shops, and the beautiful view over the bay. At the W end are the **Casino** and the **Old Harbour**.

To the W of the town is **Mont Chevalier** (alt. 67 m), with a 12th c. tower 22 m high which served as a watch-tower from which to look out for Saracen raids and also offered a measure of protection (magnificent *view). Beside the tower is a *museum* with archaeological material from many different countries.

SURROUNDINGS. – Boat trips to the offshore ***Iles de Lérins**.

Above Cannes (alt. 325 m), 8 km N, is the observatory of **Super-Cannes** (lift to top of tower), with unexcelled **views, occasionally extending as far as Corsica.

Excursions to other places on the Côte d'Azur, including **Nice** (p. 161), **Monaco** (p. 154), **Juan-les-Pins**, **Cap d'Antibes** and *Vallauris*, the important centre of ceramic production, where Picasso worked at one time.

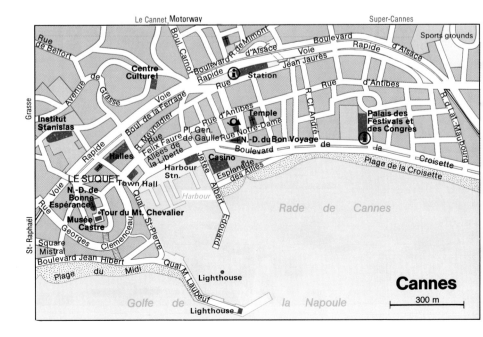

Carcassonne

Region: Languedoc-Roussillon.
Department: Aude.
Altitude: 110 m. – Population: 46,000.
Post code: F-11000. – Dialling code: 68.
ⓘ **Office de Tourisme,**
Boulevard Camille-Pelletan;
tel. 25 07 04.

HOTELS. – IN UPPER TOWN: *Cité*, I, 57 r.; *Donjon*, II, 16 r. – IN LOWER TOWN: *Terminus*, II, 110 r.; *Auriac*, II, 22 r.; *Résidence*, II, 23 r.; *Bristol*, III, 54 r.; *Central*, III, 25 r.; *Royal*, III, 26 r.; *Paris*, III, 15 r.; *Bernard*, IV, 23 r.; *Vitrac*, IV, 26 r.

Carcassonne, chief town of the department of Aude and the see of a bishop, lies in the foothills of the Pyrenees. Its ** old town is the most complete example of a medieval fortified town to have been preserved intact, making it an increasingly popular tourist attraction. The River Aude flows between the Ville Basse or lower town in the plain and the Cité which lies above the right bank.

HISTORY. – The Romans fortified the town, which lay on the road from the Atlantic to the Mediterranean, in the 1st c. B.C. and built its first ramparts; then in the 6th c. the Visigoths erected defensive towers which still survive. In the 8th c. the town was taken by the Franks, and thereafter its defences were steadily improved and perfected by the Counts of Carcassonne, Louis IX (St Louis) and Philip the Bold in the 13th c. The fortress was then regarded as impregnable. Thus work on its defences continued for some 1400 years, and even the newest parts which the present-day visitor sees are 600 years old. Restoration carried out in the mid 19th c. gave the town its present well-preserved aspect.

SIGHTS. – The **Cité (alt. 148 m), elliptical in plan, is surrounded by a double circuit of walls and towers respectively 1100 and 1500 m in length. Within the walls are the strongly fortified castle and the houses of the town, in narrow winding lanes. In case of need the castle could be defended by itself. There are only two entrances to the town, the *Porte Narbonnaise and the *Porte d'Aude.

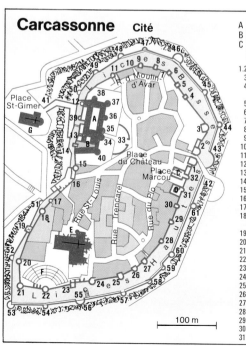

Carcassonne Cité

A Great courtyard
B Small courtyard
C Church of St-Sernin
(destroyed)

1,2 Tours Narbonnaises
3 Tour du Trésor
4 Tour du Moulin
du Connétable
5 Tour de Vieulas
6 Tour de la Marquière
7 Porte du Bourg
8 Tour de Samson
9 Tour du Moulin d'Avar
10 Poterne d'Avar
11 Tour de la Charpenterie
12 Tour de la Chapelle
13 Tour Pinte
14 Poterne Pinte
15 Tour de Justice
16 Porte d'Aude
17 Tour Wisigothe
18 Tour ronde de l'Evêque
(Tour de l'Inquisition)
19 Tour carée de l'Evêque
20 Tour de Cahuzac
21 Tour Mipadre
22 Tour du Moulin de Midi
23 Tour St-Nazaire
24 Tour St-Martin
25 Tour des Prisons
26 Tour du Castéra
27 Tour du Plo
28 Tour de Balthazar
29 Tour de Davejean
30 Tour St-Laurent
31 Tour du Trauquet

D Addition to Tour du
Trauquet (destroyed)
E Cathedral of St-Nazaire
F Open-air theatre
G Church of St-Gimer

32 Tour du Sacraire St-Sternin
33 Barbacane de l'Est
34, 35 Tours de la Porte orientale
36 Tour des Casernes
37 Tour du Major
38 Tour du Degré
39 Tour de la Poudre
40 Tour St-Paul
41 Barbacane d'Aude
(Barbacane de l'Ouest)
42 Avant-porte Narbonnaise
43 Barbacane St-Louis
44 Tour de Bérard
45 Tour de Bénazet
46 Barbacane Notre-Dame
(Poterne Notre-Dame)
47 Tour de Moreti
48 Tour de la Glacière
49 Tour de la Porte Rouge
50 Echauguette de l'Ouest
51 Tour du Petit Canissou
52 Tour du Grand Canissou
53 Tour du Grand Burlas
54 Tour d'Ourliac
55 Barbacane Crémade
56 Poterne du Razès
57 Tour Cautière
58 Tour Pouleto
59 Echauguette de l'Est
60 Tour de la Vade
61 Tour de la Peyre

100 m

Within the town is the former Cathedral of *St-Nazaire, built between the 11th and 14th c. and later considerably restored. The W front was part of the Visigothic fortifications. The Gothic choir contains 22 statues, 14th–15th c. windows and a number of fine tombs.

Two bridges (one of them the 13th c. Pont Vieux) lead into the **Ville Basse** or lower town, which is laid out on a regular grid plan and ringed by boulevards. Although not comparable in interest with the Cité, it contains two notable churches – *St-Vincent*, in the Mediterranean Gothic styles of the early 14th c., and the late 13th c. former **Cathedral** (*St-Michel*), with a valuable treasury.

SURROUNDINGS. – To the NE is the Montagne Noire, an outlier of the Cévennes, with the industrial town of *Mazamet* (47 km from Carcassonne), the starting point for the climb of the *Pic de Nore* (1210 m).

Castelnaudary, on the Toulouse road, with the 14th c. church of St-Michel and, 8 km away, **St-Papoul** (former cathedral, cloister).

Cévennes

The Cévennes, which form part of the Massif Central, are one of the French upland regions little known outside France. Bounded in the SW by Mont Aigoual (1567 m) and in the NE by Mont Lozère (1702 m), they are not a coherent chain in the ordinary sense. They lie between the valleys of the Ardèche and the Hérault, and the whole region shows much evidence of erosion by rivers, most strikingly in the famous **Gorges of the Tarn, which rises on Mont Lozère.

The Cévennes form the climatic boundary between the mild Mediterranean region and the harsher Massif Central, so that they have a very varied pattern of vegetation. The forest clearance which took place during the 18th and 19th c. to supply the charcoal needed by the numerous glass-blowing establishments came to an end 100 years ago, and since then much reafforestation has been carried out. The landscape of the Cévennes shows great variety, with its alternation of forests, barren grassland, bare moorland and deeply indented valleys, a region of solitude and tranquillity. A fine scenic road, the *Corniche des Cévennes*, runs through the mountains for 50 km from Florac in the NW to St-Jean-du-Gard in the SE (continuing towards Nîmes), offering views of the two highest points, which lie some distance off the road.

HISTORY. – During the 16th c. Wars of Religion, and still more after Louis XIV's revocation of the Edict of Nantes, these inaccessible mountains offered a place of refuge for the Huguenots. The persecution of the Huguenots led to the "Guerre des Cévennes" (1702–10), a rising by the Huguenots, who became known as the "Camisards" from the shirts they wore. Finally the killing was ended by an amnesty. The population of the Cévennes is still largely Protestant, even though Protestants were not granted equal rights in France until 1804, under the Code Napoléon. The clearance of the Cévennes forests was halted by Georges Fabre, the local director of forestry, by a series of well-conceived measures from 1875 onwards.

SIGHTS. – *Mont Lozère, a granite crag reaching its highest point in the *Pic de Finiels* (1702 m), accessible only on foot, which offers magnificent views of the whole Cévennes region. To reach it, take D 20 from Le Bleymard in the direction of Le-Pont-de-Montvert; the starting point of the climb is the *Col de Finiels* (1540 m).

*Mont Aigoual (1567 m) is reached from the Meyrueis–Millau road by a side road off D 269 or D 55. On the top is an observatory (1887). There are impressive all-round views, extending in favourable conditions to the Alps, the Pyrenees and the Mediterranean, and sometimes from Mont Blanc to Maladetta.

Anduze, SE of St-Jean-du-Gard, was around 1625 a base for the Protestant forces led by the Duc de Rohan. The picturesque old town (clock-tower of 1320) is, with the nearby pass, the *Porte des Cévennes*, a good starting point for hill walks and climbs.

**Gorges of the Tarn: see p. 118.

Chamonix

Region: Rhône-Alpes.
Department: Haute-Savoie.
Altitude: 1035 m. – Population: 9000.
Post code: F-74400. – Dialling code: 50.
ⓘ **Office de Tourisme,**
   Place de l'Eglise;
   tel. 53 00 24.

HOTELS. – *Symond-Carlton*, I, 50 r., SP; *Novotel*, Bossons, II, 90 r., SP; *Mont-Blanc*, II, 60 r.; *Sapinière*, II, 40 r.; *Croix Blanche*, II, 35 r.; *Le Prieuré*, III, 80 r.;

Richmond, III, 54 r.; *Hermitage et Paccard*, III, 30 r.; *Park*, III, 75 r.; *Albert-Premier et Milan*, III, 40 r.; *Pointe Isabelle*, III, 23 r. – *Auberge du Bois Prin*, Moussoux, II, 12 r.

WINTER SPORTS. – Skiing mainly on slopes W of town (numerous lifts); ski-jumps 3½ km SW at Les Bossons and at Praz-Conduit; skating (summer and winter) in the Stade (sports stadium) on the left bank of the Arve.

SPORT and RECREATION in summer. – Swimming in the Lac du Bouchet, N of the town, and SW of the town centre; golf-course at Les Praz.

Casino in town centre.

Chamonix (officially known as Chamonix-Mont-Blanc), situated at the foot of the highest peak in the Alps, is a health and winter sports resort and a climbing centre of international reputation. The resort area, which extends from Les Houches to Argentière in the *Vallée de Chamonix, 23 km long, also includes the resorts of Les Bossons, Les Praz de Chamonix, Les Tines and Argentière.

The high valley of the *Arve*, flanked on the SE by the Mont Blanc chain with its mighty glaciers and on the NW by the Aiguilles Rouges, does not quite equal the Bernese Oberland in scenic beauty, but vies with Zermatt in the magnificence of its glaciers and possesses in the Aiguilles mountain pinnacles which are unique in their rugged grandeur. From 1091 the valley, under the name of "Campus munitus", belonged to a Benedictine priory. From the mid 18th c. onwards it became more widely known through the writings of the English travellers Pococke and Windham and the Genevese scientists Saussure and Bourrit.

SIGHTS. – The central point of Chamonix is the intersection of the main street (Rue Dr-Paccard and Rue J.-Vallot), which runs along the whole length of the town, with the *Avenue de la Gare* (formerly Avenue Foch). Near the junction is the **Town Hall**. A short distance S, on the banks of the Arve, is the **Saussure Monument** (by J. Salmson, 1887),

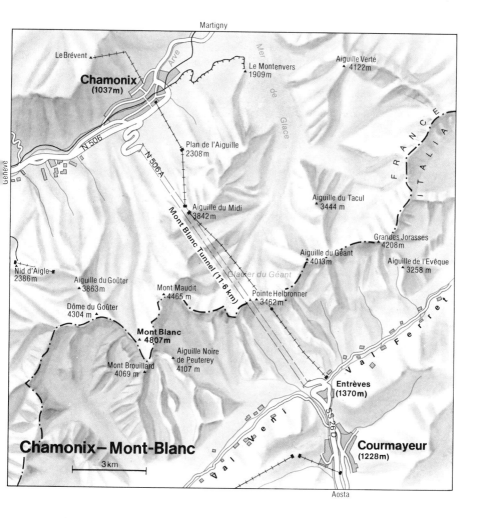

commemorating the first scientific ascent of Mont Blanc; it shows the guide, Balmat, pointing out the route to Saussure.

MOUNTAIN RAILWAYS and CABLEWAYS. – A rack railway (lower station opposite the railway station; May–Oct. only; journey time 20 min.) runs up to the summit of *Montenvers (1913 m: restaurant with extensive views). From this mountain there is a magnificent view of the Mer de Glace ("Sea of Ice"), a river of ice 7 km long and 1–2 km wide formed by three converging glaciers. Immediately opposite is the overhanging W wall of the Aiguille du Dru (a climb noted for its difficulty); beyond it, to the left, is the rounded snow-covered top of the Aiguille Verte; on the extreme left is the Aiguille à Bochard; to the right the Aiguille du Moine, farther back the Grandes Jorasses, extreme right the pinnacle of Grand Charmoz. From the upper station of the rack railway there is a cableway (2 min.) down to a tunnel 100 m long driven into the glacier (admission charge). – For experienced climbers with good heads there is a good return route by way of the Chapeau to Les Tines (2½ hrs): across the Mer de Glace (¾ hr) to the right-hand lateral moraine, then the "Mauvais Pas" up a steep rock face (¾ hr) to the *Chapeau (1601 m: inn), a projecting crag at the foot of the Aiguille à Bochard (2669 m) with a magnificent view of the lower reach of the Mer de Glace; from here a mule-track leads in ¾ hr to the Hôtel Beau-Séjour (1243 m); then left to Les Tines (20 min.).

To the **Aiguille du Midi (Courmayeur). – Cableway 5·4 km long from station at Praz-Conduit (1040 m), on the SW edge of the town, by way of an intermediate station at Plan de l'Aiguille (2308 m), with magnificent views en route, to the upper station (3790 m: 20 min.), under the summit of the Aiguille du Midi (3842 m: lift to top), with a view of Mont Blanc. – From the upper station there is a **cabin cableway (5 km; 20 min.) by way of the Gros Rognon (3533 m) and the Pointe Helbronner (3462 m; passport control) to the Rifugio Torino (3322 m: *view) in Italy, below the Col du Géant (3369 m). From here there is a third cableway leading down by way of the Pavillon del Monte Frety (2130 m) to the Italian town of Entrèves (1306 m: station in La Palud district). The whole trip from Chamonix to Entrèves (c. 15 km) takes about 1½ hrs and offers a memorable experience. – A cableway constructed as long ago as 1926–30 ascends in 15 min. to the top of **Le Brévent (2525 m). The lower station is in La Molaz (La Molard, 1090 m). From here it takes 8 min. to reach the intermediate station of Planpraz (1993 m), where it is necessary to change. The upper section, 1350 m long, climbs in 7 min., without any intermediate supports, to the upper station (2505 m), just below the summit (restaurant). From here there are magnificent views of the Mont Blanc group immediately opposite, the Bernese Alps to the NE and the mountains of Dauphiné to the SW.

Cableway up Flégère and from there to the Col de Fout: see below under "Walks and Climbs". – Cableway from Les Houches to the Pavillon de Bellevue. – Rack railway (the "Mont Blanc tram") from Le Fayet to the Nid d'Aigle.

WALKS and CLIMBS. – From Les Bossons, 4 km SW of Chamonix, in ¾ hr (chair-lift available) to the Pavillon des Bossons (1298 m: restaurant), on the left-hand lateral moraine of the Glacier des Bossons, with a fine view of the glacier and Mont Blanc du Tacul (4248 m) looming over it; to the left can be seen the Aiguille du Midi and the Aiguille du Plan

(3673 m). – There is a cableway (2205 m long; lower station 1509 m, upper station 1894 m) up *Flégère. The bridle-path (2½–3 hrs) leaves the road to Argentière on the left 800 m above the Chamonix church and in 1 hr reaches the Chalet de la Floriaz (1337 m: fine views). From here it is 1¾–2 hrs to the Croix de la Flégère (1877 m), a projecting spur of the Aiguilles Rouges, with a *view which has long been famous, almost as fine as the view from Le Brévent. – From Flégère there is a cabin cableway ("Télécabine de l'Index") to the Col du Fout (2385 m).

**Mont Blanc (4807 m), the highest peak in the Alps, over which the French–Italian frontier runs, was first climbed in 1786 by a village doctor named Michel Paccard with Jacques Balmat of Chamonix, and in the following year by the scientist Horace-Bénédict de Saussure with Balmat and 16 porters. To experienced climbers with a guide the climb offers no particular difficulties, but is extremely strenuous (danger of mountain sickness). From Les Houches the climb takes 10–12 hrs, taking the cableway to the Pavillon de Bellevue and continuing on the "Mont Blanc tram" to the Glacier de Bionnassay and from there on foot to the Chalet-Hôtel de Tête-Rousse (3167 m: 2 hrs). From here it is 3 hrs to the Refuge de l'Aiguille du Goûter (3817 m), and another 5 hrs to the summit. There are magnificent wide-ranging views, but the view from a mountain which is higher than the whole surrounding area is inevitably less impressive than the view of that mountain itself.

Of great importance to tourist traffic is the *Mont Blanc Tunnel, constructed 1958–64. It begins above the hamlet of Les Pèlerins at an altitude of 1274 m and runs through the mountain for a distance of 11·6 km to Entrèves (1381 m). The carriageway is 7 m wide, the total width including footway and buffer strip 8·15 m, the greatest height 5·98 m. The tunnel (toll charge), which is open all year round, shortens the distance from northern and central France and western Switzerland into Italy during the period when the high Alpine passes are closed (Oct.–June) by several hundred kilometres.

Champagne

The landscape of Champagne, lying between Lorraine and the Ile de France and bounded on the N by Belgium, on the S by Burgundy, has many different aspects – the cheerful aspect offered by its vineyards and valleys, in tune with the cheerfulness promoted by its most famous product, champagne; and the gloomier aspect resulting from

Mont Blanc (4807 m)

its situation – open and undefended in all directions – and reflected in the names of battles like Reims, Verdun and Chemin des Dames. The name Champagne comes from the Latin *campania*, an expanse of level country, and its derivative in English, "champaign", is an old word for battlefield.

In spite of the reputation of its wine, and notwithstanding the fine old buildings to be seen in such towns as Reims, Laon and Troyes, relatively few tourists make Champagne the object of their journey though many pass through it on the way to some other part of France. It is that Champagne does not offer scenery of the majestic beauty to be found in some other

Champagne – the Wine

(Note that in French *la Champagne* is the region, *le champagne* the wine.)

The production of wine in Champagne began in Gallo-Roman times – though it is recorded that a Roman governor of the 1st c. A.D. had all the vines torn out lest the grapes should attract an enemy. By A.D. 280, however, the Roman legions were again engaged in planting vines. St Remi, Archbishop of Reims in the 5th c., referred expressly to the vineyards of the region in his will. During the Middle Ages the fame of the wine of Champagne was spread far and wide by the trade fairs of the day.

In a champagne cellar, Reims

It was not until the late 17th c., however, that *Dom Pérignon* (after whom a particularly fine make of champagne is named), cellarer of Hautvillers Abbey, succeeded in achieving a natural fermentation in which the wine effervesced but still preserved its clarity. With the help of the *cuvée* system, blending grapes of different kinds, the champagne was given a richer bouquet. Thereafter champagne succeeded malmsey and sherry as the favourite drink of the European aristocracy. It still remained to solve the technical problems of making the bottles strong enough and finding the right kind of cork, but this was achieved in the time of Napoleon, who made a personal visit to Champagne in 1807.

After the Napoleonic wars the great days of the champagne export trade began, and millions of bottles went out from Reims and Epernay to countries all over the world. And yet the vine-growing area of Champagne is not particularly large, covering a strip of hilly land 150 km long and between 300 and 2000 m wide – only a fiftieth of France's total vine-growing area. In Champagne, too, only the finest kinds of grapes – small ones with few pips – are used; and no wine can be called champagne unless it comes from certain statutorily defined areas with a particular quality of soil.

Strict provisions prescribe that 8818 lb of grapes are to yield no more than two-thirds that amount (i.e. 704 gallons) of wine-must; and no more than this quantity can go through the rest of the wine-making process and be called champagne. The wine must be left in the cellars for five years, fermenting and dropping its sediment, before it can be sold. – Visitors passing through Champagne should make a point of calling in at one of the large champagne firms and seeing the process of producing champagne going on in their extensive cellars.

The terms *demi-sec* (semi-dry), *sec* (dry) and *brut* ("raw") refer to the quantity of "liqueur" (sugar dissolved in old champagne) added to the champagne to give the desired taste. – The produce of the 27,200 acres of vineyards is stored in cellars, which may be as much as 30 m underground, in the champagne-producing region. Since the name champagne can be applied only to wine produced in this region, other French sparkling wine must be sold – at much lower prices – either as *vin mousseux* or as wine made by the *méthode champenoise*. Nor may sparkling wines produced in other countries be described as champagne.

regions, and that it is short of popular holiday resorts; but it has much to offer the visitor, both in "Champagne sèche" ("dry" Champagne), whose permeable chalky soil and sunny hillsides provide the right conditions for the growth of the vines which produce champagne, and in "Champagne humide" ("wet" Champagne) with its prosperous stock-farms. And it is unfair to think of Champagne only as the scene of fighting in three Franco-German wars. Fortunately time has obliterated most of the traces of these wars, apart from those remains which have been preserved as memorials and the military cemeteries with their serried ranks of crosses, to be seen in so many places.

HISTORY. – Much of the history of France has been written in Champagne. When Caesar conquered Gaul in 57 B.C he made the chief town of a Belgic people, the *Remi*, a local capital, since eight trading routes met here; the town was then known as *Durocortorum*. After the collapse of the Roman Empire at the beginning of the 5th c. Archbishop St Remi baptised the Frankish king Clovis in Reims (496), establishing the city as the place of coronation of the French kings. In subsequent centuries authority lay in the hands of the Archbishops of Reims and the Counts of Champagne. In the Middle Ages Champagne, within which important fairs and markets were held, enjoyed great prosperity – a prosperity which was reflected in its architecture. In 1147 St Bernard launched his call for the Second Crusade in Châlons. Later centuries saw many vicissitudes in Champagne – the devastation wrought by the Hundred Years War, the crowning of the French king by Joan of Arc in 1429, the 16th c. Wars of Religion, another great building period in the 18th c., further destruction during the French Revolution, a period of war extending from the battle of Valmy in 1792 to Napoleon's battles of 1814, an economic upswing in the 19th c., and then the further setbacks caused by the war of 1870–71 and the two world wars.

SIGHTS. – The **Route du Champagne** runs through the vine-growing areas which produce the grapes used in making champagne. Starting from Reims, there are three sections of this route – the blue, red and green tours. There are four vine-growing areas, three producing black grapes and one white grapes, both colours being used together. The routes are signposted with special signs and are linked by D 1, the road running along the Marne. The total length of the circuit is about 120 km.

Reims: see p. 226. – **Troyes:** see p. 249.

Epernay (pop. 28,000) is, together with Reims, the chief centre of champagne production. In the Avenue de Champagne are to be seen the establishments of world-renowned champagne firms, and the Musée du Champagne displays old wine-presses and other items illustrating the history of champagne, along with archaeological material from the early historical period.

In **Hautvillers** (6 km NW of Epernay) is the abbey in which Dom Pérignon, the "inventor" of champagne, was cellarer. His tombstone is in the abbey. From the abbey garden there is a very beautiful view.

Soissons (pop. 32,000), on the Aisne, has been the see of a bishop since the 3rd c. The town suffered heavy damage in both world wars, but has long since been rebuilt. There are many military cemeteries in the surrounding area. In Place Centrale is the Gothic *Cathedral of St-Gervais-et-St-Protais (12th and 13th c.; well restored). To the S of the town are remains of the abbey of St-Jean-des-Vignes (13th–14th c.), including two 15th c. spires, respectively 70 and 75 m high, and the Gothic *façade of the church between them, together with a beautiful Gothic cloister.

Laon (pop. 30,000), NE of Soissons, the Roman *Laudunum* and now chief town of the department of Aisne, has an attractive *situation on a low hill. In the upper town stands the **Cathedral of Notre Dame with its seven towers, one of the

Laon Cathedral

Meuse valley

finest early Gothic churches in France (late 12th–early 13th c.). This handsome building, which has an external length of 121 m and an internal length of 110 m, provided the model for other large cathedrals. The W front, with three deep-set and richly decorated doorways, is flanked by two towers 56 m high. The *interior, 24 m high, is notable for its old stained glass, an 18th c. choir screen and a valuable treasury. Behind the choir is the former Bishop's Palace, now the Palais de Justice (Law Courts), with remains of a Gothic cloister. Near the Cathedral is a museum of archaeological and historical interest, in the garden of which is a Romanesque chapel of the Templars with a Gothic dome. Former abbey church of St-Martin (12th–13th c.), near which are the ruins of the 13th c. Porte de Soissons, linked by a wall with a leaning tower of the same period.

Châlons-sur-Marne (pop. 54,000) is chief town of the department of Marne, the see of a bishop and a centre of the wine trade. Its finest building is the early Gothic church of *Notre-Dame-en-Vaux, with four towers, one of the most beautiful churches in Champagne, notable particularly for the splendid 16th c. stained glass in the choir. The *Cathedral of St-Etienne (13th c.) also has stained glass of several different periods.

Bar-le-Duc (pop. 20,000), on the Rhine-Marne Canal, has two fine churches, Notre-Dame (15th and 18th c.) and St-Pierre (14th c.), and many picturesque old houses in Rue du Bourg, Rue des Ducs de Bar and Place St-Pierre. In the upper town are a ruined château, and a clock-tower which is a local landmark.

St-Amand-sur-Fion, near Vitry-le-François, is a typical Champagne village, with numerous half-timbered houses and an ochre-coloured medieval church.

L'Epine, near Châlons-sur-Marne, has a pilgrimage church of the 15th–16th c. with three late Gothic doorways (sculptured figures) which is like a miniature edition of Reims Cathedral.

Brienne-le-Château, near Bar-sur-Aube, has a late 18th c. château which belonged to the Brienne family. Napoleon spent five years at the military school here; there is a Musée Napoléon.

Visitors who want to see the **battlefields** should drive from Bar-le-Duc to **Verdun** (see p. 250) on the *Voie Sacrée*, the Sacred Way. Here, extending towards Lorraine, is the famous *Forêt d'Argonne*, the scene of heavy fighting during the First World War. Many places in Champagne – *Langres*, *Château-Thierry*, the *Chemin des Dames* and the *Marne*, to name only a few – recall the bloody battles of the past between Allied and German armies. There are organised excursions to the forts of *Vaux* and *Douaumont*, through the Forêt d'Argonne and along the Meuse to such places as *Eparges*, *Hattonchâtel*, *Apremont* and *St-Michel*.

Chartres

Region: Centre.
Department: Eure-et-Loir.
Altitude: 142 m. – Population: 45,000.
Post code: F-28000. – Dialling code: 37.
ⓘ **Office du Tourisme,**
  7 Cloître Notre-Dame;
  tel. 21 54 03.

HOTELS. – *Grand Monarque*, II, 48 r.; *France*, III, 40 r.; *Bœuf Couronné*, III, 26 r.; *Jehan de Beauce*, III, 46 r.; *Poste*, III, 56 r.; *Sports*, IV, 12 r.; *Métropole*, IV, 26 r.; *St-Jean*, IV, 15 r.

EVENTS. – *Students' pilgrimage* (April–May); *Musical Saturdays* (June and Sept.). *Organ recitals in the cathedral.*

Chartres, situated above the River Eure 100 km SW of Paris, is world-famed for its cathedral, but it is also the chief town of the department of Eure-et-Loir, the see of a bishop and the centre of the fertile agricultural region of Beauce, which extends NE towards Paris.

HISTORY. – Chartres seems to have been a religious centre from an early period, with a cave in which Druidic ceremonies took place. The first Christian church was built on the same site in the 4th c.; but the early churches were destroyed by a series of devastating fires (743, 858, 1020, 1194). The building of the present Cathedral began in 1195 and was completed in 1220, although the church was not consecrated until 1260. The early Gothic façade (1140–60) of the previous church, which still shows Romanesque features, was incorporated in the new building, and the Cathedral's most precious relic, the Virgin's veil, also escaped the fire. The building of the new church was begun in a demonstration of Christian unity, in which the whole community – high and low, rich and poor – shared in the work and hauled the carts bringing stone to the building site. Symbolically, too, the work was begun at Christmas. Since then, down to our own day, this incomparable Cathedral has suffered no serious damage in all the wars that have been fought over the centuries.

SIGHTS. – The **Cathedral is a master-piece of Gothic architecture, one of the earliest demonstrations of a new style and a new building technique. Of the six most famous French cathedrals (Amiens, Bourges, Chartres, Laon, Paris and Reims) "Chartres is the most austere and the

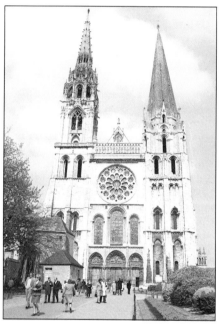

Chartres Cathedral

grandest" (Distelbarth). The great French sculptor Rodin set Chartres beside the Acropolis. But the names of the artists and craftsmen who created the Cathedral's extraordinary wealth of images in sculpture and stained glass remain entirely unknown.

The oldest parts of the CATHEDRAL (12th c.) are the *Royal Doorway (Portail royal), the S tower with its spire soaring to a height of 103 m and the lower part of the N tower. The façade also gives some impression of the previous building. The crypt, the largest in France, is also old (11th c.), and indeed incorporates an earlier structure dating from the 9th c.

The Cathedral was given its present form in the 13th c., and its architect (whose name is unknown) exerted

a decisive influence on the development of Gothic architecture in Europe. The building combines grandeur and elegance, and is quite without peer for its wealth of *sculpture and its abundance of **stained glass (over 2500 sq. m). – The dimensions of the church (130 m long, 32–46 m wide and over 36 m high) are evidently far beyond the needs of Chartres, but were justified by the large numbers of pilgrims who visited it from the earliest times. Many pilgrims still come to do honour to the graceful "Vierge du Pilier" (1507).

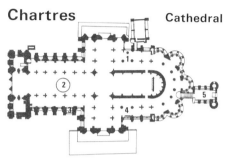

Chartres   Cathedral

1 Vierge du Pilier   4 Notre-Dame de la
2 Labyrinthe   Belle Verrière
3 Chapelle Vendôme   5 Chapelle St-Piat

Compared with the Cathedral the other buildings of Chartres inevitably pale into relative insignificance. The former **Bishop's Palace** (17th c.) now houses a museum (Flemish tapestries, pictures). Chartres also has a beautiful Gothic church, *St-Pierre*, and a number of old houses dating from the 13th and 15th c. A view of the Cathedral in all its majesty can be had from the bridges over the Eure.

Clermont-Ferrand

Region: Auvergne.
Department: Puy-de-Dôme.
Altitude: 410 m. – Population: 160,000.
Post code: F-63000. – Dialling code: 73.
ⓘ **Office de Tourisme,**
   69 Boulevard Gergovia;
   tel. 93 80 85.

HOTELS. – *Arverne*, I, 58 r.; *Frantel*, II, 124 r.; *Montjoly*, II, 32 r.; *Galliéni*, II, 80 r.; *Colbert*, III, 68 r.; *Midi*, III, 42 r.; *Excelsior*, III, 39 r.; *Albert-Elisabeth*, III, 38 r.; *Lyon*, III, 35 r.; *Bordeaux*, III, 32 r.; *Bristol*, III, 30 r.; *Fleury*, IV, 25 r.

Clermont-Ferrand, capital of Auvergne and its largest town by a considerable margin, is also chief town of the department of Puy-de-Dôme, a university town and the see of a bishop. It lies on rising ground in the fertile Limagne, bounded on the W by the Monts Dômes.

In spite of Clermont-Ferrand's considerable industrial activity the old town has preserved its old-world aspect, particularly in the area between the Cathedral and Notre-Dame-du-Port, where there are many houses dating from the 16th to the 18th c. The principal streets are Rue du Port, Rue Pascal, Rue du Terrail and Rue des Chaussetiers. The use of the local volcanic stone gives many of the houses a rather sombre colour, earning Clermont-Ferrand the name of "Ville Noire" ("Black Town").

HISTORY. – The name of the town, originally *Nemessos*, was changed in Roman times to *Augustonemetum*, and later still became *Castrum Claremunte* or *Clair-Mont*. The early prosperity of Clermont is reflected in the legend that when St Martin arrived in the town on his donkey he was greeted by such fashionably dressed local dignitaries that he forthwith turned about and departed. But however this may be the town was certainly Christianised in the 3rd c., and after suffering devastation at the hands of various invaders was the scene of the council at which Pope Urban II proclaimed the First Crusade in 1095. – The philosopher and mathematician Blaise Pascal (1623–62) was born here. – In 1630 Clermont was amalgamated with its neighbour and rival *Montferrand* to form the present-day town with its double-barrelled name. – In the 19th c., more or less by accident, Clermont-Ferrand became the main centre of the French tyre industry (Michelin).

SIGHTS. – From the spacious and imposing *Place de Jaude* Rue du 11-Novembre and *Rue des Gras* (old houses) lead to the **Cathedral**, one of France's finest Gothic cathedrals, built between 1248 and 1295 (with 19th c. spires and W front). The lightness of the structure was achieved by the use of volcanic stone (not found in any other cathedral). Much *stained glass of the 13th and 14th c. – Of earlier date is the church of *Notre-Dame-du-Port**, the main structure of which is 11th–12th c., with some even earlier work. The harmoniously conceived nave is a masterpiece of the Auvergnat Romanesque style. Richly carved capitals (human figures and animals). – The *Musée du Ranquet*, in the Renaissance mansion known as the Maison des Architectes (House of the Architects), with a charming courtyard, contains material of local and folk interest and mementoes of Pascal.

SURROUNDINGS. – The nearby town of **Royat** is a popular spa resort. – **Mozac**, to the N, has a former abbey church with capitals which are among the finest achievements of Romanesque sculpture. The adjacent little town of **Riom** has a fine Palais de Justice (Law Courts) and a late 14th c. *Sainte-Chapelle

Colmar

Region: Alsace.
Department: Haut-Rhin.
Altitude: 190 m. – Population: 67,000.
Post code: F-68000. – Dialling code: 89.

ⓘ **Office de Tourisme,**
   4 rue d'Unterlinden;
   tel. 41 02 29.

HOTELS. – *Terminus-Bristol*, II, 100 r.; *Champ de Mars*, II, 72 r.; *Novotel*, II, 60 r.; *Park*, II, 60 r.; *Colbert*, III, 30 r.; *Majestic*, III, 30 r.; *Kempf*, III, 28 r.; *Centre*, IV, 51 r.; *Beau Séjour*, IV, 28 r.; *Motel Azur*, on the Strasbourg road, IV, 19 r.

EVENTS. – *Alsace Wine Fair* (Aug.); *Sauerkraut Festival* (Sept.). – Every Tuesday during July and August there are *folk performances in the old town*, and every Thursday *serenade concerts in the Dominican convent*.

*Colmar, chief town of the department of Haut-Rhin in Upper Alsace and the third largest town in Alsace (after Strasbourg and Mulhouse), lies near the vine-covered foothills of the southern Vosges, in a situation which gives it a very agreeable climate. Lying near two major valleys in the Vosges, it is an excellent point from which to explore the High Vosges. With its picturesque old burghers' houses of the 16th and 17th c. and its wealth of outstanding works of art it is also one of the principal tourist attractions of Alsace in its own right.

Apart from the tourist trade, Colmar's economy depends on the textile industry (to the NW, along the banks of the Logelbach), on the production of foodstuffs and on metal-working (in the industrial zone to the N), together with market gardening (vegetables) and wine-production (of which Colmar is Alsace's principal centre). – 20 km SE is the Rhine port of Colmar-Neuf-Brisach.

HISTORY. – The town, first recorded in 823 under the name of *Columbarium* ("Dovecot"), was surrounded by walls in 1220. The Emperor Frederick II granted it the status of a free imperial city, which soon became the most important market town in Upper Alsace and a centre of art and learning. In 1354 Colmar joined the "Decapolis", the league of ten imperial cities in Alsace. The town was closely involved in the Reformation. During the Thirty Years War it was occupied by the Swedes and in 1673 by the French, and thereafter shared the destiny of Alsace. – Colmar was the birthplace of the painter and engraver *Martin Schongauer* (c. 1445–91), and the painter *Matthias Grünewald* (c. 1470/83–1528), the last and greatest master of the late Gothic period, also worked here.

SIGHTS. – On the W side of the old town, extending along the busy *Avenue de la République*, is the **Champ de Mars**, a long tree-planted open space which until 1804 was a military parade ground and then became a *municipal park*. On its W side is the *Head Post Office*, to the S is the *Prefecture* (1865–90), and $\frac{1}{2}$ km to the SW is the *railway station* (1905). To the N of the Champ de Mars, in Place du 18-Novembre, is the *Municipal Theatre* (1840).

Immediately E of the theatre is the former *Dominican convent of Unterlinden*, founded in the early 13th c., which became a great centre of mystical thought in the 14th and 15th c. It has preserved a beautiful early Gothic cloister. The conventual buildings and the early Gothic church (consecrated by Albertus Magnus in 1269) now house the **Unterlinden Museum*.

The CHAPEL contains fine paintings by early German artists, including **Passion scenes* by Martin Schongauer and works by Isenmann and other masters. Its chief treasure, however, is Matthias Grünewald's ****Isenheim Altar**, one of the greatest and most moving masterpieces of German painting, a work of glowing colour and great imaginative power (painted *c.* 1515 for the convent of Isenheim or Issenheim near Guebwiller; statues by Nicolas de Haguenau). There is a good general view of the painting from the gallery. – The *rooms round the cloister* contain a lapidarium and works of religious art (Romanesque and Gothic sculpture, stained glass, goldsmith's work) and an Alsatian wine-cellar. The beautiful *convent cellar* (13th c.) contains prehistoric, early historical, Gallo-Roman and Merovingian material. – On the *first floor* are collections of folk interest, furniture, weapons, pottery, porcelain, stained glass, engravings and modern paintings.

In the **old town*, with its narrow and winding streets, are many burghers' houses of the 16th and 17th c. S of the Unterlinden Museum, at 19 rue des Têtes, is the **Maison des Têtes** ("House of the Heads"), a handsome Renaissance build-

Kaysersberg, Sélestat, Strasbourg

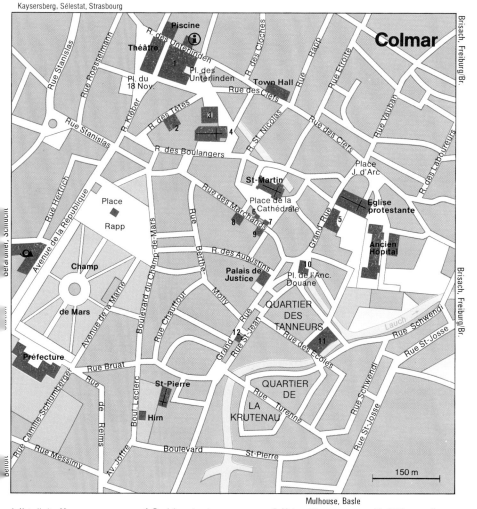

Mulhouse, Basle

1 Unterlinden Museum	4 Dominican church	7 Maison Pfister	10 Old Customs House
2 Maison des Têtes	5 Maison des Arcades	8 Bartholdi Museum	11 Market Hall
3 Municipal Library	6 Guard-House	9 Schongauer House	12 Hôtel des Chevaliers

Martin Schongauer's "Virgin of the Rose-Garden"

In *Place de la Cathédrale*, in the centre of the old town, is the church of **St-Martin**, originally Gothic but largely rebuilt in the 18th c. Noble High Gothic choir (1350–66); richly decorated St Nicholas Doorway in S transept; stained glass (15th c.) and fine carving in choir.

On the S side of the church is the former *Guard-House* (Corps de Garde, 1575), with an oriel window from which the decisions of the town council used to be announced. Adjoining this building is the Gothic *Maison Adolph* (14th c.), the town's oldest surviving private house. – Close by, at the corner of the picturesque *Rue Mercière* and *Rue des Marchands*, is the ***Maison Pfister** (1537: wooden

Maison Pfister, Colmar

ing (1609) decorated with numerous heads and figures; it is now occupied by a famous wine restaurant. – Farther S, in *Rue des Boulangers* and *Rue des Serruriers* (Bakers' Street and Locksmiths' Street), are other picturesque old half-timbered houses. Also in Rue des Serruriers is the early Gothic **Dominican church** (13th c.), a good example of the Dominican style of architecture. The interior, its roof supported by extraordinarily slender pillars, contains fine stained glass (14th–15th c.) and altars from Marbach Abbey, near Egisheim. Temporarily housed in the choir is the famous ***"Virgin of the Rose-Garden", Martin Schongauer's earliest painting (1473). Adjoining the church on the N is the former Dominican monastery, with a 15th c. cloister (serenade concerts) and the *Municipal Library* (manuscripts of the 8th–15th c., incunabula).

NE of the Dominican monastery, in Rue des Clefs, the main shopping street of the old town, is the 18th c. **Town Hall**. – SE of the Town Hall, in the *Grand Rue*, is a former *Franciscan church* (begun 1292), which has been used as a Protestant church since 1575: rood-screen and high choir. Immediately S of the church is the *Maison des Arcades*, with arches and oriel windows, which was built in 1606 to house the Protestant pastor. To the E of this house is the former *Municipal Hospital* (1735), now occupied by an Institute of Technology.

galleries), one of the finest houses in old Colmar. On the opposite side of the street is a house which is said to have been occupied by Martin Schongauer (who in fact lived in the house *"Au Cygne"*, in the adjoining Rue Schongauer). – Also in Rue des Marchands is the *Bartholdi Museum*, with mementoes of the famous French sculptor (1834–1904), creator of the statue of Liberty in New York and the Lion of Belfort, who was born here.

A little way S of the Maison Pfister, in *Place du Marché-aux-Fruits* (Fruitmarket Square), is the **Old Custom House** (*Ancienne Douane* or *Koifhus*), built in 1480, with 16th and 18th c. additions. This was once the economic and political centre of the town: the ground floor was used as a warehouse for goods awaiting payment of duty, and on the first floor is the handsome council chamber of the league of imperial cities, with coats of arms of the ten cities. On the E side of the Custom House is the *Place de l'Ancienne Douane*, with the *Schwendi Fountain* (by Bartholdi) commemorating the imperial general Lazarus von Schwendi (1552–84), who is said to have brought Tokay vines from Hungary during the Turkish wars and introduced them into Alsace. – To the SE is the QUARTIER DES TANNEURS (tanners' quarter), splendidly restored from 1968 onwards, with beautiful half-timbered houses. At the W corner of the *Market Hall* is the unusual *Fontaine du Vigneron* or Wine-Grower's Fountain (by Bartholdi, 1869).

SW of the Custom House is the 18th c. *Palais de Justice* (Law Courts). Still farther SW is the Venetian-style *Hôtel des Chevaliers de St-Jean* (House of the Knights of St John, 1608), one of the most striking Renaissance houses in Alsace. – To the SE extends the KRUTENAU QUARTER, traversed by the *Rue Turenne*.

The Krutenau quarter is bounded on the S by the *Boulevard St-Pierre*, from which the *Pont St-Pierre* crosses the River Lauch, with picturesque views of the old houses bordering the river and the tower of St-Martin. – Near the W end of Boulevard St-Pierre is the *church of St-Pierre*, a handsome Baroque structure erected by the Jesuits in the mid 18th c. on the site of a Carolingian royal fortress. In the gardens to the W of the church is a monument to the Colmar physicist G. A. Hirn (1815–90), by Bartholdi. – SW of this, in the *Parc du Château d'Eau*, is the *Natural History Museum*.

Les Corbières

This upland region to the S and SE of Carcassonne, still little frequented by tourists, was for centuries of great strategic importance as a bulwark of the French kingdom against Spain, its natural strength being reinforced by Carcassonne and five other fortified posts.

The Corbières region forms an area of transition between the Massif Central and the Pyrenees, reaching its highest point in the *Pic de Bugarach* (1231 m) E of Quillan. The Mediterranean climate favours the growth of cedars and cypresses as well as firs and oaks. The lower-lying parts of Corbières are a wine-growing area which was already well known in Roman times. – Since the region offers only limited hotel resources visitors will be well advised to make Carcassonne, Perpignan or Quillan their base.

SIGHTS. – **Quillan**, a little town with remains of fortifications and an 18th c. Town Hall.

Lagrasse, a village with remains of fortifications and an abbey built at various periods from the 11th to the 18th c.; 11th–13th c. cloister.

Fontfroide, a Cistercian abbey situated in a romantic upland valley, with a simple Romanesque church (13th c.) and a fine cloister and chapterhouse. The refectories and dormitories for monks and guests have been preserved.

The impressive ruins of the five strong points which together with Carcassonne formed the French defensive system – including the castles of *St-Martin*, *Termes* and *Arques* – lie along N 613, which runs through the Corbières region.

Along the N 117 (Quillan–Perpignan), perched on bare rocky crags, can be seen the Albigensian fortresses of *Puilaurens* (near Axat) and *Quéribus* (near the wine village of Maury). N of *Maury*, beyond Quéribus, is the particularly imposing Albigensian citadel of *Peyrepertuse* ("cleft rock").

NW of Quillan, on a sheer crag between *Bélesta* and *Lavelanet*, are the massive ruins of **Montségur**, which was the scene of horrifying events during the Albigensian wars. After a siege of the castle in 1244 200 Albigensians were burned alive in a field at the foot of the hill which became known as Prat dels Cremats (Meadow of the Burned). Some people believe that Montségur is the fabled Montsalvat where the Holy Grail containing Christ's blood is hidden. It is now the symbolic centre of the movement which seeks independence for "Occitania", the old *langue d'oc*-speaking region.

* * **Carcassonne:** see p. 89.

Corsica

*Corsica (Corse), France's largest island and the fourth largest in the Mediterranean, lies nearer Italy than the French mainland. It has an area of 8722 sq. km and is 183 km long by up to 84 km wide, with a total coastline of some 1000 km. It is a mountainous island, reaching its highest point in Monte Cinto (2717 m). The population is 280,000, with an average density of only 23 to the sq. kilometre. It is the sixth largest of the French departments, with its capital at Ajaccio.

The island, which has been christened the "island of light" and the "island of beauty", offers its visitors a great variety of scenery and occupation, combining sub-tropical vegetation with scope for climbing and even skiing in the hills of the interior, as well as a whole range of sandy beaches round the coasts. The luxuriant growth of vegetation – forest, scrub (macchia), olive-trees, orange-groves, vineyards and an abundance of flowers – led Napoleon, a native of the island, to say: "I would recognise Corsica with my eyes closed from its perfume alone."

CLIMATE. – The nature of its topography gives the island a wide range of climatic variations. Visitors tend to think in the first place of its hot dry Mediterranean summer and its rainy autumn; and indeed the winter temperatures in the coastal regions of Corsica, averaging 14 °C (57 °F), are distinctly higher than on the Côte d'Azur, the climate of which is most nearly comparable. At the height of summer, in spite of Corsica's insular situation, it can be very hot (average 25 °C (77 °F)), so that the best time for a visit is in May, June or September. Spring comes to the S coast as early as the end of February or the beginning of March. In the hills, however, the climate is considerably harsher, and the pattern of snowfall and snow-melt is similar to that of the Alps, so that many roads in the mountains may be impassable from October until May. In summer heat, however, the cooler climate of the mountainous regions of the interior can be agreeable.

HISTORY. – The original inhabitants of Corsica were a mixture of Iberians and Ligurians. In 564 B.C. Phocaeans settled on the E side of the island, followed by Etruscans and Carthaginians. The Romans landed in Corsica in 259 B.C. and had considerable difficulty in subduing the inhabitants. Later the island became a place of exile, and the philosopher Seneca, among others, was confined here for eight years. The fall of the Western Roman Empire was followed by the arrival successively of Vandals, Ostrogoths, Byzantines, Franks and Saracens, so that the island was always falling into the hands of new masters. In 1070 Pisa annexed Corsica, but lost it in 1284 to Genoa, which pursued a harsh policy of repression and exploitation. There were various risings against the oppressors, during one of which the Corsican freedom fighter Sampiero di Bastelica was murdered by the Genoese (1527); but until the 18th c. these had no success. At last, in 1735, the Corsicans succeeded in breaking free from Genoa, and a German adventurer named Theodor von Neuhof became king. In 1746 Corsica declared its independence, and Pasquale Paoli (1725–1807) showed himself a skilled and successful politician. But although the Genoese had been worsted they still held out in Bastia, and this led them in 1768 to cede the island to France. There was some resistance, but the cession went through, and in the following year Napoleon Buonaparte was born in Ajaccio. Nevertheless the conflict between the Corsicans, the French (particularly during the Revolution) and the British, to whom the Corsicans had appealed for aid, continued until 1796, when Napoleon, now famous and powerful, made "his" island finally part of France, after the British forces had withdrawn without a fight. During the Second World War Corsica was occupied by Italian and German forces until 1943.

COMMUNICATIONS. – Corsica can be reached either by sea or by air. There are air services (Air France) from Paris, Marseilles and Nice to Ajaccio and Bastia. The flight takes 100 minutes from Paris and 30 minutes from Nice. There are daily services only from June to October; during the rest of the year there is a reduced service from Paris. Air Inter also flies services from Paris, Marseilles and Nice to Ajaccio, Bastia and Calvi; the service between Marseilles or Nice and Calvi operates throughout the year. – There are boat services from both France and Italy. The shortest crossing is from Livorno (Italy) to Bastia (7 hours); from Genoa it is about the same. The crossing from the French ports of Marseilles, Toulon and Nice to Ajaccio, Bastia or Calvi takes between $6\frac{1}{2}$ and $11\frac{1}{2}$ hours. – Car ferries: see box.

Car Ferries to Corsica

From France

Marseilles–Bastia	daily
Nice–Ajaccio	daily
Nice–Bastia	daily
Nice–Calvi	daily
Nice–Ile Rousse	daily
Nice–Propriano	several times weekly
Toulon–Bastia	several times weekly

These services are run by the **SNCM** line. Agent in Britain: P & O Normandy Ferries, Arundel Towers, Portland Terrace, Southampton SO9 4AE (tel. 0703-34141).

From Italy

Genoa–Bastia	several times weekly
Livorno–Bastia	several times weekly
Piombino–Bastia	several times weekly
San Remo–Bastia	several times weekly
San Remo–Calvi	several times weekly

These services are mainly run by the **Corsica** Line of Genoa.

There are also services between Bonifacio in Corsica and Santa Teresa Gallura in Sardinia.

Within Corsica there are *air services* between Ajaccio, Bastia, Calvi and Propriano. There is a very attractive *rail* connection (rail buses) between Ajaccio, Corte, Bastia, L'Ile-Rousse and Calvi. There are *bus services* on the most important roads, and during the holiday season there are regular coach excursions from Ajaccio, Bastia and other places. A circuit of Corsica *by car* (self-drive hire facilities available in the towns), including detours, involves a journey of some 1100 km. The roads are good, but sometimes narrow, winding and hilly, so that the average speed is low and a trip of 200 to 250 km is the maximum that can be managed in a day. It should be remembered, too, that outside the towns petrol stations are sometimes few and far between. It would be wise to allow a week for the round trip; Ajaccio makes a good starting point. The height of summer is not perhaps the best time for the trip, even though part of the route runs through the cooler mountainous regions.

CIRCUIT OF CORSICA. – From **Ajaccio** (see p. 53) S to **Olmeto** (pop. 1300), situated amid olive-groves, with the ruins of the *Castello della Rocca* looming over it. – On to **Propriano** (pop. 2800), a popular bathing and health resort with a beautiful beach near the town. – **Sartène** (pop. 5500), in the Sartenais district, with a picturesque *old town of medieval aspect whose narrow streets are entered under the arch of the Town Hall. The *Sartenais* contains much unspoiled scenery typical of southern Corsica. – Farther S to **Bonifacio** (pop. 2640), a picturesque little fortified town in a magnificent **situation on a limestone peninsula 1500 m long with cliffs rising sheer from the sea to a height of 64 m. It faces Sardinia, only 11·5 km away across the strait called the Bouches de Bonifacio. Bonifacio is a town of old houses flanking medieval lanes. The Citadel can be visited by special arrangement. The most notable of the churches is Ste-Marie-Majeure (originally 12th c. but several times rebuilt); the tower is 15th c. St-Dominique (13th–14th c.) is one of the finest Gothic churches on the island; in the interior are interesting groups of figures of carved wood which are carried in procession.

From Bonifacio the road runs N to **Porto-Vecchio** (pop. 7000), on the gulf of the same name, a centre of the cork trade. It still preserves parts of its old walls and a 16th c. Genoese citadel. In the vicinity are beaches of fine sand. – Through the *Forêt de l'Ospedale* (oaks, pines) to **Zonza** (784 m; pop. 1030), set amid chestnut trees. – Over the **Col de Bavella (1242 m) to **Solenzara**, with remains of a Roman road (a unique feature in Corsica). – **Ghisonaccia** (pop. 1020), near which is a Genoese watch-tower, the Torre di

Vignale. – **Zicavo** (pop. 1240), a popular summer resort, from which *Mont l'Incudine* (2136 m) can be climbed (with guide and mule); from the top there is a magnificent view of Corsica. – **Vivario** (620 m), in a very beautiful *situation, with a handsome bridge over the Vecchio and a fountain with a figure of Diana the Huntress. – Through the ***Forêt de Vizzavona** (the village of that name being a popular summer resort) and over the Col de Vizzavona (1161 m) to **Corte** (pop. 6000), in the centre of the island. Above the town, on a rocky ridge, stands the 15th c. Citadel. Corte has played an important part in the history of Corsica: from 1755 to 1769 it was the island's capital, with a university which continued in existence until 1790. The Citadel, which is occupied by the Foreign Legion, is not open to visitors. The Palais National is of interest for its associations with Pasquale Paoli, the champion of Corsican independence, and for an instructive museum devoted to the history of the island. Beside the 17th c. church of the Annunciation stands a Baroque bell-tower. – From Corte a detour can be made to the ***Gorges de la Restonica** below *Monte Rotondo* (2625 m).

Beyond Corte, at *Francardo*, turn W and continue via *Calacuccia*, below the island's highest peak, ***Monte Cinto** (2707 m), and the ***Forêt de Valdo-Niello** with its laricio pines, then over the *Col de Vergio* (1464 m) to **Porto** (pop. 350), a popular bathing resort, with the

The Calanche on the west coast of Corsica

bathing station of Marine de Porto on the bay of the same name. – Above the bay, between Porto and *Piana*, are the curious rock formations known as the **Calanche**, granite pinnacles worn into bizarre forms resembling fabulous animals. Similar formations are to be seen on the road which continues N over the *Col de la Croix* (272 m) and the *Col de Palmarella* (374 m) and through the lonely *Balagne Déserte*, with the ruins of a silver-mine, to **Calvi** (pop. 3600), the port situated nearest France. During the period of Genoese rule Calvi was the principal place on the island, and from this period dates the fortress-like upper town. The town was completely destroyed in 1794 by a British naval expedition commanded by Nelson. There is an attractive palm-fringed promenade besides the harbour, and near this is the church of Santa Maria, originally founded in the 4th c. but rebuilt in the 14th. In the upper town is the Cathedral of St-Jean-Baptiste, originally built in the 13th c., destroyed in 1553 and soon afterwards rebuilt; it contains a celebrated crucifix and other fine pieces of carving. The house in Rue Colombo which is described as Columbus's birthplace (the "Maison Colomb") is probably not authentic, since there are other alleged birthplaces of the great discoverer in Italy and Spain. The situation and appearance of Calvi are striking, and in the Gulf of Calvi is a flat sandy beach 4 km long, the attraction which draws so many visitors to this holiday resort with its numerous hotels.

Beyond Calvi the route runs E through the fertile *Balagne* area (or alternatively on the shorter coastal route via *Algajola*) to **Belgodere** (pop. 530), in a picturesque *situation on the slopes of a hill, with a 13th c. castle. – **Ile-Rousse** (pop. 2500), on the coast, is not an island, as its name suggests: the name comes from the red rocks of La Pietra. Like Calvi, this is a very popular resort, though on a more modest level, with no luxury hotels. It was founded only in 1758 by Pasquale Paoli on the site of an earlier Roman settlement as a complement to Calvi. The climate has the reputation of being particularly mild. – Then into the hills and over the *Col de Lavezzo* (312 m) to **St-Florent** (pop. 830), charmingly situated on the gulf of the same name, with an old castle. Nearby are the remains of the medieval *Nebbio*, with the Romanesque Cathedral of Santa Maria dell'Assunta (12th c.), built of

limestone. Either from here or from Bastia visitors should make the trip (130 km) round the **Cap Corse** peninsula, the northernmost tip of the island, an area of typically Corsican scenery which will complete their impression of the island. Along the peninsula runs the *Serra* range of hills, reaching heights of up to 1305 m, while on the W side fertile valleys run down to the coast, offering favourable conditions for the growing of vines, olives and fruit, which are cultivated on a considerable scale. For much of the way the road is narrow, with poor visibility, and plenty of time should therefore be allowed for the trip. The principal places on the peninsula are the following:

Nonza (pop. 200), with an old defensive tower, in a magnificent *situation E of *Monte Stello* (1305 m).

Canari, with two medieval churches; large asbestos workings.

Pino (pop. 1000), in a picturesque *situation, with a former Franciscan friary (1486). The Torre di Seneca, on the Col Ste-Lucie, 5 km away, is said to have been the philosopher's prison in the years A.D. 43–49.

Centuri (pop. 600) is an attractive place, consisting of a number of different settlements between the road and the harbour. Several churches. From the mill at Mattei, on the road to the **Col de la Serra** (362 m), there are extensive views.

Rogliano, with the fishing village of *Macinaggio* (pop. 500), is made up of a number of separate hamlets. Napoleon landed here in 1793. Old Genoese watch-towers. From the Franciscan friary at Vignale (now in ruins) and from Cagnano Christianity spread out over Corsica.

Erbalunga has old patrician houses. Interesting Good Friday processions here and in the surrounding area.

Brando (pop. 1000) has, near the village, a stalactitic cave from which there is a fine view. At Castello is a charming Romanesque church, Notre-Dame-des-Neiges (13th–14th c.).

SPORT and RECREATION. – Excellent facilities for *water sports*; 1800 boat moorings in Ajaccio, Bastia, Bonifacio, Calvi, Cargèse, Campoloro, Macinaggio, Porto-Vecchio, Propriano, Sant'Ambrogii, St-Florent and Solenzara; more than 20 sailing clubs and ten sailing schools (in addition to private schools); wide scope for scuba diving. – *Riding*: 300 km of bridle-paths; riding clubs or stables in Ajaccio, Bastia, Calvi, Piedicroce, Calacuccia, Venaco, Porto-Vecchio, Serra di Scopamene and Propriano. – *Shooting* between the end of August and beginning of January; wildfowling on the E coast. Permits issued by 130 shooting clubs. – *Fishing*: permits for river fishing issued by angling clubs. – *Rifle ranges* (April–Sept.) at Afa (10 km from Ajaccio), Bastia, Ponte Leccia, Olivese, Propriano, Porto-Vecchio and Ghisonaccia. – *Caving*: information from Association Spéléologique, 1 rue Major-Lambroschini, Ajaccio. – *Flying clubs* at Ajaccio, Marana, La Balagne and Calvi; at Calvi also parachute jumping. – *Hill walking and climbing*: Corsica offers excellent opportunities, with more than 50 peaks over 2000 m. Trips organised by the club I Montagnoli Corsi, 11 Boulevard Sampiero, Ajaccio. – *Skiing*, with lifts, at Haut-Asco, Ghisoni, Col de Vergio; *ski trekking* at Evisa (hotels), Bastelica, Zicavo and Quenza.

Côte d'Argent

Côte d'Argent ("Silver Coast") is the name applied to the stretch of coast between Arcachon in the N and Bayonne in the S. Its particular attraction lies in its beautiful sandy beaches (with only an occasional jarring note in the remains of the "Atlantic Wall" defences of the Second World War) and the expanses of forest which border them. The beauty of the region is enhanced by a number of attractive lakes lying just inland and by lines of dunes, at Pyla reaching heights of over 100 m. The name Côte d'Argent comes from the silvery sand of the beaches, along which several modern holiday centres are under construction, promising a considerable expansion of the tourist facilities of the region.

HISTORY. – For many centuries the masses of sand which were deposited along the coast at the rate of 15 cubic metres a year for every metre of coastline were carried west by the wind to form travelling dunes which extended far inland and moved forward at the rate of anything up to 25 metres annually. The land lying just in from the coast became a mixture of sandy steppe and heathland, which blocked the flow of the rivers and created barren and unhealthy expanses of marsh and bog. Towards the end of the 18th c. steps were taken to stabilise the dunes by planting coniferous trees, and by 1867 7400 acres of coastal dunes and 198,000 acres of inland dunes had been consolidated in this way, converting the barren landscape of earlier days into a green girdle of pines and oak-trees. By 1939 there were 2.2 million acres of forest, but a third of this area was destroyed by devastating fires between 1943 and 1950. These losses have now been made good by further planting.

SIGHTS. – **Arcachon** (pop. 16,000), which is both a bathing and a health resort, is made up of a "summer town", 5 km long, on the Bassin d'Arcachon and a "winter town" in the wooded duneland to the S. Arcachon and the Ile aux Oiseaux in the middle of the Bassin are noted centres of oyster culture. – At **Pyla** (SW of Arcachon) is a dune 114 m high.

The harbour of **Mimizan** was of importance in the Middle Ages but silted up in the 18th c. On the coast is the resort of *Mimizan-Plage*.

Hossegor is a fashionable bathing resort, with numbers of villas built along the shores of a salt coastal lagoon.

Capbreton, which can also be reached from Hossegor by boat, was formerly an important port and the home of seamen who found their way to Newfoundland as early as 1392. It is now a popular bathing resort.

Côte d'Azur

The ****Côte d'Azur** ("Azure Coast"), also known as the French Riviera, extends along the Mediterranean coast of France from Marseilles to the Italian frontier at Menton. In recent years it has developed on a scale which has produced a great wave of new building and an overwhelming increase in tourist traffic, particularly during the main summer holiday season, and has destroyed much of its former charm in the process. Visitors who want to get to know it properly should go at the less busy times of year, in spring or autumn, or in winter when the climate is pleasantly mild.

The varied aspect of this coastal region is conditioned by the bays opening off the sea and the offshore islands, and also by the hills just inland, which shut out the cold N winds. From Toulon the Massif des Maures, rising to barely 800 m, extends eastwards to the River Argens, with the Iles d'Hyères lying off the coast. From St-Raphaël, which marks the beginning of the French Riviera in the narrower sense, the Esterel hills, rising to just over 600 m, extend for 20 km to just short of Cannes, with a maximum width of 12 km. Farther

Massif de l'Esterel at Anthéor on the Côte d'Azur

NE the Maritime Alps draw steadily closer to the coast, and rise steeply from the coastal strip immediately behind the principality of Monaco.

The Côte d'Azur is one long succession of holiday resorts. Whether on the coast, in the hinterland or in the hills, visitors have a great choice which offers something for every taste. There are some 50 resorts on the coast and almost a hundred in the hinterland at varying distances from the sea, from Fréjus (alt. 8 m) to the Alpine skiing resort of Isola 2000 near the Italian frontier. Over the years the popularity of the coastal resorts has varied according to the dictates of fashion. Nice, the leading resort in the 19th c., was later obliged to relinquish its position in favour of Cannes. Since the end of the last war St-Tropez has developed from a small fishing village into a fashionable rendezvous for artists and film stars. New roads – particularly the motorway which runs just inland from the coast – have been built in an attempt to provide easy access to the resorts and at the same time prevent the steadily increasing traffic from affecting their amenities; but at the height of the season the popular tourist routes on the Corniches are, and long have been, quite inadequate for meeting the double requirement of speeding the traffic and yet enabling tourists to enjoy the scenery they have come to see.

CLIMATE. – The sheltered situation of the Côte d'Azur produces an equable climate without severe fluctuations. In summer it is not too hot (July average

24°C (76°F)) and in winter the day temperatures are not unduly low (6–15°C (42–59°F)), although it can become quite cool at night. Rainfall is not heavy, and occurs mainly in spring and autumn, so that summer and winter are usually sunny. In winter the sea is not warm enough to allow bathing, which begins in May and lasts well into autumn. In the area SW of Cannes the cold mistral can sometimes be troublesome, while in summer the sirocco will occasionally waft in hot air from the S. The mild climate naturally affects the vegetation pattern: among the plants found along the Côte d'Azur are palms, olives, oranges and lemons, pines, cypresses, eucalyptus and other species, such as cacti and agaves from warm regions, as well as flowers of all kinds which are exported from this region (and from its continuation, the Italian "Riviera dei Fiori").

HISTORY. – There were *Ligurian* settlers here at the beginning of the 1st c. B.C. Marseilles was founded even earlier (*c.* 600 B.C.) by *Greeks*, under the name of *Massalia*, and became a considerable trading centre, as did Nice (*Nicaea*). The 4th c. B.C. saw the arrival in Provence of the *Celts*, who in 122 B.C. were defeated by the *Romans*. In 102 B.C. Marius halted the advance of the Teutons near Aix. After Caesar had conquered Gaul he founded *Forum Julii* or Fréjus (49 B.C.). Other Roman settlements established in the early centuries A.D. were Nice and Antibes; and in the 4th and 5th c. Christianity extended its hold along the coastal region.

In the first half of the 8th c. the *Saracens* reached the Mediterranean coast of France. Having established themselves in the Massif des Maures, they harassed the whole coastal region in the 9th and early 10th c. (The name Maures, however, has nothing to do with the Moors, but comes from the Provençal word *maouro*, meaning "dark forest".) Along with the rest of Provence the coastal regions frequently changed their national allegiance in subsequent centuries. In 1486, however, Provence was finally incorporated in France, apart from Nice, which had been joined to Savoy in 1388.

Among the various vicissitudes of French history two events particularly concerned the Côte d'Azur. On 1 March 1815 Napoleon, returning from Elba, landed at Golfe-Juan and began his march on Paris; and in

Port-Grimaud (Var)

August 1944 Allied troops landed on the Mediterranean coast of France and within two weeks had
freed the whole of Provence, only Nice holding out
until 30 August. – After a transitional period from
1815 to 1860 when the territory round Nice belonged
to the kingdom of Sardinia the final return of the Côte
d'Azur to France took place in 1860.

SIGHTS. – The main features of interest
are described below in geographical
rather than alphabetical order, following
the line of the road which runs E or NE
from **Marseilles** (see p. 150) to the
Italian frontier.

Toulon: see p. 245.

Hyères (pop. 38,000), situated slightly
inland, is the oldest winter resort on the
Côte d'Azur. Picturesque old lanes round
the Place St-Paul in the old town; 13th c.
house, well restored, in Rue Paradis.
Municipal Museum, with Greek and
Roman material from the region. From
here (or from Toulon, La Tour Fondue, Le
Lavandou, Cavalaire or La Londe) a trip
can be made to the **Iles d'Hyères,
known during the Renaissance period as

the "golden islands". The largest and
most westerly is *Porquerolles* (7·5 km
long, 2 km wide). S of the harbour is a tall
lighthouse (96 m high: view), whose light
can be seen 63 km away. – E of
Porquerolles is the island of *Port-Cros*
(4·5 km long, 2 km wide, highest point
197 m), which together with the smaller
neighbouring islands is a nature reserve. –
Immediately E of Port-Cros is the small
rocky *Ile du Levant*, in the western part of
which, at the village of Héliopolis, is a
naturist colony.

The **Massif des Maures**, a range of
wooded hills, lies between Hyères and St-
Raphaël, reaching its highest point in *La
Sauvette* (779 m); the Iles d'Hyères
originally belonged to the same range.
The hills, once lonely and deserted, now
attract increasing numbers of tourists. –
The *Corniche des Maures* runs close to
the coast from Hyères to *Le Lavandou*,
Cavalière, *Cavalaire-sur-Mer* and *Croix-
Valmer*, where the road turns inland
towards St-Tropez and continues along
the coast to St-Raphaël. – A beautiful *trip
through the Massif des Maures* (rather
more than 100 km) is from Lavandou by
way of the *Col de Babaou* (415 m:
extensive views), the ruins of the *Chartreuse de la Verne*, **Grimaud**, the *Col du
Canadel* (267 m) and the rocky mass of
the *Pierre d'Avenon*.

St-Tropez, once a small fishing port, has
become the haunt of artists and the jet set.
In the Musée de l'Annonciade is a
collection of pictures presented by

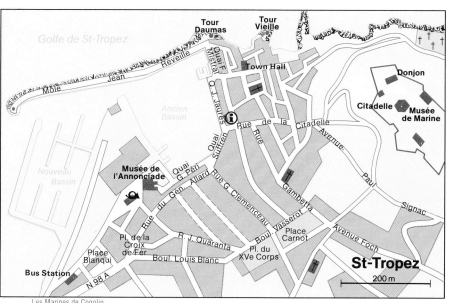

Les Marines de Cogolin
St-Raphaël

Boat harbour, St-Tropez (Var)

Georges Grammont covering the period from 1890 to 1940, with works by numerous modern painters and sculpture by Maillol and Despiau. Within the Citadel (16th–17th c.) is a Maritime Museum, with an exhibit illustrating the Allied landings of 1944. The harbour is always full of yachts and sailing boats.

Fréjus (pop. 31,000) lies on a rocky plateau in the plain between the Massif des Maures and the Esterel hills. Its Roman remains include the oldest amphitheatre in Gaul (113 m long by 85 m across – rather smaller than those of Nîmes or Arles), one of the town gates, a badly ruined theatre and some fragments of an aqueduct. The Roman harbour originally covered an area of 54 acres, with 2 km of quays, and was linked with the sea by a channel 500 m long and 30 m wide. Once a fortified episcopal town, Fréjus preserves its Cathedral, a cloister and the Bishop's Palace. The town's oldest building, by a considerable margin,

Malpasset Dam, near Fréjus, after the 1959 breach

is the 4th–5th c. *baptistery, a square structure (11 by 11 m) adjoining the Cathedral. Fréjus suffered a major disaster in 1959 when a dam burst above the town and drowned 421 people; there is a commemorative monument near the Roman amphitheatre.

The port town of **St-Raphaël** (pop. 21,500), which also dates from Roman times, is a popular winter resort. Napoleon's arrival here on his return from Egypt in 1799 is commemorated by a pyramid in the Avenue du Commandant-Guilbaud. The 12th c. Templars' church also served as a fortress. There is a museum containing archaeological finds from the sea, including many Greek amphoras of the 5th c. B.C.

Harbour, St-Raphaël

The **Massif de l'Esterel** which begins at St-Raphaël was opened up in 1903 by a coastal road, the **Corniche d'Or**. The highest point is *Mont Vinaigre* (618 m). The forests which formerly covered the hills were almost completely destroyed by fire in 1964, and the process of replanting is slow and difficult. – The **Corniche de l'Esterel** runs from St-Raphaël to **Cannes** (see p. 87), passing through all the coastal resorts. A return route from Cannes to St-Raphaël is by N 7, which runs inland, passing close to Mont Vinaigre (which must be climbed on foot: magnificent views). Other roads take in the *Pic du Cap Roux* (*c.* 40 km) and the *Pic de l'Ours* (rather over 50 km). From the Pic de l'Ours (496 m) and the Pic du Cap Roux (452 m) there are incomparable views of the coast and the hills.

EXCURSION. – 17 km N of Cannes on N 567 (the "Route Napoléon"), in a sheltered situation on the slopes of *Roquevignon*, is the old town of **Grasse** (alt. 206–526 m; pop. 35,000), whose mild climate makes it a popular winter resort. The town is famous for its extensive fields of flowers, providing the raw material which makes Grasse the principal centre of the European perfume industry (distillation of rose,

View of Vence (Alpes-Maritimes)

jasmine, lavender, etc., essences). The town was the see of a bishop from 1244 to 1790. The manufacture of perfume began in the 16th c., in the time of Catherine de Médicis. In the SE of the old town is the former Cathedral of Notre-Dame (12th c., enlarged in the 17th and 18th), which has a fine interior. Opposite it, in the former Bishop's Palace (originally 13th c.), is the Town Hall. An 18th c. mansion houses the Musée d'Art et d'Histoire de Provence (history of the town, furniture, ceramics, etc.). In the chapel of the Hôpital de Petit-Paris are three early paintings by Rubens. Fine views from the Cours Honoré-Cresp, the town's principal promenade.

The *Cap d'Antibes forms the tip of a peninsula which projects into the sea at Juan-les-Pins and Antibes. On the cape is a very powerful lighthouse. The *Jardin Thuret, named after the scientist who began to establish exotic trees here in 1856, offers a general survey of the subtropical trees and plants which grow in this region. A walk or drive round the cape affords splendid views. – Antibes, facing Nice across a long bay, is a great flower-growing centre (particularly roses, pinks and anemones). Cathedral, with Romanesque choir; narrow old streets; Château Grimaldi (16th c., with a rect-angular Romanesque tower from an earlier structure), now housing a Picasso Museum (pictures, lithographs, sketches, ceramics).

Cagnes-sur-Mer (pop. 30,000), set in a hilly landscape gay with flowers, consists of an upper town, Haut-de-Cagnes, dominated by a medieval castle, and the fishing village of Gros-de-Cagnes on the coast. The castle was built by Raynier Grimaldi, lord of Monaco, from 1309 onwards and considerably extended and embellished by his successor Henri Grim-aldi in 1620. Much restoration work has been carried out over the past 100 years, and the castle now houses a museum covering various fields of interest, includ-ing in particular a rich collection of

modern Mediterranean art. There is also a Renoir Museum, with the painter's studio and living quarters (he spent the last 12 years of his life here).

EXCURSION. – D 36 runs N into the hills towards Vence. 8 km from Cagnes is St-Paul-de-Vence (alt. 182 m; pop. 1600), a *picturesque little town perched on a hill which has preserved its medieval character; home of the painter Marc Chagall. The 16th c. town walls are well preserved; 13th c. Gothic church with a valuable treasury. A kilometre from the town is the *Maeght Foundation, an art and open-air museum, together with a group of artists' studios: works by Arp, Bonnard, Braque, Chagall, Giacometti, Kandinsky, Miró and Tal-Coat. – 4 km beyond St-Paul is the old town of Vence (alt. 325 m; pop. 12,000), still partly surrounded by its walls, a popular resort in both summer and winter (flower-growing). The former Cathedral of St-Véran (10th–15th c.) has fine choir-stalls and an altar made from a Roman sarcophagus. In the NW outskirts is the *Chapelle du Rosaire (1950), with frescoes by Matisse. Modern paintings in "Les Arts" gallery. Small open-air museum of Gallo-Roman remains; old oil-presses. Just outside the old town is the 15th c. Chapelle des Pénitents Blancs.

Maeght Foundation, St-Paul-de-Vence

There are three corniche roads along the coast between Nice (see p. 161) and Menton – the *Petit Corniche, which keeps close to the coast; the **Moyenne Corniche, half-way up the slope; and the **Grande Corniche, the highest of the three, which offers continually changing views of the coast and the hills. The distance in each case is about 30 km. It is a good idea to drive along a stretch of each of the corniche roads, since the outlook from each is different. The Grande Cor-niche was built in the time of Napoleon, replacing the old Roman Via Aurelia.

Eze (alt. 0–427 m; pop. 2000), in a strikingly picturesque **situation S of the Moyenne Corniche, is made up of two parts, one inland, the other on the coast. In the narrow lanes are numerous work-shops producing craft articles (pottery, pewterware, olive-wood carving) and perfume. Eze-Village, picturesquely situated on a crag crowned by a ruined

Eze-Village

castle (magnificent view), is still surrounded by 17th c. walls. Museum of local history and religious art. The Chapelle des Pénitents Blancs contains modern frescoes by J.-M. Poulin. From the interesting *Jardin Exotique, a botanical garden, there are wide views. – On the coast is the fishing village of *Eze-Bord-de-Mer*, now a popular holiday resort.

Roquebrune-Cap-Martin (pop. 11,000) lies between **Monaco** (see p. 154) and Menton. Its great attraction is the charming old village with its narrow arched lanes and its castle keep. The castle of *Roquebrune* is an example, unique in France, of the Carolingian strongholds which preceded by two centuries the castles of the feudal period. It was built at the end of the 10th c. as a means of defence against Saracen raids. The keep, with walls between 2 and 4 m thick, towers to a height of 26 m above the surrounding lanes.

Menton (pop. 25,000), in Italian *Mentone*, the last French town before the Italian frontier, is another major resort. Until 1848 it belonged to the principality of Monaco, and after a period under the protection of the king of Sardinia was purchased by France in 1861. It is credited with the mildest climate on the Côte d'Azur and is accordingly a very popular winter resort. Lemon-trees and other subtropical species flourish here. An international Festival of Chamber Music is held annually in August. The old town and the Promenade Georges-V are attractive features of Menton. Near the harbour is the Cocteau Museum, and inland is an interesting Botanic Garden.

In addition to the endless variety of coastal scenery, the capes and bays and hills, the picturesque towns and villages, the interesting little harbour towns and the old local capitals farther inland, the Côte d'Azur offers another attraction in the form of the numerous **Villages Perchés** (hilltop villages) or *nids d'aigle* (eagles' eyries), built on inaccessible sites on hills, crags or ridges of rock in order to escape the attentions

Menton

of foreign raiders or conquerors. The limited space available on these sites made it necessary to build houses of small surface area but considerable height, huddled closely together. Although these villages are increasingly being abandoned by their original inhabitants because of the difficulty of access and often the shortage of water, they are popular places of resort for artists and modern practitioners of the *vie de bohème*. Typical examples of these villages are Castellar, Gorbio, Roquebrune, Peillon, Eze, Vence, Tourette-sur-Loup and Gourdon.

Côte des Basques

The Côte des Basques (Basque Coast), 35 km long, is the continuation to the SW of the Côte d'Argent. Beyond the Spanish frontier it extends as far as San Sebastián. Within France it runs from Bayonne to Hendaye. The two principal bathing resorts on this stretch of coast are Biarritz and St-Jean-de-Luz, which, like the inland towns and villages though to a lesser degree, show distinctively Basque characteristics, reflected both in place-names and in the local way of life.

A glimpse of the spires of Bayonne Cathedral

HISTORY. – The **Basques**, who call themselves *Euskaldunak* in their own very distinctive language, live on both sides of the Pyrenees, some 100,000 in France and 500,000 in Spain. Although the Spanish Basques are still fighting stubbornly for self-government the French Basques, while preserving their own characteristics and customs, are integrated into French society. It is supposed that the French Basques originally came from the Spanish side of the Pyrenees, and that those living in the lower country became assimilated into the local population, while those who stayed in the hills preserved their distinctive characteristics. The origin of the Basques and of their language (which is non-Indo-European) is still a mystery.

SIGHTS. – **Bayonne** (pop. 45,000), chief town of the French Basque country, lies at the point where the Côte d'Argent merges into the Côte des Basques. In this busy port town Basque and Gascon characteristics are combined. The Musée Basque, housed in a building dating from the 15th c., gives a comprehensive survey of the Basques and their way of life, and is an essential preliminary to any visit to Basque territory, whether along the coast or inland. The Bayonne Festival, held at the beginning of August and lasting a week, offers an agreeable introduction to local folk traditions and customs. Another interesting occasion is the Ham Fair, held from Thursday to Saturday of Holy Week; for Bayonne ham, like Bayonne chocolate, is widely famed. The *Cathedral of

Ste-Marie (13th–14th c.) is one of the finest churches in SW France. The original spire, 80 m high, was matched by a second in the 19th c.; 14th c. cloister, from which the famous stained glass windows (1531) can be seen. Also of interest are the old town walls and remains of Gallo-Roman fortifications. Above the town is the Citadel, built in 1680, which offers a good general view of Bayonne. – *Anglet* is a garden city between Bayonne and Biarritz, with attractive and well-planned holiday facilities on the coast and in the immediate hinterland.

From **Biarritz** (see p. 73) N 10 runs SW by way of the little resort of *Bidart* (with a popular bathing beach) and the pretty little town of *Guéthary*, situated on rising ground above the Atlantic, a fashionable bathing and health resort which has nevertheless managed to preserve its distinctively Basque character, to St-Jean-de-Luz.

St-Jean-de-Luz (pop. 17,000) has been since the Middle Ages an important fishing port, from which as early as the 13th and 14th c. boats sailed as far afield as Newfoundland and Hudson Bay, Greenland and Spitzbergen. Since the last war the main activity of the port has been tunny-fishing. The town is also a popular bathing and winter resort. In Place Louis-XIV is the Maison Lohobiague, in which Louis XIV lived when he came here to marry Marie-Thérèse, daughter of Philip

Côte des Basques near St-Jean-de-Luz

IV of Spain. The church of St-Jean-Baptiste, originally built in the 13th c. but altered several times in subsequent centuries, still preserves a typically Basque interior. – Opposite St-Jean-de-Luz on the left bank of the Nivelle, which flows into the sea here, is *Ciboure*, with old houses set along narrow streets and the interesting church of St-Vincent. The composer Maurice Ravel was born in a house at 12 Quai Ravel, on the harbour.

From St-Jean-de-Luz the *Corniche Basque*, which offers, particularly at *Socoa*, fine views of the wild and rugged coast, continues SW to the resort of **Hendaye** and the Spanish frontier.

Côte Vermeille

Côte Vermeille ("Red Coast") is the name given to the stretch of the Mediterranean coast of France, some 50 km in length, which extends from Perpignan to the Spanish frontier. It is a region of rugged crags of rock and vine-clad hillsides. The name comes from the reddish colour of the soil.

The road along the Côte Vermeille is an alternative to the more inland route to Spain via the frontier post on the Col de Perthus. Along the coast are a number of picturesque bathing resorts, which unfortunately suffer from the steady flow of through traffic.

SIGHTS. – **Perpignan** (pop. 120,000) is the chief town of the department of Pyrénées-Orientales, the see of a bishop and the old capital of *Roussillon* (see p. 232).

Elne, once the see of a bishop, declined in importance after the bishop moved to Perpignan in 1602. The old Cathedral of

Ste-Eulalie has a S tower dating from the 11th c. and a 19th c. N tower; the adjoining *cloister dates from the 12th and 14th c.

Argelès-sur-Mer has a sandy beach some 6 km long backed by a fine pine-forest. The church was built in the 14th c. and contains late Renaissance panel paintings.

*Collioure is a picturesque bathing resort with a harbour and an old castle which attracted such artists as Matisse, Derain, Braque, Picasso and Dufy. The harbour was known to the Phoenicians. The Château des Templiers was the summer residence of the kings of Majorca and the queen of Aragon. The fortified church dates from the 17th c.; the tower formerly served as a lighthouse. There are remains of the town's walls and ramparts.

Banyuls-sur-Mer, on the Côte Vermeille

Port-Vendres, a commercial port and bathing resort, has the Fort du Fanal, part of the fortifications built by Vauban. – **Banyuls-sur-Mer** is noted both as a seaside resort and for its wine. On the *Ile Grosse*, which is linked with the mainland by a causeway, is a war memorial by Aristide Maillol. – **Cerbère** is the last town in France and the frontier station for entry into Spain. From the *Tour de Ker'Roig* (built 55 B.C.) there are wide-ranging views.

Dauphiné

The Dauphiné is an area of some 20,000 sq. km in the southern part of the French Alps, taking in the departments of Isère and Hautes-Alpes and part of the department of Drôme. It does not possess any geographical unity, and can be understood only in the light of history. From 1349 onwards the eldest son of the French king received the Dauphiné as his appanage, bore the title of Dauphin and had a dolphin in his coat of arms. The Dauphiné is bounded in the E by the Italian frontier, in the W by the Rhône; its northern boundary runs approximately at the latitude of Grenoble, and its southern boundary is marked by the passes into Haute Provence and such places as Gap and Barcelonnette. The dominant mountain range is the Pelvoux massif SE of Grenoble, which rises to 4100 m. To the E is the high Alpine *Upper Dauphiné*, to the W the pre-Alpine *Lower Dauphiné*, an agricultural region in which high plateaux alternate with valleys.

In the Dauphiné as in Savoy (see p. 238) the Alpine regions are made easily accessible by deeply indented river valleys running in different directions: no other Alpine area has so many good roads running over passes. Briançon (alt. 1326 m) is probably the highest town in Europe. The capital of the Dauphiné is Grenoble, which ranks with Innsbruck as one of the only two major cities in the Alps. In the area around Grenoble are a number of well-known winter sports resorts (Alpe d'Huez, Chamrousse, Villard-de-Lans). Like the rest of the Alps, the Dauphiné has a dual character: in summer it is walking and climbing country, in winter the haunt of skiers, with some roads which are used in summer and others used in winter. The best-known road in the Dauphiné, open throughout the year, is the "Route Napoléon" between Grenoble and the Mediterranean, the route followed by Napoleon after his return from Elba. Coming from Cannes by way of Sisteron, it enters the Dauphiné at Gap and from there runs N to Grenoble.

HISTORY. – In the 6th c. B.C. a Celtic tribe, the *Allobroges*, occupied the territory between the Rhône and the Isère. In 121 B.C. this area was conquered by the *Romans*, after which the Allobroges came to an accommodation with Rome and assimilated Roman culture. The region was converted to Christianity at the end of the 2nd c. About 443 the territory was captured by the *Burgundians*, coming from the E, but in 532 the Burgundians were in turn conquered by the *Franks*. During subsequent centuries the only stable factor was the Church.

At the beginning of the 11th c. the Dauphiné as we know it began to take shape, when Count Guigues I was granted four estates as his fief. At the end of the 12th c. André Guigues, founder of a new dynasty, added three further estates to the Dauphiné, including the area round Gap. One of his successors, Humbert II, negotiated the sale of the territory to the king of

France. From the mid 15th c. onwards the Dauphin Louis II (later king as Louis XI) promoted trade and established a parliament in Grenoble. The strategic importance of the Dauphiné was demonstrated during the wars between France and Italy at the turn of the 15th and 16th c. In the second half of the 16th c. the Reformation made headway in this region – the apostle of the Reformation in the Dauphiné being Guillaume Farel – and as a result it became involved in the fierce religious wars of the period. In 1628 Richelieu abolished the last remains of self-government in the Dauphiné.

The first stirrings of the French Revolution were felt in Grenoble and Vizille in 1788, and in 1791 the old province was divided between the departments of Isère, Drôme and Hautes-Alpes. Napoleon's return in 1815 and his passage through the Dauphiné aroused first agitation and then enthusiasm in the region: the troops stationed here came out in his support, and the people of Grenoble unbarred the town's gates to let him in. Napoleon himself says in his memoirs: "Until I came to Grenoble I was an adventurer; in Grenoble I became a prince." – During the Second World War the Resistance forces in the Vercors region, particularly in 1944, played a leading part in the fight for the liberation of France.

SIGHTS. – **Grenoble:** see p. 119. – ***Vercors:** see p. 249.

***Alpe d'Huez** (SE of Grenoble: alt. 1860 m) is both a summer and a winter resort with facilities for walking and climbing, skiing in summer and sunny ski-runs in winter. Splendid panoramic views from the *Dôme des Petites Rousses* (2813 m) and the *Pic du Lac Blanc*.

Bourg d'Oisans (alt. 720 m), a small health resort in the valley of the Romanche,

Chambon reservoir, near Bourg d'Oisans

chief town of the district of *Oisans*, in which is **Mont Pelvoux**, an imposing Alpine massif rising to a height of just over 4100 m, the most impressive mountain in France after Mont Blanc (National Park: glaciers, high valleys, tremendous panoramic views). Bourg d'Oisans, a lively agricultural market town (butter, cheese, etc.), is a good base from which to explore the Dauphiné. Near the town is the *Cascade de la Sarennes*, which is particularly impressive in spring.

Briançon (alt. 1200–1326 m; pop. 10,500) is a picturesque little town, the centre of the Briançonnais district. The old town, lying above the Guisane and Durance valleys, is surrounded by a double girdle of walls with several gates. The strategic importance of Briançon, situated as it is near the Italian frontier, was reflected in the construction of a powerful fortress by Vauban at the end of the 17th c., and this was put to the test on a number of occasions: in 1815 it withstood attack by an Austrian force twenty times the size of the garrison, and in 1940 it held out against Italian attacks. Vauban also built the church of Notre-Dame (beginning of 18th c.). Below the old town the *Pont d'Asfeld (56 m long) spans the gorge of the Durance. The new town lower down has fewer features of interest. – Near Briançon are the winter sports resorts of *Serre-Chevalier* and *Mont-Genèvre.*

In the **Massif de Chamrousse**, E of Grenoble, are **Chamrousse** itself (alt. 1650–1750 m: winter sports) and the spa of **Uriage-les-Bains** at the foot of the Belledonne range. The highest point is the *Croix de Chamrousse* (2255 m: cableway), from which there are wide-ranging *views in all directions.

Embrun (870 m), situated E of Gap 80 m above the Durance valley, was the seat of a Prince-Bishop and is now a summer and winter resort. The church of Notre-Dame (late 12th c.), considered the most beautiful church in the Dauphiné, has fine examples of Lombard sculpture, 15th c. stained glass, one of the oldest organs in France and a valuable treasury.

The ****Col du Galibier**, on N 202 in the northern Dauphiné, reaches a height (in the tunnel) of 2556 m and ranks with the *Col de l'Iseran, 200 m higher, among the highest passes in France; splendid

views on both the ascent and the descent. It may, however, be impassable on account of snow from October until the end of May. It is possible, before entering the tunnel, to climb or take the chair-lift to the highest point on the pass (2704 m), the panoramic **view from which is one of the best in the French Alps. – The Col du Galibier is one of the most gruelling sections of the famous cycle race, the Tour de France. At the S entrance to the tunnel is a memorial to Henri Desgranges, who initiated the Tour de France in 1903.

Gap (pop. 29,000) is, after Grenoble, the liveliest town in the Dauphiné and an important point on the Route Napoléon. The Departmental Museum contains a 17th c. mausoleum of black marble, and Alpine and historical collections. – Near the town, below *Mont Charance* (1902 m), is the *Château de Charance*, set in a beautiful park, formerly residence of the Bishop of Gap.

La Grave (alt. 1526 m), in the upper valley of the *Romanche*, is a good centre for mountain walks and climbs, particularly in the *Meije*, with its mighty glaciers, which rears above the village.

La Meije (Hautes-Alpes)

The four **lakes** of *Laffrey, on the Route Napoléon not far from Grenoble, are the main features of the barren *high plateau of Matésine*. Here Napoleon won over a battalion which had been sent to stop him from advancing any farther. – From **Corps**, on the Route Napoléon between

Gap and Grenoble, a visit can be made to the *pilgrimage church of Notre-Dame-de-la-Salette*, situated at an altitude of 1770 m amid magnificent Alpine scenery. The church was built in honour of the Virgin, who appeared weeping, to two children on 19 September 1851, and is visited by some 100,000 pilgrims every summer.

The district of *Queyras, in the eastern Dauphiné near the Italian frontier, extends for a distance of some 45 km in the valley of the *Guil*, a tributary of the Durance. Dominated by the peak of *Monte Viso (3841 m), in Italy, it is one of the most unspoiled parts of the Dauphiné, and has a number of resorts (*Abriès, Aiguilles, Guillestre*, etc.) which are frequented in both summer and winter. – The **Château Queyras**, above the village of the same name, was built in the 13th c. and restored by Vauban; the original keep has been preserved.

The artificial *lake of Serre-Ponçon, created in the mid 1970s as part of a hydroelectric scheme, covers an area of some 7400 acres (about the same as the Lac d'Annecy), fitting perfectly into the landscape.

Vallouise, so named in the 15th c. in honour of Louis XI, is a side valley of the Durance, to the W of Briançon. In this expanse of lush green pastureland under a southern sky is the holiday resort of *Ailefroide* (alt. 1510 m), a good centre for walkers and climbers. The Cézanne Hut above the village is at the beginning of the Pelvoux National Park (32,000 acres).

Villard-de-Lans, situated above Grenoble at an altitude of 1050 m, is a popular health and winter sports resort (many children's holiday homes).

The small industrial town of **Vizille** would be of little importance were it not for the *Château du Connétable de Lesdiguières. The nobleman who built the château was a leading Protestant but renounced his faith in 1662 in order to obtain the title of Connétable. The building was begun in 1611 and completed in 1627 with the construction of a flight of steps leading down to the Renaissance-style park. The French Revolution can be said to have begun here with a meeting of the Estates of the Dauphiné in 1788 at which a claim was put forward for the personal freedom of all Frenchmen.

Dijon

Region: Bourgogne.
Department: Côte-d'Or.
Altitude: 250 m. – Population: 157,000.
Post code: F-21000. – Dialling code: 80.
ⓘ **Office de Tourisme et Accueil,**
Place Darcy;
tel. 32 18 54.

HOTELS. – *Chapeau Rouge*, II, 36 r.; *Central*, II, 90 r.; *Morot et Genève*, II, 100 r.; *Terminus*, II, 30 r.; *Novotel*, on the Beaune road, II, 120 r.; *Poste*, III, 60 r.; *Continental*, III, 36 r.; *Ducs*, III, 56 r.; *Nord*, III, 27 r.; *Provence*, IV, 25 r.; *France*, IV, 43 r.; *Sauvage*, IV, 23 r.

Dijon has many handsome buildings recalling the time when it was capital of the Duchy of Burgundy, and these alone will repay a visit; but it is also chief town of the department of Côte-d'Or, a university town and the see of a bishop, as well as a considerable industrial town and an important centre of the wine trade.

Place Rude, Dijon

HISTORY. – In Roman times Dijon (*Dibio*) was a fortified post on the road from Lyons to Mainz. After many centuries of vicissitudes it became part of the Duchy of Burgundy in the 11th c. It was devastated by fire in 1137 and was then completely rebuilt. In the 14th and 15th c., under Dukes Philip the Bold (1364-1404), John the Fearless (1404–19), Philip the Good (1419–67) and Charles the Bold (1467–77), Dijon enjoyed a first cultural flowering. It is related that during a siege of the town in 1513 by a superior force of Swiss, Germans and Franche-Comté troops the defenders asked for a parley and began the process of negotiation by sending out whole waggon-loads of wine, which induced the previously bellicose Swiss to call off the attack. The French king, to whom Burgundy had belonged since 1477, was not entirely satisfied with the terms of the treaty thus arrived at. Even after becoming part of France Dijon remained an important administrative centre, and its citizens erected some of the handsome buildings which can still be seen today. At the end of the 18th c. the English traveller Arthur Young wrote: "Dijon, on the whole, is a handsome town; the streets, though old built, are wide and very well paved, with the addition, uncommon in France, of *trottoirs*." At that time Dijon had no more than 20,000 inhabitants. It was only in the mid 19th c., with the increase in trade and traffic, that Dijon began to develop into the city we see today.

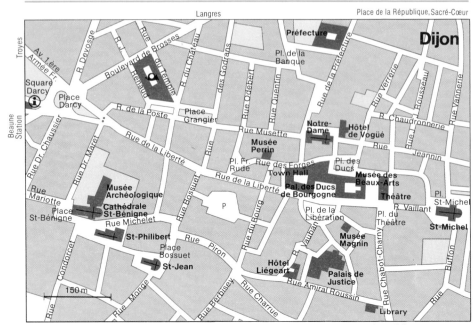

SIGHTS. – The central feature of the old town is the semicircular colonnaded square, the *Place de la Libération*, which was laid out in 1682, at the same time as the Ducal Palace, by the architect responsible for Versailles. The Baroque *Palais des Ducs de Bourgogne* incorporates parts of the earlier medieval structure. To the rear of the palace is the *Tour de Philippe le Bon* (46 m high), which dates from the same period; from the platform (316 steps) there are fine views in all directions. The E wing of the Ducal Palace is now occupied by the **Musée des Beaux-Arts**, one of France's leading art museums, which no visitor should miss. On the ground floor is a collection of sculpture; the former kitchen contains six handsome fireplaces. On the first floor, in the former *Salle des Gardes* (Great Hall), are a number of tombs, including the **tomb of Philip the Bold; and on this and the second floor is a valuable collection of *pictures (Rubens, Schongauer, Frans Hals, etc.).

Near the palace is the **Town Hall** (14th c.), once the lodgings occupied by the French kings when visiting Dijon. – NW of the palace is the church of *Notre-Dame, a beautiful Gothic building (13th c.) with an attractive clock-tower (1382) with mechanical figures; originally there was only one male figure, but in the course of time a woman and two children were added (the most recent in 1881). Inside, in a chapel on the right, is an 11th

c. "Black Virgin", one of the oldest pieces of wood sculpture in France. The church also contains a fine tapestry altar-cloth and a modern tapestry depicting the two occasions on which the town was liberated, in 1513 and in 1944.

There are charming old houses to the E of Notre-Dame, in *Rue Verrerie*, Rue Chaudronnerie and *Rue Vannerie*, and also in the characteristic *Rue des Forges* between the Ducal Palace and Notre-Dame.

E of the Ducal Palace is the church of *St-Michel* (16th c.), in Flamboyant style, with three richly decorated doorways. – S of the palace is the **Palais de Justice** (Law Courts), of the 16th and 17th c. – W of the palace is the twin-towered Gothic Cathedral of *St-Bénigne*, originally an abbey church, built on the site of an earlier church which incorporates a Romanesque doorway and a large crypt containing the tomb of St Bénigne (Benignus) from an earlier church on the same site. Adjoining the church, in a Gothic hall which belonged to the old Benedictine abbey, is an **Archaeological Museum** with an outstanding collection of Roman and medieval material.

On the western outskirts of the town are the remains of the **Chartreuse de Champmol** (church doorway and Moses Fountain of 1404), where the Dukes of Burgundy used to be buried; the site is now occupied by a psychiatric hospital.

Gascony

Gascony (Gascogne) forms a kind of continuation of the Basque region, which it bounds on the SW; for, as the name suggests, it was settled in the 7th c. by Basques from beyond the Pyrenees who advanced beyond the main area of settlement in France. Not surprisingly, therefore, the Gascons have a reputation for enterprise and courage, personified in the figure of d'Artagnan in "The Three Musketeers". Gascony occupies the area between Béarn in the Pyrenean foreland (which includes the Basque territory) and the River Garonne to the SE and NE, and is bounded on the W by the Landes, with the Côte d'Argent extending southward along the Atlantic.

Gascony includes an extensive area of flat country which makes good agricultural land; but there is one part of the region known to connoisseurs of good living the world over – the old county of Armagnac, centred on the town of Auch, producer of the amber-coloured liquid which has been called the "soul of Gascony". In the three areas where it is produced – Haut-Armagnac round Auch, Ténarèze round Condom and Bas-Armagnac round Eauze – life revolves round Armagnac. But Gascony is also a maize-growing country and along with the Agenais – the area round Agen which forms a transition to Périgord – the home of succulent prunes, which grow ripe and sweet under its sunny sky.

Gascony takes in the departments of Landes (chief town Mont-de-Marsan) and Gers (chief town Auch), together with parts of Hautes-Pyrénées, Haute-Garonne, Gironde and Lot-et-Garonne; but its boundaries cannot be narrowly confined, since the stretch of sea off the French coast between Hendaye and Bordeaux is known as the Gulf of Gascony.

HISTORY. – Gascony was part of the Roman province of *Aquitania*, into which the Basques penetrated in the 7th c. Gascony then became an almost independent duchy within the Frankish kingdom, which when the ducal line died out in the mid 11th c. passed to the Aquitanian duchy of *Guyenne*. Along with the county of *Armagnac*, and thanks to the valour of the men of Armagnac, Gascony temporarily controlled almost the whole of France in the time of Count Bernard VII (1391–1418). The exposed situation of Gascony, however, meant that it was frequently ravaged by war, as the many ruined castles bear witness. As a part of the French kingdom Gascony was one of the country's largest provinces, until the Revolution divided the old historical units into the modern departments.

SIGHTS. – **Auch** (pop. 24,000) was the capital and is still the main centre of Gascony, as well as chief town of the department of Gers and the see of an archbishop. The old town is built on high ground above the River Gers and is reached by a flight of more than 200 steps. The *Cathedral of St-Pierre (late 15th to 17th c.) is one of the finest churches in southern France, notable particularly for its 113 splendid carved *choir-stalls. The narrow lanes (*pousterles*) round the Cathedral are lined with old houses. The Maison du Tourisme, the oldest house in the town (late 15th c.), contains a Gascon folk museum.

Condom (pop. 8000) has an Armagnac folk museum, an early 16th c. church (formerly a cathedral) with a late Gothic doorway, and a number of old patrician houses of the 17th and 18th c.

Mont-de-Marsan, the third of Armagnac's principal towns and chief town of the department of Landes, has two interesting museums, an art museum and a museum of prehistory (in a Romanesque house of the 12th c.). There are remains of a 14th c. watch-tower.

Simorre (8 km S of Saramon on the Auch–Foix road) has a fortified church (14th–15th c.) with fine stained glass and choir-stalls which are well worth a visit.

The former episcopal town of **Lectoure**, standing above the Gers valley, has magnificent distant views of the Pyrenees from a promenade laid out on an old bastion. It also has a Gothic church and an archaeological museum (early medieval altars). – A short distance away, also in the Gers valley, is **Fleurance**, with a fine church in southern French Gothic style (14th c.) and arcades round the main square. The plan of the old fortified settlement (*bastide*) laid out in 1280 can still be distinguished.

Vic-Fezensac is noted for a great annual event, the bullfights which take place at Whitsun.

Those who like Armagnac will want to visit **Montesquiou**, whose name appears on many bottles. Now a small

The Tarn gorge at Castelbouc

village, in the past it played an important part in the history of Gascony, and has preserved from its past a number of interesting old buildings. – From here it is only 12 km to **Mirande**, which has an arcaded square, a 15th c. church with an unusual tower and the Delort Museum, with charming pictures of Gascony.

Gorges du Tarn

The****Gorges du Tarn (Gorges on the River Tarn), which are at their most impressive between Ste-Enimie and Les Vignes, and are continued by the fine *Gorges de la Jonte between Meyrueis and Le Rozier, are undoubtedly one of the most striking scenic features in France. Their canyon-like scenery can be seen either by road or (in some stretches) by boat.**

The Tarn, rising on Mont Lozère in the Cévennes, follows a winding course hewn deep in the limestone of the Causses. The valley was carved out in a number of different phases, the last of which extended over something like a million years, forming sheer cliffs which tower above the valley bottom to heights of up to 500 m and offer a constantly changing succession of views to tempt the photographer.

Coming from N 107, *Florac* (alt. 545 m; pop. 2000), at the foot of the Causse Méjean, is the obvious starting point of a *TRIP THROUGH THE GORGES DU TARN, as well as a link with an exploration of the Cévennes. From here N 107 bis runs parallel with the river to **Ste-Enimie**, an old-world little *town at a bend in the Tarn, with a Romanesque church and a hermitage above the town. – From Ste-Enimie N 586 goes N to *Mende* and S to the ****Aven Armand**, a magnificent stalactitic cave (with stalagmites up to 30 m high) which was discovered in 1897 but not opened to the public until 1926.

The next place in the Tarn valley is *La Malène*, the starting point of a boat trip through the narrow *Détroits ("Straits"), which cannot be reached from the road, to the ***Cirque des Baumes**; the return trip can be made by bus. – The road then runs past the *Pas de Souci*, where the river disappears under a tumble of rocks.

From the small village of *Les Vignes* a side road winds steeply up to the most impressive viewpoint in the Gorges, the **Point Sublime** (400 m above the river-bed); the finest views are at sunset. – From Les Vignes it is possible to take a boat trip to **Le Rozier**, at the junction of the Tarn and the Jonte; but the beauties of this stretch can also be seen from the road. Le Rozier takes its name from the roses grown by monks in the 11th c.; there was a potter's workshop here in Roman times. Above the village is the crag of Capluc, with a ruined castle and magnificent views.

From here it is possible to continue S towards **Millau** (alt. 379 m; pop. 24,000), in the Tarn basin, a glove-manufacturing town with an arcaded square and a Gothic church. It is well worth while, however, to turn E through the *Gorges de la Jonte, which are less imposing than the Tarn gorges but equally romantic. The Jonte rises on Mont Aigoual. The gorges are particularly impressive between Le Rozier and Meyrueis; the best viewpoint in the Gorges de la Jonte is the *Belvédère des Terrasses*, just off the road.

From Le Rozier or Millau there is a rewarding 12 or 18 km run to the rock labyrinth of *Montpellier-le-Vieux, a series of bizarre rock formations which in places looks like a ruined town. A walk round the site (signposted) takes about $1\frac{1}{2}$ hours. From some of the higher points there are fine views of the Causses.

Near Meyrueis is a very interesting cave, the *Grotte de Dargilan** (alt. 850 m), 1600 m long, with magnificent stalactites.

Grotte de Dargilan

1 Entrance
2 Salle du Chaos
3 Salle de la Mosquée
4 Salle Rose (Pink Chamber)
5 Descent
6 Petrified Waterfall
7 Salle du Lac
8 Labyrinth
9 Salle des Gours (Chamber of Gullies)
10 Salle du Clocher (Bell-tower)

Grenoble

Region: Rhône-Alpes.
Department: Isère.
Altitude: 210 m. – Population: 170,000.
Post code: F-38000. – Dialling code: 76.
(i) **Office de Tourisme et Accueil,**
    Maison du Tourisme,
    Rue de la République;
    tel. 54 34 36.

HOTELS. – *Sofitel Jacques Borel*, I, 100 r.; *Sofitel Park*, I, 75 r.; *Angleterre*, II, 70 r.; *Grand Hôtel*, II, 76 r.; *Terminus*, II, 50 r.; *Savoie*, II, 83 r.; *Alpes*, III, 40 r.; *Bristol*, III, 46 r.; *Europe*, III, 44 r.; *Napoléon*, III, 50 r.; *Suisse et Bordeaux*, III, 75 r.; *Beausoleil*, IV, 23 r.; *Clé d'Or*, IV, 35 r.; *Saint-Bruno*, IV, 26 r.

Grenoble, capital of the Dauphiné, lies in a valley surrounded by mountains towering up to heights of 3000 m. It is the administrative centre of the department of Isère, the see of a bishop and a university town. The city attracted the eyes of the world when the Winter Olympics were held here in 1968, leading to a great increase in tourist traffic. Important contributions are made to the city's economy by glove manufacture and the walnuts which are grown in the lower Isère valley between Tullins and St-Marcellin.

HISTORY. – The name of the city comes from the Roman *Gratianopolis*, named in honour of the Emperor Gratian in A.D. 379, on the site of a much earlier Gallic settlement. It became the see of a bishop, fell successively under Burgundian and Frankish rule, and in the 12th c. came into the hands of the Counts of Albon, who bore the style of "Dauphin" and thus gave the region its name. The last Dauphin of Viennois, Humbert II, ceded his territory to king Philip VI of France in 1349, after which the title of Dauphin was held by the heir to the French throne. The first stirrings of the French Revolution were felt at Grenoble in 1788. In the 19th c. the city prospered as a result of the development of industry.

SIGHTS. – The best general view of the city is to be had by taking the cableway up to the *Fort de la Bastille*, on the slopes of *Mont Rachais* (1045 m). There is also a good view from the *Tour Perret* (86 m high: lift) in the Parc Paul-Mistral. 2 km S of the park is the *Olympic Stadium*, built in 1967, with seating for 70,000. – Other notable new buildings are the *Town Hall*, also built in 1967, and the *Maison de la Culture* (1968), with three large halls and fine modern works of art.

Grenoble's charming OLD TOWN centres on the streets between its two major churches, the Cathedral of **Notre-Dame** (12th–13th c.), which contains a 15th c.

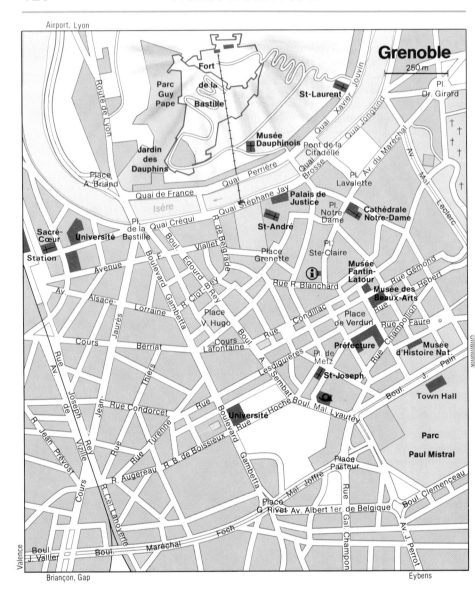

tabernacle in Flamboyant style 14 m high, and the 13th c. church of **St-André**, originally the Dauphin's private chapel. At 14 rue Jean-Jacques-Rousseau is the birthplace of the great 19th c. novelist Stendhal (1783–1842). Near St-André is the handsome **Palais de Justice** (Law Courts), partly dating from the 15th c., with a charming early Renaissance façade; the interior (conducted tour by porter) contains fine carved wood.

The city is rich in gardens and in museums. The *Jardin de Ville* is reached from *Place Grenette*, the hub of the city's traffic, through a vaulted passage. On the far side of the Isère, below the Fort de la Bastille, are the *Jardin des Dauphins* (orientation table) and the *Parc Guy-Pape*, both with views of Fort Rabot, built

on a rocky crag. The *Parc Paul-Mistral*, in the SE of the city, contains a number of modern buildings. Another park extends along the banks of the Isère, opposite the medieval church of *St-Laurent* on the Bastille hill, towards the Ile Verte.

Among the city's museums the **Museum of Painting and Sculpture** in Place de Verdun is outstanding, and houses one of France's finest collections of pictures. This is true particularly of the museum's collection of modern art, which was begun after the First World War and has been steadily developed. The old masters are well represented, with works by Rubens, Tintoretto, Velázquez, Murillo, Goya, Dürer, Cranach and many others. In the same building is the *Municipal Library*, which has an almost complete

Grenoble, with the splendid mountains of the Dauphiné in the background

collection of Stendhal's manuscripts. There is also a Stendhal Museum in the former Town Hall. Other interesting museums are the *Musée Dauphinois*, the *Musé Hébert* (devoted to the work of this fine local painter) and the *Natural History Museum* (Alpine fauna, mineralogy).

SURROUNDINGS. – There are excursions into the *Vercors (see p. 249) by way of the attractive winter sports resort of *Villard de-Lans* (alt. 1043 m), to the **Pelvoux massif (p. 114), to **Chamrousse** (p. 114) and through the *Chartreuse* forest to the **Grand Chartreuse** (alt. 961 m), mother house of the Carthusian order, founded in 1084, in a magnificent setting. Unfortunately the monastery is not open to visitors.

Grand Chartreuse monastery, near Grenoble

Le Havre

Region: Haute-Normandie.
Department: Seine-Maritime.
Altitude: 1–5 m. – Population: 216,000.
Post code: F-76600. – Dialling code: 35.

(i) **Office de Tourisme,**
Place de l'Hôtel-de-Ville;
tel. 21 22 88.

HOTELS. – *France et Bourgogne*, II, 33 r.: *Normandie*, II, 65 r,; *Marly*, II, 34 r.; *Astoria*, III, 34 r.; *Foch*, III, 33 r.; *Angleterre*, III, 31 r.; *Marignan*, III, 28 r.; *Pharès*, IV, 22 r.; *Ile de France*, IV, 16 r.; *Paris*, IV, 16 r.

Le Havre, France's second largest port after Marseilles, situated at the mouth of the Seine (here 9 km wide), **suffered heavy destruction during the Second World War and had to be almost completely rebuilt, so that it is now a city of very modern aspect. It is the principal French Atlantic port.**

HISTORY. – The town was founded only in 1509. Six years later Francis I ordered a harbour to be built, and the first warship put into port in 1518. Later Le Havre developed into an important commercial port, mainly involved in the North American traffic. In 1850 the *Franklin*, driven by sails and paddlewheels, made the crossing to New York in 15 days, and in 1864 the first steamship, the *Washington*, came into service. After the American War of Independence Le Havre became the main centre for the import of colonial products such as coffee, tobacco, cotton, sugar and exotic woods. During the Second World War the city suffered 146 air raids, and in September 1944 it was besieged by Allied forces.

SIGHTS. – Since practically no old buildings are left, the features of tourist interest are all modern. It is well worth while making a tour of the **port installations**, still in course of development, with several railheads. The city contains some interesting examples of contemporary architecture, such as the spacious *Place de l'Hôtel-de-Ville*, with tower blocks and a series of lower

Avenue Foch, Le Havre

buildings. The *Avenue Foch* is a magnificent promenade which has been compared with the Champs-Elysées in Paris. The modern church of *St-Joseph* is a reinforced concrete structure with an octagonal tower 106 m high from which there are splendid views. Also worth seeing is the 160 m long *escalator* in Rue Aristide-Briand which climbs 50 m to the upper town (which can also be reached from the Cours de la République through the *Tunnel Jenner*).

From the W end of Avenue Foch the *bathing beach* extends N along the *Boulevard Albert-1er* to the villa suburb of STE-ADRESSE and the outer suburb (4 km away) of NICE HAVRAIS (the "Nice of Le Havre").

The *Musée des Beaux-Arts* is notable particularly for work by modern painters, including Dufy. The *Musée du Vieux Havre* also contains much of interest. – In the old church of *Ste-Honorine de Graville* (11th–13th c.: "Black Virgin") and the adjoining cloister is a museum of sculpture, with works of the 12th–16th c.

Ile de France

The Ile de France is the area round Paris which takes in the departments of Seine-et-Marne, Yvelines, Essone, Hauts-de-Seine, Seine-St-Denis, Val-de-Marne and Val-d'Oise – the part of France in which the French language and French art and civilisation had their origin. It is the very quintessence of French culture with its historic towns, its magnificent forests, its fine châteaux set in beautiful parks and gardens and its great Gothic cathedrals. Much of what is thought of as typically French and peculiar to the French character is to be found, if not in Paris then in the Ile de France, at Versailles or Fontainebleau, Chartres or St-Denis.

The name Ile de France goes back to the 10th c., and gives expression to the idea that this area in the Paris basin, surrounded by the plains of Normandy, Champagne and Beauce and the district of Caux, is both geographically and symbolically a part of France which can stand for the whole. But within the Ile de France the 14 separate territories which form a girdle round Paris are very different from one another; and all the time the conurbation of Paris and its suburbs is reaching out ever farther into the open country which surrounds it. Agriculture and industry both make their contribution to the economy of the Ile de France, though the tourist is more likely to think first of the scenic and historical interest which it offers. The principal attractions are described below under four headings – churches, abbeys, châteaux and towns.

Churches

Beauvais (N of Paris) was once an important episcopal city, with a Cathedral which was planned as the largest in France, although the plan was never carried out in its entirety. Only the choir and transepts were built, but in dimensions and artistic achievement these are of magnificent effect. Even as it stands the Cathedral is the tallest in France (68 m). Outstanding features are the stained glass (14th–16th c,), still as vivid as if it had just been made, the tapestries and the treasury. Adjoining the Cathedral is the nave of the earlier Carolingian cathedral.

The church of *St-Etienne (Romanesque and late Gothic) should also be seen.

**Chartres: see p. 96.

Laon (NE of Paris), strikingly situated, with an upper town surrounded by walls and towers, has a magnificent **Cathedral. The choir dates from the turn of the 12th c.; the towers flanking the W front are very fine. On the corner turrets are 16 figures of oxen, recalling the use of oxen as draught animals in medieval times. The Cathedral (interior dimensions: 100 m long, 24 m high) reflects the transition from Romanesque to Gothic. See also p. 95.

Morienval (NE of Paris) has one of the finest Romanesque churches in the Paris area, *Notre-Dame, originally belonging to a Benedictine abbey, which shows what is probably the earliest use of Gothic rib-vaulting.

Noyon (NE of Paris), an episcopal city since the 6th c. to which its brick-built houses give a distinctive character, has a massive**Cathedral (Notre-Dame), built at the turn of the 12th and 13th c., which shows a mingling of Romanesque and Gothic. Noyon was the birthplace of the great Reformer Jean Calvin (1509–64), and has a Calvin Museum.

St-Denis (in the northern outskirts of Paris) recalls the legend of the martyred St Denis, who after being beheaded is said to have carried his severed head here from Montmartre before giving up the ghost. A chapel was built on the site, and this was followed in the 7th c. by a Benedictine abbey. The present *Cathedral, built in the mid 12th c., became the model for the great churches of Chartres, Senlis and Meaux. Having fallen into ruin, it was rebuilt in the 19th c.

St-Sulpice-de-Favières, a picturesque village S of Paris, has a Gothic pilgrimage church (13th–14th c.) which is claimed to be France's most beautiful village church.

Senlis (NE of Paris) has not only one of the best preserved circuits of Roman walls in France (840 m in length, with 16 towers still surviving) but also a royal castle and a Cathedral which shows all the successive phases of Gothic architecture between the 12th and the 16th c. The 12th c. spire is 78 m high, and the central

doorway, which also dates from the 12th c., is the earliest in France to be devoted entirely to honouring the Virgin and is a landmark in the development of Gothic sculpture.

Soissons (NE of Paris), an old episcopal city, has remains of important abbeys and a 13th c. *Cathedral (St-Gervais-et-St-Protais). The W front was altered in the 18th c. Its finest feature is the 15th c. rose window in the N transept. The S transept is also notable. See also p. 95.

Abbeys

Châalis (NE of Paris) has a beautiful park and remains of a Cistercian abbey founded in 1136. There is a small museum in one of the monastic buildings (1740).

Jouarre (E of Paris) preserves the crypts of an abbey founded in 630, which are among the oldest sacred buildings in France. A tower survives from the abbey church. The present buildings of the Benedictine convent date from the 18th c.

Longpont (NE of Paris), in a beautiful setting, has considerable remains of a Cistercian abbey founded in the 12th c., with a fortified gatehouse and the impressive ruins of the church (105 m long).

Le Moncel (N of Paris), just outside Pont-Ste-Maxence on the Oise, is a convent of Poor Clares founded in 1309. The buildings are well preserved.

Ourscamp (NE of Paris) is an *abbey founded in 1129, enlarged in the 18th c. and still occupied by monks. Only ruins of the church are left. The main feature is the fine infirmary of 1260, now used as a chapel, with three vaulted aisles 30 m long.

Port-Royal-des-Champs (SW of Paris) has remains of an important 13th c. Cistercian abbey which has associations with Pascal and Racine. The buildings were demolished on the orders of Louis XIV.

Prémontré (NE of Paris), in the Forêt de Coucy, was the mother house of the Premonstratensian order, founded in 1120. The abbey was rebuilt in the 18th c.

Royaumont (N of Paris, near Asnières-sur-Oise), a Cistercian abbey founded in 1228, has suffered much destruction but still preserves a number of notable buildings, including a Gothic *refectory.

Soissons (NE of Paris) possesses, in addition to its Cathedral, remains of three abbeys – St-Léger (13th c. church with 14th c. doorway), St-Jean-des-Vignes (church with fine *W front, cellar vaulting) and St-Médard (pre-Romanesque crypt).

Châteaux

Anet (W of Paris) has remains of a 16th c. château built for Diane de Poitiers (tympanum by Benvenuto Cellini).

Breteuil (SW of Paris), in the Chevreuse valley, has a beautifully decorated and furnished 17th c. château with a fine park laid out by Le Nôtre.

Champs (E of Paris) has an early 18th c. château sumptuously decorated by Mme de Pompadour which was acquired by the State in 1935. Splendid interior.

Chantilly (N of Paris), on the edge of a forest well stocked with game, has a château begun in 1560 and later enlarged. The *château is a magnificent pile, with its stables, valuable collections and beautiful *park, now owned by the Institut de France. In the Grand Château is the Musée Condé, with rich collections of *paintings. The Petit Château or Châtelet, the first part of the château to be built, contains a valuable library (1500 manuscripts). – With its château, its forest and its racecourse Chantilly is the centre of a fashionable and popular holiday area. Among products associated with the town are lace, china and whipped cream (*crème Chantilly*).

Châteaudun (SW of Paris) is a picturesque town dominated by an imposing *château dating from the 15th c. In the Sainte-Chapelle are 12 fine 15th c. statues. In some of the rooms are Gobelin tapestries.

Compiègne (N of Paris) is a town of art and history. In 1430 Joan of Arc was taken prisoner here by the Burgundians and handed over to the English. The *château, which was occupied by all the rulers of France from the earliest days of the kingdom, was a favourite residence of Napoleon III and the Empress Eugénie. The armistice which ended the First World War was signed in a railway carriage in the Forest of Compiègne on 11 November 1918. The château, built for Louis XIV by J.-A. Gabriel, is now a national museum,

splendidly decorated and furnished and rich in historical associations.

Coucy-le-Château (NE of Paris) was the largest and finest medieval castle in France, with a keep which is now destroyed. The round towers are still impressive, as is the little town with its walls and 28 towers dating from the 13th c.

Courances (S of Paris) has a château built in 1630 on the foundations of a medieval castle. The park, designed by Le Nôtre, has a profusion of *fountains and cascades.

La Ferté-Milton (NE of Paris), birthplace of Racine (1639–99), has the ruins of a 14th c. castle above the town. The castle has an impressive façade with a rectangular tower containing living quarters and three round towers. On the monumental gateway is a carving of the "Coronation of the Virgin".

***Fontainebleau** (SE of Paris) is of all France's châteaux the one with the richest historical associations. From Louis VII to Napoleon III the rulers of France lived here and contributed to the enlargement and embellishment of the palace.

The **layout** of the palace is rambling and irregular, almost the whole of it having only one storey above the ground floor. It is built round five courtyards. The large forecourt, enclosed by a railing, is known as the *Cour du Cheval Blanc* or *Cour des Adieux* because Napoleon said farewell to his Guard here after abdicating. A horseshoe-shaped *double staircase* (1634) leads up to the first floor of the main building. A passage on the right leads into the *Cour de la Fontaine*, which opens on to the park and the *carp-pond*. On the left-hand (N) side of this is the *Galerie de François I*. – Passing through the E wing and a corner pavilion, with the *Porte Dorée* (1528), one enters the *Cour Ovale*, an arcaded courtyard which is an outstanding example of French Renaissance architecture. At the far end is the *Porte du Baptistère*, and opposite this, beyond a Baroque railing, is the *Cour des Offices*.

The *INTERIOR of the château (conducted tour, 1 hr) is magnificently decorated by Italian and French artists (the Fontainebleau school). – To the left of the main entrance is the 17th c. *Chapelle de la Ste-Trinité*. – On the first floor, looking on to the Jardin de Diane, are *Napoleon I's Apartments*, with Empire furniture. Beyond these are the *Salle du Conseil*, dating from the reign of Louis XV, and the *Salle du Trône*, and beyond these again are the *Queen's Apartments*, splendidly furnished (Sèvres porcelain). The *Galerie de Diane* contains the library. – Opposite the Queen's Apartments, looking on to the Cour Ovale, are the **King's Apartments**, with ceiling paintings and stuccowork by Primaticcio and beautiful Gobelin tapestries. In the *Escalier du Roi* (King's Staircase) are scenes from the the life of Alexander the Great. – On the S side of the Cour Ovale is the ***Salle de Bal** (30 m long, 10 m wide), built by Francis I and splendidly decorated (paintings by Primaticcio) by Henry II for his mistress Diane de Poitiers. – In the *Galerie de François I* (54 m long), with a terrace overlooking the Cour de la Fontaine, are 14 large pictures by Rosso de' Rossi. – In the wing which runs S from the W end of the gallery are the *Apartments of the Queen Mother* and the *Apartments of Pope Pius VII*, and at the far end is a pavilion containing the *Musée Chinois* (valuable collection of Chinese porcelain).

The **gardens** are very beautiful. W of the carp-pond is the *Jardin Anglais*, laid out in the time of Napoleon I, and to the E is the *Parterre*, designed by Le Nôtre, with ornamental ponds and statues. – To the NE, beyond the canal constructed during the reign of Henry IV, is the *park*, with the *Labyrinthe* (Maze) and the *Treille du Roi* (vine-covered trellises).

The *Forest of Fontainebleau* (17,000 hectares), bounded on the NE by the windings of the Seine, ranks as France's most beautiful forest. It is a hilly region, mainly of sand and sandstone. The magnificent stands of tall trees and the wild gorges offer a varied range of scenic beauty which has attracted many painters (the Babizon school), and a network of paths opens up the forest to walkers.

Gisors (NW of Paris), strategically situated at the meeting of three valleys, has a ruined castle which was one of the strongest fortresses in France. It was begun in 1097 and completed in the 12th and 13th c. There are remains of its 12 towers and keep (28 m high).

Maintenon (SW of Paris) has a château, originally built in the Middle Ages, which Louis XIV acquired for Mme de Maintenon. In the park, which was designed by Le Nôtre, is an unfinished *aqueduct designed by Vauban to convey water from the Eure to Versailles.

Maisons-Laffitte (NW of Paris) is noted both for its racecourse and for its 17th c. *château, one of France's most exquisite châteaux, with a sumptuous interior.

Malmaison (W of Paris) was a privately owned *château which Napoleon bought for Joséphine in 1799. It was her favourite residence, and she died here in 1814. It is now a museum, offering a comprehensive survey of the history and the art of the Napoleonic era. The park still preserves rose-beds and other features as they were in Joséphine's time.

Le Marais (SW of Paris), originally a fortified castle, was rebuilt in 1770 as a château typical of the time of Louis XVI.

Pierrefonds (NE of Paris) was originally a medieval castle, begun in 1390. It was slighted by Richelieu and later restored by Napoleon III as a fortified *castle, complete with massive round towers and picturesque battlements.

Rambouillet (SW of Paris), situated in a forest, dates back to the 8th c. It is now the summer residence of the President of the Republic (open to visitors when he is not in residence). Other features of interest are the Laiterie de la Reine (Queen's Diary), the Bergerie (sheep-farm) and the House of the King of Rome, built by Napoleon in 1811–14 for his son. The forest, once much larger, is a game reserve.

Rosny-sur-Seine (W of Paris) has a magnificent château which belonged to one of Henry IV's ministers, with beautiful furniture and a large park gay with flowers.

St-Cloud (on the western outskirts of Paris) is a place pregnant with history. The château which once stood here has not been preserved, but the beautiful *park, designed by Le Nôtre, merits a visit in its own right; cascade and fountain 42 m high.

St-Germain-en-Laye (W of Paris) was once an important royal residence, and still possesses a splendid Renaissance château (with later alterations). Beautiful *terrace, 2 km long, with extensive views. The château, which was restored in 1862, now houses the *Musée des Antiquités Nationales. There are extensive forests in the surrounding area.

Sceaux (on the SW outskirts of Paris) has a château built for Colbert by Perrault, much of which was destroyed in 1798. The park, designed by Le Nôtre, is one of the finest in the Paris area. The château, rebuilt in the 19th c., now houses the Musée de l'Ile de France (history, art, literature, folk traditions).

Thoiry (W of Paris) has a beautifully proportioned 17th c. château with a charming interior. The park contains a *Réserve Africaine, in which several hundred wild animals roam freely; visitors can drive through it in their cars.

Vaux-le-Vicomte (SE of Paris) was built in the middle of the 17th c. for Fouquet, Louis XIV's finance minister, and delighted the young king when he visited it in 1661. He then invited the artists responsible to work at Paris and

Versailles, and transported some of the works of art to Versailles. The *château with its four corner pavilions is a beautiful and impressive sight. The park was Le Nôtre's first great masterpiece, surpassed only by Versailles.

Vaux-le-Vicomte: the château and its gardens

Versailles: see p. 252.

Villers-Cotterets (NE of Paris) has a fine Renaissance château (1520), much altered in later centuries. Splendid receptions and hunting parties were held here in the 18th c.

Vincennes (on the eastern outskirts of Paris) has a *château which was a kind of forerunner of Versailles. The site, in the *Bois de Vincennes, was occupied in the 9th c. by a royal castle, which itself replaced an earlier hunting lodge. Louis IX (St Louis) and the Capetian kings used the castle as a residence, and it later served as a fortress, a prison (in which Diderot and Mirabeau were confined) and barracks. The château (which now houses a historical museum) occupies a total area of 320 by 178 m and is surrounded by walls and a moat. – A porcelain manufactory was established at Vincennes in 1738, working in the manner of Chantilly. In 1756 this was moved to Sèvres, where it still is. – The Forest of Vincennes, laid out in the 19th c. as a park in the English style, is now a favourite recreation area for the people of Paris.

Towns

In addition to the places already mentioned in connection with churches, abbeys or châteaux, the following towns have much of interest to offer the visitor.

Auvers-sur-Oise (N of Paris) was a popular resort of painters in the 19th c. Van Gogh died here and is buried, with his brother Théo, in the cemetery.

Barbizon (S of Paris), on the edge of the Forest of Fontainebleau, is famous for the Barbizon school of painters (Corot, Millet, Daumier, etc.). Millet's studio can be visited.

Blérancourt (NE of Paris) has a Museum of French-American Cooperation.

Bonneval (SW of Paris) is a little town of medieval aspect, with old houses and town walls.

Le Bourget (in the NE outskirts of Paris) has one of Paris's three airports. Charles Lindbergh landed here in 1927 after his famous transatlantic flight.

Champlieu (NE of Paris), on the edge of the Forest of Compiègne, has Gallo-Roman remains (a theatre with a diameter of 70 m and seating for 4000; baths) and Christian catacombs.

Château-Landon (S of Paris) has a medieval air and possesses a number of fine old buildings (Romanesque church, remains of an abbey).

Château-Thierry (E of Paris) has a ruined castle, old houses, a gate in the town walls, a 15th–16th c. bell-tower and a hospital founded in 1304. There is a museum devoted to the 17th c. poet La Fontaine ("Fables"), who was born here in 1621.

Conflans-Ste-Honorine (SW of Paris), on the Seine, is a centre of the shipping traffic on the canals of northern France and Belgium, with much lively activity on the quays.

Crépy-en-Valois (NE of Paris) has a number of picturesque medieval buildings. The Château de Valois houses a Museum of Archery.

Dreux (W of Paris), in the Blaise valley, has 15th–16th c. half-timbered houses, a tall belfry and a museum (art and archaeology) in a disused chapel.

Enghien-le-Bains (N of Paris) is noted for its thermal springs and its racecourse.

Ermenoville (NE of Paris) is a village on the edge of the forest in which Rousseau died in 1778. English-style *park, zoo and "Mer de Sable" (dunes) in the forest.

Etampes (S of Paris) is an old royal town and one of the great treasurehouses of art of the Ile de France. 12th c. church with a Romanesque tower and statues in the style of Chartres; Tour Guinette, a keep with a ground plan in the form of a four-leaved clover; old houses and Renaissance mansion; interesting Municipal Museum.

L'Hay-les-Roses (S of Paris) has a Rose Museum and a rose-garden with 8000 varieties which flower in June.

Larchant (S of Paris) is an old fortified town with a church (12th–13th c.) dedicated to St Mathurin which became a place of pilgrimage. The church contains remarkable works of art in Romanesque and Gothic style, including 12th c. wall paintings. – Near the town are sandstone rocks which are popular with climbers.

Mantes-la-Jolie (W of Paris), on the left bank of the Seine, is the place where Henry IV recanted his Protestant faith for the second time ("Paris is worth a mass"). Fine collegiate *church showing similarities with Notre-Dame in Paris and other older buildings.

Marly-le-Roi (W of Paris) was a favourite residence of Louis XIV's and later a popular resort for writers and artists (Dumas, Sardou, Sisley, Pissarro, Maillol). Of the royal château nothing is left but the lines of the foundations, but the park has largely been preserved.

Meudon (on the SW outskirts of Paris) has preserved only two orangeries and the "Château Neuf" of its 17th c. château. Museum on the history of the châteaux. Musée Rodin (in a house which once belonged to the sculptor), with casts and sketches. Musée de l'Air, an important museum of flying.

Montmorency (N of Paris), situated on the fringes of the forest, gave its name to one of the great French families. Jean-Jacques Rousseau lived here from 1757 to 1762 and wrote three of his major works; there is a Rousseau Museum.

Provins (SE of Paris) was the trading centre of Champagne in the Middle Ages, with a population of some 80,000, and has numerous historic old buildings. The upper town has several such buildings, including the *"Tour de César", an old watch-tower 44 m high, the Porte St-Jean and the Grange aux Dîmes (Tithe Barn). There is an interesting archaeological museum. – In the lower town are several old churches and a medieval tower. – To the N of the town is the old Hôpital Général, in a Franciscan convent of 1246 with two cloister galleries. – The town is a centre of rose-growing, and fields of roses extend along N 19 round the villages of *Villecresnes*, *Brie-Comte-Robert*, *Grisy-Suisnes*, *Guignes-Rabutin* and *Nangis*, earning this road the name of "Route des Roses".

Sèvres (in the western outskirts of Paris) is the home of the world-famed National Porcelain Manufactory and the *National Museum of Ceramics, with more than 30,000 exhibits illustrating ceramics of the past and present.

SPORT and RECREATION in the Ile de France. – The Valois country is the traditional home of *archery*. The Forest of Fontainebleau offers opportunities for *rock-climbing*. There is also ample scope for *riding* in the forests, and riding events are held at Barbizon, Chantilly, Compiègne and Fontainebleau. *Horse-racing* at Chantilly, Maisons-Lafitte, St-Cloud (gallops), Vincennes (trotting), Enghien (steeplechasing), Compiègne, Fontainebleau and Rambouillet. There is plenty of scope for *water sports* on the Seine and its tributaries. Rowing at Lagny; sailing at Draveil, Les Mureaux, Poissy, St-Fargeau, Ponthierry, Triel and Villennes-sur-Seine. *Fishing* at many places on rivers and lakes. Information about *golf* and *tennis* can be obtained from the clubs and associations concerned.

Jura

The *French Jura, officially the region of Franche-Comté, is a part of France relatively unknown to tourists, though it borders in the W on Burgundy, a very popular tourist area, and in the N on the Vosges. The Jura proper is a range of mountains lying between France and Switzerland and continued beyond the Swiss border by the Swiss Jura.

Although the climate of the Jura may sometimes show the rawness of an upland region – its highest peaks rise above 1600 m – there is a good deal of exaggeration in the joking claim that it has eight months of snow and two months of wind but the rest of the year is wonderful. Goethe, Lamartine and Ruskin all spoke

In the upper Doubs valley

enthusiastically about the Jura, referring to one of its greatest attractions, the magnificent views of the snow-covered Alps to be had from so many places in the region.

But it is not only the distant views of the mountains that appeal to the visitor in the Jura. It has its wine-growing areas like Arbois, its agriculture, with great herds of cattle and a wide variety of cheeses, its beautiful valleys and numerous lakes (of which no fewer than 70 have been counted) and its extensive forests (1·2 million acres) covering more than 40% of its area.

Two great Frenchmen were born in the Jura – the biologist Pasteur and the painter Courbet. The principal towns are Besançon, Dole and Lons-le-Saunier, together with Belfort in the northern Jura, already under the influence of the Vosges. Also worth visiting are the numerous villages, with country-style buildings which preserve indigenous cultural traditions. Thanks to the limited inroads which tourism has so far made on this region, visitors can discover in the Jura something of an older France. And though they may encounter rain and snow they will remember that the rain gives the fields their fresh green colour and the snow provides excellent facilities for winter sports.

The main holiday areas in the Jura are the Doubs and Loue valleys, the forests of Joux, the high valley of the Ain with its reservoir lakes, and the Bienne and Valserine valleys. There are something like 40 places above 600 m with accommodation for holiday visitors, the most popular winter sports resorts being the Col de la Faucille, Les Hôpitaux-Neufs, Jougne, Mijoux and above all Les Rousses. Below 600 m there are some 60 other holiday resorts, among the leading ones Arbois, Baume-le-Dames, Champagnole, Montbéliard, Nantua, Poligny, St-Claude and Vesoul.

HISTORY. – The Jura was already peopled in the time of the Gauls, with its chief town at Besançon (*Vesontio*). In 58 B.C. Caesar drove back the advancing Germanic tribes and occupied the region, which remained Roman in spite of a series of risings. Under Roman rule the towns of Besançon, Salins, Dole, Lons-le-Saunier and Pontarlier flourished, and in A.D. 180 Christianity came to Besançon. In 457, however, the Jura became part of the Burgundian kingdom. The 10th c. brought troubled times, and many castles and fortresses were built. The area was ruled by counts and dukes appointed by the Burgundian kings who soon acquired hereditary rights. When Burgundy was divided up the Jura region formed the *Comté de Bourgogne*, or Comté for short, while the territories on the Saône became the Duchy of Burgundy. In 1032 the Jura fell under the influence of the German emperors, but in 1295 it was purchased by Philippe le Bel of France. In the mid 14th c. the population was decimated by plague. The name **Franche-Comté** appears in an official document for the first time in 1366. For a century the Jura belonged to Burgundy, until its occupation by Louis XI in 1477. Soon afterwards, however, in 1491, it fell into the hands of the Emperor Maximilian, and this led to a growth of Spanish influence in the Jura, which in 1556 passed directly to the Spanish crown. Then in 1678, in spite of local resistance, the Comté was finally annexed by France and since then has shared its destiny, including the German occupation of 1940 and the liberation of 1944 (which in this region was not achieved until November of that year).

SIGHTS. – **Arbois** (pop. 4500) is picturesquely situated amid vineyards (opportunities for visiting wine-making establishments), and owes its fame to the fact that Louis Pasteur, who was born in Dole, spent his early years in Arbois and frequently returned there, visiting it for the last time in the year before his death in 1895. His parents' house has been preserved as it was and is open to visitors, who can even see specimens which were originally planted by him. Other features of interest are the 18th c. houses in Place de la Liberté, the Town Hall (formerly a monastic house), the church of St-Just (12th–13th c.) and the Wine Museum. – 2 km from the town, on the right of N 83, is Pasteur's vineyard, the produce of which served for his research into alcoholic fermentation in 1878.

Arc-et-Senans is noted for the former royal salt-works on the banks of the Loue, with imposing 18th c. neo-classical buildings intended as the nucleus of a salt-producing town which never came into being. The salt-works ceased to operate at the end of the 19th c.

The industrial town of **Audincourt** (pop. 14,000), on the Doubs, has an interesting modern church designed by Novarina (1951), with stained glass windows by F. Léger and mosaics by Bazaine.

Baume-les-Dames (pop. 5500), formerly known as Baume-les-Nonnes, owes its name to a convent founded in the 7th c. for ladies of noble birth. The former abbey church is not open to visitors. The church of St-Martin in the Place de la République was built in the 17th c.

Baume-les-Messieurs (pop. 230), the male counterpart of Baume-les-Dames, dates back to the 6th c., when it was founded by the Irish monk St Columban. The abbey of Cluny was founded in 910 by twelve Benedictines from the town. The abbey (which was closed down in 1793), with its 12th–13th c. church (15th c. façade), still has something of the atmosphere of monastic life. – 3 km S is the Cirque de Baume, a rocky corrie.

The hill of **Colomby de Gex** (1689 m) is one of the highest points in the Jura. It is a two hours' climb (there and back) to the summit, starting from a forestry road which runs S from the Col de la Faucille. From the top there are tremendous views, extending over Lake Geneva to the Alps, a distance of more than 200 km.

The **Crêt de Chalame** (1545 m) is the highest peak in the range of hills above the Valserine. It is a 90 minutes' climb (there and back), with magnificent views of the Jura, extending in clear weather as far as Mont Blanc.

Divonne-les-Bains (pop. 3300) is a popular spa with springs which were already being used in Roman times. It lies near the Swiss frontier between Lake Geneva and the Jura hills, and is the only resort in the Jura with luxury hotels, a golf-course and a racecourse. Its nearness to Switzerland offers the possibility of trips to Geneva, Lake Geneva and the Swiss Jura peak of Dôle.

Dole (pop. 30,000) was the birthplace of Louis Pasteur, who left the town at the age of five. The house in which he was born in Rue Pasteur (formerly Rue des Tanneurs) is now a museum. Other features of interest are the 16th c. church of Notre-Dame, with a spire 74 m high, the old town, with houses dating from the 15th–18th c., which lies round the church, the Hôtel Froissard (16th–17th c.) and the former Jesuit Collège de l'Arc, now a school and museum of painting.

The **Col de la Faucille** (1323 m), between Gex and La Cure, is the most important pass in the Jura, carrying the road to Switzerland (N 5). Near the pass is *Mont-Rond* (1614 m), one of the finest viewpoints in the Jura (cableway).

Faverney (pop. 1100) has a former abbey, with a church which is said to have been the scene of a miracle in 1608.

Ferney-Voltaire (pop. 3050), lying close to the Swiss frontier and the Geneva airport of Cointrin, was from 1760 onwards the favourite residence of Voltaire, who enlarged and improved the château and the park. The château contains mementoes of the philosopher.

The **Génissiat Dam** on the Rhône has created an artificial *lake* 23 km long, extending to the Swiss frontier, which supplies hydroelectric power. The dam is 140 m long, 104 m high and 100 m thick at the base, and impounds some 53 million cubic metres of water. It is one of the greatest examples of French engineering skill.

Gex (alt. 628 m; pop. 3200) is a popular medium-altitude resort 12 km below the Col de la Faucille, conveniently close to the mountains and Geneva. In consequence of its nearness to the frontier it has for the past 150 years been a duty-free zone for the inhabitants. From Place Gambetta there is a view of Mont Blanc.

The ***Grand Colombier** (1531 m) is one of the finest viewpoints in the Jura, within 200 m of the Croix du Colombier on a motor road (D 1204 bis).

***Joux** is a wooded region with one of the finest fir forests in France. The forest covers an area of 2659 hectares to the W of Pontarlier and has trees ranging up to 45 m high and 1·25 m in diameter. – The *"Route des Sapins"* ("Fir Road") which runs from Champagnole to Villers-sous-Chalamont (34 km), with its various side roads, offers a convenient way of seeing the best parts of the forest. Where the road divides (signpost "Par les Crêtes"), bear right to reach a viewpoint and the "President's Fir" (over 230 years old, 45 m high, 3·85 m in girth).

Lons-le-Saunier (pop. 25,000) is both a tourist centre and a health resort. Clock-tower in Place de la Liberté; in Rue du Commerce picturesque arcades and two churches, of which St-Désiré has one of the oldest crypts in the Jura (11th c.). – In the surrounding area are a number of charming châteaux, including the Château d'Arlay and the Château du Pin.

Montbéliard (pop. 33,000) was once the capital of a duchy which for almost 400 years, under the name of Mömpel-gard, belonged to Württemberg. An industrial centre (Peugeot works in Sochaux-Montbéliard), it still has a large proportion of Protestants. The main feature of interest is the castle built by Henrietta of Württemberg in the 15th c., of which only part remains. One room in the museum is devoted to the work of Etienne Oehmichen, who in 1924 invented the helicopter. In Place St-Martin are the Town Hall (1776, with later alterations), the Hôtel Beurnier, the Maison des Princes and the Protestant church of St-Martin, founded in the early 17th c. by a Württemberger named Schickhardt.

Montbenoît is a village in the Saugeais valley with a charming abbey: 12th c. nave, 16th c. choir, bell-tower rebuilt in early 20th c. The 15th c. cloister shows

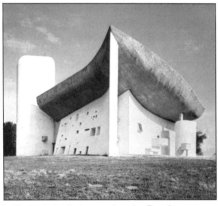
Le Corbusier's pilgrimage chapel at Ronchamp

the influence of the Flamboyant style of the late Gothic period.

Mont-Rond has two peaks, the lower one 1534 m (observation tower) and the higher 1614 m, offering between them the most comprehensive *view of the Jura. The lower peak is reached by cabin-lift from the Col de la Faucille.

Morez (pop. 6750), in the Bienne valley, is a town of watchmakers and spectacle-manufacturers (the latter trade having been practised here for almost 200 years).

Nantua (pop. 4000), on the *Lac de Nantua* (2·5 km long, 650 m wide), owed its origin to a Benedictine abbey, founded in the 12th c., which was destroyed during the French Revolution. All that is left is the church of St-Michel, with a beautiful doorway.

Nozeroy (pop. 420) has an old-world aspect, with old houses in the Grande Rue, an ancient town gate (the Clock Gate) and a 15th c. church.

Ornans (pop. 4300) was the birthplace of the painter Courbet; the house in which he was born is now a museum. It is an attractive little town, with old houses, in the Loue valley. The church, originally Romanesque (12th c.), was rebuilt and enlarged in the 16th and 17th c. and is richly furnished.

Poligny (pop. 5000) lies in the middle of a fertile agricultural region and is noted for its wine and its Gruyère cheese. The church of St-Hippolyte is notable particularly for its statues of the Burgundian school (15th c.). Behind the church is a convent of Poor Clares founded in 1415. In the Grande Rue are charming old houses with carved doors (17th c.).

Pontarlier (pop. 20,000) is of more importance as a centre from which to explore the surrounding region than for its own sights – a triumphal arch dating from the time of Louis XV, the church of St-Bénigne and a chapel.

Ronchamp is world-famed for the *chapel of Notre-Dame-du-Haut by Le Corbusier (1955), situated on a hill 150 m high above the industrial area of Ronchamp, which it dominates with its white walls and striking lines.

St-Claude (pop. 13,500), noted for the manufacture of pipes, is one of the leading tourist centres of the Upper Jura. Its main feature of interest is the Cathedral of St-Pierre (14th–15th c., with a square tower and neo-classical façade added in the 18th c.); the interior contains fine *choir-stalls of the mid 15th c. The church, one of the finest in the Jura, belonged to an abbey which was destroyed during the French Revolution.

Salins-les-Bains, in the narrow valley of the Furieuse, is noted for its salt-mine, which was already being worked in Roman times. The salt is now used only for medicinal purposes. A tour of the workings, 250 m underground, is an impressive experience.

RIVERS and VALLEYS. – One of the great attractions of the Jura is the striking and constantly varying scenery of its valleys, including those of the Ain, Doubs, Dessoubre, Loue and Valserine. Visitors to the Jura should make a point of exploring one or other of these valleys, or the deep mountain valleys known as *reculées*.

The valley of the **Ain** traverses the Jura for a distance of 190 km, offering a series of rapids, waterfalls and picturesque gorges. This attractive scenery can be enjoyed by driving down the upper Ain valley from Nozeroy (near the source of the river) to its junction with the Seine, or along the lakes formed by a succession of dams between Pont-de-Poitte and Poncin, a distance of some 100 km.

The **Dessoubre** is one of the least known but most attractive of the Jura rivers. There is a pleasant drive of 30 km along its course from the source in the Cirque de Consolation to its junction with the Doubs at St-Hippolyte. In the cirque is the former monastery of Notre-Dame de Consolation. From here the lonely road, flanked by trees, runs down through beautiful scenery to St-Hippolyte.

The little Dessoubre is very different from the majestic valley of the *Doubs, which rises near Mouthe (alt. 937 m) and flows into the Saône after a winding course of 430 km, though the distance as the crow flies is only 90 km. The road down the Doubs valley descends the upper valley from the source to Morteau, through the impressive Doubs gorges to Montbéliard and from there to Besançon, after which the Doubs

leaves the Jura near Dole. Among the principal attractions of this road are the gorge of Cluse-et-Mijoux (of which there is a fine view from Les Rosiers); the Lac de Chaillexon, with a fall 28 m high on the Doubs; the Corniche de Goumois near the Swiss frontier, with magnificent views of the mountains; and the little town of L'Isle-sur-le-Doubs, divided by the river into three parts.

The *Loue was often painted by Courbet; and indeed it is a very picturesque river, its banks lined by trees. It is also attractive to canoeists. From its *source at Ouhans it follows a winding course to its junction with the Doubs. Its main attractions are its source, in a large cave which has been shown to be connected with the Doubs, its numerous viewpoints like the Moine de la Vallée and Mouthier, and the Nouailles gorges. Particularly picturesque is the stretch between Cléron and the mouth of the Lison.

The **Valserine** is a high valley of great romantic charm, extending for a distance of some 60 km from near the Col de la Faucille to Bellegarde, where it flows into the Rhône. On either side of the valley rise the highest peaks in the Jura, with stretches of mountain pasture between them. A striking feature is the Pont des Pierres, which spans the river between Montanges and Mulaz in an arch 80 m wide. The finest viewpoint is at Mijoux, on the way up to the Col de la Faucille.

The "**reculées**" are the steep-sided valleys which are found, for example, on the *Cuisance*, the *Seille* and the *Vallière*. They extend from Arbois by way of the Cirque de Baume to Lons-le-Saunier and Pont-de-Poitte, a road distance of 80 km. These very attractive valleys cut their way through the hills to end in a cirque or corrie with sheer rock faces which often contain caves. The *Reculée des Planches* or Reculée d'Arbois, SE of the town of Arbois, contains the two sources of the River Cuisance and ends in the impressive *Cirque du Fer à Cheval*. Another striking cirque is the *Cirque de Ladoye*, but the finest of all is the *Cirque de Baume*, with magnificent *views from its crags. From the top of this steep path runs down to the caves at the foot, formerly one of the sources of the River Dard, which after heavy rain emerges here in the form of a waterfall. The amphitheatre-like *Creux de Revigny*, between Lons-le-Saunier and Pont-de-Poitte, also contains many caves.

Languedoc
See under Roussillon
(Languedoc-Roussillon)

Lille

Region: Nord–Pas de Calais.
Department: Nord.
Altitude: 1–23 m. – Population: 177,000.
Post code: F-59000. – Dialling code: 20.
ⓘ **Office du Tourisme,**
   Palais Rihour;
   tel. 54 21 46.

HOTELS. – *Grand Hôtel Bellevue*, II, 80 r.; *Carlton*, II, 70 r.; *Royal Concorde*, II, 111 r.; *Terminus*, III, 65 r.;

Nord-Motel, III, 80 r.; *Paix*, III, 36 r.; *Moderne*, III, 69 r.; *Chopin*, IV, 28 r.; *Continental*, IV, 32 r.; *Coq Hardi*, IV, 30 r.; *Faidherbe*, IV, 43 r.

EVENTS. – *International Trade Fair* (April); *Summer Carnival*, with parade of giant figures (Whitsun).

Lille, situated near the Belgian frontier, lies in the centre of an industrial conurbation with a population of a million. It is the chief town of the Nord department and the metropolis of French Flanders, a modern city with few memories of the past. It was the birthplace of General de Gaulle (1890–1970). The city has large textile, engineering and chemical industries.

HISTORY. – Until 1713 Lille was in Dutch Flanders, but under the treaty of Utrecht which ended the War of the Spanish Succession it was ceded to France. The old capital of Flanders was called L'Isle (which became Lille) because it lay on an island between the rivers Deule and Lys.

SIGHTS. – Lille has a number of fine medieval buildings – the Gothic church of *St-Maurice, with two lateral aisles on each side of the nave and a spacious interior with 36 columns; the 16th c. church of *Ste-Catherine*, which was enlarged in the 17th c. (*"Martyrdom of St Catherine" by Rubens in N aisle); the 15th c. *Palais Rihour*; the 12th c. *Hospice Comtesse*; and a 15th c. *bell-tower*. The **Cathedral** (*Notre-Dame-de-la-Treille*) was begun only in 1854 and has not yet been completed; in the apsidal chapel is a fine marble statue of the Virgin (11th c.).

Among more recent buildings are the imposing **Citadel** (originally 16th c.), Vauban's finest fortification; the **Porte de Paris**, a triumphal arch (France's second largest after the Arc de Triomphe in Paris) erected in honour of Louis XIV in the late 17th c.; and the Flemish-style **Old Exchange** (mid 17th c.), in the courtyard of which is a monument to Napoleon, erected in 1854. – The *Theatre* was built shortly before the First World War, the *New Exchange* shortly after it. The *Town Hall*, near the Porte de Paris, was built between 1925 and 1933; it has a slender tower 106 m high.

The outstanding feature of Lille, however, is the **Palais des Beaux-Arts**, which houses one of France's finest museums, with sculpture, decorative art, ethnographical material, 3000 Italian and French *drawings and a very fine collection of **paintings, including works by Flemish, Dutch, Italian and Spanish masters and paintings by Watteau, Poussin and other French artists.

Limoges

Region: Limousin.
Department: Haute-Vienne.
Altitude: 290 m. – Population: 147,000.
Post code: F-87000. – Dialling code: 55.
ⓘ **Office de Tourisme,**
   Boulevard Fleurus;
   tel. 32 52 80.

HOTELS. – *Frantel Royal Limousin*, I, 76 r.; *Novotel*, I, 90 r.; *Luk*, II, 59 r.; *Jeanne-d'Arc*, II, 55 r.; *Caravelle*, II, 31 r.; *Richelieu*, II, 27 r.; *Bordeaux-Terminus*, III, 60 r.; *Faisan*, III, 80 r.

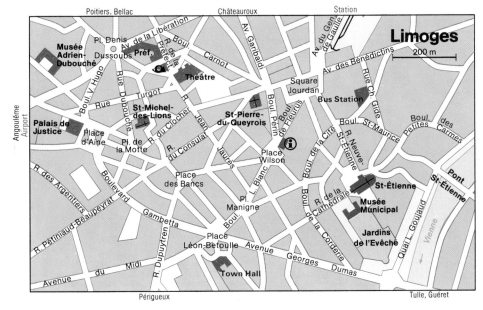

Limoges, capital of the Limousin and chief town of the department of Haute-Vienne, lies in hilly country at a ford on the River Vienne which was of importance in earlier times. Its name is now mainly associated with the china which has been produced here since the late 18th c.; but still older is the fame of Limoges enamel, which has been made since the 12th c. The city's other main industry is shoe manufacture.

Pont St-Etienne, Limoges

SIGHTS. – The most important building is the *Cathedral (St-Etienne), the only piece of Gothic architecture in Limoges, which was begun in 1273, continued in various later periods and completed only in the 19th c. The Flamboyant doorway dates from about 1525. The bell-tower is 62 m high, the three lower storeys being Romanesque, the top four Gothic. In the choir are three impressive memorials to church dignitaries of the 14th and 16th c. There is a valuable treasury with fine *enamels. – Other features of interest are two more churches, the old-world Boucherie quarter with its narrow lanes and the two medieval bridges. – The Musée National Adrien-Dubouché contains archaeological material and a large collection of china from different countries.

Enamel casket from Limoges

Visitors interested in Limoges enamel will want to visit the Enamel Workshop at 31 rue des Tanneries, where the techniques of enamel-working are explained. The Municipal Museum in the former Bishop's Palace also has a collection of *enamel from the Limousin covering the period from the Middle Ages to the present day. – From the terraced gardens of the Bishop's Palace above the Vienne there are attractive views of the town.

Limousin

The Limousin, which takes its name from Limoges, embraces an extensive area in the departments of Creuse, Haute-Vienne and Corrèze. Its capital, Limoges, is in the NW part of the region. Limousin is associated in visitors' minds with Périgord, which bounds it on the SW, and Quercy, which lies to the SE.

Still rather off the beaten track of tourism, Limousin has preserved much unspoiled natural beauty. Its upland regions, outliers of the Massif Central nowhere exceeding 1000 m in height, are broken up by high plateaux and river valleys, the most important of which is the valley of the Vézère. It is an area well supplied with water; and fishermen and water sports enthusiasts will find plenty of entertainment on its numerous streams and on the Lac de Vassivière (2470 acres) between Limoges and Aubusson.

HISTORY. – Although many standing stones and megalithic tombs are to be found in Limousin, there is less evidence of prehistoric settlement here than in the neighbouring province of Périgord. There was a great flowering of Romanesque art between the 11th and 13th c., to such an extent that Gothic made relatively little headway. The 14th c. was a time of trial for Limousin, with famine, plague, exploitation and plunder; and yet it was during this period that a French Pope, Clement VI (Pierre de Rosiers), declared: "I shall plant in God's church a rose-bush from Limousin which will still produce roots and buds in a hundred years." And indeed within 30 years, through his efforts and those of his nephew and successor (Pierre-Roger de Beaufort, who became Gregory XI), Limousin gave the church a dozen patriarchs, some 40 cardinals and more than 300 bishops – thus confirming the prophecy by St Martial, who brought Christianity to this region about 250, that this "land of saints" would prove a fertile soil for the church. – The china industry which has given Limousin, and Limoges in particular, international fame was brought to the region from Sèvres about 1770. It was little affected by the Revolution, and after the First Empire centred increasingly on Limoges, which thus acquired a virtual monopoly. The great Impressionist Renoir (1841–1919) began his artistic career as a porcelain painter in Limoges.

SIGHTS. – **Ahun**, which was already a place of some importance in Gallo-Roman times, has at Moutier d'Ahun a 12th c. abbey church (rebuilt after destruction at the beginning of the 17th c.) with fine carved woodwork of 1673–81.

The church at **Ambazac**, a little town surrounded by hills rising to 700 m, contains a magnificent reliquary of 1123.

Aubusson, in the Creuse valley, appeals to visitors with its attractive narrow lanes, but is known mainly for its *tapestries, whose fame dates back to the 15th c., when the craft of tapestry-making was brought here from Flanders. In the 18th c. works by Watteau, Boucher and other artists were woven in tapestry. Aubusson still has large tapestry and Gobelins workshops (some of which can be visited). Every summer there is an exhibition of new work in the Town Hall. In the "Maison du Vieux Tapissier" an old Gobelins workshop can be seen. – From Aubusson visitors can have pleasant trips into the beautiful valley of the Creuse.

Bellac, on the borders of Poitou, is a beautifully situated little town, birthplace of the playwright Jean Giraudoux (1882–1944: memorial), who is commemorated by a Festival of Drama and Music held every year at the end of June and beginning of July. In his novel "Suzanne et le Pacifique" Giraudoux celebrated the beauty of the Limousin.

Bourganeuf stands on a hill at the meeting of three valleys. Of its château there remains the "Tour de Zizim", with a striking three-storey timber structure (oak); fine view from top. The Town Hall contains Gobelins of the late 18th c. from Aubusson.

Brive is called Brive la Gaillarde ("sturdy") in recognition of its stubborn resistance in numerous sieges during the wars of earlier days. It lies on the Corrèze near the borders of Périgord, and has a number of handsome old houses such as the Hôtel de Labenche as well as the 16th c. Tour des Echevins (Magistrates' Tower). The Musée Ernest Rupin, in an elegant mansion of the time of Louis XIII, has much material of regional interest and mementoes of distinguished citizens of the town.

Chambon-sur-Voueize has one of the finest Romanesque churches in Limousin, Ste-Valérie (12th c., restored 1850). Its total length is 87 m, its width 38 m. The square tower dates from the 13th c. – 2 km away is the spa of *Evaux-les-Bains*, which was already frequented in Roman times, with some 30 springs (14–60 °C). Romanesque church of St-Pierre-et-St-Paul.

The River **Creuse**, on its way down from the Massif Central, has carved out a picturesque valley with impressive gorges between *Fresselines* and *Argenton*. Here too is the *artificial lake of Eguzon* (15 km long). In one of her novels George Sand remarked that "the Creuse in April is surely the most beautiful river in the world." Many painters, including Claude Monet, have worked here.

The ***Dordogne**, one of France's longest rivers, is also held to be its most beautiful. Between *Bort-les-Orgues* and *Beaulieu-sur-Dordogne* it flows through the Limousin and then on into Périgord, frequently harnessed to supply hydro-electric power. There are large *dams in the Limousin at *Bort-les-Orgues* and *Marèges*, and smaller ones like the *Barrage de l'Aigle, Barrage du Chastang* and *Barrage du Sablier* near Argentat. These various dams, extending over a distance of more than 100 km like a giant staircase, have transformed the landscape. Between Bort and the Barrage du Sablier the river falls some 400 m, regulated by five dams. The total volume of water thus impounded is 935 million cubic metres. – The Dordogne is formed at the foot of the Puy de Sancy by the junction of the Dore and the Dogne, which also combine to give it its name. Leaving the volcanic region of Auvergne, it enters the granite hills of the Limousin, and after a course of almost 500 km joins with the Garonne to form the Gironde, which flows into the Atlantic at Royan.

The **Millevaches Plateau**, between the upper valleys of the Vienne and the Vézère, reaches a height of just under 1000 m and is known as the "roof of the Limousin". The name has nothing to do with *vaches* (cows), but is derived from the Celtic word *batz*, "spring" – of which there are many in this region. The plateau is sparsely populated. It has a number of picturesque lakes formed by dams (Lac de Vassivière, Lac de Faux-la-Montagne, Lac de Viaman, Lac du Chamet), and is at its most beautiful in spring and autumn. –

Felletin, in the northern part of the area, is a centre of tapestry-weaving, like nearby Aubusson. **Meymac**, to the S, has an 11th c. church which belonged to a Benedictine abbey (some buildings of which have been restored). – The highest point is Mont Bessou, above Meymac. From the top of the *Signal d'Audouze* (854 m), half-way between Felletin and Meymac on D 36, there are magnificent panoramic views, extending as far as the volcanic cones of Auvergne. This mountain is also the watershed between the Loire and the Dordogne. Adjoining the Millevaches plateau are the *Monts de Monédières* (911 m), from which also there are very fine views.

Oradour-sur-Glane acquired tragic fame on 10 June 1944, when the village was destroyed and its entire population killed by 200 S.S. men. The ruins of the village, including the church (in which the villagers perished) have been preserved as they were, and a new village with the same name built nearby.

Pompadour is famous for the château which Louis XV presented to Mme de Pompadour. He also founded (1761) the stud farm which has made Pompadour a centre of horse-breeding (Anglo-Arab horses) and racing (annual horse-shows and races). The National Stud (Haras National) can be visited.

St-Junien has a fine Romanesque church (11th–12th c.), typically Limousin in style, and many 14th and 15th c. houses.

St-Léonard-de-Noblat is a charming little town with picturesque old houses (13th–16th c.), birthplace of the physicist Gay-Lussac (discoverer of the law of volumes). The town, situated on a hill, has a beautiful Romanesque church (11th c.); the bell-tower has fine capitals.

St-Yrieix-la-Perche, in the middle of a stock-farming region, had the kaolin deposits which gave the first impulse to the manufacture of china in Limoges. The collegiate church known as the Moûtier (12th–13th c.), with the austere aspect of a fortified church, occupies the site of an abbey founded in the 6th c. The Tour du Plô once formed part of the town walls.

La Souterraine, on the site of a Gallo-Roman settlement, is also of medieval aspect. The Porte St-Jean, a town gate

dating from the 14th–15th c., has two turrets. The church (12th–13th c.) stands over an early 11th c. crypt.

Tulle, extending for over 3 km along the narrow Corrèze valley, became the see of a bishop in 1317, which led to a long period of disputes with Limoges. The town was involved in many warlike events during the 14th–16th c., and again in 1944. The main features of interest are in the old parts of the town around the Cathedral, where, among a maze of narrow lanes and steps, stands the 15th c. Maison de Loyac with its beautiful façade and handsome staircases. The finest part of the Cathedral is the 14th c. bell-tower (75 m high), which was damaged by lightning in 1645 but rebuilt in the original style. Visitors can also see a cloister, adjoining which is a museum.

Ussel (alt. 631 m) has a number of 15th–17th c. buildings in the centre of the town and a large Roman eagle found at the Peuch mill, the original site of the town.

Uzerche (pop. 3500), by virtue both of its *situation and its architecture, is one of the most attractive little towns in the Limousin. There is a saying that if you have a house in Uzerche you can claim to have a château in the Limousin. Apart

Uzerche

from the general impression, the town's main features are the Romanesque church of St-Pierre, the Porte Bécharie (the only one of the town's old gates to survive) and the view from the Esplanade de la Lunade.

SPORT and RECREATION in Limousin. – *Water sports* and *riding* are well catered for. There are numerous rivers and a number of lakes which offer scope for anglers. The rivers offer attractive canoe and kayak trips. Information about facilities for riding can be obtained from the Ligue du Limousin de la Fédération Française de Sports Equestres in Brive. A popular riding centre is Pompadour, where the Club

Méditerranée has an establishment. – For *walkers* there are large numbers of unfrequented footpaths running through beautiful scenery. A number of the trails known as "Sentiers de grande randonnée" pass through the region – GR 4, from Aubusson to Angoulême (way-marked throughout); GR 44, from Bort-le-Orgues to Vassivière; GR 46, from Aubusson to Rocamadour (not yet completely way-marked).

Château de Chenonceaux, on the Cher

Loire Valley

The Loire is France's longest river, with a course of 1020 km from its source 'on the Gerbier de Jonc in Vivarais to the Atlantic. Its name is particularly associated with the many **châteaux which are the special attraction of the *Loire valley, making it one of the most popular tourist areas in France. Many of these châteaux are not actually on the river but in the beautiful surrounding countryside.

As a navigable waterway the Loire is of importance only in its lowest reaches, and in comparison with previous centuries the traffic it carries is small. This is because of the considerable variations in level to which it is subject, making any regular use impossible. From the 12th c. onwards frequent efforts were made to control the spates and flooding, which at times could reach serious proportions (for example in 1846, 1856, 1866 and 1910), by the construction of dams; and it was thanks to these dams that the Loire valley increased in importance and prosperity.

The Loire valley in the narrower sense is thought of as extending from Giens to somewhere short of Nantes (perhaps Ancenis), since the river's most westerly stretch belongs to Brittany. It passes through the four departments of Loiret, Loir-et-Cher, Indre-et-Loire and Maine-et-Loire, which have replaced the older territorial designations of Orléanais, Blésois (the area round Blois), Touraine and Anjou. All these areas have two things in common – the alluvial soil deposited by the Loire and the plateau, ranging in height between 50 and 200 m, which borders the river. Fruit, vines and vegetables flourish in this fertile region, with a climate influenced by the nearby ocean. The less fertile areas are occupied by forests. The principal towns in the Loire valley are situated on the river – **Orléans** (see p. 171), **Blois**, **Tours** (p. 248) and

Angers (p. 63), together with **Nantes** (p. 159) in Brittany – their economic importance depending on their industry.

The various *tributaries of the Loire* resemble the Loire in their geographical pattern and scenery, and also in their possession of fine old buildings and places of historical interest. The most important are the *Cher*, the *Indre*, the *Vienne* and the confusingly similar *Loir* (without an e).

The ****châteaux of the Loire**, which for most tourists are the principal attraction of the Loire valley, all date from different periods. Those of *Angers*, *Chinon, Langeais, Loches* and *Sully* go back to medieval times. The most famous and the most beautiful were built at the Renaissance, the most important being *Amboise, Azay-le-Rideau, Blois, Chambord, Chaumont, Chenonceaux, Ussé* and *Villandry*. Other châteaux, in neo-classical style, were built in the 17th and 18th c., such as *Cheverny* and *Valençay*. Nowhere else in the world can such a range of splendid mansions and palaces be seen within such a relatively small area. But no visitor, of course, can see more than a selection of them in the time he is likely to have available. Although the distances between them are not great, sufficient time must be allowed for seeing and enjoying the châteaux themselves.

Château d'Amboise, on the Loire

To get any idea of at least the principal châteaux and other places of interest a full week is required. – There are "Son et Lumière" performances at many châteaux during the summer.

HISTORY. – Although the Romans were able to establish their hold on the Loire valley, the first risings against Caesar's forces took place here. Christianity came to the region in the 3rd c., and later St Martin was active in propagating the Gospel. He died in 397, and his tomb in Tours became a place of pilgrimage in Merovingian times. In subsequent centuries Huns, Saracens and Norsemen thrust into the Loire valley, fighting and plundering. Thanks to the weakness of the Carolingian kings wealthy nobles became sovereign rulers of their own territories, each constantly at odds with his neighbours. There was particularly bitter hostility between the Counts of Anjou and Blois; and when the rulers of Anjou, the Plantagenets, also became kings of England (1154) their domains extended from the borders of Scotland to the Pyrenees. The Capetian kings of France were nevertheless able to establish their authority from 1216 onwards; but the English then returned and the Hundred Years War began. The English forces advanced steadily farther into France, until on 9 March 1429, in the château of Chinon on the Loire, the Dauphin (Charles VII) gave supreme command to Joan of Arc, who on 8 May in the same year freed Orléans. Although Joan was tried and burned at the stake in Orléans, the Loire valley thereafter formed a secure barrier against hostile attack and became a favourite residence of the French kings. Louis XI built the little château of Plessis-lès-Tours and the splendid château of Langeais; Amboise was built in the time of Charles VIII; Louis XII built a wing of Blois; Francis I added another, and also built Chambord. Following the example of the kings, the nobility began to build their country houses here, too. But the great days of the Loire valley lasted little more than 150 years: the last king to reside here was Henry III (d. 1589), and with Henry IV the glory of the Loire châteaux departed. Thereafter the Loire region entered a period of economic difficulties, which became worse in the 18th c.; and the industry and trade of such towns as Orléans, Amboise, Tours and Saumur suffered accordingly. During the French Revolution there was fighting in Anjou, but the population of this fertile region soon settled down to more peaceful pursuits. The Loire valley is now one of France's major tourist areas, appealing to both French and foreign visitors with its mild climate and the splendours of its châteaux.

SIGHTS. – Apart from the châteaux which are its main attraction the Loire valley has many charming old towns and fine churches.

Amboise (pop. 11,500) presents its most picturesque aspect when seen from the right bank of the Loire or from the bridge. The *château then appears to dominate the town. It is one of the oldest and most beautiful of the royal residences in the Loire valley, although after the French Revolution considerable parts of it were pulled down for lack of money to maintain them. The heyday of Amboise lay between the beginning of the 16th c., when Francis I brought Leonardo da Vinci (who died and was buried in Amboise) to work here, and the year 1560, in the reign of Francis II, when a Protestant conspiracy was brought to light and the conspirators hanged within the château. In the time of Louis XIV the château was used as a prison. – The château was built from 1492 onwards in the reign of Charles VIII, who also laid out an Italian-style garden. Among its finest features are the terrace (view), the beautifully proportioned *chapel of St-Hubert, the Tour des Minimes (21 m in diameter, with a spiral ramp up which horses could be ridden) and the even more massive Tour Hurtault (24 m in diameter, with walls 4·3 m thick). – In the town are two medieval churches, a 16th c. Town Hall and a clock-tower dating from the time of Charles VIII.

Max Ernst Fountain, Amboise

On the Loire embankment is a striking modern fountain by Max Ernst (1968). – Just outside the town is the 15th c. manor-house of Le Clos-Lucé, in which Leonardo da Vinci lived and in which he died in 1519. Although altered by later owners, the house has now been restored to something like its original condition.

Angers, with its *château and *Cathedral, is one of the principal towns and one of the main tourist centres of the Loire valley: see p. 63.

The contemporary world is represented by **Avoine-Chinon** (11 km NW of Chinon),

Château de Chambord, on the Loire

with France's first atomic power station, which can be seen from an observation tower.

Azay-le-Rideau (pop. 2700) is notable for its Renaissance *château, a building of fairytale charm and elegance on the banks of the Indre. It was built between 1518 and 1529 by a financier of the day who later had to flee the country and died in exile; it is now the property of the State. Externally the château shows some Gothic features, but the layout of the old moats, designed for ornament rather than use, shows the emergence of a new spirit. Fine state apartments.

Beaugency (pop. 7000) had what was for many centuries the only bridge over the Loire between Orléans and Blois, and accordingly was frequently subject to hostile attack. In the 12th c. two councils were held here to solve marital problems within the royal family. The town still has a medieval aspect, with its rectangular keep (11th c.), a clock-tower which formed part of the old fortifications, the Tour du Diable (Devil's Tower) which defended the bridgehead, the 15th c. château (now housing a regional museum) built by Dunois, the "Bastard of Orléans", and the rather later Renaissance Town Hall, which contains panels of 17th c. embroidery. The church of Notre-Dame originally belonged to an abbey, and the

Tour St-Firmin is also part of a church which no longer exists. Dramatic performances are given here in July.

Blois (pop. 50,000) is the market centre for a flourishing agricultural area, but is principally known for its magnificent **château. Originally a strong point defending the bridge over the Loire, the château was built in successive stages between the 13th and 17th c. It was, in a sense, the forerunner of Versailles, a favourite residence of Louis XII and Francis I during the 16th c. During the reign of Henry III the king's rival Duke Henry of Guise was murdered here in 1588; and only eight months later the king himself suffered the same fate. Later Louis XIII exiled his mother Marie de Médicis to Blois. – The different parts of the château are not difficult to distinguish. The tour starts from the Place du Château (the outer ward of the medieval castle). The various wings were built by successive rulers – Charles d'Orléans (gallery), Louis XII, Francis I, Gaston d'Orléans. The Duke of Guise was murdered on the second floor of the Francis I wing (on the first floor of which are the apartments of Catherine de Médicis), although the interior of the wing was altered in later periods. A striking feature of the château is the *staircase tower built by Francis I. The Louis XII wing houses a museum with furniture and objets d'art of the 15th–18th

c. – It is well worth while also looking round the town of Blois, which has a picturesque old quarter with interesting houses between the Cathedral (restored in the 17th c.) and the Loire. The church of Notre-Dame de la Trinité is a modern structure with a bell-tower 60 m high and a carillon of 48 bells (rung on Sundays and public holidays from Easter to 1 November at 4.30 p.m.). – Denis Papin, inventor of the steam engine, was born in Blois in 1648. There is a monument to him in the town.

Brissac, one of the châteaux not so well known to visitors, was built at the beginning of the 17th c. in place of an old castle with two 15th c. towers. The park and the interior of the château are both worth seeing.

**Chambord, another forerunner of Versailles, is the largest of the Loire châteaux, measuring 117 by 156 m, with no fewer than 440 rooms. The view when approaching the château is strikingly impressive. It was built for Francis I from 1519 onwards, regardless of expense: indeed the Loire was diverted to enhance the effect. Here in 1552 the German princes signed the agreement ceding the bishoprics of Metz, Toul and Verdun to France. Later kings of France, except Henry III and Henry IV, liked to stay at Chambord. Louis XIV frequently came here, and Molière wrote a number of his plays here, including "Le Bourgeois Gentilhomme". Louis XV granted the château to Maurice of Saxony as a residence in the 18th c.; but thereafter it fell into disrepair, and during the French Revolution the furniture and furnishings were destroyed. It became the property of the State in 1930. – The park, which has an area of 13,600 acres, four-fifths of it forest, is surrounded by a wall 32 km long (the longest in France), with six gates giving access to six avenues leading to the château. The terrace – reflecting Italian influence – is very attractive, and was a central feature of the château under the monarchy. The château itself has an impressive *grand staircase.

Chaumont-sur-Loire, standing above the Loire, offers a fine view of the valley from its terrace, reminiscent of Amboise. The *château, built between 1465 and 1510 on the site of earlier fortified castles, is approached through a park planted with cedars. Its original warlike aspect was relieved by the insertion of new

windows. In the interior are fine Gobelin tapestries. The stables are worth visiting to see the luxury in which horses were housed in those days.

**Chenonceaux, built over the Cher, is a "must" for every visitor. It was built about 1520 by Thomas Bohier, treasurer to three French kings, and later presented by Henry II to his favourite, Diane de Poitiers, who was later forced by Henry's widow Catherine de Médicis to exchange it for Chaumont. Thereafter it was the scene of splendid entertainments. In the 18th c. the château became the property of a tax-farmer named Dupin, and Jean-Jacques Rousseau lived here for some time as tutor to his son. The château is still in private ownership, but is open to visitors. It is

approached by a fine avenue of plane-trees, at the end of which a drawbridge leads on to a terrace in front of the entrance. The original structure of the château is square, with four corner turrets, and stands out in the river. Beyond this is a two-storey terrace built by Catherine de Médicis, also with the river flowing below it. The two lower floors, which are shown to visitors, contain pictures and Gobelin tapestries. On both sides of the château are gardens laid out by Diane de Poitiers and Catherine de Médicis.

*Cheverny is built in the classical style of the 17th c., and has preserved its original decoration. The château, which is in private ownership, contains a Hunting Museum (in an annexe), with 2000 stags' antlers, and large kennels.

Chinon (pop. 9000) offers an image of the Middle Ages to which both the town and the château contribute. Rabelais spent his early years here at 15 rue de la Lamproie. The most interesting parts of the old town are Rue Voltaire, with its old houses, and the Place du Grand Carroi, the centre of medieval Chinon, which has associations with such different characters as Richard Cœur-de-Lion and Joan of Arc (who stayed in the inn here while waiting to be received by the king). The crag on which the château stands was already fortified in Roman times. The castle ward, measuring 400 by 70 m, contains three separate fortifications, now partly in ruins – the Fort St-Georges, the Château du Milieu and the Château du Coudray – and is entered by way of a 35 m high clock-tower which houses a Joan of Arc Museum. There are fine views from the ramparts on the S side. Joan of Arc stayed on the first floor of the Tour du Coudray. Until 1450 Chinon was a royal residence, and in 1498 Louis XII received Cesare Borgia here. Later the château passed into the hands of Richelieu. In the 18th and 19th c. it fell into disrepair, but was finally acquired and restored by the department of Indre-et-Loire.

Cléry-St-André (pop. 1850) has a 15th c. church in which Louis XI and Dunois were buried. Richly carved choir-stalls.

Cunault is notable for a *church* which belonged to a Benedictine abbey (11th and 13th c.). Its main features are the bell-tower (with a squat 15th c. spire), the interior, the 223 carved capitals and the remains of medieval wall paintings.

Fontevrault-L'Abbaye: see p. 64.

Gien (pop. 14,000) is for many visitors the beginning of the real Loire valley. In spite of heavy destruction during the Second World War it is an attractive little town. The château is an unpretentious building of 1484, and houses a Museum of Hunting and Falconry as well as a selection of the characteristic Gien earthenware. (There is a manufactory on the banks of the Loire, founded 1820, covering an area of 6 hectares.) The church of Ste-Jeanne-d'Arc is a modern brick structure (rebuilt after destruction in 1940) with a 15th c. tower. Near the town is the *Château de la Bussière* (originally 13th c., later rebuilt), surrounded by a moat, which contains a Fishing Museum.

Langeais (pop 3900) has a *château which was completed more quickly (in 4–5 years) than most of the Loire châteaux. Although it is less splendid than some of the others, it is particularly worth

visiting because it has preserved its form without alteration and still has its original decoration. It was built by Loius XI between 1465 and 1469. In the park is a 10th c. keep, the oldest in France, built by Foulques Nerra, Count of Anjou.

Loches (pop. 6500), on the banks of the Indre, makes an attractive medieval picture with its castle and old houses. Although it lies off the main road, it is well worth a detour. The town is dominated by the **castle on its hill. This is entered through the 13th c. Porte Royale, which is flanked by two 15th c. towers. It contains a regional museum, with 19th c. paintings, and a museum of Far Eastern art. In the richly decorated Logis Royal are the oratory of Anne de Bretagne and the tomb of Charles VII's favourite Agnès Sorel. The castle proper has two 15th c. towers, the Tour Ronde and the Martelet, designed to reinforce the original massive 11th c. keep. A walk round the fortifications reveals their impressive strength, with only two gates interrupting the 2 km of walls. – In the town are the 12th c. *church of St-Ours, with a Romanesque doorway; several town gates; the Tour St-Antoine, a 16th c. water-tower; and the *Town Hall, also 16th c. – In nearby *Beaulieu-lès-Loches* are a Romanesque church and the ruins of the medieval abbey to which it belonged.

Orléans: see p. 171.

St-Benoît-sur-Loire has a Romanesque *church built between 1067 and 1218 which is one of the finest in France. Originally the towers were higher than they now are, and there were also two bell-towers. The outstanding feature is the porch-tower (originally free-standing), with its richly carved capitals. Beautifully proportioned choir. To the S of the church is a new abbey, replacing the buildings destroyed during the French Revolution.

Saumur (pop. 36,000) is a town of many facets, noted for its wine, for the manufacture of rosaries and other devotional articles, and for its famous Cavalry School. The main features of interest are the Romanesque church of Notre-Dame-de-Nantilly, with fine 15th–17th c. tapestries; the château, built at the turn of the 14th c., which houses a *Museum of Decorative Art (mainly medieval and Renaissance work) and a Museum of the Horse; the old town, with the Maison du Roi; the Quartier des Ponts (rebuilt after the last war), on an island between two arms of the Loire, with the 15th c. Maison de la Reine de Sicile; and a number of churches.

Suèvre (pop. 1200), NE of Blois near the N bank of the Loire, is an ancient little town with two (originally Romanesque) churches, St-Lubin and St-Christophe.

Sully-sur-Loire (pop. 5100) is picturesquely situated on the Loire. The château was damaged in 1940, but the unique medieval timber roof of the upper chamber in the keep survived in good condition. The building was erected before 1360, and its defences were made more formidable by four corner towers. The young Voltaire lived for some time in Sully, and his early plays were performed here. The castle gave its name to Henry IV's minister Maximilien de Béthune when he was created a duke.

Tours: see p. 248.

Ussé is the most romantic and fanciful of all the Loire châteaux, and is said to have given Charles Perrault, the 17th c. writer of fairytales, the idea of the Sleeping Beauty's castle. The best view of the château is to be had from the bridge over the Loire, a few hundred metres away. The château (which is in private ownership) was built in stages between the 15th and 17th c., and shows a mingling of late Gothic and Renaissance features. In the park is a chapel in pure Renaissance style (1520–38).

Valençay lies S of Chambord, over 50 km from the Loire, but the affinities of this 16th c. château to Chambord are unmistakable. It was built by Jacques d'Estampes, a *nouveau riche* anxious to display his wealth, and in 1805 was acquired by Talleyrand. Only part of the château, furnished in Empire style, is open to visitors. There is a Talleyrand Museum in an annexe.

Villandry is of even greater interest for its *gardens than for the *château itself, which dates from the 16th c. and contains a fine collection of pictures. The French-style gardens as we see them today were laid out in the 16th c. but were replaced in the 19th c. by gardens in the English style then fashionable, only to be restored to their original form by a later owner. They consist of three terraces on different levels: a water garden with 7000 sq. metres of water basins and ponds on the highest level, below this an ornamental garden, and below this again a vegetable garden. The geometrically patterned beds are marked out by carefully clipped and constantly tended yew and box hedges.

SPORT and RECREATION. – The Loire valley offers scope for a great variety of activities. There are some 30 places with *sailing clubs*, and a dozen or so with facilities for water skiing, including Tours, Blois and Gien. There are numbers of *swimming pools*, open-air, heated and indoor. The only *golf-courses* are at Tours (18 holes), Donnery (near Orléans), La Ferté-St-Aubin and Sully-sur-Loire (all 9 holes). There are *tennis courts* in some 100 places and facilities for *riding* in 70. More specialised interests like *clay-pigeon shooting* (6 places), *archery* (10 places) and *karting* (11 places) are also catered for. There are facilities for *flying* in over 20 places.

Lorraine

Lorraine is usually associated with Alsace; and the term Alsace-Lorraine has an emotional impact derived from past history, although these border regions have long since ceased to be disputed between France and Germany. Compared with Alsace it must be admitted that Lorraine has less to offer the tourist. While Alsace has the contrasting scenery of the Rhine plain and the Vosges, Lorraine is a gently rolling plateau whose main economic importance lies in its minerals – coal, iron ore, rock salt.

Lorraine takes in the departments of Meurthe-et-Moselle, Meuse, Moselle and Vosges – although only the western part of the Vosges themselves are in Lorraine, the eastern part falling into Alsace. The chief towns of the departments are Nancy, Metz, Epinal and Bar-le-Duc; but many other places, like Verdun, Douaumont and the Argonne Forest, are well known for their associations with the two world wars.

Lorraine's attractions for the tourist are not confined to tours of the battlefields. It is true that the devastation of war has left Lorraine with few places still bearing the patina of the past; but it has a number of notable churches, and the western slopes of the Vosges have a wide range of scenic beauty to offer – for example the lakes round Gérardmer and the Moselle valley.

HISTORY. – The treaty of Verdun in 843 brought about a division of the Frankish empire which had important consequences for the future. Under the treaty the western part of the empire fell to Charles the Bald, the middle section, including Lorraine, to Lothair, and the eastern part to Ludwig (Louis) the German. In 870, however, Lorraine also passed to Ludwig. In 959 the duchies of Upper and Lower Lorraine (Lotharingia) were created, the latter, with its capital at Nancy, becoming known as Lorraine *tout court*. In 1552 France acquired the towns of Metz, Toul and Verdun, and in 1766 the Duchy of Lorraine also became French. After the Franco-Prussian War of 1870–71 a large part of Lorraine, mainly German-speaking, including in particular Metz and the surrounding area, was incorporated in the newly established German Empire, becoming part of the province of Alsace-Lorraine. After the First World War it returned to France, and has since then remained French except for a brief interruption in 1940–44.

SIGHTS. – **Bains-les-Bains** (pop. 2000) is a popular spa (heart, nerves, blood pressure) with eleven springs which were already being used in Roman times. The Bain Romain is built on the foundations of a Roman bath.

Bitche (pop. 7000) lies amid extensive forests, dominated by a fort built by Vauban in 1680.

La Bresse (alt. 630–1366 m; pop. 5600) lies on the Moselotte, a tributary of the Moselle, and is one of the leading winter sports resorts in the Vosges, also popular in summer.

Dabo (pop. 3200) is a popular summer holiday resort. On the Rocher de Dabo (664 m) is a chapel from which there are wide views; it occupies the site of a former castle belonging to King Dagobert.

Domrémy-la-Pucelle (pop. 300) was the birthplace of Joan of Arc (1411–31) and attracts many visitors on that account. The house in which she was born, near the church, is open to visitors; opposite it is a museum.

Lunéville (pop. 25,000) was from 1702 to 1737 the residence of the Dukes of Lorraine. It has an 18th c. château and the twin-towered church of St-Jacques (mid 18th c.).

Epinal (pop. 43,000), surrounded by forests, is the chief town of the department of Vosges, famous since the 18th c. for the coloured prints, *images d'Epinal*, which for a period enjoyed world-wide sales. Examples of these prints can be seen in the Vosges Departmental Museum (along with sculpture and pictures) and in an International Museum of Folk Art. The

church of St-Maurice dates from the 14th c., its tower from the 11th; in the transept is a 14th c. Virgin. The ruins of a château, destroyed in 1670, are to be seen in the park.

Gérardmer (alt. 666–1100 m; pop. 10,000) lies in the High Vosges, below the *Col de la Schlucht*, with a number of beautiful lakes in the surrounding area. It is a popular resort both in summer and winter, offering facilities for both water sports and winter sports. The *Lac de Gérardmer* has a perimeter of $5\frac{1}{2}$ km. Near the town are the Lac de Longemer and the Lac de Retournemer, and there is excellent walking in the surrounding area. Numerous hotels.

Metz: see p. 153.

Nancy: see p. 158.

Neufchâteau (pop. 9600), situated above the Meuse, was a place of some consequence in the Middle Ages, a free city within the Duchy of Lorraine. Churches of St-Christophe (13th–14th c.) and St-Nicolas (12th–13th c.); Renaissance Town Hall.

Phalsbourg (pop. 4000) was built about 1570 as a fortified town. In 1662 it was acquired by France, and in 1680 the fortifications were considerably strengthened by Vauban. The richly decorated Porte de France and Porte d'Allemagne belonged to these fortifications. There is a museum devoted to the history of the town.

Plombières-les-Bains (pop. 4000) is a spa, with 28 thermal springs (13 to 81 °C) which were already in use in Roman times. There is a very beautiful park containing the spa establishment; Gothic church.

Rambervillers (pop. 7500), in the western Vosges, is a picturesque little town with a 16th c. Town Hall, old houses of the same period and remains of fortifications.

Remiremont (pop. 11,400), situated on the Moselle near the inflow of the Moselotte, had until the Revolution a convent founded in the 11th c. for women of good family. Their tombs are in the church of St-Pierre (13th–16th c.). There are a number of buildings, including the Abbess's Lodging, belonging to the former abbey. Fine arcades in the Grande Rue; interesting regional museum.

St-Dié (pop. 27,500) suffered heavy damage during the last war, but no trace of this now remains. A book published here in 1507 was the first to give the name of America to the land discovered by Columbus. The Cathedral is Romanesque (12th–13th c.), with a Gothic choir and a tower added in 1711; charming Gothic cloister (14th c.).

St-Maurice-sur-Moselle (pop. 2000), lying below the *Ballon d'Alsace* and the *Rouge-Gazon*, is a popular summer resort which also offers facilities for winter sports on the surrounding hills.

Sarrebourg (pop. 15,000), situated on the fringe of the Vosges on the right bank of the River Sarre (Saar), has a large military cemetery of the First World War (13,000 graves). In a former Franciscan chapel is a museum of antiquities.

Sarreguemines (pop. 26,000), on the River Sarre (Saar) near the German frontier, is an industrial town (ceramics). There are fine views from the ruined castle on the Schlossberg.

Sedan (pop. 25,000), a fortified town on the Meuse, in the Ardennes, was the scene of Napoleon III's surrender in 1870. The town suffered heavy damage during the Second World War. 17th c. church; monument to Marshal Turenne (1611–75), who was born here.

Thillot (pop. 5000), a popular holiday resort throughout the year, lies below the *Ballon d'Alsace* (1250 m), the most southerly peak in the Vosges.

Toul (pop. 15,000), in the upper Moselle valley, was a place of considerable importance in the Middle Ages as the see of a bishop and a free imperial city (until 1648). The town is still surrounded by its 17th c. walls, with four gates. The *Cathedral of St-Etienne (13th–14th c.) has a late Gothic façade and two octagonal towers 65 m high. The 16th c. cloister is a very beautiful example of the Flamboyant style. Old houses, particularly in Rue Général-Gengoult, some of them dating from the 14th c.

Vittel (pop. 7000) has been since the mid 19th c. one of the best known spas in Lorraine, and its mineral water enjoys a wide market. The town's reputation goes back to Roman times. Church of St-Rémy (late Gothic); spa establishment and casino.

SPORT and RECREATION in Lorraine. – *Water sports* mainly on the Moselle; many swimming pools of all kinds. – *Golf-courses* at Nancy, Bar-le-Duc and Metz. – *Tennis* and *riding* at over 30 places each. *Casinos* at Contrexéville, Gérardmer, Plombières-les-Bains and Vittel. – Nature-lovers will find in the *Lorraine Nature Park* (457,000 acres) ample scope for watching wild life and walking.

Lot Valley

The Lot is a river relatively little known outside France. Rising at an altitude of 1400 m on Mont Goulet in the Cévennes, it flows through the whole of the southern Massif Central and after traversing Quercy joins the Garonne in the Agenais (the region round Agen) after a total course of 480 km. In earlier times it was an important navigable waterway, linking Auvergne and the wine-trading town of Cahors with Bordeaux. It is now popular with canoe and kayak enthusiasts, who find excitement in traversing the gorges between Espalion and Entraygues – though the less expert will do well to keep below Entraygues.

The scenery of the Lot valley alternates between the gently beautiful and the wild and rugged. The roads which run through the valley (N 120, N 601, N 111, N 662) give visitors an excellent opportunity of enjoying the scenery of this most characteristic of French rivers and making the acquaintance of its towns and villages.

The most striking section of the valley is in the *Gorges du Lot**, the succession of gorges which – particularly between Estaing and Pont de Coursavy – challenge comparison with the gorges of the Tarn. Here the valley is caught between walls of rock some 300 m high. At Entraygues-sur-Truyère the Lot is joined by the Truyère, with the impressive **Gorges de la Truyère**, which cut through the Auvergne hills to the *Viaduc de Garabit, interrupted by a number of imposing dams and beautiful artificial lakes; for much of the way, however, the road runs at some distance from the river. Near Estaing in the Gorges du Lot is the Golinhac dam.

SIGHTS. – **Mende** (alt. 730 m; pop. 11,000), in the upper valley of the Lot, is a good starting point either for an exploration of the Lot valley or the **Gorges du Tarn** (see p. 118). The Cathedral is mainly 14th c., though the towers took another 200 years to build. In the Middle Ages Mende possessed the largest bell in Christendom, weighing 20 tons, but this was destroyed in 1579 by militant Protestants; a fragment 2·15 m high is preserved in the little church. – The narrow Pont de Notre-Dame over the Lot dates from the 14th c., having successfully withstood the river's annual spates.

Espalion (pop. 4800), in a beautiful situation, has an old Renaissance mansion on the banks of the Lot which forms a harmonious group with the 13th c. sandstone bridge over the river.

Estaing (pop. 1000), at the beginning of the Lot gorges, has a 15th–16th c. château, a 15th c. bridge and picturesque old houses.

Entraygues-sur-Truyère (pop. 1600) lies in a fertile hilly region at the junction of the Truyère and the Lot. It is a charming old town, particularly the Rue Basse, which has preserved its medieval aspect almost intact. There is a 13th c. bridge over the Lot.

Conques (pop. 500), standing above the little River Ouche some distance from the Lot, is of outstanding interest for the *Church of Ste-Foy, one of the supreme achievements of Romanesque art, particularly notable for the sculptured *Last Judgment, in the style of Auvergne, in the tympanum of the W doorway. The church was begun in the 11th c. and mostly built in the 12th. The interior is very fine, and there is a valuable treasury containing works of religious art of the 9th to 16th c. The abbey to which this church belonged was between the 11th and 13th c. an important staging post on the "Way of St James", the pilgrim road to Compostela. After the destruction of the abbey by Protestants in 1561 the church, partly destroyed by fire, was neglected and fell into disrepair, until it was discovered in the mid 19th c. by the writer Prosper Mérimée and restored after he had made its plight public.

Figeac (pop. 10,500), situated on the River Celé a short distance from the Lot,
was also on the pilgrim road which passed through Conques. The town has preserved some charming old quarters. The Hôtel de la Monnaie, a fine Gothic building, houses a museum of local history. Figeac was the birthplace of Jean-François Champollion (1790–1832) who, early in the 19th c., was the first to decipher Egyptian hieroglyphics.

*St-Cirq-Lapopie (pop. 240), magnificently situated on a crag above the Lot, is a picturesque little village of carefully restored old houses. – Near here is the cave of *Pech-Merle, discovered in 1922, with evidence of the people who lived here 20,000 years ago – painted or incised figures of bisons, mammoths (of the Aurignacian period) and horses.

Ste-Foy of Conques: a figure in the church treasury

Cahors (pop. 21,000), in a bend on the Lot, was the old capital of Quercy, an important centre of medieval trade, with a university. Beautifully situated on the Lot, with the imposing medieval *Pont Valentré, defended by three towers 40 m high, spanning the river, Cahors possesses a number of other notable monuments of the past. The *Cathedral of St-Etienne was built in the 11th c. in the style of a fortified church and added to on several occasions down to the 14th c. The Flamboyant cloister was built in the early 16th c. The finest part of the Cathedral is the N doorway, originally on the W front, with a beautiful Romanesque sculpture of the Ascension in the tympanum. In spite of the damage it has suffered, the cloister still preserves much of its rich sculptured decoration. – There are considerable remains of the old town walls, including several towers. In the highest part of the old town is the 14th c. church of St-Barthélemy. The Tour de Jean XII, 34 m high, is all that remains of a palace which once stood here. The late 15th c. Maison de Roaldès was restored in 1912; Henry IV is said to have stayed in this house during the siege of Cahors in 1580. In the former Bishop's Palace is the Municipal Museum, with mementoes of the politician Léon Gambetta, who was born in Cahors and spent his early years in the town.

Near **Duravel**, some distance from the Lot, is the *Château de Bonaguil*, still impressive in spite of the damage it suffered during the French Revolution. It is an outstanding example of the type of fortified castle built from the late 15th c. until well on in the 16th.

Villeneuve-sur-Lot (pop. 25,000), in the Middle Ages one of the most important fortified towns in this region, has preserved two town gates dating from this period. The bridge over the Lot was built by the English in the 13th c.

SPORT and RECREATION in the Lot valley. – *Water sports* and *fishing* are among the principal attractions of the Lot valley, in addition to the usual sports facilities found in the larger places.

Lourdes

Region: Midi-Pyrénées.
Department: Hautes-Pyrénées.
Altitude: 410 m. – Population: 18,000.
Post code: F-65100. – Dialling code: 62.
ⓘ **Office de Tourisme,**
4 Place de l'Eglise;
tel. 94 15 64.

HOTELS. – *Grand Hôtel de la Grotte*, I, 95 r.; *Impérial*, I, 100 r.; *Christina*, II, 210 r.; *Galilée-Windsor*, II, 120 r.; *Jeanne d'Arc*, II, 86 r.; *Espagne*, II, 88 r.; *Saint-Louis-de-France*, II, 98 r.; *Albion*, III, 51 r.; *Angleterre*, III, 22 r.; *Biarritz*, III, 30 r.; *Central*, III, 50 r.; *Golgotha*, III, 81 r.; *Vatican*, III, 31 r.; *Esplanade-Eden*, IV, 150 r.; *Cimes*, IV, 48 r.

Lourdes, beautifully situated at the foot of the Pyrenees, owes its fame and its prosperity to Bernadette Soubirous, who had a vision of the Virgin in 1858 and was guided by her to the spring which now supplies healing water to large numbers of pilgrims. The impression which Lourdes makes on a visitor depends

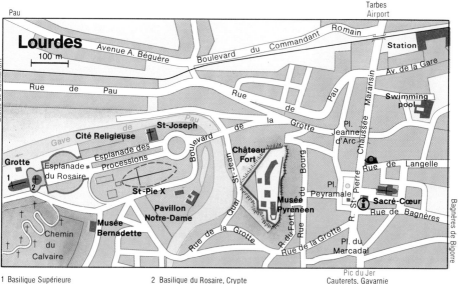

1 Basilique Supérieure   2 Basilique du Rosaire, Crypte

entirely on his attitude to the pilgrimages which bring millions of people to the shrine every year. The spring which is credited with healing powers flows out of the Grotte de Massabielle, and its water is not only drunk by the pilgrims but despatched to those who cannot come to Lourdes.

SIGHTS. – In the **Grotte de Massabielle** (12 m across, 10 m deep), in the "Cité Religieuse", is a *figure of the Virgin*, lit by worshippers' candles. – The story of Bernadette is explained in the "Cachot", SW of the grotto in *Place Peyramale*, the former prison in which the six members of the Soubirous family lived. In Rue Bernadette-Soubirous is the *birthplace of Bernadette*, the Moulin de Boly in which her father worked as a miller. – 80 m above the town is a **castle** (13th–17th c.), reached by a lift. Extensive views from the terrace. The castle now houses a *Museum of the Pyrenees*.

St-Pie-X is the largest church in Lourdes, completed in 1958, it has an area of 12,000 sq. m and can accommodate 20,000 pilgrims. The altar stands in the middle of the church. – The *Esplanade des Processions* leads on to the *Place du Rosaire*, where the daily procession of the sacrament (with blessing of the sick) ends; the procession starts from the grotto at 4.30 p.m. On the W side of the square is the **Basilica of the Rosary**, built in 1885–89, which can accommodate a congregation of 5000. Above the grotto is the **Basilica**, built 1864–71 and consecrated in 1876, with a bell-tower 70 m

high. From the Basilica the Chemin du Calvaire (*Stations of the Cross*) leads up to a **Calvary** with 14 bronze figures. – *Musée de Notre-Dame-de-Lourdes*, with mementoes of Bernadette and evidence of miraculous cures. *Musée Bernadette*, with dioramas and film shows on the life of the saint.

SURROUNDINGS. – The most impressive time to visit Lourdes is during one of the processions, with candles, from the grotto to the Place du Rosaire which take place every evening from April to October. – There are a number of interesting *caves* in the surrounding area – the *Grotte des Sarrazins*, the *Grotte du Loup*, the *Grotte du Roy*.

16 km from Lourdes are the fascinating *Grottes de Bétharram (open only in summer), with large rock chambers and an underground river (boat trips).

Lyons

Region: Rhône-Alpes.
Department: Rhône.
Altitude: 170 m. – Population: 463,000.
Post code: F-69000. – Dialling code: 78.
ⓘ **Office de Tourisme,**
Place Bellecour;
tel. 42 25 75.

HOTELS. – IN THE CENTRE: *Sofitel*, L, 200 r.; *Royal*, L. 94 r.; *Grand Hôtel*, I, 143 r.; *Beaux-Arts*, II, 80 r.; *Carlton*, II, 96 r.; *Etrangers*, II, 52 r.; *Artistes*, II, 53 r.; *Globe et Cecil*, III, 65 r.; *Moderne*, III, 31 r.; *Paix*, III, 51 r.; *Russie*, III, 60 r.; *Central Aixois*, IV, 22 r.; *Pax*, IV, 22 r.; *Croix-Paquet*, IV, 20 r. – IN PERRACHE: *Terminus*, I, 122 r.; *Bordeaux et Parc*, II, 88 r.; *Bristol*, II, 126 r.; *Tourinter*, II, 122 r.; *Verdun*, II, 32 r.; *Angleterre*, III, 86 r.; *Continental*, III, 104 r.; *Simplon*, III, 38 r.; *Dubost*, III, 50 r.; *Alexandra*, IV, 24 r.; *Genève*, IV, 36 r.; *Vaubecour*, IV, 17 r.

EVENTS. – *International Trade Fair* (from Saturday after Easter); *Folk Festival* with illuminations (8 December).

Lyons (in French spelling *Lyon*), France's third largest city (after Paris and Marseilles), is well situated at the junction of the Rhône and the Saône. It is the chief town of the Rhône department and the see of an archbishop, with a University and a College of Technology, Lyons is the principal centre of the French textile industry, and particularly of silk production, but has a variety of other industries, whose products are displayed at the Lyons Trade Fair, held annually in spring.

The main part of the city lies on an island between the two rivers, 5 km long and between 600 and 800 m across. Recently it has been reaching steadily farther out

Pilgrims in Lourdes

Lyons: general view

towards the E, where the industrial suburb of Villeurbanne already has a population of over 100,000.

HISTORY. – Lyons was originally a Celtic settlement (*Lugdunum*), which in 42 B.C. became a Roman colony and in the time of Augustus capital of the province of Gallia Lugdunensis. At the end of the 2nd C. A.D. there was a ruthless persecution of the Christians in the town. In 1033 Lyons, along with the rest of Burgundy, became part of the Holy Roman Empire. At the beginning of the 14th c., however, the County of Lyonnais (the present-day departments of Loire and Rhône) passed to France. During the French Revolution much of Lyons was destroyed and 6000 of its citizens were killed.

SIGHTS. – On the hill of **Fourvière** (294 m: from the Latin *Forum vetus*) are the imposing remains, excavated from 1933 onwards, of the Roman city of Lugdunum (a large theatre and a small odeon, a temple of Cybele, a paved Roman road, remains of baths, aqueducts, mosaics) and a magnificent new Gallo-Roman Museum. A short distance away is the massive basilica of *Notre-Dame-de-Fourvière* (late 19th c.), with a richly decorated interior and crypt. From the NE tower (48·5 m high; 278 steps) there are very fine *views of Lyons and the surrounding area, extending as far as Mont Blanc, 160 km away, and Auvergne.

Adjoining the basilica is a Chapel with a figure of the Virgin and votive tablets.

The hub of the city's life is the *Place Bellecour*, with an *equestrian statue of Louis XIV* by a local sculptor, erected in 1825. The façades along the E and W sides of the square were built after the destructions of the French Revolution. From the N side there is a view of the hill of Fourvière. – The principal business and shopping street, *Rue de la République*, runs N from the square, parallel to the Saône on the left and the Rhône on the right. To the left is the Place des Jacobins, from which Rue Mercière, with old Gothic and Renaissance houses, runs N. At the end of this street is the church of **St-Nizier**, formerly the cathedral, a beautiful Gothic structure (15th c.) with a Renaissance doorway and a crypt under the choir dating from the 6th c. but decorated in modern times. Farther N is the *Place des Terreaux*, with a *monumental fountain*. During the Revolution the guillotine stood here, but later mass executions were carried out by drowning in the Rhône. Also in this square is the 17th c. *Town Hall** (restored in 1702 and again from 1853 onwards), with a tower 50 m high. Behind it is *Place de la Comédie*,

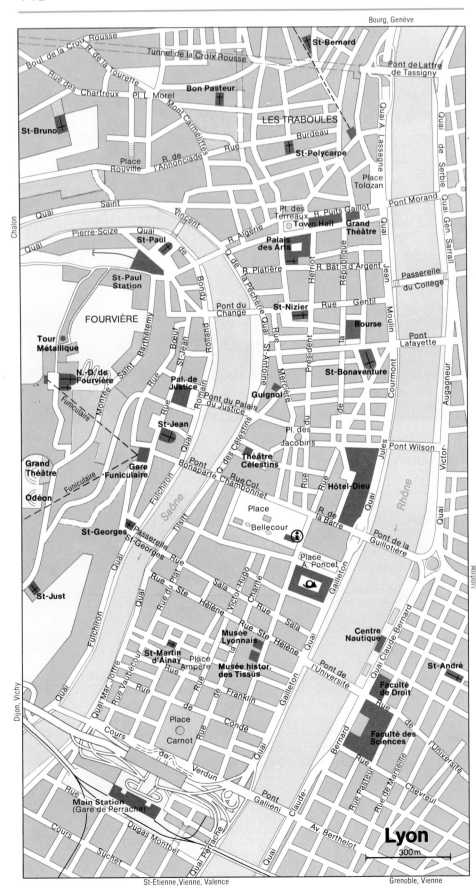

Lyon

with the *Grand Théâtre*. On the S side of Place des Terreaux is the Palais des Arts, in a 17th c. Benedictine convent, with the richly stocked *Museum of Fine Arts* (collection of inscriptions unique in France, sculpture, medieval art, pictures by Rubens and Perugino, works by 19th c. French artists).

From Place Bellecour the Rue Victor-Hugo runs S to *Place Ampère* and beyond this *Place Carnot*, with a *Monument to the Republic* erected in 1890. A little way W of Place Ampère is the church of *St-Martin-d'Ainay* (11th c.), Lyons' oldest church, originally belonging to a Benedictine abbey; the mosaic floor in the choir was laid in the 12th c. In Rue de la Charité, E of Place Ampère, are the *Textile Museum (Musée Historique des Tissues)* and the **Museum of Decorative Art** (*Musée Lyonnais des Arts Décoratifs*).

From the NE corner of Place Bellecour the Rue de la Barre runs down to Quai Jules-Courmont and the extensive complex of the **Hôtel-Dieu**, founded in 542. The 17th and 18th c. hospital buildings flank the Rhône for a distance of 325 m. – Beyond the Saône is the *Cathedral of St-Jean* (12th–15th c.), with a late Gothic W front and a rose window of 1393; 13th and 14th c. stained glass. To the N is the OLD TOWN with its narrow streets and picturesque old houses, particularly in Rue St-Jean, Rue du Bœuf, Rue de Gadagne and Rue Juiverie.

The newer parts of the city are on the left bank of the Rhône. In the district of LES BROTTEAUX (Boulevard des Belges) is the *Parc de la Tête d'Or, laid out from 1856 onwards, with a lake, a *Zoological Garden* and a *Botanical Garden*.

Le Mans

Region: Pays de la Loire.
Department: Sarthe.
Altitude: 51 m. – Population: 155,000.
Post code: F-72000. – Dialling code: 43.
ⓘ **Office de Tourisme,**
38 Place de la République;
tel. 28 17 22.

HOTELS. – *Concorde*, I, 60 r.; *Moderne*, II, 32 r.; *Central*, III, 51 r.; *Saumon*, III, 41 r.; *Escale*, III, 44 r.; *Pommeraie*, III, 32 r.

EVENTS. – *24-hours motor-race* (June); *motor-cycle racing* (Sept.).

Le Mans – a place of some importance in Roman times, the see of a bishop from the 4th c., chief town of the medieval County of Maine and now of the department of Sarthe – lies half way between Paris and Nantes on both banks of the Sarthe. A smaller river, the Huisne, flows into the Sarthe in the southern part of the town.

SIGHTS. – In the centre of Le Mans is the large *Place de la République*, on the W side of which are the *Palais de Justice* (Law Courts), in an old monastic building, and the *church of the Visitation* (1730), with a beautiful interior. – SE of the square is the former abbey church of **Notre-Dame-de-la-Couture** (originally 10th c.; present structure mainly 13th and 14th c.). The W front has a porch and a richly sculptured *doorway. The richly decorated interior has tapestries and some good pictures, including *"Elijah's Dream" by Philippe de Champaigne. Opposite the pulpit is a beautiful white marble *Virgin by Germain Pilon. 10th c. crypt. – S of the church, in the former abbey (18th c.), is the *Prefecture*, with a handsome staircase.

NW of Place de la République, on a hill above the Sarthe, is the OLD TOWN, with many ancient houses. In the main street, the *Grande Rue*, is the Renaissance *Maison d'Adam et d'Eve* (No. 71), of 1525. – From here we can find our way NE through a tunnel to the old-world *Rue de la Reine-Bérengère*, on the right-hand side of which, at No. 13, is the *Maison de la Reine Bérengère* (1440–1515), with two beautiful courtyards; it now houses a *Pottery Museum*.

At the N end of Rue de la Reine-Bérengère is the *Cathedral, dedicated to St Julien, first bishop of Le Mans in the 3rd c., with a Romanesque nave (11th–12th c.), Gothic choir (13th c.) and late Gothic transepts (14th–15th c.). On the S side is a 12th c. doorway with statues, reminiscent of the Royal Doorway at Chartres, with a porch (Porche du Cavalier). The interior is impressive. The **choir has splendid *stained glass (13th–14th c.), beautiful tapestries (15th–16th c.), two fine *monuments (on left) and a 17th c. terracotta "Entomb-ment" (on right). In the N transept are a magnificent rose window (15th c.) and (on left) the tomb of Berengaria

(Bérengère), Richard Cœur-de-Lion's widow (13th c.). The apsidal Lady Chapel has fine 14th c. frescoes.

Opposite the W end of the Cathedral is the *Hôtel du Grabatoire* (1530). – To the W, running parallel with Rue Denfert-Rochereau, Rue St-Hilaire and Rue de la Porte-Ste-Anne on the edge of the old town, are remains of the Gallo-Roman **town walls**, with ten towers still standing.

Behind the choir of the Cathedral is the spacious *Place des Jacobins*, on the E side of which is the *Theatre*, built in 1842 on the site of a Gallo-Roman amphitheatre and reconstructed in 1960. Beyond it is the pleasant *Promenade des Jacobins*. – Immediately NE, in a park, is the former Bishop's Palace, which now houses the interesting **Musée de Tessé**, with a rich collection of pictures. Among other items of interest is an *enamel tablet (made in Verdun 1145–50) from the tomb of Geoffroy Plantagenêt.

To the W of the old town, on the right bank of the Sarthe, is the former abbey church of **Notre-Dame-du-Pré**, a fine Romanesque structure (11th and 12th c.; restored) with an impressive crypt.

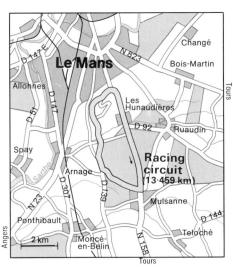

SURROUNDINGS. – Just S of the town is the famous **car-racing circuit** used in the Le Mans 24-hour race ("Les 24 Heures du Mans"), held annually in June. Here too is the *Bugatti Circuit*, a training circuit 4½ km long. Interesting Automobile Museum with cars of up to about 1937.

Marseilles

Region: Provence–Alpes–Côte d'Azur.
Department: Bouches-du-Rhône.
Altitude: 0–160 m. Population: 915,000.
Post code: F-13000. – Dialling code: 91.
ⓘ **Office de Tourisme,**
4 La Canebière;
tel. 33 69 20.

HOTELS. – **Résidence du Petit Nice et Marina Maldormé*, Corniche Kennedy, L, 20 r.; **Sofitel Vieux-Port*, 36 Boulevard Charles-Livon, L, 222 r., SP; *Frantel*, Rue Neuve-St-Martin, I, 200 r.; *Concorde – Palm Beach*, 2 Promenade de la Plage, I, 160 r., SP; *Concorde – Prado*, 11 Avenue Mazargues, I, 100 r.; *Noailles*, 66 Canebière, I, 80 r.; *P.L.M. Beauvau*, 4 rue Beauvau, I, 71 r.; *Ribotel*, 50 Boulevard Verne, I, 45 r.; *Novotel Marseille Est*, in St-Menet, II, 131 r., SB; *Rome et St-Pierre*, 7 Cours St-Louis, II, 70 r.; *Sélect*, 4 Allé Léon-Gambetta, II, 69 r.; *Genève*, 3 bis rue Reine-Elisabeth, II, 48 r.; *Petit Louvre*, 19 Canebière, II, 40 r.; *Paris*, 11 rue Colbert, III, 90 r.; *Breton*, 52 rue Mazenod, III, 44 r.; *Européen*, 115–117 rue Paradis, III, 43 r.

RESTAURANTS (*bouillabaisse* a speciality) in the hotels; also *Calypso*, 2 rue des Catalans; *New York* – *Vieux Port*, 7 Quai des Belges; *Au Pescadou*, 19 Place Castellane; *Jambon de Parme*, 67 rue de la Palud; *Miramar*, 12 Quai du Port; *Michel – Brasserie des Catalans*, 6 rue des Catalans; *Chez Caruso*, 158 Quai du Port.

EVENTS. – *International Trade Fair* (middle of April and second half of Sept.).

Marseilles (in French spelling *Marseille*), situated on the Mediterranean 790 km from Paris, is France's second largest city and its largest port, with a very beautiful natural harbour. It is also the oldest city in France, combining the charm of its southern situation with the bustling activity of a great international city. It is the chief town of the department of Bouches-du-Rhône and the see of an archbishop, with three faculties of the University of Aix-Marseilles. A good general view of the city can be had from the church of Notre-Dame-de-la-Garde, which stands on a limestone hill 160 m high.

HISTORY. – The town was founded by the Phoenicians in the 8th c. B.C., and two centuries later was renamed *Massalia* by Greek settlers; later still it became the Roman *Massilia*. A road link with Rome was provided by the construction of the Via Aurelia in A.D. 117. After the fall of the Roman Empire the town was occupied by the Visigoths and later by the Franks, subsequently becoming part of the kingdom of Arles. It was destroyed by the Saracens and rebuilt in the 10th c. It was at first subject to the Vicomtes of Marseilles but later became independent. As the main port of embarkation for the Crusades it grew in importance and prosperity, and about 1250 was seized by Charles of Anjou. In 1481 it passed to

The Vieux Port, Marseilles

France. The population was decimated by plague in 1720–21. At the beginning of the French Revolution a band of local revolutionaries marched from Marseilles to Paris, taking with them the "Marseillaise" (originally composed in Strasbourg as the "Chant de guerre pour l'Armée du Rhin"), which became the French national anthem. Later, however, following a rising in Marseilles, the guillotine was erected in the Canebière and claimed many victims. During the Second World War the city suffered damage in air raids, and in 1943 almost the whole of the old town was demolished by the Germans. After the war the city acquired an impressive example of contemporary architecture in Le Corbusier's "Cité Radieuse".

SIGHTS. – Every visitor to Marseilles must take a stroll along the *Canebière, a street lined with shops, hotels and cafés which has become the living – and lively – symbol of the city. Its name comes from *cannabis* (hemp) and is thought to refer to the ropeworks once to be found here. At its western end is the *Vieux Port (Old Harbour), a natural inlet reaching far into the town (ferries, tunnel) which has been used as a harbour since the time of the Greek settlers. The Quai des Belges at the head of the harbour is now used only by fishing boats and excursion vessels. All the restaurants round the Vieux Port serve the famous *bouillabaisse* (fish soup). At the mouth of the harbour are two 17th c.

forts. Beyond Fort St-Nicolas is the *Parc du Pharo*, with a 19th c. château from the terrace of which there are fine *views of the old town and the harbours. – On the N side of the harbour is the *Quai du Port*, with the **Town Hall** (1663–83) and, a short distance away, the *Musée des Docks Romains* and *Musée du Vieux Marseille* (Museum of Old Marseilles).

N of the Vieux Port is what remains of the old town, and beyond this are the city's two cathedrals – the handsome newer **Cathédrale de la Major** (1852–93), the largest church built in the 19th c., 141 m long, with two domed towers, a dome 16 m high over the crossing and a profusion of marble in the interior; and, E of this, the old *Cathédrale St-Lazare*, built in the 11th–12th c. but originally founded in the 4th c. (no longer used for services). Adjoining the Cathedral is the *New Harbour (Port Moderne), which has 25 km of quays and covers an area of over 200 hectares; work on this harbour was begun in 1844. The Bassin de la Grande Joliette is used by passenger ships; the *Harbour Station* is at the end of Boulevard des Dames. At weekends a view of the

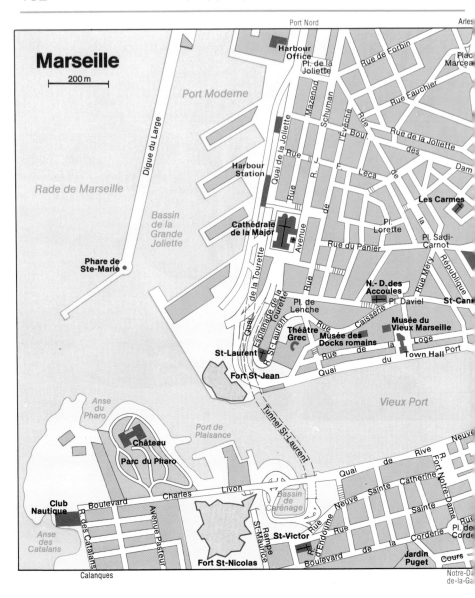

harbour can be obtained from the 5 km long breakwater. Boat tours of the harbour area from the Vieux Port.

From the *Quai de Rive Neuve* on the S side of the Vieux Port it is a short distance up to the church of *St-Victor, which originally belonged to an abbey founded in the 5th c. and in its present form dates from the 11th and 14th c. – Marseilles is dominated by the church of **Notre-Dame-de-la-Garde** (1853–54), which replaced an earlier pilgrimage chapel. The tower (46 m high) with its gilded figure of the Virgin is the very emblem of Marseilles. There is a fine *view of the city from the terrace in front of the church.

Marseilles has numerous *museums*. Of particular interest are the *Museum of Fine Arts* (pictures and sculpture) in the ***Palais Longchamp**, the *Grobet-Labadié Museum*, in an old patrician mansion, and the *Shipping Museum* (Musée de la Marine), in the Stock Exchange (Bourse), near which are the excavated remains of the old *Greek harbour walls* (3rd–2nd c. B.C.).

A popular EXCURSION from Marseilles is a motor-boat trip from the Vieux Port to the **Château d'If**, which is famous for its association with Dumas's "Count of Monte Cristo". The fortress was built in 1529 and served as a state prison. There are fine views from the crag on which the castle is built. There are other islands in the vicinity.

Metz

Region: Lorraine.
Department: Moselle.
Altitude: 170 m. – Population: 117,000.
Post code: F-57000. – Dialling code: 87.
ⓘ **Office de Tourisme,**
Porte Serpenoise;
tel. 75 62 20.

HOTELS. – *Frantel*, I, 115 r.; *Sofitel*, I, 110 r.; *Royal-Concorde*, I, 76 r.; *Carlton*, II, 44 r.; *National "Le Globe"*, II, 88 r.; *Métropole*, III, 73 r.; *Bristol*, III, 64 r.; *Metz*, III, 60 r.; *Moderne*, III, 43 r.; *Foch*, III, 42 r.; *Gare*, III, 40 r.; *Central*, IV, 75 r.; *Terminus*, IV, 47 r. – *Novotel Metz Hauconcourt*, II km N of the town, II, 64 r.

EVENTS. – *International Trade Fair* (first half of Oct.); *Mirabelle Plum Festival* (first Sunday in Sept.); *Festival of Contemporary Art* (first half of Nov.).

Metz, originally the Gallo-Roman city of *Metis* and now chief town of the Moselle department and the see of a bishop, lies on the River Moselle. In the 6th c. it was a residence of the Merovingian kings; later it became a free imperial city, and in 1552 was incorporated in France. It was capital of Lorraine when Alsace and Lorraine were annexed to the German Empire between 1871 and 1918. It is a lively town, with ancient buildings but living in the modern world.

SIGHTS. – Round the *Place d'Armes* is the picturesque old town, whose narrow lanes and old houses form a suitable frame for the two main buildings in the square, the Cathedral and the Town Hall. The *Cathedral (*St-Etienne*) is a Gothic structure (1250–1380) with two towers; in one of them, the Tour de Mutte, is the bell known as Dame Mutte (1605). The Cathedral incorporates an older church built on the same site. Facing the Place d'Armes is the Portail de la Vierge (Virgin's Doorway), with 13th c. sculpture. The right-hand side is decorated with copies of work by the Master of Naumburg Cathedral, who was also employed here.

The INTERIOR of the Cathedral, just under 42 m high, is bathed in radiance from the splendid**stained glass windows, with their large areas of brilliant colour, particularly the 14th c. *rose window* at the W end and the windows in the 16th c. choir and transepts. – In the choir ambulatory is stained glass by Marc Chagall, in a side chapel glass by Jacques Villon, dating in both cases from about 1960. – The marble **bishop's throne** in the choir is Merovingian. The *treasury*, in spite of the losses it has suffered, still contains many beautiful and valuable items.

The **Town Hall** is 18th c. Nearby are the **Municipal Museums**, with Gallo-Roman material recovered by excavations, sculpture, pictures and zoological collections. Outstanding among Metz's many churches is **St-Martin** (1202), with 15th and 16th c. stained glass and a Louis XV organ. From the charming *Esplanade there are beautiful views of the Moselle valley. To the S of the Esplanade is the ruined church (now being restored) of *St-Pierre-aux-Nonnains*, which is thought to be France's oldest church. It dates from the 7th c. and originally belonged to a Benedictine abbey, but was later rebuilt in Gothic style for a convent of nuns.

Rue des Allemands leads to the ***Porte des Allemands** (Germans' Gate), a relic of the medieval fortifications, with two 13th c. round towers and two gun

Porte des Allemands, Metz

bastions of the 15th c. – To the NW of the town is a *military cemetery* of the First World War, with the graves of those who fell in the fighting for Metz. – A modern airport is being constructed on the banks of the Moselle.

Monaco

Principality of Monaco. – Area: 1·8 sq. km. Altitude: 0–65 m. – Population: 25,000. Vehicle registration letters: MC. – Dialling code: (00 33) 93.

ⓘ **Direction du Tourisme et des Congrès,** Monte-Carlo, 2 bis Boulevard des Moulins; tel. 50 60 88.

HOTELS. – IN LA CONDAMINE: *Bristol*, 25 Boulevard Albert-1er, I, 49 r.; *Siècle*, 10 Avenue Prince-Pierre, III, 39 r.; *Cosmopolite*, 4 rue de la Turbie, IV, 26 r.; *France*, 6 rue de la Turbie, IV, 27 r.; *Helvetia*, 1 bis rue Grimaldi, IV, 31 r.; etc. – IN MONTE-CARLO: *Hermitage*, Square Beaumarchais, L, 210 r., SP; *Loews*, 12 Avenue des Spélugues, L, 650 r., SP; *Métropole*, Avenue de la Madone, L, 150 r., SP; *Mirabeau*, 1–3 Avenue Princesse-Grace, L, 100 r., SP; *Paris*, Place du Casino, L, 275 r., SP; *Balmoral*, 12 Avenue de la Costa, L, 65 r.; *Alexandre*, 35 Avenue Princesse-Charlotte, II, 55 r.; *Europe*, 6 Avenue des Citronniers, II, 46 r.; *Splendid*, 4 Avenue Roqueville, II, 65 r.; *Palmiers*, 26 Boulevard de Suisse, III, 38 r.; *Poste*, 5 rue des Oliviers, IV, 24 r. – IN LARVOTTO: *Holiday Inn*, 10 Avenue Princesse-Grace, I, 316 r., SP; *Berne*, 21 rue de Portier, III, 16 r.; *Résidence des Moulins*, 27 Boulevard des Moulins, III, 14 r.

RESTAURANTS in most hotels; also IN MONACO: *Castelroc*, Place du Palais; *Aurore*, 8 rue Princesse-Marie-de-Lorraine; *International*, 6 rue de l'Eglise. – IN MONTE-CARLO: *Rampoldi*, 3 Avenue des Spélugues; *Bec Rouge*, 6 Avenue St-Charles; *Brazil*, 2 bis Boulevard des Moulins; *La Calanque*, 33 Avenue St-Charles; *Costa Rica*, 40 Boulevard des Moulins; *Quicksilver*, 1 Avenue J.-F.-Kennedy.

Casinos. – *Casino de Monte-Carlo; SBM-Loews Casino.*

EVENTS. – *Grand Prix* (May), qualifying for the drivers' world championship.

The independent principality of Monaco, one of Europe's smallest states, has a magnificent situation on the Côte d'Azur, near the Italian frontier.

Only about a sixth of the population, which is predominantly Roman Catholic, consists of native Monégasques (as the people of Monaco are called); roughly a half are French, a fifth Italian, and the rest from many other countries. The official language is French, but a local dialect (Monegasco) and Italian are also spoken. – Monaco is a hereditary constitutional monarchy governed, subject to the authority of the Prince, by a National Council of 18 members (the legislature) and a Minister of State (the executive) assisted by a Government Council. There are also a State Council and a Crown Council with advisory functions. Monaco has close relationships with France in both internal and external matters (customs and currency union, assimilation of tax law).

HISTORY. – Archaeological evidence has revealed the existence of human settlement here earlier than the Stone Age. About 900 B.C. the Phoenicians dedicated a rock to the god Baal of Tyre (cult of Melkart). A Greek trading post was established here, and this later became a Roman port, under the name of *Herculis Monoeci Portus*. Its later history was affected by the great migrations and the incursions of the Saracens. Later it fell into the hands of the Genoese, and in 1215 a castle was built, the ruins of which can still be seen. In 1297 it passed into the hands of the Genoese family of *Grimaldi*, which acquired the title of Prince in 1614. After a period when it was under Spanish protection Monaco passed to the French line of Goyon de Matignon-Grimaldi in 1731. In 1793 it was united with France, but in 1814 was restored to Prince Honoré IV. From 1815 to 1860 it was under the protection of the kingdom of Sardinia. In 1861 the role

of protector was taken over by France, and in return Prince Charles III was obliged to give up Menton and Roquebrune. In 1866 the town of Monte-Carlo was given independent urban status, with a casino, an opera-house and a luxury hotel. In 1911 Prince Albert promulgated a constitution, and in 1918 the relationship with France was re-defined. Louis II (1922–49) was succeeded by *Rainier III*, who in 1956 married the American film actress *Grace Kelly*.

SIGHTS. – The oldest part of the principality, **Monaco-Ville**, a huddle of narrow lanes, is picturesquely situated on a rocky peninsula 60 m high jutting out into the sea, with numerous remains of earlier fortifications. At the western end is the *Place du Palais* (wide views), with the 13th c. **Palais du Prince** (changing of the guard daily at 11.55 a.m.). This contains sumptuous state apartments (Throne Room in Empire style, 18th c. York Room) and beautiful 17th c. Genoese frescoes. The *Palace Museum* has a fine *collection of stamps. Concerts in the courtyard in summer.

From the Palace the Rue du Tribunal leads to the *Cathedral* (1897), which contains

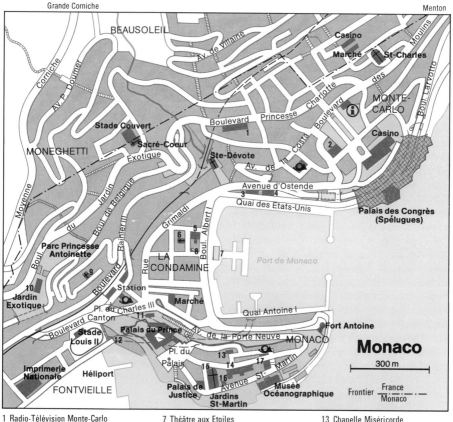

1 Radio-Télévision Monte-Carlo
2 Sporting-Club International
3 Maison de la Culture
4 Bureau Hydrographique
5 Centre Administratif et Bibliothèque Municipale
6 Eglise Réformée

7 Théâtre aux Etoiles
8 Sûreté
9 Chapelle Saint-Martin
10 Musée d'Anthropologie Préhistorique
11 Bibliothèque Caroline
12 Centre d'Acclimatation Zoologique

13 Chapelle Miséricorde
14 Town Hall
15 Cathedral
16 Bishop's Palace
17 Musée de l'Egypte et du Monde

Prince Albert I of Monaco

an altarpiece by Bréa (*c.* 1500) and the tombs of Princes and bishops. Near-by are the *Historial des Princes*, a historical museum, and the *Chapelle de la Miséricorde*.

At the end of the *Jardins de St-Martin*, which extend along the S side of the peninsula, is the *Oceanographic Museum, rising to a height of 87 m above the sea, with massive underbuilding. This contains important scientific collections (material gathered on Prince Albert I's research expeditions, items contributed by Jacques Cousteau, specimens of marine plants and animal life), a fine *aquarium*, a laboratory, a library and exhibitions of model ships and modern technical apparatus; screening of instructional and documentary films. – Opposite the Oceanographic Museum is the *Museum of Egypt and the Ancient World. From *Fort Antoine*, at the tip of the peninsula, there are magnificent views. – At the W end of the peninsula, on the slopes to the S, is the *Centre d'Acclimatation Zoologique* (acclimatisation centre, zoo and animal training school).

Below the crag to the N is the **Harbour**, constructed in its present form between

1901 and 1926 (numerous yachts), with the *Stade Nautique Rainier-III* (stadium for water sports). – Along the W side of the harbour runs the *Boulevard Albert-1er*, the main street of the district of **La Condamine**, with shops, railway station, library, market, etc. – In a gorge-like valley at the NW corner of the harbour is the *church of Ste-Dévote*, dedicated to the town's patron saint, with a beautiful 18th c. marble altar.

A series of long flights of steps and winding lanes climb up the E face of the *Tête de Chien* to the *Moyenne Corniche*, which is in French territory (N 564), giving access to the fine villas and beautiful gardens of the district of **Mone-ghetti**, built in a succession of terraces on the hillside. In the western part of this district, above the Boulevard Rainier-III, are the **Exotic Garden** (*Jardin Exotique*), with stalactitic caves and a *Museum of Prehistoric Anthropology*, and the *Parc Princesse-Antoinette*.

The favourable climatic conditions in the **Exotic Garden**, laid out on the warm, moist slopes of the hill, enable a great variety of delicate tropical plants to flourish. – The **caves** contain stalactites, stalagmites and other interesting rock formations. – The **Museum of Prehistoric Anthropology** displays human remains found in the surrounding area, together with coins, jewellery, etc., of the pre-Roman and Roman periods.

In the Casino, Monte-Carlo

The town of **Monte-Carlo** lies on a rocky promontory N of the harbour. In the higher part are business and shopping streets – *Boulevard Princesse-Charlotte* (with the headquarters of Radio-Télévision Monte-Carlo at the W end),

Boulevard des Moulins (Office de Tourisme at SW end; church of St-Charles just off the N side) and *Avenue de la Costa*, with numerous luxury shops. There are fine views from beautiful gardens such as the *Allées des Boulingrins* (column commemorating Prince Albert I) and the *Jardins du Casino*. In the gardens are magnificent buildings, among them the famous *Casino (built in 1878 by Charles Garnier, architect of the Opéra in Paris), run by the Société Anonyme des Bains de Mer (SBM), founded in 1863.

At the E end of this district is the *Monte-Carlo Congress Centre (*Les Spélugues*), opened in 1978, a massive complex on a hexagonal plan, incorporating a luxury hotel and a hundred flats, built over the Boulevard Louis-II.

In the SW of the **Larvotto** district is the *Hall du Centenaire* (Centenary Hall). Near this, in Avenue Princesse-Grace, is the *National Museum of Automata and Dolls* (Musée National des Automates et Poupées d'Autrefois), with several hundred dolls, over 80 automata and more than 2000 miniature objects of the 18th and 19th c.

Mont St-Michel

Region: Basse-Normandie.
Department: Manche.
Altitude: 3–80 m. – Population: 110.
Post code: F-50116. – Dialling code: 33.
ⓘ **Office de Tourisme,**
   Corps de Garde des Bourgeois;
   tel. 60 14 30.

HOTELS. – *Mère Poulard*, II, 30 r.; *Digue*, II, 36 r.; *Guesclin*, III, 14 r.; *Mouton Blanc*, III, 36 r.; *Confiance*, III, 18 r.; *K Motel*, III, 60 r.

The ** Mont St-Michel, rising out of the sea off the coast of Normandy, is one of the most striking sights that France has to offer. Perched on its rocky islet and surrounded by walls and bastions, this old abbey has the appearance of a fortified castle. At this point in the English Channel the tides have a very considerable rise and fall (up to 14 m): at low tide it is possible to walk round the island on foot, while at high tide the waves surge up to its very walls and may even wash over the car park at the foot of the hill. It is a particularly impressive sight at the spring tides (three days after the new moon or

Mont St-Michel Abbey at low tide

full moon). There are pilgrimages on 29 September (the Feast of the Archangel Michael) and 16 October.

HISTORY. – Legend has it that after an apparition of the Archangel Michael in the year 708 Archbishop Aubert of Avranches founded an abbey dedicated to St Michael on the island, and from then until the 16th c. a succession of buildings in Romanesque and later in Gothic style were erected here. Thanks to the strength of its defences the abbey was never conquered by an enemy; but the nature of the site and its inaccessible situation must have created difficulties in the provision of materials for the buildings. Pilgrims flocked to the shrine from the early medieval period onwards, as they still do today. In 1790 the abbey was dissolved, and in 1811 the buildings began to be used as a prison; but in 1863 this use was discontinued, and thereafter the abbey was gradually restored, making Mont St-Michel the major tourist attraction it is today.

SIGHTS. – From the mainland a causeway 1·8 km long, constructed in 1879, leads to the foot of the rock, where there is a car park (beware of high tide!). From here we pass through the outer *walls at the Porte du Roi and walk up the Grande Rue, the island's only street, lined by shops, restaurants and hotels. Here too is a small Historical Museum. The street, and indeed the island as a whole, is liable to be crowded in summer. On the highest point is the **Abbey, built in the 11th–13th c. The bell-tower of the church rises to a height of 87·5 m, and the statue of St Michael which tops the spire reaches 155·5 m above sea-level. Visitors entering the abbey pass through the guard-room to reach the N wing, known as the *Merveille (Marvel). The conducted tour begins in the Aumônerie (Almonry), where pilgrims used to be given a night's lodging without payment, and leads through a number of fine rooms. The *cloister (1225–28), on the second floor, has 220 graceful granite columns. The adjoining *abbey church was begun in 1020 and has a Romanesque nave which contrasts effectively with the 15th c. Gothic choir. From an external gallery 120 m above the sea there are magnificent *views. The abbey garden can also be visited.

Visitors who want to walk round the island should enquire when the tide begins to come in. Since it will be fairly wet underfoot, rubber boots should be worn, or none at all.

Nancy

Region: Lorraine.
Department: Meurthe-et-Moselle.
Altitude: 210 m. – Population: 112,000.
Post code: F-54000. – Dialling code: 83.
ⓘ Office de Tourisme,
   14 Place Stanislas;
   tel. 35 22 41.

HOTELS. – Grand Hôtel Concorde, I, 62 r.; Jacques Borel, I, 100 r.; Frantel, II, 200 r.; Novotel Nancy Ouest, II, 121 r.; Novotel Nancy Sud, II, 86 r.; Bon Coin, III, 30 r.; Mercure, III, 100 r.; Univers, III, 90 r.; Albert-1er, III, 112 r.; Mapotel du Palais, III, 68 r.; Académie, IV, 28 r.; Choley, IV, 25 r.; Clair-Séjour, IV, 11 r.; Poste, IV, 47 r.; Guise, IV, 50 r.; Sources, IV, 20 r.

EVENTS. – European Fair (first two weeks of June).

Nancy, situated on the River Meurthe and on the Rhine–Marne Canal, is the old capital of Lorraine, and now chief town of the department of Meurthe-le-Moselle. It is an industrial and a university town, but its main glory is its magnificent 18th c. *Baroque architecture.

HISTORY. – In the 12th c. Nancy became capital of the Duchy of Lorraine. About 1475 Duke René became involved in hostilities with Charles the Bold of Burgundy, during which Charles was killed outside the walls of Nancy. Following the War of the Polish Succession (1733–38) Stanislas Leszcýnski, the dethroned king of Poland, was compensated for the loss of his kingdom by receiving Lorraine, and with it Nancy, in exchange. He brought architects and artists to the city, who erected many fine buildings. After his death (1766) the duchy reverted to France.

SIGHTS. – Although the old town is centred on the so-called "Point Central", the intersection of the three main traffic

Nancy, the city of Baroque architecture

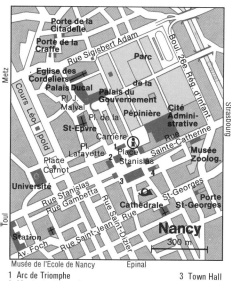

Musée de l'Ecole de Nancy   Epinal
1 Arc de Triomphe
2 Musée des Beaux-Arts
3 Town Hall
4 Préfecture

arteries (Rue St-Dizier, Rue St-Georges and Rue St-Jean), most visitors are drawn first to the **Place Stanislas (Place Royale)** N of the Cathedral, a square of grandiose effect which is unmatched in France. In the middle is a *statue of King Stanislas*, and flanking the square are five handsome palaces. – The largest of the palaces is the **Town Hall**, which has a grand staircase with very fine wrought-iron banisters. On the W side of the square is the *Museum of Fine Arts*, with a collection of fine paintings of the 16th–19th c. Adjoining the Museum is a *triumphal arch*, erected for Louis XV in 1757, which leads into *Place de la Carrière*, an elongated square in which are other palaces and fine town houses. At the far end is the **Palais du Gouvernement**. The principal architect of this fine piece of urban design was Emmanuel Héré. Beyond the Palais du Gouvernement, to the left, is the former *Ducal Palace* (Palais Ducal), in late Gothic style (1502–44), which now houses the *Historical Museum of Lorraine*. Just beyond it is the *Eglise des Cordeliers* (Franciscan Church), with the tombs of Dukes of Lorraine. At the far end of the street is the **Porte de la Craffe**, one of the 14th c. town gates and Nancy's oldest surviving buildings. Until the French Revolution it was used as a prison. – As they walk about the town visitors will see a variety of interesting features, including the fountains and grilles of the Place Stanislas. If time permits, it is worth seeing the twin-towered Baroque *Cathedral* (1703–42) in Rue St-Georges. At the end of the street is the *Porte St-Georges* (1608).

Nantes

Region: Pays de la Loire.
Department: Loire-Atlantique.
Altitude: 8 m. – Population: 264,000.
Post code: F-44000. – Dialling code: 40.
ⓘ Office de Tourisme,
Place du Change;
tel. 47 04 51.

HOTELS. – *Jacques Borel*, I, 100 r.; *Astoria*, II, 45 r.; *Central*, II, 143 r.; *Frantel*, II, 150 r.; *Vendée*, II, 90 r.; *Supmotel*, II, 41 r.; *Paris*, III, 56 r.; *Colonies*, III, 24 r.; *Concorde*, III, 34 r.; *Grand Hôtel de Nantes*, III, 40 r.; *Graslin*, III, 46 r.; *Résidence*, III, 21 r.; *Atlantique*, IV, 20 r.; *Belgique*, IV, 10 r.; *Grand Monarque*, IV, 22 r.; *Santeuil*, IV, 32 r.; *Trianon*, IV, 20 r.

Nantes, the largest town in Brittany, is not purely Breton but is also orientated along the Loire valley towards inland France. It is in other ways too a town of many different aspects in which art and architecture, industry and shipping all play a part. Wartime destruction and postwar reconstruction affected many parts of the town but left the old medieval quarters largely untouched.

HISTORY. – After the Gallic and Roman periods, the early Middle Ages were a time of strife for Nantes, which came under attack from the Norsemen and other enemies. In the later medieval period Nantes vied with Rennes for the status of capital of Brittany. In 1598 the town submitted to Henry IV, who in the Edict of Nantes issued in that year, proclaimed freedom of religious belief for the first time. Between the 16th and 18th c. Nantes prospered on the trade in sugar and ebony, so that by the end of the 18th c. it was France's leading port. The town went through some bad times during the French Revolution, but the problems of economic recession in the 19th c. were

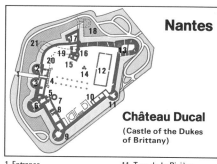

Nantes

Château Ducal
(Castle of the Dukes of Brittany)

1 Entrance
2 Tour du Pied-de-Biche
3 Tour de la Boulangerie
4 Grand Gouvernement (Ducal palace, with Folk Museum)
5 Tour de la Couronne d'Or
6 Tour des Jacobins
7 Well
8 Grand Logis (barracks, with Museum of Decorative Art)
9 Tour du Port
10 Petit Gouvernement (smaller palace)
11 Tour de la Rivière
12 Harnachement (harness room)
13 Tour du Fer-à-Cheval
14 Remains of original castle
15 Loge du Concierge (porter's lodge)
16 Vieux Donjon (Old Keep)
17 Bastion Mercoeur
18 Tour au Duc
19 Vieux Logis (barracks)
20 Chapel
21 Tour des Espagnols

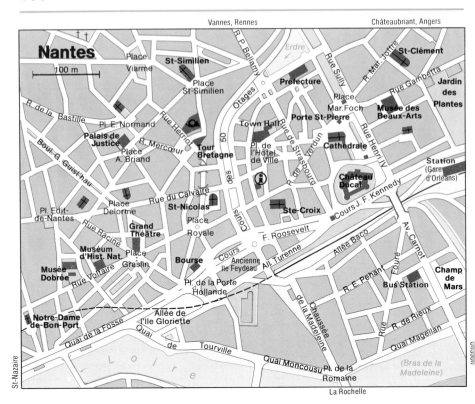

perhaps even worse. Ships were now growing larger and could no longer reach Nantes, so that it became necessary to build an outer harbour at St-Nazaire and develop new industries in Nantes. At the outbreak of the Second World War Nantes was France's sixth largest port; during the war it suffered less damage than Brest, Lorient or St-Nazaire.

SIGHTS. – The *Cathedral (*St-Pierre-et-St-Paul*) had a long building history, extending from 1434 to 1893, but the unity of its Gothic style shows surprisingly little sign of this. The W front, with three doorways and two towers, is very fine.

THE INTERIOR of the Cathedral is still more impressive. The nave is 102 m long, 32 m wide and 37·5 m high – higher even than Notre-Dame in Paris. In the S transept is the *tomb of François II, last Duke of Brittany, a masterpiece of Renaissance sculpture (beginning of 16th c.) which by a fortunate chance escaped destruction during the French Revolution.

The *Ducal Castle (*Château Ducal*), a stronghold of the Dukes of Brittany, was originally built in the 10th c., rebuilt in 1466 and enlarged in the 16th c. The Edict of Nantes was signed here in 1598. In the Grand Logis in the SW wing is the *Museum of Decorative Art*, and a short distance away is the interesting *Breton Folk Museum*, a visit to which is a good preparation for a tour of Brittany.

Nantes also has a *Museum of Fine Arts*, one of the best in France outside Paris, with a rich collection of French paintings of the 19th c. and later periods down to the present day. Visitors interested in shipping and fishing will want to visit the *Musée de la Marine* in the "Harnachement" in the Ducal Castle, which is particularly good on the 18th c.

Finally there is the **Dobrée Museum**, in the palace built by a 19th c. collector named Dobrée and in the adjoining 15th c. *Manoir de la Touche*, which has a very varied collection of antiquities, sculpture, paintings and other works of art. – In the *Porte St-Pierre*, N of the Cathedral, is a collection of material illustrating the history of the town.

No visit to Nantes should omit a walk through the 18th c. part of the town. The Place Royale, Rue Crébillon, Place Graslin and Cours Cambronne will give a good impression of the older Nantes, while Le Corbusier's "Cité Radieuse" in the suburb of REZÉ represents the modern town. The **Harbour**, downstream from the town, is also worth a visit.

SURROUNDINGS. – In *La Jonelière*, N of the town, are a Zoo and an *Automobile Museum*, with more than 50 veteran and vintage cars. – An attractive excursion, very popular with the people of Nantes, is a boat trip up the *valley of the Erdre*, which flows into the Loire at Nantes. These trips are run during the summer, and can be extended if desired.

Nice

Region: Provence–Alpes–Côte d'Azur.
Department: Alpes-Maritimes.
Altitude: 1–20 m. – Population: 347,000.
Post code: F-06000. – Dialling code: 93.

ⓘ **Office de Tourisme,**
32 rue de l'Hôtel-des-Postes;
tel. 85 25 25.
13 Place Masséna;
tel. 85 47 89.

HOTELS. – *Négresco*, L, 175 r.; *Méridien*, L, 434 r.;
Plaza, L, 175 r.; *Frantel*, I, 205 r.; *Atlantic*, I, 120 r.;
Parc, I, 150 r.; *Aston*, I, 157 r.; *Royal*, I, 140 r.; *Beau
Rivage*, II, 170 r.; *Cecil*, II, 130 r.; *Albert-1ᵉʳ*, II, 74 r.;
Ambassador, II, 45 r.; *Chatham*, II, 45 r.; *Marina*, II, 40
r.; *Napoléon*, II, 83 r.; *Grand Hôtel de Noailles*, II, 72 r.;
Vendôme, II, 60 r.; *Albion*, III, 85 r.; *Astor*, III, 30 r.;
Athéna, III, 21 r.; *Berne*, III, 57 r.; *Choiseul*, III, 43 r.;
Flandres, III, 39 r.; *Régence*, III, 40 r.; *Suisse*, III, 39 r.;
Vichy, III, 47 r.; *William's*, III, 73 r.; *Ann-Margaret*, IV,
30 r.; *Calais*, IV, 49 r.; *Astrid*, IV, 19 r.; *Gavotte*, IV, 12 r.;
Escurial, IV, 100 r.; *Interlaken*, IV, 40 r.; etc.

RESTAURANTS in the hotels; also *Chantecler*, *La
Poularde chez Lucullus*, *Périgord*, *St-Moritz*, etc.

Casinos: *Casino Ruhl*, Promenade des Anglais;
Casino Club, 2 rue St-Michel; *Palais de la Méditerranée*, 15 Promenade des Anglais.

EVENTS. – *Carnival*, with parades, cavalcades,
balls, dancing in the streets and a concluding firework
display; *International Trade Fair* and *International
Book Fair* (both in spring); *International Folk Festival*
(July); important *tennis tournaments*.

Carnival, Nice

Nice, chief town of the department
of Alpes-Maritimes and capital of
the Côte d'Azur, is a very popular
resort in both summer and winter,
with a beautiful situation and an
agreeable climate. The principal
event of the year is the Carnival, in
the last eleven days before Lent,
with a full programme of parades
and celebrations of all kinds.

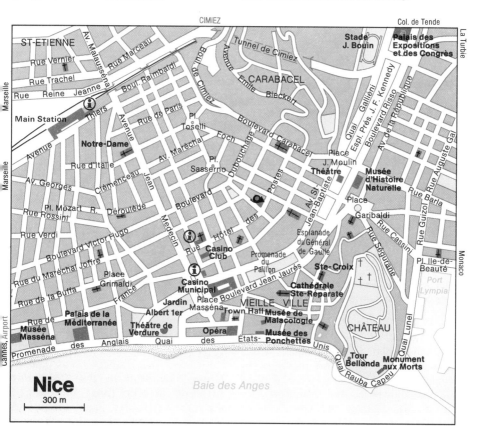

Seafront promenade, Nice

HISTORY. – In 350 B.C. Greeks from Marseilles founded a settlement which they named *Nicaea* in honour of the goddess of victory Nike. The Romans showed little interest in the town. From the 10th c. onwards, under the Counts of Provence, it increased in importance. In 1388 it was incorporated in the Duchy of Savoy, which was united with Sardinia; then in 1712 it passed to France, in 1814 to the kingdom of Sardinia, and finally in 1860 returned to France. The hero of Italian liberation, Garibaldi, was born in Nice in 1807, and the painters Matisse and Dufy are buried in the town. In 1966 Nice became a university town.

SIGHTS. – The main attractions of Nice lie in its townscape – *Place Masséna* in the centre of the town, with the *Municipal Casino*; the **Promenade des Anglais*, the lively seafront promenade, lined with magnificent palms; and the *flower market* in the old town (1 to 4 p.m.).

The **Château** is a hill (92 m) adjoining the harbour, once surrounded by the old town; it can be climbed by a flight of 198 steps. The castle which once stood here was destroyed in 1706, leaving only the *Tour Bellanda*. The hill is now laid out as a park, with a terrace from which there are very fine **views*. – Another popular park is the *Jardin du Roi Albert 1er*, just off the Promenade des Anglais.

Nice has a number of fine art museums – the **Chagall Museum* (Musée National Message Biblique Marc Chagall), with a comprehensive collection of works by Chagall, including the series of Biblical scenes known as the "Message Biblique"; the *Matisse Museum*, with an excellent cross-section of the painter's

work; the *Masséna Museum*, with mementoes of Napoleon's marshal, and also paintings by the Impressionists; and the *Chéret Museum*, containing the municipal art collection.

SURROUNDINGS. – It is well worth while going up to the villa suburb of **Cimiez**, the site of a Roman colony, with remains of an *amphitheatre* (65 by 57 m), *baths*, etc. There is also a *museum* containing material recovered by excavation.

Nîmes

Region: Languedoc-Roussillon.
Department: Gard.
Altitude: 39 m. – Population: 134,000.
Post code: F-30000. – Dialling code: 66.
ⓘ**Office de Tourisme,**
6 rue Auguste;
   tel. 67 29 11.

HOTELS. – *Impérator*, I, 60 r.; *Jacques Borel*, I, 100 r.; *Cheval Blanc*, II, 48 r.; *Mercure*, II, 100 r.; *Novotel*, II, 96 r.; *Midi*, II, 70 r.; *Carrière*, III, 55 r.; *Empire*, III, 45 r.; *Parc*, III, 15 r.; *Louvre*, III, 37 r.; *Michel*, III, 29 r.; *Provence*, III, 40 r.; *Château*, III, 15 r.; *Couronne*, IV, 18 r.; *France*, IV, 10 r.; *Central*, IV, 19 r.; *Menant*, IV, 30 r.; *Moderne*, IV, 24 r.

EVENTS. – *Spring Fair; Craft Exhibition* (Sept.–Oct.); *Antiques Fair* (Dec.).

SUMMER COURSES IN ARCHAEOLOGY: *Ecoles antiques de Nîmes*, Musée Archéologique, Boulevard Amiral-Courbet.

Nîmes, situated in the Cévennes foreland, attracts large numbers of visitors with its well-preserved Roman remains – though perhaps it

hardly deserves the title of the
"French Rome" which is sometimes
claimed for it. It is the chief town of
the Gard department, the see of a
bishop and a centre of the wine and
fruit trade, with clothing and footwear industries. It was the birthplace of the 19th c. writer Alphonse
Daudet (1840–97).

HISTORY. – The town grew up round a sacred spring,
the haunt of the god *Nemausus* who gave Nîmes its
name. With the coming of the Romans in 121 B.C. the
town began to prosper, and handsome public
buildings were erected. At the end of the 1st c. B.C. the
town was surrounded by walls. By the 2nd c. A.D.
Nîmes had reached a high pitch of prosperity, helped
by the fact that it lay on the road from Italy to Spain.
The advance of the Visigoths prevented the spread of
Christianity, which did not reach the area until the 8th
c. Thereafter Nîmes was ruled by its own Vicomtes
until 1185, when it came into the hands of the Counts
of Toulouse. In the 16th c. much of the population
accepted the Reformed faith, and the town became a
stronghold of the Calvinists. Religious strife continued until the French Revolution, and was particularly bitter in the early 18th c.

Roman amphitheatre, Nîmes

SIGHTS. – In the centre of the town is the
Amphitheatre (*Arènes*), built in the
early 1st c. A.D., at about the same time as

the one in Arles. It measures 131 by 100 m
and could accommodate 21,000 spectators. It is one of the best preserved of the
70 or so known Roman amphitheatres,
and in terms of size it takes 20th place. The
Visigoths made it into a fortress. In the

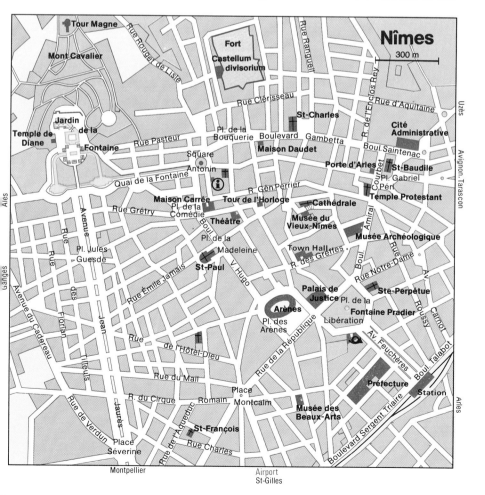

19th c. the structure (which had been buried under 6 m of earth) was restored to its original condition. It is still sometimes used for bullfights.

Another important Roman building is the *Maison Carrée ("Square House"), an excellently preserved temple dating from the time of Augustus. It served a variety of purposes before being restored after the French Revolution. It now houses a *museum of antiquities containing a variety of interesting material recovered by excavation, including a large statue of Apollo. – Less well preserved are the Temple of Diana, which was associated with Roman baths, and the Tour Magne (end of 1st c. B.C.) on Mont Cavalier, the original function of which is unknown. The top of the hill, with an *observation platform, is reached by climbing 140 steps. At the foot of the hill is the beautiful *Jardin de la Fontaine, laid out in 1750.

Other buildings in the town include the Cathedral, built in the late 11th c. and considerably altered in later periods, most recently in the 19th c. – At 20 Boulevard Gambetta is Daudet's birthplace.

Nîmes museums include the Archaeological Museum, in the former Jesuit College, the Museum of Old Nîmes and the Museum of Fine Arts. – In the N of the town is the 18th c. Fort, beside which is the Castellum divisorium, a distribution chamber at the end of the Roman aqueduct which brought water from Uzès to Nîmes by way of the Pont du Gard.

Normandy

As its name indicates, Normandy is the part of France in which the Norsemen from Scandinavia settled in the 11th c. – a peaceful settlement based on an agreement with the French king. This coastal region, bounded by Brittany in the W, Picardy in the E and the Ile de France in the S, is one of the most fought-over parts of France, most recently in 1944. It is also a thriving agricultural region, notable particularly for its stock-farming, and a land of fine buildings, with cathedrals which show affinities with those of the Ile de France; and finally it has some of

France's leading bathing resorts, among them Deauville, Trouville and Dieppe.

Normandy includes the departments of Seine-Maritime and Eure in Upper Normandy and Calvados, Orne and Manche in Lower Normandy. The most important towns in Upper Normandy are Rouen and Le Havre, in Lower Normandy Caen. The main industrial towns are Rouen and Le Havre. Stock-farming concentrates on cattle (butter, cheese) and horses. Large areas of Normandy belong to the "Bocage Normand" – a well-watered landscape of woodland and pasture crisscrossed by countless hedges. An area round the River Orne is given the name of the "Norman Switzerland" – although the highest point in the whole of Normandy reaches no more than 417 m. Between Upper and Lower Normandy lies the Pays d'Auge, with a very distinctive landscape pattern – a chalk plateau traversed by river valleys (the Dives, the Touques) which produces Calvados (apple brandy), cider and Camembert cheese and contains some of the most picturesque spots in Normandy, with typically Norman farmhouses.

Chalk cliffs near Etretat

Normandy also has no fewer than 29 military cemeteries – British, American, Canadian, Polish and German.

HISTORY. – After the arrival of the Romans there were invasions by Germanic peoples in the 2nd and 5th c. In the 6th c. Normandy became part of the Merovingian kingdom. From the 9th c. onwards there were incursions by Vikings from Denmark, the Norsemen (Normans), who in the year 911 established a Norman duchy which soon expanded to take in the Cotentin peninsula. From here William the Conqueror crossed to England, won the battle of Hastings and united England and Normandy. The Duchy of Normandy did not become part of France until 1204, with the capture of Château Gaillard and the town of Rouen. In 1315, however, Normandy received a charter recognising its special legal status. The Hundred Years War, symbolised by the figure of Joan of Arc, ravaged Normandy from 1337 onwards, and for a short time it was annexed to England again. In 1431 the trial of the Maid of Orléans took place in Rouen. In 1450, three years before the end of the Hundred Years War, Normandy was finally reunited with France, and thereafter shared its destiny during the Wars of Religion and the French Revolution. From 1940 to 1944 Normandy was occupied by German forces; then in June 1944 came the Allied landings and the battle for Normandy; and after winning this battle in July and August the Allies were able to begin their advance towards Germany. Normandy suffered severely from the effects of the war: 586 of its 3400 communes had to be provided with completely new communications and services, and 200,000 dwellings were destroyed or badly damaged. 640,000 German soldiers were killed, wounded or taken prisoner during the fighting. All trace of the ten weeks of destruction have now been removed apart from the memorials which recall these historic events.

Château de Tocqueville (Manche)

SIGHTS. – **Alençon** (pop. 40,000), in the upper Sarthe valley in southern Normandy, has been a lace-making centre since the 17th c., and still has a lace-making school. Its finest building is the *church of Notre-Dame (1444), in Flamboyant style, with an elegant porch; the tower and choir were rebuilt in the 18th c. The museum in the Town Hall has a display of lace-making; the Lace-Making School (Ecole Dentellière) has showrooms in which lace can be bought

Les Andelys (pop. 10,000), in the Seine valley, has the imposing ruins of *Château Gaillard overlooking the town. The castle dates from the time of Richard Cœur-de-Lion, who built it at the turn of the 12th c. to bar the French king's way to Rouen. In spite of its strength, however, it was taken by French forces in 1204. The outer walls have almost completely disappeared, but much of the keep and its surrounding walls has survived. – There are two churches in the town, the more notable of which is Notre-Dame, with a 13th c. nave and 16th–17th c. façade and a fine *organ and *stained glass.

Anet, in the Eure valley on the borders of the Ile de France, is regarded as the most elegant and expressive of France's Renaissance châteaux, although it has suffered at the hands of later owners. It was begun in 1548, and the greatest artists of the day contributed to its construction and decoration. Among them were Benvenuto Cellini and the tapestry-weavers of Fontainebleau, who together represent the style of Henry II's reign. The goddess Diana provides a constantly recurring decorative theme, referring to the owner of the château, Henry's mistress Diane de Poitiers (who is not directly represented by any portrait).

Argentan (pop. 18,000), once an important lace-making centre, suffered heavy damage in 1944. Church of St-Germain (15th–17th c.), restored.

Arromanches-les-Bains (pop. 340) is a little seaside resort NE of Bayeux, famous since 1944 for the "Mulberry harbour" used in the British landings (museum).

Avranches (pop. 11,000) was the scene in 1172 of a council at which Henry II of England, having done penance, received absolution for the murder of Thomas Becket. The Cathedral was destroyed during the French Revolution; its site is marked by a tablet in the gardens of the Sous-Préfecture in Place Daniel-Huet. Avranches was in the thick of the fighting in 1944, and was the starting point of General Patton's advance in July of that year. Fine views from the Jardin des Plantes. Museum, with important manuscripts of the 8th–15th c.

Bagnoles de l'Orme (pop. 640), along with **Tessé-la-Madeleine**, is a popular spa, beautifully situated at the mouth of a gorge and on a lake. It is a good base from which to visit several châteaux and explore the "Norman Switzerland".

Bayeux (pop. 15,000) was the first French town to be liberated in the Second World War (7 June 1944), and suffered no damage. The *Cathedral of Notre-Dame (11th and 13th c.) is typical of the Gothic style of Normandy. The W towers,

Bayeux Cathedral

fort, with museum of the Second World War and the Liberation), 3 km from the town centre. The naval harbour is closed to foreign visitors. The Thomas Henry Museum has a number of fine pictures (Botticelli, Millet).

The **Cotentin peninsula**, with *Cap de la Hague* and the town of Cherbourg, projects NW from western Normandy. The lonely country in the interior, with its intricate pattern of hedges, is less frequented by tourists than the coasts but is of striking scenic beauty. On the W coast is *Carteret*, on the Cap de Carteret, from which there is a ferry service to Jersey.

Nez de Jobourg, Cotentin peninsula

built in the 11th c., have Gothic spires. The *tower over the crossing is 80 m high. In the museum facing the S side of the Cathedral is the famous **Bayeux Tapestry ("Tapisseries de la Reine Mathilde"), actually a work of embroidery (11th c.) on a band of linen 70 m long, which shows a kind of strip cartoon of the Norman conquest of England. – There are interesting old houses in Rues St-Martin, St-Malo, Bienvenue and Franche.

Cabourg (pop. 3000) is one of the most popular and fashionable of Normandy's seaside resorts. It dates from the Second Empire.

Caen: see p. 86.

Cherbourg (pop. 40,500), on the N coast of the Cotentin peninsula, is France's third largest naval base and an important port for the Atlantic shipping traffic. In 1853 the harbour was protected by a breakwater 3·6 km long, with two piers; later two other piers were built, separating the large and the small harbour. In 1944 Cherbourg became the main landing point of heavy military equipment and played a vital part in the Allied victory. The advantages of the harbour had been recognised two centuries earlier by Vauban. – A fine general *view of the town and the harbour can be had from the *Montagne de Roule* (112 m:

Coutances (pop. 12,000), on the Cotentin peninsula, was severely damaged by bombing in 1944. Its *Cathedral of Notre-Dame (1251–74), which came through the war relatively undamaged, is a fine example of Norman Gothic. The *W front has two towers 77·5 m high, and there is a domed tower 57 m high over the crossing, from the top of which there is a view extending to Jersey and St-Malo.

Deauville (pop. 5600 – multiplied six-fold during the season) is a resort of international renown, with its high season in July and August (like the neighbouring resort of Trouville). It lies on the *Côte Fleurie*, which extends NE to Honfleur and SW to Cabourg, with a total length of more than 30 km.

Dieppe (pop. 40,000), on the Channel coast, is the seaside resort nearest Paris and the one which has been popular for longest. It was the scene of the first Allied landing (by Canadian forces) in occupied France on 19 August 1942 – a reconnaissance raid in considerable strength (7000 men) which was successfully beaten off by the Germans but which misled them about Allied invasion plans. – From the busy harbour there are ferry

Evreux Cathedral

ficent views and a constantly changing play of colour. In the town is a handsome old market hall. – On the cliffs to the NE is a monument to the pioneer fliers Nungesser and Coli.

Evreux (pop. 50,000) is chief town of the department of Eure and an important agricultural market town. The damage it suffered during the last war has been well repaired. The *Cathedral of Notre-Dame preserves some remains of the original structure, which was rebuilt in the 12th c. The choir is 13th c., the chapels 14th c. In spite of the damage it has suffered down the centuries (most recently in June 1940) the Cathedral has still some beautiful *stained glass and fine grilles on the chapels. – The church of St-Taurin contains a fine 13th c. *reliquary of St Taurin (Taurinus), a masterpiece of the French goldsmith's art.

Falaise (pop. 10,000), which suffered much destruction during the last war, has a handsome castle with a keep and a massive 15th c. round tower (35 m high, with walls 4 m thick).

Fécamp (pop. 23,000) is the principal French cod-fishing port. Guy de Maupassant stayed here for a time and used Fécamp as the setting of some of his stories. The main feature of the town,

services to Newhaven on the English S coast. Lively fishing harbour. – The beach is some 2 km long. A castle built in 1433 (museum) stands on a chalk crag above the town.

Etretat (pop. 1600) is a popular seaside resort, with rocky *coastal scenery on both sides of the bay (Falaise d'Aval, Falaise d'Amont) which offers magni-

Fishing harbour, Honfleur (Calvados)

Ruins of Jumièges Abbey

apart from the harbour, is the church of
*Ste-Trinité, originally belonging to an
abbey, which was built in the 12th–13th
c. and altered in a later period. With a
length of 127 m, it is only 3 m shorter than
Notre-Dame in Paris, although there is a
certain lack of harmony between the nave
and the W front. Norman tower 64 m high.
The richly decorated interior contains a
15th c. "Death of the Virgin". – The first
Bénédictine liqueur, distilled from herbs
growing on the coastal cliffs, was produced in Fécamp in 1510. The distillery is
open to visitors, and there is a museum.
Only a few fragments of the abbey have
been preserved.

Granville (pop. 15,000) is a popular
seaside resort with a busy harbour. The
upper town is still surrounded by its old
walls, and visitors can make a complete
circuit of the walls and the town. Within
the walls are the church of Notre-Dame
(15th and 17th c.) and an informative
Municipal Museum in the Grande Porte.
On the Pointe du Roc are a lighthouse
(fine view) and an aquarium. – A boat trip
can be taken from Granville to the rugged
Iles Chausey.

Le Havre: see p. 121.

Honfleur (pop. 10,000), at the mouth of
the Seine, is given a distinctive and
colourful character by the older parts of
the town and harbour. This was the home
port of the 16th c. seamen who made their

famous voyages to Canada, making that
country almost a Norman colony. On the
N side of the harbour is the 16th c.
Lieutenance, the old governor's house.
The church of *Ste-Catherine has a free-
standing bell-tower. The church itself is of
wood, and was built by local shipwrights
after the Hundred Years War.

Jumièges (pop. 1500), in the Seine
valley, has a ruined *abbey which has
been called the "finest ruin in France".
The remains of two churches and the
abbey buildings can be seen; museum.
The smaller church of St-Pierre dates in
part from the Carolingian period, and
shows early Norman work of the 10th c.

Lisieux (pop. 25,000), situated at the
junction of the Touques and Orbiquet
valleys, is the chief town of the Pays
d'Auge. Unfortunately the old town,
formerly famed for its Gothic and Renaissance houses, fell a victim to the war
in 1944. The Rue aux Fèvres was completely destroyed, and Lisieux was left
only with its Cathedral and its associations with *St Thérèse*. The Cathedral
was built between 1170 and the middle of
the 13th c. There are still a few old houses
in Rue du Dr-Lesigne, Rue Henry-Chéron
and Rue Banaston – poor fragments of the
town's former rich heritage from the past.
– St Thérèse was born Thérèse Martin in
1873, entered a convent in 1888, died in
1897 and was canonised in 1925. There
are large *pilgrimages* to her shrine,
particularly on 15 August, the last Sunday
in September and 30 September. There
are many places associated with the saint
in the town.

Mont St-Michel: see p. 157.

Basilica of Ste-Thérèse, Lisieux

Rouen: see p. 231.

The **Seine valley** is the great tourist attraction of inland Normandy. The river flows through Normandy from Vernon by way of Rouen to Le Havre, with numerous bends which in spite of its gentle gradient (with a fall of only 16 m from Vernon to its mouth, more than 100 km away as the crow flies), almost double its length. For those who wish to see the scenery on both sides of the river, there are bridges at Rouen, at Caudebec-en-Caux (where there is also a ferry) and at Tancarville (near the mouth). The *"Route des Abbayes"* from Rouen to Le Havre along the right bank of the Seine is particularly attractive.

"**Norman Switzerland**" is the beautiful area in and around the Orne valley extending between *Thury-Harcourt* (S of Caen) in the N, *Flers-de-l'Orne* in the S and *Falaise* in the E. The bends of the river, the rocky bluffs along its banks and the isolated hills standing farther back combine with the intricate pattern of hedges to give the scenery a particular charm. The most striking features are the **Roche d'Oëtre*, in the hilliest part of the area, above the gorges of the Rouvre (fine views), the Vère and Noireau valleys, and the 27 km long stretch of the Orne between Thury-Harcourt and Pont d'Ouilly.

Tancarville, at the mouth of the Seine, has the ruins of an 11th c. castle and a *road bridge opened for traffic in 1959. This is a suspension bridge which crosses the Seine at a height of 48 m above the water, with a total length of 1400 m and a middle span 608 m wide.

Le Tréport, a small port on the English Channel, at the mouth of the River Bresle, is a resort much favoured by Parisians.

SPORT and RECREATION in Normandy. – The coast is lined with *seaside resorts* of varying size and varying standards of amenity. In the department of Seine-Maritime in eastern Normandy there are 24 resorts, 11 of which have beaches of fine sand. Calvados, farther W, has 27 resorts, all with good sandy beaches. In western Normandy the Manche department, including the Cotentin peninsula, has 25 resorts. – There are over 50 *sailing schools* in Normandy, and more than 45 *yacht harbours*. In addition to the beaches there are numerous *swimming pools* of all kinds. – There are facilities for *tennis* and *riding* in almost all resorts.

The **Normandy-Maine Nature Park** (*Parc naturel régional de Normandie-Maine*), in Lower Normandy and the Loire country, has an area of 578,000 acres.

Tancarville Bridge

Of this area 111,000 acres are forest, but there is also ample scope for canoe and kayak enthusiasts on rivers and lakes. – There is also the **Brotonne Nature Park**, an area of 123,000 acres in the departments of Seine-Maritime and Eure, centred on the *Forest of Brotonne* (16,800 acres). – An attractive and specially signposted tourist road is the "Route du Cidre" (Cider Road) in the Cambremer area (Pays d'Auge), which runs through a region of apple orchards; the signposts bear the symbol of an apple. It is possible to visit the cellars of the cider-producers and to sample and buy their cider and Calvados.

Orange

Region: Provence–Alpes–Côte d'Azur.
Department: Vaucluse.
Altitude: 46 m. – Population: 26,000.
Post code: F-84100. – Dialling code: 90.
ⓘ **Office du Tourisme**,
　Cours St-Martin;
　tel. 34 06 00.

HOTELS. – *Arène*, II, 30 r.; *Louvre et Terminus*, II, 40 r.; *Princes*, II, 48 r.; *Glacier*, III, 30 r.; *Commerce*, IV, 20 r.; *Gare*, IV, 14 r.; *Arts*, IV, 16 r.

EVENTS. – *Performances in Roman theatre* (July); *Agricultural Show* (mid Oct.).

Orange, in the Rhône valley, was once the flourishing Roman colony of *Arausio Secundanorum*, and its

Statue of Augustus in the Roman theatre, Orange

today. In the 16th c., surprisingly, the town – then capital of the little principality of Orange – passed to the Dutch House of Nassau. (This is why the Queen of the Netherlands still bears the title of Princess of Orange-Nassau.) In 1713, under the Treaty of Utrecht, Orange became part of France.

SIGHTS. – The road from Lyons passes the *Triumphal Arch, erected after Caesar's victory in 49 B.C., the third largest of its kind in the Roman world and the finest in France.

In the S of the town is the **Roman Theatre, beyond question the finest and best preserved of the ancient world. It was built at the end of the 1st c. B.C. and renovated in the 2nd c. The stage wall is 103 m long and 38 m high, and still preserves remains of its elaborate decoration. It can accommodate 7000 spectators and has excellent acoustics. It is the only Roman theatre to have preserved a statue of Augustus (3·55 m tall; restored). – Adjoining the theatre are the sparse remains of earlier buildings, including a *stadium* and a *temple*. There is a *museum* containing material recovered by excavation.

The former *Cathedral of Notre-Dame* dates from the 11th–12th c. The *Town Hall* is 17th c. – There is a good *view of the town and its Roman structures from the *Colline St-Eutrope*, the hill behind the theatre.

principal tourist attractions are a Roman theatre and a Roman triumphal arch.

HISTORY. – The first encounter between Roman forces and the Germanic tribes, the Cimbri and the Teutons, took place outside Orange in 105 B.C., when 100,000 Romans were killed. Three years later Marius revenged this defeat at Aix. During the "Pax romana" Orange had a population four times as large as it has

A bend on the River Ardèche

SURROUNDINGS. – Some 35 km NW are the impressive **Ardèche Gorges**, 30 km long. A road runs through the gorges, and there are boat trips on the river. To the S of the gorges, at the village of *Orgnac*, is a magnificent stalactitic cave, the **Aven d'Orgnac** (conducted tours, 1 hr).

Orléans

Region: Centre.
Department: Loiret.
Altitude: 110 m. – Population: 110,000.
Post code: F-45000. – Dialling code: 38.
Office de Tourisme,
  Place Albert-1er;
  tel. 53 05 97.

HOTELS. – *Novotel*, II, 120 r.; *Terminus*, II, 45 r.; *Cèdres*, II, 32 r.; *Moderne*, II, 38 r.; *Ibis*, III, 108 r.; *Martroi*, III, 14 r.; *Marguerite*, III, 25 r.; *Central*, III, 20 r.; *Berry*, IV, 25 r.; *Grand Hôtel*, IV, 28 r.; *Châtelet*, IV, 9 r.; *Blois*, IV, 20 r.

EVENTS. – *Feast of Joan of Arc* (7 and 8 May).

The name of Orléans is inseparably bound up with that of Joan of Arc, the Maid of Orléans; but it is also the chief town of the department of Loiret and see of a bishop, and has had a University since 1309. It lies at the most northerly point in the course of the Loire. The town's industries are dependent on the agriculture of the surrounding area.

HISTORY. – In Gallic times the site of Orléans was occupied by the settlement of *Cenabum*, which was destroyed by Caesar in 52 B.C. From the 3rd c. the town, situated at the junction of important roads, began to be known as *Aurelianum*, from which its present name is derived. In 451 the town was besieged by Attila; in 498 it was captured by Clovis, king of the Franks. But Orléans made its real appearance in history when the town, then under siege by the English, was relieved by Joan of Arc. In the course of this operation she first advanced along the wrong bank of the Loire, so that she had to send her forces back to Blois and herself cross the river by boat. She achieved success by rousing the French forces in the beleaguered town to fresh ardour which enabled them to beat off the English. In the course of the fighting she was wounded, and for a time was believed by the English to have been killed; and it was her reappearance that decided the battle. The date of this victory, 8 May, is still remembered and enthusiastically celebrated. – During the Second World War Orléans suffered considerable destruction.

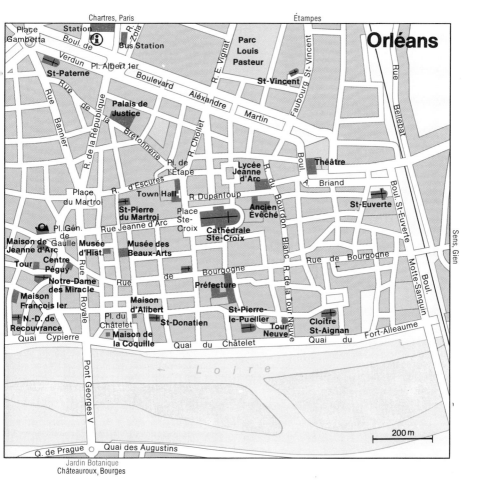

Panoramic view of Orléans

SIGHTS. – In *Place du Martroi* is an *equestrian statue of Joan of Arc*, erected in 1855. Rue Royale, which runs S from the square, was rebuilt after the war in its original 18th c. style; it leads to the *Pont Georges-V*, a bridge over the Loire 333 m long, constructed in 1760. – The town's dominant building is the *Cathedral (Sainte-Croix)*, built between the 13th and 16th c., and partly destroyed by Protestants in 1567. Henry IV restored it in Gothic style, replacing the Romanesque towers by new ones, also "Gothic". The Cathedral is almost as large as Notre-Dame in Paris. The interior contains a handsome 17th c. organ and splendid *wood-carving in the choir (early 18th c.). Traces of three earlier churches on the site can be seen in the crypt.

In the **Town Hall**, built in 1530, King Francis II died in 1560. – There is a very good **Museum of Fine Arts** in the Hôtel des Créneaux (formerly the Town Hall), mainly devoted to pictures from the 15th c. to the present day.

Paris

Region: Ile de France.
Departments: Ville de Paris; Yvelines, Essonne, Hauts-de-Seine, Seine-St-Denis, Val-de-Marne, Val-d'Oise.
Altitude: 60 m.
Population: 2·3 million (Ville de Paris)
8·4 million (conurbation)
9·9 million (Région Parisienne).
Post code: F-75000 (Ville de Paris). – Dialling code: 1.

ⓘ **Office de Tourisme de Paris**,
Syndicat d'Initiative et Accueil de France,
127 Avenue des Champs-Elysées
(9 a.m. to 8 or 10 p.m.);
tel. 7 23 61 72.
Hôtesses de Paris (City Hostesses) at main railway stations:
Gare du Nord, tel. 5 26 94 82;
Gare de l'Est, tel. 6 07 17 73;
Gare de Lyon, tel. 3 43 33 24;
Aérogare des Invalides, tel. 7 05 82 81.
Palais des Congrès,
Porte Maillot;
tel. 7 58 22 45.

Automobile-Club de France (ACF),
6–8 Place de la Concorde;
tel. 2 65 34 70.
Touring-Club de France (TCF),
65 Avenue de la Grande-Armée;
tel. 5 02 14 00.

EMBASSIES. – *Australia*, 26 rue de la Pépinière; *Canada*, 35 Avenue Montaigne; *New Zealand*, 7 ter rue Léonard-de-Vinci; *South Africa*, 59 Quai d'Orsay; *United Kingdom*, 35 rue du Faubourg St-Honoré; *United States of America*, 2 Avenue Gabriel.

HOTELS. – BETWEEN THE PLACE DE LA CONCORDE AND THE ETOILE: *George V*, 29–31 Avenue George-V, L. 300 r.; *Plaza-Athénée*, 23–27 Avenue Montaigne, L, 225 r.; *Royal-Monceau*, 35 Avenue Hoche, L. 230 r.; *Prince de Galles*, 33 Avenue George-V, L, 203 r.; *Bristol*, 112 rue du Faubourg St-Honoré, L, 220 r.; *Crillon*, 10 Place de la Concorde, L, 217 r.; *Lancaster*, 7 rue de Berri, L, 70 r.; *California*, 16 rue de Berri, L, 177 r.; *Trémoille*, 14 rue de la Trémoille, L, 112 r.; *Terminus-St-Lazare-Concorde*, 108 rue St-Lazare, I, 335 r.; *Napoléon*, 40 Avenue de Friedland, I, 140 r.; *Belford*, 17 rue de l'Arcade, I, 142 r.; *Castiglione*, 40 rue du Faubourg St-Honoré, I, 107 r.; *San Régis*, 12 rue Jean-Goujon, I, 42 r.; *Royal Alma*, 35 rue Jean-Goujon, I, 84 r.; *Celtic*, 6 rue Balzac, I, 79 r.; *Roblin*, 6 rue Chaveau-Lagarde, I, 67 r.; *Vernet*, 25 rue Vernet, I, 63 r.; *Queen-Elisabeth*, 41 Avenue Pierre-1er-de-Serbie, I, 68 r.; *Royal*, 33 Avenue de Friedland, I, 57 r.; *Astor*, 11 rue d'Astorg, I, 144 r.; *Château-Frontenac*, 54 rue Pierre-Charron, I, 100 r.; *Atlantic*, 44 rue de Londres, II, 94 r.; *Elysées-Marignan*, 12 rue de Marignan, II, 70 r.; *Printemps*, 1 rue de l'Isly, II, 70 r.; *Powers*, 52 rue François-1er, II, 60 r.; *West-End*, 7 rue Clément-Marot, II, 60 r.; *Céramic*, 34 Avenue Wagram, II, 59 r.; *Bradford*, 10 rue St-Philippe-du-Roule, II, 48 r.; *Arcade*, 7 rue de l'Arcade, II, 47 r.; *Rond-Point des Champs-Elysées*, 10 rue de Ponthieu, II, 46 r.; *Franklin-Roosevelt*, 18 rue Clément-Marot, II, 42 r.; *Opal*, 19 rue Tronchet, II, 40 r.; *Florida*, 12 Boulevard Malesherbes, II, 49 r.; *Ouest*, 3 rue du Rocher, III, 62 r.

BETWEEN THE PLACE DE LA CONCORDE AND THE BASTILLE: *Ritz*, 15 Place Vendôme, L, 170 r.; *Intercontinental*, 3 rue de Castiglione, L, 492 r.; *Meurice*, 228 rue de Rivoli, L, 186 r.; *Lotti*, 7 rue de Castiglione, L, 130 r; *Westminster*, 13 rue de la Paix, L, 101 r.; *Louvre-Concorde*, Place du Théâtre-Français, I, 230 r.; *France et Choiseul*, 239 rue St-Honoré, I, 142 r.; *Normandy*, 7 rue de l'Echelle, I, 140 r.; *Madeleine Palace*, 8 rue Cambon, I, 114 r.; *Edouard-VII*, 39 Avenue de l'Opéra, I, 100 r.; *Mayfair*, 3 rue Rouget-de-l'Isle, I, 53 r.; *Cusset*, 95 rue Richelieu, II, 114 r.; *François*, 3 Boulevard Montmartre, II, 81 r.; *Brighton*, 218 rue de Rivoli, II, 69 r.; *Etats-Unis-Opéra*, 16 rue d'Antin, III, 52 r.; *Métropole-Opéra*, 2 rue Grammont, II, 50 r.; *Normandie*, 3 rue de la Banque, II, 44 r.; *Richepanse*, 14 rue Richepanse, II, 43 r.; *Molière*, 21 rue Molière, II,

Bird's-eye view of the Etoile

30 r.; *Cambon*, 3 rue Cambon, II, 50 r.; *France*, 4 rue du Caire, III, 51 r.; *Roubaix*, 6 rue Grenéta, III, 48 r.; *Montpensier*, 12 rue Richelieu, III, 43 r.

BETWEEN THE MADELEINE AND THE GARE DU NORD: *Grand Hôtel*, 2 rue Scribe, L, 608 r.; *Ambassador*, 16–18 Boulevard Haussmann, I, 300 r.; *Pavillon*, 36–38 rue de l'Echiquier, I, 214 r.; *Franklin et Brésil*, 19 rue Buffault, I, 62 r.; *Commodore*, 12 Boulevard Haussmann, I, 180 r.; *Chamonix*, 8 rue d'Hauteville, I, 35 r.; *Terminus-Nord*, 12 Boulevard Denain, II, 240 r.; *Carlton*, Boulevard Rochechouart, II, 100 r.; *Normandie*, 4 rue d'Amsterdam, II, 71 r.; *Richmond*, 11 rue du Helder, II, 58 r.; *Haussmann*, 6 rue du Helder, II, 57 r.; *Hélios*, 75 rue de la Victoire, II, 53 r.; *London-Palace*, 32 Boulevard des Italiens, II, 49 r.; *Gare du Nord*, 33 rue de St-Quentin, II, 48 r.; *Morny*, 4 rue de Liège, II, 42 r.; *Caumartin*, 27 rue Caumartin, II, 40 r.; *Blanche Fontaine*, 34 rue Fontaine, II, 41 r.; *St-Pétersbourg*, 33 rue Caumartin, II, 120 r.; *Mondial*, 5 Cité Bergère, II, 60 r.; *Paris-Est*, Gare de l'Est, II, 32 r.; *Amiot*, 76 Boulevard de Strasbourg, III, 70 r.; *Français*, 13 rue du 8-Mai-1945, III, 70 r.; *Royal-Magenta*, 7 rue des Petits-Hôtels, III, 53 r. *Laffon*, 25 rue Buffault, III 47 r.; *Victor-Massé*, 32 bis rue Victor-Massé, III, 47 r.; *Hollandais*, 16 rue Lamartine, III, 46 r.

IN THE N AND E: * *Méridien*, 81 Boulevard Gouvion-St-Cyr, L, 1023 r.; *Concorde Lafayette*, Place de la Porte des Ternes (in Congress Centre: 34 floors, 120 m high), I, 1000 r.; *Terrass'*, 12 rue J.-de-Maistre, L, 108 r.; *Splendid*, 1 bis Avenue Carnot, I, 60, r.; *Novotel*, 1 Avenue de la République (in Bagnolet, on eastern outskirts of city), II, 608 r., SP; *Mercure Etoile*, 27 Avenue des Ternes, II, 56 r.; *Balmoral*, 6 rue Gén.-Lanrezac, II, 57 r.; *Regent's Garden*, 6 rue P.-Demours, II, 42 r.; *Banville*, 166 Boulevard Berthier, II, 138 r.; *Régence-Etoile*, 24 Avenue Carnot, II, 38 r.; *Laumière*, 4 rue Petit, III, 54 r.; *Luxia*, 8 rue Seveste, III, 48 r.; *Astrid*, 27 Avenue Carnot, III, 40 r.; *Palma*, 77 Avenue Gambetta, III, 34 r.; *Unic*, 6 rue Dupont-de-l'Eure, IV, 36 r.

LEFT BANK OF THE SEINE, BETWEEN THE EIFFEL TOWER AND THE JARDIN DES PLANTES (INCLUDING THE QUARTIER LATIN): *Sofitel-Bourbon*, 32 rue St-Dominique, L,

112 r.; *Pont Royal*, 5–7 rue Montalembert, L, 75 r.; *Relais Bisson*, 3 rue Christine, L, 39 r.; *Lutétia-Concorde*, 45 Boulevard Raspail, I, 315 r.; *Victoria-Palace*, 6 rue Blaise-Desgoffe, I, 120 r.; *Littré*, 9 rue Littré, I, 120 r.; *Cayré*, 4 Boulevard Raspail, I, 140 r.; *Montalambert*, 3 rue Montalembert, I, 61 r.; *Bourdon-nais*, 111 Avenue de la Bourdonnais, II, 60 r.; *Madison*, 143 Boulevard St-Germain, II, 60 r.; *Résidence de Saxe*, 9 Villa de Saxe, II, 52 r.; *Paris-Dinard*, 29 rue Cassette, II, 51 r.; *Colbert*, 7 rue de l'Hôtel-Colbert, II, 40 r.; *Bourgogne et Montana*, 3 rue de Bourgogne, II, 35 r.; *Université*, 22 rue de l'Université, II, 28 r.; *France*, 102 Boulevard de La Tour-Maubourg, III, 60 r.; *Albe*, 1 rue de la Harpe, III, 43 r.; *St-Pierre*, 4 rue de l'Ecole-de-Médecine, III, 51 r.

IN THE S AND W: *Sheraton-Paris*, 10 rue du Commandant-Mouchotte, L, 1000 r.; *Hilton-Suffren*, 18 Avenue Suffren, L, 487 r., with "Le Toit de Paris" roof-top restaurant; *Raphaël*, 17 Avenue Kléber, L, 85 r.; *Sofitel-Paris*, 2 rue Grognet, L, 630 r., SP; *Nikko*, 68 Quai de Grenelle, L, 780 r., SP; *Majestic*, 29 rue Dumont-d'Urville, L, 28 r.; *P.L.M. St-Jacques*, 17 Boulevard St-Jacques, I, 812 r.; *Alexander*, 102 Avenue Victor-Hugo, I, 64 r.; *Résidence du Bois*, 16 rue Chalgrin, I, 20 r.; *Paris-Lyon-Palace*, 158 Boulevard Brune, II, 90 r.; *Victor Hugo*, 19 rue Copernic, II, 74 r.; *Azur*, 5 rue de Lyon, II, 70 r.; *Terminus-Lyon*, 19 Boulevard Diderot, II, 59 r.; *Modern Lyon*, 3 rue Parrot, II, 53 r.; *Aiglon*, 232 Boulevard Raspail, II, 49 r.; *Régina de Passy*, 6 rue de la Tour, II, 62 r.; *Pacific*, 11 rue Fondary, III, 66 r; *Carlton Palace*, 207 Boulevard Raspail, III, 65 r.; *Marceau*, 13 rue Jules-César, III, 56 r.; *Midi*, 4 Avenue René-Coty, III, 50 r.; *Slavia*, 51 Boulevard St-Marcel, III, 49 r.; *Viator*, 1 rue Parrot, III, 47 r.; *Bois*, 11 rue du Dôme, III, 41 r.; *Rubens*, 35 rue du Banquier, IV, 68 r. – IN NEUILLY: *Paris-Club-Méditerranée*, 58 Boulevard Victor-Hugo, I, 320 r.; *Charlemagne*, III, 38 r.; *Home du Roule*, III, 34 r. – IN COURBEVOIE: *Paris-Penta*, 18 rue Baudin, II, 494 r. – AT ORLY AIRPORT: *Hilton-Orly*, I, 390 r.; *Motel P.L.M.-Orly*, I, 194 r.; *Air Hôtel*, I, 56 r. – AT ROISSY AIRPORT: *Sofitel Jacques Borel*, I, 352 r., SP. – IN VÉLIZY-VILLACOUBLAY: *Ramada*, I, 208 r., SP. – CAMPING SITES in *Bois de Boulogne*, at *Champigny-sur-Marne* (Paris-Est-Le-Tremblay, 15 km E of Paris), *Maisons-Lafitte* and *Ermenonville* (in *park*).

RESTAURANTS in most of the hotels listed. Also BETWEEN THE PLACE DE LA CONCORDE AND THE ETOILE: *Ledoyen*, Carré Champs-Elysées; *Lasserre*, 17 Avenue F.-D.-Roosevelt; *Lucas-Carton*, 9 Place Madeleine; *Régence-Plaza*, 25 Avenue Montaigne; *Taillevent*, 15 rue Lamennais; *Maxim's*, 3 rue Royale; *Fouquet's*, 99 Avenue des Champs-Elysées; *Au Vieux Berlin*, Avenue George-V; *Chez Tante Louise*, 41 rue Boissy-d'Anglas; *La Pergola*, 144 Avenue des Champs-Elysées. – BETWEEN THE PLACE DE LA CONCORDE AND THE BASTILLE: *Grand Véfour*, 17 rue Beaujolais; *Prunier*, 9 rue Duphot; *Drouant*, Place Gaillon; *Vert Galant*, 42 Quai des Orfèvres; *Chez Pauline*, 5 rue Villedo; *Coconnas*, 2 Place des Vosges; *Brasserie Bofinger*, 5 rue de la Bastille; *St-Antoine*, Rue des Prêtres-St-Germain-l'Auxerrois; *Drugstore*, 133 Avenue des Champs-Elysées, near the Arc de Triomphe (American-style).

BETWEEN THE MADELEINE AND THE GARE DU NORD: *Aux Ducs de Bourgogne*, 2 Place Anvers; *Nicolas*, 12 rue Fidélité; *Chez Michel*, 10 rue Belzunce; *Taverne d'Alsace*, 42 rue Rochechouart.

IN THE N AND E: *La Coquille*, 6 rue Débarcadère; *Grand Veneur*, 6 rue P.-Demours; *Mère Cathérine*, 6 Place du Tertre.

LEFT BANK OF THE SEINE BETWEEN THE EIFFEL TOWER AND THE JARDIN DES PLANTES: *Tour d'Argent, 15 Quai de la Tournelle (a famous old restaurant; specialty roast duck); Plein Ciel and Panoramique, in Eiffel Tower; La Bourgogne, 6 Avenue Bosquet; Récamier, 4 rue Récamier; Champ de Mars, 17 Avenue de la Motte-Picquet; Source, 35 Boulevard St-Michel.

IN THE S AND W: Jamin, 32 rue de Longchamp; Train Bleu, 20 Boulevard Diderot; Les Marronniers, 52 bis Boulevard Arago; Bocage Fleuri, 19 rue Duranton; Rhône, 40 Boulevard Arago.

FOREIGN RESTAURANTS. – ITALIAN: San Francisco, 1 rue Mirabeau; Stresa, 7 rue Chambiges. – NORTH AFRICAN: Timgad, 21 rue Brunel.

CAFÉS. – de la Paix, 12 Boulevard des Capucines; Rond-Point, des Champs-Elysées, corner of Avenue Matignon; Marignan, 27 Avenue des Champs-Elysées; Le Madrigal, 32 Avenue des Champs-Elysées; Deux Magots, 170 Boulevard St-Germain; La Coupole, 102 Boulevard Montparnasse; Dôme, 108 Boulevard Montparnasse.

EVENTS. – Horse-racing at Vincennes (Jan.); Festival International du Son (March); horse-racing at Auteuil (Palm Sunday); Printemps Musical ("Musical Spring": April, May); Foire de Paris (Trade Fair), in Parc des Expositions (end of April and beginning of May); International Air Show at Le Bourget Airport (beginning of June in odd-numbered years); Festival des Quartiers du Marais (June, July); Summer Festival (July, Aug., Sept.); Chamber Music Festival in the Orangery, Sceaux (summer months); Motor Show, in Parc des Expositions (beginning of Oct. in even-numbered years); International Film Festival (Oct.); Autumn Festival (Oct., Nov.).
For information about theatres, concerts, exhibitions and other events see the programme "Saison de Paris" issued by the Office de Tourisme. There is also a very useful weekly publication, "Une semaine de Paris – Pariscope", which can be obtained at newspaper kiosks.

Theatres, concerts and cabarets. – Visitors with sufficient time at their disposal should make a point of going to one of the Paris theatres – though for plays it is advisable to have some knowledge of French. Paris has some 60 theatres, some of which are world-famed. – The Paris cabarets (the first of which was the Cabaret du Chat Noir founded by Rodolphe Salis in 1884) were originally the haunt of artists, but have now lost much of their character and are mainly aimed at tourists.

Of the Paris theatres the most famous are the **Opéra** (Théâtre National de l'Opéra: grand opera and ballet) and the **Comédie Française** (classical French plays). Others are the Opéra-Comique (now called the Opéra-Studio or Salle Favart) the Théâtre National Populaire in the Palais de Chaillot (well-produced modern and classical plays); the Théâtre de France in Place de l'Odeon; the Châtelet, a large theatre specialising in operettas which is about to become the Municipal Opera-House; the Théâtre des Ambassadeurs, 1 Avenue Gabriel; the Atelier, Place Dancourt; the Comédie des Champs-Elysées, 15 Avenue Montaigne; the Gaîté Lyrique, Square des Arts-et-Métiers; the Grand Guignol, 20 rue Chaptal; the Mogador, 25 rue Mogador; the Michodière, 4 rue de la Michodière; the Palais-Royal, 33 rue de Montpensier; and the Théâtre de la Ville, formerly the Théâtre Sarah-Bernhardt, in Place du Châtelet. – Other celebrated establishments are the Folies-

Bergère, 32 rue Richer (spectacular revues); the Casino de Paris, 16 rue de Clichy (music hall); and Olympia, Boulevard des Capucines (music hall).

Numerous Symphony orchestras (Orchestre de Paris, Orchestre de l'Opéra, Orchestre National de France, Nouvel Orchestre Philharmonique de Radio-France, Orchestre des Concerts Lamoureux, Orchestre des Concerts Colonne, Orchestre Pasdeloup, Orchestre Symphonique de l'Ile de France), with conductors and soloists of international reputation, combine with numerous chamber music groups and choirs to consolidate Paris's reputation as one of the great musical capitals of Europe. – Concerts of classical music are given mainly in the Salle Pleyel, 252 rue du Faubourg St-Honoré (3000 seats); the Salle Gaveau, 45 rue La Boëtie; the Théâtre du Châtelet, Place du Châtelet; the auditorium of Radio France in Avenue du Président-Kennedy; the Théâtre des Champs-Elysées, 13–15 Avenue Montaigne (2200 seats); the Conservatoire, 14 rue de Madrid; and occasionally also in the Palais Chaillot, Palais des Congrès (Porte Maillot) and Théâtre de France (Odéon). Concerts of avant-garde music are organised in the Beaubourg Centre by IRCAM, the musical institute which has its headquarters there; performances are given by the Ensemble Intercontemporain and other groups.

Most of the cabarets (which frequently require clients to buy champagne and have very high charges) are in Montmartre, around the Champs-Elysées and the Etoile, the Madeleine and the Opéra, St-Germain-des-Prés and the Odéon. The main artists' haunts are on the Butte Montmartre, in the Quartier Latin and in the Montparnasse area. – Typical establishments are the **Lido**, 78 Avenue Champs-Elysées (music hall turns, revues, cabaret); Shéhérazade, 3 rue de Liège; Monseigneur, 94 rue d'Amsterdam; Mimi Pinson, 79 Avenue des Champs-Elysées; Club des Champs-Elysées, 15 Avenue Montaigne; Folies-Pigalle, Eve and Narcisse, all in Place Pigalle; Pigall's, 77 rue Pigalle; Lapin Agile, 22 rue des Salues (a typical Montmartre cabaret); Chez Patachou, 13 rue du Mont-Cenis (songs); Caveau des Oubliettes, rue St-Julien-le-Pauvre (old French songs); Club St-Germain-des-Prés, 13 rue St-Bénoît; Villa d'Este, 4

The **Métro** (Chemin de Fer Métropolitain de Paris), the Paris underground railway system, came into operation in 1900, and now has 15 lines and a total length of some 200 km, with rubber-tyred coaches which give a smooth ride. It is the fastest means of public transport in Paris. Trains (which have 1st and 2nd class) run from 5.30 a.m. to 1.15 a.m., at intervals of between $1\frac{1}{2}$ and 10 minutes. Tickets are cheaper if bought in carnets of 10 tickets (valid also on the buses), and there are also tourist tickets at reduced rates for foreigners. The stations – many of them still preserving their original Art Nouveau entrances – are usually about 500 m apart. Tickets are at a flat rate for the whole system, and any number of changes can be made. Connections (often involving a long walk through tunnels which sometimes run on three levels, one above the other) are indicated on the platform by a yellow illuminated sign, "Correspondance". Exits to the street are indicated by blue signs, "Sortie". – There is also an Express Métro system (RER) reaching out to the suburbs, for which special tickets are required.

The Conciergerie

rue Arsène-Houssaye; *La Tête de l'Art*, 5 Avenue de l'Opéra; the famous *Moulin Rouge* (cinema and dance-hall with floor shows); and there are many others.

Shopping. – Paris is, of course, a paradise for the shopper; but it is impossible within the framework of this guide to give even the most general survey of the possibilities. Visitors will find a great wealth of information about shops and shopping in the "Nouveau Guide de Paris Gault-Millau", which also has useful lists of hotels and restaurants.

Buses. – The municipal buses run from 6.30 a.m. to 0.30 a.m. (with some night services as well). Bus stops are indicated by posts with yellow and red signs. A new ticket is required for each fare stage; it is advisable, therefore, to buy a *carnet* of tickets.

Parking in the *Zone Bleue* which takes in the whole of the city centre is permitted only with a parking disc (obtainable from tobacconists, petrol stations or the Office du Tourisme) or at a parking meter. There are numerous underground car parks.

Boat trips on the Seine are run by "Bateaux Mouches" all year round.

Paris's six **railway stations** are all terminuses, carrying traffic to different parts of France.

There are three **airports** – the *Aéroport Charles-de-Gaulle* at Roissy (25 km NE: rail connection with Gare du Nord, "Roissy Rail", 30 min.), *Aéroport d'Orly* and *Aéroport Le Bourget*.

**Paris is truly an incomparable city. The capital and focal point of France – by virtue of its situation, its charm, its art and culture, its economic and political importance – it enjoys an international reputation as the most attractive city in the world. Even though by the outbreak of the last war Paris had lost something of its traditional character as a result of new building, the constant flood of traffic and the swarms of tourists, a visit to Paris is still a unique experience, wherever the particular visitor's interests may lie. It should be remembered, however, that although you must know Paris if you want to get a complete picture of France you do not know France if you have only seen Paris. It is also an error to suppose that Paris is a city of frivolity and enjoyment. There is, of course, an element of truth in this – though to a much lesser extent than some prospective visitors like to imagine – but this side of Paris is only one small part of a much greater whole. – Even a brief visit is enough to give some impression of Paris; but to get any real idea of what it has to offer – its treasures of art and architecture, the atmosphere of its streets, the everyday life of the city, the variety of human interest it offers – enough time should be allowed.

Paris – capital of France, the seat of government, the see of a Cardinal Archbishop, with the headquarters of all the main government departments and of numerous international organisations – lies in a wide basin on both banks of the *Seine*, which here receives its principal tributary, the *Marne*. It is also France's largest inland port, with facilities for handling container traffic as well as ordinary freight and oil. The *view of the city, extending over both banks of the Seine, the low hills of Montmartre (127 m) and the Buttes Chaumont (101 m) in the N and the Montagne de Ste-Geneviève (60 m) in the S, is one of particular charm. The boulevards with their never-ending streams of traffic and after dark their brilliant neon signs − in striking contrast to the parks and the quiet side streets − the long lines of streets and spacious squares, the brilliance of the Champs-Elysées, the magnificent public buildings and churches (often illuminated at night), the views to be had from the higher points in the city and the busy activity of the boats on the Seine: all this, combined with the splendours of its museums, contributes to the fascination of Paris and the unforgettable impression it makes on every visitor.

The *population* of Paris (the inner area known as the Ville de Paris) is 2,300,000, including many foreigners. At the beginning of the 12th c. it was just under 100,000; by 1860, after taking in some suburban areas, it had reached some 1,500,000 within the then existing fortifications. With an area of 105 sq. km, of which 1764 acres are occupied by the Seine, Paris is the most densely populated of the world's capitals. If the new departments of Hauts-de-Seine, Seine-St-Denis and Val-de-Marne (established in 1965 in the Paris conurbation) and parts of the departments of Val-d'Oise, Yvelines, Essonne and Seine-et-Marne are included the *Région Parisienne* has a population approaching 10 million.

HISTORY. − The oldest part of Paris is on the Ile de la Cité, which in Caesar's time was occupied by a fortified Gallic settlement, *Lutetia Parisiorum*. This became the centre of Roman and later of Frankish Paris, with only a small settlement, surrounded by forest and swamp, on the left bank of the Seine. Here, too, in Frankish times the Church established its headquarters. − In the later medieval period the town spread increasingly on to the right bank. By the 12th c. Paris had become a great centre of Western culture, with a university to which students flocked from many countries to study under the leading teachers of the day. The town's favourable situation and the royal protection it enjoyed promoted craft industry and trade, and this in turn led to much building activity.

The growth of the town can be measured by successive enlargements of its circuit of walls. The *Wall of Philippe Auguste*, built about 1200, which extended from Rue Etienne-Marcel, near the Head Post Office, to the present Luxembourg Gardens, had become much too small by 1356, when *Etienne*

Marcel began the building of a new wall on the right bank which extended northward from the Seine to Porte St-Denis on the line of the present-day Grands Boulevards.

In the 15th c. the growth of Paris was hampered by the Hundred Years War. There was a fresh burst of building activity in the reign of *Francis I* (rebuilding of Louvre, Tuileries and Hôtel de Ville), but the real development of Paris began in the time of *Henry IV*, after the end of the Wars of Religion.

Under *Louis XII* (1633–36) the extension of the town walls along the whole length of the Grands Boulevards W of the Porte St-Denis, which had been begun under the last Valois rulers, was carried through to completion. The Ile St-Louis was created and built up from 1614 onwards. − In the reign of *Louis XIV* many new monumental structures were built (Louvre Colonnade, Hôtel des Invalides, numerous churches, Place Vendôme) and the outer districts of the town extended in all directions. It was not until shortly before the Revolution, however, that the new districts were enclosed within the *Enceinte des Fermiers-Généraux*, a wall designed to facilitate the collection of taxes on goods brought into the city, which extended along the line of the outer boulevards on both banks of the Seine from the Place de l'Etoile in the W to the Place de la Nation in the E.

During the *French Revolution* and its aftermath (1789–1804) the centralisation of France reached its peak, and this period also saw the disappearance of most of Paris's religious houses, which occupied large areas of land in excellent situations.

Under the *First Empire* (1804–14) Paris was the centre of Europe. The treasures of art and learning which Napoleon brought back from his victorious campaigns went to embellish his capital. He began the N linking wing between the Louvre and the Tuileries, the construction of the Rue de Rivoli, the building of the Bourse, the Madeleine and much else besides; but most of this remained unfinished at the time of his fall, and his masterpiece of civic architecture, the Arc de Triomphe de l'Etoile, was not completed until the reign of Louis-Philippe.

Paris had a great upsurge of vigour during the *Restoration* (1814–30), when French literature, art and science began the great advance which led towards the reconquest of their world supremacy, and French society reached a peak of elegance and refinement. Under the *July Monarchy* (1830–48) this progress was continued. Louis-Philippe enthusiastically resumed the development of Paris which had been planned by Napoleon, spending more than 100 million gold francs on new streets, churches, government buildings, bridges, embankments and public gardens. Once again Paris was surrounded by a new circuit of walls, the *Enceinte de Thiers*, which took in 13 adjoining communes.

All previous building activity, however, was surpassed in the reign of *Napoleon III*. In 1853 he appointed *Georges-Eugène Haussmann* (1809–91) Prefect of the Seine department, and Haussmann made Paris − which hitherto, apart from the old boulevards, had preserved its cramped medieval street pattern − into a modern city whose layout became a model for other towns both in France and abroad. The process began with the construction of a new N–S traffic artery formed by the Boulevards de Strasbourg and de Sébastopol on the right bank and the Boulevards du Palais and St-Michel on the Ile de la Cité and the left bank. Then came the Boulevard Haussmann and Boulevard de Magenta on the right bank, the Boulevard St-Germain on the left bank, the extension of the Rue de Rivoli, the Avenue de l'Opéra and the Champs-Elysées district. Among public buildings erected during this period were the new wings of the Louvre and the Opéra.

Under the *Third Republic* work in progress was completed and new streets and squares were laid out. Sculpture purchased at the annual art exhibitions ("Salons") was set up in public parks and gardens, making them into miniature open-air museums. The city's public transport was improved by the construction of an underground railway, the Métro. New residential areas surrounded by gardens and playgrounds were built on the site of the former fortifications, which had been purchased by the city. Here too were laid out the Exhibition Grounds (Parc des Expositions) and a Cité Universitaire containing students' residences. A succession of international exhibitions (in 1855, 1867, 1878, 1889, 1900 and 1937) led to the erection of many new buildings, among them the Eiffel Tower (1889), the Palais de Chaillot (1937) and the Museum of Modern Art.

During the *First World War* Paris was saved from German occupation by the "Miracle of the Marne". During the *Second World War* it was occupied from 1940 to 1944, but fortunately came through the war almost completely unscathed.

From 1945 onwards, under the *Fourth* and *Fifth Republics*, many notable buildings were erected in Paris – the UNESCO building (1958), the CNIT exhibition hall in the new district of La Défense (1959), the *Maison de la Radio* (1963), the Tour Maine-Montparnasse and the Centre International de Paris (a congress centre) in 1974, the Centre Beaubourg in 1977. The tower blocks of La Défense to the NW of the city – an area still in course of development – are also altering the skyline of Paris. In 1971 the famous "Halles" were pulled down, the market which they had housed having been moved to Rungis in 1969, and in September 1979 a new shopping and leisure complex, the Forum des Halles, was opened on part of the site. – The movement of traffic has been eased by the construction of through roads along the Seine and a ring motorway, the Boulevard Périphérique (1973). A new Express Métro, the Réseau Express Régional or RER, was brought into service in 1970, and a new international airport named after General de Gaulle was opened at Roissy in 1974.

In 1977 the city acquired its first elected Mayor in this century (Jacques Chirac), replacing the government-appointed Prefect.

ADMINISTRATIVE DIVISIONS OF THE CITY. – The city of Paris proper, i.e. the department of Ville-de-Paris, is divided into 20 administrative districts, officially styled *cantons* but universally known as *arrondissements*. The arrondissements numbered I to VIII are centrally situated on both banks of the Seine, while those numbered from IX to XX are strung round the city centre in a wide arc. Each *arrondissement* is divided into four *quartiers*, numbered from 1 to 80. The *arrondissements* and *quartiers* are listed below:

I. Louvre
1–4: St-Germain-l'Auxerrois, Les Halles, Palais-Royal, Place-Vendôme.
II. Bourse
5–8: Gaillon, Vivienne, Mail, Bonne-Nouvelle.

III. Temple
9–12: Arts-et-Métiers, Enfantes-Rouges, Archives, Ste-Avoie.
IV. Hôtel-de-Ville
13–16: St-Merri, St-Gervais, Arsenal, Notre-Dame.
V. Panthéon
17–20: St-Victor, Jardin-des-Plantes, Val-de-Grâce, Sorbonne.
VI. Luxembourg
21–24: Monnaie, Odéon, Notre-Dame-des-Champs, St-Germain-des-Prés.
VII. Palais-Bourbon
25–28: St-Thomas-d'Aquin, Invalides, Ecole-Militaire, Gros-Caillou.
VIII. Elysée
29–32: Champs-Elysées, Faubourg-du-Roule, Madeleine, Europe.
IX. Opéra
33–36: St-Georges, Chaussée-d'Antin, Faubourg-Montmartre, Rochechouart.
X. Enclos St-Laurent/Porte-St-Denis
37–40: St-Vincent-de-Paul, Porte-St-Denis, Porte-St-Martin, Hôpital-St-Louis.
XI. Popincourt/République
41–44: Folie-Méricourt, St-Ambroise, Roquette, Ste-Marguerite.
XII. Reuilly
45–48: Bel-Air, Picpus, Bercy, Quinze-Vingts.
XIII. Gobelins
49–52: Salpêtrière, Gare, Maison-Blanche, Croule-barbe.
XIV. Observatoire/Montparnasse
53–56: Montparnasse, Parc-Montsouris, Petit-Montrouge, Plaisance.
XV. Vaugirard
57–60: St-Lambert, Necker, Grenelle, Javel.
XVI. Passy
61–64: Auteuil, La Muette, Porte-Dauphine, Chaillot.
XVII. Batignolles-Monceau
65–68: Ternes, Plaine-Monceau, Batignolles, Epinettes.
XVIII. Butte-Montmartre
69–72: Grandes-Carrières, Clignancourt, Goutte-d'Or, Chapelle.
XIX. Buttes-Chaumont
73–76: Villette, Pont-de-Flandre, Amérique, Combat.
XX. Ménilmontant
77–80: Belleville, St-Fargeau, Père-Lachaise, Charonne.

In the fields of *culture* and the *economy*, too, Paris plays a central role, controlling almost the whole of the country's life. For long the unchallenged leader of France in art and learning and its principal industrial and commercial centre, with almost every type of industrial and economic activity carried on within its bounds, Paris still occupies a leading position in many fields and is the country's most influential financial market. – For centuries Paris has ruled the world of European **fashion**. Its most famous *couturiers*, who present their newest models at shows held in the first week of February and the end of July or beginning of August, are to be found, along with world-renowned *parfumiers*, in the streets N and S of the Champs-Elysées and around the Rue de la Paix and Place Vendôme. – Most of the **art**

galleries are near the Rue de Seine on the left bank of the river in the Faubourg St-Honoré and the Rue La Boëtie on the right bank. *Antique-dealers* are also to be found in these areas. – *Car-dealers* have their showrooms mainly on the Champs-Elysées. The *furniture industry* is established in the Faubourg St-Martin (E of the Place de la Bastille), with furniture shops jostling one another in the Rue du Faubourg-St-Martin, and to the S of the Gare de l'Est. The *leather industry* has its main centre on the left bank of the Seine, along an old stream, the Bièvre, which is now covered over. – Most of the *newspaper* and *magazine publishers* have their offices near the Bourse (Rue Réaumur, Rue des Italiens, etc.), while the **book trade** is centred on the left bank, around the Boulevard St-Germain. Here, too, along the quays on both banks of the Seine, are the stalls of the *bouquinistes* who sell old books and prints. – On the Quai de la Mégisserie and Quai de Gesvres, on the right bank, are shops selling *seeds* and *birds*. Opposite, on the Ile de la Cité, is the *flower market*. – The **Foire de Paris**, held in the Parc des Expositions near the Porte de Versailles in SW Paris, is one of Europe's leading trade fairs. – A great international *Air Show* is held in alternate (odd-numbered) years at Le Bourget.

Museums

Paris has a wealth of richly stocked and frequently world-famous museums (usually closed on Tuesdays and on public holidays), and the programme of even a brief visit should include at least the **Louvre** and the **Cluny Museum**. The following list can give only a general impression of what each museum has to offer and draw attention to some of the outstanding exhibits. For a thorough visit to the larger museums the catalogue which is usually available will be found helpful. – See also the descriptions in the following section.

*Armée, Musée de l',
in Hôtel des Invalides;
open daily 10 a.m. to 6 p.m.
The Army Museum, probably the finest of its kind in the world, is made up of two sections. On the W side of the courtyard is the **Arms and Armour Section*, with some 40,000 items of European and Oriental equipment, including some outstanding masterpieces of Renaissance work. On the second and third floors of this wing are rich collections of material from the

two world wars. There is also a collection of prints. – On the E side of the courtyard is the *Historical Section*, devoted to the great exploits of the French army and its generals. *Museum of relief maps and plans.*

**Art Moderne, Musée National d',
in Beaubourg Centre;
open 12 noon to 10 p.m., Sat. and Sun. 10 a.m. to 10 p.m., closed Tues.
A collection of some 2000 20th c. paintings and works of sculpture (Arp, Brancusi, Chagall, Dali, Ernst, Kandinsky, Léger, Matisse, Miró, Picasso).

Art Moderne de la Ville de Paris, Musée d',
11 Avenue du Président-Wilson;
open 10–5.30, closed Mon. and Tues.
Paintings of the 20th c. Paris school (Modigliani, Utrillo, etc.). Temporary exhibitions.

*Arts Africains et Océaniens, Musée des,
293 Avenue Daumesnil (at Parc de Vincennes);
open 9.45–12 and 1.30–5.15, closed Tues.
A comprehensive display of material from former French colonies (history, art, economy, etc.). In the basement are a *tropical aquarium* and *terrarium*.

Arts Décoratifs, Musée des,
in the New Louvre,
107–109 rue de Rivoli;
open 10–12 and 2–5, closed Tues.
Applied art, interior decoration, furniture.

Arts et Traditions Populaires, Musée des,
in the Jardin d'Acclimatation;
open 10–5.15, closed Tues.
Temporary special exhibitions of French folk traditions (house interiors, trades and crafts, costumes, folk art).

*Carnavalet, Musée (*Musée historique de la Ville de Paris*),
23 rue de Sévigné;
open 10–5.45, closed Sun., Mon., Tues.
History of the city (particularly 16th–20th c.: furniture, pictures, dress, etc.) and of the Revolution.

Centre National d'Art et de Culture Georges Pompidou (Centre Beaubourg), Rue Rambuteau;
open noon to 10 p.m., Sat. and Sun. 10 a.m. to 10 p.m., closed Tues.
Modern art; exhibitions.

Cernuschi, Musée,
7 Avenue Vélasquez;
open 10–5.30, closed Sun., Mon., Tues.
A collection of Chinese and Japanese works of art, of great importance for the study of early Chinese art, from the beginnings to the 10th c.

Cinéma, Musée du,
in E wing of Palais de Chaillot;
seen only by prior arrangement.
Showing of films from the archives (some 60,000 films) of the *Cinémathèque Française*.

**Musée de Cluny,
6 Place Paul-Painlevé;
open 9.45–12.45 and 2–5.15, closed Tues.
The Cluny Museum, founded in 1833 on the basis of a collection of medieval and Renaissance objects assembled by the antiquary Alexandre du Sommerard, is perhaps the leading Paris museum after the Louvre. In 24 rooms it gives a magnificent survey of medieval European applied and decorative art. In addition to fine examples of wood and stone sculpture, valuable

The Centre Beaubourg

examples of goldsmith's, copper, bronze and enamel work, ivory carvings, old fabrics and embroidery, and French, Italian and Hispano-Mauresque faience (mainly 15th–18th c.), the museum is notable for its fine French and Brussels *tapestries*. Particularly beautiful (in Room XI, on the first floor) are the *Tapisseries de la Dame à la Licorne* ("Lady with the Unicorn" tapestries), from the château of Boussac in the department of Creuse (*c.* 1500), with representations of the five senses and a reference to the medieval legend of the unicorn which can be tamed only by a pure maiden, and (in the chapel) French tapestries from Auxerre church (*c.* 1500) depicting the life of St Stephen and the finding of his relics. – In Room XIX, on the first floor, is a fine *gold altar frontal from Basle Cathedral, probably Lombard work, presented by the German emperor Henry II (d. 1024). The late Gothic *chapel on the first floor has richly ornamented canopies. – Inside and around the museum (also visible from the Boulevard St-Michel) are imposing remains of **Roman baths**, including the vaulted frigidarium or cold bath (18 m high, 20 m long, 11·5 m wide).

Cognacq-Jay, Musée,
25 Boulevard des Capucines;
open 10–5.45, closed Mon. and Tues.
French and English pictures, sculpture and drawings; 18th c. furniture.

*Conservatoire National des Arts et Métiers, Musée National des Techniques,
292 rue St-Martin;
open 12–5.30, Sun. 10–5.30.
One of the most important museums of technology in Europe, originally founded in the priory of St-Martin-des-Champs in 1798 as the Musée des Techniques, based on a collection of machinery and tools assembled by an engineer named Vaucanson for the instruction of the working classes. The 40 rooms, including the early Gothic *church, contain numerous pieces of apparatus, models, inventions, etc., in many different fields of technology (mining, engineering, optics, building, general physics, chemical industry, meteorology, geodetics, astronomy, photography, printing).

*Découverte, Palais de la,
1 Avenue Franklin-Roosevelt;
open 10–6, closed Mon.
An important collection of material illustrating research, discovery and invention in every scientific field, including the latest developments in nuclear physics. In the Palais and the adjoining *Planetarium* lectures and demonstrations are given in non-technical language.

Ecole Nationale des Beaux-Arts, Musée de l',
17 Quai Malaquais and 14 rue Bonaparte.
In this museum, particularly in the courtyards opening off Rue Bonaparte, are displayed fine architectural fragments from French buildings dating from Gallo-Roman times to the 16th c., left over from the Musée des Monuments Français which was formerly housed here. The main building has a noble Renaissance façade of 1830.

Ennery, Musée d',
59 Avenue Foch;
open Sun. 1–4 or 5, closed in August.
A collection of East Asian art (statuettes, vases, ivory and lacquer), largely articles of inferior quality produced for export.

Grévin, Musée,
10 Boulevard Montmartre;
open 2–7; on Sun., public holidays and during school holidays 1–8 (admission charge).
A wax museum founded in 1882 by a caricaturist named Grévin.

*Guimet, Musée,
6 Place d'Iéna;
open 9.45–12 and 1.30–5.15, closed Tues.
A rich collection of Oriental works of art presented to the State by the Lyons industrialist Emile Guimet (d. 1918), together with a library on the religions of the Far East. Apart from Oriental ceramics the museum includes Egyptian antiquities and excavation material from Afghanistan.

Histoire de France, Musée de l',
60 rue des Frances-Bourgeois;
open 2–5, closed Tues.

Histoire Naturelle, Muséum National d'.
In the wider sense this is the Jardin des Plantes with all its buildings and grounds; in the narrower sense the term is applied to the *Galerie d'Histoire Naturelle* on the W and S side of the gardens (open 1–5, closed Tues.).
In the SW corner is the *Galerie de Zoologie*, and adjoining this on the S is the rich library. Along the S side of the gardens, from W to E are the *Galerie de Géologie et de Minéralogie*, the *Galerie de Botanique* and, in the SE corner, the *Galerie d'Anatomie, de Paléontologie et d'Anthropologie*.

*Historique de la Ville, Musée: see Carnavalet.

*Homme, Musée de l',
in the Palais de Chaillot;
open 10–6, Sat. and Sun. 10–8, closed Tues.
The museum, arranged in geographical and comparative order, gives a vivid survey of man on earth (ethnography, anthropology, prehistory, palaeontology).

*Jaquemart-André, Musée,
158 Boulevard Haussmann;
open 1.30–5.30, closed Mon. and Tues.
In rooms containing fine 18th c. furniture and

tapestries and Venetian ceiling paintings, the museum displays a collection of old and modern pictures (including works by Rembrandt, Ruisdael, Carpaccio and Tiepolo), sculpture, small objets d'art, pottery and porcelain.

**Jeu de Paume, Musée du,
Place de la Concorde;
open 9.45–5.15, closed Tues.
French Impressionists.

**Louvre, Musée du,
Place du Carrousel;
open 9.45–8, closed Tues.
The Louvre Museum, opened in 1793, which brings together art treasures from royal palaces, churches and abbeys, later acquisitions obtained by purchase and excavation material from Egypt and the East, is in many respects Europe's finest museum. There are so many rooms that even to walk through them takes two hours. A detailed description is given in the official guides, with plans, sketches and photographs; but those who have time for only one visit to the Louvre – with its six departments covering the art of every period from the Egyptians and Babylonians to the end of the 19th c. – should confine themselves to the items of outstanding importance which are mentioned in the following description, arranged by departments. (It should be remembered that on certain days whole departments may be closed in rotation.)

**Greek and Roman antiquities (*Antiquités grecques et romaines*), on the ground and first floors. Entering the Tuileries wing, on the S side along the Seine, by the Porte Denon, turn left into the *Galerie Denon*, with a rich collection of carved Roman sarcophagi, and continue down the Escalier Daru into the *Salle des Reliefs Funéraires* (grave-stones, lecythi). Then into the *Salle du Parthenon* in the SW corner of the Old Louvre. On the rear wall of this room is a **fragment of a frieze from the Parthenon (erected under the direction of Phidias, 447–438 B.C.). Opposite the middle window is the figure of a *suppliant (*c.* 400 B.C.) from the Palazzo Barberini in Rome. In the next room are two *metopes (*c.* 460 B.C.) from the Temple of Zeus at Olympia. – Then into the *Salle Archaïque*, containing sculpture of the 6th and 5th c. B.C. In the third room beyond this, on the courtyard side of the Old Louvre, stands the celebrated **Venus of Milo, the most famous piece of sculpture in the Louvre, found in a cave on the island of Melos (Milo) in 1820. Although the figure itself dates from the 2nd c. B.C. it is based on an earlier representation of the 4th c., showing Aphrodite holding a shield in front of her with both hands to serve as a mirror.
In the next room are three *reliefs from the island of Thasos, fragments from an altar of the Nymphs and the Graces dating from the 5th c. B.C.
After passing through two other rooms, turn right into the large *Salle des Caryatides*, with a figure of *Diana with the hind, known as the Versailles Diana (a copy of a work of the 4th c. B.C.), the Venus of Arles, the Aphrodite of Cnidos, the *Apollo Sauroctonus ("Lizard-Killer") and the *Diana of Gabii – all four good copies after Praxiteles (4th c. B.C.) – together with four *caryatids by Jean Goujon (d. *c.* 1565).
On the upper landing of the Escalier Daru, on the E side, is the **Nike of Samothrace, a winged goddess of victory (Hellenistic, *c.* 200 B.C.).

**Egyptian antiquities (*Antiquités égyptiennes*), in the SE part of the ground floor and the S wing of the first floor in the Old Louvre. From the Pavillon des Arts on the river side of the Old Louvre go E into the *Salle du Mastaba*, with the *mastaba (funerary chapel) of an official named Ekhet-hotep, of the 5th Dynasty, when Egyptian carving reached its peak. Farther on, in the *Salle Archaïque*, is the *tombstone of King Zet ("Snake"), from the earliest period of Egyptian history (*c.* 3000 B.C.). In the next room but one is the **Scribe, the seated figure of an official making notes (*c.* 2700 B.C.). In the large *Salle du Nouvel Empire* is a painted bas-relief of King Sethos I and the goddess Hathor. On the first floor are smaller Egyptian antiquities, including a *bust of King Amenophis IV and wood and stone *statuettes.

*Oriental antiquities (*Antiquités orientales*), in the northern half of the Old Louvre, on the ground floor. Important finds from Mesopotamia, Persia and Syria (French expeditions). Particularly notable items are colossal *winged bulls with crowned human heads, in the *Grande Galerie Chaldéo-Assyrienne* (E wing); two life-size *lions of brilliantly coloured glazed terracotta (11th c. B.C.), in the N wing; and the famous *Stele of Hammurabi, a block of greenstone inscribed with the laws of Hammurabi, king of Babylon (*c.* 1750 B.C.).

*Medieval, Renaissance and modern sculpture (*Sculptures du Moyen-Age, de la Renaissance et des Temps modernes*), on the ground floor of the S Tuileries wing.
Outstanding items are the Burgundian *tombstone of Philippe Pot (d. 1494) and the **"Chained Slaves", marble figures by Michelangelo (1475–1564). The French sculpture of the 17th c. includes fine works by Puget, Girardon and Coysevox.

*Applied and decorative art (*Objets d'art*), on the first floor of the E and NW wings of the Old Louvre and in the Galerie d'Apollon.
A rich collection of faience, carved ivory, bronzes, ceramics, glass, furniture, etc. At the E end of the S Tuileries wing is the **Galerie d'Apollon, the finest room in the Louvre and one of the most magnificent rooms in the world, built in the reign of Louis XIV by Louis le Vau to replace an earlier gallery of Henry IV's time which was burned down in 1661. The famous *ceiling painting of "Apollo fighting the serpent Python" was the work of Eugène Delacroix (1850–51). The room contains gems, enamels, goldsmith's work and jewellery, including what is left of the French crown jewels (the rest having been sold in 1887). Among them is the *"Regent", a diamond weighing some 28 grams (137 carats).

**Pictures (*Peintures*), on the first floor of the Tuileries wing and the second floor of the Old Louvre. The Louvre picture gallery, with over 5000 pictures (of which perhaps half are on show), is one of the richest and finest in the world. A complete rearrangement of the collection has been under way since 1968, and the previous arrangement under stylistic periods is giving place gradually to an arrangement in national schools. In the first place the works of French painters, including many not previously exhibited, are being brought together into a magnificent display of French art. A distinction is also being made between the rooms containing the great masterpieces and those with less important works, intended for study. From the Escalier Daru go through the *Salle des Sept Mètres* (so called because of its width), which at present contains Dutch and Flemish works but will later show 19th c. French pictures, and turn right into the *Grande Galerie*, a lofty room 375 m long which after restoration and rearrangement now contains a splendid display (in the eastern part of the gallery) of 17th and 18th c. French painting, including large and showy works by Nicolas Poussin, some fine Watteaus and numerous pictures, not previously exhibited, by lesser-known artists like Louis Le Nain, Charles Le Brun and Claude Lorrain. In the western part of the gallery are works by early Italian masters, including Cimabue, Giotto and Fra Angelico. Adjoining the Grande Galerie to the right is the *Salle des Etats*, which contains some of the great masterpieces of Italian painting – Leonardo da Vinci's **"Mona Lisa" or "La Gioconda" (1506), the Louvre's best known picture, and his **"Virgin of the Rocks", Paolo Veronese's **"Marriage in Cana", the largest picture in the Louvre (6·66 m high by 9·90 m long), painted in 1562–63, and several works by Titian. In the smaller room beyond are two pictures by Raphael, a **portrait of the courtier and writer Baldassare Castiglione and a "Holy Family", known as the "Belle Jardinière". In the adjoining rooms are works by 19th c. French painters. In the room which adjoins the Grande Galerie on the W and in smaller rooms on the right are masterpieces of Flemish and Dutch painting, including Van Dyck's **portrait of Charles I and Rembrandt's **"Disciples at Emmaus". Rubens's works are mainly in the *Galerie Médicis*, but are to be moved to the northern half of the second floor, along with the Flemish, Dutch, English and German schools. Beyond this are more Italian pictures and the *Béistegui* collection. The southern part of the second floor contains 18th and 19th c. French painting. – The *Pavillon de Flore*, at the W end of the Tuileries wing, contains 19th c. sculpture on the ground floor and works by Spanish masters (Velázquez, El Greco, Murillo, Zurbarán, Ribera, etc.) on the first floor.

Marine, Musée de la,
in the Palais de Chaillot;
open 10–5 or 6, closed Tues.

Marmottan, Musée,
2 rue Louis-Boilly (Métro station La Muette, near Bois de Boulogne);
open 10–6, closed Mon.
Rich collection of Impressionists, including many works by Monet and his friends.

Mode et du Costume, Musée de la,
in Palais Galliéra,
10 Avenue Pierre-1er-de-Serbie;
open 10–5.45, closed Mon. and Tues.
The museum, housed in a Renaissance-style palace built in 1878–88, is devoted to clothing from 1735 to the present day.

*Monuments Français, Musée des,
in the Palais de Chaillot;
open 9.45–12.30 and 2–5.15, closed Tues.
An impressive collection of casts (many in the original size) of architectural features such as doorways and chapels and copies of stained glass and wall paintings from medieval to modern times: worth seeing before visiting the French cathedral cities.

*Nissim de Camondo, Musée,
63 rue de Monceau;
open 10–12 and 2–5, closed Mon. and Tues.
The museum, housed in a mansion built by Comte Moïse de Camondo in 1911–14, is a branch of the Museum of Decorative Arts, with a collection of select items (18th c. furniture, sculpture, pictures, tapestries, etc.).

Opéra, Musée de l',
Place Charles-Garnier;
open 10–5, closed Sun.

*Petit Palais,
Avenue Winston-Churchill;
open 10–6, closed Tues.
The Petit Palais houses the municipal art collection, the *Musée des Beaux-Arts de la Ville de Paris*, which has grown in size since 1875, largely by purchases from the "Salons" (art exhibitions). Temporary exhibitions of 19th and 20th c. sculpture and painting. In the N wing is the **Tuck Collection* (old pictures, tapestries, furniture, Meissen and Chinese porcelain, sketches and drawings). The S wing contains the **Dutuit Collection*, with old and modern pictures, decorative art, rare books and Dutch drawings, including examples by Rembrandt and Van Dyck.

*Picasso, Musée,
in the Hôtel de Juigné (1656), Place de Thorigny (in the Marais).

*Rodin, Musée,
77 rue de Varenne;
open 10–6, closed Tues.
The museum, in the former Hôtel Biron (1728–30), displays either the originals or casts of the whole of Rodin's work.

Victor Hugo, Musée,
6 Place des Vosges;
open 10–5, closed Mon. and Tues.

If you are pressed for time, you should confine your sightseeing to the most important things, rather than destroy your pleasure by trying to see too much and exhausting yourself. The shorter your time is, the more you should concentrate on those parts of the city where you can see the splendours of the great capital alongside the everyday activities of ordinary people going about their daily business. The best plan is to use the excellent public transport (the Métro, the buses, the boats on the Seine) or the relatively cheap taxis rather than your own car. But if you have not even enough time for this, you can get at least a fleeting impression of Paris from the following tour by car (1$\frac{1}{2}$–2 hrs).

Lightning tour of Paris: From *Place de la Concorde* along the right bank of the Seine to the *Louvre* and the *Hôtel de Ville*; on to *Place de la Bastille*, then along the Grands Boulevards to the *Opéra* and *Madeleine*, then back to *Place de la Concorde*. From there, up the *Champs-Elysées* to the *Etoile*, along Avenue Kléber to the *Palais de Chaillot*, then over the *Pont d'Iéna* to the *Champ de Mars* and the *Eiffel Tower*. From here to the *Dôme des Invalides*, then W to the *Palais du Luxembourg* and the *Panthéon*, down the *Boulevard St-Michel*, passing the *Sorbonne* and the *Hôtel de Cluny*, to the *Pont St-Michel* and the *Ile de la Cité*, with the *Palais de Justice* and *Notre-Dame*. Then continue over the Seine to the *Hôtel de Ville*, and back along *Rue de Rivoli* to *Place de la Concorde*.

If you have a little more time you should walk along some of the main streets (in particular from Place de la Concorde to the Opéra or the Etoile), visit one of the parks, and watch from the terrace of a café the bustling activity of the street.

City tours are run by various travel agencies.

Sightseeing in Paris

The Tuileries and Champs-Elysées

Paris has a prestigious centre in the splendid **Place de la Concorde**, one of the world's largest and most beautiful squares. Lying on the magnificent long artery which extends from the Louvre to the Etoile, it offers a series of tremendous vistas – to the W the Arc de Triomphe de l'Etoile at the top of the Champs-Elysées; to the E the Tuileries Gardens, flanked by handsome buildings; to the N, at the end of Rue Royale, the Madeleine; and to the S, across the Seine, the Palais Bourbon. Between 1793 and 1795 the guillotine claimed 2800 victims in this square. It received its present layout in 1854 at the hands of an architect from Cologne named Hittorff.

In the middle of the square stands the granite *Obelisk of Luxor*, just under 23 m high, which originally came from the porch of a temple at Thebes erected by Ramesses II in the 13th c. B.C. in Upper Egypt (near the present town of Luxor) and which was presented to King Louis-Philippe by Pasha Mohammed Ali in 1831. On either side of the obelisk are two *fountains* designed by Hittorff. – Along the N side of the square are the *Ministère de la Marine* (Admiralty: on right), the *Automobile Club* and the *Hôtel de Crillon*. – On the S side of the square is the **Pont de la Concorde** over the Seine, built 1787–91 and reconstructed 1935–39, from which there are magnificent *views upstream to the square towers of Notre-Dame and downstream to the Eiffel Tower.

On the E side of the Place de la Concorde is a wide gateway, its pillars crowned by handsome winged horses with Mercury and Fama (by Coysevox) – the entrance to the *Jardin des Tuileries, once the pleasure garden of the French kings, mainly laid out in 1664, with numerous statues and two formal ponds. – To the left of the entrance, on the *Terrasse des Feuillants*, is the **Musée du Jeu de Paume** (in a building formerly used for an early form of tennis, the *jeu de paume*). The museum is a branch of the Louvre containing its collection of Impressionists (Van Gogh, Renoir, Cézanne, Gauguin, Degas, Monet, etc.). To the right of the

entrance to the Tuileries, on the *Terrasse du Bord de l'Eau*, is the *Orangerie*, which houses pictures (mainly Impressionists) from the collection of G. Walter, and two rooms with eight large paintings by Claude Monet, "Les Nymphéas" ("The Water-Lilies"). Temporary exhibitions are also held in the Orangerie.

In the eastern part of the Tuileries Gardens, beyond the Avenue du Général-Lemonnier, is an enclosed area of gardens between the wings of the New Louvre. This was the site of the Tuileries Palace, built in 1564 on land previously occupied by tile-works (*tuileries*), which was the residence of French kings and emperors until the time of Napoleon III but was destroyed in May 1871, during the Paris Commune. – In the centre of the gardens is the **Arc de Triomphe du Carrousel** (14·6 m high), once the main entrance to the courtyard of the Tuileries. A smaller version of the Arch of Severus in Rome, it was erected for Napoleon I in 1806–08 to commemorate his victories over Austria. On top of the arch is a quadriga or four-horse chariot by Bosio, set there in 1828 to symbolise the triumph of the Restoration; before 1815 the arch had been crowned by four ancient bronze horses removed from St Mark's in Venice. – Until the mid 19th c. the area to the E, extending from the *Place du Carrousel* over the *Square du Carrousel* to the Old Louvre, was filled with a maze of narrow streets and old houses.

The eastern end of the Tuileries Gardens is closed off by the **Louvre**, Paris's finest and most important public building, both for its architecture and for the valuable collections it contains (see under *Museums*, above).

The earliest structure on the site was a fortified castle built in the reign of Philippe Auguste (1180–1223), which Charles V (1364–80) extended and embellished. During the 15th c. the Louvre was neglected by the French kings and served as an arsenal and prison. In 1546 Francis I (1515–47) resolved to build a new palace here and commissioned Pierre Lescot, the finest architect of the early Renaissance period in France, to build it. Lescot was responsible in particular for the southern part of the *courtyard façade of the W wing, which, with sculpture by Jean Goujon and Paul Ponce, shows the full splendour of Renaissance architecture and ranks as the finest building of that period in France. Under later kings the building of the "Old Louvre" was continued by a number of different architects, including Claude Perrault, who between 1667 and 1674 completed most of the magnificent Colonnade on the E front. Meanwhile the building of the Tuileries Palace which adjoined the Louvre on the W had been proceeding since 1564. In the reign of

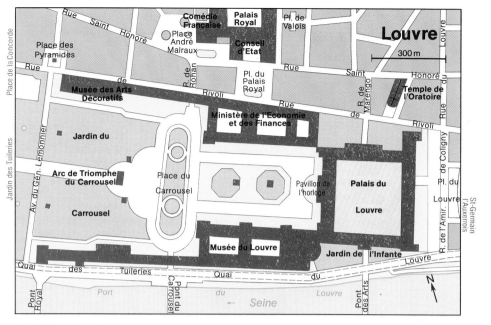

Louis XIV, who no longer lived in the Louvre after 1662 and was interested only in Versailles, the half completed buildings fell into disrepair. In 1793 a museum was opened in the Louvre, and from 1805 onwards a complete restoration was carried out on the orders of Napoleon. During his reign, too, and in that of Napoleon III two imposing wings crowned by domes and sumptuously decorated were built along the N and S sides of the gardens to link the Louvre and the Tuileries Palace.

The whole complex of buildings, which cover an area of some 198,000 sq. m including the courtyards – more than three times as much as the Vatican and St Peter's – thus falls into two main parts: the **Old Louvre**, whose four wings enclose the large E courtyard, and the **New Louvre**, consisting of two palaces on the N and S sides of the Square du Carrousel, with wings extending westward to the Tuileries pavilions at the end. The palace on the N side is now occupied by the *Ministry of Finance*. The *Pavillon de Marsan*, at the W end of the N wing, houses the **Musée des Arts Décoratifs** (see above under *Museums*), and the whole of the Old and New Louvre is also used, or due to be used, as a museum.

Along the N side of the Tuileries Gardens and the Louvre runs the * **Rue de Rivoli**, continuing E to the Hôtel de Ville. This is one of Paris's finest traffic arteries, built between 1811 and 1856, with a uniform façade along the whole of the western section (arcades on the ground floor, rows of balconies on the upper floors). – Along the S side of the Tuileries Gardens is the **Quai des Tuileries**, with three bridges across the Seine, all offering fine views of Paris – from W to E the *Pont de Solférino*, the *Pont Royal* (1685–89) and the *Pont du Carrousel* (1831–34).

Off the W side of the Place de la Concorde open the famous ** **Champs-Elysées**, a splendid avenue 1·9 km long laid out at the end of the 17th c. which carries a constant stream of traffic, particularly in the afternoon and evening. At the beginning of the eastern section, which runs through a park-like area 300–400 m wide to the Rond-Point des Champs-Elysées, are two figures of "Horse-Tamers" by Guillaume Coustou (brought here in 1795 from the Château de Marly).

In this first section, on the left, is the * **Petit Palais** or *Palais des Beaux-Arts de la Ville de Paris*, built for the International Exhibition of 1900, with an imposing main entrance topped by a dome and rich sculptural decoration; it now houses a valuable art collection (see above under *Museums*). Immediately W of the Petit Palais is the **Grand Palais**, a large exhibition hall built 1897–1900 which is used for temporary exhibitions. Built on to its W side, in the Avenue Franklin-D.-Roosevelt, is the *Palais de la Découverte* (see under *Museums*).

Between the Petit Palais and the Grand Palais the Avenue Alexandre-III runs S to the * *Pont Alexandre-III* (107·5 m long), built in 1896–1900 for the International Exhibition and richly decorated with allegorical sculpture, which offers fine views, particularly of the Invalides. – Opposite the Grand Palais on the N side of the Champs-Elysées is the attractive *Théâtre Marigny*, and beyond this, set in a large garden, is the *Palais de l'Elysée* (1718), residence of the President of the Republic.

Arc de Triomphe at night

The park-like south-eastern part of the Champs-Elysées ends at the **Rond-Point des Champs-Elysées**, a round-about forming the intersection with the *Avenue Franklin-D.-Roosevelt* and the *Avenues Montaigne* and *Matignon*. – The section of the Champs-Elysées beyond the Rond-Point is lined on both sides by hotels, restaurants (with tables set out in the open air), cinemas, banks, newspaper offices and luxury shops, including many car showrooms.

The Avenue des Champs-Elysées ends in the circular **Place Charles-de-Gaulle** (until 1970 **Place de l'Etoile**), com-mandingly situated on high ground at the centre of the "star" (*étoile*) formed by twelve radiating avenues. In the middle of the square stands the *****Arc de Triomphe de l'Etoile**, the largest triumphal arch in the world and one of France's great national monuments, 49 m high, 45 m wide and 22 m deep. Designed by Chalgrin (d. 1811), it was intended, like its smaller counterpart in the Place du Carrousel, to proclaim the glory of Napoleon's victories; but in fact this

massive structure – one of the finest achievements of the classical style of the Empire – was not completed until 1836, during the reign of Louis-Philippe.

The piers are decorated with colossal pieces of **sculpture**: on the E side, the *rising of the people in 1792, known as "The Marseillaise", by Rude (right), and Napoleon crowned with laurel at the Peace of Vienna in 1810, by Cortot (left); on the W side, the resistance of the French people in 1814 (right) and the blessings of peace in 1815 (left), both by Etex. The scenes carved above these and on the ends of the arch depict battles of the Republic and Empire. Under the cornice is a frieze depicting the departure and return of the army, and on the inner faces of the arch are inscribed the names of 172 battles and 386 generals (those who fell being underlined).

Under the arch is the **tomb of the Unknown Soldier**, a nameless French soldier of the First World War who fell at Verdun and whose remains were deposited here on 11 November 1920. An *eternal flame* burns at the head of the slab. – From the platform on top of the Arc de Triomphe (admission charge; lift; closed Tues.) there are magnificent **views. Under the platform is a small **museum** (history of the construction of the arch; mementoes of Napoleon and the First World War).

The most important of the avenues radiating from the Etoile are the *Avenue Friedland* to the NE and its continuation the Boulevard Haussmann (with the Jacquemart-André Museum: see above under *Museums*), which leads to the Place St-Augustin; the *Avenue Hoche*, which leads to the Parc Monceau; the *Avenue de Wagram*; the *Avenue de la Grande-Armée*, which runs NW to the *Porte Maillot*, with the **Centre International de Paris** (1973: *Palais des Congrès*; tower block of *Hôtel Concorde-La Fayette*, 120 m high), and continues as the *Avenue Charles-de-Gaulle* (formerly Avenue de Neuilly) to the *Pont de Neuilly* and the imposing new complex of tower blocks, *La Défense, with the CNIT (National Centre for Industry and Technology) Exhibition Hall; the *Avenue Foch* and *Avenue Victor-Hugo*, which run SE to the Bois de Boulogne; the *Avenue Kléber*, which runs down to the Place du Trocadéro and the Palais de Chaillot; and the *Avenue Marceau*, which runs SE to the Pont de l'Alma.

The Grands Boulevards

From the Place de la Concorde the wide *Rue Royale* runs N to the *Madeleine church, begun under the Empire (1806) as a Temple of Fame (designed by P. Vignon, following ancient models) but not completed until 1842 (by Huvé). This imposing building, surrounded by a Corinthian colonnade, is 108 m long, 43 m wide and over 30 m high. In the tympanum of the main façade is a sculptured Last Judgment by Lemaire, and there is much fine sculpture in the interior. On the high altar is a marble group by Marochetti representing the Magdalene being borne up to heaven by angels. In the apse is a mosaic of Jesus and other New Testament figures by Gilbert-Martin, and above this is a large fresco by J. Ziegler representing Christianity in the East and in the West (below, Napoleon I and Pius VII). The church is renowned for its music (particularly on Sunday at 11) and its organ.

The Madeleine is the starting point of the *Grands Boulevards, which run round the older part of the city for a distance of 4·3 km to the Place de la Bastille, with a width of 30 m. They date from the enlargement of the city in the reign of Louis XIV, when the old ramparts (*boulevards* = "bulwarks") were pulled down. The name was also applied to the "outer boulevards" which formed the city boundary until 1860, and to the "ring bou-

levards" which run along the line of the now demolished fortifications; and from 1852 onwards it was applied to numerous avenues which had no connection with the city's defences. – The Grands Boulevards, with numerous elegant shops, cinemas and cafés, rank along with the Champs-Elysées as the city's main traffic arteries, particularly busy in the late afternoon and brilliantly illuminated by neon lights after dark.

Going E from the Madeleine, the first section of the Grands Boulevards is the **Boulevard de la Madeleine**. Its continuation, the **Boulevard des Capucines** (at No. 25, on right, the *Cognacq-Jay Museum*: see above under *Museums*), runs into the *Place de l'Opéra, one of Paris's busiest traffic intersections. Immediately on the left is the Grand Hôtel, with one of the city's leading cafés, the famous Café de la Paix, now a scheduled national monument. On the N side of the square is the *Opéra (*Théâtre National de l'Opéra*), built 1862–74 to the design of Charles Garnier, the world's largest (11,237 sq. m) and most magnificent theatre, though in terms of the number of seats (2167) it falls short of other theatres like the Metropolitan Opera of New York (3800 seats), the Châtelet and the Milan La Scala (3600 seats each) or San Carlo in Naples (2900 seats).

In the *entrance hall*, with its profusion of statues, note particularly, to the left of the last arch on the right, "The Dance", by Carpeaux (original in the Louvre). – The interior can be seen only during performances. Beyond the vestibule with its statues is the splendid *Grand Staircase (*Escalier d'honneur*), one of Garnier's finest achievements. Notable also are the richly gilded *auditorium, with five tiers of boxes decorated in red and a ceiling painted by Marc Chagall in 1964, and the *Foyer du Public* (54 m long) with its adjoining *Loggia* (fine views). – In the Pavillon de l'Empereur in Rue Scribe are the **Musée de l'Opéra** (see above under *Museums*), with an interesting collection on theatrical history, and the well-stocked *library* of the Opéra.

In the eastern section of the Boulevard des Capucines, beyond Place de l'Opéra, and its continuation the **Boulevard des Italiens** are some of the most elegant shops in the whole of the Grands Boulevards. On the right-hand side of the Boulevard des Italiens, with its façade facing Place Boïeldieu, is the *Opéra-Comique* or Salle Favart, rebuilt after a fire in 1887, with 1500 seats. Originally devoted mainly to Italian and French lyrical and romantic operas, it is now also used for performances of experimental music and for the discovery and training of promising young performers (*Opéra-Studio*).

Beyond the intersection with the *Boulevard Haussmann*, which comes in on the left from the Place de l'Etoile, is the **Boulevard Montmartre**. – On the right of this boulevard is Rue Vivienne, which runs S to the *Place de la Bourse* (reached direct from the Place de l'Opéra by the busy Rue du Quatre-Septembre). In this square stands the **Bourse** (Exchange), an imitation of the Temple of Vespasian in Rome (by Brongniart and Lambarre, 1808–26), with a Corinthian colonnade.

The Boulevard Montmartre is continued by the **Boulevard Poissonnière** and the **Boulevard de Bonne-Nouvelle**, with more moderate traffic and more modest shops. At the far end of the Rue d'Hauteville, which leaves the Boulevard de Bonne-Nouvelle on the left, can be seen the church of St-Vincent-de-Paul. – The Boulevard de Bonne-Nouvelle ends at a major intersection with the *Rue du Faubourg-St-Denis* (left) and *Rue St-Denis* (right), one of the oldest streets in Paris and for long one of the most important. On the left stands the **Porte St-Denis** (by Blondel, 1673), a triumphal arch 25 m high, with allegorical figures and sculpture glorifying Louis XIV's victories in Holland.

The **Boulevard St-Denis**, which begins at the Porte St-Denis, cuts across another important traffic artery, formed by the *Boulevard de Sébastopol* (right) and *Boulevard de Strasbourg* (left). Along the Boulevard de Sébastopol can be seen the dome of the Tribunal de Commerce; at the far end of the Boulevard de Strasbourg is the Gare de l'Est. – The Boulevard St-Denis then ends at an intersection with *Rue St-Martin* (right) and *Rue du Faubourg-St-Martin* (left), with another triumphal arch glorifying Louis XIV, the **Porte St-Martin** (17·5 m high; by Bullet, 1674–75), which has allegorical reliefs commemorating the capture of Besançon and Limburg and French victories over German, Spanish and Dutch forces. – To the S, in Rue St-Martin, is the *Conservatoire National des Arts et Métiers*, a museum of technology (see above under *Museums*) housed in the former priory of St-Martin. In the beautiful refectory of the priory (now a library)

are modern paintings by Steinheil and Gérôme.

The **Boulevard St-Martin**, which begins at the Porte St-Denis, runs past three theatres – the *Renaissance, Porte St-Martin* and *Ambigu* – and ends in the spacious **Place de la République**, laid out in 1880, the meeting place of numerous streets. In the middle of the square, on a stone base 15·5 m high, is the *Monument de la République* (1883), which stands 9·5 m high to the tip of the olive branch in the figure's right hand; in front are a bronze lion and urn symbolising universal suffrage.

From Place de la République the *Boulevard du Temple, Boulevard des Filles-du-Calvaire* and *Boulevard Beaumarchais* continue to the Place de la Bastille, offering little of interest to the tourist.

From the Opéra to the Bastille

From the Place de l'Opéra there are two routes to the Place du Théâtre-Français – either direct by the imposing *Avenue de l'Opéra*, laid out between 1854 and 1879, with its elegant shops, or by going SW down the wide *Rue de la Paix*, one of the more distinguished of the older streets, with famous fashion houses, jewellers, parfumiers and other luxury shops, and then turning SE from the Place Vendôme along Rue St-Honoré.

The ***Place Vendôme**, one of the world's finest squares, was designed in severely classical style by Jules Hardouin-Mansart (1708). In the centre stands the **Vendôme Column** (43 m high), an imitation (by Gondouin and Lepère) of Trajan's Column in Rome, with sculptured scenes running spirally round it. Cast from the metal of 1200 Austrian and Russian cannon, it depicts the war with Austria and Russia in 1805, and is topped by a statue of Napoleon in the garb of a Roman emperor. At No. 12 in the square, with a commemorative inscription, is the house in which Chopin (1810–49) died.

On the left-hand·side of Rue St-Honoré is the church of **St-Roch** (by Jacques Lemercier, built 1653–1740), the finest Baroque church in Paris. In the beautiful interior are numerous tombs, many of them from other churches now destroyed, and some fine sculpture, including a marble *Nativity by Michel Anguier. The fourth chapel on the left commemorates Frenchmen deported to Germany during the Second World War. The church is noted for its fine music (Sundays at 10).

At the S end of Rue St-Honoré is the *Place du Théâtre-Français*, with two fountains. On the E side of the square is the **Théâtre Français** (*Comédie Française*, with seating for 1500: classical plays and comedies), built 1787–90 and completely renovated after a fire in 1900; in the foyer is a seated *figure of Voltaire by Houdon (1781), a masterpiece of realistic portraiture.

The N and E sides of the Théâtre Français adjoin the **Palais Royal**, long a royal residence, from which an armed mob set off for the Bastille on 14 July 1789. All that remains of the original Palais Cardinal built for Richelieu by L. Lemercier (1624–39) is the Galerie des Proues (Gallery of Prows) on the E side of the courtyard, named after its nautical decoration. The other parts of the building were erected or altered in the 19th c. The Palais Royal is now occupied by the *Conseil d'Etat*, the supreme administrative court, and the *Directorate of Fine Arts*. – N of the Palais Royal is the attractive *Jardin du Palais Royal*, surrounded by colonnades (by Victor Louis, 1781–86).

N of the Palais Royal, on the site of a palace acquired by Cardinal Mazarin in 1649, is the ***Bibliothèque Nationale** (National Library), with one of the world's richest collections of books. Most of the building dates from the 19th c.; the entrance is on the W side. Since several copies of every book published in France must be deposited in the library, its stock is constantly increasing. On the first floor is the Galerie Mazarine, a relic of Mazarin's palace, with fine ceiling paintings by Romanelli (1654). Here too is the *Cabinet des Médailles et Antiques* (not at present open), with a rich collection of medals, cameos, jewellery, small objets d'art and other precious items.

A little way E of the Bibliothèque Nationale is the famous pilgrimage church of *Notre-Dame-des-Victoires* (1629–1740). To the S of the church is the **Banque de France**, the French national bank, founded in 1800. – From the N end of the Bank it is a short distance E to the circular *Place des Victoires*, with an equestrian statue of *Louis XIV* erected in

1822, and beyond this to the massive **Head Post Office** (*Hôtel des Postes*, built 1880–84), the entrance to which is on the W side.

SE of the Head Post Office is **St-Eustache**, one of Paris's largest churches, noted for its music. Begun in 1532 but not completed until 1637, it has a wholly Gothic plan but Renaissance forms. The W front (1754–88) is a masterpiece of French Baroque, still reflecting classical traditions. The "Festival of Reason" was celebrated here in 1793, and from 1795 to 1803 the church was a "Temple of Agriculture". Notable features of the spacious interior (88 m long, 34 m high) are a *statue of the Virgin by Pigalle in the Lady Chapel (built 1640) behind the high altar and the tomb of the great 17th c. statesman Colbert in the chapel to the left. Above the main entrance is a world-famed Ducroquet organ, several times restored.

Immediately S of St-Eustache is the site of the famous **Halles**, the old central market for fruit and vegetables, meat and flowers, built 1854–59 (one of the earliest and largest iron structures of its kind) and pulled down in 1971, after the transfer of the market to Rungis. The site has been redeveloped to provide a huge underground car park and a new shopping and leisure centre, the "Forum des Halles", opened in September 1979. – To the W of the site is the circular **Bourse du Commerce** (Commercial Exchange), built in 1889. – To the SE, in the *Square des Innocents*, is a Renaissance fountain by P. Lescot, the *Fontaine des Innocents* (1549).

Between the Palais Royal and the Ministry of Finance (part of the Louvre complex), on Rue de Rivoli, is the *Place du Palais Royal*. – A little way SE, opposite the E front of the Old Louvre, is the fine Gothic church of ***St-Germain-l'Auxerrois** (13th–16th c.), with a late Gothic façade, a porch with sculptured figures (1435–39) and a notable interior (16th c. Flemish altar and triptych in N aisle: light can be switched on).

To the S of St-Germain-l'Auxerrois, along the river, is the *Quai du Louvre*. From the two bridges which span the river here – the *Pont des Arts* (pedestrians only) and the *Pont Neuf* (1578–1603), which in spite of its name is the oldest bridge in

Paris

250 m

St-Germain
LA DÉFENSE
Porte Maillot

Bois de Boulogne

Porte St-Cloud

Versailles

Musée Nissim
de Camondo

Conservatoire
de Musique

Pl. des
Ternes

Salle Wagram

Salle Pleyel

Musée
Jacquemart
André

St-Augustin

Pl.
St-Augustin

Gare
St-Laza

Av. des Ternes

Av. de la Gr. Armée

Place
Arc de Triomphe
de l'Etoile
Charles-de-Gaulle

Av. Foch

Friedland

Saint Honoré

Boulevard

Haussmann

St-Philippe-d.-R.
Salle Gaveau

Min. de l'Intérieur

Av. V. Hugo

Centre de
Conférences
Internationales

des
Champs-

Rue de Ponthieu

Palais de
l'Elysée

Théâtre
Marigny

British
Embassy

U.S.
Embassy

Ste-Madelei

Lauriston

Kléber

Rond-Point des
Champs-Elysées

Pal. de
la Glace

R. Royale

Min. de
Justice

Musée Guimet

Hôtel
Galliéra

Place
d'Iéna

Palais
d'Art Moderne

Théâtre des
Champs-
Elysées

Grand
Palais

Petit
Palais

Cours la Reine

Place
de la
Concorde

Orangerie

Musée
l'Impre

Jar

Place du
Trocadéro

York

Seine

Pl. de la
Résistance

Quai

Quai des

Palais
de
Chaillot

New

Min.
Commerce
Extérieur

Rue de l'Université

d'Orsay

Min. d. Aff.
Etrangères

Gare des
Invalides
Air Terminal

Palais
Bourbon

Pont
d'Iéna

Tour Eiffel

Saint

Dominique

Min. de la
Défense

Gare
du Qua
d'Orsay

Champ

Grenelle

Pl. des
Invalides

Institut
Géogr.

Ste-Clotilde

de

Mars

Hôtel des
Invalides

Min. du
Commerce

Ministère de
l'Equipeme

Palais
des Sports

Suffren

Ecole

Avenue de Tourville

Musée Rodin

Varenne

St-Léon

Militaire

Unesco

St-François-
Xavier

Rue

Babylone

Sèvres

Grenelle

Place de
Breteuil

Sécretariat
d'Outre-Mer

Avenue Emile Zola

Boulevard Garibaldi

Rue des Entrepreneurs

MONTPARNASSE

Rue de l'Eglise

Tour Maine
Montparnasse

Chartres

Gare Montparnasse

Paris – there are attractive views of the centre of the city. From here to the Pont Louis-Philippe, and on the opposite bank of the river, the stalls of the *bouquinistes* (secondhand booksellers) line the quays.

– The *Quai de la Mégisserie* continues the line of the Quai du Louvre eastward to the busy **Place du Châtelet**, on the N side of which the Boulevard de Sébastopol comes in. In the centre of the square is

the *Fontaine de la Victoire*, erected by Napoleon in 1808 to commemorate the success of his Egyptian expedition. On the W side of the square is the large *Théâtre du Châtelet* (3600 seats), on the E side the *Théâtre de la Ville* (formerly Théâtre Sarah-Bernhardt; 1700 seats). – From the S side the *Pont au Change* crosses the northern arm of the Seine to the Ile de la Cité.

In a public garden NE of the Place du Châtelet, fronting Rue de Rivoli, is the **Tour St-Jacques** (58 m high), a handsome late Gothic tower which belonged to the pilgrimage church of St-Jacques-la-Boucherie, built 1508–22 on the site of an earlier Carolingian church and pulled down in 1797. It is now a meteorological station and is not open to the public. – A short distance NE is the late Gothic church of *St-Merry*, built 1515–55, with a 15th c. crypt and good stained glass. – To the N of the church, on the *Plateau Beaubourg*, is the *****Centre National d'Art et de Culture Georges Pompidou** or *Centre Beaubourg*, opened in 1977, a futuristic building 166 m long, 60 m across and 42 m high. The Centre, designed to promote communication, houses the ****National Museum of Modern Art*, exhibition areas, a library and many other facilities. See above under *Museums*. To the S of the Centre, underground, is the *Institut de Recherche et de Coordination Acoustique/Musique (IRCAM)*.

rebuilt during the 16th c. in late Gothic style with some Renaissance features. The W front, added in 1616–21, was the earliest in France to combine the three classical orders – Doric, Ionic and Corinthian. – Nearby, on the Quai de l'Hôtel de Ville, is the *Cité International des Arts*, a cultural centre.

To the NE of the Hôtel de Ville extends the MARAIS QUARTER, which was until the 18th c. a select and fashionable part of the town and still preserves many handsome aristocratic mansions (*hôtels*), particularly in *Rue des Archives*. – In the middle section of Rue des Archives, with its main front on Rue des Francs-Bourgeois, is the former *Hôtel de Soubise* (mainly 1704–12), which since 1808 has housed the **Archives Nationales**. The Archives contain several million documents, the most interesting of which are in the *Musée de l'Histoire de France* (see above under *Museums*).

In *Rue des Francs-Bourgeois* (entrance at 23 rue de Sévigné) is the *****Carnavalet**

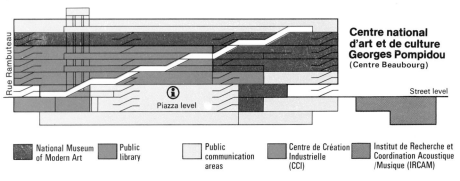

Centre national d'art et de culture Georges Pompidou
(Centre Beaubourg)

Street level

Piazza level

Rue Rambuteau

| National Museum of Modern Art | Public library | Public communication areas | Centre de Création Industrielle (CCI) | Institut de Recherche et Coordination Acoustique /Musique (IRCAM) |

From the Place du Châtelet the *Quai de Gesvres* (many shops selling caged birds) runs E, past the *Pont Notre-Dame*, to the *Place de l'Hôtel de Ville*, from the S side of which the *Pont d'Arcole* crosses to the Ile de la Cité. In this square, formerly the much smaller Place de Grève, public executions were carried out from 1310 to 1832. The square also played an important part during the French Revolution. On the E side stands the **Hôtel de Ville** (Town Hall), built 1874–82 by Ballu and Deperthes to replace an earlier building of 1533 which was destroyed during the Paris Commune in 1871. It is a handsome and imposing building in French Renaissance style, with some 200 statues and groups.

Behind the Hôtel de Ville, at the far side of a small square, is the church of **St-Gervais-St-Protais**, built in 1212 and

Museum (see under *Museums*), in a Renaissance mansion built in 1544. – From here Rue de Sévigné runs S to the former Jesuit church of **St-Paul-St-Louis** (1627–41), with a fine Baroque doorway and an impressive interior. – At the E end of Rue des Francs-Bourgeois is the *****Place des Vosges** (formerly Place Royale), once the heart of the aristocratic part of the city. The square, laid out in 1607–12, has preserved its old-world character, and offers a characteristic example of French classical architecture. In the centre of the square is an *equestrian statue of Louis XIII*, erected 1816–19. At No. 6, in which Victor Hugo lived from 1832 to 1848, is the *Victor Hugo Museum* (see under *Museums*), with mementoes of the writer.

A short distance SE of the Place des Vosges, at the end of the Grands Boulevards, is the **Place de la Bastille** (usually referred to merely as *"la Bastille"*), at the intersection of numerous streets. This was the site of the old *Bastille St-Antoine*, built 1370–83, which was left standing when the old fortifications of Paris were pulled down, and thereafter served as a prison for persons arbitrarily detained by royal authority, and earned its place in history when it was destroyed at the beginning of the French Revolution. The Place de la Bastille also played a part in the revolutions of 1830 and 1848 and in the Commune of 1871. In the centre of the square stands the **July Column** (*Colonne de Juillet*), 47 m high, which was erected in 1831–40 to commemorate those who had fought on the barricades during the July Revolution. In the circular substructure is a vault with two colossal sarcophagi containing the remains of those who died in 1830 and 1848; from the platform on top of the column (238 steps) there are wide views. – In the *Boulevard Richard-Lenoir*, which runs NE from the Place de la Bastille, the famous Foire à la Ferraille (Scrap Iron Fair), at which the most extraordinary things are sometimes offered for sale, is held during Holy Week and in October. The Foire aux Jambons (Ham Fair) is also held there in October.

From the Place de la Bastille the Rue de Lyon runs S, past the *Gare de la Bastille* (Gare de Vincennes) to the **Gare de Lyon**, with a tower 64 m high.

The Islands

From Place du Châtelet the Pont au Change leads on to the **ILE DE LA CITÉ**, the oldest part of Paris. – Immediately beyond the bridge, on the right, is the massive bulk of the **Palais de Justice** (Law Courts: the public are freely admitted; closed Sat. and Sun.), in the *Boulevard du Palais*. It occupies the site of an old royal stronghold, of which, following fires in 1618 and 1776, nothing is left but the Sainte Chapelle, four towers and parts of the foundations. At the NE corner, near the Pont au Change, is the 14th c. *Tour de l'Horloge*, with a clock which has been repaired or restored on many occasions down the centuries; along the N front on the Quai de l'Horloge are the *Tour de César*, the *Tour d'Argent* and the battlemented *Tour St-Louis* or *Tour Bon-Bec*, all three dating from the reign of Philippe le Bel (1285–1314). Most of the Palais de Justice dates from the end of the 18th c.

INTERIOR of the Palais de Justice. – From the Boulevard du Palais we pass through a wrought-iron grille (1785) into the forecourt, the *Cour du Mai*. A flight of steps leads up into the *Galerie Marchande*, from which we turn right to enter the *Salle des Pas Perdus*, the lobby of the civil courts of first instance, where barristers meet their clients when the court is not sitting. This was built in 1871 in place of the Great Hall of the old royal palace, and is 73 m long, 28 m wide and 10 m high. The courts, which sit from noon, are entered from the lobby.

From the Cour du Mai a passage on the left, the Galerie de la Sainte Chapelle, leads into the *Cour de la Sainte Chapelle*, in which is the **Sainte Chapelle**, one of the most exquisite achievements of Gothic architecture. It is in fact two chapels, one over the other, and was built as the palace chapel in 1246–48, during the reign of Louis IX (St Louis), to house the Crown of Thorns and other relics brought to France in 1239 (now in Notre-Dame); the architect was probably Pierre de Montereau. It was profaned in 1791, during the Revolution, and is no longer used for worship. Open 10–11.45 and 1.30–4.45 or 5.45, closed Tues.; admission charge. Visitors first enter the lower chapel, which was meant only for servants, and go up a spiral staircase to reach the upper chapel, which was reserved for the court. The wall surfaces of the chapel, which is 20 m high, are almost entirely taken up by windows (15 m high, 4 m wide), with vividly coloured *stained glass, some of it dating from the time of St Louis, set in graceful tracery. The late Gothic rose window, with scenes from the Apocalypse, dates from the reign of Charles VIII (1493–98).

On the Quai de l'Horloge is the entrance to the *Conciergerie, with sinister associations from its use as a prison during the French Revolution (conducted tours, admission charge; closed on Tues. in winter). Among features shown to visitors are the *Salle des Gens-d'Armes*, a magnificent Gothic hall with massive piers supporting the roof, above which is the Salle des Pas Perdus; the *Cuisines de St Louis*, a square kitchen with four large Gothic fireplaces; the prisons of Marie-Antoinette (executed 1793) and Robespierre (executed 1794); and the Salle de Girondins, formerly a chapel, which now houses the Musée de la Conciergerie.

Opposite the Palais de Justice, at the end of the Pont au Change, is the Renaissance-style **Tribunal de Commerce** (1860–66), with a dome 42 m high which is a prominent landmark. – Behind it is the *Marché aux Fleurs*, a small square in which the Paris flower-market is held on weekdays and a bird market on Sundays. On the S side of the square is the **Préfecture de Police**, the police headquarters, with a Police Museum. On the E side of the square is the *Hôtel-Dieu*, one of the oldest hospitals in Europe, originally founded as a convent for women about 660; the present buildings date from 1868–78.

The S side of the Hôtel-Dieu faces on to the *Place du Parvis-Notre-Dame* (on which important archaeological finds were made during the construction of an

The Seine and Notre-Dame

underground car park from 1960 onwards). On the E side of the square, which was much smaller before the building of the present Hôtel-Dieu, stands **Notre-Dame**, the cathedral of the Archbishop of Paris, founded in 1163 on a site which had been occupied by two earlier churches. The choir and transepts were completed by 1177, but the rest of the building, including the chapel, was not finished until the 14th c. During the French Revolution the church was severely damaged, and in 1793–94 it served as a "Temple of Reason". The finest part of the cathedral is the *W front, the oldest of its kind and the model for many other W fronts in northern France. The sculpture on the doorways was destroyed during the Revolution, but was later restored on the basis of surviving fragments or on the model of other French cathedrals. The central doorway depicts the Last Judgment, with Christ in Majesty in the tympanum; the angel on the left holding the nails is a masterpiece of 13th c. sculpture. The S doorway is dedicated to St Anne, the N doorway (c. 1210–20) to the Virgin. Above the doorways is a long row of niches containing 28 statues of the kings of Judah; and above this again is a large rose window 9·6 m in diameter. The façade is crowned by two towers 69 m high (never completed to their full height). The N tower can be climbed (376 steps; closed Tues.) to get a *view which is one of the finest in Paris, on account particularly of the vista of the Seine and its bridges. In the S tower is the "Bourdon de Paris", a bell weighing 15,000 kg which was cast in 1686. In the S transept is the Porte St-Etienne, with numerous statues; in the N transept is the Porte du Cloître, with a beautiful figure of the Virgin (latter part of 13th c.). Particularly impressive is the view of the choir, with its graceful gable windows and bold flying buttresses.

The *INTERIOR of Notre-Dame (130 m long, 48 m across, 35 m high), with its 75 round piers, is extraordinarily impressive (effective indirect lighting; open 8 a.m. to 7 p.m.; High Mass daily at 10; organ recital Sun. 5.45–6.30). Of the numerous *stained glass windows* only the great *rose window in the N transept, with 80 Old Testament scenes (c. 1270), and the windows in the S transept (1257) are old. On the right-hand pier at the entrance to the choir is *Notre-Dame de Paris, a much revered 14th c. figure of the Virgin. On the choir screen are 23 carved *scenes from the life of Christ*, painted and in some cases gilded (1319–51, by Jehan Ravy and his nephew Jehan le Bouteiller). The most notable of the *chapels* around the choir is the second on the left of the entrance to the sacristy, with the *tomb of the Comte d'Harcourt (d. 1718), by Pigalle. The Cavaillé-Coll organ, with 8500 pipes, is the largest in France.

In the **Sacristy** (closed Sun.), built on to Notre-Dame in 1845–50 on the site of the old Archbishop's Palace (demolished 1831), is the Cathedral *treasury*, with (among much else) the reliquaries containing the "great relics" from the Sainte Chapelle (the Crown of Thorns, a piece of the True Cross and a nail from the Cross).

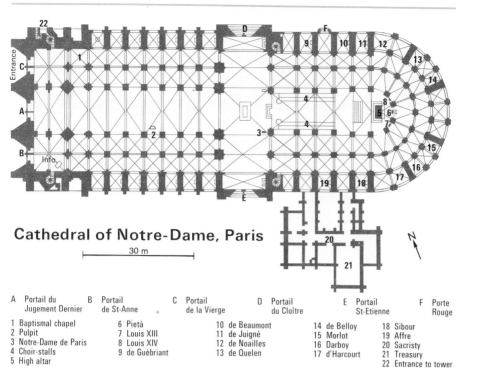

Cathedral of Notre-Dame, Paris

30 m

A	Portail du Jugement Dernier	B	Portail de St-Anne	C	Portail de la Vierge	D	Portail du Cloître	E	Portail St-Etienne	F	Porte Rouge

1 Baptismal chapel	6 Pietà	10 de Beaumont	14 de Belloy	18 Sibour
2 Pulpit	7 Louis XIII	11 de Juigné	15 Morlot	19 Affre
3 Notre-Dame de Paris	8 Louis XIV	12 de Noailles	16 Darboy	20 Sacristy
4 Choir-stalls	9 de Guébriant	13 de Quelen	17 d'Harcourt	21 Treasury
5 High altar				22 Entrance to tower

At the SE tip of the Ile de la Cité is the *Mémorial de la Déportation* (1962), an impressive monument (with crypt) commemorating the 200,000 Frenchmen who died in German concentration camps during the Second World War. – A short distance N of this is the *Pont St-Louis* (rebuilt 1969–70: pedestrians only; cars must go round by the Pont Marie), which leads on to the **ILE ST-LOUIS**, formed between 1614 and 1630 from two smaller islands. On the island are fine old mansions which have preserved the uniform character of 17th c. architecture.

In *Rue St-Louis-en-l'Ile*, the island's narrow main street, is the *church of St-Louis-en-l'Ile* (1664–1726), with a richly decorated interior. – A walk round the island on the quays offers attractive views of the river and central Paris.

The Northern districts

From the Madeleine the busy *Boulevard Malesherbes* runs NW to *Place St-Augustin*, where it intersects with the Boulevard Haussmann and other important streets. On the N side of the square is the church of **St-Augustin** with its mighty dome (1860–71), the finest achievement of the architect Victor Baltard, who made bold use of cast-iron in his imitation of early Renaissance forms. –

From here the lively *Rue de la Pépinière* runs E to the *Gare St-Lazare*, built 1886–89 (trains to W and NW France), from which *Rue St-Lazare* continues to the **Trinité church** (1861–67, by Ballu), in late Renaissance style (interior richly decorated with paintings; noted for its organ and choir). – Still farther E, in *Rue de Châteaudun*, is the church of *Notre-Dame-de-Lorette* (1823–36, by Hippolyte Lebas), in the form of an early Christian basilica, with a high Corinthian portico and a beautiful interior.

N of here, on the Butte Montmartre which extends from the outer boulevards to the city boundary, is the district of MONT-MARTRE, more famous in the past than in the present as the haunt of artists and the home of the *vie de bohème* but still the centre of Paris's night life. At the foot of the hill, to the SW, traversed by the *Boulevard de Clichy*, is **Place Pigalle**, in and around which are numerous night-spots; and a short distance W, in Place Blanche, is the famous *Moulin Rouge*.

From the *Boulevard de Rochechouart*, the eastward continuation of the Boulevard de Clichy, Rue de Steinkerque runs N to *Place St-Pierre*. From here flights of steps, steep paths and a funicular continue N up to *Montmartre (the Butte Mont-martre), a hill (127 m) rising to 101 m

Sacré-Cœur

W of the Sacré-Cœur is the old church of *St-Pierre-de-Montmartre, one of the earliest Gothic churches, built under the influence of St-Denis. It originally belonged to a Benedictine convent founded in 1147 and dissolved during the Revolution. By the 19th c. it had fallen into disrepair, but between 1900 and 1905 it was restored. The groined vaulting in the choir is the oldest in Paris.

In the surrounding area there are many old streets and squares, including the picturesque **Place du Tertre**; but the original character of this quarter has been destroyed by the development of the tourist industry with its "*auberges*", cabarets, etc., and by the extensive new building which is steadily displacing the old houses and spreading westward beyond the famous old dance-hall, the *Moulin de la Galette*, with its two old windmills.

Artists in the Place du Tertre

above the Seine which commands a view of the whole of Paris. On the summit is the huge church of the **Sacré-Cœur**, in Romanesque-Byzantine style, with a dome 83 m high. A prominent landmark visible from a long way off, it is most striking when seen from a distance. It was built in fulfilment of a vow taken by a group of Catholics after the Franco-Prussian War of 1870–71. Building began in 1875 and was completed in 1914, and the church was consecrated in 1919; the architect was Paul Abadie (d. 1884). Behind the apse is a bell-tower 84 m high erected in 1905–10, containing the "Savoyarde", a bell 3 m high weighing 18,835 kg. From the terrace in front of the church there are magnificent **views of Paris, and there are even wider views from the dome (entrance near the N doorway; 350 steps; admission charge).

The INTERIOR is notable for its imposing spatial effect, and has many beautiful *stained glass windows*. In the choir vaulting is a large *mosaic* (by L. O. Merson, 1923) depicting the glorification of the Sacred Heart (*Sacré-Cœur*). On the marble high altar is a monstrance in which the sacrament is permanently displayed. – A spacious *crypt* (admission charge) extends under the whole church.

In the western part of Montmartre, a little way N of the Boulevard de Clichy, is the **Montmartre Cemetery** (*Cimetière de Montmartre* or *Cimetière du Nord*), which has fewer monuments and famous names than the cemetery of Père-Lachaise but is well worth a visit. Among notable people buried here are the German poet Heinrich Heine (1797–1856) in the Avenue de la Cloche (W side), the composer Hector Berlioz (1803–69) in the Avenue des Carrières (E side) and the composer Jacques Offenbach (1819–80) in the Avenue des Anglais (W side), both the latter being near the northern tip of the cemetery.

1 km N of Montmartre is the **Porte de Clignancourt**, where the famous *Marché aux Puces* ("Flea-Market", origi-

nally so called because of the vermin sometimes to be found in the second-hand goods offered for sale) is held from Saturday to Monday. There are in fact five separate markets (the best known being the Marché Biron, the most picturesque the Marché Vernaison in the southern part of the area), with rows of stalls selling the most extraordinary range of objects.

The busy *Boulevard de Magenta*, which runs SE from the E end of the Boulevard de Rochechouart to Place de la République, passes the two most important railway stations in Paris. Near the N end of the boulevard is the **Gare du Nord** (trains to Belgium, Germany and the Channel Ports), built in 1864 by the Cologne architect J. I. Hittorff. Farther SE is the **Gare de l'Est** or *Gare de Strasbourg* (trains to Luxembourg, Frankfurt, Strasbourg, Basle, etc.), which was considerably enlarged in 1928–30.

A little way SW of the Gare du Nord is the church of *St-Vincent-de-Paul (1824–44: begun by Lepère, completed by Hittorff), in the style of a Latin basilica with a porch. In the tympanum is a fine sculptured group of St Vincent de Paul (1576–1660), "father of the poor", between Faith and Charity. The interior, with 86 pillars, contains noble wall paintings by Hippolyte Flandrin (1850–54), painted on a gold ground in the manner of the Ravenna mosaics, which can be appreciated only in full sunlight.

S of the Gare de l'Est, near the N end of the Boulevard de Strasbourg, is the handsome church of **St-Laurent**, one of the oldest in Paris, completely rebuilt 1862–66. – 1 km SE of the church, at the end of the Boulevard de Magenta, is the Place de la République.

The Eiffel Tower and Invalides

In the western part of the large area of Paris which lies on the left bank of the Seine, between the Ecole Militaire and the river, is the **Champ de Mars** ("Field of Mars"), originally a military parade ground, later the scene of great national celebrations and international exhibitions. Near the Seine is the ****Eiffel Tower** (*Tour Eiffel*), Paris's best known landmark, erected 1887–89 for the International Exhibition of 1889 by the engineer Gustave Eiffel (1832–1923). When it was built it was the highest man-

Eiffel Tower

made structure in the world (300 m); with the television aerial which was added in 1957 it is now 317·93 m high.

The tower is 129·22 m square at the base. The first platform (58 m from the ground: restaurant) is 65 m square; the second (café) is 116 m from the ground; the third 276 m from the ground, with a glassed-in gallery 16·5 m square which can accommodate 800 people. From the third platform a stair leads up to the lantern (24 m high), in which is a circular balcony 5·75 m in diameter. The searchlight above this has a range of 70 km. – The first and second platforms can be reached either by lift or by stairs (350 and 730 steps respectively); the third platform can be reached only by lift. The*view from the top platform extends for up to 90 km in clear weather (which is rare); the best time is an hour before sunset. When illuminated after dark (on summer evenings and on Saturdays, Sundays and public holidays throughout the year) the Eiffel Tower is a breathtaking sight.

From the Eiffel Tower the *Pont d'Iéna* (built 1806–13 to commemorate Napoleon's victory over the Prussian army at Jena in 1806; widened 1935–36) leads over the Seine to the **Palais de Chaillot**, beautifully situated above terraced gardens, built in 1937 on the site of the old Trocadéro, an exotic building erected for the International Exhibition of 1878. The two semicircular wings house five important museums (see above, *Museums*) – in the W wing the *Musée de la Marine* and the *Musée de l'Homme*, in the E wing the *Musée des Monuments Français*, the *Musée des Arts et Traditions Populaires* and the *Musée du Cinéma*. The terrace between the two wings, from which there are fine views of Paris, forms the roof of a large *theatre* (entrance in E wing; 3000 seats). – In the middle of the *Jardins du Trocadéro*, which descend in terraces to the Seine, is a large ornamental pond, and in a grotto in the eastern part of the gardens is an *aquarium* (admission charge), with a rich collection of French fresh-water fish.

On the N side of the Palais de Chaillot, at the intersection of several streets, is the **Place du Trocadéro**. From here the wide *Avenue Kléber* runs NE to the Arc de Triomphe de l'Etoile, and the *Avenue du Président-Wilson* runs E to the **Place d'Iéna**, near which are several museums (*Musée Guimet, Musée Galliéra, Musée d'Art Moderne de la Ville de Paris*). – Below the Palais de Chaillot, along the Seine, is the *Avenue de New-York*, continued to the SW by the *Avenue du Président-Kennedy*, in which is the **Maison de Radio-France** (1963, by H. Bernard), a massive circular structure with a central tower block 70 m high (conducted tours 10–12 and 2–5 except Mon.).

On the S side of the Champ de Mars is the imposing bulk of the **Ecole Militaire**, built 1752–74 to the design of J.-A. Gabriel to house the newly established Military (Cadet) Academy. In 1792 it became a barracks. Two wings were added in 1854–59, and in 1880 it became the Ecole Supérieure de Guerre, for the training of staff officers. – Behind it, in *Place de Fontenoy*, are the headquarters of *UNESCO, a Y-shaped building designed by B. Zehrfuss (French), P. L. Nervi (Italian) and M. Breuer (American) which was opened in 1958. It has a richly decorated interior, with work by contemporary artists, including Picasso (conducted tours by prior arrangement). – On the NE side of Place de Fontenoy are the *Ministère de la Marine Marchande* (Ministry of Shipping) and *Ministère du Travail* (Ministry of Labour).

NE of the Ecole Militaire is the **Hôtel des Invalides** (1671, by Libéral Bruant), built on the orders of Louis XIV to house old soldiers. It originally had accommodation for 7000 ex-soldiers, but is now occupied only by a small number of war-disabled, mostly employed as museum attendants; the rest of the building is used as government offices. – In a garden outside the N front (210 m long) are the *Batterie triomphale* of 18 guns, 20 bronze barrels from cannon captured in the 17th and 18th c. and two Second World War Panther tanks. – On the left-hand side of the Grand Courtyard (*Cour d'Honneur*: "Son et Lumière" in summer) of the Hôtel

des Invalides is the entrance to the *Army Museum** (see under *Museums*), which occupies the wings on both sides of the courtyard. – On the S side of the courtyard is the church of **St-Louis-des-Invalides**, also by Bruant, built at the same time as the main building. In the nave are two rows of flags captured in the wars of the 19th c. To the right of the choir is the Chapelle Napoléon, with mementoes of the Emperor's death and the transfer of his remains to Paris; famous organ recitals.

Adjoining the church on the S (entered from the SE corner of the Grand Courtyard by the Corridor de Metz) is the *Dôme des Invalides**, an imposing structure built 1675–1706 by Jules Hardouin-Mansart as a fitting termination to the Hôtel des Invalides and as an "Eglise Royale" in which the king could attend divine service in a setting of appropriate magnificence. The elegant gilded *dome* stands 97 m high (107 m including the cross).

In the INTERIOR of the Dôme des Invalides (closed Tues.; admission charge) is the *crypt containing **Napoleon's tomb**, designed by Visconti (23 m in diameter, 6 m deep; unroofed). Also in the crypt is the lead sarcophagus of *Napoleon II* (1811–32), the "Roi de Rome", Napoleon's only legitimate son. In the two smaller chambers which open off the central rotunda are the tombs of Marshal *Turenne* (1611–75), who commanded French troops during the Thirty Years War and later in Alsace, and the famous military engineer *Vauban* (1633–1707). In the four corner chapels, reached through narrow openings, are the tombs of Napoleon's eldest brother *Joseph Bonaparte* (1768–1844), who became king of Naples and later of Spain; his younger brother *Jérôme Bonaparte* (1784–1860), king of Westphalia, along with the heart of his wife, Princess Katharina of Württemberg (d. 1835); Marshal *Foch* (1851–1929); and Marshal *Lyautey* (1854–1934).

From the Invalides to the Luxembourg and Montparnasse

Immediately E of the Invalides is the very interesting *Rodin Museum* (see under *Museums*). – $\frac{1}{2}$ km NE is the large neo-Gothic church of **Ste-Clotilde** (1846–56, by Gau and Ballu).

To the N of the Hôtel des Invalides is the spacious *Esplanade des Invalides*, leading to the Pont Alexandre-III. Just before the bridge, on the right, are the *Aérogare des Invalides*, the air terminal for Orly Airport, and the *Gare des Invalides* (trains to Versailles, etc.). – From here the **Quai d'Orsay** runs along the Seine to the right.

Immediately on the right is the imposing building erected in 1845–53 to house the *Ministère des Affaires Etrangères*, the French Foreign Office. Immediately E is the residence of the President of the National Assembly. Beyond this, opposite the Pont de la Concorde, is the **Palais Bourbon**, named after the Duchesse de Bourbon for whom the original palace was built in 1722. Since 1795 this has been the seat of the National Assembly, the second chamber of the French Parliament. Particularly notable are the five *ceiling paintings by Eugène Delacroix (1838–47) in the Library (seen only on written application to the Prefecture). – ½ km farther E, at the Pont de Solférino, is a palace built in 1782–86 for Prince von Salm-Kyrburg, which since 1804 has been the headquarters of the Légion d'Honneur (*Palais de la Légion d'Honneur*). Adjoining this is the former *Gare du Quai-d'Orsay* (1898–1900).

Beyond this *Quai Voltaire*, with its *bouquinistes* and antique-dealers, continues along the Seine, passing the Pont du Carrousel, and runs into *Quai Malaquais*, on which is the **Ecole Nationale des Beaux-Arts** (National School of Fine Arts), with interesting collections within the School and in its two courtyards. – Farther along, at the Pont des Arts, is the **Institut de France**, an imposing building with a high dome, erected 1663–72 by Louis Le Vau at the expense of Cardinal Mazarin. Originally called the Collège Mazarin, and popularly known as the Collège des Quatre Nations, it was intended for the education of young people from the new French provinces of Roussillon, Pignerol, Flanders and Alsace. During the French Revolution it was used as a prison. Since 1805 it has been the home of various learned societies and academies, including the famous Académie Française, founded in 1629. Here too is the *Bibliothèque Mazarine* (Mazarin Library), with over 350,000 volumes. The three courtyards offer a picturesque means of access to Rue Mazarine, to the rear. – Immediately E of the Institut de France is the **Hôtel des Monnaies** (1771–75), familiarly known simply as the *Monnaie* (Mint), the first monumental building in Louis XVI style, with the *Musée Monétaire* (closed Sun.), a collection of French and foreign coins, etc.

From the Ecole des Beaux-Arts *Rue Bonaparte* runs S to the church of *St-Germain-des-Prés**, the oldest church in Paris (11th c.), built on the site of a still earlier church belonging to the famous abbey (founded 543) of St-Germain "in the Fields" in which the Merovingian kings were buried. The present church, with interior painting (1850) in the style of the 11th c., contains some fine sculpture and monuments. – The S side of the church faces on to the **Boulevard St-Germain**, over 3 km long, which was driven through older property in 1855–56. Farther W along the boulevard are the *Ministry of Works* and the *Ministry of Defence*. – The cafés round the church of St-Germain-des-Prés are favourite meeting-places of the Parisians.

At the S end of Rue Bonaparte is the *Place St-Sulpice*, with a handsome fountain (1847). On the E side of the square is the imposing church of *St-Sulpice**, built between 1646 and 1745 on the site of an earlier church. During the Revolution, in 1792, it served as a Temple of Victory, and in 1799 it was the scene of a banquet in honour of the victorious General Bonaparte. The church is 110 m long, 56 m wide and 33 m high, with an interior richly decorated with 19th c. frescoes. Behind the high altar is a beautiful Rococo *Lady Chapel. The *organ, rebuilt in 1862, has a fine organ-loft of 1777.

From Place St-Sulpice the Rue Férou runs S into the longest street in Paris, *Rue de Vaugirard*, which has a total length of almost 4½ km. A short distance along this street to the left is the **Palais du Luxembourg**, built by Salomon de Brosse in 1620–21 for Henry IV's widow Marie de Médicis, and now the seat of the Senate. Just beyond it is the old *Théâtre de l'Odéon*, built 1779–82, which was for long a branch of the Comédie Française (the "Salle du Luxembourg") but is now the independent *Théâtre de France*. – Behind the Palais du Luxembourg, to the S, extends the beautiful *Jardin du Luxembourg**, laid out in 1613, the finest and most popular park on the left bank of the Seine and the only surviving Renaissance garden in Paris, with numerous monuments and statues.

The S gate of the Luxembourg Gardens opens into the wide *Avenue de l'Observatoire*, the northern part of which is even more spacious, with a broad strip of gardens running down the middle. At the S end of this section, at the beginning

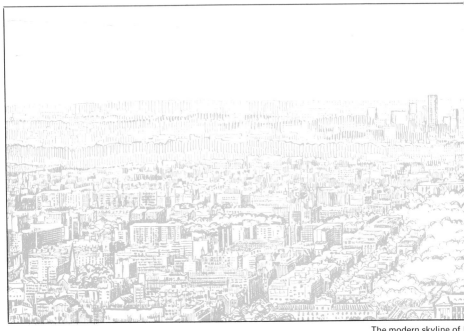

The modern skyline of

of a large road intersection, the *Carrefour de l'Observatoire*, is the large *Fontaine de l'Observatoire* (1874), with a fine bronze group by Carpeaux (the four parts of the world supporting an armillary sphere). At the S end of the Carrefour de l'Observatoire, where there is a statue, erected in 1853, of Marshal Ney (who was shot here in 1815), the Avenue de l'Observatoire cuts across the Boulevard du Montparnasse and the Boulevard de Port-Royal and comes to the **Paris Observatory** (1667–72, designed by Claude Perrault). The Observatory stands on the Paris meridian, 2° 20′ 14″ E of Greenwich. The shaft leading from the cellar 27 m underground, with a constant temperature of 11·8 °C, to the revolving dome 27 m above ground was used by the physicist Foucault for his experiments with the pendulum.

From the Carrefour de l'Observatoire the Boulevard du Montparnasse runs NE through the MONTPARNASSE quarter, which became the haunt of artists at a later period than Montmartre and has still numbers of cafés frequented by writers and artists. – Just S of the Boulevard du Montparnasse, along the *Boulevard de Vaugirard*, is the new *Maine-Montparnasse* complex, with huge blocks of offices and flats, including the gigantic 56-storey **Tour Maine-Montparnasse**, 210 m high, which was completed in 1974. The new *Gare Montparnasse*

(trains to Brittany and the SW), built 1966–69, replaced an older station on the Boulevard du Montparnasse.

A short distance to the S of the Boulevard du Montparnasse is the **Montparnasse** or **Southern Cemetery** (*Cimetière du Montparnasse, Cimetière du Sud*), the third of Paris's large cemeteries, established in 1824. Laid out on a regular plan, it has fewer notable graves than the Père-Lachaise and Montmartre cemeteries; among those buried here are the poet Charles Baudelaire (1821–67) and the novelist Guy de Maupassant (1850–93).

Quartier Latin, Jardin des Plantes and Place d'Italie

To the E of the Palais du Luxembourg, between the Seine, the Gare d'Austerlitz and the Boulevard de Port-Royal, is the **QUARTIER LATIN** (Latin quarter), which ranks with the Ile de la Cité as one of the oldest parts of Paris and has since time immemorial been noted for its universities and learned institutions. The principal street of this quarter is the **Boulevard St-Michel** (familiarly known as the *Boul' Mich'*), one of Haussmann's great new avenues, running from the Carrefour de l'Observatoire to the Ile de la Cité.

A short distance E of the Boulevard St-Michel is the **Sorbonne**, now part of the

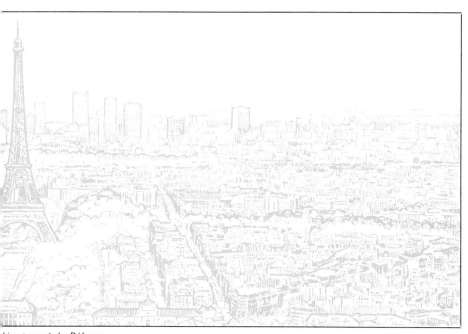

king towards La Défense

University of Paris. Originally founded in 1253 by Robert de Sorbon, Louis IX's confessor, as a theological college, it later became the theological faculty of the University, which had been founded 50 years earlier, and played a leading part in French intellectual life. In 1470 the first printing press in France was established here. The present building dates from the time of Cardinal Richelieu (1627 onwards), with extensive rebuilding and enlargement between 1885 and 1901. Since 1896 it has housed the faculty of philosophy and most of the faculty of mathematics and science of Paris University, together with three state institutes not belonging to the University. A notable feature of the interior is the *Grand Amphithéâtre* (2700 seats), with an allegorical painti g by Puvis de Chavannes, "Le Bois Sacré" (the sacred grove of learning). On the first floor is the well-stocked *Library*. In the centre of the complex of buildings is the **Sorbonne Church** (1635–53), built by Jacques Lemercier for Cardinal Richelieu, with a dome which is a prominent Paris landmark. The N façade, looking on to the Grand Courtyard, is particularly fine. The interior (for admission apply to the porter on the left of the main entrance) is bare and austere. In the S transept is the *tomb of Cardinal Richelieu (1585–1642), the most important work (1694) of the sculptor F. Girardon. – To the E of the Sorbonne is the **Collège de France**, a college founded by Francis I in 1530 for the teaching of Latin, Greek and Hebrew which became a great centre of French humanism. The present building, originally erected in 1610, has been considerably enlarged over the centuries. Here public lectures are given in all fields of knowledge.

Just S of the Sorbonne is Rue Soufflot, which runs E to the ***Pantheon**, on the "Montagne de Ste-Geneviève" (60 m), the highest point in the old part of the town on the left bank. The site was originally occupied by an earlier church built over the tomb of St Geneviève (422–512). The present building (122 m long, 84 m wide, 91 m high, height including the cross above the lantern 117 m), built between 1764 and 1790 to the design of Germain Soufflot in fulfilment of a vow made by Louis XV, was also dedicated to St Geneviève, but in 1791, by decision of the National Assembly, became a Pantheon for the burial of France's great men, and thereafter was used for worship only between 1806 and 1830 and between 1851 and 1885. On the pediment of the porch, which is borne by 22 Corinthian columns, is a famous *bas-relief by David d'Angers (1831–37) showing France distributing garlands to her great citizens.

In the *INTERIOR of the Panthéon (admission charge; closed Tues.) are numerous large pictures. Notable among them are "The Childhood of St Geneviève" (1877) in the S aisle and "St Geneviève

watching over Paris and bringing food to the city"
(1898) on the N side of the choir, both by Puvis de
Chavannes. – In 1851 the famous physicist Léon
Foucault demonstrated the rotation of the earth in a
new way by means of a pendulum suspended from the
dome. – In the N transept is a staircase leading up to
the **dome** (425 steps to the lantern; open 10–12 and
1.30–4), from which there are extensive *views. – At
the NE corner of the choir is the entrance to the **crypt**
(conducted tour, 10 a.m. to 4 p.m.), with the tombs of
Rousseau (1712–78), *Voltaire* (1694–1778), the
architect *Soufflot* (1713–80), *Victor Hugo*
(1802–85), *Emile Zola* (1840–1902) and other
notable Frenchmen.

Facing the Panthéon on the N side of
the square is the *Bibliothèque Ste-
Geneviève*, founded in 1624. – Behind
the Panthéon, to the NE, is the church of
*St-Etienne-du-Mont (15th–16th c.),
which is late Gothic in general plan but
shows strong Renaissance influence.
During the Revolution it became a
"Temple of Filial Love". Features of the
very picturesque interior are a *rood-
screen (1525–35) with rich Renaissance
decoration, a pulpit of 1640 and beautiful
16th c. windows. In the second chapel on
the right in the ambulatory is a richly
ornamented modern reliquary containing
part of St Geneviève's coffin. In the old
charnel-house (reached from the choir)
are 12 stained glass windows of
1612–22.

In Rue St-Jacques, 1 km S of the
Sorbonne, is the church of **Val-de-
Grâce**, with a magnificent dome. This
was originally built in 1645 by François
Mansart for the adjoining Benedictine
convent (which has been a military
hospital since 1793); work was continued
by Lemercier and completed by Le Duc in
1665.

The *Hôtel de Cluny** is situated N of the
Sorbonne on the site of Roman baths, of
which considerable remains have survived. This graceful late Gothic building,
erected between 1480 and 1510, replaces
an earlier residence of the Abbots of
Cluny. It now houses one of Paris's finest
museums (see above under *Museums*). –
Still farther N, at the N end of Rue St-
Jacques, is the church of *St-Séverin,
the finest late Gothic church in Paris,
mostly built in the 15th c. Beautiful
interior, with stained glass, some of it 15th
and 16th c. – A little way E is the little early
Gothic church of *St-Julien-le-Pauvre*
(altered in 1651), which since 1889 has
been a Greek Catholic (Uniate) church.

The streets which skirt the Seine to the N
of St-Julien-le-Pauvre run SE past the

massive **Faculty of Science** building
(erected in the 1960s on the site of the old
Halle aux Vins) to the **Jardin des
Plantes** (open 9 a.m. to 6 p.m., in winter
5 p.m.). This was originally laid out as a
"physic garden" in 1635, but in 1794,
with the addition of a zoological section, it
became the *National Museum of Natural
History* (see under *Museums*). The gardens, with which is associated a scientific
institute, have a total area of over 69
acres, and comprise a *Botanic Garden*
(admission free), a *Menagerie* and
Vivarium (9–12 and 2–6; admission
charge), and a number of galleries displaying scientific collections which are
among the richest in the world; there are
also a large *library*, laboratories and
lecture theatres.

Opposite the SE corner of the Jardin des
Plantes, in the *Boulevard de l'Hôpital*,
which runs SW to the Place d'Italie, is the
Gare d'Austerlitz or *Gare d'Orléans*
(trains to Orléans and SW France). To the
E of the station is the *Viaduc du Métro*,
which crosses the Seine at a height of 30
m; to the N the *Pont d'Austerlitz*, built
1804–06 and widened during the 19th c.
– On the E side of the Boulevard de
l'Hôpital is the extensive area occupied by
the *Hôpital de la Salpêtrière*, built 1657
on the site of an old arsenal (*salpêtrière*),
with a dome similar to that of the
Invalides. It is now a female geriatric
hospital.

NW of the Jardin des Plantes are the
excavated remains of a *Roman amphitheatre of the 2nd or 3rd c. A.D.,
known as the *Arènes de Lutèce*, which
could accommodate 16,000 spectators. It
is freely open to the public. – S of this, at
the W end of the Jardin des Plantes, is a
*Mosque, surrounded by other buildings
in Moorish style. This was the first
mosque built in France (1923–27), following Moroccan models. The main
entrance is in Place du Puits-de-
l'Hermite; conducted tours daily except
Friday 10–12 and 2–6. – Behind the
mosque, at the corner of Rue Daubenton
and Rue Geoffroy-St-Hilaire, is a *Turkish
bath*, with a Moorish *café*, an Arab
restaurant and a shop selling North
African and Oriental goods.

A short distance SW, near the N end of the
wide *Avenue des Gobelins*, is the late
Gothic church of *St-Médard* (15th–16th
c.). – In the Avenue des Gobelins (No.

42) are the unpretentious premises of the famous *Gobelins Manufactory, founded in 1601 by Henry IV and later transferred to the workshops of a family of dyers named Gobelin, who thus gave their family name to the tapestries made there. A visit to the *workshops* (conducted tours on Wed., Thu., Fri., 2–4) and the *museum* (open at the same times) is a rewarding experience. The museum puts on temporary exhibitions of French, Flemish, Italian, etc., tapestries from its large and valuable stock.

The Avenue des Gobelins ends in the circular **Place d'Italie** (fountain), the busiest traffic intersection in SE Paris.

Parks in the Outer Districts

From the Etoile the *Avenue Foch*, 120 m wide, runs SW to the *Porte Dauphine*, the main entrance to the *Bois de Boulogne, one of Europe's most beautiful public parks. The park, usually known simply as the *Bois*, has an area of more than 2100 acres, and is bounded by the line of the old fortifications on the E, the Seine in the W and the suburbs of Boulogne and Neuilly in the S and N. It is a relic of the old forest of *Rouvray* (from Latin *roveretum*, oak-forest) which originally covered the whole of the Seine peninsula. For long an area of waste land, it was acquired by the city in 1853 and laid out as a park in the English style. It is traversed by broad motor roads and a network of footpaths, and with its lakes, waterfalls, open-air theatre and two racecourses it is one of Paris's most frequented recreation areas.

Near the eastern boundary of the Bois are two elongated artificial lakes, the *Lac Inférieur* (with two islands) and the *Lac Supérieur*, **Auteuil Racecourse** (*Champ de courses d'Auteuil*: steeplechasing) and the *Marmottan Museum* (see under *Museums*). From the *Butte Mortemart*, at the W end of the racecourse, there are attractive views. – On the SW border of the Bois, near the Seine, is **Longchamp Racecourse** (*Hippodrome de Longchamp*: flat racing), a celebrated and fashionable course (room for 10,000). – In the western part of the Bois is the little château of *Bagatelle, built in 1777 by the Comte d'Artois (later Charles X) in 64 days for a wager. It was purchased by the city in 1905. (Charge for admission to the park, which has a famous rose-garden.)

The NW corner of the Bois is occupied by the **Jardin d'Acclimatation**, established in 1854 to promote the introduction of foreign animals and plants. It is now mainly a zoo and amusement park (open-air theatre, menagerie, circus turns, trained animals, etc.) and also contains the *Museum of Folk Arts and Traditions* (see under *Museums*).

In the S of the city, along the N side of the Boulevard Jourdan, is the **Parc de Montsouris** (39 acres), opened in 1878. On a hill beyond the ring road is the *Meteorological Observatory* of the City of Paris, housed in a copy of the Bey of Tunis's palace. At the foot of the hill, to the NE, is a small lake. – To the S of the park, beyond the Boulevard Jourdan, is the **Cité Universitaire**, founded in 1921, where there are many students' residences built by various countries.

On the SE outskirts of Paris, on both sides of the wide *Avenue Daumesnil*, is the *Bois de Vincennes, laid out in its present form in 1860–67. With an area of 2273 acres (of which 295 are under grass), it is Paris's largest park, vying with the Bois de Boulogne in the beauty of its scenery.

At the main entrance, on the W side, is the *Museum of African and Oceanian Art* (see under *Museums*), and near this is the beautiful *Lac Daumesnil* or *Lac de Charenton*, with two islands. On the NE side of the lake is the *Zoological Garden, one of Europe's leading zoos. – 1 km E of the Zoo is the lavishly planned **Centre Universitaire** (Faculty of Arts, 7500 students), opened at the end of 1968. – On the northern edge of the park, at the end of the Avenue Daumesnil and on the southern fringe of the suburb of VINCENNES (pop. 50,000), is the *Château de Vincennes or *Fort de Vincennes* (admission charge), a 14th c. castle 320 m long built by Philip VI and Charles V on the site of an earlier castle, which until the 16th c. was a favourite residence of the French kings; it is now mostly occupied by barracks. On the W side of the castle courtyard, which is entered from the N end, is the *keep* (52 m high), frequently used in the past as a state prison and now occupied by the *Musée Historique de Vincennes* (closed Tues.: conducted tour, which also includes the chapel). On the E side of the courtyard is the Sainte Chapelle, built between 1387 and 1552, with beautiful 16th c. stained glass. In the SW and SE corners of the courtyard are the Pavillon du Roi and Pavillon de la Reine, built 1654–59 by Le Vau and restored after a fire in 1944.

In eastern Paris, on the *Boulevard de Ménilmontant*, is the *Père Lachaise or **Eastern Cemetery**, the largest (44 hectares) and most famous of the three Paris cemeteries, established in 1804 and named after Louis XIV's confessor. It affords fine views of Paris, but its graves are of more historical than artistic interest; a plan can be obtained at the entrance. A tour of the cemetery takes $1\frac{1}{2}$–2 hours.

At the end of the main avenue is the *Monument aux Morts (1891–99, by Albert Bartholomé). *Bartholomé* (1848–1928) is buried at the near end of the path leading to the monument. Some 100 m S of the monument are the tombs of the composers *Luigi Cherubini* (1760–1842) and *Frédéric Chopin* (1810–49). – A short distance NE is the **Chapel**, and on the right of this is a smaller chapel with the tomb of the statesman *Adolphe Thiers* (1797–1877). – 200 m N of the Chapel is the grave of the novelist *Honoré de Balzac* (1799–1850). 150 m NW is *Georges Bizet* (1838–75), the composer of "Carmen". – 200 m SE of the Chapel are the empty tombs of *La Fontaine* (1621–95) and *Molière* (1622–73). – Near the E side of the cemetery, 100 m SE of the crematorium, is the grave of *Oscar Wilde* (1856–1900). – In the SE corner of the cemetery are four monuments commemorating Frenchmen shot or deported by the Germans during the last war.

In NE Paris, in the middle of a working-class district, is a park laid out by Haussmann (1864–67) in an old quarry, the **Buttes-Chaumont* (25 hectares). In the centre of the park, on a crag (88 m) surrounded by a lake and approached by bridges on the S and W sides, is a miniature *temple*, from which there are fine views of St-Denis and Montmartre. There are even better views from another hill (101 m: café-restaurant) at the S end of the park.

In NW Paris, ½ km NW of the church of St-Augustin, is the **Parc Monceau*, laid out from 1778 onwards by Philippe d'Orléans as a rendezvous for fashionable society but halved in size in 1861. With its palms and Asian conifers and its clumps of trees with varied colours of foliage – green, silver or coloured – it has an attraction all its own. Near the main entrance is the "*Naumachie*", an oval lake surrounded by the remains of a colonnade, dating from the 18th c.

SURROUNDINGS OF PARIS

The area round Paris offers so much scenic beauty and so much of historical and artistic interest that it is possible to refer in the following section only to a few of the major features.

Some 9 km SW of the city centre – an attractive trip on one of the Seine boats in good weather – is the suburb of **Meudon** (alt. 30–153 m; pop. 55,000), rising in terraces above the left bank of the Seine. To the W, above the old town (alt. 100 m), which has a beautiful church of the 16th and 18th c., is the **Terrasse de Meudon* (open until dusk), which affords beautiful views of the Seine valley and Paris; to the E, beyond the little *Val Fleury* ("valley of flowers"), a large orphanage forms a prominent landmark. At the SW corner of the terrace is an astrophysical *observatory*, housed in a converted château. From the W end of the terrace a flight of iron steps leads up to the château *park*, which in turn leads into the *Bois de*

Meudon, a favourite weekend resort of Parisians, with beautiful little lakes (Etang de Villebon, Etang de Trivaux, etc.). – Near the NE outskirts of Meudon is the *Villa des Brillants*, where the sculptor Auguste Rodin lived for the last 20 years of his life; it now houses a *Rodin Museum* (Sat., Sun., Mon. 1.30–6; closed in winter), with sketches, preliminary models and casts.

Immediately NW of Meudon, on a terrace above the Seine, is the villa suburb of **Bellevue**, with beautiful views from a terrace a short distance NW of the station. – Still farther NW, on the left bank of the Seine, is the suburb of **Sèvres** (pop. 20,000), which lies on the road from Paris to Versailles. On the N side of the Grande Rue, near the bridge over the Seine, is the famous *Porcelain Manufactory*, founded at Vincennes in 1738, moved to Sèvres in 1756 and installed in its present premises in 1876 (conducted tours 2–3.30 on first and third Thursday in month; closed July and Aug.). On the ground and first floors is the rich **Musée Céramique* (9.30–12 and 1.30–5); one particularly notable item is the 3·15 m high Neptune Vase (1867).

Upstream from Sèvres, still on the left bank of the Seine, is the beautifully situated suburb of **St-Cloud** (pop. 28,000), with the headquarters of Interpol, established here in 1967. Between Sèvres and St-Cloud, above the river, is the **Parc de St-Cloud* (1100 acres); there is an attractive view of Paris from the "Lanterne de Diogène" on a terrace at the E end of the park. ½ km N of this terrace are the Grande Cascade (1734) and a fountain called the Grand Jet, which on certain Sundays (alternating with Versailles) shoots its water up to a height of 42 m. To the SE, below the terrace, is the *Pavillon de Breteuil*, now housing the International Bureau of Weights and Measures, which keeps the standard measures (in platinum) of the metre and the kilogram (not open to the public). – A short distance N of the Grande Cascade the Paris–Versailles motorway (Autoroute de L'Ouest) runs through a tunnel 832 m long.

From St-Cloud the *Pont de St-Cloud* crosses the Seine into the industrial suburb of **Boulogne-Billancourt** (pop. 115,000). On the Quai du 4-Septembre beyond the bridge is the entrance to the **Jardins Albert Kahn* (open 2–6, closed in winter), laid out by the banker of that name at the beginning of the 20th c., with examples of different types of garden; particularly attractive is the Japanese garden in the SW part.

5 km NW of St-Cloud, near the SW fringe of the suburb of *Rueil-Malmaison* (pop. 65,000), is the *Château de Malmaison, built at the beginning of the 17th c. and enlarged in 1799. The château, which now belongs to the State, was a favourite residence of Napoleon in 1803–04, when he was First Consul, and from 1809 to 1814 was the home of the Empress Joséphine, whom Napoleon divorced in 1809. From 1861 it was also a favourite residence of the Empress Eugénie, wife of Napoleon III. The château is now a museum (conducted tours; closed Tues.), decorated and furnished as it was in the time of Joséphine.

From Rueil-Malmaison the road from Paris runs SW, passing close to the château, and soon comes to the Seine. 9 km from Rueil is the suburb of **St-Germain-en-Laye** (alt. 86 m; pop. 40,000), in a beautiful situation, the summer residence of the French kings from the 12th c. onwards. On the E side of the town, near the railway station, is the 16th c. **Château**, on a site previously occupied by a medieval castle destroyed during the wars with England; the chapel of the older building (1230–38) survives. The treaty of St-Germain between the Entente powers and Austria was signed in the Château on 10 September 1919. The Château houses the *Museum of National Antiquities* (closed Tues.), with a comprehensive collection of prehistoric and early historical antiquities from all parts of France which gives an excellent survey of Gallic, Gallo-Roman and Frankish culture. – A walk through the beautiful *park* ("*Parterres*") leads to the famous *Terrace laid out by Le Nôtre, which runs high above the Seine for a length of 2·4 km along the edge of the beautiful Forest of St-Germain (*c.* 4400 hectares), affording beautiful views of the park-like plain below.

10 km N of Paris city centre, on the road to Chantilly and Compiègne, is the large suburb of **St-Denis**, with a population of over 97,000. On the E side of the town is the *Basilica* or Cathedral of St-Denis, begun in 1137 and substantially completed by the end of the 13th c., on the site of a 5th c. church and abbey built over the grave of St Denis (Dionysius). This was the first monumental Gothic structure to be built in France, still showing some Romanesque features (e.g. on the W front). After Louis IX (St Louis) had erected the first royal tombs in the choir to commemorate his ancestors, the church became the burial place of all the French kings and of princes and other great persons. During the French Revolution, in 1793, the church and the tombs it contained were devastated, and attempts at restoration were unhappy. Only when Viollet-le-Duc took over responsibility for the work in 1847 was the venerable old building restored to its former splendour. The *interior is 108 m long and 29 m high, with a width of 39 m in the transepts, and is of impressive effect with its tall pillars and its 37 windows (10 m high: mostly modern). Of the numerous (now empty) tombs in the choir (conducted tours from 1 April to 30 Sept., 10–12 and 1–4; closed Sunday mornings) the most notable are the following: in the N transept the *tomb of Louis XII (d. 1515) and his wife Anne de Bretagne (d. 1514), erected 1517–31, and the *tomb of Henry II (d. 1559) and his wife Catherine de Médicis (d. 1589), completed in 1573, with a smaller and simpler monument adjoining; to the right of the high altar the tomb of Dagobert I (13th c.), with a *statue of Queen Nantilde (nearby, a 12th c. painted Virgin). – The former *abbey* adjoining the church, an imposing 18th c. building, has been since 1809 a girls' boarding school for daughters and other relatives of members of the Légion d'Honneur.

Few visitors will want to leave Paris without making the 20 km trip to **Versailles** (see p. 252) to see the splendid palace on which Louis XIV lavished so much money and care. Particularly impressive features of the palace itself are the Grands Appartements and the Hall of Mirrors, but the beautiful park is an additional attraction. A whole day should be allowed for the visit.

Périgord

Périgord, with its capital at Périgueux, corresponds roughly to the department of Dordogne. Its many attractions include its varied scenery, its generally mild climate,

Hunting for truffles, Périgord

the extensive forests which cover a quarter of its area, its caves with their fascinating prehistoric remains, its picturesque castles and country houses and – not least – its rich and delicate cuisine, with the local specialities of truffles and foie gras.

Geographically there are two different Périgords – *Périgord Blanc* (White Périgord), the plateau region N of the Dordogne and Vézère valleys, and *Périgord Noir* (Black Périgord) to the S of this. The names refer to the different kinds of forest: "Black" Périgord is more densely forested and therefore appears darker in colour. Even in "white" Périgord, however, there are considerable areas of forest. Roughly a quarter of Périgord is covered with coniferous and deciduous forest, the chestnut forests having a particular charm of their own.

HISTORY. – Few areas have such early traces of human occupation as Périgord. The caves have produced evidence dating back to the time of *Cro-Magnon* Man (named after a site in the Vézère valley), and altogether no fewer than 200 prehistoric sites have been identified in Périgord, at least half of them in the Vézère valley. In historical times the region was occupied by the *Petrocorii*; thereafter it was conquered by the Romans under Caesar, although the local people never lost their hankering for independence. During the wars with England castles and fortifications were built to withstand English attacks, and in the 15th c. Périgord became part of the kingdom of France. The French Revolution left

Périgord with its old boundaries almost intact in the new department of Dordogne.

SIGHTS. – **Bergerac**, on the Dordogne SW of Périgueux, is a centre of agriculture (tobacco, wine) and the chemical industry. The interesting Tobacco Museum on the second floor of the Town Hall is the only one of its kind in France.

Beynac-et-Cazenac has a magnificently situated medieval castle dominating the little village and offering breathtaking views of the Dordogne valley.

The castle of **Bonaguil** is a characteristic example of the art of fortification of the 15th–16th c.

Brantôme, in the Dromme valley, has a beautiful situation and an old abbey which make it one of the most popular tourist attractions in Périgord. The abbey dates back to the time of Charlemagne (769), but was rebuilt in the 11th c. and much altered in later centuries.

Cadouin has a church dating from 1154. The cloister was begun in the late 15th c. in Flamboyant style and completed, with some Renaissance features, in the mid 16th c.

Domme offers (from the Belvédère de la Barre) an enchanting view of the Dordogne valley, here at its most typical. – Under the town are *caves* in which animal bones were found, and there are attractive walks round the old town walls, with the twin-towered town gate, and along the rocky banks of the river.

Les Eyzies-de-Tayac, at the junction of the Vézère and the Beune, lies in the centre of a group of important prehistoric sites, including the *Grotte du Grand Roc*, the *Cro-Magnon* rock shelter and other caves and sites where discoveries have been made. A general survey is offered by the *National Museum of Prehistory* in the old castle above the little town. This medieval stronghold, restored in the 16th c., belonged to the Barons of Beynac. – Prehistoric drawings of animals can be seen in the *Grottes des Eyzies*, the *Grotte de Combarelles*, the *Grotte de la Mouthe* and above all in the *Grotte de Font-de-Gaume*.

Near **Gourdon**, on the borders of Périgord and Quercy, are the interesting *Grottes de Cougnac*, also with cave paintings.

Rocamadour

with its major buildings and its streets of old houses all contributing to the effect. Once the see of a bishop, Sarlat competed for many centuries with Périgueux and Cahors. Its most important church is St-Sacerdos, founded in the 8th c., though the present building dates from the 16th and 17th c.; only the tower on the W front survives from its Romanesque predecessor. – A walk round the old town takes rather over an hour and reveals many handsome aristocratic mansions and burghers' houses of the 14th–17th c. The Hôtel de Malleville (Hôtel de Vienne) has two beautiful Renaissance façades. The Hôtel Plamon or Hôtel des Consuls dates from the 14th c.; it is well preserved, though the façade shows later alterations. A round tower of the 12th c. is known as the Lanterne des Morts ("Lantern of the Dead"). Also worth seeing are the Maison La Boëtie (which belonged to the 16th c. writer of that name), the Hôtel de Grezel and the narrow little Rue des Trois-Conils.

Near *Montignac*, on the Vézère, with a tower belonging to an old castle now destroyed, is one of the most remarkable prehistoric sites in Périgord, the * ***Grotte de Lascaux**, notable for the magnificent cave paintings discovered in 1940. Unfortunately the cave has been closed to the public since 1963, but there is an information centre showing films which are an authentic record of the paintings.

* ***Rocamadour**, on the borders of Quercy, is one of France's most unusual places of pilgrimage. During the Middle Ages pilgrims flocked here to see the Black Virgin of Roc-Amadour (12th c.). Built on a rock face in the gorge of the Alzon, Rocamadour is dominated by its 14th c. castle, which is reached from the village by a steep flight of steps with the Stations of the Cross. It is not known with certainty who St Amadour was – perhaps a hermit named Zacchaeus. – Rocamadour is notable both for its situation and its historic old buildings. The "holy of holies" is the Chapelle Miraculeuse. During the season the village, with its single street, is overrun by visitors, and it is pleasanter to see it in spring or autumn, when the commercialisation of the shrine is less obtrusive.

* **Sarlat** (pop. 11,000), formerly the capital of Périgord Noir, is one of the most attractive little towns in the whole region,

Périgueux

Region: Aquitaine.
Department: Dordogne.
Altitude: 85 m. – Population: 38,000.
Post code: F-24000. – Dialling code: 53.
ⓘ **Office de Tourisme**,
1 Avenue d'Aquitaine;
tel. 53 10 63.

HOTELS. – *Domino*, II, 37 r.; *Boule d'Or*, II, 33 r.; *Bristol*, II, 30 r.; *Arènes*, III, 19 r.; *France*, IV, 44 r.; *Régina*, IV, 38 r.

Périgueux, on the right bank of the River Isle, has preserved much of the atmosphere of the past. Chief town of the department of Dordogne and the see of a bishop, it is the main tourist centre of Périgord, whose culinary specialities are exported from here to countries all over the world.

SIGHTS. – The town's principal attraction is the * **Cathedral of St-Front**, one of the largest churches in SW France and one of the most striking in the whole country. Built in the 12th c., it is Romanesque in style with Byzantine influences. Notable features are the five high domes (which can be seen at close quarters by climbing up to the roof) and the four-storey Romanesque * bell-tower. The original effect of the exterior is spoiled by 17 turrets added during a 19th c.

restoration. On the S side of the Cathedral is a *cloister* (Romanesque, with several Gothic features) containing a number of Merovingian sarcophagi. – The church of *St-Etienne, which was the cathedral until 1669, was built in the 12th c. and largely destroyed in 1577, leaving only the W tower and two bays of the original building. A notable feature of the interior is the carved reredos of the high altar.

An attractive part of old Périgueux has been preserved between the Cathedral and the Allées de Tourny, in which is the *Musée du Périgord, with much pre-historic materials and a collection of pictures. – Remains of the Roman period include the imposing **Tour de Vésone** (24 m high, interior diameter 17 m) and fragments of an *amphitheatre* which could accommodate 20,000 spectators. – The late 15th c. *Tour Mataguerre* is a relic of the fortifications of Puy-St-Front.

Picardy and the North

Northern France, an area relatively little visited by tourists, consists of the old provinces of Picardy, Flanders and Artois. The landscape is flat, and traversed by numerous canals and streams. The economic wealth of Artois and Flanders is based on coal, and there are more factories than anywhere else in France, in such industrial towns as Lille, Roubaix, Cambrai, Valenciennes and Armentières. The coastal area which extends from the adjoining province of Normandy, in the SW, to the Belgian frontier forms a complement and a contrast to the industrial zone, with the ports of Boulogne, Calais and Dunkirk and a string of seaside towns, continuing the line of resorts on the Belgian side of the frontier.

These northern territories are in many respects – scenery, population, economy, culture – more similar to the neighbouring countries than to the southern parts of France. But the series of great Gothic cathedrals extends without a break from the Ile de France into this region, marked by such names as Laon, Amiens, St-Quentin and many more; and this wealth of Gothic architecture, in particular the cathedrals of Picardy, is one of the great attractions of the North. Besides there is much truth in the saying that the history of Picardy is the history of France; and in northern France every town and every village has memories of warlike events of the past – a past which extended right down to the events of the Second World War.

SIGHTS. – **Abbeville**, lying near the coast, suffered heavy damage in both world wars but has preserved the late Gothic church of St-Vulfran (with a Renaissance doorway) and an 18th c. château, the Folie de Bagatelle.

Amiens: see p. 61.

Arras (pop. 55,000), between Amiens and Lille, is the chief town of the department of Pas-de-Calais and the see of a bishop. The *Grand'Place and Place des Héros are distinctly Flemish in style. The town was formerly famed for its tapestries (hence the English word "arras"). There was heavy fighting here in the First World War, and there are many British and Commonwealth military cemeteries in the surrounding area (information from the Commonwealth War Graves Commission, Place du Maréchal-Foch). The Town Hall (15th–16th c.), with its 75 m tower, was destroyed in 1914 but was restored after the war. The Cathedral is classical in style. Nearby are the Palais St-Vaast (museum) and the house in which Robespierre was born.

Bavay has remains, excavated from 1942 onwards, of the Roman town of *Bagacum* (mid 2nd c. A.D.).

Bergues is a town of very Flemish type, with 17th c. ramparts and moat. Of its old buildings the 17th c. Town Hall, a Mont-de-Piété (municipal pawnshop) of 1629, a massive gateway and two towers are particularly notable. – It is well worth while making an excursion from here to *Hondschoote*, which has a Renaissance Town Hall and the 12th c. mill of Nordmolen.

Boulogne-sur-Mer (pop. 50,000) is France's principal fishing port and an important commercial harbour (services to Dover and Folkestone). The damage it suffered during the last war has been made good. The upper town still preserves

Rodin's "Burghers of Calais"

its old walls and towers, with four gates. 17th c. Town Hall; church of Notre-Dame, with an 11th c. crypt and a miraculous image of the Virgin.

Calais (pop. 75,000) situated opposite Dover at the narrowest point in the English Channel, is a major ferry port (services to Dover and Folkestone: 34 km, fastest crossing 75 min., by hovercraft 20 min.). It is also a popular seaside resort, with one of the finest beaches in northern France. Its main feature of interest is the Place du Soldat-Inconnu, with Rodin's group of the Burghers of Calais (1895), commemorating the 200 years of war between France and England. – Near the town is the *Plage Blériot*, where Blériot took off in 1909 for the first flight across the Channel to Dover.

Cambrai (pop. 40,000), on the Escaut (Scheldt), was the home of the fine fabric known as cambric, first made here in the 15th c. Its most important building is the 18th c. church of St-Géry, with a bell-tower 76 m high and a Renaissance rood-screen. Relics of the town's former fortifications are two gates and the 16th c. citadel. The 17th c. theologian and writer Fénelon, Archbishop of Cambrai, is buried in the Cathedral of Notre-Dame.

Cap Blanc-Nez and **Cap Gris-Nez** (Capes "White Nose" and "Grey Nose"), between Calais and Boulogne, afford extensive *views, extending in clear weather as far as the English coast, 35 km away.

Le Cateau was the birthplace of the painter Henri Matisse; there is a Matisse Museum in the Town Hall. 18th c. church and Archbishop's Palace.

Douai (pop. 52,000), S of Lille, did not finally become part of France until 1713. It is an industrial town largely centred on coal, and until 1889 possessed a university founded by the Spaniards. The principal building is the 15th c. *Town Hall, with a defensive tower 54 m high (the interior of which is open to visitors). In spite of losses due to fire during the last war the museum has some fine pictures and a notable 16th c. altar, the Anchin Altar of 1520.

Dunkirk (in French *Dunkerque*), France's most northerly town, is an important ferry port (services to Newhaven in Sussex), and earned its place in history when the British Expeditionary Force was evacuated from here in 1940. During the evacuation the town suffered heavy damage. There is a memorial on the seafront. In the centre of the town is the Place Jean-Bart, with a monument to its most famous seaman (1651–1702). Church of St-Eloi (Gothic), severely damaged in 1940; defensive tower of 1440, 58 m high, formerly the church's bell-tower. The busy port, restored after war damage, is an impressive sight; lighthouse, affording very fine *views.

Montreuil-sur-Mer has fortifications built by Vauban in the 17th c. and a rather older citadel. The church of St-Saulve is one of the finest Gothic churches in the Pas-de-Calais.

Noyon is dominated by its Gothic **Cathedral, with its 62 m high towers. Its architecture shows the transition from Romanesque to Gothic. Adjoining the church are a 13th c. chapterhouse and cloister. The chapter library (4000 volumes) is unusual, being built on timber piles. There is a local museum in the former Bishop's Palace and another museum in the birthplace of the Reformer Jean Calvin. – 6 km S is *Ourscamp Abbey*, with the ruins of a church (originally Gothic) destroyed during the French Revolution.

Péronne has a 12th c. castle, built in sandstone, in which Charles the Bold held

Louis XI prisoner. It is an imposing structure, with four round towers. Equally impressive are the remains of the town's fortifications (parts of the 17th c. walls and the Porte de Bretagne). The town is surrounded by lakes formed by the River Somme (water sports, fishing).

Pierrefonds has an impressive and many-towered castle which was restored by Napoleon III.

Le Quesnoy has fortifications built by Vauban, beautiful parks and gardens, and facilities for water sports.

Roubaix, 12 km NE of Lille but forming part of the same conurbation, is the centre of the textile industry of northern France. It has a 15th c. Gothic church (St-Martin).

St-Omer lies between Calais and Lille, in Artois. Its finest building is the church of Notre-Dame (13th–15th c.), with a bell-tower 50 m high, a notable S doorway and a rich interior. Near the church is a well-stocked art museum.

St-Quentin has a number of fine buildings round the Grand'Place, including the late Gothic Town Hall (with carillon) and the spacious *collegiate church (late 12th–15th c.). Nearby are two interesting museums – a collection of 600,000 butterflies and the first children's museum in France (1956).

St-Riquier has a church which belonged to an important medieval abbey (at present under restoration), a fine late Gothic building with a richly decorated doorway, an unfinished tower and a notable interior.

Le Touquet one of the most fashionable resorts on the "Opal Coast", lies in 800 hectares of woodland at the mouth of the River Canche. It came to the fore during the 19th c. It has a wide range of sports facilities and an attractive seafront promenade.

Tourcoing, near the Belgian frontier, is a rapidly growing industrial town, which with Roubaix and other places forms a conurbation round Lille with a population of 250,000.

Valenciennes is an industrial town, formerly the centre of an important lace-making industry, which suffered considerable damage during the last war. The

On the beach, Le Touquet

painter Antoine Watteau was born here. There are a fine *art museum and a number of interesting churches. There is a procession to the church of Notre-Dame-du-Saint-Cordon in September.

SPORT and RECREATION in Picardy and the North. – Plenty of scope for *walking* and *riding*. *Boat trips* on the Somme and Marne; cabin cruisers on the Oise and Aisne. – *Water sports* on the rivers and the coast. – There are a number of *nature parks* and *leisure parks*, e.g. at Ham the Domaine des Iles leisure park and at Ermenonville a country park with a zoo and Wild West shows.

A popular attraction is the underground town (9th–14th c.) at the *Grottes de Naours*, between Amiens and Doullens. – There are also many visitors to the *battlefields of the First World War* on the Somme.

Poitiers

Region: Poitou-Charentes.
Department: Vienne.
Altitude: 120 m. – Population: 85,000.
Post code: F-86000. – Dialling code: 49.
(i) **Office de Tourisme**,
  Hôtel de Ville, Place Maréchal-Leclerc;
  tel. 41 21 24.

HOTELS. – *France*, I, 95 r.; *Relais de Poitiers*, II, 95 r.; *Bois de la Marche*, II, 32 r.; *Royal Poitou*, II, 32 r.; *Europe*, III, 44 r.; *Chapon Fin*, III, 48 r.; *Terminus*, III, 26 r.; *Paix*, IV, 16 r.; *Moderne*, IV, 20 r.; *Belle Aurore*, IV, 18 r.; *Renaissance*, IV, 15 r.

Poitiers, capital of Poitou, chief town of the department of Vienne, the see of a bishop and a university town, is strikingly situated on a rocky plateau above two river valleys. It is one of France's leading art cities, notable in particular for its early Romanesque churches, although its qualities do not reveal

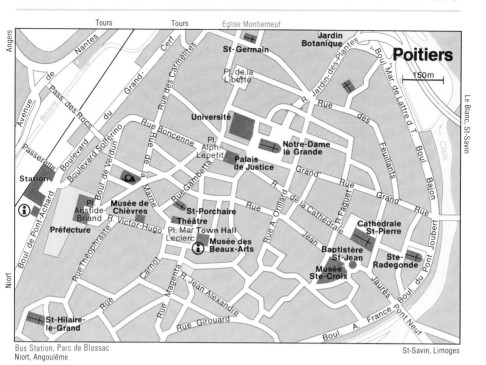

themselves to the visitor at first glance. Its economy depends on the thriving agriculture of the surrounding region.

HISTORY. – Poitiers was the Roman *Limonum*. The first Christians gathered here in the 3rd c., and the Baptistery is France's oldest Christian building. The city's first great bishop was St Hilarius (St Hilaire), St Martin's teacher. It was perhaps no accident, therefore, that the battle in which Charles Martel defeated the Arabs and halted the advance of Islam took place near Poitiers in 732. In the 12th and 14th c. Poitiers twice came under English rule. With the founding of the University in 1432 the town became an important intellectual centre. At this time, too, it

possessed no fewer than 67 churches. In 1569 the town was besieged by Protestant forces, but ten years later it was the scene of the "grands jours de Poitiers", a meeting aimed at putting an end to religious strife.

SIGHTS. – Of the town's many churches the finest is **Notre-Dame-la-Grande** (11th–12th c.), one of the most richly decorated Romanesque churches in France. Particularly impressive is the **W front, flanked by two low towers. Notable features of the interior are the capitals in the choir and a 12th c. fresco on the choir vaulting.

The **Cathedral** (*St-Pierre*), begun at the end of the 12th c., is an imposing building with an interior length of 90 m, already largely Gothic in style. Here too the main feature is the W front, with three fine doorways; the upper part and the towers· date from the 14th and 15th c.

The church of *St-Hilaire-le-Grand (11th c.) is purely Romanesque, though it has suffered from a 19th c. restoration carried out after the collapse of the tower (1590).

The church of **Ste-Radegonde**, originally founded in 560, has a Romanesque apse and tower (with a Flamboyant doorway added in the 15th c.) and an aisleless Gothic nave. Beautiful 13th and 14th c. windows. In the crypt is the black marble sarcophagus of St Radegund (Radegonde: d. 587), wife of Lothair I.

Notre-Dame-la-Grande, Poitiers

A little way S of the Cathedral is the **Baptistery, probably the oldest religious building in France (second half of 4th c.). The apse was added in the 7th c. and the porch in the 11th, after a fire. The interior has frescoes of the 11th–14th c.

There are also a number of interesting old secular buildings. The **Palais de Justice** (Law Courts) incorporates the keep and parts of the old Ducal Palace, including the timber-roofed Great Hall of the 12th–13th c. – The *Hôtels Fumée, Jean-Beaucé* and *Berthelot* are charming old aristocratic mansions. – The **Town Hall**, in *Place Maréchal-Leclerc*, contains a fine *art museum* with exhibits ranging in time from a Roman Minerva of white marble to works by Maillol.

Poitou-Charentes and Vendée

Inland from the coast between the rivers Loire and Gironde extend the regions of Vendée, Poitou and the Charentes. The largest of these, taking in the old provinces of Angoumois, Aunis and Saintonge, is the Charentes – Charente Maritime, the part of the River Charente's basin nearest the sea, and the inland department of Charente. Poitou and the Charentes merge into one another without any significant differences. Poitou takes in the departments of Vienne and Deux-Sèvres, and is, correspondingly, divided into Upper Poitou (Haut-Poitou: E of Thouet) and Lower Poitou (Bas-Poitou: W of Thouet).

For the tourist this region offers two different kinds of attraction. The first consists of the "Jade Coast", running S from the borders of Brittany, with Les Sables d'Olonne and other seaside resorts, and the "Côte de Beauté" N of Royan, where the light of the South begins to shine and the offshore islands gleam like arabesques in the sun. The second is centred on a little town in Charente, its best known and most famous name – Cognac, the town but also the name of the characteristic and distinctive product of this vine-growing area.

This is a region of varied landscape pattern – flat country with patches of woodland separating the meadows which provide grazing for cattle, marshland along the coast, the "Marais" from which ponds have been formed for the cultivation of oysters. The best known of these marshland areas is the Marais Poitevin (75,000 hectares), a network of watercourses on either side of the Sèvre Niortaise. The pattern of agriculture varies according to the nature of the soil – stock-farming, fruit-growing, vegetables, wine or tobacco. Although most of the land is flat the hills of the Vendée rise to heights of up to 285 m. The coastal regions with their offshore islands add a further touch of variety.

HISTORY. – Christianity came to this region in the 3rd and 4th c. In 732 Charles Martel defeated the Arabs at Poitiers. About 820 Saintes and Angoulême were destroyed in raids by the Norsemen. During the 11th and 12th c. SW France was ruled by the Counts of Poitiers and Angoulême. Poitou was incorporated in the French kingdom of 1204; but under the treaty of Brétigny in 1360 Aunis, Saintonge and Angoumois passed to the English king, and did not revert to France until 1455. In the 16th c. the region was ravaged by the Wars of Religion. Between 1793 and 1795 Vendée was the scene of a rising against the Convention in Paris, in protest against the execution of Louis XVI and the persecution of priests. In 1815 Napoleon spent his last days on French soil on the Ile d'Aix, off La Rochelle.

SIGHTS. – **Angoulême** (pop. 52,000), chief town of the department of Charente and the see of a bishop, is an industrial town, lying above the River Charente. Its finest building is the *Cathedral of St-Pierre (1105–28, restored *c*. 1650, rebuilt *c*. 1875), which, like St-Front in Périgueux and Notre-Dame in Poitiers, shows a mingling of Romanesque and Byzantine styles. The *W front has over 70 sculptured figures. – A walk (or drive) round the old town walls and towers is interesting in itself and also affords beautiful *views of the surrounding countryside. There are also several aristocratic mansions of the 18th c.

Aulnay has a magnificent Romanesque *church (St-Pierre), with a beautiful dome and fine capitals. In the churchyard is a 15th c. Hosanna cross.

Brouage has *fortifications (1630–40) typical of the pre-Vauban period: 13 m high walls, seven bastions and two gates.

The River **Charente**, which has a total length of 360 km, traverses a wide valley between Angoulême and Saintes, a distance of just under 100 km. The main features of interest in this stretch are

The Château de Labrède, home of the Montesquieu family

Bassac Abbey, the charming Romanesque churches of *Chaniers*, *Châteauneuf-sur-Charente* and *Châtre*, the town of *Cognac*, the château and dolmen of *Garde-Epée*, *Jarnac* and the notable Romanesque church of *Trois-Palis*.

Chauvigny has the beautiful 12th c. Romanesque church of St-Pierre, with particularly fine *capitals, and the imposing ruins of three castles.

Cognac (pop. 23,000) is the centre of a wine-growing area where cognac has been distilled since the 17th c. The chalky soil and the climate provide the right conditions for the vines, which cover some 173,000 acres. The trade was originally carried on by Dutch and English merchants. There are two wine-growing areas – Grande Champagne round Segonzac and Petite Champagne round Jonzac, Barbezieux and Jarnac – the best quality coming from the former area. The town has a picturesque old quarter with a number of 16th and 17th c. patrician houses and a Valois castle with parts dating from the 13th, 14th and 16th c. A visit to one of the cognac producers' establishments is recommended.

Confolens is a picturesque old town at the junction of the Vienne and the Goire,

with a Romanesque church, an old bridge and narrow lanes of houses dating from the 15th to the 18th c.

Cordouan has a *lighthouse* which can be reached from Royan at low tide. It was built in several stages between the 14th and 18th c. and now stands 66 m high; magnificent views.

Coulon is a good starting point for a boat trip into the *Marais Poitevin* (1–2 hrs).

Fenioux, N of Saintes, has a small country church with walls dating from the Carolingian period; the façade and bell-tower are Romanesque. Interesting *lanterne des morts* ("dead man's lantern").

Lichères, N of Angoulême, is a Romanesque church, standing by itself in the fields. It has a beautiful doorway.

Ligugé, S of Poitiers, has an abbey whose origins go back to the 4th c. Since 1853 it has again been occupied by Benedictine monks. The present abbey incorporates older work, and excavations carried out since 1953 have revealed interesting remains dating from the 6th c. The monks produce charming enamelled articles, which can be purchased. The church of St-Martin was rebuilt in Flamboyant style in the 16th c.

Loudun, N of Poitiers, has some charming old streets with ancient half-timbered and stone-built houses. In the Middle Ages it had a population of 20,000, three times the present population. A square tower of the 11th c., from which there are extensive views. Church in Flamboyant style.

Luçon, N of La Rochelle, is an old episcopal city, with the Cathedral of Notre-Dame (1317), in which Richelieu and Colbert were bishops. Adjoining the church are the Bishop's Palace, with a 16th c. façade, and a cloister of the same period which shows a happy blending of Gothic and Renaissance features. Charming gardens, the Jardin Dumaine, laid out in the reign of Napoleon III.

Lusignan has an old ruined castle said to have been built by the fairy Melusine.

Maillezais, N of La Rochelle, has the ruins of an abbey founded in the 10th c., with remains of the church and monastic buildings.

The **Marais Poitevin** *can* be seen by car, if you are content with a general impression; but to get to know it properly you must travel by boat – from Coulon, Arcais, La Garette or St-Hilaire-la-Palud. A distinction is made between the more attractive *marais mouillé* ("wet marsh"), known as "Venise verte" ("Green Venice"), and the drained *marais desséché* near the coast.

Melle, between Poitiers and La Rochelle, has two churches in Poitevin Romanesque style, St-Hilaire and St-Pierre.

Montmorillon, on the River Gartempe, has interesting frescoes dating from the turn of the 12th c. in the crypt of the church of Ste-Catherine.

Niort (pop. 40,000), on one of the two arms of the River Sèvre, has a castle built by Henry II Plantagenet and Richard Cœur-de-Lion whose keep dominates the town. Other features of interest are the old houses in and around Rue St-Pierre, the former Town Hall (16th c.) and two museums, one of them an attractive art museum.

Nouaillé-Maupertuis, near Poitiers, has an old abbey surrounded by walls. The church (11th–12th c., restored) contains a tomb of the 10th or 11th c.

Oiron, NW of Poitiers, has a particularly charming Renaissance château with a fresco-painted gallery, and a very fine Renaissance church (16th c.).

Parthenay, W of Poitiers, is supposed, like the castle of Lusignan, to have been built by the magic arts of the fairy Melusine. During the Middle Ages it was a staging post for pilgrims travelling to Santiago de Compostela. The Rue de la Vaux-St-Jacques has preserved much of its medieval appearance, and the town is still entered by way of the 13th c. Pont St-Jacques and Porte St-Jacques. Particularly attractive is a walk through the 13th c. citadel with its old walls and clock-tower (clock of 1454). – Above *Parthenay-le-Vieux*, 2 km away, is the Romanesque church of St-Pierre, with an octagonal tower, well restored, which has a carved figure of the fairy Melusine. – Parthenay is now an important agricultural market town.

Pornic is a little fishing port and a popular seaside resort on the "Jade Coast", with sandy beaches. The old town, with the harbour and a 13th–14th c. castle, is very attractive. Along the Jade Coast remains of the German "Atlantic Wall" can be seen.

La Rochecourbon, NW of Saintes, is a 15th c. castle which was rescued from its derelict state and restored by the novelist Pierre Loti in the 1920s. It is an imposing structure, surrounded by beautiful gardens in the French style.

Rochefort-sur-Mer (pop. 35,000), on the Charente 15 km above its mouth, was founded by Colbert in 1666 as a port. Pierre Loti (1850–1923) lived (and died) here. The old arsenal was entered through the Porte du Soleil (1830). In Place Colbert are a handsome fountain (1750), the Town Hall and the church of St-Louis. The Hôtel des Cheusses (17th c.) houses the Municipal Museum and Naval Museum.

La Rochefoucauld, near Angoulême, is notable for its fine château, built in 1622, which is reminiscent of the châteaux of the Loire; the keep dates from the 11th c. The *Grand Courtyard, which shows Italian influence, is one of the finest in France.

La Rochelle: see p 229.

Royan (pop. 18,000) was almost completely destroyed in 1945 but was rebuilt in contemporary style and is now one of France's best equipped seaside resorts, capital of the "Côte de Beauté". It has a fine beach, and there is also good bathing in the beautiful bays W of the town, served by a "panoramic road". The church of Notre-Dame, in reinforced concrete, has a tower 60 m high. Only the Pontaillac quarter in the W of the town preserves something of the tranquil atmosphere of old Royan.

Les Sables d'Olonne is one of the best known and most popular of France's large family seaside resorts, with a magnificent *beach more than 2 km long. The great rendezvous for holidaymakers is the Promenade du Remblai. Les Sables d'Olonne is also a fishing town, and the fishermen's houses are to be found in the La Chaume quarter, around the Tour d'Arundel and Fort St-Nicolas.

*St-Emilion, E of Bordeaux, is best known for its red wine, but it also has a church of the 9th–12th c. hewn out of the rock, and the 13th c. Chapelle de la Trinité, under which is the cave occupied by the hermit St Emilion, with his stone "bed"; free-standing bell-tower 67 m

Ruins of the friary, St-Emilion

high. There is a picturesque market square which is a scene of lively activity on market days. Above the square is the 13th c. Château du Roi. The fragmentary but still imposing remains of a Franciscan friary and cloister are now surrounded by vineyards.

St-Savin-sur-Gartempe, on the left bank of the River Gartempe, is noted for its Romanesque *church with magnificent **wall paintings. The finest are those on the vaulting of the nave, covering an area of 412 sq. m and illustrating the Biblical story from the Creation onwards. There are also fine paintings in the crypt. The church itself is 76 m long and has a spire 77 m high.

Saintes (pop. 28,000), on the left bank of the Charente, has fine medieval and later buildings and also notable *Roman remains. The church of St-Pierre, formerly the Cathedral, was built between 1117 and the 15th c., destroyed by the Calvinists in 1568 and soon afterwards rebuilt. Notable features are the Gothic doorway and the 15th c. tower. Equally important is the church of St-Eutrope (1096; tower 1496), a pilgrimage church which was partly destroyed during the French Revolution. The fine crypt is almost a church within the church. The church and abbey of *Ste-Marie-aux-Dames, founded in 1047, were for a time diverted to other purposes and were restored only in the course of this century. The church is Romanesque, with a richly sculptured doorway. – The old town has preserved many interesting 17th and 18th c. buildings. – Saintes was the birthplace of Dr J. I. Guillotin (1738–1814), inventor of the guillotine. – The Roman *amphitheatre is one of the earliest structures of its kind (1st c. A.D.); it is of medium size, with seating for some 20,000 spectators. The Arch of Germanicus, which is now on the right bank of the Charente, stood until 1842 in the middle of the bridge over the river; it was originally erected in A.D. 19. Nearby is an Archaeological Museum with other Roman remains. Other museums in Saintes are the Musée Mestreau (material of local and regional interest) and an art museum. – Saintes is a good starting point for a tour (some 60 km) of Romanesque churches in the style of Saintonge in the surrounding area.

The Islands

Aix has associations with Napoleon, who stayed here from 8 to 15 July 1815 before leaving for St Helena. The house in which he lived is now a museum. The island was fortified by Vauban.

*Noirmoutier, to the S of the Loire estuary, is 19 km long. It can be reached

Romanesque church, Talmont

by car over a causeway constructed at the end of the 19th c., the Passage du Gois, which at high tide is 4 m under water. The principal place on the island is *Noirmoutier-en-l'Ile*, whose main street, the Grande-Rue, opens off the Place d'Armes beside the harbour. The castle is surrounded by a rectangle of walls 100 m by 50 m; within the walls are the Governor's House and a square keep which now contains a museum. The church of St-Philibert (Romanesque and Gothic) originally belonged to a Benedictine abbey; under the choir is an 11th c. crypt – Features which appeal to holiday visitors are the Bois de la Chaize (60 hectares of woodland), the Plage des Dames, a beach of fine sand, and the adjoining Promenade des Souzeaux, from which there are views of the "Jade Coast".

* **Oléron**, with an area of 180 sq. km and a population of 15,000, is the largest French island after Corsica. It is a popular summer holiday resort, with its beautiful beaches, forests and, particularly in the N, wooded dunes. It is reached from the mainland by a *bridge 3 km long (45 piers). The principal place on the island is the little port of *Château d'Oléron* on the E coast, with a 17th c. castle. – The island's economic centre is the township of *St-Pierre-d'Oléron*, with a church (viewpoint) and a 20 m high *lanterne des morts* ("dead man's lantern") in the market square. – The most popular bathing place is *St-Trojan* (which offers only limited accommodation for visitors). – There are extensive oyster beds, particularly on the E side of the island.

Ré is 25 km long by 5–7 km wide and has an area of 85 sq. km. It can be reached by a car-ferry (15 min.) from La Pallice, near La Rochelle, and has a road (N 735) running across the island from E to W. The most popular bathing beaches are on the S coast (Ars, La Couarde, Le Bois-Plage and Ste-Marie). – The capital of the island is *St-Martin-de-Ré*, with charming old narrow streets and an old-world atmosphere. The fortifications date from the early 15th c. and were remodelled by Vauban from 1627 onwards. The circuit is interrupted by two massive gates. The former fortified church of St-Martin (15th c.) is known as the Grand Fort. – *Ars* is another charming little place, with narrow lanes and the church of St-Etienne, which has a slender spire, a beautiful Romanesque doorway and a Gothic choir. – Lighthouse 55 m high (1854).

Yeu, 10 km long by 4 km wide, is an attractive island (reached by boat from Fromentine) with a romantic castle, a rugged S coast and a fishing harbour (lobsters). Marshal Pétain was confined in a cell in the citadel from 16 November 1945 to 29 June 1951, and died at the age of 96 on 23 July 1951. He is buried in the cemetery of *Port-Joinville*, where the boat from the mainland puts in.

Provence

** **Provence, the Roman *Provincia*, owes its special charm to its clear light and brilliant sun. It is the part of France most favoured by nature and most popular with visitors – though most of those who come to Provence confine themselves to a relatively small number of places of well-established attractions. With all its variety of scenery, Provence has one common element – its beautiful climate, with an average annual temperature of 15 °C (59 °F), a long warm summer and a mild winter. From June onwards there is practically no rain throughout the summer. The only disagreeable feature is the mistral, a dry, cold wind which blows violently from the N between three and nine days at a time in spring and autumn, bringing sharp falls in temperature.**

Although Provence in the wider sense extends along the Mediterranean coast of France from the Italian frontier to the region of Montpellier, thus including the departments of Var and Alpes-Maritimes (see under *Côte d'Azur*), in the narrower sense it can be taken as including the departments of Bouches-du-Rhône and Vaucluse, along with Alpes-de-Haute-Provence (Upper Provence). Much of Provence lies within a greater or lesser distance of the *Rhône*, on both the E and W banks. A tributary of the Rhône, the *Durance*, forms a link with the Alpine part of Provence. The frontiers of Provence can be set at Barcelonnette in the NE, Montpellier in the SW, Montélimar in the NW and Marseilles in the S.

The roofs of Aigues-Mortes

HISTORY. – Provence made its appearance in history with the founding of *Massilia* (Marseilles) by Greek settlers, although it had undoubtedly been inhabited long before that period. When threatened by Celtic invaders the Greeks sought help from the Romans, who in 122 B.C. established the province of *Gallia Narbonensis*, with Narbonne and Aix as their first bases. In the reign of Augustus the province flourished, and in the early centuries A.D. Nîmes and Arles became major centres of Roman culture. In the 5th and 6th c. the vandals, Burgundians, Visigoths, Ostrogoths and Franks all successively pressed into Provence, and in 536 it became part of the Frankish kingdom. Between the 8th and 10th c. it suffered from the incursions of the Saracens. Under the treaty of Verdun in 843 Provence, together with Burgundy and Lorraine, passed to Lothair, who in 855 set up the kingdom of Provence for his son Charles. In the 10th c. Provence became part of the Holy Roman Empire. The Counts of Arles, however, had other ideas, and asserted their independence. Thereafter Provence passed from them to the Counts of Toulouse, and in 1125 to the Counts of Barcelona. In 1246 Charles became Count of Provence by his marriage, and for 200 years Provence was ruled by the House of Anjou. During this period (1309–1403) Avignon became the residence of Popes and Anti-Popes. In 1486 Provence was incorporated in France, and thereafter shared its destiny, including the 16th c. Wars of Religion. In 1720 the Nassau fief of Orange fell to France, in 1791 Avignon. In 1792 Provence sent the "Marseillaise" to Paris. But even after becoming part of France Provence preserved its own characteristics, and in the 19th c. produced an outstanding representative of Provençal language and poetry (which had flourished many centuries earlier in the age of the troubadours) in Frédéric Mistral, who was awarded the Nobel Prize for literature in 1904. During the Second World War Provence was occupied by German forces in 1942.

SIGHTS. – **Aigues-Mortes** was the port from which Louis IX (St Louis) set out on his first Crusade in 1248 with a fleet of 38 ships. The town, with its **walls and towers, was founded by Louis and further developed by his son Philip the Bold. It has preserved its medieval aspect, surrounded by its high walls. The most massive of its towers is the *Tour de Constance, for centuries used as a prison. There is a fascinating walk round the walls. – 6 km away is the old fishing port of **Le Grau-du-Roi**, now a popular holiday resort, with the new holiday centre of **Port-Camargue** and its fine marina.

Aix-en-Provence: see p. 52. – **Arles**: see p. 65. – **Avignon**: see p. 69.

Les Baux-de-Provence is a deserted village with a great historical past, strikingly situated on a great crag of rock in the *Alpilles. In the Middle Ages the lords of Les Baux made their castle a hospitable resort for the troubadours, and on occasion there were as many as 6,000 people living here. Later Les Baux became a stronghold of Protestantism, and in 1632 the castle and the walls were destroyed on the orders of Louis XIII. Then in 1822 the mineral which yields aluminium was discovered here and was given the name of bauxite.

The charm of Les Baux, now a major tourist attraction, lies in the appeal which this ruined village with its great past makes to the imagination. The main features of interest, in addition to the ruined castle with its keep and the views it offers, are the church of St-Vincent (midnight mass on Christmas Eve, with Festival of the Shepherds, which attracts a large congregation) in Place St-Vincent, the Chapel of the White Penitents, the former Town Hall (17th c.), two 16th c. aristocratic mansions and a museum. There is a monument to the Provençal poet Charloun Rieu; views extending to Arles, Aigues-Mortes and the Camargue.

Beaucaire was known until the 19th c. for its busy July market, which might attract anything up to 300,000 people. Visitors now go to see the remains of the 11th c. castle, rebuilt in the 13th c. and later pulled down by Richelieu. Within the ruined walls are a triangular tower (very fine *views), courtyards and a Romanesque chapel.

Les Baux

The *Calanques, SE of Marseilles, are deep narrow arms of the sea enclosed by rugged white limestone cliffs. Some of them are used as natural yacht harbours, and they offer endless scope for rock climbers. They can be visited from the little port of *Cassis* either on foot or (in good weather only) by boat.

The *Camargue is one of the best known – though not perhaps the most beautiful – parts of Provence. The ordinary visitor sees nothing of the famous wild horses and bulls of the Camargue (whose territory is steadily being reduced by the expansion of the rice-fields and vine-yards): they can be seen only with special

Calanque d'en Vau

Idyll in the Camargue

permission and under the guidance of one of the keepers. The Camargue occupies an area of some 138,000 acres in the Rhône delta between the Grand Rhône and the Petit Rhône. Round the Etang de Vaccarès is a nature reserve of 33,000 acres in which both the native wildlife and wintering migrant birds are protected (Camargue Museum; information centre at Ginès). From the road visitors can see the flocks of pink flamingoes which spend the summer here. There are facilities for pony-trekking on the light-coloured Camargue horses and for boat tours. – The principal place in the Camargue is **Saintes-Maries-de-la-Mer** (see below), which was painted by Van Gogh and is the venue of a famous gipsy pilgrimage. – It is perhaps worth adding a word of warning: visitors who go to the Camargue with exaggerated ideas of what they are going to see may be disappointed, particularly if they go during the dry and dusty summer.

Carpentras has a Roman triumphal arch of about the same date as the one at Orange, and the former Cathedral of St-Siffrein (15th c.), in Flamboyant style, with a treasury chapel containing wood statues (14th–16th c.).

Châteauneuf-du-Pape is the name of a famous wine and of the little town in the Rhône valley from which it comes. The wine became famous after the Popes, during their stay in Avignon, caused the vineyards to be planted. There is a small wine museum in the Caves du Père Anselme.

Fontaine-de-Vaucluse, in a picturesque *situation in a rocky cirque (vallis clausa), with a ruined castle of the Bishops of Cavaillon looming over it, is one of the most popular sights in Provence. Petrarch lived here for 16 years after his unrequited passion for Laura, who died of the plague in 1348, during his stay here. He is commemorated by a column in the square and by a museum. The *Fontaine de Vaucluse* is not a spring but the *resurgence of an underground river, swollen by rain.

Gordes, on the edge of the Vaucluse plateau N of Mont Ventoux, has a graceful Renaissance château containing a museum devoted to the contemporary painter Vasarély. There is a good view of the château from the Cavaillon road (D 15). – Near the town is the "Black Village", a long abandoned settlement of

Grignan

bories (primitive beehive-shaped houses in drystone construction).

Grignan, 45 km W of Orange, is a little town picturesquely situated on a hill, with a magnificent 16th c. château (fine views from the terrace) where the famous 17th c. letter-writer Mme de Sévigné died in 1696. Her tomb is in the town's 16th c. church.

Marseilles: see p. 150.

Montélimar is brought to the visitor's notice long before he reaches the town by the advertising for its famous white nougat. It has a ruined castle dating from the 12th–14th c.

*Montmajour** has remains of a medieval abbey with 18th c. additions; church of Notre-Dame (12th c.: crypt), cloister (Romanesque and some Gothic capitals), 14th c. keep (view).

*Mont Ventoux** (*mons ventosus*, "windy hill") is an imposing pyramidal hill which rises above the Rhône to a height of 1909 m (snow from winter into spring). There is a road to the top, where there are a telecommunications tower, a meteorological observatory and a radar station. Both the *road and the *summit afford extensive views; the road passes the *Chalet Reynard* (1460 m), a winter sports centre.

The **Moulin de Daudet** (Daudet's Mill), between Arles and Les Baux, is the setting of Daudet's "Lettres de mon moulin" (1869) – actually written in Paris. The mill contains a small museum.

Nîmes: see p. 162. – **Orange:** see p. 169.

The **Pont du Gard**, near Remoulins on the road to Uzès, is one of the most remarkable sights in Provence – a magnificent Roman aqueduct, built towards the end of the 1st c. B.C., which carried the Nîmes water supply from Uzès over the River Gardon. It is possible to walk across it at the various levels. The statistics of the structure are astonishing: lowest level, with 6 arches, 142 m long, 6 m wide and 22 m high; middle tier, with 11 arches, 242 m long, 4 m wide and 20 m high; third tier (carrying the water channel), with 35 arches, 275 m long, 3 m wide and 7 m high.

Pont Saint-Esprit is named after the bridge built over the Rhône between 1265 and 1309, some 1000 m long, with 25 arches (19 of them dating from the original construction). There is a good view of the bridge from the terrace beside the 17th c. church of St-Pierre.

Roussillon (not to be confused with the district of that name at the foot of the Pyrenees) is a village strikingly situated on a hill between the Coulon valley and the Vaucluse plateau. From the "Castrum" there are views of the ochre-coloured rocks of the surrounding area. Near the village is the "Giants' Road", with the rock formations known as the "Fairies' Needles".

St-Gilles, known as the "gateway to the Camargue", has a *church which is one of the supreme achievements of Romanesque art in Provence. The three doorways on the W front (1180–1240) are richly decorated with *sculpture. The oldest of the three is the central one (school of Toulouse), but the side doorways, with work by sculptors from the Ile

Alphonse Daudet's mill

The Roman aqueduct of Pont du Gard

de France (scenes from the life of Christ), are more interesting. Crypt (50 m by 25 m); fine spiral staircase in N tower.

St-Rémy-de-Provence has important Roman remains and excavations. Just above the town are a mausoleum and the oldest triumphal arch (early Augustan period), which is unfortunately not completely preserved. Nearby are the remains of the Greek and later Roman town of **Glanum**, dating from the 2nd c. B.C., which have been excavated since 1921. The town was destroyed by Germanic tribes in the 3rd c. Remains of the forum and of baths, a nymphaeum, temples and houses have been revealed by excavation.

Saintes-Maries-de-la-Mer is the name of a fortified church built in the 12th c. on the site of an earlier pre-Romanesque church of the 9th c. Legend has it that the three Marys and their servant Sarah, fleeing from persecution in Judaea, landed here, and the statue of Sarah has long attracted a *gipsy pilgrimage on 24–25 May and the Saturday and Sunday after 22 October. The little town has now become a popular seaside resort, and in recent years has lost much of its original

character, as depicted in Van Gogh's pictures. The Caroncelli Museum contains material illustrating the life of the Camargue.

Salon-de-Provence is an attractive little Provençal town, dominated by a castle of the 10th–15th c., with the church of St-Laurent (14th–15th c.), the church of St-Michel (Romanesque doorway) and an unusual fountain in front of the Town Hall.

Sénanque is a Cistercian abbey founded in 1148 which was occupied, with some interruptions due to the vicissitudes of history, until 1969, and has now been restored for use as a cultural centre. It has preserved monastic buildings of the 12th c. and fine cloister columns. Collection of material from the Sahara.

Silvacane is a former Cistercian abbey founded in 1144, which fell into disrepair during the Middle Ages, was used for some time as a farmhouse and has since been partly restored. It has a simple church (12th–13th c.), a late 13th c. cloister and various monastic buildings, including the refectory.

Tarascon, the home of a fabulous monster of Provençal tradition, became more widely known through Daudet's novel "Tartarin de Tarascon". It is now a market town for fruit and vegetables. It has a 12th c. church (Ste-Marthe), a 17th c. Town Hall and a monumental castle built between the 12th and the 15th c. The castle was used as a prison until 1926 but has now been restored to the condition it was in 500 years ago and is open to visitors. From the terrace there are magnificent views of the Alpilles, the Rhône, Beaucaire and Tarascon.

Uzès is one of the most striking little towns in Provence, formerly the seat of the premier French duke. The Ducal Palace (*Duché*) shows work dating from many centuries – several towers, a Renaissance façade of 1550, a Gothic chapel, a series of furnished rooms. Close by is a 2nd c. crypt, an early Christian place of worship. Cathedral of St-Théodorit (17th c.), with the 12th c. Tour Fénestrelle, 42 m high (six storeys); the circular form of the tower is unique in France. Other features of interest are a number of old mansions, another 12th c. bell-tower and a collection of old cars in the Museon di Rodo (Museum of the Wheel).

Vaison-la-Romaine, a little *town picturesquely situated on the Ouvèze, has 12 acres of excavated Roman remains. They include a theatre of the early 1st c. A.D. (rather smaller than those of Arles and Orange), a portico, a nymphaeum and a number of large houses (the House of the Silver Bust, the House of the Dolphin, etc.), which give an excellent idea of the life led by the inhabitants of the town. There is also a Roman bridge 17 m high, still carrying the road over the Ouvèze as it did 2000 years ago. – The former Cathedral of Notre-Dame (11th–13th c.) has a pre-Romanesque high altar and a fine cloister.

The ****Grand Canyon du Verdon,** one of the most magnificent gorges in Europe, lies SW of the little town of *Castellane* in the *Verdon* valley. In places the river has cut down into the Jurassic rocks to a depth of over 600 m. The valley bottom ranges between 6 and 100 m wide, while the distance across the top varies between 200 and 1500 m. For most of the way the sides of the gorge fall sheer down to the river.

Tarascon Castle

Grand Canyon du Verdon

A rewarding **round trip* of some 120–140 km (about 5 hours) would be as follows, starting and finishing in Castellane: 12 km, *Pont-de-Soleils*: cross to right bank of river. – 16 km, *Comps*, a small hamlet. Take road to right, then 13 km to the *Balcons de la Mescla, with an impressive view into the deep gorge of the Verdon. – Along the *Corniche Sublime to *Pont de l'Artuby* (3 km); then through the *Tunnels de Fayet* (view) and continue high above the *Falaises des Cavaliers* (1210 m). – Then a magnificent stretch of road round the *Cirque de Vaumale* and over the Col d'Illoire (963 m). – 21 km, *Aiguines*. – After another 8 km cross the Verdon, here dammed to form a lake 12 km long, and continue uphill. – In 3 km, road junction 2½ km S of the ancient little town of Moustiers-Ste-Marie (pottery; Romanesque-Gothic church). – Now SE above the N side of the canyon. – 18 km, La Palud (alt. 890 m: information centre). From here there is a detour (recommended) to the *Belvédères de la Maline*, to the S. – 8 km NE of La Palud is the viewpoint of *Point Sublime, 180 m above the river. Beyond this, on the right (1250 m off the road) is the *Belvédère du Couloir Samson*. – 6 km, *Pont-de-Soleils*. – 12 km, Castellane.

Villeneuve-lès-Avignon lies across the river from *Avignon* (see p. 69). The town grew up around *Fort St-André, built in the second half of the 14th c., and its development was promoted by the presence of the Popes in Avignon. It became the residence of cardinals and later of the nobility, and in consequence acquired some handsome mansions. It has a 14th c. church and cloister; in the sacristy are a 14th c. ivory figure of the Virgin and other works of art. The town's earliest work of fortification was the Tour de Philippe le Bel, built 1292–1307 and heightened by the addition of a second storey in the 14th c. (fine views from terrace). Church of the Chartreuse du Val de Bénédiction (14th c.), with the tomb of Pope Innocent VI. In the Papal chapel are fine 14th c. frescoes showing the influence of the school of Giotto.

Viviers is an old episcopal city with a history going back to the 5th c. The old town has a number of notable buildings, including a tower from the original fortifications, the Maison des Chevaliers (Renaissance façade) and the Romanesque Cathedral of St-Vincent (tapestries). There are other attractive old buildings between Place Riquet and the Grand-Rue.

FESTIVALS in Provence. – There are numerous local and regional festivals and other celebrations. In addition to those already mentioned (such as the pilgrimage at Saintes-Maries-de-la-Mer), there are the *Festival of the Tarasque* in Tarascon (last Sunday in June), the *Festival of the Ancient Theatre* at Vaison-la-Romaine (July–Aug.), the *Olive Festival* at Nyons (July) and *Christmas Fairs* at Les Baux, Allauch, Fontvieille, Séguret and Ventabren (24 Dec.).

RECREATION and SPORT. – *Bathing* in the Mediterranean and at many other places with swimming pools. – Ample scope for *tennis, riding* and *walking*. – *Fishing* in the sea and in lakes and rivers. – With so much to see in Provence, however, visitors may find that they have little leisure left for anything else.

Le Puy

Region: Auvergne.
Department: Haute-Loire.
Altitude: 630 m. – Population: 29,000.
Post code: F-43000. – Dialling code: 71.
ⓘ Office de Tourisme,
23 rue des Tables;
tel. 09 27 42.

HOTELS. – *Chris'tel*, I, 30 r.; *Régina*, II, 40 r.; *Bristol*, II, 33 r.; *Cygne*, III, 43 r.; *Parc*, III, 40 r.; *Val Vert*, IV, 23 r.; *Voyageurs*, IV, 15 r.

**Le Puy can claim, without fear of challenge, to have the most unusual topographical pattern of any town in France, with some of its principal buildings set on top of the volcanic cones which rear up within its boundaries. Situated on the eastern fringe of Auvergne, it is the chief town of the department of Haute-Loire and the see of a bishop. It is noted for its lace-making industry.

HISTORY. – The town's history goes back to the 6th c., but its great days began in the 13th c., when Louis IX (St Louis), returning from a crusade, brought back from Egypt a "Black Virgin" which became an object of pilgrimage. – Lace-making came to Le Puy in the late medieval period, and its development was promoted by a Jesuit father in the 17th c.

SIGHTS. – Although the principal monument of Le Puy is the Cathedral, at the foot of the **Rocher Corneille**, the visitor's eye is inevitably first caught by the huge *statue of the Virgin* (staircase to top) on the summit of the crag (755 m) and the *chapel of St-Michel d'Aiguilhe* (10th–11th c.) on the neighbouring pinnacle, the * **Rocher St-Michel** (flight of steps to top).

The * * **Cathdral** (*Notre-Dame du Puy*) is a 12th c. building in Romanesque style, with some Byzantine influence as a consequence of the Crusades. A broad flight of steps leads up to the façade, with further steps into the porch. A structure on the left is part of the 13th c. fortifications. Passing the beautifully carved doors of the side chapels, we come to the old main entrance, which was walled up in 1780: the present main entrance is in the S aisle.

INTERIOR. – On the high altar is the **Black Virgin**. In the sacristy is the *treasury*, with the Carolingian * *Bible de Théodulfe* (c. 795). In the *Chapel of the Relics* is a fresco of the Seven Liberal Arts. – Romanesque * **cloister**, with mosaics of coloured stones, richly carved capitals and beautiful grilles. Above the W wing is a *Museum of Religious Art*.

From the *Place du Breuil*, in the centre of the town, there is an interesting walk, passing fountains and fine old houses, to the *Place des Tables* and the **Hôtel-Dieu** with its Gothic façade. – The * **Musée Crozatier**, at the S end of the *Jardin Vinay*, is concerned with local history and the lace-making industry since the 15th c. – The finest old aristocratic mansions are in Rue Pannessac, Rue du Chamarlenc and Rue du Cardinal-de-Polignac.

SURROUNDINGS. – 5 km W, on a hill, are the ruins of the *Château de Polignac* (13th–14th c.). – 5 km S, by way of the *Pépinière de Taulhac* (view of a bend in the Loire), is a crater lake situated at an altitude of 1208 m, the **Lac du Bouchet** (106 acres).

Pyrenees

The *Pyrenees, with peaks rising to over 3000 m, are France's finest mountains after the Alps – in some respects, indeed, they rival the Alps – and form a natural frontier with Spain. On the French side they can be divided into three mountain massifs – the Pyrénées Orientales (Eastern Pyrenees) rising above the Mediterranean; the Hautes Pyrénées (High Pyrenees) extending from the Ariège valley, between Ax-les-Thermes and the Col du Puymorens, to the Vallée d'Ossau, roughly on a line from Pau to the Col du Puymorens, with the highest peaks round Bagnères-de-Luchon; and the Basses Pyrénées (Lower Pyrenees) falling towards the Atlantic and covering part of the Basque region. The total length of the range is about 450 km. On the Spanish side the Pico de Aneto reaches a height of 3404 m, but on the French side the peaks are rather lower (*Le Canigou, 2785 m).

In spite of the beauty of the mountains and valleys and the attraction of their southern climate the Pyrenees are less popular with visitors from northern Europe than other tourist regions in France, no doubt as a result of their greater distance. The best way to "discover" the Pyrenees is to follow the *"Route des Pyrénées"* (N 618), which runs from Argelès-sur-Mer on the Mediterranean to St-Jean-de-Luz on the Atlantic, a distance of something over 700 km, and affords opportunities for many attractive excursions. Plenty of time should be allowed for this tour, which runs through high valleys and involves difficult winding ascents and descents on either side of the mountain passes. The best time to make the trip is from mid May onwards, since before then – depending on snow conditions – the highest passes may be closed. This applies particularly to the Col d'Aubisque (1710 m) and the Col du Tourmalet (2115 m).

There are no large towns in the Pyrenees, though Pau in Béarn, the pilgrimage centre of Lourdes and the industrial town of Tarbes – all three situated at the foot of the mountains – are places of some consequence. There are numerous holiday resorts, including popular and old-established spas and, more recently, increasing numbers of winter sports resorts. Thanks to the more southerly situation of the Pyrenees the sun reaches comparable strength a good four weeks earlier here than in the Alps, so that January in the Pyrenees corresponds to February in the Alps.

HISTORY. – Evidence of prehistoric settlement in the Pyrenees was yielded by the caves at *Aurignac* (22 km from St-Gaudens) which gave their name to the Aurignacian culture. In historical times the region was settled by Ligurians and later (6th c. B.C. onwards) by Iberians. Between 60 and 50 B.C. it was conquered by the Romans, who established the first mineral baths. An Iberian tribe pressed forward over the Pyrenees and settled in Gascony, but the Basques remained in the Pyrenees and have preserved to this day their cultural independence and their language, on both the French and Spanish sides of the mountains. In 719 the Arabs pushed through the Pyrenees, but their advance was brought to a halt by Charles Martel's victory at Poitiers in 732. The story of Roland, which crops up at many places in the Pyrenees, dates from this period. When Charles the Bald drew his western frontier in 865, after the division of the Carolingian empire, the Pyrenees, including Roussillon, fell into Spanish Catalonia; and this remained the position until 1659, when a treaty between France and Spain made the Pyrenees the frontier between the two countries. During this period the Pyrenees were for the most part ruled by various counts, with authority over such areas as Béarn, Foix and Bigorre – though some of these had already been incorporated in France before 1659. Since the establishment of the new frontier in the 17th c. the French Pyrenees have shared the destinies of the rest of France.

SIGHTS. – **Amélie-les-Bains**, in the Tech valley, is a popular spa, open all year round. The waters were used for curative purposes in Roman times, and a Roman bath, restored, is still in use. The local festivals, such as the traditional masquerade on Shrove Tuesday and the blessing of the mules on 25 June, attract many visitors.

Argelès-sur-Mer, on the stretch of the Mediterranean coast known as the "Côte Vermeille", has a beautiful beach fringed by a pine forest. It is the starting point of the **"*Route des Pyrénées*" (N 618).

Argelès-Gazost (pop. 4000) lies at an altitude of 457 m in the High Pyrenees, between Lourdes and Cauterets. It is a popular spa (sulphurous springs) with a beautiful park. From the Tour Mendaigne in the upper town there are very fine views (orientation table). In the district of *St-Savin* is a notable church belonging to a former Benedictine abbey of the 12th–14th c., with a Romanesque doorway, a 16th c. organ and a small museum.

Arles-sur-Tech is a historic and picturesque little town in the Tech valley, with narrow lanes and wrought-iron balconies. The abbey church of Ste-Marie is one of the oldest in Roussillon (11th c.). To the left of the main doorway is the "Sainte Tombe", a 4th c. sarcophagus. Gothic cloister with leaf capitals. Church of St-Sauveur (Romanesque and Gothic).

Aulus-les-Bains (alt. 762 m) is a small spa and winter sports resort on the *Col de Latrape* (1336 m), with four mineral springs and waterfalls in the surrounding area.

Ax-les-Thermes (alt. 720 m), in the Ariège valley 15 km from the Spanish frontier, is a well-known and old-established spa, with springs which were frequented in Roman times. The "Bassin des Ladres" was used in the Middle Ages for the treatment of crusaders suffering from leprosy. There are altogether 80 springs, serving four spa establishments. Ax is a good centre for mountain walking and climbing in the summer. Near the town are the skiing areas of *Ax 1400* and *Ax 2300*, reached by cableways.

Bagnères-de-Bigorre (alt. 550 m) is a spa and holiday resort in the Adour valley. It is a picturesque old town, with the 15th c. Tour des Jacobins and remains of a cloister belonging to an earlier church. Church of St-Vincent (15th–16th c.). Salies Museum, with pictures and material of local interest. – Near the town (2 km) is the *Grotte de Médous*, with beautiful stalactites (boat trip on underground river).

Bagnères-de-Luchon (alt. 630 m) is a fashionable spa lying under the highest peak in the Pyrenees, with the winter sports resort of *Superbagnères* (1800 m) 19 km away. The springs were frequented in Roman times, and three Roman baths have been excavated. Later the spa was made fashionable by Cardinal Richelieu. The springs have one of the highest sulphur contents and one of the highest degrees of radioactivity in the world. The town offers a wide range of amenities, including a casino; regional museum. – Nearby are the fine Romanesque churches of Montauban (with crypt) and St-Aventin (two square towers, doorway with figured capitals).

Cambo-les-Bains (alt. 65 m), situated in Basque territory in the valley of the

Solar energy station, Odeillo

Nive, with *Bas-Cambo*, a village-like quarter of the town which is typically Basque, and a health resort to which the 19th c. dramatist Edmond Rostand retired (museum in his villa).

Cauterets (alt. 932 m), a spa and winter sports resort in a beautiful *situation amid the peaks of the High Pyrenees. Skiing on the *Lys plateau* (1850–2300 m), reached by cableway. Starting point for the 10 km walk to the *Lac de Gaube*, by way of the *Pont d'Espagne* (waterfall), and for other mountain walks.

Céret (alt. 171 m) is a little town situated at the point where the Tech valley enters Roussillon, with a war memorial by Maillol and a Museum of Modern Art containing works by the "Fauves", who established a school of painting here which played an influential role in modern French art (Picasso, Matisse, Dufy, Marquet, etc.). – 14th c. "Pont du Diable" over the Tech (a single arch with a span of 45 m).

Foix (alt. 400 m), formerly capital of the old county of Foix, is dominated by the castle, with three massive towers, built on a hill above the town. Foix was independent from 1001 to 1290, when it fell to Béarn. Church of St-Volusien (12th and 15th c.), with a Romanesque doorway and an unfinished square tower. Near the church are a number of old half-timbered houses and the curious Goose Fountain. – In the surrounding area are many Romanesque churches of the 11th and 12th c. – *Bénac, Loubens, Mercus, St-Jean-de-Verges, Serres-sur-Arget, Vernajoul* – and a number of caves with prehistoric rock paintings (*Grotte de Niaux, Grotte du Portel*). 6 km from the town is the underground river of *Labouiche*, with interesting rock formations (boat trip).

Font-Romeu–Odeillo–Via (alt. 1800 m) is a fashionable health and winter sports resort in a sunny *situation, surrounded by 25,000 acres of forest. *Solar Power Research Centre*, with a solar power station. Winter sports and mountain training area. With a high average sunshine level, this is a favourite resort for families with children. – Hermitage, with a chapel and a miraculous statue of the "Vierge de l'Invention" (pilgrimages on third Sunday after Whitsun, 15 August and 8 September); beautiful Calvary, with Stations of the Cross. – 6 km away is a viewpoint with magnificent distant views, Belvédère 2000.

Cirque de Gavarnie

Gavarnie (alt. 1357 m) is a small village (church of Notre-Dame-des-Neiges) which is the starting point for mountain walks and climbs, and particularly for the imposing **Cirque de Gavarnie**. The track follows a stream (1 hr walk: mules can be hired), passing the Hôtel du Cirque, to the head of the valley, surrounded by sheer rock faces with numerous waterfalls. The *Grande Cascade, which has its source in Spanish territory, is the highest waterfall in Europe, with a drop of 422 m. A short distance away is the *Brèche de Roland* (2804 m), a gash in the rocks which is said to have been hewn by Roland with his sword Durandal.

La Mongie (alt. 1800 m) is one of the leading Pyrenean winter sports resorts, 4 km from the Col du Tourmalet and 25 km from *Bagnères-de-Bigorre*. Magnificent ski runs; lifts and cableways.

Les Eaux-Bonnes (alt. 750 m) is a spa in a forest setting. Nearby, at 1385 m, is the rising winter sports resort of *Gourette*.

Les Eaux-Chaudes (alt. 656 m) is a health resort in a steep-sided wooded gorge, 4 km S of Laruns.

Lourdes: see p. 145.

Luz-St-Sauveur (alt. 730 m) is a spa and holiday resort in a sheltered situation on the Gave de Pau in the High Pyrenees. It has a fortified church of the 12th and 14th c. (not a Templars' church as is sometimes said). The resort became fashionable in the 19th c., when it was frequented by the imperial court. It is a good base for visits to many features of interest in the Pyrenees. S of the town is the Pont Napoléon (built 1860), with a span of 47 m.

Mont-Louis (alt. 1600 m) is a holiday and winter sports resort on a high plateau near Font-Romeu, with a citadel and walls built by Vauban.

Oloron-Ste-Marie (alt. 250 m) is a lively little town at the junction of the Gave d'Aspe and Gave d'Ossau. Church of Ste-Marie, with some 12th c. work and a 14th c. choir. *Romanesque doorway, with bas-reliefs in the arch depicting the capture of Jerusalem by the Comte de Béarn. Above the old town is the Romanesque church of Sainte-Croix. In the old town itself are picturesque 15th and 17th c. houses.

Orthez (alt. 62 m), on the Gave de Pau, is an attractive old town. Pont-Vieux (13th c.), with a defensive tower; Tour Moncade (13th–14th c.); Maison de Jeanne d'Albret (1500); the 14th c. Hôtel de la Lune, formerly the guest-house of the Comte de Foix; numerous burghers' houses. The medieval church of St-Pierre, restored after the Wars of Religion, formed part of the town's defences.

Pau (alt. 207 m; pop., with surrounding area, 135,000) is the capital of Béarn, a health resort popular in both summer and winter, and an important economic centre. Originally a village which grew up

around the old *hunting-lodge of the Counts of Béarn, it developed into a town which became the capital of Béarn in 1464. It was the residence of Jeanne d'Albret, Queen of Navarre and a convert to Protestantism, whose son became king of France as Henry IV in 1589. The town, which had barely 8000 inhabitants at the end of the 18th c., was "discovered" by British visitors in the 1820s and thereafter developed rapidly. Between the castle and the Parc Beaumont runs the *Boulevard des Pyrénées, just under 2 km long, which was laid out on the orders of Napoleon and affords magnificent *views of the Pyrenees. The castle, originally built

Pau (Pyrénées-Atlantiques)

between the 12th and 15th c., was extended in later centuries and has a modern entrance. It contains fine *tapestries, the apartments of Jeanne d'Albret and Henry IV, and a Museum of Béarn. The art museum is of more than regional interest, with pictures by Tintoretto, El Greco, Rubens and Degas. There is a Bernadotte Museum commemorating Marshal Bernadotte, later King of Sweden, who was born in Pau. The park contains remains of the gardens which surrounded the castle in the 16th c.

Prades (alt. 350 m), in the Têt valley, became widely known as the home of the cellist Pablo Casals. It has a Gothic church (St-Pierre), with a Romanesque tower and Spanish-style altar furnishings (17th c.). – 7 km away is the health resort of **Molitg-les-Bains**. – E of Prades, reached by N 116 and N 618, is the *Prieuré de Serrabone*, with fine carved decoration. – 3 km SE is the abbey of *St-Michel-de-Cuxa*. Some of the capitals from the cloister were sold to the United States in 1925 and are now in the Cloisters Museum in New York. Half the cloister has been rebuilt with fragments which were left or were found in the area.

St-Bertrand-de-Comminges

***St-Bertrand-de-Comminges** (alt. 446 m) is a half deserted village with a great past. It was the site of the Roman town of *Lugdunum Convenarum*, which at one time had a population of 60,000. Excavations have brought to light the forum, a temple, baths, a theatre, an amphitheatre and many other buildings. The Galerie du Trophée, in a former Benedictine abbey, contains statues of the 1st and 2nd c. – Church of *Notre-Dame, built on the site of an earlier Romanesque cathedral. The little Romanesque cloister has a famous pillar with the four Evangelists, and affords a beautiful view of the Pyrenees. – The church of *St-Just-et-St-Pasteur in the neighbouring village of Valcabrère, surrounded by a churchyard, dates from the 8th–9th c.

St-Jean-Pied-de-Port (alt. 160 m) is a picturesque old town on the Nive, with a 17th c. citadel, old houses, an old bridge, the Porte d'Ugange and the fortified church of Notre-Dame-du-Pont. – Near the town are the **Oxocelhaya and Isturits caves*, with prehistoric rock engravings and stalactites, and the *Forest of Iraty*, one of the finest in the Basque country.

Tarascon-sur-Ariège (alt. 480 m) is a little town on the Ariège, with the Tour St-Michel and a Gothic church with a fine doorway, both 14th c.

Tarbes (alt. 320 m), an industrial and commercial town with a history going back to Roman times. It was the birthplace of Marshal Foch; the house in which he was born is open to visitors. The Jardin Massey, with a 40 m high observation tower, was laid out by a director of the gardens of Versailles for his own pleasure. Museum of Bigorre; re-erected cloister (15th–16th c.) from St-Sever-de-Rustan; exhibition devoted to horse-breeding in Tarbes. National Stud (for military horses). Cathedral of Notre-Dame-de-la-Sède (13th c.), with modern pictures.

Villefranche-de-Conflent (alt. 435 m), with town walls, old houses and the 12th–13th c. church of St-Jacques.

RECREATION and SPORT in the Pyrenees. – Endless scope for *walking* and *climbing*. – *Bathing* in the Mediterranean and the Atlantic, and many swimming pools (some of them heated), both outdoor and indoor. – *Golf-courses* at Pau, Bagnères-de-Luchon, St-Jean-de-Luz and elsewhere. – *Fishing* (trout and salmon) in mountain streams. – The principal *winter sports* resorts are Ax-les-Thermes, Bagnères-de-Bigorre and Superbagnères, Barèges, Cauterets, Font-Romeu, La Mongie, Mont-Louis, Porté-Puymorens, St-Lary-Soulan and Gourette.

Reims

Region: Champagne-Ardenne.
Department: Marne.
Altitude: 83 m. – Population: 184,000.
Post code: F-51100. – Dialling code: 26.

(i) **Office de Tourisme**,
3 Boulevard de la Paix;
tel. 47 25 69.

HOTELS. – *Frantel, I, 116 r.; *Bristol*, II, 38 r.; *Paix*, II, 100 r.; *Mercure*, II, 98 r.; *Novotel*, II, 125 r.; *Continental*, III, 55 r.; *Anvers*, III, 28 r.; *Crystal*, III, 28 r.; *Nord*, III, 50 r.; *Univers*, III, 44 r.; *Alsace*, IV, 24 r.; *Arcades*, IV, 35 r.; *Auberge de France*, IV, 20 r.; *Horloge*, IV, 26 r.; *Royal*, IV, 12 r.

The **cellars** of various champagne firms can be visited.

The historic city of Reims (in the traditional English spelling Rheims), the place of coronation of the French kings, the see of a bishop since the 4th c. (and now of an archbishop), owes its fame to its Cathedral, one of the supreme achievements of Gothic architecture, and to its champagne. Here past and present combine to form a memorable whole.

HISTORY. – The city takes its name from a Celtic tribe, the *Remi*, who lived here before the coming of the Romans. Later it became the Roman *Durocortorum*, then a more important place than Paris. After the

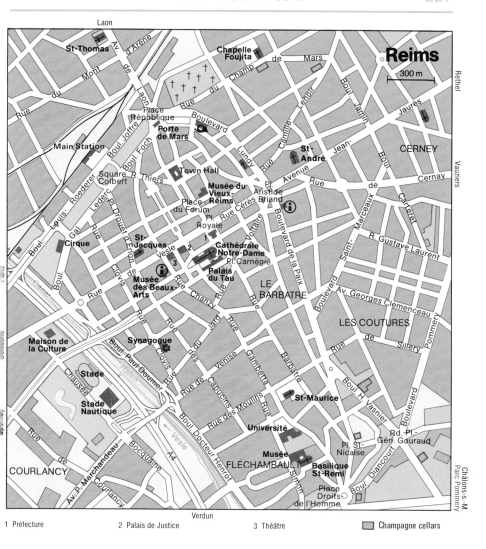

1 Préfecture   2 Palais de Justice   3 Théâtre   ▢ Champagne cellars

baptism of Clovis, king of the Franks, by the local bishop, St Remi (Remigius), in 496, which was followed by the conversion of the Franks, the status of the bishops of Reims was enhanced. Thereafter it fell to them to crown successive kings of France, and in consequence the town grew steadily in importance between 988 and 1825. On 17 July 1429 Joan of Arc accompanied Charles VII to the Cathedral for his anointing. During the First World War Reims suffered heavy damage in the first battle of the Marne and throughout the later course of the war, four-fifths of its buildings, including the Cathedral, being either wholly or partly destroyed. The city suffered further damage, though on a lesser scale, during the Second World War, which ended with the German surrender in Reims in May 1945.

SIGHTS. – The **Cathedral (*Notre-Dame*) stands in the centre of the city in *Place du Cardinal-Luçon*. It is one of the great masterpieces of Gothic architecture, even though much of the sculpture is badly weathered and requires a continuing programme of restoration and repair. It occupies the site of the church in which Clovis was baptised in the 5th c. and in which the early kings of France were crowned. The building as we see it today was begun in 1211 and finished by 1294, apart from the towers, which were completed in 1428. The tower over the crossing was destroyed in 1914. The finest features of the Cathedral are the three *doorways on the W front, with the great *rose window (12 m in diameter) above the central doorway, the gallery of royal statues above this again and finally the two towers rising to a height of 82·5 m. A profusion of medieval sculpture adorns both the exterior and interior of the Cathedral. The sculpture on the *central doorway depicts the life of the Virgin. On the left doorway is the guardian angel with the famous "Sourire de Reims" ("Smile of Reims"). – The Cathedral is 138·5 m long, just under 50 m wide in the transepts and 38 m high. Unfortunately the stained glass has been almost completely destroyed; a few windows have

Interior of Reims Cathedral

with many kilometres of underground galleries hewn from the chalk (conducted tours).

As reminders of its Roman past Reims has the remains of its *forum* (partly excavated) and a triumphal arch, the ***Porte de Mars** (2nd c. A.D.), which served as a town gate until 1544; it was fully exposed to view by the removal of adjoining buildings in 1817.

Rennes

Region: Bretagne.
Department: Ille-et-Vilaine.
Altitude: 30 m. – Population: 205,000.
Post code: F-35000. – Dialling code: 99.
ⓘ **Office de Tourisme,**
Pont de Nemours;
tel. 30 73 24.

HOTELS. – *Frantel*, II, 140 r.; *Novotel*, II, 104 r., SP; *Du Guesclin*, II, 75 r.; *Central*, II, 44 r.; *Président*, II, 34 r.; *Cheval d'Or*, III, 42 r.; *Astrid*, III, 30 r.; *Voyageurs*, III, 24 r.; *Brest*, IV, 30 r.

RESTAURANTS in the hotels; also *Rôtisserie Le Coq-Gadby, Ti-Koz*.

Rennes, situated at the junction of the canalised Ille and the Vilaine, is chief town of the department of Ille-et-Vilaine, a university town and the see of an archbishop. The old capital of Brittany, Rennes is still its economic and cultural centre.

Rennes is now almost entirely a modern city, in consequence partly of a great fire in 1720, which burned for a week and destroyed most of the old town, and partly of bombing during the last war which severely damaged other parts of the city.

SIGHTS. – In the centre of the older part of the town is the *Place de la Mairie*, with the handsome **Town Hall** (*Hôtel de Ville*), built in 1734 by Louis XV's architect Gabriel, and the *Theatre* (1831–35). – A little way E of the Theatre is the 16th c. church of *St-Germain*.

To the N is the *Place du Palais*, surrounded by elegant 18th c. houses. On the N side of the square is the ***Palais de Justice** (Law Courts), built 1618–54, formerly the seat of the Breton Parliament. Richly decorated interior; particularly notable is the *Grand'Chambre, with a beautiful wooden ceiling and magnificent tapestries.

been restored, and there are six new ones by Marc Chagall (1974). There is a rich treasury.

In the SE of the town is the church of *St-Remi, formerly belonging to an abbey. The nave and transepts are Romanesque; all the rest is Gothic. In the choir is the tomb of St Remi.

The main square of the city is the *Place Royale*, with buildings in classical style and an equestrian statue of Louis XIV. There are three important museums: the Museum of Fine Arts, with *tapestries and a fine collection of pictures; a Cathedral Museum, with sculpture from the Cathedral which has been replaced by replicas; and the Museum of Old Reims. – At the Rond-Point Pommery is the entrance to the famous *Pommery Champagne Cellars*,

½ km NE of the Palais de Justice is the former abbey church of **Notre-Dame** (*St-Mélaine*, 11th–13th c.), with a richly sculptured façade. To the left of the church are the old monastic buildings, now housing the City Planning Department, with a beautiful *cloister*. Behind the church, to the E, extends the *Jardin du Thabor*, formerly the abbey gardens and now the city's finest park, with the *Botanic gardens* adjoining.

W of the Place de la Mairie is the attractive church of *St-Sauveur* (1725). Beyond this is the **Cathedral** (*St-Pierre*), a very old foundation which was almost completely rebuilt in the 19th c. It has a W front in classical style, with two towers built between 1541 and 1703, and a spacious interior; in the last chapel in the S aisle is a very beautiful altar (German school, 15th c.).

In the narrow streets S of the Cathedral many old houses have been preserved, like the 18th c. *Hôtel de Blossac* at 6 rue du Chapitre. A short distance W of the Cathedral is the *Porte Mordelaise*, a relic of the town's 15th c. defences.

To the S of Place de la Mairie and the Cathedral the canalised River Vilaine flows from E to W, flanked on either side by busy streets with new blocks of flats. These streets cut across the animated *Place de la République*, laid out in quite recent times over the Vilaine. On the S side of the square, in the newer part of the city on the left bank of the Vilaine, is the massive *Palais du Commerce* (Chamber of Commerce: 19th–20th c.), also housing the *Head Post Office*.

To the E, on Quai Emile-Zola, is the *Palais des Musées. The *Museum of Fine Arts* has, among much else, fine French, Italian and Dutch paintings, sculpture and ceramics. The *Museum of Brittany* is devoted to archaeology and folk art, and has much excavated material from Brittany and the Mediterranean countries, together with applied art, furniture, costumes and pictures, mainly from Brittany and Italy. – Opposite the museum building, to the SW, is the old Jesuit church of *Toussaints* (1624–57), with a richly decorated interior.

Visitors who have enough time at their disposal will find it rewarding to walk through some of the well-preserved little streets of old Rennes which escaped the 1720 fire. They are mostly to be found S of the Cathedral, e.g. in Rue des Dammes and Rue du Chapitre.

La Rochelle

Region: Poitou-Charentes.
Department: Charente-Maritime.
Altitude: at sea level. – Population: 80,000.
Post code: F-17000. – Dialling code: 46.
(i) **Office de Tourisme,**
　 10 rue Fleuriau;
　 tel. 41 14 68.

HOTELS. – *Brises*, II, 46 r.; *Yachtman*, II, 36 r., SP; *Champlain*, II, 35 r.; *France et Angleterre*, II, 75 r.; *François*, III, 34 r.; *Terminus*, III, 27 r.; *Savary*, III, 27 r.; *Atlantic*, IV, 29 r.

The interesting port town of La Rochelle, formerly capital of the district of Aunis and now chief town of the department of Charente-Maritime and the see of a bishop, lies between Nantes and Bordeaux in a bay on the Atlantic which is sheltered on the seaward side by the islands of Ré and Oléron. The fishing harbour to the S of the old town is the second largest in France (after Boulogne); the largest seagoing ships use the outer harbour of La Pallice.

HISTORY. – Between the 14th and the 18th c. La Rochelle was one of France's leading maritime towns, carrying on an independent trade with North America from an early period. During the Wars of Religion, as a stronghold of the Huguenots, it was the scene of much fighting. In 1628 it was besieged by Richelieu's forces and starved into surrender. The revocation of the Edict of Nantes in 1683 and the loss of Canada in 1763 ended La Rochelle's great days; but with its old harbour defences and its arcaded houses the town has preserved much of the character of the Huguenot period. During the Second World War the German garrison in La Rochelle held out until the final surrender on 8 May 1945. – The famous physicist René-Antoine de Réaumur (1683–1757), inventor of the Réaumur temperature scale, was born in La Rochelle.

SIGHTS. – In the centre of La Rochelle is the *Place de l'Hôtel de Ville*, with the *Hôtel de Ville** (Town Hall), a richly decorated Renaissance building mainly dating from 1595 to 1606, surrounded by a defensive wall completed in 1498. In *Rue des Merciers*, an arcaded street which runs from the NE corner of the Town Hall to the market square, are many picturesque old houses (particularly Nos. 3, 5, 8, 17 and 23).

From the Town Hall the Rue Dupaty runs W into the town's main N–S axis – to the

Panoramic view of La Rochelle

left Rue du Palais, lined by arcades of the 14th–18th c., to the right *Rue Chaudrier*, which runs N into the *Place de Verdun*. – At the far end of Rue Chaudrier, on the left, is the **Cathedral** (*St-Louis*), a building in classical style (1742–62) with a 15th c. tower. – A short distance SW of the Cathedral is the *Musée d'Orbigny* (local history, ceramics, East Asian art). To the S of the Museum is *Rue de l'Escale*, lined with handsome Baroque houses. – A little way W of the Place de Verdun, in Rue Gargoulleau, is the former Bishop's Palace (18th c.), which now houses the **Musée de Peinture** (the municipal art gallery) and the *Municipal Library*. Notable among the pictures in the Museum are a landscape by Corot and an "Adoration of the Shepherds" by E. Le Sueur.

In *Rue Albert-Ier*, the northward continuation of Rue Chaudrier, is the **Jardin des Plantes** (*Botanical Garden*), with the *Fleuriau Museum* (natural history) and *Lafaille Museum* (oceanography and ethnography).

In Rue du Palais, on right, are the *Palais de Justice* (Law Courts: 1789) and the *Bourse* (Exchange: 1785), with a beautiful courtyard. – At the end of the street is the **Porte de la Grosse-Horloge** (14th–15th c.), the only surviving town gate; the top portion dates from 1746. –

Beyond the gate, flanked by *Quai Duperré* and *Cours Wilson*, is the **Old Harbour**, a busy and picturesque scene with its crowded fishing boats (boat trips round the harbour). The entrance from the *outer harbour* is guarded by the massive *Tour St-Nicolas* (1384: view) on the E side and the *Tour de la Chaîne* on the W. The Tour de la Chaîne (which contains an interesting relief model of the town) is named after the chain which was drawn across

Salt-pans, La Rochelle

the mouth of the harbour at night during the Middle Ages. From the S side of the outer harbour there is a magnificent *view of the main harbour and the towers of the town.

From Cours Wilson *Rue St-Jean-du-Pérot* runs SW, with the *fish-market* on the right and the 17th c. *Tour St-Jean*, a relic of a church which once stood here. Farther on, to the left, is the **Tour de la Lanterne**, built 1445–76 as a lighthouse (*view). – At the far end of Rue St-Jean-du-Pérot is the beautiful **Parc Charruyer**, which runs alongside the old *fortifications*. Beyond the park it is continued by the *Mail*, a promenade, much frequented in summer, which runs past the bathing beach (casino) and along the seafront.

SURROUNDINGS. – 7 km W is the little town of **La Pallice**, with La Rochelle's New Harbour (1883–90), which can accommodate large ships. Here too can be seen the important German submarine base established during the last war.

2½ km offshore, lying across the N end of a spacious bay, the *Pertuis d'Antioche*, is the **Ile de Ré** (25 km long, 5–7 km wide, area 85 sq. km), with extensive vineyards, salt-pans and oyster-beds. See p. 214.

Rouen

Region: Haute-Normandie.
Department: Seine-Maritime.
Altitude: 10 m. – Population: 118,000.
Post code: F-76000. – Dialling code: 35.
ⓘ Office de tourisme,
   25 Place de la Cathédrale;
   tel. 71 41 77.

HOTELS. – *Dieppe*, II, 42 r.; *Frantel*, II, 125 r.; *Poste*, II, 84 r.; *Astrid*, III, 40 r.; *Nord*, III, 60 r.; *Bordeaux*, III, 43 r.; *Viking*, III, 37 r.; *Chapeau-Rouge*, IV, 30 r.; *Petit Palais Royal*, IV, 36 r.; *Escargot*, IV, 16 r.; *Carillon*, IV, 15 r.; *France*, IV, 95 r.; *Rochefoucauld*, IV, 34 r.; *Chantilly*, IV, 10 r.

Rouen, capital of Upper Normandy and an important port, lies on the right bank of the Seine, 86 km E of its mouth. The city suffered heavy damage by fire in 1940 and bombing in 1944, and after reconstruction takes pride in its status as a "museum town" (*Ville Musée*) **and as the most attractive to tourists of the large cities of northern France. It is a major centre of the cotton industry.**

HISTORY. – The Gallic town of *Rotomagus*, capital of the Vellocasses, flourished under the Romans and became the see of a bishop in the year 260. In 911

Rollo, a leader of the invading Norsemen, became Duke of Normandy as Robert I. From 1066 to 1204 Rouen, along with the rest of Normandy, belonged to England, and from 1419 to 1449, during the Hundred Years War, it was again in English hands. The trial and burning of Joan of Arc took place here in 1431. In 1449 Charles VII recaptured the town, and thereafter it prospered until the outbreak of the Wars of Religion. The 16th and 17th c., however, brought further trials, and after the revocation of the Edict of Nantes in 1683 over half the population of Rouen left the town. Then in the 18th c. the textile industry brought a further period of prosperity. The novelist Gustave Flaubert, author of "Madame Bovary", was born in Rouen in 1821. The Second World War meant a purely temporary setback to the city's fortunes.

View of Rouen

SIGHTS. – The ***Cathedral** (*Notre-Dame*), in the centre of the old town, is one of France's most beautiful Gothic cathedrals. It was begun in the early 13th c. (transept 1280) but not completed until the 16th c. The *W front dates from 1509 to 1530, and is flanked by two towers. The lower part of the N tower was built in the 12th c.; the S tower, the *Tour de Beurre* (Butter Tower), was built between 1485 and 1507, and is 77 m high. (The Butter Tower is so called because it was paid for by offerings from the faithful, who in return were permitted to eat butter during Lent.) The spire over the crossing is the highest in France (151 m); it is made of cast-iron, and replaces an earlier stone spire destroyed by lightning in 1822. The side doorways as well as the central one are richly decorated with sculpture. The *interior is of majestic dimensions (136 m long, transepts 51·6 m across). Its finest feature is the choir, but it also contains a number of notable tombs and stained glass of various periods including the present day. The Cathedral was extensively restored after the last war to make good the damage it had suffered.

The site of the old town is now occupied by modern blocks of flats extending down to the Seine. Only one Renaissance building, the Fierté St-Romain (1542),

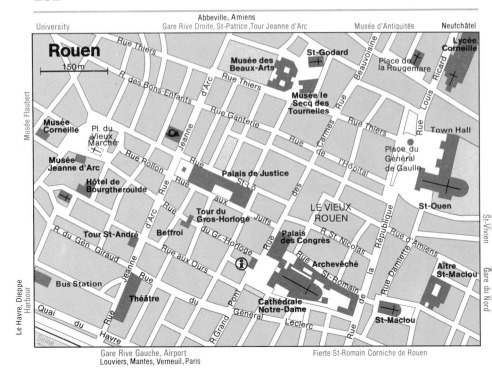

has been preserved. The bridges over the Seine are new, replacing those destroyed during the war.

The second most important church in Rouen is *St-Ouen, a late Gothic church which originally belonged to an abbey; the W doorway is 19th c. The top of the striking tower over the crossing (early 16th c.) is known as the "Crown of Normandy". The interior is also very fine. – A third notable church is *St-Maclou (1437–1517), in Flamboyant style. It has an impressive W front, with three *doorways, two of which have fine Renaissance doors; the spire is modern. A short distance away is the **Aître St-Maclou** (from Latin *atrium*, "courtyard"), one of the few surviving medieval charnel-houses, with wooden galleries running round the central courtyard; it is now occupied by the School of Fine Arts.

Rouen's best-known secular building is the ***Great Clock-Tower** (*Gros-Horloge*), a gateway of 1527 flanked by an earlier tower. It spans the Rue du Gros-Horloge, in which are a number of old houses. – Other notable buildings are the *Hôtel de Bourgtheroulde* (16th c.), the Gothic* **Palais de Justice** (Law Courts), and the *Tour de Jeanne d'Arc* (a relic of a castle which once stood here), in which Joan of Arc was tortured. – The *Place du Vieux-Marché* is the place where Joan of Arc was burned at the stake on 30 May 1431, at a spot marked in the roadway (though the square has been much changed since 1431).

The *museums* of Rouen deserve a day to themselves. There is a *museum on the life of Joan of Arc*, and museums devoted to *Corneille* (his birthplace in Rue de la Pie) and *Flaubert*. The ***Museum of Fine Arts** contains an excellent collection of pictures and notable examples of local ceramics. The ***Le Secq des Tournelles Museum** has a remarkable collection of wrought-iron work. The **Museum of Antiquities** is housed in a former convent. There is also a *Museum of Natural History, Ethnography and Prehistory*.

Roussillon (Languedoc-Roussillon)

*Roussillon, in the extreme south of France, is a region particularly favoured by nature in terms of climate and vegetation. It extends westward from Perpignan along the northern flanks of the Pyrenees, taking in considerable areas of the range. From Roussillon come the early vegetables and fruit which supply the markets of France year by year. The early establishment of human

settlement in this region was reflected in an early flowering of art;
and the earliest sculptured figures in
the whole of Western art, dating
from 1020, are to be found in the
church of St-Genis-des-Fontaines,
to the S of Perpignan between Céret
and Argelès-sur-Mer.

The coast of Languedoc, which immediately adjoins the "Côte Sablonneuse" (Sandy Coast) of Roussillon,
has gained greatly in tourist attraction over the last ten years or so
through the development of elaborately planned holiday centres, extending eastward into Provence.
This whole stretch of coast is commonly referred to under the joint
name of Languedoc-Roussillon
(strictly, Littoral du Languedoc-
Roussillon).

SIGHTS. – **Perpignan** (pop. 120,000) is
the most important town in Roussillon
and its agricultural market centre. The
name – which is first recorded in the 12th
c. – is said to come from a cowherd named
Père Pinya from Mont-Louis in the
Pyrenees who came down to the coast
and settled here. Between 1278 and 1344
Perpignan was capital of the kingdom of
Majorca, which took in the Balearics,
Roussillon, Cerdagne and the coastal area
round Montpellier. The town developed
rapidly after the middle of the 19th c.,
expanding beyond its old walls; and its
population has increased threefold since
1914. The citadel, with the royal castle

Le Castillet, Perpignan

(restored), recalls Perpignan's heyday as
capital of the Majorcan kingdom. The
present fortifications date from the time of
Vauban. The royal palace, a masterpiece
of southern French medieval architecture,
is the town's most important building,
begun in 1284 but not completed until the
16th c. The main tower, in the middle of
the E front of the grand courtyard,
contains two chapels, one above the
other; the upper one, the Chapelle de la
Sainte-Croix (the royal chapel), has a
13th c. marble doorway. Nearby is the
entrance to the Great Hall (32 m long, 13
m wide and 13 m high). – The particular
charm of Perpignan, with its Spanish
flavour, can best be appreciated by a walk
through the old town, starting from the
Place de la République (Theatre) and
continuing by way of Place de la Loge
(with the *Loge de Mer, built in 1397 and
enlarged in the 16th c.) and the Town Hall
(13th, 16th and 17th c.) to the Cathedral
of St-Jean. Built between 1324 and
1509, this shows all the characteristics of
southern French Gothic. The *interior is
notable for its beautiful reredoses. Under
the passage leading to the chapel of
Notre-Dame-dels-Correchs (11th c.) are
remains of the original church of St-Jean-
le-Vieux. In the Chapelle du Christ
is a finely carved *crucifix known as
the "Dévot Christ" (1307), one of the
supreme achievements of medieval sculpture, probably from the Rhineland. –

Gruissan (Aude)

Other notable churches in the town are St-Jacques (14th and 18th c.), starting point of the famous Good Friday procession, and the 14th c. Notre-Dame-la-Réal, court church of the queen of Majorca. The Tour du Castillet (1370), a relic of the old town walls, affords wide views of Roussillon and the Pyrenees and, with the Casa Pairal, houses a museum of Roussillon art and folk traditions. The Rigaud Museum contains work by Hyacinthe Rigaud, court painter to Louis XIV, and also works of Catalan art.

15 km N of Perpignan is **Salses**, with an imposing 15th c. castle built by the Spaniards to defend Roussillon. The road to Salses passes close to *Rivesaltes*, which is noted for its excellent wines; the Muscatel of Rivesaltes ranks as one of the best such wines in France. Other well-

Cap d'Agde holiday centre (Hérault)

Salses Castle (Roussillon)

known wines are produced at *Baixas*, W of Rivesaltes, and *Thuir*, to the S, which also makes a world-famed apéritif. In Baixas it is worth looking into the 17th c. church, which has a magnificent altar. – 10 km E of Perpignan is the lively seaside resort of *Canet-Plage*, with a beach of fine sand.

Along the coast N and NE of Perpignan are a series of modern *holiday centres* offering every facility for visitors, particularly for water sports enthusiasts – *Port-Barcarès*, **Port-Leucate**, *Gruissan*, *Valras-Plage*, **Cap d'Agde**, *Carnon* and **La Grande Motte**, with a total of some 1660 moorings for boats. Between the Spanish frontier and the borders of Provence there are no fewer than 8000 moorings. There is an observation and rescue station at Cap d'Agde. To the N of Cap d'Agde, too, is the largest naturist centre in the Mediterranean, with an extensive beach. The various holiday centres, promoted and planned by government agencies, vary in style and

layout, and great care has been taken to fit them into the landscape. These new developments have opened up a whole region which previously had few attractions for holidaymakers. There is also one of these new centres SE of Perpignan at *St-Cyprien*, adjoining Canet-Plage.

Agde, at the mouth of the Hérault between Sète and Béziers, was originally a Phoenician settlement. The name comes from the Greek *Agathe (Tyche)*, "good fortune". It is a town of narrow streets, with three churches, including the Cathedral of St-Etienne (12th c., originally founded in the 5th c.), a fortified church with thick walls of black volcanic stone. The Musée Agathois contains objects recovered by underwater excavation and local material of folk interest.

Béziers (pop. 90,000) is a centre of the southern French wine trade. The town was completely destroyed during the Albigensian wars, but in the 17th c. it prospered as a result of the construction of the Canal du Midi linking the Mediter-

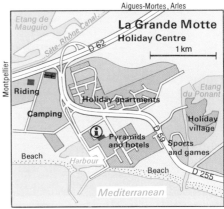

Béziers (Hérault)

ranean and the Atlantic. The beautiful Allées Paul-Riquet are named after the 17th c. nobleman who directed the building of the canal. The *Cathedral of St-Nazaire (13th and 14th c.) has a cloister containing pieces of sculpture and various fragments. The Museum of Fine Art near the Cathedral has works by medieval Flemish and German masters, including Holbein, and other artists down to the 19th c. There are remains of a Roman theatre. The Arena, with seating for more than 13,000 spectators, is also used for bullfights, earning Béziers the title of the "French Seville". – 14 km SW is the **Oppidum d'Ensérune**, with the excavated remains of an Iberian and Greek settlement of the 4th–3rd c. B.C. and a museum; there is also a Wine Museum.

Elne was once the see of a bishop, and for a time was capital of the whole of Roussillon. In 1602 the bishop moved to Perpignan, and Elne declined. The Cathedral of Ste-Eulalie dates from the 11th c. (with some later work, including the N tower) and has a magnificent cloister, the first gallery dating from the 12th c. and the second from the 13th–14th (fine Romanesque capitals with animal decoration).

Montpellier (pop. 200,000), capital of southern Languedoc, is a noted art centre, the see of a bishop, a university town and the chief town of the department of Hérault. The central feature of the town is the *Place de la Comédie* (Theatre), with the Esplanade, a spacious promenade laid out in the 18th c., opening out to the N. In the *Promenade du Peyrou on the W side of the town are a triumphal arch erected in 1691 in honour of Louis XIV and an

equestrian statue of the king. At the W end of the Promenade is a water tower with an 800 m length of the aqueduct built 1753–66 to bring water from a spring 14 km away. – The Jardin des Plantes was France's first botanical garden (1593). – The Cathedral of St-Pierre dates mainly from the 14th c. (Gothic porch and nave), but was not completed until the 19th c. – Montpellier has many patrician and merchants' houses of the 17th and 18th c. with fine decorated façades. Most of them are in the University quarter, e.g. in Rue du Cannau, Place Aristide-Briand and Rue Jean-Moulin. The 17th c. Hôtel de Lunaret houses the Archaeological Museum. The city's principal museum is the richly stocked *Fabre Museum (pictures and sculpture). The Atger Museum, in the former Bishop's Palace (16th c.), has a collection of Baroque drawings.

Montpellier Cathedral

Narbonne (pop. 41,000) vies with Béziers as a centre of the wine trade of southern France. The *Cathedral of St-Just consists only of a choir (13th–14th c.), which, with a height of 41 m, rivals the cathedrals of northern France and is surpassed only by Amiens and Beauvais. The Chapelle de l'Annonciade, added in the 15th c., contains the Cathedral treasury (beautiful 17th–18th c. tapestries). Adjoining the Cathedral is the fortress-like *Archbishop's Palace, built between the 10th and 17th c., which now houses the Town Hall and two museums, the Museum of Art and History (pottery and ceramics, pictures) in the Palais Neuf and the Archaeological Museum in the Vieux Palais. Between the Cathedral and the Palace is a fine 14th c. cloister. The Maison des Trois Nourrices (House of the

Three Nurses) is a 16th c. house in Renaissance style in which Cinq-Mars, one of the conspirators in a plot against Richelieu, was arrested. – On the coast is *Narbonne-Plage*, with a sandy beach. – SW of Narbonne (N 113 and N 613) is the Cistercian abbey of *Fontfroide, situated in a wild and romantic valley, with a 13th c. Romanesque church and the finest cloister in southern France.

Sète (pop. 42,000) became an important port for trade with North Africa after the harbours of Narbonne and Aigues-Mortes silted up. The old harbour dates from the time of Louis XIV; from the Môle St-Louis there is a fine view of the town and *Mont St-Clair with the Fort Richelieu. The writer Paul Valéry is buried in the cemetery (the "Cimetière marin" of his best-known poem), and there is a room devoted to him in the Municipal Museum. the museum also contains works by modern painters and costumes, etc., associated with the traditional fishermen's festival, the Joutes Sètoises, held annually on 25 August.

SPORT and RECREATION in Languedoc-Roussillon. – The long stretch of coast from the Spanish frontier to the borders of Provence offers facilities for a wide range of activities; the new **holiday centres** in particular are well equipped to cater for every kind of **water sport**, with many sailing schools, water skiing, scuba diving and boating. All the holiday centres also have tennis courts and facilities for riding and other sports. – There are also a variety of interesting **folk events**.

The boating harbour, Sète (Hérault)

St-Malo

Region: Bretagne.
Department: Ille-et-Vilaine.
Altitude: at sea level. – Population: 46,000.
Post code: F-35400. – Dialling code: 99.

(i) **Office de Tourisme,**
Esplanade St-Vincent;
tel. 40 84 67.

HOTELS. – *Central*, II, 44 r.; *Duguesclin*, II, 23 r.; *Univers*, II, 74 r.; *France et Chateaubriand*, III, 80 r.; *Digue*, III, 55 r.; *Bristol-Union*, III, 26 r.; *Alba*, III, 24 r.; *Continental*, III, 25 r.; *Hostellerie Grotte aux Fées*, III, 40 r.; *Jacques Cartier*, IV, 29 r.; *Louvre*, IV, 47 r.; *Commerce*. IV, 29 r. – IN PARAMÉ: *Thermes*, III, 72 r.; *Chateaubriand*, III, 17 r.; *Surcouf*, III, 16 r.; *Courtoisville*, III, 40 r.; *Charmettes*, IV, 18 r.; *Bains de Rochebonne*, IV, 22 r.; *Manoir*, IV, 20 r.; *Rochebelle*, IV, 33 r. – IN ST-SERVAN: *Servannais*, III, 47 r.; *Rance*, IV, 20 r.

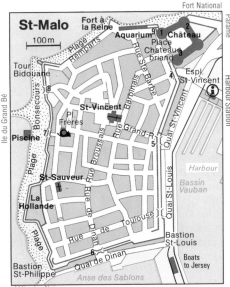

1 Galerie Quic-en-Groigne
2 Town Hall
3 Musée
4 Porte St-Vincent
5 Grande Porte
6 Porte de Dinan
7 Porte des Bés
8 Porte Champs Vauverts
9 Porte St-Thomas

The Breton port of St-Malo has a magnificent *situation on a former island now joined to the mainland at the mouth of the broad River Rance, facing the town of Dinard across the river to the W. Still surrounded by its old walls, it preserves the aspect of a fortified coastal town of the Middle Ages.

St Malo's heyday was between the 16th and 18th c., when a native of the town, Jacques Cartier (1491–1557), discovered Canada (1534) and established some of his fellow citizens as its first settlers, and when other daring seamen

The harbour, St-Malo

from St-Malo were sailing the seas in all directions. The French writer and statesman Chateaubriand (1768–1848) was born in St-Malo. – During the Second World War the *old town was largely destroyed, with the exception of the walls, but has since been rebuilt in its original style, with narrow little streets and tall granite houses.

SIGHTS. – Inside the walls at the NE corner of the old town, near the handsome *Porte St-Vincent*, is *Place Chateaubriand*, a busy traffic intersection. The Hôtel France et Chateaubriand occupies the site of the house in which Chateaubriand was born. On the E side of the square is the massive **Castle** (14th and 15th c.), with four towers. In one of the towers, the Tour Quic-en-Groigne at the NW corner, is the *Galerie Quic-en-Groigne*, with interesting displays (including wax figures) illustrating events in the history of the town. In the SW wing of the castle is the *Municipal Museum*, also mainly devoted to the history of the town; from here visitors can gain access to the towers, from which there are fine views. – To the W, in Place Vauban, is an interesting *aquarium*. SW of the castle is the parish church of *St-Vincent*, formerly the Cathedral (14th and 15th c.; W front 1713).

From the *Porte St-Thomas*, immediately N of Place Chateaubriand, and from the other town gates, steps lead up to the *ramparts. A walk round the complete circuit takes between half an hour and an hour. From the ramparts, and particularly from the projecting bastions on the N and W sides, there are magnificent views of the town, the mouth of the Rance, with Dinard on the opposite bank, and the sea and offshore islands. The views are particularly fine at high tide, which is usually 7 or 8 m above low tide but at the spring-tides may be over 15 m above. Below the W side of the ramparts is the *Bonsecours* bathing beach, with a swimming pool. – From the Castle the *Grande Plage* extends eastwards to PARAMÉ. On an island off its western end is *Fort National*, built by Vauban in 1689 (accessible on foot only at low tide).

To the E of the old town is the **Harbour**, with several basins.

SURROUNDINGS. – $\frac{1}{2}$ km NW of the town, on the island of **Grand Bré** (a 20 minutes' walk through the shallows at low tide), is the lonely tomb of Chateaubriand. – 300 m W is the smaller island of *Petit Bré*.

$\frac{1}{2}$ km S of St-Malo, beyond the harbour, is the district of **St-Servan**, with the church of Sainte-Croix (18th–19th c.: fine interior). – $\frac{1}{2}$ km W of the church, on the S side of a peninsula, is *Port St-Père*. On the SE side of this natural harbour is the massive *Tour Solidor*, formerly used as a prison. From the N side of the harbour a magnificent promenade, the **Corniche d'Aleth*, encircles the peninsula, offering wide-ranging views. At the NW corner of the peninsula, on the site of the Gallo-Roman city of *Aleth*, is the *Fort de la Cité*, which was strengthened and stubbornly defended by German forces during the last war.

The **boat trip up the Rance*, passing Dinard and the tidal power station, to **Dinan** and back is strongly to be recommended. The return trip, without disembarking takes about 4 hours.

Savoy

Savoy and the Dauphiné (see p 112) lie in the French Alpine region, and the Savoy Alps have the highest peak not only in France but in the whole of Europe – Mont Blanc (4810 m). Savoy takes in the departments of Haute-Savoie and Savoie (chief towns Annecy and Chambéry) and extends from the southern shore of Lake Geneva to a line running between Chambéry and Grenoble from Les Echelles to the Col du Galibier. Most of this region is occupied by the Savoy Alps with an adjoining pre-Alpine area of lakes, including the Lac d'Annecy and the Lac du Bourget. Here the mountains rise to heights of up to 1800 m. Savoy forms

Megève in winter

the northern part of the French Alps, bounded on the S by the Dauphiné and on the E by Switzerland and Italy.

The Savoy Alps have long attracted climbers and winter sports enthusiasts, and Balmet, the Chamonix guide who climbed Mont Blanc for the first time in 1786, has had many followers. Winter sports resorts like Chamonix, Megève, Morzine and Val d'Isère enjoy an international reputation, as do such spas as Aix-les-Bains, Thonon and Evian. But Savoy is also an important agricultural region (cattle-rearing, dairy-farming, wine-growing, fruit). – The **Mont Blanc Tunnel, 11·6 km long, provides a direct link between Savoy (and Europe N of the Alps) and Italy.

HISTORY. – The history of Savoy has followed a different course from that of the Dauphiné. Early traces of human settlement have been found on the shores of the Lac du Bourget and the Lac d'Annecy. The region was occupied by a Celtic tribe, the Allobroges, who were conquered by the Romans in 121 B.C. In later centuries Savoy was ruled successively by Burgundians, Franks and the Carolingian kings. Shortly after the year 1000 the County of Savoy, under Count Humbert I ("Humbert of the White Hands"), became part of the Holy Roman Empire. Thereafter, secure in its possession of the Alpine passes, Savoy sought to extend its power into Italy and France and consequently became involved in bitter warfare. In 1564, after the Wars of Religion, it was compelled to cede Geneva, Vaud and the Valais to the Swiss Confederation. Savoy saw further fighting during its wars with Louis XIV and was twice occupied by French troops, but was liberated after Prince Eugene's victory at Turin in 1706. Under the Peace of Utrecht in 1713 Savoy acquired the kingdom of Sicily, but soon afterwards exchanged it for Sardinia. Savoy and Sardinia together formed the kingdom of Sardinia, which belonged to the Holy Roman Empire; but after 1815 the House of Savoy recovered its independence and in 1848 put itself at the head of the movement for Italian unification. France, under Napoleon III, supported the movement, and in recognition of its help in freeing Italy from the Austrians received the heartland of Savoy, together with Nice, in 1859. In a plebiscite held in 1860 there were 130,533 votes for union with France and only 235 against. Savoy was thus the last territory in France – leaving aside the special problem of Alsace and Lorraine – to become part of the country as we know it today.

SIGHTS. – **Aix-les-Bains**, situated under *Mont Revard* on the **Lac du Bourget* (France's largest lake, 18 km long, 2–3 km across, 60–100 m deep), has an international reputation as a spa with a mild and equable climate. The springs were already being used for curative purposes in Roman times. – Up to 45,000 people come here every year to take the cure. The *Thermes Nationaux* (two spa establishments, the older one dating from 1864, the newer one from 1934, with an extension in 1972: remains of Roman baths) are open to visitors. Other Roman remains are the Arch of Campanus (9 m high) and the Temple of Diana. Musée du Dr-Faure, with pictures (including particularly Impressionists) and sculpture. The Town Hall is in a 16th c. château which belonged to the Marquis d'Aix; the elegant staircase is built of stone from Roman structures. – Attractive drives round the lake and boat trips, for example to *Hautecombe Abbey, with the tombs of the kings and princes of Savoy. The elaborately decorated church was restored in the 19th c.; the doorway originally dated from the 16th c.

Lac d'Annecy (Haute-Savoie)

Annecy (alt. 448 m; pop. 60,000) is attractively situated on the lake and has a considerable amount of industry, including the bell foundry which made the bell known as the "Savoyarde" for the Sacré-Cœur church in Paris. – There are a number of churches in the old town, among them the 16th c. Cathedral of St-Pierre. The Bishop's Palace, built 1784, now houses the police headquarters. The principal street is Rue Ste-Claire, with attractive arcades and houses of the 16th–18th c. Annecy has associations with the early days of Jean-Jacques Rousseau. Along the very beautiful shores of the *Lac d'Annecy runs the Avenue d'Albigny, shaded by plane-trees, which offers fine views over the lake. The Château, once the residence of the

Counts of Geneva, was given its present form in the 15th and 16th c. There is a very attractive drive round the lake; cableway to the top of *Mont Veyrier (1252 m), from which there are magnificent views.

Chambéry (alt. 270 m; pop. 60,000) was from 1232 until the 16th c. capital of the independent state of Savoy, and the town is dominated by the castle which was successively occupied by the lords of Chambéry, the Counts and Dukes of Savoy and the Kings of Sardinia. The castle dates from the 14th to the 15th c. but suffered damage in two fires during the 18th c. From Place du Château the oldest parts can be seen. The conducted tour takes in the Sainte Chapelle (Gothic, 1408), the Tour Trésorerie (exhibition on the history of the castle) and the re-erected doorway, in Flamboyant style, of the church of St-Dominique, originally belonging to a Dominican abbey. – The best known monument in the town is the Elephant Fountain commemorating General Comte de Boigne (1751–1830). In close proximity to one another are the Cathedral, the former chapel (15th–16th c.) of a Franciscan friary and the old Bishop's Palace, which now houses the *Savoy Museum (prehistoric material, folk traditions, mementoes of the House of Savoy). The finest old mansions are in Rue Croix-d'Or. Interesting Museum of Fine Arts. – 2 km away is **Les Charmettes**, where Jean-Jacques Rousseau lived from 1735 to 1740.

Chamonix: see p. 90.

Evian-les-Bains (alt. 375–500 m; pop. 6400) has a beautiful situation on *Lake Geneva, the S shore of which belongs to France. The lake is 72 km long and up to 14 km wide, giving it a total area of 582 sq. km; its greatest depth is 310 m. Evian is popular both as a spa and as a holiday resort. On a sail round the lake the boat calls in at 46 places in France and Switzerland, taking about 10 hours (4 hours for the part known as the *Haut-Lac* or Upper Lake E of Evian). There is also a boat service between Evian and Lausanne, which lies opposite it on the northern shore.

Grenoble: see p. 119.

Megève (alt. 1113 m; pop. 5000) is one of France's leading winter sports resorts, but is also a popular holiday resort,

Avoriaz (Haute-Savoie)

2100 m), a popular summer and winter resort which has one of the highest modern winter sports centres in France, and for the huge dam built to supply a hydroelectric power station, of which there is a good view from an artificial terrace on N 202. From the Lac de Tignes there are cableways up to heights of over 3000 m (e.g. to the Grande Motte, 3459 m), so that skiing is possible even in summer.

Val d'Isère (alt. 1850 m; pop. 1000) has long been a favourite skiing area, with a network of pistes reaching heights of up to 3750 m.

Valloire (alt. 1430 m; pop. 1000) is a popular tourist centre in both summer and winter. It has a 17th c. church which is one of the most richly decorated in Savoy.

SPORT and RECREATION in Savoy. – *Walking* and *climbing* in summer and *winter sports* are the main attractions, but there are other possibilities as well, for example *fishing* in the mountain streams and lakes (particularly for salmon in the lakes, where they are sometimes also netted). Many resorts have *tennis courts* and facilities for *riding* and *bathing*. There are *golf-courses* at Aix-les-Bains, Annecy, Chamonix and Evian.

particularly for families with children. The famous French Alpine skiing technique was developed here by Emile Allais.

****Mont Blanc:** see p. 92.

Morzine-Avoriaz (alt. 1000–1800 m; pop. 3300) lies at the meeting of six valleys and offers tremendous scope for mountain walking and climbing in summer and skiing in winter. Near here are the *Lac de Montriond* (alt. 1049 m) and the Ardent waterfall, which is particularly impressive when the thaw sets in.

St-Gervais-les-Bains (alt. 900 m; pop. 4800) has been for the last hundred years one of the best known health resorts in Savoy. It is a good point from which to climb Mont Blanc, either on foot or by means of the cableways. With its high skiing slopes it is also a favourite winter sports resort.

Thonon-les-Bains (alt. 425 m; pop. 27,000), on a terrace above Lake Geneva, with magnificent views, is popular both as a tourist centre and as a health resort. The Place du Château marks the site of a stronghold of the Dukes of Savoy which was destroyed in 1589. The 17th c. Château de Sonnaz houses a museum devoted to the folk traditions of the Chablais region round Thonon. – A few kilometres W are the attractive lakeside resorts of *Excenevex* (beautiful beach), at the point of transition between the wider Grand-Lac to the E and the Petit-Lac to the W, and *Yvoire*, which still preserves its old 14th c. walls (with two gates) on the landward side as well as a number of medieval houses.

Tignes (alt. 1810 m; pop. 1000) is notable both for the *Lac de Tignes* (alt.

Strasbourg

Region: Alsace.
Department: Bas-Rhin.
Altitude: 136 m. – Population: 260,000.
Post code: F-67000. – Dialling code: 88.
ⓘ **Office de Tourisme**,
10 Place Gutenberg;
tel. 32 57 07.

HOTELS. – *Sofitel, 4 Place St-Pierre-le-Jeune, L, 180 r., with the Chateaubriand restaurant; *Grand Hôtel*, 12 Place de la Gare, I, 95 r.; *Terminus Gruber*, 10 Place de la Gare, I, 84 r.; *Holiday Inn*, 20 Place de Bordeaux, II, 180 r., SP; *Nouvel Hôtel Maison Rouge*, 4 rue des Francs-Bourgeois, II, 136 r.; *Monopole-Métropole*, 14 rue Kuhn, II, 110 r.; *France*, 20 rue du Jeu-des-Enfants, II, 70 r.; *Hannong*, 15 rue du 22-Novembre, II, 70 r.; *Bristol*, 4 Place de la Gare, II, 40 r.; *Rohan*, 17–19 rue du Maroquin, II, 36 r.; *Pax*, 24–26 rue du Faubourg National, 111, 110 r.; *National*, 13 Place de la Gare, III, 85 r.; *Carlton*, 15 Place de la Gare, III, 70 r.; *Rhin*, 7–8 Place de la Gare, III, 64 r.; *Europe*, 38–40 rue du Fossé-des-Tanneurs, III, 60 r.; *Gutenberg*, 31 rue des Serruriers, III, 50 r.; *Lutétia*, 2 rue du Général-Rapp, III, 43 r. – *Motel Pont de L'Europe*, at the Rhine bridge, II, 93 r.; *Mercure Strasbourg-Sud*, II, 98 r., SP, and *Novotel Strasbourg-Sud*, II, 76 r., SP, both 10 km S on N 83.

RESTAURANTS in most of the hotels; also *Crocodile*, 10 rue de l'Outre; *Valentin-Sorg*, 6 Place de l'Homme-der-Fer; *Gourmet sans Chiqué*, 15 rue Ste-Barbe; *Maison Kammerzell*, 16 Place de la Cathédrale; *Ancienne Douane*, 6 rue de la Douane; *Gerwerstub*

Strasbourg: view over "Little France" to the Cathedral

(Maison des Tanneurs), 42 rue du Bain-aux-Plantes; *Zimmer*, 6 rue du Temple-Neuf; *Buerehiesel*, 4 Parc de l'Orangerie.

WINE BARS. – *Hailich Graab* (Saint-Sépulcre), 15 rue des Orfèvres; *Muensterstuewel Pfifferbrieder*, 8–9 Place du Marché-aux-Cochons-de-Lait; *Bourse aux Vins*, 2 Petite Rue de l'Eglise; *Cave d'Ammerschwihr*, 9 rue des Tonneliers.

EVENTS. – *Foire de Printemps* (Spring Fair: 10 days in April–May); *International Musical Festival* (*c.* 16 days in June); *Foire-Kermesse de la St-Jean* (Midsummer Fair: *c.* 3 weeks in June–July); *Foire Européenne* (*c.* 12 days in Sept.).

Strasbourg – capital of Alsace, a university town, the see of a bishop, seat of the Council of Europe, the European Commission of Human Rights and the European Science Foundation, and as the meeting-place of the European Parliament the germ of a future united Europe – lies at the intersection of important traffic routes on the left bank of the Rhine, which at this point is joined by the River III, the Rhine-Marne Canal and the Rhine-Rhône Canal. With its soaring Cathedral and its many burghers' houses of the 16th and 17th c., Strasbourg still retains something of the character of an old free city of the Holy Roman Empire, but is also typically French with its handsome buildings in Louis XV style, dating from the time of the French Cardinal-Bishops of the 18th c., and its numerous mansard roofs.

The city's principal industries are metal-working, the manufacture of building materials and the production of foodstuffs (brewing, pâté de foie gras), followed by paper-making, textiles and tanning. The port of Strasbourg is the largest on the Upper Rhine, and is particularly active in the export trade. – Tourism has now also become an important element in the economy of Strasbourg, which attracts increasing numbers of visitors as the principal tourist centre of Alsace and the venue of numerous congresses and conferences.

HISTORY. – About A.D. 16 the Romans established a fortified post which they called *Argentoratum* beside an earlier Celtic settlement situated on important traffic routes. In the 4th c. the Alemanni built a new settlement on its ruins, and this appears in the records in the 6th c. under the name *Strataburgum* ("the fortified town on the roads"). – Strasbourg became the see of a bishop in 1003 and rose to considerable prosperity through its shipping and its trade. In 1262, after a conflict with the bishop and the nobility, it achieved independence as a free Imperial city, which for a time was the wealthiest and most brilliant in the Holy Roman Empire. Art and learning flourished in the city. In the 14th c. the Dominican preachers and mystics *Meister Eckhart* and *Johannes Tauler* lived in Strasbourg, and between 1434 and 1444 *Gutenberg* developed the art of printing here. After the coming of the Reformation in 1520 Strasbourg numbered

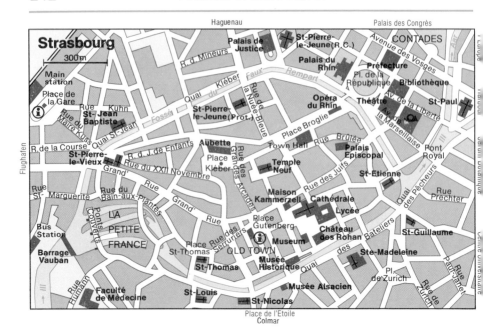

among its citizens the Protestant writer and satirist *Johannes Fischart* (1546–90) and the educationalist *Johannes Sturm* (1507–89), rector of the Protestant grammar school and founder of a theological academy which was the forerunner of the University. In 1681, taking advantage of the weakness of the Holy Roman Empire, Louis XIV occupied Strasbourg and soon afterwards had it fortified by Vauban. Until 1793, however, the town retained a degree of autonomy, and French cultural influence did not assert itself until the time of Napoleon. After the Franco-Prussian War of 1870–71 Strasbourg returned to German sovereignty as capital of the province of Alsace-Lorraine, and remained German until the end of the First World War. The establishment of the Council of Europe in Strasbourg in 1949, together with its history and geographical situation, seemed to make it a pre-destined future capital of Europe.

SIGHTS. – The hub of the city's traffic is *Place Kléber*, named after General J. B. Kléber, born in Strasbourg in 1753; in the square is a statue of Kléber, under which is a vault containing his remains. On the N side of the square is the *Aubette* (Orderly Room), built 1765–72 by Blondel.

From the SE corner of Place Kléber the busy *Rue des Grandes-Arcades* runs S to *Place Gutenberg*, with the spire of the Cathedral towering over the NE side of the square. In the middle of the square is a *statue of Gutenberg* (1840). On the SW side of the *Chamber of Commerce* (with the Tourist Office), the finest Renaissance building in Lower Alsace, erected in 1582–85 as the Town Hall. – From the SE corner of Place Gutenberg *Rue Mercière*, offering a magnificent view of the W front of the Cathedral, runs into the *Place de la Cathédrale*.

The **Cathedral of Notre-Dame**, begun in 1015 on the foundations of an earlier Romanesque church, has long been famed as one of the noblest achievements of Western architecture and reflects the organic development of the whole range of styles from Romanesque to late Gothic (12th–15th c.). The choir and transepts, begun in 1176, are Romanesque, while the nave, built 1250–90, is Gothic. The W front was the work of Master Erwin of Steinbach (1277–1318) and his successors; the delicately articulated octagon of the N tower was built by Ulrich von Ensingen from Ulm (1399–1419), the openwork spire, 142 m high, by Johannes Hültz of Cologne (1420–39). In 1793 235 statues and countless ornaments fell victim to the fanaticism of the French Revolution. There was even a plan to demolish the spire, since it towered above other buildings and thus offended against the principle of equality; but saner counsels prevailed, and the spire suffered nothing worse than having a lead Jacobin cap set on its tip. The Cathedral itself became a "Temple of Reason". In 1878–89 a Romanesque dome was built over the crossing. – On the splendid *W front, built of red sandstone from the Vosges, are a large rose window ($13\frac{1}{2}$ m in diameter) and a profusion of sculptural ornament (most of it restored in the 19th c.). – In the tympana of the **doorway in the S transept are sculptured representations of the Coronation and Death of the Virgin (the latter being the original) which rank among the highest achievements of medieval art. On either side are two other masterpieces the famous allegorical figures of the Church and the Synagogue (by a German sculptor, *c.* 1230). – The *façade of the chapel of St-Laurent (1495–1505), which is built on to the N transept, is one of the most splendid achievements of German late Gothic art.

Strasbourg Cathedral

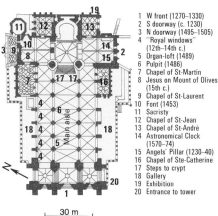

1 W front (1270–1330)
2 S doorway (c. 1230)
3 N doorway (1495–1505)
4 "Royal windows"
  (12th–14th c.)
5 Organ-loft (1489)
6 Pulpit (1486)
7 Chapel of St-Martin
8 Jesus on Mount of Olives
  (15th c.)
9 Chapel of St-Laurent
10 Font (1453)
11 Sacristy
12 Chapel of St-Jean
13 Chapel of St-André
14 Astronomical Clock
  (1570–74)
15 Angels' Pillar (1230–40)
16 Chapel of Ste-Catherine
17 Steps to crypt
18 Gallery
19 Exhibition
20 Entrance to tower

30 m

The *INTERIOR (103 m long, 41 m wide, 31·5 m high) contains beautiful *stained glass (12th–15th c.), including representations of 21 German emperors and kings in the N aisle, a late Gothic *pulpit* (1484–85) and an organ (1714–16) by Andreas Silbermann (d. in Strasbourg 1734). In the S transept are the *"*Angels' Pillar*" (Pilier des Anges, 1230–40) and the famous *Astronomical Clock (case, 18 m high, made between 1547 and 1574; works 1838–42). Other notable features are the *chapel of Ste-Catherine* (1331 and 1563) in the S aisle, the *font* (1453) and a sculptured group, *"Jesus on the Mount of Olives"* (15th c.) in the N transept. Entered from the N transept (but not always open) is the *chapel of St-Jean* (*c.* 1240), with the tomb of Bishop *Konrad von Lichtenberg* (d. 1299). There is a three-aisled *crypt*.

It is well worth while making the effort to climb the **tower**, from which there are magnificent views of the city, the Rhine plain, the Black Forest and the Vosges.

On the N side of Place de la Cathédrale is the *Maison Kammerzell* (restaurant), the finest old burgher's house in the city, with a stone-built ground floor (1467) and a half-timbered superstructure (1589). At the corner of Rue Mercière is a half-timbered building of 1567 housing a *pharmacy* which has been on this site since 1268.

On the S side of the Cathedral is *Place du Château*, with the *Lycée Fustel de Cou-langes* on its E side and the **Château des Rohan** (1728–42) on the S. Until the

Revolution the Château was the re-sidence of the Cardinal-Bishops of the great house of Rohan. From the terrace on the main front, facing the River III, there are attractive views. On the ground and first floors are the *Bishop's Apartments,* in Rococo style, with a library, a print room and a chapel. In the basement is the **Archaeological Museum**. On the first and second floors of the central block is the *Museum of Fine Arts*, with works by Italian, Spanish, Flemish, Dutch and French masters from the Middle Ages to modern times. In the right-hand wing of the Château is the *Museum of De-corative Arts* (principally ceramics and porcelain).

At the SW corner of Place du Château is the **Maison de l'Oeuvre Notre-Dame**, which has housed the Oeuvre Notre-Dame (the authority responsible for the maintenance of the Cathedral) since 1349. The E wing dates from 1347 (renovated in the 16th c.), the W wing from 1579 to 1585. It contains the *Musée de l'Oeuvre Notre-Dame, with the originals of sculpture from the Cathedral and a number of paintings, mainly by artists from the Upper Rhine region.

To the SW, behind the Maison de l'Oeuvre Notre-Dame, is the picturesque *Place du Marché-aux-Cochons-de-Lait* (Sucking Pigs Market). Beyond this is the **Grande Boucherie**, built 1586–88 as a meat market, which now houses the *Municipal Historical Museum*. Across the street to the W is the **Ancienne Douane** (Old Custom House), the oldest part of which dates from 1358. It now contains the **Museum of Modern Art**, with 19th and 20th c. pictures and sculpture, includ-ing works by Hans Arp (born in Stras-bourg), Braque, Klee, Max Ernst, Rodin, Renoir and Degas; temporary exhibitions; restaurant. – From the Ancienne Douane the *Pont du Corbeau* leads over the III to *Place du Corbeau*, with an old inn, the *Hôtellerie du Corbeau* (14th c.: pictur-esque courtyard), once a post-house, where many notable people stayed be-tween the 16th and 18th c. (including Frederick the Great in 1740). – W of Place du Corbeau, in a patrician house dating from 1620, is the *Musée Alsacien (folk art, furniture, costumes, domestic equip-ment, etc.).

From Place Gutenberg the Rue des Serruriers (Street of the Locksmiths) runs

SW to the church of **St-Thomas**, the only hall-church in Alsace, which has a Romanesque W work (1230–50), a Gothic nave (c. 1330) and an octagonal tower over the crossing (1348), with a clock which for 400 years has struck the hours 4 minutes too soon, in order to make itself heard before the Cathedral clock strikes. In the apse is the tomb of the French marshal Maurice de Saxe (of Saxony: d. 1750), an allegorical marble group by J.-B. Pigalle (1777). The church has a Silbermann organ (1737–40) on which Albert Schweitzer frequently played.

A short distance NW of St-Thomas is the old *QUARTIER DES TANNEURS (Tanners' Quarter), with picturesque half-timbered buildings lining its narrow streets. This is the area known as "Little France" (la Petite France). In Rue du

Picturesque half-timbered houses, Strasbourg

Bain-aux-Plantes is the old *Gerwerstub* ("Tanners' Room": restaurant). To the SW are the **Ponts Couverts**, four bridges, formerly roofed, crossing the River Ill, which is here divided into four arms. Four at the medieval defence towers are also preserved here. The best view (and also a fine *view of the town) can be had from the *Grande Ecluse*, a dam built by Vauban.

N of the Ponts Couverts, on the W side of the old town, is the church of **St-Pierre-le-Vieux**, a handsome building of the 14th and 15th c. From the S side of the church the old-world *Grand'Rue* leads back to Place Gutenberg.

To the E of Place Kléber extends the elongated rectangle of *Place Broglie*, laid out in 1742 on the site of the old horse market. Along the S side of this square are a number of imposing 18th c. buildings, with their main fronts on Rue Brûlée – the **Old Town Hall**, built 1730–36 as the

residence of the Landgrave of Hesse and used as a town hall from 1805 to 1976, and to the E, in a garden, the *Hôtel du Gouvernement Militaire* (c. 1760). At the E end of the square is the **Opéra du Rhin**, the *Municipal Theatre* (1804–22). On the N side of the square (No. 5) is the *Banque de France*, on the spot where Rouget de Lisle sang the "Marseillaise" for the first time on 26 April 1792.

Beyond the Theatre, on the far side of the old town moat, is the *Place de la République*, surrounded by public buildings, with a *monument* commemorating the dead of the First World War. On the NW side of the square is the *Palais du Rhin* (1883–89), formerly a German imperial palace. On the SE side is the *National and University Library* (1889–94: c. 3 million volumes), with the *Conservatoire de Musique* (1889–94) to the right. A little way NW of the Palais du Rhin is the Roman Catholic church of *St-Pierre-le-Jeune* (1889–93), with an imposing dome.

To the E of the old town, beyond the Ill, is the **University** (1879–85), with various University *institutes*, an *Observatory* and a *Botanical Garden*. Farther S, beyond the Boulevard de la Victoire, is the new *Centre Universitaire*, with the *Academy of Engineering*, the 15-storey *Institute of Chemistry* and the *Faculty of Letters*.

To the S and E of the new University buildings extends the *Esplanade* district, which has been developed since 1962, with tall blocks of flats. – Farther E, towards the river port, is the old **Citadel**, built 1682–84 as the central element in Vauban's system of fortifications. It is now an attractive park, laid out in 1967. – 1 km W of the University is the large complex of buildings occupied by the **Hôpital Civil**, one of France's largest teaching hospitals. About 500 m SE of this is the **Administrative Centre** of the Strasbourg conurbation (Centre Administratif de la Communauté Urbaine de Strasbourg).

A kilometre or so N of Place de la République, on the E side of the spacious *Place de Bordeaux*, is the *Maison de la Radio*, the Strasbourg headquarters of the French radio and television service, with a lattice aerial mast 110 m high. – 500 m farther N, in a large park, is the new international **Congress Centre** (*Palais de la Musique et des Congrès*), built 1973–75. This is a hexagonal building designed to serve a variety of purposes (with a number of halls seating a total of 3200 people) which caters for something like a hundred congresses, conferences, cultural events, exhibitions and concerts every year. – NE of the Congress Centre are the **Exhibition Grounds** (*Terrain d'Exposition*), with an exhibition hall and an ice-rink. To the E and W extend *sports and recreation grounds*.

Some 500 m SE, beyond the III, is the new *Palais de l'Europe, built in 1972–77 near the older Maison de l'Europe. This is a fortress-like structure of 9 storeys (30 m high, 105 m along each side) with an interior courtyard containing the tent-like chamber in which the Council of Europe and the European Parliament meet. – NE of the Palais de l'Europe is the *Palais des Droits de l'Homme*, the headquarters of the Commission of Human Rights. – To the SE of the Palais de l'Europe extends the beautiful Parc de l'Orangerie, laid out in the early 19th c., with the *Orangery* built for the Empress Joséphine, now used for exhibitions and receptions.

To the E and S of the city are the extensive installations of the **Port** (sightseeing boat trips), with 12 docks and a total area of 2643 acres, making it the second largest port on the Rhine (after Duisburg) and the largest river port in France. 90% of its turnover is concerned with export (mainly mineral ore, building materials, petroleum products and grain). The old port was considerably enlarged from 1882 onwards, and the port area now extends for more than 100 km along the French bank of the Rhine from Marckolsheim to Lauterbourg.

Toulon

Region: Provence–Alpes–Côte d'Azur.
Department: Var.
Altitude: 1–10 m. – Population: 185, 000.
Post code: F-83000. – Dialling code: 84.
(i) **Office de Tourisme,**
    Boulevard Général-Leclerc;
    tel. 92 37 64.

HOTELS. – *Grand Hôtel*, I, 31 r.; *Tour Blanche Frantel*, II, 100 r.; *Corniche*, II, 22 r.; *Réserve*, III, 20 r.; *Europe*, III, 30 r.; *Amirauté*, III, 63 r.; *Napoléon*, III, 53 r.; *Dauphiné*, IV, 62 r.; *Rex*, IV, 40 r.; *Lutétia*, IV, 37 r.; *Molière*, IV, 20 r.; *Provence*, IV, 14 r.

Toulon, beautifully situated on the S coast of France, is the leading French port and the base of the

French **Mediterranean fleet. The bay in which it lies is divided into an inner anchorage, the Petite Rade, and a larger outer one, the Grande Rade, with a breakwater 1250 m long between the two.**

HISTORY. – In Roman times Toulon was famed for the purple dye it produced from shellfish. It was fortified at the end of the 16th c., and its defences were later strengthened by Vauban. During the 17th and the first half of the 18th c. it was the home port of the royal galleys. In 1793 the Royalists handed the town over to British forces under Admiral Hood, but it was subsequently recaptured by the Revolutionary army in an action in which the young Napoléon Bonaparte distinguished himself. The town was threatened with destruction as a punishment for its surrender to the British but was spared at the last moment. Toulon was again the scene of dramatic events in 1942, when the French fleet was scuttled in the harbour on the orders of the Vichy government. Until its liberation in August 1944 Toulon suffered heavy damage, now completely made good.

In Toulon harbour

SIGHTS. – Between the harbour and the Boulevard de Strasbourg is the **old town**, with the picturesque Place Puget, Rue d'Alger and *Vieille Darse* (Old Harbour). Among the new buildings along *Quai Stalingrad* is the *Musée Naval* (Shipping Museum), with *caryatids* by Puget (1656) on the façade. – The **Cathedral** (*Ste-Marie-Majeure*) is early Gothic, with 17th c. additions and an 18th c. tower. – Charming Provençal-style *fish-market* and *vegetable market* (Cours Lafayette). – The **Naval Arsenal** cannot be entered by foreigners. – The early 16th c. *Tour Royale*, part of the town's fortifications, was used for many years as a prison. There are museums devoted to Old Toulon, art and archaeology.

SURROUNDINGS. – The finest view of Toulon is from *Mont Faron (542 m), in the range of hills which encircles the town; there is a steep road to the top (8 km). On the hills are the *Tour Beaumont* (also reached by cableway) and a *monument*, erected in 1964, commemorating the Allied landing in August 1944.

Toulouse

Region: Midi-Pyrénées.
Department: Haute-Garonne.
Altitude: 146 m. – Population: 385,000.
Post code: F-31000. – Dialling code: 61.
ⓘ **Office de Tourisme**,
Donjon du Capitole;
tel. 23 32 00.

HOTELS. – *Frantel*, L, 100 r.; *Concorde*, I, 97 r.; *Caravelle*, II, 32 r.; *Sofitel Jacques Borel*, II, 100 r.; *Mercure-St-Georges*, II, 170 r.; *Novotel*, II, 124 r.; *Bordeaux*, III, 22 r.; *Capoul*, III, 110 r.; *Europe*, III, 34 r.; *France*, III, 59 r.; *Riquet*, III, 75 r.; *Terminus*, III, 53 r.; *Antoine*, IV, 19 r.; *Argente*, IV, 30 r.; *Astrid*, IV, 20 r.; *Lutétia*, IV, 16 r.; *Unic*, IV, 20 r.; *Chez Tony*, IV, 22 r.

Toulouse, France's fourth largest city, situated on the Garonne and the Canal du Midi, is the cultural and economic centre of southern France. It is the see of an archbishop, a university town, the capital of Languedoc and chief town of the department of Haute-Garonne. Known as the "red city" because of its numerous brick buildings, it is rich in art and architecture, and is also the centre of the French aircraft industry.

HISTORY. – Originally a Ligurian and Iberian settlement (*Tolosa*), Toulouse is supposed to have been founded even earlier than Rome. In the 3rd c. St Saturninus (Sernin) brought Christianity to the area. After the Roman period the town was from 419 to 506 the capital of the Visigothic kingdom, and later became the principal place in Aquitaine. From 845 to 1249 it was ruled by the Counts of Toulouse. Under the treaty of Paris in 1229 Toulouse passed to the French crown along with the rest of Languedoc. The University was founded by Pope Gregory IX after the Albigensian wars. The town prospered after being granted a monopoly of the production of pastel colours for dying cloth. The Académie des Jeux Floraux was founded by Louis XIV.

SIGHTS. – The church of **St-Sernin** is the largest and best preserved Romanesque church in southern France, a brick-built structure erected in the 11th and 12th c. and dedicated to the first bishop of Toulouse. Its most striking feature is the

St-Sernin, Toulouse

six-storey tower over the crossing (65 m high), which was much imitated in Languedoc and Gascony. It has imposing doorways, in particular the *Porte Miégeville in the S aisle, with magnificent 12th c. Romanesque sculpture (King David, Apostles, the Ascension). The church is 115 m long and 21 m high, with two aisles on either side of the nave and nine chapels round the choir.

The **Cathedral** (*St-Etienne*) shows many varieties of Gothic, reflecting the long period over which its construction extended (11th–17th c.). The 13th c. rose window in the W front is similar to the one in Notre-Dame in Paris. The church is dominated by its mighty bell-tower. In the 12th c., when it was constructed, the 19 m span of the nave vaulting was the widest of its kind in Europe. Fine windows, tapestries and choir-stalls.

The *Church of the Jacobins (recently restored) is a masterpiece of southern French Gothic (13th c.; *cloister 1307). The tower (44 m high) was modelled on St-Sernin. The remains of St Thomas Aquinas (1225–74) were deposited in the church in 1974. – Other fine churches are *Notre-Dame-la-Daurade* and *Notre-Dame-de-la Dalbade*. Toulouse has many fine mansions dating from the 16th c. and later periods, among them the *Hôtel de Bernuy*, the *Hôtel Béringuier-Maynier* (in

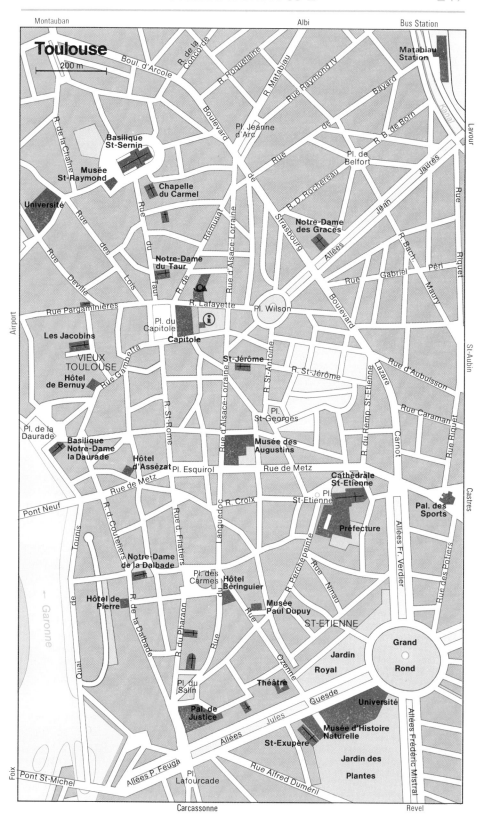

Toulouse

Montauban Albi Bus Station

200 m

Boul. d'Arcole

R. de la Concorde

R. Roquelaine

R. Matabiau

Rue Raymond IV

Bavard

Matabiau Station

Lavour

Basilique St-Sernin

Musée St-Raymond

Chapelle du Carmel

Pl. Jeanne d'Arc

Rue

de

R. D. Rochereau

Strasbourg

Pl. de Belfort

Jean

R. B. de Born

Jaurès

Rue

Riquet

St-Aubin

Université

Rue de la Chaîne

Rue

des

Rue

du

Rue

Lois

Remusat

Rue d'Alsace-Lorraine

Notre-Dame des Graces

R. Bach

Péri

Maury

Notre-Dame du Taur

Rue Deville

Rue

du

Taur

Rue

de

R. Lafayette

Pl. Wilson

Rue

Gabriel

Rue Pargaminières

Pl. du Capitole

Les Jacobins

Capitole

St-Jérôme

R. St-Antoine

R. St-Jérôme

Boulevard

Rue d'Aubuisson

VIEUX TOULOUSE

Rue Gambetta

Hôtel de Bernuy

R. d'Alsace-Lorraine

R. St-Etienne

Lazare

Rue d'Aubuisson

Rue Caraman

Pl. de la Daurade

Basilique Notre-Dame la Daurade

R. St-Rome

Pl. St-Georges

Musée des Augustins

Carnot

Castres

Hôtel d'Assézat

Pl. Esquirol

Rue de Metz

Cathédrale St-Etienne

Pal. des Sports

Rue de Metz

R. d'Alsace-Lorraine

R. Croix

Pl. St-Etienne

Pont Neuf

R. d. Couteliers

Rue d. Filatiers

Languedoc

Préfecture

Allées Fr. Verdier

Garonne

Notre-Dame de la Dalbade

Pl. des Carmes

Hôtel Béringuier

R. Perchepinte

Rue Ninau

Rue des Potiers

Hôtel de Pierre

R. de la Dalbade

Musée Paul Dupuy

ST-ETIENNE

R. du Pharaon

Rue

Grand Rond

Pl. du Salin

Théâtre

Ozenne

Jardin Royal

Allées Frédéric Mistral

Foix

Pont St-Michel

Pal. de Justice

Allées

Jules

Guesde

Université

Musée d'Histoire Naturelle

Allées P. Feuga

Pl. Lafourcade

Rue Alfred Duméril

St-Exupère

Jardin des Plantes

Carcassonne Revel

Airport

Toulouse Renaissance style) and – most elegant of all – the *Hôtel d'Assézat*; there are many other charming 16th–18th c. houses in the same area.

Musée du Vieux-Toulouse; *** Musée des Augustins**, with a cloister belonging to the old monastery and some notable pictures (Rubens, Delacroix, Toulouse-

Lautrec, etc.) and early sculpture. – In the **Capitole** (Town Hall: mid 18th c., with a tower of 1529) are pictures by noted citizens of the town and works by the local painter Henri Martin (1860–1943).

Tours

Region: Centre.
Department: Indre-et-Loire.
Altitude: 55 m. – Population: 146,000.
Post code: F-37000. – Dialling code: 47.
(i) **Office du Tourisme**,
    Place de la Gare;
    tel. 0 50 58 08.

HOTELS. – *Méridien Relais des Trois Rivières*, II, 125 r., SP; *Univers*, II, 90 r.; *Grand Hôtel*, II, 75 r.; *Métropole*, II, 65 r.; *Bordeaux*, II, 53 r.; *Central*, II, 42 r.; *Royal*, II, 32 r.; *Europe*, III, 51 r.; *Terminus*, III, 50 r.; *Armor*, III, 42 r.; *Châteaux*, III, 30 r.

RESTAURANTS. – *Barrier; Lyonnais; Tourangelle.*

EVENTS. -- *Fêtes Musicales de Touraine* (June); *Western European Agricultural Show* (Sept.).

Tours, capital of Touraine and centre of an agricultural and wine-growing region but also an industrial city, is a lively and attractive town, and a good base from which to see the Loire châteaux, lying as it does in the middle of the château region.

HISTORY. – Tours has been known since the 4th c. as the city of St Martin, the saint who shared his cloak with a beggar but was also one of Gaul's leading bishops, who fought vigorously for Christianity and against paganism. He died in 397, and the church which was built over his grave in 470 became a place of pilgrimage and a centre of healing comparable with Lourdes in our own day. The abbey in consequence quickly became wealthy. Alcuin, the monk and scholar whom Charlemagne summoned to his court from York, was abbot in the 8th c., and promoted the production of important illuminated manuscripts here. Tours was ravaged by the Norsemen (who burned down St Martin's church, the abbey and 28 other churches), and again during hostilities between the Counts of Blois and Anjou. In the 15th and 16th c. silk-weaving brought the town prosperity: at one time no fewer than 8000 looms were at work in the town, employing 20,000 weavers and 40,000 assistants – altogether three-quarters of the population (80,000). Tours became a stronghold of Protestantism, and as a result was the scene of a horrifying massacre by the Catholics ten years before the massacre of St Bartholomew's Day in Paris. This threw the town into economic decline, and by 1801 the population had fallen to only 20,000. Since then Tours has recovered its prosperity, receiving a considerable stimulus from the coming of the railway in the 19th c.

SIGHTS. – The **Cathedral* (*St-Gatien*), begun in the 13th c. and completed 300 years later, bears the mark of all the different phases of Gothic, while the upper parts of the towers are already Renaissance in style. The finest feature of the Cathedral is its stained glass (13th–15th c.). – The former *Archbishop's Palace* (17th–18th c.) is notable both for its sumptuous interior decoration and its fine collection of *pictures, which include a Rembrandt. The large cedar in the courtyard was planted in 1808. – From the Cathedral are entered the elegant 15th–16th c. *cloister and the ruins of the 16th c. cloister of the older church, which was devastated by the Huguenots in 1562 and fell into a state of dilapidation after the French Revolution. The present Rue des Halles crosses the site of the earlier church, the centre of which lay between the bell-tower and the Tour Charlemagne. The tomb of St Martin was placed in the crypt of the new church, built in place of the old, and is still a place of pilgrimage (first Sunday in July, 11 November and the Sunday following).

A walk through the OLD TOWN (Place Foire-du-Roi, Place Plumereau, etc.) reveals fine old mansions and picturesque half-timbered houses of different periods. The **Hôtel Gouin**, a very typical Renaissance mansion, was partly destroyed by fire in 1940, but has been excellently restored and now houses an *Archaeological Museum* (medieval and Renaissance art). – The *Musée du Gemmail* contains works in a kind of glass mosaic technique. – Other notable buildings are a number of old churches and the *Tour de Guise* (now in the Caserne Meusnier), the last relic of the castle built by Henry Plantagenet in the 12th c. to defend the river crossing, in which Charles VII received Joan of Arc after the liberation of Orléans. – Tours has many parks and gardens, with old trees and exotic plants.

SURROUNDINGS. – Within easy reach of Tours are the ruined abbey of **Marmoutier** (founded by St Martin); the *priory of St-Côme*, of which Ronsard was titular abbot for 20 years before his death here in 1585; Anatole France's house, *La Béchellerie*, shown to visitors as it was in his lifetime; *La Grenadière*, where Balzac lived for a time; and Henri Bergson's house, *La Gaudinière*.

Troyes

Region: Champagne-Ardenne.
Department: Aube.
Altitude: 113 m. – Population: 75,000.
Post code: F–10000. – Dialling code: 25.
ⓘ **Office de Tourisme,**
16 Boulevard Carnot;
tel. 43 01 03.

HOTELS. – *Grand Hôtel*, II, 70 r.; *Royal*, II, 42 r.; *France*, III, 60 r.; *Paris*, III, 26 r.; *Thiers*, III, 38 r.; *Gare*, III, 18 r.; *Monnaie*, IV, 31 r.; *Cirque*, IV, 16 r.; *Grammont*, IV, 15 r.

Troyes, capital of Champagne and chief town of the department of Aube, lies on the Seine, here divided into a number of arms, and has some fine Gothic and Renaissance buildings. Its main industry is hosiery.

HISTORY. – In Roman times the town was called *Augustobona*; its present name comes from that of the local Gallic tribe, the *Tricasses*, which later became *Trecae*. It was the see of a bishop from the 4th c. During the battle of the Catalaunian Fields in 451 Troyes successfully held out against the Huns. In the 10th c. the town passed to the Counts of Champagne, and in 1304 became part of France.

View of Troyes Cathedral

SIGHTS. – Troyes has six churches of artistic importance. The *Cathedral (St-Pierre-et-St-Paul)* dates from the 13th–16th c. and has a richly ornamented Renaissance façade. Notable features are the "Beau Portail" ("Beautiful Doorway") in the N transept and the fine 13th and 14th c. *stained glass. In spite of the unfinished state of its towers it ranks among the finest achievements of Gothic architecture in Champagne. – The church of St-Nizier is late Gothic, with a Renaissance façade (mid 16th c.). – The church of *St-Urbain, built in the second half of the 13th c., is another of the great masterpieces of Gothic architecture in Champagne. The structure of the windows enhances the elegance of the whole building. In a chapel on the S side of the choir is the famous Renaissance "Virgin of the Grapes" (16th c.). – The church of **Ste-Madeleine** has a 12th c. nave, a Renaissance choir, a Flamboyant *roodscreen (early 16th c.) and a doorway in Flamboyant style. – The church of **St-Jean**, near a street of half-timbered houses, the *Rue des Chats*, was built between the 13th and 16th c.; it has a beautiful Renaissance choir and a 17th c. high altar. – The church of **St-Nicolas** is a late Gothic structure (16th c.) with Renaissance additions; Calvary Chapel, approached by a flight of steps with sculptured decoration.

St-Urbain, Troyes

The former **Abbey of St-Loup**, near the Cathedral, houses a large and valuable *Library* (200,000 volumes, 3000 manuscripts, 700 incunabula) and the **Museum of Fine Arts**, with pictures ranging in date from the 15th c. to the present day. – In the 16th c. **Hôtel de Vauluisant** are the *Historical Museum* (medieval sculpture) and a museum illustrating the development of the local hosiery industry.

The OLD TOWN is traversed by *Rue Emile-Zola*, with the late Gothic church of *St-Pantaléon*. In this area are several little streets with picturesque old houses – Rue Champeaux, Rue des Chats, Rue Bruneval, Rue de la Trinité.

Vendée
See under Poitou-Charentes

Vercors

The district of *Vercors, SW of Grenoble, which forms part of the Dauphiné, has a landscape of rather different pattern from the Alpine regions of France. During the

Second World War its forests and gorges were a centre of the French Resistance, the *maquis*, and in the course of the fighting the villages of St-Nizier, Vassieux and La Chapelle were destroyed. Part of the 1968 Winter Olympics took place in Vercors (Autrans, St-Nizier, Villard-de-Lans).

It is well worth while making a special tour of Vercors, the itinerary of which must certainly include the Combe Laval road and the gorges on the Bourne, W of Villard-de-Lans, which are typical of the unusual scenery of Vercors. This area still lies off the usual Alpine tourist track, with the exception of Villard-de-Lans, which is now a kind of outpost of Grenoble.

SIGHTS. – **Combe Laval** is the name of a mountain road constructed in 1897 and originally intended for the transport of timber from the Forest of Lente to St-Jean-en-Royans. The finest part of the road begins at the Col de la Machine on the way down to St-Jean-en-Royans, affording magnificent aerial views of the country below.

The *Gorges de la Bourne** are between Pont-en-Royans and Choranche on N 531. Interesting caves can be reached from the road, the *Grotte de Bournillon* and the *Grottes de Choranche*.

The *Grands Goulets** are the most impressive natural feature in Vercors – a gorge on the River Vernaison lined with high rock walls, through which the road finds its way with the help of a series of tunnels and galleries.

Léoncel has a Romanesque church which originally belonged to a Cistercian abbey founded in 1137; it contains a carved wood figure of Christ by a local artist (1860).

St-Jean-en-Royans is one of the best places – the other good centre being Villard-de-Lans – from which to explore Vercors.

St-Nizier-du-Moucherotte lies below *Moucherotte* (1901 m: lift) and is a popular summer and winter resort. From the village, and even more from the summit of Moucherotte, there are magnificent *views* of the mountains and of Grenoble. There is a cemetery with the graves of those who fell in the Resistance.

Vassieux-en-Vercors was completely destroyed in 1944 but has been rebuilt. The deeds of the Resistance are commemorated by a memorial and by the National Cemetery of Vercros.

Villard-de-Lans (alt. 1043 m), 30 km from Grenoble, is a holiday and winter sports resort in a wide expanse of Alpine meadows. There is a cabin-lift up to *Côte 2000* (i.e. an altitude of 2000 m), where there are magnificent views and good skiing. – 8 km from Villard-de-Lans is the Calvary of *Valchevière*, with 14 Stations of the Cross (the last being a chapel), commemorating the destruction of the village in July 1944.

SPORT and RECREATION in Vercors. – Endless scope for *walking*, *climbing* and *winter sports*.

Verdun

Region: Lorraine.
Department: Meuse.
Altitude: 199 m. – Population: 35,000.
Post code: F-55100. – Dialling code: 29.
(i) **Office de Tourisme**,
Place de la Nation;
tel. 86 12 16.

HOTELS. – *Bellevue*, II, 72 r.; *Coq Hardi*, III, 45 r.; *St-Paul*, III, 34 r.; *Pergola*, III, 23 r.; *Paris*, IV, 40 r.; *Pai*, IV, 18 r.; *Metz*, IV, 23 r.

This fortress town has made two appearances in history – the first in 843, when the treaty dividing up the Frankish kingdom was signed here, and the second in 1916, when it was the centre of bloody fighting which cost the lives of more than half a million men. Its main interest to the tourist is as a staging post or a base from which to visit the battlefields.

HISTORY. – The Roman town on this site was called *Virodunum*. It became the see of a bishop in the 3rd c. Under the treaty of Verdun in 843 Charlemagne's Frankish empire was split up into the three territories of France, Germany and Lorraine. Verdun was at first included in Lorraine, but in 870 passed to the East Frankish kingdom and then, as *Virten*, became a free imperial city in the Holy Roman Empire. In 1552 Henry II of France occupied the town, and in 1648 it was permanently incorporated in France. Thereafter its defences were built up, particularly by Vauban. During the First World War it was the pivot of the French front line, and between 21 February and 12 July 1916 withstood all German attempts to take it. The number of dead on both sides is estimated at between 500,000 and 800,000, and the name of Verdun has become a synonym for senseless slaughter.

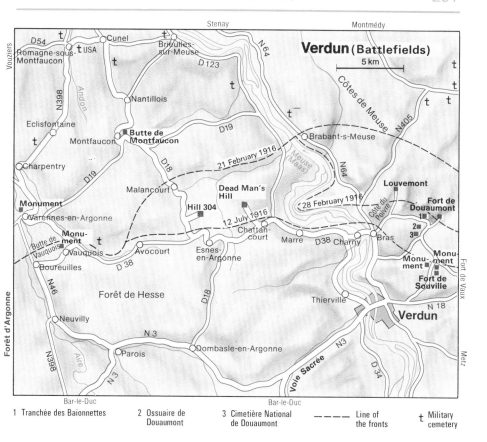

1 Tranchée des Baïonnettes   2 Ossuaire de   3 Cimetière National   – – – – Line of   † Military
                       Douaumont   de Douaumont   the fronts   cemetery

SIGHTS. – In Rue Mazel, in the centre of the town, is a massive **Victory Memorial** (1929), in the crypt of which is a book containing the names of all those who took part in the fighting.

Verdun's finest building is the **Cathedral** (*Notre-Dame*), in the Romanesque style of the Rhineland, with a beautiful crypt. Late Gothic cloister (16th c.). On the N side is the 12th c. Lion Doorway. – Above the Cathedral is the **Citadel**, with a network of chambers and passages hewn from the rock.

On the N side of the town, in front of the Porte St-Paul, is a sculpture by *Rodin* symbolising the *Defence of Verdun*. – On the Quai de la République is a *war memorial*, and on the opposite bank of the Meuse is the 14th c. *Porte Chaussée*, with two round towers.

The *battlefields of the First World War* lie on both banks of the Meuse, but those pressed for time can confine themselves to the right bank – **Fort de Vaux**, **Fort de Souville** (memorial to André Maginot, after whom the Maginot Line was named; museum), the **Ossuaire de Douaumont** (containing the

remains of unidentified soldiers), **Fort de Douaumont** and the **Tranchée des Baïonnettes** (the trench in which a section of infantry was buried alive). – On the left bank are **Dead Man's Hill** (*Mort-Homme*), **Hill 304** (*Côte 304*) and the **Butte de Montfaucon**, which all featured prominently in the fighting.

Douaumont, near Verdun

Versailles

Region: Ile de France.
Department: Yvelines.
Altitude: 132 m. – Population: 98,000.
Post code: F-78000. – Dialling code: 1.
(i) **Office de Tourisme**,
    7 rue des Réservoirs;
    tel. 9 50 36 22.

HOTELS. – *Trianon Palace*, L, 140 r.; *Versailles*, II, 48 r.; *Royal*, II, 30 r.; *Bellevue*, II, 24 r.; *Cheval Rouge*, III, 42 r.; *France*, III, 13 r.; *Richaud*, III, 39 r.; *Printania*, III, 30 r.; *Eden*, IV, 23 r.; *Chasse*, IV, 15 r.; *Berry*, IV, 41 r.; *Palais*, IV, 24 r.

Versailles, 20 km SW of Paris, is chief town of the department of Yvelines and the see of a bishop; but its great glory is the splendid royal ****Palace with its beautiful** ***gardens – a splendour which is also reflected in the layout and architecture of the town itself.**

HISTORY. – From 1682 onwards Versailles was the regular residence of the French court, and in consequence was closely associated with the history of France. In 1789 the French States-General were summoned to meet in Versailles, and the third of the three Estates (nobility, clergy and people) formed itself into a National Assembly and thus took the first step towards the Revolution. On 5–6 October 1789 Louis XVI, suspected of planning reactionary measures, was forced by the Paris mob to leave Versailles and move to the Tuileries in Paris. Thereafter Versailles lost its importance. – During the Franco-Prussian War of 1870–71 Versailles was occupied by German troops (19 September 1870) and was the German headquarters until 6 March 1871. On 18 January 1871 the new German Empire was proclaimed in the Hall of Mirrors. – After the First World War the Treaty of Versailles was signed in the Hall of Mirrors (28 June 1919). – In June 1978 Breton separatists exploded a bomb in the Palace, causing serious damage.

SIGHTS. – The town's main traffic artery is the wide *Avenue de Paris*, which meets the Avenue de St-Cloud and Avenue de Sceaux in the *Place d'Armes* in front of the Palace. – A little way S of the Place d'Armes is the *Salle du Jeu de Paume* (Tennis-Court), built for the king and the court in 1686, in which the National Assembly met in 1789. – Farther S is the 18th c. **Cathedral** (*St-Louis*). – In Rue de l'Indépendance-Américaine, W of the Place d'Armes, are the *Grand-Commun*, built by Mansart in 1682 to accommodate persons attached to the court (now a military hospital), and the *Municipal Library*, with a beautifully decorated interior. – To the N of the town are the church of *Notre-Dame* (Mansart, 1684–86) and the *Lambinet Museum* (18th c.), which contains furniture, pictures, prints, etc.

On the E side of the spacious Place d'Armes are the *Royal Stables* (Ecuries Royales), built by Mansart and now used as barracks, which could accommodate 2500 horses and 200 carriages. – On the W side of the square is the ****Palace of Versailles**, the largest and most magnificent ever built, and with its terraced gardens and park the finest achievement of the reign of Louis XIV.

The BUILDING of the Palace. – In 1624 Louis XIII built a hunting lodge here, the wings of which enclosed what is now the Cour de Marbre. The present palace is largely the work of Louis XIV, who at first confined himself to making a number of improvements; but later, when he found St-Germain no longer adequate to his needs, he planned a vast extension in order to make it possible to have not only

The Palace of Versailles floodlit

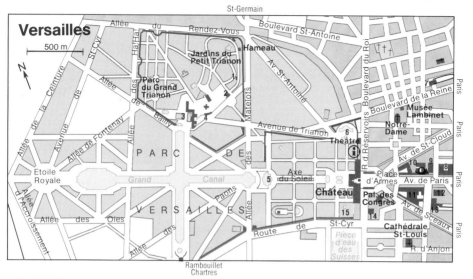

Versailles

1 Temple de l'Amour
2 Le Petit Trianon
3 Le Grand Trianon
4 Musée des Voitures
5 Bassin d'Apollon
6 Bassin de Neptune
7 Station (Gare Rive Droite)
8 Préfecture
9 Palais de Justice
10 Les Grandes Ecuries Royales
11 Les Petites Ecuries Royales
12 Town Hall
13 Station (Gare Rive Gauche)
14 Bibliothèque
15 Orangerie

the government and administration of the country but the whole nobility of the court more or less permanently round him, in a setting of great sumptuousness and artistic splendour. To begin with the original hunting lodge was enlarged by the addition of the two E wings, designed by *Le Vau* (d. 1670). Le Vau was succeeded in 1676 by *J. Hardouin-Mansart*, who added another storey to Le Vau's wings and built the Hall of Mirrors and the long N and S winds on the garden front of the palace. Last of all came the two pavilions in classical style at the outer end of the Cour Royale, built by *Gabriel* (18th c.) and *Dufour* (1820). – The whole gigantic structure, 580 m long on the garden front and with accommodation for 10,000 people, is said to have cost 500 million gold francs, not counting the forced labour of the peasants, and to have required the labour of anything up to 36,000 men and 6000 horses at any one time.

VISITING THE PALACE, including the gardens, requires at least one full day ("Son et Lumière" presentations). – The *Avant-Cour* (Forecourt) is entered through a tall lattice. On either side is a range of buildings, separate from the Palace, occupied by the king's ministers. Beyond this is the *Cour Royale*, with an equestrian statue of Louis XIV (1832), and beyond this again the *Cour de Marbre*, with busts of Roman emperors.

The **INTERIOR of the Palace (entrance on right-hand side of Cour Royale), which is a National Museum, contains the *state apartments* and *residential apartments* of Louis XIV and his successors – themselves a unique museum of decorative art – and the *Musée des Gloires de la France*, with an overwhelming profusion of pictures and sculpture.

In the *N wing* (conducted tours) begins the *Galerie d'Histoire*, with pictures of kings and their courts. At the end of the gallery is a staircase leading to the foyer of the *Theatre* (Gabriel, 1770). – On the upper floor are the continuation of the Galerie d'Histoire and the entrance to the *Chapel* (begun by Mansart 1669, completed by de Cotte 1710).

In the *central section* of the Palace are the state and residential apartments, which have preserved the original gilded stucco decoration of the walls and ceilings, panelling, doors and chimneypieces, and in spite of the absence of furniture still convey a vivid impression of the sumptuous High Baroque style of Louis XIV's reign. A frequently recurring theme in the decoration is the sun which symbolises the "Roi Soleil". – Passing through a vestibule, with the entrance to the chapel on the left, and the *Salon d'Hercule* (colossal ceiling painting by Lemoyne), we enter the **Grands Appartements**, six splendid state apartments with large mythological paintings on the ceilings. From the *Salon de la guerre* (allegorical ceiling painting) we come into the world-famous **Hall of Mirrors** (*Galerie des Glaces*), which

Hall of Mirrors, Versailles

together with the Salon de la Guerre and the *Salon de la Paix* occupies the whole of the W front of the central section of the Palace, looking out on to the gardens. The decoration, by Charles Lebrun and the leading artists of the day, is of extreme splendour. Seventeen large round-headed windows afford magnificent views of the gardens and a vista of the park stretching out into the distance, and on the other side are 17 large mirrors, in those days a very costly feature. – Behind the Hall of Mirrors are the *Apartments of Louis XIV*. Here, exactly in the centre of the Palace, is the *bedroom* in which he died in 1715, with the balustrade behind which the bed formerly stood. – Adjoining the Salon de la Paix are the *Queen's Apartments*, with beautiful decoration and paintings. – Also in the central section of the Palace are the smaller residential apartments known as the *Petits Appartements*.

The *S* wing contains a further section of the Musée des Gloires de la France. In the 120 m long *Galerie des Batailles* are portraits and busts of French generals.

The **gardens** behind the Palace (freely open to the public throughout the day), once the scene of splendid festivals and entertainments, were laid out by *Le Nôtre*, the most celebrated landscape gardener of his day, from 1667 onwards, in complete harmony with the architecture of the Palace. As far as the Allée d'Apollon they have been preserved in their original state, with their regularly planned shrubberies, paths and ornamental ponds and their hundreds of statues and vases. They are seen at their finest from the topmost terrace when the *fountains (the Grandes Eaux)* are playing (on the first and third Sundays in the month from May to September). – From the *Parterres du Midi* two flights of steps lead down to the *Orangery (Mansart, 1684–86), with 1200 orange trees. The central path, the *Tapis Vert*, leads to the *Bassin d'Apollon* and beyond this the *Grand Canal*, 62 m wide and 1588 m long, with arms extending to left and right in the shape of a cross.

The Avenue de Trianon, to the right, leads to the Petit Trianon and Grand Trianon, two charming smaller châteaux set in gardens on the N side of the park.

The *Petit Trianon* (conducted tour), with an attractive English-style garden, was built by Louis XV in 1766 for Mme du Barry; the architect was Gabriel. This was a favourite residence of Marie-Antoinette's. The interior (which contains mementoes of Marie-Antoinette) is much more simply decorated than Versailles. In the *garden*, planted with rare trees, is the *Hameau* (Hamlet), a group of cottages set round a small lake where the ladies of the court liked to dress up as peasants and play at the simple life.

At the end of the Avenue de Trianon is the *Grand Trianon*, built by Louis XIV for Mme de Maintenon. Having bought the little village of Trianon in 1663, he built first a modest country cottage and then the present château (Mansart, 1687–88). The house, now used for the accommodation of distinguished visitors to France, has been tastefully redecorated in period style and contains paintings by Mignard, Lebrun, Boucher and other French artists. – The *park*, with numerous ornamental ponds, was laid out by Le Nôtre. – At the entrance to the Grand Trianon, on the right, is the *Musée des Voitures* (Carriage Museum), with a collection of state coaches, sleighs, sedan chairs and harness of the Baroque period.

Vichy

Region: Auvergne.
Department: Allier.
Altitude: 260 m. – Population: 35,000.
Post code: F-03200. – Dialling code: 70.

(i) **Office de Tourisme et de Thermalisme**,
19 rue du Parc;
tel. 98 71 94.

HOTELS. – *Ambassadeurs*, I, 160 r.; *Elysée-Palace*, I, 63 r.; *Pavillon Sévigné*, I, 55 r.; *Astoria*, II, 57 r.; *Paix*, II, 80 r.; *Régina*, II, 80 r.; *Ermitage du Pont-Neuf*, II, 65 r.; *Séville et Lisbonne*, II, 88 r.; *Balmoral*, III, 50 r.; *Masséna*, III, 49 r.; *Europe*, III, 77 r.; *Foch et Centre*, III, 66 r.; *Midland*, III, 57 r.; *Splendid*, III, 100 r.; *Alexandra*, IV, 68 r.; *Alsace-Lorraine*, IV, 18 r.; *Angleterre*, IV, 45 r.; *Barcelone*, IV, 54 r.; *Palais*, IV, 50 r.; *Sport*, IV, 23 r.

Vichy, situated on the Allier on the northern fringes of Auvergne, is France's most renowned spa (for the treatment of liver, stomach, intestines and kidneys). Between 1940 and 1944 it was the seat of Marshal Pétain's government. Vichy water was prized by the Romans and is still a popular drink all over France. The springs have temperatures ranging between 16 and 43 °C (61–109 °F).

Spa establishment, Vichy

SIGHTS. – The life of Vichy is centred on the *Parc des Sources*, with its hotels, two spa establishments and casinos. The **Grand Etablissement Thermal** is the largest of its kind in Europe. – The older part of the town still preserves a number of old buildings, such as the *Clock-Tower*, a relic of a 15th c. castle, the *Pavillon Sévigné*, dating from the time of Louis XIII, and the *Maison du Bailliage* (Chastel Franc: 16th c.), which houses a museum of local art and archaeology. – Along the banks of the Allier and the shores of the *Lac d'Allier* (an artificial lake formed by a dam) extends the beautiful *Parc de l'Allier.*

Vienne

Region: Rhône-Alpes.
Department: Isère.
Altitude: 158 m. – Population: 30,000.
Post code: F-38200. – Dialling code: 74.
ⓘ **Office de Tourisme,**
  3 Cours Brillier;
  tel. 85 12 62.

HOTELS: – *Résidence de la Pyramide*, I, 15 r.; *Nord*, II, 43 r.; *Central*, II, 25 r.; *Poste*, III, 40 r. – *Pyramide* restaurant (cuisine of outstanding quality).

Vienne lies in the lower Rhône valley 30 km S of Lyons, on the important traffic route between Burgundy and the Mediterranean. In Roman times it was the second capital of southern Gaul and during the Middle Ages capital of the Dauphiné, and preserves major monuments of architecture dating from both of these periods.

SIGHTS. – In the centre of the town is the *Place de l'Hôtel-de-Ville*, with the *Town Hall*. A little way SE is the *Portique des Thermes Romains*, part of the colonnade

Roman portico, Vienne

round the Roman forum. To the SW, in *Place du Palais*, is the **Temple of Augustus and Livia** (25 B.C.), which was used as a church during the Middle Ages and became a "Temple of Reason" during the Revolution. To the S is the twin-towered church of **St-Maurice** (12th–16th c.), formerly the Cathedral, with a Flamboyant W front (Romanesque sculpture in the interior, 16th c. Flemish tapestries, fine glass). The *Museum of Fine Arts* contains much Roman material.

A short distance SW, near the Rhône, is the church of *St-Pierre, one of the oldest early medieval churches in France (6th–10th c.), now deconsecrated and housing a *Musée Lapidaire* (sculptural and architectural fragments from Vienne). – In the *Jardin Public*, to the S, is a short section of *Roman road*. – 500 m farther S is the *Aiguille*, an obelisk 16 m high which formerly stood in the Roman circus on this site.

SE of the Place de l'Hôtel-de-Ville is a large **Roman theatre** (1st c. A.D.), at the foot of *Mont Pipet*, on which are a statue of the Virgin and a modern chapel (view).

In the N of the town, on the banks of the Rhône, is the mainly Romanesque church of **St-André-le-Bas** (beautiful capitals); in the 12th c. cloister is a *Museum of Christian Art.*

On the right bank of the Rhône is the suburb of STE-COLOMBE, with the *Tour de Philippe de Valois* (14th c.), which stood at the end of a Roman bridge destroyed in 1651. Here too is the recently excavated Roman site of St-Romain-en-Gal (mosaics). – On the road to St-Etienne are the *stadium* and the *swimming pool.*

Vosges

The Vosges are a range of mountains running parallel to the Rhine valley and the Black Forest on the far side of the Rhine, rising to their highest point in the Grand Ballon (1423 m). They extend for a distance of some 170 km from N to S and for up to 20 m from E. to W. The highest peaks are in the S; to the N they fall away gradually, merging into the Haardt hills in the German Palatinate to the

E. The Vosges form the higher part of Alsace, above the rift valley of the Rhine.

The hotel resources and tourist facilities of the Vosges are still relatively limited, although much progress has been made in the last few years. Nature-lovers and walkers, however, will appreciate the scenery and the solitude of the region.

WALKING in the Vosges. – Three long-distance trails have been way-marked by local clubs. No. 1 runs from Wissembourg to Masevaux (marked with red rectangles: 388 km); No. 2 from Lembach to Masevaux (blue rectangles: 282 km); No. 3 from Obersteinbach to Masevaux (yellow rectangles: 324 km). There are also linking paths (red rectangles with a white stripe) from railway stations and villages to route No. 1.

SIGHTS. – The *Ballon d'Alsace (1250 m) is the most southerly of the Vosges peaks. The plateau-like summit is treeless and affords wide views. On the top are a statue of the Virgin, a monument to Joan of Arc and a monument to the *démineurs* (mine-clearance and bomb-disposal experts).

Bruyères (alt. 500) lies in a wooded region in the western Vosges; Romanesque church of Champ-le-Duc.

Bussang (alt. 599) is a little resort with a mineral spring in the upper Moselle valley, on the road to the *Col de Bussang* (731 m) in the High Vosges. Nearby is the *source of the Moselle* (monument).

The *Champ du Feu (1110 m) is the highest point in the central Vosges, with a plateau which attracts many winter sports enthusiasts (ski-lift). There is an observation tower 20 m high, from which there are views extending in clear weather as far as the Alps.

*Le Donon (1009 m) is a much visited mountain in the central Vosges, with the *Col du Donon* (727 m) in a treeless area on its southern slopes. Extensive views from the top. The mountain was a Celtic religious shrine, and a Temple of Mercury was built on it in Roman times. There is a museum in the form of a temple, built in 1869, with Roman and other remains; lower down are Roman memorial stones. On the pass is a copy of a Jupiter column.

Ferrette (alt. 470 m) is a little town in the Alsatian Jura, under the ruins of Hohenpfirt castle (1125: alt. 613 m). Charming medieval half-timbered houses; Gothic church (13th c.).

The *Grand Ballon (1423 m), above the town of Guebwiller, is the highest peak in the Vosges, with views extending as far as the Alps (Säntis to Mont Blanc); good country for winter sports. There was a shrine to the sun god here in early historical times. Monument commemorating the defence of the hill by French Chasseurs Alpins in the First World War. – 400 m below the summit, in the midst of the forest, is the *Lac du Ballon* (area 75 hectares, 23 m deep), which was dammed by Vauban in 1699 and now serves industrial purposes. Hotel below the summit, with facilities for winter sports.

Grand Ballon, Vosges

Hartmannswillerkopf (956 m) is a hill, with a 22 m high cross on the summit, which was the scene of bitter fighting during the First World War. There are cemeteries and memorials for the 60,000 men who fell here and a crypt containing the remains of 12,000 unknown soldiers, with a French war memorial over it. Some of the old German positions can still be recognised.

*Haut-Koenigsbourg (755 m), a prominent landmark overlooking the Rhine plain, is a medieval castle (restored) which belonged to the Hohenstaufens. It fell into ruin in the 17th c. but was restored at the beginning of this century by Kaiser Wilhelm II, and now looks more or less as it did in 1479. It is entered through the Lion Gate (Porte des Lions). Conducted tours (recommended for the explanations of fortification techniques and the views of the surrounding countryside). – Near the castle is a monkey enclosure.

*Hohneck (1362 m) is one of the highest peaks in the central Vosges, which lay on the Franco-German frontier between 1870 and 1918. It offers magnificent views and excellent skiing in winter. 4 km from the summit is the *Col de la

Schlucht; below it is *Klein-Hohneck* (1287 m).

Le Hohwald (alt. 643 m) is a village on the Andlau, attractively situated among fir forests, which is popular as a health and winter sports resort. Some of the firs, which are anything up to 250 years old, reach heights of 45 m and girths of 5 m.

The **Markstein** (1176 m), on the *Route des Crêtes* (see below), a saddle from which there are wide views, offers good opportunities for walking and skiing. Below it is the *Lac de la Lauch* (alt. 924 m, area 11 hectares), an artificial lake formed by a dam.

Masevaux (alt. 405 m) is a little industrial town and health resort in a very attractive setting in the Doller valley. It has burghers' houses of the 16th and 17th c. and an 18th c. fountain. Above the town is the *Rossberg* (1191 m), with a number of easy routes to the top. A road runs up the Doller valley, in which is the artificial Lac d'Alfeld, to the Ballon d'Alsace.

Plombières-les-Bains (alt. 456 m) has mineral springs (temperature 12 to 81 °C) which have been known since Roman times. During the 19th c. it developed into a fashionable spa. Beautiful park; casino; Gothic church; museum devoted to the work of the painter Louis Français.

St-Amarin (alt. 420 m), a little place at the beginning of the upper St-Amarin valley, one of the most beautiful in the Vosges, at the head of which is the Rainkopf. In the parish church is a reliquary containing the remains of St Amarin, who came here in the 8th c. and gave his name to the village and the valley.

Ste-Marie-aux-Mines (alt. 360 m; pop. 1200), a prominent silver-mining town in the Middle Ages, now has textile industries. Town Hall, now a museum, built in 1634. Conducted tours of the old St-Barthélemy mine. Carneval des Paysans, with cavalcade, on the Sunday after Ash Wednesday. Collectors of minerals will find much to interest them in the surrounding area.

Mont Ste-Odile (762 m) is one of the most interesting places in the Vosges. This wooded ridge is surrounded by a prehistoric defensive wall, some 10 km in extent, known as the *Mur païen* (Heathens' Wall). In places the wall, 2 m thick, still stands to a height of 2–3 m; the stones were originally bonded together with oak dowels. A walk round the entire circuit takes 4–5 hours. The Romans built a fort on top of the hill, and in Merovingian and Carolingian times there was a convent of nuns here. The convent was destroyed by the Huns, but in 1049 Pope Leo IX, who came from Alsace, founded a new convent and church dedicated to St Odile, patron saint of Alsace. The convent flourished in the 12th and 13th c., but was destroyed by fire in 1546. In the middle of the 19th c. the Bishop of Strasbourg revived the pilgrimage to the shrine of St Odile. – The present church dates from 1092 and has an altar dedicated to St Odile. Chapelle de la Croix (11th c.); *Chapelle Ste-Odile*, with the saint's sarcophagus, the goal of the pilgrimages; other chapels; large statue of the saint blessing the countryside below. The main pilgrimages are at Easter and Whitsun, on the first and second Sundays in July and on 13 December. – The highest point on Mont Ste-Odile is the **Bloss (823 m: *view). Below the convent is the *Source Ste-Odile* (St Odile's Spring), which is believed to cure eye ailments, since Odile was born blind and gained her sight when she was baptised.

Schirmeck (alt. 311 m) is a popular summer resort in a wooded setting in the Bruche valley, at the foot of Le Donon. Above the village is a hill with the ruins of an episcopal castle and a museum.

Struthof, 5 km SE of Schirmeck, is a former concentration camp, preserved as a memorial to the 40,000 people who were imprisoned here between 1941 and 1944 (conducted tours; museum; cemetery; memorial).

Les Trois-Epis (alt. 658 m) is an old-established place of pilgrimage, with the 17th c. chapel of Notre-Dame des Trois-Epis ("Our Lady of the Three Ears of Corn"). The Virgin is said to have appeared here in 1491 to a local blacksmith, called on the people of the district to give up their sinful ways and promised them a rich harvest in return.

Of the various tourist routes which pass through the Vosges or run close to them, the most important are the ***Route des Crêtes** and the **Route des Vosges**. The Route des Crêtes (75 km) constructed during the First World War, runs from the *Col du Bonhomme* by way of the **Col de* *la Schlucht*, the *Markstein*, the *Grand Ballon* and *Hartmannswillerkopf* to *Mulhouse*. The Route des Vosges runs from *Klingenthal* (near Obernai) to *Mont Ste-Odile* and then continues via *Hohwald* and *Andlau* to *Sélestat*.

SPORT and RECREATION in the Vosges. – In summer there is plenty of *walking*; in winter *skiing* is becoming increasingly popular (ski-lifts). – There are a variety of interesting *folk events* and pilgrimages. – The lakes offer facilities for *water sports*. – Also *tennis* and *riding*.

Military cemetery, Hartmannswillerkopf

Practical Information

ATTENTION AU FEU

Warning!

During the long dry summer period there is grave danger of **forest fires** in many parts of France.

It is therefore strictly forbidden to light fires within 200 metres of a wooded area, to smoke in forests or to throw away lighted cigarette ends or other inflammable articles. Camping is permitted only on specially designated sites.

Safety on the road

When to go, Weather, Time

Travel documents

Customs regulations

Currency

Postal rates

Travelling to France

Travelling in France

Language

Accommodation

Food and drink

Recreation and sport

Taking the cure

Son et lumière, châteaux

National parks

Caves

Winter sports

Folk traditions

Calendar of events

Shopping and souvenirs

Information

Emergency calls

Index

Some Alsatian specialties

Safety on the Road. Some Reminders for the Holiday Traveller

When to go

France likes to call itself the "land of four seasons"; and it is true that with its varied pattern of landscape, extending from the Channel coast by way of the Pyrenees and the Alps to the Côte d'Azur and the island of Corsica, and its consequent variety of climate, France offers attractions to visitors at every time of year. It is worth remembering, however, that accommodation is more easily and cheaply available outside the main holiday season (August).

Spring is a good time to visit Alsace, the châteaux in the Loire valley, Provence, the Côte d'Azur (particularly between Cannes and Menton), the Basque coast and the coasts of Corsica, where there is good bathing early in the year.

In *summer* there is a wide choice: the upland regions and mountains – the Vosges, the Jura, Auvergne, the Cévennes and the Tarn gorges, the Pyrenees, the Alps and the hills of Corsica – and the coastal regions and resorts of Flanders, Normandy and Brittany, the coast between Les Sables d'Olonne and Royan, the Côte d'Argent and the Basque coast, the whole of the Mediterranean coast and Corsica.

Autumn is the time to visit Burgundy and the other wine-growing regions on the fringes of the Vosges and round Bordeaux; but all the areas mentioned above are attractive, particularly in early autumn.

In *winter* the upland and mountain regions – particularly, of course, the Alps, but also the Pyrenees, Auvergne, the Cévennes and the Jura – offer excellent skiing, and the winter resorts on the Riviera and in Corsica attract many visitors with their mild climate.

And of course Paris, France's principal tourist attraction, has something to offer at every time of year. In winter it has its brilliantly lit streets, its theatres and concerts; in spring and autumn the surrounding countryside is at its most beautiful; and in summer, when many Parisians are away from Paris on holiday, visitors may have an opportunity of exploring the city at a more leisurely pace.

Weather

France lies within the northern temperate zone, a region of mild climate with winds blowing predominantly from the west and with a fairly regular alternation between areas of low and high pressure determining the weather pattern throughout the year. Lying on the western edge of the European continent, France is exposed to maritime influences which extend far to the east and modify the continental features of the climate.

At certain points on the Channel coast, at any rate within a narrow coastal strip, the winter, under the influence of the Gulf Stream, is as mild as on the Mediterranean coast. Throughout France as a whole the growing season begins early, though in the course of the summer the rest of Europe tends to catch up.

Southern France lies within the Mediterranean climatic zone, with the rain falling almost exclusively in autumn and spring, and summers which are often completely rainless. In this region the abundance of sunshine offers an additional attraction to the holidaymaker.

For a more detailed account of the French climate see p. 17.

Time

France is in the Central European time zone, one hour ahead of Greenwich Mean Time. From the beginning of April to the end of September *summer time* is in force, and France is then two hours ahead of GMT and one hour ahead of British summer time.

Travel Documents

Visitors from Britain and most Western countries require only a valid **passport** (or a British Visitor's Passport) to enter France.

British and other Western **driving licences** and **car documents** are accepted in France. Although nationals of EEC countries do not need an *international insurance certificate* ("green card"), it is desirable to have one, since otherwise only third-party cover is provided. You are advised to consult your insurers prior to any overseas visit to confirm that your cover is adequate. All foreign cars visiting France must display an *international distinguishing sign* of the approved pattern and design. *Failure to do so can result in a fine.*

Health insurance cover is available to nationals of EEC countries on the same basis as for French citizens, covering insured persons and pensioners. You should apply to the Department of Health and Social Security, well before your date of departure, for leaflet SA30 which gives details of reciprocal arrangements for medical treatment and contains an application form for a certificate of entitlement (Form E111). Under the French health insurance system patients pay for treatment received at prescribed rates and receive reimbursement from the health insurance authorities. Since the reimbursement is not usually 100%, it is advisable to take out supplementary private insurance.

Dogs and cats can be taken into France if they have a certificate of vaccination against rabies not less than a month nor more than a year old. (In view of the quarantine regulations on re-entry into Britain most British visitors will of course leave their pets at home.)

Customs Regulations

Personal effects and such things as camping and sports equipment are admitted without formality. For outboard motors of over 92 cc a *triptyque* or *carnet de passage* is required.

In addition visitors are allowed the usual duty-free allowances of alcohol and tobacco, etc. For goods bought in the ordinary shops in Britain or another EEC country (i.e. duty and tax paid) the allowances are 300 cigarettes *or* 150 cigarillos *or* 75 cigars *or* 400 grammes of tobacco; $1\frac{1}{2}$ litres of alcoholic drinks over 38·8° proof (22° Gay-Lussac) *or* 3 litres of alcoholic drinks not over 38·8° proof *or* 3 litres of fortified or sparkling wine, *plus* 4 litres of still table wine; 75 grammes of perfume; and 375 cc of toilet water. For goods bought in a duty-free shop, on a ship or on an aircraft the allowances are two-thirds of these amounts (250 grammes of tobacco); the allowances of tobacco goods are doubled for visitors from outside Europe.

The duty-free allowances on return to Britain are the same as those from British visitors to France.

Currency

The unit of currency is the French **franc** (*F*), which is made up of 100 *centimes*.

There are banknotes for 10, 50 and 500 francs, and coins in denominations of 5, 10 and 20 centimes and $\frac{1}{2}$, 1, 5 and 10 francs.

Exchange rates fluctuate. The rates at the end of 1981 were approximately as follows:

1 pound sterling=10·50 francs
1 franc=9·6p
1 US dollar=4·10 francs
1 franc=24 cents
1 Canadian dollar=3·60 francs
1 franc=28 cents

There are no restrictions on the import of French or foreign currency. The export of foreign currency in cash is permitted up to a value of 5000 francs or to any higher amount which has been declared on entry into France. Up to 5000 French francs may be exported. It is advisable to take travellers' cheques and/or Eurocheque cards. Credit cards may also be used.

Postal rates

Postage on letters (up to 20 g (0·7 oz)) to the United Kingdom is 1·90 francs; to Canada airmail postage on letters is 2·15 francs up to 5 g; 2·70 francs from 5 to 10 g; 3·25 francs from 10 to 15 g; 3·80 francs from 15 to 20 g.

To the United States airmail postage on letters is 2·85 francs up to 5 g; 3·40 francs from 5 to 10 g; 3·95 francs from 10 to 15 g; 4·50 francs from 15 to 20 g.

Stamps can be bought in tobacconists' shops more conveniently than in post offices. They are also usually sold by shops, kiosks, etc., selling postcards.

Post-boxes are coloured yellow. They are usually fixed to walls; there are no pillar-boxes of the British type.

Travelling to France

By car. – There are *Sealink* car ferries between Dover and Boulogne, Dover and Calais, Folkestone and Boulogne, Folkestone and Calais, Newhaven and Dieppe, and Weymouth and Cherbourg. Other services are run by *Townsend-Thoresen* (Dover–Calais, Portsmouth–Le Havre, Southampton–Le Havre, Southampton–Cherbourg), *P & O Ferries* (Dover–Boulogne, Southampton–Le Havre), *Brittany Ferries* (Plymouth–St-Malo and Roscoff, Portsmouth–St-Malo, Cork–Roscoff), the *Olau Line* (Ramsgate–Dunkirk) and the *Irish Continental Line* (Rosslare–Cherbourg and Le Havre). There are also services between St-Malo and the Channel Islands.

There are hovercraft services (carrying cars) from Dover to Boulogne and Calais and from Ramsgate to Calais. The crossing takes between 30 and 40 minutes, but the timetable can be upset by weather and tide conditions.

The onward journey in France can be shortened by using one of the French motorail services (see below).

By air. – There is a wide choice of air routes between the *United Kingdom* and France. Most of the traffic goes between London (Heathrow and Gatwick) and the major French airports, particularly Paris (Roissy and Orly), but there are also services from many other airports in Britain, including Aberdeen, Birmingham, Bradford/Leeds, Bristol, Cardiff, Edinburgh, Glasgow, Manchester, Newcastle,

Plymouth, Southampton and Swansea. The main French airports served, apart from Paris, are Basle/Mulhouse, Bordeaux, Lyons, Marseilles, Nice, Strasbourg and Toulouse, but there are also services to many smaller French airports, from Cherbourg and Calais in the north to Perpignan, Nîmes and Montpellier in the south. Apart from the national airlines, **British Airways** and **Air France**, the carriers include British Caledonian, UK Air, Dan-Air and a number of smaller airlines. – From **Ireland** there are services by **Aer Lingus** from Dublin and Cork to Paris and Lourdes. – From the *United States* and *Canada* there are services by **Air France**, **Pan Am**, **TWA**, **Air Canada** and other airlines.

By rail. – Apart from the normal train services linking up with the Channel ferries, through carriages run overnight between London and Paris.
For rail services within France, see below.

By coach. – There are regular coach services from London and certain other towns in ·Britain to Paris and other destinations in France: e.g. Manchester, Birmingham, London and Dover to Calais and Paris (Godfrey Abbot, 151 Charles Street, Stockport SK1 3JU, tel. 061–429 6144); London to the Pyrenees, to Perpignan and to Nice (Clipper Coaches, Continental House, Royal Parade, Chislehurst, Kent, tel. 01–467 0106); London to Paris, Bordeaux and south of France (European ·Express, 60 King Street, Twickenham, Middlesex TW1 3SH, tel. 01–891 0771); Paris to the Côte d'Azur (Europabus: British Rail Travel Centres

and selected stations); London to Paris and Lyons (Euroways, 8 Park Lane, Croydon CR9 1DN, tel. 01–462 7733); London to Caen, Calais, Rouen and Paris (National Travel, Victoria Coach Station, London SW1, tel. 01–730 0202); Cheltenham, Bristol, Bath, Salisbury and Southampton to Paris (National Travel, Coach Station, Cheltenham GL50 4DX, tel. 0242–38331).

Travelling in France

Motoring

France is served by a dense network of roads, and even minor roads are usually in excellent condition. The **motorways** (*autoroutes*), which have been developed in recent years and now have a total length of some 4000 km, mainly radiate from Paris to the N (Roubaix), NW (Rouen and Caen), SW (Tours and Poitiers), SE (Auxerre, Lyons and Avignon) and E (Metz and Strasbourg), and also run parallel to the Mediterranean coast. Tolls are payable except on a few short, stretches near large cities. You should ensure that you have sufficient currency to cover the cost of toll charges which can be exceedingly expensive.

Most of the traffic, however, is still carried by the excellently engineered **routes nationales**, which are marked by red and white kilometre stones bearing the number of the road, prefixed by the letter N. Frequently these have only three lanes for traffic in both directions, the middle lane being used for overtaking. The extensive network of roads means that as a rule the roads are not too crowded, though there may be considerable holdups during the holiday season (particularly at the beginning and end of the month) on the roads radiating from Paris. – Roads of lesser importance are classified as **routes départementales**. They have yellow and white kilometre stones bearing a number prefixed by the letter D. A free road map giving details of less congested alternative "holiday" routes, plus information centres and petrol stations open for 24 hours, is available from service stations displaying the *Bison Fute* poster (a Red Indian chief in full war bonnet).

Driving in France. – As in the rest of continental Europe, traffic goes on the right. The wearing of *safety belts* is compulsory.

In general *priority* at road junctions belongs to the vehicle coming from the right, and warnings are often given by the sign *Priorité à droite*. Roads which have priority are indicated by signs before junctions, reading *Passage protégé*. – Parking is permitted on the left-hand side of the road within built-up areas, but in narrow streets parking is often prohibited on either side alternately (either on alternate days or in each half of a month). This is indicated by the sign *Stationnement alterné*, with an indication of the pattern of alternation – on even-numbered days (*jours pairs*) on one side and on odd-numbered days (*jours impairs*) on the other, or on days 1–15 and 16–31. The centres of towns are often

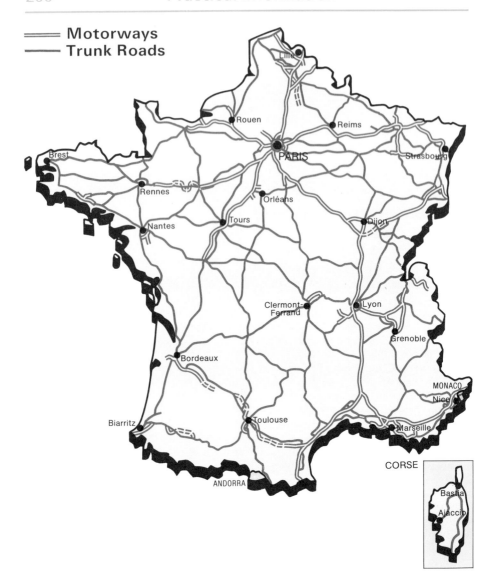

=== Motorways
—— Trunk Roads

designated as "blue zones" (*zones bleues*), within which parking (for a limited period) is allowed only with a parking disc (*disque*, obtainable from the police and motoring organisations). Special provisions apply in Paris, where there are many underground car parks. – Dipped headlights must be used between dusk and dawn both inside and outside built-up areas. Warning signals at night must be given by flashing your headlights, not by the use of the horn. Yellow headlights are normal in France and although visitors are not required to fit amber lens converters this is recommended as a courtesy measure.

Since the French have a very individual style of driving, particular care should be

Domestic air service

— Air France
— Air Inter

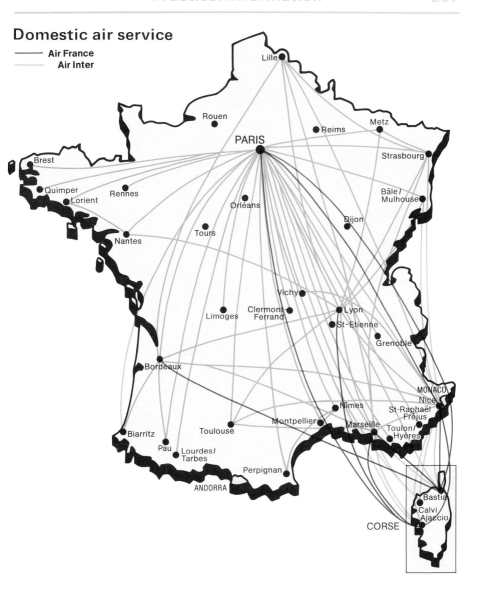

Air services

The French national airline, **Air France**, flies not only international routes but also the most important domestic services. *Air Inter* serves also the smaller airports of purely regional importance.

Railways

The French railways, offering high standards of service and comfort, are run by a State corporation, the *Société Nationale des Chemins de Fer Français* (*SNCF*). The main routes are served by Trans-European Expresses (TEE), fast express trains and through expresses (*rapides*).

exercised by visiting drivers. The consequences of an accident are unpleasant and may be protracted. If you do become involved in an accident be sure to follow the instructions issued with your "green card" as to recording and reporting particulars of the incident.

The present **speed limits** are **130 km per hour** on motorways, **110 km per hour** on expressways, **90 km per hour** on national and departmental roads and **60 km per hour** in built-up areas unless otherwise signposted. Drivers who have held a licence for less than a year are limited to 90 km per hour. *Warning* Heavy on-the-spot fines are likely to be imposed in France for relatively minor traffic offences.

Railways

—— Main lines
—— Branch lines

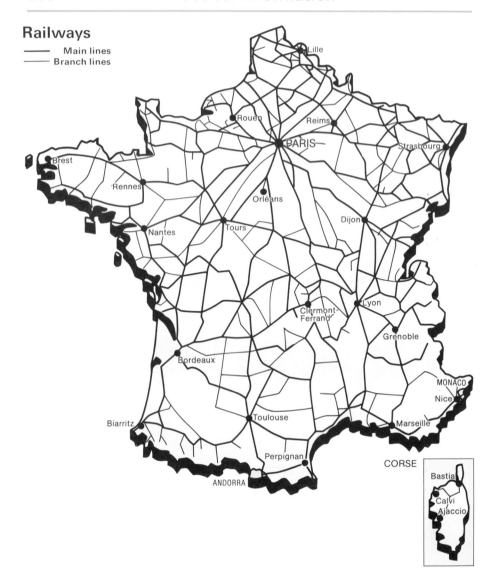

Tickets are not now checked at the entrance to the platform. Passengers must themselves validate their ticket in a date-stamping machine at the entrance, and failure to do so entails a surcharge of 20%. (This does not, however, apply to tickets bought outside France.)

Concession fares are available for tourists (20% reduction for journeys of at least 1500 km), old age pensioners (with the "Carte Vermeil", from age 65 for men and 60 for women, 30% reduction – a reduction also available to holders of a British "Senior Citizen's Railcard" for journeys booked in Britain), families (for journeys of over 300 km, 30–75% reduction according to number of children), "France Vacances" rail rover card (available for 7 days, 15 days or a month), groups of ten or more, students and school-children. – Children under 4 accompanied by adults travel free; children over 4 and under 10 (under 12 for tickets issued in any European country other than France) pay half fare.

Car hire at railway stations ("*Train+Auto*"). – Cars can be hired at some 200 stations in France; advance booking necessary.

Bicycle hire at railway stations ("*Train+Vélo*") – Bicycles can be hired at almost 100 stations on production of a passport or other identity document; charge 15 francs per day.

Motorail

The journey to the south of France can be shortened by using one of the motorail services which convey cars and their passengers quickly and comfortably from one end of the country to the other. There are motorail service from Dover and Folkestone to Avignon, Biarritz, Fréjus-St-Raphaël and Narbonne, and also services within France (Calais to Lyons, Fréjus-St-Raphaël and Nice; Boulogne to Fréjus-St-Raphaël, Avignon, Narbonne and Biarritz; Paris to Avignon, Biarritz, Grenoble, Lyons, Narbonne, Nice, St-Gervais, Fréjus-St-Raphaël and Toulon).

Information about services can be obtained from railway stations and travel agencies.

Bus services

The rail services are supplemented by a network of bus services, run either by the SNCF or by local bus companies. – The SNCF runs popular coach excursions, which are listed in their timetable, "Indicateur Tourisme".

Boat services

There are regular services (including car ferries) from Marseilles, Toulon and Nice to Corsica; the crossing takes 9–12 hours.

Many of the islands off the Atlantic and Mediterranean coasts are served by local shipping companies.

Language

French developed out of Vulgar Latin, the colloquial form of classical Latin, which was spoken by the Celtic peoples of Gaul after their conquest by the Romans. Although incorporating many words of Celtic and later Germanic origin, it preserved its Romanesque character and was for centuries the most important of the Romance languages, widely spoken in educated circles throughout Europe and in diplomatic intercourse. Although it is the mother tongue of no more than 80 million people it is one of the leading languages of the world, taught in schools all over the world and used over large areas as the language of commerce and communication.

Although English is widely spoken in France, particularly by those concerned in any way with the tourist trade, visitors will get more out of their holiday if they know at least some French. A small dictionary or phrase-book will be found helpful; the following paragraphs of this Guide can give only the essential minimum of vocabulary.

There are **summer language courses** in French for foreigners at the universities of Aix-en-Provence, Amiens, Annecy, Avignon, Besançon, Bordeaux, Dijon, Grenoble, Lille (courses at Boulogne), Lyons, Montpellier, Nancy, Nice, Paris (Sorbonne and Université de Paris III), Pau, Perpignan, Poitiers, Quimper, Reims, Strasbourg and Toulouse (courses at Bagnères-de-Bigorre in the Pyrenees). Other courses are run in association with universities at La Rochelle, Montpellier, Paris, St-Malo, Tours, Ustaritz and Vichy, and by various higher educational establishments in Angers, Cannes, Menton, Montpellier, Nice, Paris

(several courses), Perpignan and Strasbourg. Addresses are given in the booklet, "Loisirs en France", published by the Secrétariat d'Etat au Tourisme.

In southern France the *Provençal* language (*langue d'oc*, distinguished from the language of the north, *langue d'oïl*) is still spoken by many people. This differs considerably from French; its principal characteristics are the maintenance of *a* in an open syllable (*pra*, compared with French *pré*, from Latin *pratum*), the change of this *a* to *ié* where French has *é* (*marchié*, compared with French *marché*, from mercatum), the existence of four terminal vowels (*a, e, i* and *o*, with Provençal *a* and *e* corresponding to French *e*), the ending -*o* in the first person of the verb, the regional distinction between nominative and accusative and the development of certain sounds peculiar to Provençal.

In Alsace and parts of Lorraine a dialect of German (*Elsässerditsch*) is widely spoken, in Corsica a Central Italian dialect peculiar to the island, in Brittany the Breton language (*brezonnek*), an off-shoot of the British branch of the Celtic languages, and in the extreme SW of France the non-Indo-European Basque language (*euskara*).

Pronunciation of French. – Characteristic features are the placing of the stress towards the end of the word and the frequent nasalisation of vowels. – *Vowels* (always pronounced without dipthongisation): *ai* like English *ay*; *ais* an open *e* as in "bed"; *é* like *ay*; *è* and *ê* an open *e*; *an, en, em* at the end of a syllable like a nasalised *on* (not quite *ong*); *un, im, in, ein* at the end of a syllable like a nasalised *un* (not quite *ung*); *eu* a little like the *u* in "fur"; *oi, oy* like *wa*; *ou* like *oo*; *u* a sound obtained by pronouncing *ee* with rounded lips.

– *Consonants*: c before *e, i* or *y* and *ç* before other vowels, like *s; c* before *a, o* or *u* like *k; j,* and *g* before *e, i* or *y,* like *zh; g* before *a, o* or *u* like a hard English *g; ch* like *sh; gn* usually like *ny* in "canyon"; *h* always silent; *ll* between vowels often palatalised to a *y* sound, but sometimes a light *l* (e.g. in *elle*); *q, qu* like *k; x* between vowels like *z.* – The following letters are usually silent at the end of a word (and often also at the end of a syllable): *b, c, d, e, p, r* (only after *e*), *s, t, x* and *z.*

Numbers

0	zéro	21	vingt et un
1	un, une	22	vingt-deux
2	deux	30	trente
3	trois	40	quarante
4	quatre	50	cinquante
5	cinq	60	soixante
6	six	70	soixante-dix
7	sept	71	soixante et onze
8	huit	80	quatre-vingt(s)
9	neuf	81	quatre-vingt-un
10	dix	90	quatre-vingt-dix
11	onze	91	quatre-vingt-onze
12	douze	100	cent
13	treize	101	cent un
14	quatorze	153	cent cinquante-trois
15	quinze	200	deux cent(s)
16	seize	300	trois cent(s)
17	dix-sept	400	quatre cent(s)
18	dix-huit	500	cinq cent(s)
19	dix-neuf	1000	mille
20	vingt	1001	mille un
		2000	deux mille
		1,000,000	un million

Ordinals

1st	premier, première
2nd	deuxième; second(e)
3rd	troisième
4th	quatrième
5th	cinquième
6th	sixième
7th	septième
8th	huitième
9th	neuvième
10th	dixième
11th	onzième
100th	centième

Fractions

$\frac{1}{2}$	demi(e)
$\frac{1}{3}$	tiers
$\frac{1}{4}$	quart
$\frac{3}{4}$	trois quarts

Vocabulary

When addressing anyone it is usual to add the polite *Monsieur, Madame* or *Mademoiselle*; and any request or enquiry should be accompanied by *s'il vous plaît* ("please").

Good morning, good day!	Bonjour!
Good evening!	Bonsoir!
Good night!	Bonne nuit!
Goodbye	Au revoir
Do you speak English?	Parlez-vous anglais?
I do not understand	Je ne comprends pas
Yes	Oui
No	Non
Please	S'il vous plaît
Thank you	Merci
Yesterday	Hier
Today	Aujourd'hui
Tomorrow	Demain
Help!	Au secours!
Have you a single room?	Avez-vous une chambre à un lit?
Have you a double room?	Avez-vous une chambre à deux lits?
Have you a room with private bath?	Avez-vous une chambre avec bain?
How much does it cost?	Combien (est-ce que) ça coûte? Quel est le prix de . . .?
Please wake me at 6	Veuillez me réveiller à six heures, s'il vous plaît
Where is the lavatory?	Où sont les toilettes?
Where is the chemist's?	Où est la pharmacie?
Where is the post office?	Où est le bureau de poste?
Where is there a doctor?	Où y a-t-il un médecin?
Where is there a dentist?	Où y a-t-il un dentiste?
Is this the way to the station?	Est-ce le chemin de la gare?

Road and traffic signs

Attention!	Caution
Au pas!	Slow
Centre ville	To town centre
Chantier	Road works
Danger (de mort)	Danger (of death)
Douane	Customs
Fin de limitation de vitesse	End of speed restriction
Garage	Parking; passing place
Gravier, gravillons	Loose stones, gravel
Halte!	Stop
Impasse	No through road; cul-de-sac
Limitation de vitesse	Speed restriction
Passage interdit	No entry, no thoroughfare

Passage protégé	You have priority at junction ahead
Priorité à droite	Priority for traffic coming from right
Prudence!	Drive with care
Ralentir, ralentissez!	Reduce speed now
Route barrée	Road closed
Sens unique	One-way street
Serrez à droite!	Keep in to the right
Sortie de camions	Lorries crossing
Stop!	Stop
Tenez vos distances!	Keep your distance
Toutes directions	All directions
Travaux	Road works
Virage (dangereux)	(Dangerous) bend
Voie unique	Single-lane traffic
Zone bleue	Parking only with parking disc
Zone rouge – Mise en fourrière immédiate	No parking: parked cars liable to be towed away immediately

Rail and air travel

Airport	Aéroport
All aboard!	En voiture!
Arrival	Arrivée
Baggage	Bagages
Baggage check	Bulletin de bagages
Bus station	Gare routière
Couchette	Couchette
Departure	Départ
Flight	Vol
Halt	Arrêt
Information	Information, renseignements
Lavatory	Toilette(s)
Line (railway)	Voie
Luggage	Bagages
Non-smoking	Non-fumeurs
Platform	Quai
Porter	Porteur
Restaurant car	Wagon-restaurant
Sleeping car	Wagon-lit
Smoking	Fumeurs
Station	Gare
Stewardess	Hôtesse (de l'air)
Stop	Arrêt
Ticket	Billet, ticket
Ticket collector	Contrôleur
Ticket window	Guichet
Timetable	Horaire
Train	Train
Waiting room	Salle d'attente
Window seat	Coin fenêtre

Months

January	Janvier
February	Février
March	Mars
April	Avril
May	Mai
June	Juin
July	Juillet
August	Août
September	Septembre
October	Octobre
November	Novembre
December	Décembre

Days of the week

Sunday	Dimanche
Monday	Lundi
Tuesday	Mardi
Wednesday	Mercredi
Thursday	Jeudi
Friday	Vendredi
Saturday	Samedi
Day	Jour, journée
Public holiday	Jour de fête

Festivals

New Year	Nouvel an
Easter	Pâques
Ascension	Ascension
Whitsun	Pentecôte
Corpus Christi	Fête-Dieu
Assumption	Assomption
All Saints	Toussaint
Christmas	Noël
New Year's Eve	Le Saint-Sylvestre

At the post office

Address	Adresse
Express	Exprès
Letter	Lettre
Letter-box	Boîte à lettres
Parcel	Paquet, colis
Postcard	Carte postale
Poste restante	Poste restante
Postman	Facteur
Registered	Recommandé
Small packet	Petit paquet
Stamp	Timbre (-poste)
Telegram	Télégramme
Telephone	Téléphone
Telex	Télex

Glossary
of topographical terms

Abbaye	Abbey
Aiguille	Pinnacle, crag
Anse	Bay
Archevêché	Archbishop's Palace
Archipel	Archipelago
Arènes	Amphitheatre
Auberge	Inn
Autoroute	Motorway
Avenue	Avenue
Bac	Ferry
Baie	Bay
Bain	Bath(s)
Banlieue	Suburb(s)
Barrage	Dam
Basilique	Church (usually one of particular dignity)
Bassin	Dock; ornamental lake, pond
Belvédère	Viewpoint
Bibliothèque	Library
Bois	Wood
Boulevard	Boulevard, avenue
Bourse	(Stock) exchange
Butte	Low hill, bluff
Calvaire	Calvary
Camping	Camping site

Capitainerie	Harbourmaster's office	Forteresse	Fortress
Carrefour	Road intersection	Fosse	Pit; grave
Carrière	Quarry	Fossé	Ditch; moat
Cascade	Waterfall	Gare	Railway station
Cathédrale	Cathedral	Gare routière	Bus station
Causse	Limestone plateau	Gave	Mountain stream (in
Cave	Cellar		Pyrenees)
Caverne	Cave	Glacier	Glacier
Chaîne	Chain, ridge (of hills)	Golfe	Gulf, bay
Chalet	Chalet; mountain hut or	Gorge	Gorge
	hotel	Gouffre	Chasm, swallow-hole
Champ	Field	Grotte	Cave
Chaos	Tumble of rocks	Gué	Ford
Chapelle	Chapel	Halle	Market hall
Chartreuse	Charterhouse	Hameau	Hamlet
Château	Château (covering the	Hauteur	Height, hill
	whole range from	Hippodrome	Racecourse
	fortified castles to	Hôpital	Hospital
	country houses and	Horloge	Clock
	small manor-houses)	Hôtel	Hotel; aristocratic
Château-fort	(Fortified) castle		mansion
Chemin	Road, track	Hôtel de ville	Town hall
Chemin de fer	Railway	Ile	Island
Cimetière	Cemetery	Ilot	Islet
Citadelle	Citadel	Impasse	Cul-de-sac
Cité	City (often the old part	Jardin	Garden
	of a town)	Jardin des plantes	Botanic garden
Cité universitaire	University residence(s)	Lac	Lake
Clocher	(Bell-) tower	Lagune	Lagoon
Cloître	Cloister	Lande	Heath
Clos	Enclosure, field,	Logis	Lodging
	vineyard	Lycée	Grammar school
Cluse	Gorge	Mairie	Town hall
Col	Pass	Maison	House
Collégiale	Collegiate church	Manoir	Manor-house
Colline	Hill	Maquis	Scrub(land)
Colonne	Column	Marais	Marsh, bog
Combe	Valley, combe	Marché	Market
Comté	County	Mare	Pool
Corniche	Corniche road (along	Marécage	Marsh, bog
	side of hill)	Mas	Farmhouse (in
Côte	Coast; slope (of hill)		Provence)
Côté	Side	Menhir	Standing stone
Coteau	Slope, hillside	Mer	Sea
Cour	Courtyard	Monastère	Monastery
Cours	Avenue	Monnaie	Mint
Cours d'eau	River, watercourse	Mont	Mount(ain)
Couvent	Convent, religious house	Montagne	Mountain
Crête	Crest, ridge (of hill)	Moulin	Mill
Défilé	Defile, gorge	Mur, muraille	Wall
Dent	Crag, pinnacle (of	Musée	Museum
	mountain)	Nef	Nave (of church)
·Dolmen	Megalithic tomb	Nez	Nose, cape
Dôme	Dome, rounded hill	Nord	North
Donjon	Keep	Oratoire	Oratory
Ecluse	Lock (on canal)	Ouest	West
Ecole	School	Palais	Palace
Ecole normale	Teachers' training	Palais de justice	Law courts
	college	Parc	Park
Embouchure	Mouth (of river)	Passerelle	Footbridge
Escalier	Staircase	Pays	Country
Est	East	Phare	Lighthouse
Estuaire	Estuary	Pic	Peak
Etablissement thermal	Spa establishment	Piscine	Swimming pool
Etang	Pond, lake	Place	Square
Evêché	Bishop's Palace	Plage	Beach
Falaise	Cliff	Plaine	Plain
Faubourg	Suburb, outer district of	Plateau	Plateau
	town	Pointe	Peak (of hill); cape,
Fleuve	River (flowing into the		point
	sea)	Pont	Bridge
Fontaine	Fountain	Porche	Porch
Forêt	Forest	Port	Port, harbour
Forêt domaniale	State forest	Portail	Doorway
Fort	Fort	Porte	Door

Poste	Post office	Source	Spring; source of river
Prairie, pré	Meadow	Square	Public square with
Presqu'île	Peninsula		gardens
Prieuré	Priory	Stade	Stadium
Promontoire	Promontory	Station	Resort; station
PTT	Post Office	Station thermale	Spa, health resort
Puits	Well	Sud	South
Quai	Quay; embankment	Syndicat d'Initiative	Tourist information
Quartier	Quarter, district (of a		office
	town)	Téléférique	Cableway
Rade	Anchorage, roadsteads	Télésiège	Chair-lift
Refuge	Traffic island; mountain	Téléski	Ski-lift
	hut	Temple	Temple; Protestant
Remparts	Ramparts		church
Rivière	River (not flowing into	Thermes	Baths
	sea)	Tombe, tombeau	Tomb
Roc, roche, rocher	Rock	Torrent	Mountain stream
Rond-point	Roundabout	Tour	Tower
Route	Road	Trésor	Treasure, treasury
Ru	Stream	Tribunal	Law court
Rue	Street	Trou	Hole
Ruisseau	Stream	Tunnel	Tunnel
Sable	Sand	Université	University
Saline	Salt-pan	Val, vallée, vallon	Valley
Salle	Hall, room	Viaduc	Viaduct
Saut	Waterfall	Village	Village
Sente, sentier	Path	Ville	Town, city

Accommodation

Hotels

French hotels are usually good, and well up to the standards laid down for their particular category. Outside the larger towns the rooms almost invariably have a *grand lit*, the large French double bed, and the charge for two people is only slightly higher than for one. Most of the good-class hotels are approved and classified by the Commissariat Général au Tourisme as *hôtels de tourisme* and display a sign recording their classification. Details can be found in the official Hotel Guide published annually and in the local and regional lists issued free of charge by Offices de Tourisme and Syndicats d'Initiative.

A considerable number of hotels in various categories, mainly in areas where it was desired to promote tourism, have been modernised with assistance from the Fédération Nationale des Logis de France, and these **Logis de France** offer modern standards of comfort and amenity at reasonable prices. There are also the **auberges rurales**, offering a family atmosphere and traditional country cooking at even more moderate rates. Both types of establishment are listed in a booklet published annually.

Many hotels, particularly off the main roads, are known as **relais** (a term which originally meant posting station) – *relais de campagne*, *relais du silence*, etc. These are usually excellent establishments, often with a distinct personality of their own.

Information: **Fédération Nationale des Logis de France,**
25 rue Jean-Mermoz,
F-75008 **Paris**;
tel. (1) 3 59 86 67.

Hotels with **facilities for the handicapped** (*handicapés physiques*) are indicated by the wheel-chair symbol in the official Hotel Guide – the "Guide National Officiel de l'Hôtellerie Française – Les Hôtels de France" (94 Boulevard Beaumarchais and 83 rue Amelot, F-75011 Paris, tel. (1) 7 00 56 30).

French hotels are classified in five categories – one, two, three and four stars and luxury.

Category		Tariff for one night (in francs)	
official	in this Guide	1 person	2 persons
★★★★L	L	140–600	250–800
★★★★	I	90–300	130–500
★★★	II	60–200	80–250
★★	III	50–120	60–170
★	IV	40–90	50–130

The prices shown include service and taxes, but not breakfast.

Youth Hostels

France has over 300 **youth hostels** (*auberges de jeunesse*), which can be used by foreign visitors with an international youth hostel card (obtainable from the youth hostels association in their own country). Advance booking is advisable in July and August; the maximum stay permitted is usually three nights.

Information: **Fédération Unie des Auberges de Jeunesse,**
6 rue Mesnil,
F-75116 **Paris;**
tel. (1) 2 61 84 03.

Holiday Apartments and Chalets

There are numerous chalets and holiday apartments (*appartements de vacances*) available for renting, particularly in the newer holiday centres in the winter sports areas and popular coastal resorts. They can be booked through the French Government Tourist Office or through local estate agents. It is advisable to have a written rental agreement.

Country Holidays

The term **Tourisme vert** covers a wide range of holidays all over France, in farmhouses and little country inns (*auberges rurales*) which offer simple but entirely adequate and comfortable accommodation and on quiet little *camping sites*. Standards of amenity are indicated by symbols – one, two or three ears of corn.

Information: **La Maison du Tourisme Vert,**
Rue Godot-de-Mauroy,
F-75009 **Paris;**
tel. (1) 0 73 25 43 and 0 73 23 16.

Association Française des Stations Vertes de Vacances,
Préfecture,
F-72000 **Le Mans.**

Camping and Caravanning

Camping holidays are more popular and better catered for in France than in other European countries. Almost every place of tourist interest has at least one, and often more than one, camping site (*terrain de camping,* or *camping* for short). Sites are classified, according to the standard of amenities provided, with from one to four stars. The camps run by the Touring Club de France (TCF), or by other bodies on their behalf, are particularly well equipped.

Two particular types of camping site are the *Castels et Camping* sites, laid out in the grounds of châteaux and country houses, and the small remote sites on farms classified as *Camping rural.* There are also a number of naturist camping sites (*camps naturistes*).

During the main holiday season the camping sites along the main tourist routes and the favourite holiday areas are usually full (*complet*), but as a rule room can be found on sites a little farther from the beaten track.

Information: **Fédération Française de Camping et de Caravaning** (*FFCC*),
78 rue de Rivoli,
F-75004 **Paris;**
tel. (1) 2 72 84 08.

Food and Drink

French cuisine is world-famed both for its quality and its variety. Since the average Frenchman attaches importance to a well-chosen menu and sets aside between one and two hours for his meals, eating plays an important part in daily life and cooking has developed into an essential component of French culture.

A concern with the quality and variety of meals is believed to have been brought to the French court by

Henry II's wife Catherine de Médicis, and like all courtly fashions to have spread from there to the ordinary French household. Henry IV, seeking to better the lot of the people of France, declared that he wanted every peasant to have a chicken for his Sunday dinner. The French Revolution brought with it not only civil liberties but also a higher standard of cuisine for ordinary people. In 1825 Anthelme Brillat-Savarin wrote his "Physiologie du goût" ("Physiology of Taste"), which still provides a philosophical basis for the enjoyment of good food.

Typical features of the highest standard of French cooking (**haute cuisine**) are the use of fresh ingredients – anything canned or preserved is anathema! – and of plenty of butter and cream (*crème fraîche*). Herbs and spices are used on a large scale and in a variety of combinations. French sauces are famous. – In recent years there has been much talk of **la nouvelle cuisine**, which avoids over-elaboration but relies on the very best ingredients. – There are also various **cuisines régionales** which are much esteemed by the most discriminating gourmets.

Visitors to France should not ignore this side of French culture, even though it may sometimes occupy a good deal of valuable sightseeing time. Some experience of this essential element in the famous French *savoir vivre* is necessary for anyone who really wants to get to know France.

Even some quite modest-looking **restaurants** can offer a choice of memorable dishes. In such places it is usual, and advisable, to discuss the menu with the host or hostess before deciding what to have. If there is no menu it is as well to enquire about prices, since the abundance and quality of the fare offered is likely to be reflected in the cost of a meal. In general, however, restaurant prices in France are not unduly high when measured against the quality of the meal. Frequently there are special "tourist menus" which are particularly good value. – Visitors who want a cheap snack should not go to a restaurant: they will find what they want in more modest establishments calling themselves *rôtisseries*, *bistros* or *brasseries*. In Paris there are numerous *self-service restaurants* where excellent cheap meals can be had. In holiday resorts there are likely to be stalls and kiosks selling *pommes frites*, hot dogs, *merguez* (highly spiced sausages), *crêpes* (pancakes) and sandwiches.

Cafés are by no means confined to selling coffee but offer a choice of alcoholic and non-alcoholic drinks and ices as well, remaining open all day and sometimes late at night. In the larger towns there are *salons de thé* (tearooms), which may offer a variety of cakes and pastries. These can also be obtained in *pâtisseries*, though usually not for consumption on the premises.

Meals (*repas*). – The simple French *petit déjeuner* (breakfast), with white or black coffee, tea or chocolate and croissants or rolls, is often taken in a café. – Lunch (*déjeuner*) is served in restaurants between 12 and 2.30, and may be either a set meal (*menu*) consisting of an hors d'œuvre, main course and cheese and/or dessert, followed by coffee, or an *à la carte* meal selected from the full menu (*carte*). – The evening meal (*dîner* or *souper*) is similar to lunch, except that the hors d'œuvre is usually replaced by soup. – White bread is the regular accompaniment to a meal, cut either from the long crisp *baguettes*, the shorter *flûtes* or some other of the wide range of French loaves.

The meal is accompanied by wine almost as a matter of course. On the various wines of France, some of which are world-famous, see below. For everyday drinking the ordinary local wine is recommended, in a *carafe* (about ½ litre) or *carafon* (about ¼ litre). It may be diluted with water if desired. When ordering wine in bottle – either a full bottle (*bouteille entière*) or half bottle (*demi-bouteille*) – it is a good idea to ask the waiter's advice. – There are also good French *beers*, now increasingly popular, from Alsace (Pêcheur, Kronenbourg, Kanterbräu, Mutzig) and Lorraine (Champigneulles, Vézélise). Beer is either bottled (*cannette*) or draught (*bière pression*). A small glass of draught beer is called a *demi*, a half litre usually a *véritable*, a litre a *formidable*. Regional variations may be encountered. – France has a wide range of *mineral waters*, either still (*eau minérale*) or containing carbonic acid (*eau gazeuse*). The best known brands are Perrier, Vichy, Evian, Vittel and Contrexéville.

Reading a French Menu (*Carte*)

The following glossary may help in deciphering the complexities of a French menu.

The table-setting. – Couvert, the place-setting (knife, fork, spoon, etc.). – Knife *couteau*; fork *fourchette*; spoon *cuiller*; glass *verre*; cup *tasse*; napkin *serviette (de table)*; corkscrew *tire-bouchon*.

Hors d'œuvres. – Artichauts artichokes; *huîtres* oysters (among the best being Belons, Fines de Claires and Portugaises from the Atlantic coast); *bouchées* pasties; *canapés* small open sandwiches, canapés; *cornichons* pickled gherkins; *foie gras*, goose liver; *crudités*, a selection of salad vegetables; *jambon cru*, raw ham; *saumon fumé* smoked salmon.

Soups (soupes, potages). – Bouillon clear meat soup; *consommé* clear soup; *potage* soup containing a variety of ingredients.

Egg dishes. – Œufs au plat fried eggs; *œufs pochés* poached eggs; *œufs brouillés* scrambled eggs; *œufs à la coque* soft-boiled eggs; *omelette* omelette; *omelette aux champignons* mushroom omelette; *omelette aux fines herbes*, omelette with mixed herbs; *omelette au fromage* cheese omelette; *omelette au jambon* ham omelette.

Fish (poisson). – Aiglefin haddock; *anchois* anchovy; *anguille* eel; *barbeau* barbel; *barbue* brill; *brochet* perch; *cabillaud* cod; *carpe* carp; *carrelet* plaice; *colin* hake; *congre* conger-eel; *féra* dace; *flétan* halibut; *hareng* herring; *limande* dab; *maquereau* mackerel; *merlan* whiting; *ombre* grayling; *ombre chevalier* char; *perche* perch; *plie* plaice; *raie* ray, skate; *sardine* sardine; *saumon* salmon; *sole* sole; *tanche* tench; *thon* tunny; *truite* trout; *turbot* turbot. – Crevettes shrimps; *écrevisses* crayfish; *homard* lobster; *huîtres* oysters; *langouste* spiny lobster; *moules* mussels; *palourdes*, *clams, clovisses* different kinds of shellfish; *oursin* sea-urchin. – *Cuisses de grenouille* frogs' thighs; *escargots* snails; *tortue* turtle.

Meat (viande). – *Agneau* lamb; *bœuf* beef; *cochon de lait* sucking pig; *mouton* mutton (*pré-salé*, from the salt meadows of Brittany); *porc* pork; *veau* veal. – *Cuts of meat: cervelle* brain; *côte* rib; *entrecôte* steak cut from the ribs; *escalope* fillet (of veal); *filet* fillet (of beef); *foie* liver; *gigot* leg of mutton; *jambon* ham; *langue* tongue; *pieds* feet; *poitrine* breast; *ris* sweetbread; *rognons* kidneys; *selle* saddle (of mutton), baron (of beef); *tête* head; *tournedos* fillet steak; *tripes* tripe. – *Methods of cooking: carbonnade* meat grilled on charcoal; *cassoulet* stew made in an earthenware dish; *chaudfroid* in aspic; *civet* stew (of venison, etc.); *civet de lièvre* jugged hare; *émincé* thinly sliced meat served in sauce; *galantine* galantine; *rôti* roast; *soufflé* soufflé; *terrine* potted meat, pâté.

Poultry (volaille). – Domestic poultry from Brittany and the Lyonnais, wildfowl from Gascony: *bécasse* snipe; *caille* quail; *canard* duck; *caneton* duckling; *coq* cock; *dindonneau* turkey; *faisan* pheasant; *oie* goose; *perdreau* partridge; *pigeon* pigeon; *pintade* guineafowl; *poulet* chicken; *poularde* fattened pullet. – Game (*gibier*): *cerf* venison (red deer); *chevreuil* roedeer; *lapereau* rabbit; *lièvre* hare; *sanglier* wild boar.

Vegetables (légumes). – *Ail* garlic (from the Yffiniac area in Brittany); *artichauts* artichokes; *asperges* asparagus; *betterave* beetroot; *cardon* cardoon; *carotte* carrot; *céleris* celery; *chicorée* endive; *chou (blanc)* cabbage; *chou rouge* red cabbage; *chou-fleur* cauliflower; *chou-rave* kohl-rabi; *concombre* cucumber; *endive* chicory; *épinards* spinach; *fenouil* fennel; *haricots blancs* haricot beans; *haricots verts* French beans; *laitue* lettuce; *lentilles* lentils; *oignon* onion; *petits pois* peas; *poireau* leek; *salade verte* green salad; *salsifis* salsify; *tomato* tomato. – *Cèpes* boletus mushrooms; *champignons de Paris* mushrooms (cultivated in the Loire valley); *chanterelles, girolles* chanterelles; *helvelles* turban-top mushrooms; *morilles* morels; *truffes* truffles (particularly from Périgord). – *Pommes de terre* potatoes; *pommes frites* chips; *pommes-allumettes* thin ("match-stick") fried potatoes; *pommes paille* potato straws; *purée de pommes de terre* potato purée, mashed potatoes; *pommes-croquettes* potato croquettes; *pommes à la dauphine* dauphine potatoes; *riz* rice.

Methods of cooking: Braisé braised; *farci* stuffed; *glacé* glacé; *gratiné* au gratin; *grillé* grilled; (*à la*) *meunière* fried in butter; *poché* poached; *sauté* sauté.

Sweets (desserts). – *Biscuits* biscuits; *coupe glacée* ice-cream sundae; *crème* cream; *crème Chantilly* whipped cream; *crêpes* pancakes; *crêpes Suzette* dessert pancakes, flambé; *flan* custard; *gâteau* cake; *gaufrettes* waffles; *glace* ice; *sorbet* water ice; *tarte* tart; *vermicelles à la Chantilly* chestnut mousse with whipped cream.

Fruit (fruits). – *Abricots* apricots (particularly from Roussillon); *amandes* almonds; *avelines* hazelnuts; *cerises* cherries (grown round Yonne in Burgundy); *citron* lemon; *fraises* strawberries; *framboises* raspberries; *marrons* chestnuts (from Lyonnais, Provence and Alsace); *melon* melon (from Cavaillon); *noisettes* hazelnuts; *noix* walnuts (from Périgord); *orange* orange; *pastèque* water-melon; *pêche* peach; *poire* pear; *pomme* apple; *prune* plum; *pruneau* prune (from Agen); *raisin* grapes.

Cheese (fromage). – Only a selection from the enormous range of French cheeses can be given here.

– *Roquefort* a ewe's-milk cheese from Roquefort (Aveyron), matured in natural caves (conducted tours); *Camembert* a famous soft cheese from Normandy; *Brie* a delicate soft cheese from the Ile de France; *Munster Géromé* a strong-smelling cheese made in Alsace and Lorraine; *Pyrenean cheeses* ewe's-milk cheeses with a light rind and cow's-milk cheeses with a dark rind; *Bleu de Bresse* a mild creamy blue cheese from the Lyonnais; *nut cheese* a soft cheese containing walnuts or almonds produced in various areas, particularly Savoy, which has recently become very popular. – From Normandy and Brittany come very good *salt butter* and *crème fraîche* a sourish-tasting cream with a fat content of 40%. – *Yaourt* yoghourt; *fromage blanc* cream cheese.

Regional Specialties

Cassoulet a rich stew containing beans, knuckle of pork, preserved goose, bacon and sausage (in Toulouse region); *potée auvergnate* vegetable stew; *soupe à l'oignon* onion soup with bread and cheese gratiné (Paris). – *Andouilles* chitterling sausages (Brittany, Loire valley); *confit d'oie* goose preserve (Périgord); *foie gras d'oie* goose-liver pâté (Alsace, Périgord); *saucissons de Lyon* large meat sausages (Lyonnais); *rillettes* pork pâté (Brittany, Loire valley). – *Choucroute garnie* sauerkraut with sausages, etc. (Alsace, Lorraine); *choucroute au riesling, choucroute au champagne*, with wine or champagne (highly recommended); *escargots* snails (Alsace, Burgundy); *fondue bourguignonne* meat fondue with sauces (Burgundy); *quiche lorraine* an open flan containing bacon (Lorraine); *tripes à la mode de Caen* a highly spiced tripe stew (Normandy); *tripoux* lamb's tripe with herbs (Limousin). – *Bêtises de Cambrai* a peppermint sweet (Cambrai); *dragées de Verdun* glacé almonds and hazelnuts (a local specialty since the 13th c.); *gugelhupf* (Alsace); *madeleines de Commercy* (Burgundy); *marrons* chestnuts, candied, roasted, purée or boiled as a vegetable garnishing or a desert (Lyonnais); *nonnettes de Dijon* gingerbread (Dijon). – *Moutarde* mustard, either from Meaux (large-grained, mild) or Dijon (sharp).

Provençal cooking stands on its own. Unlike French cuisine, it makes much use of olive oil and tomatoes. The herbs mainly used are garlic and onion, rosemary, thyme, basil, sage and saffron. – *Bouillabaisse* fish soup with garlic, rosemary and saffron; *aigo-boulido* herb soup with cheese; *aigo-saou* fish soup; *soupe au pistou* pumpkin soup with basil; *sea-urchin soup.* – *Aïoli* garlic mayonnaise; *anchoiade* a slice of white bread spread with anchovy and garlic pâté; *pan-bagnat* a huge roll sandwich; *pissaladière* an onion tart with olives and anchovies; *ratatouille* a stew of mixed vegetables; *salade niçoise* a substantial salad of raw vegetables, egg, tunny and olives. – *Calissons* honey and almond biscuits; *candied fruit; nougat* from Montélimar.

Drinks (*boissons*). – *Café* coffee; *café crème* coffee with cream; *café au lait* coffee with milk; *thé* tea; *thé au citron* tea with lemon; *lait* milk; *chocolat* chocolate; *bière* beer; *cidre* cider (Brittany and Normandy); *eau minérale* mineral water; *sirop de menthe* a sweet peppermint drink; *vin blanc* white wine; *champagne* champagne; *vin rouge* red wine. – *Spirits:* Cognac a brandy from the Charentes which is matured for many years in oak casks and comes in various grades (*** or VSOP, Extra, XO and Napoléon or Hors d'Age – all matured for some 50 years); *Armagnac* a brandy made

Oysters

in Gascony; *Calvados* an apple brandy from Normandy, commonly drunk during a meal to stimulate the appetite (a practice known as the *trou normand*, the Norman hole or gap); *Quetsch* (made from plums), *Kirsche* (cherries) and *Mirabelle* (mirabelle plums), fruit brandies made in Alsace, Lorraine and Franche-Comté; *Chartreuse* a herb liquer made by monks in the Dauphiné (green Chartreuse made since 1735, using 130 herbs; the lighter yellow Chartreuse since the mid 19th c.); *Cointreau* an orange liqueur from Anjou; *Cassis* a blackcurrant liqueur (Burgundy); *Bénédictine*, from Fécamp, famous since the 16th c.; *pastis* or *anisette* an aniseed brandy drunk in a large glass of iced water (Provence); *Brou*, *Ratafia* and *Eau de Noix* walnut liqueurs from Périgord; *Grand Marnier* a mandarine liqueur based on cognac; *Kir* an aperitif of white wine and Cassis; *Mauresque* an aperitif of pastis and orgeat (almond milk).

Wine

The Language of the Wine Label

Appellation (d'origine) contrôlée (*A.O.C.*)	An indication of the place of origin (the right to which is strictly controlled)
Blanc de blancs	A white wine (particularly a sparkling wine) made from white grapes fermented without their skins
Brut	Extra dry (of champagne or quality sparkling wines)
Cave, caveau	Wine cellars; the establishment in which the wine is made
Cépage	Type of vine
Château	Wine-making establishment (only for quality wines)
Clos	Vineyard
Crémant	Quality sparkling wine
Cuvée	Blending; also a classification of Côte d'Or wines (Premières Cuvées, etc.)
Domaine	"Estate": wine-making establishment (quality wines only)
Méthode champenoise	The "champagnisation" of wine by natural fermentation in bottle
Mis(e) en bouteille	Bottled, bottling
Nouveau	A young, fresh red wine
Sigille	Seal of quality
Vendange tardive	Late-gathered grapes
Vin délimité de qualité supérieure	A wine of high quality from a particular area
Vin de pays	Local wine, country wine
Vin de table	Table wine

Calvados (apple brandy)

French Wines at a Glance

(Source: Comité National des Vins, Paris)

NAME	AREA	COLOUR	CHARACTERISTICS	YEARS IN CELLAR	DRINKING TEMPERATURE (C/F)
Alsace	Alsace	white rosé	dry, distinguished dry, light	2–5 2–5	10°/50° 10°/50°
Arbois	Jura	white red	dry, flowery vigorous, elegant	2–8 5–10	10°/50° 16°/61°
Banyuls	Languedoc-Roussillon	red	a fruity dessert wine, semi-sweet to sweet	6–15	5°/41°
Beaujolais	Burgundy	red	light, palatable	1–2	12°/54°
Beaune	Burgundy	red	full-bodied, elegant	6–12	16°/61°
Bergerac	SW France	white rosé red	from dry to sweet dry, light vigorous, elegant	2–5 1–2 3–6	8–6°/46–43° 10°/50° 18°/64°
Blanquette de Limoux	Languedoc-Roussillon	white	a light sparkling wine, from extra dry (brut) to sweet (doux)	3–5	6°/43°
Bordeaux	Bordeaux	white red	mostly sweet, fruity vigorous, slightly dry	4–6 5–10	6°/43° 18°/64°
Bourgogne (Burgundy)	Burgundy	white red	dry, distinguished full-bodied, rich bouquet	2–5 5–10	10°/50° 16°/61°
Cahors	SW France	red	very full-bodied, dry	5–10	16°/61°
Chablis	Burgundy	white	dry, distinguished	3–15	10°/50°
Champagne	Champagne	white	an elegant sparkling wine	1–4	6°/43°
Châteauneuf du Pape	Rhône valley	red	very full-bodied	3–8	16°/61°
Clairette de Die	Rhône valley	white	a light sparkling wine, from extra dry (brut) to a sweet muscatel taste	1–2	6°/43°
Corbières	Languedoc-Roussillon	red	full-bodied	2–3	16°/61°
Coteaux Champenois	Champagne	white red	dry, distinguished vigorous, elegant	1–3 2–5	10°/50° 18°/64°
Coteaux du Languedoc	Languedoc-Roussillon	rosé red	dry, semi-light vigorous, fresh	2–3 2–3	10°/50° 16°/61°
Côte de Beaune	Burgundy	red	full-bodied, elegant	6–12	16°/61°
Côtes de Provence	Provence/Côte d'Azur	rosé red	dry, vigorous vigorous, fresh	1–2 2–5	10°/50° 16°/61°
Côtes du Jura	Jura	white rosé red	dry, flowery dry, light vigorous, elegant	2–8 2–6 5–10	10°/50° 10°/50° 16°/61°
Côtes du Rhône	Rhône valley	red	full-bodied, rich bouquet	2–3	16°/61°
Côtes du Roussillon	Languedoc-Roussillon	white rosé red	dry, distinguished dry, vigorous full-bodied	2–5 1–2 3–5	10°/50° 10°/50° 16°/61°
Côtes du Ventoux	Rhône valley	red	vigorous, fresh	2–3	16°/61°
Crémant d'Alsace	Alsace	white	a light sparkling wine, from extra dry (brut) to sweet (doux)	1–4	6°/43°
Crémant de Bourgogne	Burgundy	white	a light sparkling wine, from extra dry (brut) to sweet (doux)	1–4	6°/43°
Crémant de Loire	Loire valley	white	a light sparkling wine, from extra dry (brut) to sweet (doux)	1–4	6°/43°
Crozes-Hermitage	Rhône valley	red	full-bodied, elegant	3–10	16°/61°

NAME	AREA	COLOUR	CHARACTERISTICS	YEARS IN CELLAR	DRINKING TEMPERA-TURE (C/F)
Entre-deux-Mers	Bordeaux	white	dry, fresh	2–3	8°/46°
Fitou	Languedoc-Roussillon	red	full-bodied, rich bouquet	3–6	16°/61°
Gaillac	Languedoc-Roussillon	white	dry, fresh	1–2	8°/46°
		white	sparkling	1–2	6°/43°
		rosé	dry, fresh	1–2	10°/50°
		red	vigorous, fresh	2–5	16°/61°
Gevrey-Chambertin	Burgundy	red	full-bodied, rich bouquet	8–15	16°/61°
Gigondas	Rhône valley	red	full-bodied	3–5	16°/61°
Graves	Bordeaux	white	dry, distinguished	5–10	10°/50°
		red	full-bodied, elegant	7–15	18°/64°
Graves de Vayres	Bordeaux	white	sweet, fruity	4–6	6°/43°
Graves Supérieures	Bordeaux	white	sweet, flowery	5–10	6°/43°
Jurancon	SW France	white	dry, distinguished	2–5	10°/50°
Mâcon	Burgundy	white	dry, fruity	1–3	10°/50°
		rosé	dry, semi-light	1–2	10°/50°
		red	light, fruity	2–3	12°/54°
Mèdoc	Bordeaux	red	full-bodied, elegant	5–10	18°/64°
Meursault	Burgundy	white	dry, distinguished	5–20	10°/50°
Minervois	Languedoc-Roussillon	red	full-bodied	2–3	16°/61°
Monbazillac	SW France	white	sweet, well-rounded	5–15	6°/43°
Muscadet	Loire valley	white	dry, fresh	1–3	8°/46°
Muscat d'Alsace	Alsace	white	dry, distinguished, muscatel taste	2–4	10°/50°
Muscat de Rivesaltes	Languedoc-Roussillon	white	a sweet dessert wine with a muscatel taste	2–3	5°/41°
Pomerol	Bordeaux	red	full-bodied, rich bouquet	10–20	16°/61°
Rivesaltes	Languedoc-Roussillon	white	a sweet dessert wine	6–10	5°/41°
Rosè d'Anjou	Loire valley	rosé	sweet, fruity	1–2	8°/46°
Saint-Emilion	Bordeaux	red	full-bodied, rich bouquet	10–20	16°/61°
Sancerre	Loire valley	white	dry, distinguished	1–2	10°/50°
Saumur	Loire valley	white	semi-dry	1–5	10°/50°
			sparkling wine	1–4	6°/43°
Sauternes	Bordeaux	white	sweet, well-rounded	10–20	6°/43°
Tavel	Rhône valley	rosé	dry, full-bodied	1–2	10°/50°
Touraine	Loire valley	white	dry to sweet	1–10	8–6°/46–43°
		red	light, flowery	1–5	12°/54°
Vin de Corse	Corsica	rosé	dry, full-bodied	3–6	10°/50°
		red	very full-bodied	3–6	16°/61°
Vin de Pays	Languedoc-Roussillon, Corsica	red	light, fruity	1–2	12°/54°
Vin de Savoie	Savoy	white	dry, fruity	2–5	10°/50°
		rosé	dry, light	1–2	10°/50°
		red	semi-light, flowery	2–5	12°/54°
Vouvray	Loire valley	white	sweet, well-rounded	1–25	6°/43°
		white	sparkling wine	1–4	6°/43°

Zwicker and Edelzwicker are blended wines made in Alsace. Both are white wines, fresh and aromatic in character. They should not be drunk too cold.

Map of the French wine-growing areas: see next page.

Types of Grape

(Source: Comité National des Vins de France, Paris)

Aligoté. – A regional grape grown in Burgundy.

Aramon. – A regional grape grown in Languedoc.

Auxerrois. – A regional grape grown round Cahors.

Breton: see Cabernet Franc.

Cabernet Franc. – The grape which produces the great red wines of Bordeaux. Also grown in the Loire valley under the name of *Breton* and used in making the red wines of Bourgueil, Chinon and Saumur-Champigny.

Cabernet-Sauvignon. – A grape grown in the Bordeaux region, particularly in Médoc and Graves, which produces 50–70% of the great wines of the area. It makes full-bodied, full-coloured red wines rich in tannic acid which improve with age.
In Anjou it is used along with Cabernet Franc to produce semi-dry rosé wines.

Cardinal. – A favourite table grape.

Carignan. – The principal grape of the Mediterranean region. Along with Cinsaut and Grenache it produces substantial highly coloured red wines of high alcohol content which improve with age.

Chardonnay. – A grape used in the great white wines of Burgundy (Montrachet, Meursault, Chablis, Pouilly-Fuissé) and Champagne (Blanc de Blancs). It produces light, fruity, transparent wines.

Chasselas. – Used in Alsace, under the name of *Gutedel*, to produce light white wines. Also a good table grape.

Chenin. – Also known as *Pineau de la Loire*. Grown in Anjou and Touraine, it produces in some years full-bodied but mild white wines which keep well.

Cinsaut. – A grape grown in the Mediterranean region which produces delicate, soft, aromatic wines.

Clairette. – A white grape grown in the S of France. It produces wines of high alcohol content which tend to take on a taste of "age". Also a table grape.

Cot. – A regional grape grown in the Loire valley.

The French Wine-Growing Areas

Folle Blanche. – Also known as *Gros Plant du Pays Nantais*. An even older grape than Melon, from the Charentes and Gers; it was formerly used to produce cognac and armagnac in the Nantes area.

Gamay. – This black grape with white juice does best on the granitic soils of Beaujolais. The wines it yields are light, fruity, palatable and full of charm. It is also found in the Mâconnais and in some wines of Auvergne, St-Pourçain, Châteaumeillant, etc.

Gewürztraminer. – A grape grown in Alsace which produces a strong, full-bodied white wine with a delicate bouquet and full aroma.

Grauklevner: see Tokay.

Grenache. – Grown in the S of France (Châteauneuf du Pape; dessert wines of Banyuls and Rivesaltes). In combination with Cinsaut, Mourvèdre and Syrah it produces the delicate wines of Languedoc.

Grolleau. – A regional grape grown in the Loir valley.

Gros Plant du Pays Nantais: see Folle Blanche.

Gutedel: see Chasselas.

Jacquère. – A regional grape grown in Savoy.

Knipperlé. – A regional grape grown in Alsace. Little aroma.

Maccabéo. – A regional grape grown in Roussillon.

Malbec. – A regional grape grown in the Bordeaux area.

Malvoisie. – A regional grape grown in Roussillon.

Manseng. – A regional grape grown in the Pyrenean foreland.

Mauzac. – A regional grape grown round Gaillac and Limoux.

Melon. – Formerly grown in Burgundy, it is now used to produce the fresh, dry, fruity white wines of Muscadet in the area round Nantes.

Merlot. – A black grape which is used to supplement the Cabernet grapes of the Bordeaux area. It is the dominant element in Pomerol and St-Emilion, giving fire and fullness to the wine.

Meunier. – A regional grape grown in Champagne.

Mondeuse. – A regional grape grown in Savoy.

Mourvèdre. – A grape grown in the southern Côtes du Rhône (Châteauneuf du Pape), E of the Rhine (Côteaux du Tricastin, Côtes du Ventoux) and in Côtes de Provence. It is found at its best round Bandol, giving the wine soul, distinction and keeping quality.

Muscadelle. – A regional grape grown in the Bordeaux area.

Muscat. – There are many kinds of muscatel grapes, used both as table grapes and for the production of wine, which all have a strong and unmistakable aroma of muscatel but produce very different kinds of wine: *Muscat d'Alsace* is a dry fruity wine. *Muscat de Hambourg* is both a table grape and (in S and SW France) a wine grape.

Harvesting grapes at Vertus (Champagne)

Muscat doré à petits grains (small-berried golden muscatel) produces the famous dessert wines Muscat de Frontignan, Muscat de Rivesaltes, Muscat de Lunel and Muscat de Beaumes de Venise.
In the Die area, E of the Rhône, Muscat is used along with Clairette to produce a popular sparkling wine, Clairette de Die.
Muscat d'Alexandrie is used in Roussillon to produce excellent dessert wines.

Neilluccio. – A regional grape grown in Corsica.

Pécoui-Touar. – A regional grape grown in Provence.

Picpoul. – A regional grape grown in Languedoc.

Pineau de la Loire: see Chenin.

Pinot Blanc. – Grown in Alsace, under the name of *Weissklevner* or *Weissburgunder*, to produce a dry, flowery white wine.

Pinot Gris: see Tokay.

Pinot Noir. – Produces the great red wines of Burgundy; also grown in Champagne. It is also found in Alsace, under the name of *Spätburgunder*, in the Mâconnais and in the rosé wines of Sancerre and Alsace.

Poulsard. – Grown in the Jura, and used in combination with Trousseau, Pinot or Chardonnay to produce red and rosé wines.

Riesling. – The best known of the grapes grown in Alsace. It produces a distinguished dry white wine, fruity and with a delicate bouquet.

Roussanne. – A regional grape grown in the Rhône valley.

Roussette. – A regional grape grown in Savoy.

Sauvignon. – An excellent white grape which produces wines of some distinction. It is grown in the Bordeaux area (Graves) and in the Loire valley (Pouilly-Fumé, Sancerre, Quincy, Reuilly, etc.).

Savagnin. – A late-ripening grape which is sometimes not harvested until November. It gives the "ice wines" or *vins jaunes* (yellow wines) of the Jura,

Château-Chalon, L'Etoile and Côtes du Jura their distinctive character.

Sciaccarello. – A regional grape grown in Corsica.

Semillon. – The commonest white grape of the Bordeaux area, the basis for the great white wines of Bordeaux, either dry like Graves or sweet like Sauternes, Barsac, etc.

Spätburgunder: see Pinot Noir.

St-Emilion des Charentes: see Ugni Balnc.

Sylvaner. – Grown in Alsace. It produces fresh, fruity white wines.

Syrah. – An aromatic grape grown in the northern Côtes du Rhône (red Hermitage, Cornas). The wine has a beautiful ruby colour and a characteristic tang. Syrah is also used to add quality to the wines of Languedoc.

Tannat. – A regional grape grown in the Pyrenean foreland.

Terret. – A regional grape grown in Languedoc.

Tilbouren. – A regional grape grown in Provence.

Tokay. – Grown in Alsace, where it is also known as *Grauklevner* or *Pinot Gris*. It produces a full-bodied dry white wine.

Tressot. – A regional grape grown in Burgundy.

Ugni Blanc. – This grape is widely grown in Provence, and gives the wines of southern Languedoc the tannic acid which they often lack. It is also used in western France, under the name of *St-Emilion des Charentes*, to produce cognac.

Vermentino. – A regional grape grown in Corsica.

Viognier. – A regional grape grown in the Rhône valley.

Weissburgunder, Weissklevner: see Pinot Blanc.

Recreation and Sport

Bathing

There are well-known bathing resorts on the *Channel coast*, in *Brittany*, on the *islands* off the Atlantic coast (Belle-Ile, Ile d'Yeu, Oléron, Noirmoutier, etc.) and along the *Mediterranean coast*. The flat sandy beaches of the *Landes*, between the mouth of the Gironde and the Spanish frontier – often extending for kilometres along the coast – are very popular; the Bassin d'Arcachon is also famous for its large oyster-beds. – In Languedoc-Roussillon (between Montpellier and Perpignan) on the Mediterranean coast large new *holiday and recreation centres* have been developed.

On the Atlantic coast the water is kept clean by the constant movement of the tides and currents. In the Mediterranean, however, the quality of the water has suffered from industrial and other pollution, and the beaches of Brittany and the Channel are constantly exposed to the possibility of oil pollution from the large tankers which pass close to the coast.

Walking

Systematically maintained and way-marked footpaths and trails are found mainly in the **Vosges**. There are three main long-distance trails laid out by the Club Vosgien: No. 1 (390 km, red markings) from Wissembourg to Masevaux, No. 2 (280 km, blue markings) from Lembach to Masevaux, and No. 3 (325 km, yellow markings) from Obersteinbach to Masevaux. In the rest of France there are a number of trails (*sentiers de grande randonnée*) way-marked by the Comité National des Sentiers de Grande Randonnée; elsewhere walkers are left to work out their own routes.

There are a number of *European long-distance trails* passing through France. *E 2* runs S from the Luxembourg frontier through Lorraine and the Vosges and then cuts through the Jura and the Alps, running parallel to the Swiss and later the Italian frontier to end at Nice. *E 3* runs E

Bathing safety. – The larger bathing resorts have beach guards and a *warning system* to indicate whether weather and current conditions are safe for bathing. Coloured flags are flown, as follows:

green: *bathing possible without restriction*;

yellow: *bathing dangerous*;

red: *bathing prohibited*.

Care should be taken, particularly on the Atlantic coast, not to underestimate the force of the waves even on a perfectly calm day. The considerable rise and fall of the tides in the Channel (e.g. a difference of up to 14 m between high and low tide at Mont St-Michel) makes special caution necessary.

from Royan on the Atlantic coast to Limoges and Clermont-Ferrand, and then turns N, crosses the Loire and runs E of Paris to the Luxembourg frontier. *E 4* runs from Bourg-Madame on the Spanish frontier along the northern flank of the Pyrenees, then via Carcassonne into the Cévennes and high above the Ardèche gorge, through Vercors and via Grenoble and Chambéry to the Swiss frontier.

Information: **Comité National 'des Sentiers de Grande Randonnée**,
92 rue de Clignancourt,
F-75883 **Paris**;
tel. (1) 2 55 86 73.

Club Vosgien,
4 rue de la Douane,
F-67000 **Strasbourg**;
tel. (88) 32 57 96.

Climbing and Hill Walking

Climbers will find plenty of scope not only in the Alps and Pyrenees but in many lower ranges. The Club Alpin Français has branches in many towns all over France.

Information: **Club Alpin Français**,
7 rue La Boëtie,
F-75008 **Paris**;
tel. (1) 2 65 54 45.

Shooting

With its wide topographical variety France offers ample scope for the sportsman – deer, wild pig, pheasants, wild duck, hares, etc.

Foreigners who desire to shoot in France must have a *permis de chasser* or a *licence de chasse* valid for 48 hours (issued only on presentation of a game licence from the visitor's own country), which can be obtained from the Prefecture for the area where they are staying. For the *permis de chasser* the applicant must present a police certificate of character. A shooting insurance policy must also be taken out in France.

Information: **Office National de la Chasse**,
85 bis Avenue de Wagram,
F-75017 **Paris**;
tel. (1) 2 67 57 40.

Office National des Forêts,
4 Avenue de St-Mandé,
F-75012 **Paris**;
tel. (1) 3 44 46 33.

Regional offices throughout France.

Fishing in Corsica

Fishing

Fishing is perhaps the Frenchman's favourite recreation, and the country's numerous rivers, streams and lakes offer ample scope for coarse fishing, spinning and fly-fishing. Fishing waters are classified in two categories, Category I (mainly salmon and trout) and Category 2 (mainly other species). To fish in any of France's inland waters it is necessary to have a *fishing permit* issued by the local angling club (*société de pêche*), and for private water the permission of the owner or tenant. – Sea-fishing from the shore is free to all (maximum of two rods per person); but there are certain closed areas, about which enquiry should be made. Special regulations apply to fishing from boats or with nets.

Information: **Conseil Supérieur de la Pêche**,
10 rue Péclet,
F-75010 **Paris**;
tel. (1) 8 42 10 00.

Office National des Forêts,
4 Avenue de St-Mandé,
F-75012 **Paris**;
tel. (1) 3 44 46 33.

Riding

There are opportunities for riding practically everywhere in France. Many private agencies offer pony treks lasting several days. In many places horse-drawn carriages can be hired.

Information: **Association Nationale pour le Tourisme Equestre** (*ANTE*),
12 rue du Parc-Royal,
F-75003 **Paris**;
tel. (1) 2 77 48 56.

Regional associations (ARTE) in many French towns.

Golf

There are something like 100 golf-courses in France, most of them open to visitors.

Information: **Fédération Française de Golf,**
          11 rue de Bassano,
          F-75016 **Paris**;
          tel. (1) 7 20 26 15.

Water Sports

Sailing. – There are facilities for sailing on the inland lakes and round the coasts of France (particularly in the Mediterranean). There are sailing clubs and schools and boats for hire in many places.

Information: **Fédération Française de Yachting à Voile,**
          7 rue St-Lazare,
          F-75009 **Paris**;
          tel. (1) 5 26 00 30.

Canoeing. – There are plenty of peaceful stretches of river, but also many areas of wild water which call for a high standard of fitness and experience.

Information: **Fédération Française de Canoë-Kayak,**
          87 Quai de la Marne,
          F-94340 **Joinville**;
          tel. (25) 8 73 79 25.

Scuba diving. – France has long taken a leading place in the field of scuba diving, oceanography and underwater archaeology. The Mediterranean coast and Corsica are still the favourite places for these activities, though the immediate coastal areas have lost much of their former wide variety of fauna as a result of over-fishing and pollution. On the Atlantic coast careful regard must be had to the tides and currents. For underwater hunt-

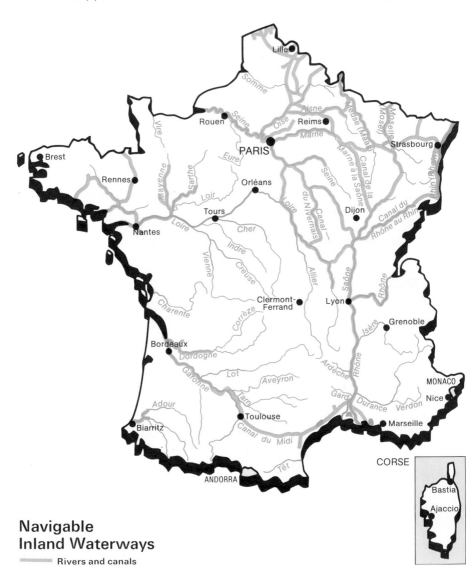

Navigable
Inland Waterways

Rivers and canals

ing a permit (obtainable from local diving clubs) is required.

Information: **Fédération Française d'Etudes et de Sports sous-marins,-** 24 Quai de Rive-Neuve, F-13007 **Marseille**; tel. (91) 33 99 31.

Water skiing. – There are water skiing clubs in many resorts.

Information: **Fédération Française de Ski nautique,** 9 Boulevard Péreire, F-75017 **Paris**; Tel. (1) 2 67 15 66.

Surfing. – This is practised on the Atlantic coast between the mouth of the Gironde and the Spanish frontier.

Information: **Fédération Française de Surf,** Cité Administrative, Avenue Edouard-VII, F-64200 **Biarritz.**

Wind-surfing. – This very new sport is practised in Aquitaine and Brittany.

Information: **Association Française de Wind-Surf,** 29 rue du Général-Delestraint, F-75016 **Paris.**

Canal and river cruising. – A trip in a cabin cruiser or barge on some of France's quieter rivers and canals is an excellent way of seeing the country. Numerous agencies offer boat hire and package tours. Normally a "driving licence" is not required, and after a brief demonstration the boats are not difficult to manoeuvre. Information can be obtained from local tourist information offices or from travel agencies.

Motor-boating. – A licence is required to navigate a motor-boat in French inland or coastal waters.

Information: **Fédération Française Motonautique,** 8 Place de la Concorde, F-75008 **Paris**; tel. (1) 0 73 89 38 and 2 65 34 70.

Caving

France can claim to have played a pioneering role in the field of speleology. There are still large numbers of caves not fully explored, particularly in the karstic country of Périgord. There are caving clubs in many towns.

Information: **Fédération Française de Spéléologie,** 130 rue St-Maur, F-75011 **Paris**; tel. (1) 3 57 56 54.

Flying

Gliding. – There are excellent facilities for gliding, particularly in the upland regions.

Information: **Fédération Française de Vol à Voile,** 29 rue de Sèvres, F-75006 **Paris**; tel. (1) 5 44 04 78 and 5 44 05 92.

Hang-gliding. – The most popular areas for this sport are Aquitaine, Auvergne, Savoy and the Pyrenees.

Detailed information about all kinds of recreational and leisure activities, including **holiday training courses, old-time railways, summer language courses, folk and vintage festivals, museums, naturism, cycle touring, sea-water cures** and **country holidays**, is contained in a booklet produced by the Secrétariat d'Etat au Tourisme, "Loisirs en France".

Taking the Cure

France's medicinal springs were already being used for curative purposes in Roman times. There are now something like 1200 springs used in the treatment of a wide range of conditions in a hundred or so spas (often identified by the addition of "les Bains" to their name).

Practically all these resorts have preserved an agreeable flavour of earlier days, and there are few modern spa establishments – though this in no way detracts from their effectiveness.

⬤ Spas

1 **Bagnoles-de-l'Orne** (Orne)
Altitude: 222 m.
Circulatory disorders.

2 **Forges-les-Eaux** (Seine-Maritime)
Altitude: 175 m.
Circulatory disorders.

3 **Enghien-les-Bains** (Val d'Oise)
Altitude: 46 m.
Respiratory passages, lymphatic disorders.

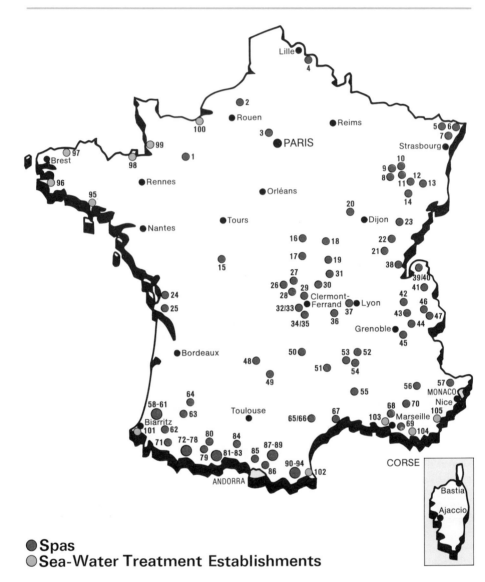

● Spas
○ Sea-Water Treatment Establishments

4 St-Amand-les-Eaux (Nord)
Altitude: 17 m.
Rheumatism, bones and joints.

5 Niederbronn (Bas-Rhin)
Altitude: 192 m.
Rheumatism, bones and joints.

6 Pechelbronne (Bas-Rhin)
Altitude: 150 m.
Rheumatism, bones and joints.

7 Morsbronn (Bas-Rhin)
Altitude: 183 m.
Rheumatism, bones and joints.

8 Bourbonne-les-Bains (Haute-Marne)
Altitude: 270 m.
Rheumatism, bones and joints.

9 Contrexéville (Vosges)
Altitude: 337 m.
Kidneys, urinary organs.

10 Vittel (Vosges)
Altitude: 335 m.
Kidneys, urinary organs.

11 Bains-les-Bains (Vosges)
Altitude: 350 m.
Circulatory disorders.

12 Plombières-les-Bains (Vosges)
Altitude: 424 m.
Digestive organs.

13 Bussang (Vosges)
Altitude: 600 m.
Circulatory disorders.

14 Luxeuil-les-Bains (Haute-Savoie)
Altitude: 300 m.
Gynaecological conditions.

15 La Roche-Posay (Vienne)
Altitude: 75 m.
Skin diseases.

16 Pouques-les-Eaux (Nièvre)
Altitude: 200 m.
Digestive organs.

17 Bourbon-l'Archambault (Allier)
Altitude: 260 m.
Rheumatism, bones and joints.

18 **St-Honoré-les-Bains** (Nièvre)
Altitude: 300 m.
Respiratory passages, lymphatic disorders.

19 **Bourbon-Lancy** (Saône-et-Loire)
Altitude: 240 m.
Rheumatism, bones and joints.

20 **Maizières** (Côte-d'Or)
Altitude: 350 m.
Rheumatism, bones and joints.

21 **Lons-le-Saunier** (Jura)
Altitude: 255 m.
Respiratory passages, lymphatic disorders.

22 **Salins-les-Bains** (Jura)
Altitude: 354 m.
Respiratory passages, lymphatic disorders.

23 **Besançon** (Doubs)
Altitude: 242 m.
Gynaecological conditions.

24 **Rochefort** (Charente-Maritime)
Altitude: 5 m.
Rheumatism, bones and joints.

25 **Saujon** (Charente-Maritime)
Altitude: 7 m.
Nervous system.

26 **Evaux-les-Bains** (Creuse)
Altitude: 460 m.
Rheumatism, bones and joints.

27 **Néris-les-Bains** (Allier)
Altitude: 350 m.
Nervous system.

28 **Châteauneuf-les-Bains** (Puy-de-Dôme)
Altitude: 390 m.
Rheumatism, bones and joints.

29 **Châtelguyon** (Puy-de-Dôme)
Altitude: 400 m.
Digestive organs.

30 **Vichy** (Allier)
Altitude: 263 m.
Digestive organs.

31 **Sail-les-Bains** (Loire)
Altitude: 300 m.
Skin diseases.

32 **La Bourboule** (Puy-de-Dôme)
Altitude: 850 m.
Respiratory passages, lymphatic disorders.

33 **Royat** (Puy-de-Dôme)
Altitude: 450 m.
Circulatory disorders.

34 **Le Mont-Dore** (Puy-de-Dôme)
Altitude: 1050 m.
Respiratory passages, lymphatic disorders.

35 **St-Nectaire** (Puy-de-Dôme)
Altitude: 700 m.
Kidneys, urinary organs.

36 **Montrond-les-Bains** (Loire)
Altitude: 370 m.
Digestive organs.

37 **Charbonnières-les-Bains** (Rhône)
Altitude: 250 m.
Circulatory disorders.

38 **Divonne-les-Bains** (Ain)
Altitude: 500 m.
Digestive organs.

39 **Thonon-les-Bains** (Haute-Savoie)
Altitude: 430 m.
Kidneys, urinary organs.

40 **Evian-les-Bains** (Haute-Savoie)
Altitude: 376 m.
Kidneys, urinary organs.

41 **St-Gervais-les-Bains** (Haute-Savoie)
Altitude: 850 m.
Skin diseases.

42 **Aix-les-Bains** (Savoie)
Altitude: 250 m.
Rheumatism, bones and joints.

43 **Aix-les-Bains-Marlioz** (Savoie)
Altitude: 280 m.
Respiratory passages, lymphatic disorders.

44 **Allevard** (Isère)
Altitude: 475 m.
Respiratory passages, lymphatic disorders.

45 **Uriage-les-Bains** (Isère)
Altitude: 414 m.
Skin diseases.

46 **La Léchère-les-Bains** (Savoie)
Altitude: 440 m.
Circulatory disorders.

47 **Brides-les-Bains** (Savoie)
Altitude: 600 m.
Metabolic disorders.

Salins-des-Brides (Savoie)
Altitude: 550 m.
Rheumatism, bones and joints.

48 **Miers-Alvignac** (Lot)
Altitude: 360 m.
Digestive organs.

49 **Cransac** (Aveyron)
Altitude: 292 m.
Rheumatism, bones and joints.

50 **Chaudes-Aigues** (Cantal)
Altitude: 750 m.
Rheumatism, bones and joints.

51 **Bagnols-les-Bains** (Lozère)
Altitude: 913 m.
Circulatory disorders.

52 **St-Laurent-les-Bains** (Ardèche)
Altitude: 840 m.
Rheumatism, bones and joints.

53 **Neyrac-les-Bains** (Ardèche)
Altitude: 390 m.
Skin diseases.

54 **Vals-les-Bains** (Ardèche)
Altitude: 250 m.
Metabolic disorders.

55 Les-Fumades-les-Bains (Gard)
Altitude: 200 m.
Respiratory passages, lymphatic disorders.

56 Digne (Basses-Alpes)
Altitude: 650 m.
Rheumatism, bones and joints.

57 Berthemont-les-Bains (Alpes-Maritimes)
Altitude: 950 m.
Respiratory passages, lymphatic disorders.

58 Préchacq-les-Bains (Landes)
Altitude: 20 m.
Rheumatism, bones and joints.

59 Dax (Landes)
Altitude: 12 m.
Rheumatism, bones and joints.

60 Tercis-les-Bains (Landes)
Altitude: 65 m.
Skin diseases.

61 Saubusse-les-Bains (Landes)
Altitude: 85 m.
Kidneys, urinary organs.

62 Salies-de-Béarn (Basses-Pyrénées)
Altitude: 54m.
Gynaecological conditions.

63 Eugénie-les-Bains (Landes)
Altitude: 85 m.
Kidneys, urinary organs.

64 Barbotan (Gers)
Altitude: 130 m.
Circulatory disorders.

65 Lamalou-les-Bains (Hérault)
Altitude: 200 m.
Nervous system.

66 Avène-les-Bains (Hérault)
Altitude: 300 m.
Skin diseases.

67 Balaruc-les Bains (Hérault)
Altitude: 2 m.
Rheumatism, bones and joints.

68 Aix-en-Provence (Bouches-du-Rhône)
Altitude: 177 m.
Circulatory disorders.

69 Camoins-les-Bains (Bouches-du-Rhône)
Altitude: 250 m.
Respiratory passages, lymphatic disorders.

70 Gréoux-les-Bains (Basses-Alpes)
Altitude: 400 m.
Rheumatism, bones and joints.

71 St-Christau (Basses-Pyrénées)
Altitude: 330 m.
Skin diseases.

72 Les Eaux-Chaudes (Basses-Pyrénées)
Altitude: 675 m.
Respiratory passages, lymphatic disorders.

73 Les Eaux-Bonnes (Basses-Pyrénées)
Altitude: 750 m.
Respiratory passages, lymphatic disorders.

74 Cauterets (Hautes-Pyrénées)
Altitude: 1000 m.
Respiratory passages, lymphatic disorders.

75 Argelès-Gazost (Hautes-Pyrénées)
Altitude: 460 m.
Circulatory disorders.

76 St-Sauveur-les-Bains (Hautes-Pyrénées)
Altitude: 730 m.
Gynaecological conditions.

77 Beaucens-les-Bains (Hautes-Pyrénées)
Altitude: 480 m.
Rheumatism, bones and joints.

78 Barèges (Hautes-Pyrénées)
Altitude: 1240 m.
Rheumatism, bones and joints.

79 Bagnères-de-Bigorre (Hautes-Pyrénées)
Altitude: 550 m.
Nervous system.

80 Capvern (Hautes-Pyrénées)
Altitude: 450 m.
Kidneys, urinary organs.

81 Luchon (Haute-Garonne)
Altitude: 630 m.
Respiratory passages, lymphatic disorders.

82 Barbazan (Haute-Garonne)
Altitude: 450 m.
Digestive organs.

83 Encausse-les-Thermes (Haute-Garonne)
Altitude: 362 m.
Digestive organs.

84 Salies-du-Salat (Haute-Garonne)
Altitude: 300 m.
Respiratory passages, lymphatic disorders.

85 Ussat-les-Bains (Ariège)
Altitude: 486 m.
Nervous system.

86 Ax-les-Thermes (Ariège)
Altitude: 720 m.
Rheumatism, bones and joints.

87 Escouloubre-les-Bains (Aude)
Altitude: 911 m.
Respiratory passages, lymphatic disorders.

88 Ginoles-les-Bains (Aude)
Altitude: 350 m.
Kidneys, urinary organs.

89 Rennes-les-Bains (Aude)
Altitude: 310 m.
Rheumatism, bones and joints.

90 Molitg-les-Bains (Pyrénées-Orientales)
Altitude: 450 m.
Skin diseases.

91 Vernet-les-Bains (Pyrénées-Orientales)
Altitude: 650 m.
Rheumatism, bones and joints.

92 La Preste-les-Bains (Pyrénées-Orientales)
Altitude: 1130 m.
Kidneys, urinary organs.

93 **Amélie-les-Bains** (Pyrénées-Orientales)
Altitude: 230 m.
Rheumatism, bones and joints.

94 **Le Boulou** (Pyrénées-Orientales)
Altitude: 78 m.
Digestive organs.   Map: p. 286

⬤ **Sea-Water Treatment
Establishments**

95 **Quiberon** (Morbihan)
Institut de Thalassothérapie de Quiberon.

96 **Douarnenez-Tréboul** (Finistère)
Centre de Cure Marine de la Baie de Tréboul-Douarnenez.

97 **Roscoff** (Finistère)
Institut Marin Rock-Roum.

98 **St-Malo-Paramé** (Ille-et-Vilaine)
Thermes Marins de St-Malo-Paramé.

99 **Granville** (Manche)
Centre de Thalasso-Réadaptation Fonctionnelle "Le Normandy".

100 **Trouville** (Calvados)
Cures Marines de Trouville.

101 **Biarritz** (Pyrénées-Atlantiques)
Institut de Thalassothérapie.

102 **Collioure** (Pyrénées-Orientales)
Centre Hélio-Marin de Réadaptation Fonctionnelle "Mer-Air-Soleil".

103 **Marseilles** (Bouches-du Rhône)
Balnéothérapie Marseillaise.

104 **Toulon** (Var)
Centre de Cures Marines de Toulon.

105 **St-Raphaël** (Var)
Institut Marin "La Calanco".

Son et Lumière

During the summer season there are many "Son et Lumière" performances in châteaux and other places of particular interest to tourists. These usually present a kind of historical pageant, with highly theatrical lighting effects, of events connected with the particular building.

⬤ **Privately Owned Châteaux**

In addition to the châteaux and other historic buildings in public ownership, such as the famous châteaux of the Loire valley and the Ile de France, there are many hundreds of châteaux, medieval castles, monastic buildings and palaces still in private hands. Many of these are open to visitors, and give an excellent impression of the aristocratic society which created them and which left its stamp on the culture of Europe. Often they are set in beautiful parks. Since the upkeep of these splendid buildings involves a heavy financial burden, some of them have been turned into hotels, in which the guests can not only see but participate in their atmosphere of gracious living. The following list includes only a selection of the many châteaux, castles and abbeys in private ownership. Over 400 of them are members of an association of owners of historic buildings, "La Demeure Historique" (55 Quai de la Tournelle, F-75005 Paris), which can supply a list of the properties and their opening times. The association also publishes a quarterly journal. Admission charges range from nothing to 8 francs or so (in exceptional cases more).

1 **Long** (18th c.)   Map: p. 290
Long (Somme)

2 **Valmont** (11th–15th c.)
Valmont (Seine-Maritime)

3 **Bailleul** (Renaissance)
Angerville (Seine-Maritime)

4 **Balleroy** (17th c.)
Balleroy (Calvados)

5 **Bizy** (18th c.)
Vernon (Eure)

6 **Royaumont Abbey** (13th c.)
Asnières-sur-Oise (Val-d'Oise)

7 **Thoiry** (16th c.)
Thoiry (Yvelines)

8 **Dampierre** (17th c.)
Dampierre (Yvelines)

9 **Gros-Bois** (Louis XIII)
Boissy-St-Léger (Val-de-Marne)

10 **Guermantes** (17th–18th c.)
Guermantes (Seine-et-Marne)

11 **Maintenon** (12th–17th c.)
Maintenon (Eure-et-Loir)

12 **Jeurre** (18th c.)
Morigny (Essonne)

13 **Vaux-le-Vicomte** (17th c.)
Maincy (Seine-et-Marne)

14 **Kintzheim** (14th c.)
Kintzheim (Bas-Rhin)

15 **Rosanbo** (12th–17th c.)
Lanvellec (Côtes-du-Nord)

16 **Malesherbes** (14th–17th c.)
Malesherbes (Loiret)

Privately Owned Châteaux

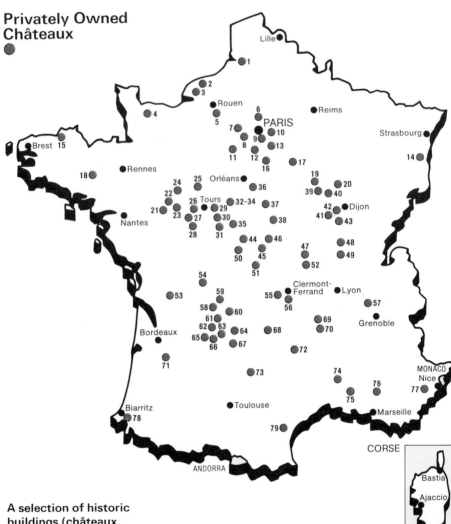

A selection of historic
buildings (châteaux,
abbeys, etc.)
open to the public

17 Fleurigny (14th–15th c.)
Fleurigny (Yonne)

18 Josselin (Renaissance)
Josselin (Morbihan)

19 Tanlay (16th–17th c.)
Tanlay (Yonne)

20 Montigny-sur-Aube (12th–19th c.)
Montigny-sur-Aube (Côte-d'Or)

21 Brissac (15th–17th c.)
Brissac (Maine-et-Loire)

22 Montgeoffroy (18th c.)
Maze (Maine-et-Loire)

23 Boumois (15th–17th c.)
St-Martin-de-la-Place (Maine-et-Loire)

24 Le Lude (15th–18th c.)
Le Lude (Sarthe)

25 Poncé (16th c.)
Poncé-sur-le-Loir (Sarthe)

26 Cinq-Mars (12th–13th c.)
Cinq-Mars (Indre-et-Loire)

27 Ussé (15th–18th c.)
Ussé (Indre-et-Loire)

28 Le Rivau (18th c.)
Lémeré (Indre-et-Loire)

29 Le Clos-Lucé (15th c.)
Amboise (Indre-et-Loire)

30 Montpoupon (13th–16th c.)
Céré-la-Ronde (Indre-et-Loire)

31 Montrésor (late 15th c.)
Montrésor (Indre-et-Loire)

32 Beauregard (16th c.)
Cellettes (Loir-et-Cher)

33 Villesavin (16th c.)
Tour-en-Sologne (Loir-et-Cher)

34 Cheverny (17th c.)
Cheverny (Loir-et-Cher)

35 Valençay (Renaissance)
Valençay (Indre)

36 Sully (16th c.)
Sully (Saône-et-Loire)

37 Blancafort (15th c.)
Blancafort (Cher)

38 **Maupas** (13th c.)
   Morogues (Cher)

39 **Ancy-le-Franc** (16th c.)
   Ancy-le-Franc (Yonne)

40 **Fontenay Abbey** (12th c.)
   Marmagne (Côte-d'Or)

41 **Thoisy** (Renaissance)
   Thoisy-la-Berchère (Côte-d'Or)

42 **Commarin** (15th–18th c.)
   Commarin (Côte-d'Or)

43 **La Roche-Pot**
   (medieval and Renaissance)
   La Roche-Pot (Côte-d'Or)

44 **Diors** (16th c.)
   Diors (Indre)

45 **Culan** (12th–15th c.)
   Culan (Cher)

46 **Ainay-le-Vieil** (Renaissance)
   Ainay-le-Vieil (Cher)

47 **Beauvoir** (13th–18th c.)
   Echassières (Allier)

48 **Brancion** (10th–14th c.)
   Martailly-lès-Brancion (Saône-et-Loire)

49 **Berzé-le-Châtel** (18th–19th c.)
   Berzé-le-Châtel (Saône-et-Loire)

50 **George Sand's House**
   Gargilesse (Indre)

51 **Boussac** (15th c.)
   Boussac (Creuse)

52 **La Palice** (13th–16th c.)
   Lapalisse (Allier)

53 **Cognac** (13th–16th c.)
   Cognac (Charente)

54 **Rochebrune** (11th–12th c.)
   Etagnac (Charente)

55 **Cordès** (15th–16th c.)
   Orcival (Puy-de-Dôme)

56 **La Batisse** (10th–18th c.)
   Chanonat (Puy-de-Dôme)

57 **Virieu** (11th–17th c.)
   Virieu (Isère)

58 **Jumilhac** (13th–17th c.)
   Jumilhac-le-Grand (Dordogne)

59 **Bonneval** (14th c.)
   Coussac-Bonneval (Haute-Vienne)

60 **Ségur** (15th c.)
   Ségur-le-Château (Corrèze)

61 **Hautefort** (14th–17th c.)
   Hautefort (Dordogne)

62 **Coulonges** (13th–15th c.)
   Montignac-sur-Vézère (Dordogne)

63 **Richemont** (16th c.)
   St-Crépin-de-Richemont (Dordogne)

64 **Turenne** (12th–13th c.)
   Turenne (Corrèze)

65 **Fages** (medieval and Renaissance)
   St-Cyprien (Dordogne)

66 **Beynac** (13th c.)
   Beynac-et-Cassenac (Dordogne)

67 **La Treyne** (14th–17th c.)
   Lacave (Lot)

68 **Anjony** (15th–18th c.)
   Tournemire (Cantal)

69 **Voûte-Polignac** (10th–18th c.)
   La Voûte-sur-Loire (Haute-Loire)

70 **Volhac** (11th c.)
   Coubon (Haute-Loire)

71 **Roquetaillade** (12th–14th c.)
   Mazères (Gironde)

72 **La Baume** (17th–18th c.)
   Prinsuéjols (Lozère)

73 **Najac** (13th c.)
   Najac (Aveyron)

74 **Le Duché** (Ducal Castle)
   Uzès (Gard)

75 **Roussan** (18th c.)
   St-Rémy-de-Provence
   (Bouches-du-Rhône)

76 **Ansouis** (11th–15th c.)
   Ansouis (Vaucluse)

77 **Gourdon** (9th–17th c.)
   Gourdon (Alpes-Maritimes)

78 **Maison de Louis XIV** (Louis XIII)
   St-Jean-de-Luz (Pyrénées-Atlantiques)

79 **Fontfroide Abbey** (11th c.)
   Narbonne (Aude)

National Parks Map:
p. 292

1 **Parc National de la Vanoise**
  Administration: Chambéry (Savoie).
  Area: 130,963 acres.
  Situation: between the high valleys of the Isère
  and the Arc in Savoy, at altitudes between 1250
  and 3850 m.
  Activities: photographic safaris, climbing, ski
  trekking, conducted tours.

2 **Parc National des Ecrins**
  Administration: Gap (Hautes-Alpes).
  Area: 222,390 acres.

Situation: departments of Isère and Hautes-Alpes
and the Pelvoux wildlife reserve, at altitudes
between 800 and 4102 m.
Activities: climbing, walking, cycle tours.

3 **Parc National des Cévennes**
  Administration: Florac (Lozère).
  Area: 208,058 acres.
  Situation: in the departments of Lozère, Gard and
  Ardèche.
  Activities: walking, ski trekking, water sports,
  caving.

National Parks

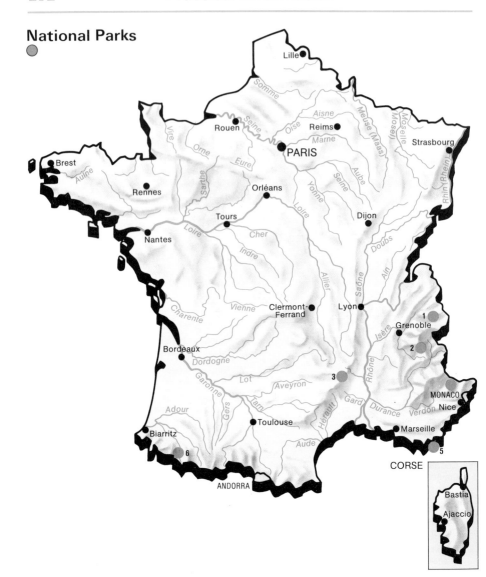

4 Parc National du Mercantour
Administration: Nice (Alpes-Maritimes).
Area: *c.* 148,260 acres.
Situation: N of St-Martin-Vésubie, between the Alpes Maritimes and the Italian frontier. Still in course of development.
Activities; walking, climbing, caving.

5 Parc National de Port-Cros
Administration: Hyères (Var).
Area: 18,137 acres.
Situation: the island of Port-Cros and the seabed round it. The park is to be extended to take in the island of Porquerolles, and will then be known as the Parc National des Iles d'Hyères.

6 Parc National des Pyrénées Orientales
Administration: Tarbes (Hautes-Pyrénées).
Area: 118,608 acres.
Situation: SW of Tarbes near the Spanish frontier, at altitudes between 1000 and 3300 m.
Activities: walking, pony trekking, climbing, fishing.

Regional Nature Parks

Parc de Lorraine
(Meuse, Moselle, Meurthe-et-Moselle)
Area: 457,135 acres.
Climbing, water sports, shooting, fishing.

Parc des Vosges du Nord
(Bas-Rhin, Moselle)
Area: 296,520 acres.
Water sports, canoeing.

Parc des Landes de Gascogne
(Gironde, Landes)
Area: 509,026 acres.
Riding, canoeing.

Parc des Volcans
(Puy-de-Dôme, Cantal)
Area: 684,467 acres.
Riding, caving, climbing, canoeing.

Parc de Morvan
(Saône-et-Loire, Côte-d'Or, Nièvre, Yonne)
Area: 427,483 acres.
Riding, canoeing, shooting, fishing.

Parc d'Armorique
(Finistère)
Area: 160,615 acres.
Riding, shooting, fishing.

Parc de la Forêt d'Orient
(Aube)
Area: 160,615 acres.
Riding, water sports, fishing.

Parc de la Montagne de Reims
(Marne)
Area: 123,550 acres.

Parc du Haut-Languedoc
(Hérault, Tarn)
Area: 358,295 acres.
Riding, canoeing.

Parc de St-Amand-Raismes
(Nord)
Riding, water sports.

Parc de Brotonne
(Seine-Maritime, Eure)
Area: 122,561 acres.

Parc Normandie-Maine
(Manche, Mayenne, Orne, Sarthe)
Area: 333,585 acres.

Parc du Marais Poitevin
(Charente-Maritime, Deux-Sèvres, Vendée)

Parc de Brière
(Loire-Atlantique)
Area: 98,840 acres.

Parc de la Camargue
(Bouches-du-Rhône)
Riding.

Parc du Lubéron
(Vaucluse, Alpes de Haute-Provence)
Area: 276,752 acres.
Riding.

Parc du Queyras
(Hautes-Alpes)
Area: 148,260 acres.
Riding, climbing, canoeing.

Parc du Pilat
(Loire)
Area: 148,260 acres.
Riding.

Parc du Vercors
(Isère, Drôme)
Area: 333,585 acres.

Parc de la Corse
(Corsica)
Area: 370,650 acres.

Parc des Ardennes
at the planning stage.

Caves Open to the Public

● Map:
p. 294

1 Cave à Margot
nr Saulges (Mayenne)
Stalactites, rock concretions.

2 Grottes d'Arcy
nr Arcy-sur-Cure (Yonne)
Rock concretions.

3 Grotte des Planches
nr Arbois (Jura)
Underground river: fossils.

3 Grotte d'Osselle
nr Roset-Fluans (Doubs)
Underground river; rock concretions.

5 Grotte de Baume
nr Baume-les-Messieurs (Jura)
Spring; rock concretions.

6 Grotte du Cerdon
nr Nantua (Ain)
Rock concretions.

7 Grotte de la Balme
nr Balme-les-Grottes (Isère)
Rock concretions.

8 Grotte de la Diau
nr Thorens-Glières (Haute-Savoie)
Erosional features.

9 Grotte des Echelles
nr Les Echelles (Savoie)
Erosional features.

10 Cuves de Sassenage
nr Sassenage (Isère)
Erosional features.

11 Grottes de Choranche
nr Choranche (Isère)
Erosional features, stalactites.

12 Grotte de la Luire
nr La Chapelle-en-Vercors (Drôme)
Erosional features.

13 Grottes de l'Observatoire
Principality of Monaco
Stalactites, rock concretions.

14 Grotte de St-Cézaire
nr Grasse (Alpes-Maritimes)
Rock concretions.

15 Fontaine de Vaucluse
nr Cavaillon (Vaucluse)
Underground river.

16 Aven de Marzal
nr Bourg-St-Andéol (Ardèche)
Stalactites, rock concretions.

17 Aven d'Orgnac
nr Orgnac-l'Aven (Ardèche)
Stalactites.

18 Grotte de Clamouse
nr Gignac (Hérault)
Stalactites, rock concretions.

19 Grotte des Demoiselles
nr Ganges (Hérault)
Stalactites, rock concretions.

20 Abîme de Bramabiau
nr Camprieu (Gard)
Underground river; erosional features.

21 Grotte de Dargilan
nr Dargilan (Lozère)
Rock concretions, stalactites.

22 Aven Armand
nr Meyrueis (Lozère)
Stalactites.

Caves Open to the Public

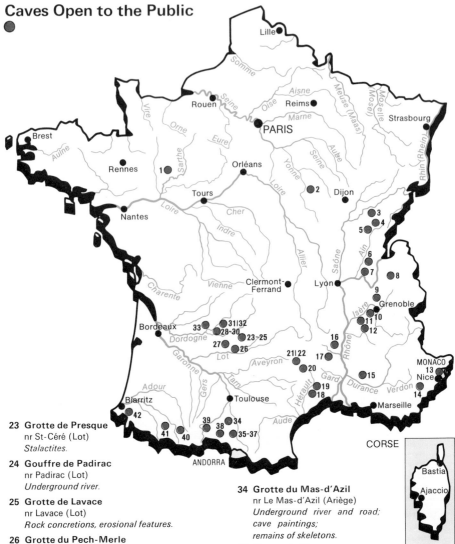

23 Grotte de Presque
nr St-Céré (Lot)
Stalactites.

24 Gouffre de Padirac
nr Padirac (Lot)
Underground river.

25 Grotte de Lavace
nr Lavace (Lot)
Rock concretions, erosional features.

26 Grotte du Pech-Merle
nr Cabrerets (Lot)
Cave paintings; rock concretions, stalactites.

27 Grottes de Cougnac
nr Gourdon (Lot)
Cave paintings; stalactites, rock concretions.

28 Grotte de Font-de-Gaume
nr Les Eyzies (Dordogne)
Cave paintings; rock concretions.

29 Grotte des Combarelles
nr Les Eyzies (Dordogne)
Cave painting.

30 Gouffre de Proumeyssac
nr Le Bugue (Dordogne)
Rock concretions.

31 Grotte de Lascaux
nr Montignac (Dordogne)
Cave paintings.
Cave closed since 1963; film shows in information
centre.

32 Grotte de Rouffignac
nr Rouffignac (Dordogne)
Cave paintings.

33 Caverne de Bara-Bahau
nr Le Bugue (Dordogne)
Cave paintings.

34 Grotte du Mas-d'Azil
nr Le Mas-d'Azil (Ariège)
*Underground river and road;
cave paintings;
remains of skeletons.*

35 Grotte de Niaux
nr Niaux (Ariège)
Cave paintings; rock concretions.

36 Grotte de Bédeilhac
nr Bédeilhac (Ariège)
Cave paintings; rock concretions.

37 Rivière souterraine Labouiche
nr Foix (Ariège)
*Underground river; rock concretions, erosional
features.*

38 Grotte de Moulis
nr Moulis (Ariège)
Rock concretions, stalactites; cave laboratory.

39 Grottes de Gargas
nr Aventignan (Hautes-Pyrénées)
Cave paintings.

40 Grotte de Médous
nr Bagnères-de-Bigorre (Hautes-Pyrénées)
Underground river; stalactites.

41 Grottes de Bétharram
nr St-Pé-de-Bigorre (Hautes-Pyrénées)
*Underground river; erosional features, rock
concretions.*

42 Grottes d'Oxocelhaya et d'Isturits
nr St-Martin-d'Arberoue (Pyrénées-Atlantiques)
Cave paintings; rock concretions.

Winter Sports

Facilities for winter sports in France are extensive and varied. In recent years new resorts have been developed in good skiing areas with guaranteed snow and have been planned from the outset to meet the needs of winter sports enthusiasts, with accommodation, ski-lifts, recreation facilities and *après-ski* provision all on an appropriate scale. Ski-lifts, etc., are provided on such an adequate scale that waiting is rarely necessary.

Useful addresses:

Comité des stations françaises de sports d'hiver,
49 rue Pigalle,
F-75009 Paris;
tel. (1) 8 74 32 84.

Fédération française du ski,
34 rue Eugène-Flachat,
F-75071 Paris;
tel. (1) 7 54 99 39.

Syndicat national de téléphériques et téléskis de France,
23 bis rue de Constantinople,
F-75008 Paris;
tel. (1) 3 87 78 07.

Syndicat national des moniteurs du ski français,
12 rue Irvoy,
F-38000 Grenoble;
tel. (76) 96 51 05.

Horloge des Neiges (snow reports),
Inter Service Neige, Paris;
tel. (1) 8 58 33 33.

In the following list of winter sports areas the term "cableways" includes all types of ski-lifts, ski-tows, chair-lifts, etc.

Winter Sports Areas

Map: p. 297

Vosges

La Bresse (630 m)
F-88250 La Bresse
Cableways to 1300 m.

Gérardmer (666 m)
F-88400 Gérardmer
Cableways to 1113 m

Jura

Metabief – Mont-d'Or (1000 m)
F-25370 Les Hôpitaux-Neufs
Cableways to 1430 m

Les Rousses (1120 m)
F-39220 Les Rousses
Cableways to 1690 m

Massif Central

Le Mont-Dore (1050 m)
F-63240 Le Mont-Dore
Cableways to 1846 m

Super-Besse (1350 m)
F-63610 Besse-en-Chandesse
Cableways to 1850 m

Super-Lioran (1240 m)
F-15300 Murat
Cableways to 1840 m

Northern Alps

SAVOIE and HAUTE-SAVOIE

Arèches-Beaufort (1080 m)
F-73270 Beaufort-sur-Doron
Cableways to 1955 m

Bellecombe – Crest-Voland (1134 m)
F-73850 Notre-Dame-de-Bellecombe
Cableways to 1800 m

Bonneval-sur-Arc (1800 m)
F-73480 Lanslebourg – Mont-Cenis
Cableways to 2500 m
Skiing in summer

Bourg-St-Maurice – Les Arcs (800–1600 m)
F-73700 Bourg-St-Maurice
Cableways to 3000 m

Les Carroz d'Araches (1140 m)
F-74300 Cluses
Cableways to 1850 m

Chamonix (1035 m)
F-74401 Chamonix
Cableways to 3842 m
Skiing in summer

La Chapelle-d'Abondance (1020 m)
F-74690 La Chapelle-d'Abondance
Cableways to 1700 m

Châtel (1200 m)
F-74390 Châtel
Cableways to 2080 m

La Clusaz (1100 m)
F-74220 La Clusaz
Cableways to 2400 m

Combloux (1000 m)
F-74700 Sallanches
Cableways to 1760 m

Les Contamines – Montjoie (1164 m)
F-74190 Le Fayet
Cableways to 2487 m

Le Corbier (1550 m)
F-73300 St-Jean-de-Maurienne
Cableways to 2266 m

Cordon (1000 m)
F-74700 Sallanches
Cableways to 1650 m

Courchevel (1850 m)
F-73120 Courchevel
Cableways to 2700 m

Flaine (1600 m)
F-74300 Cluses
Cableway to 2500 m

Flumet – Praz-sur-Arley (1000 m)
F-73590 Flumet
Cableways to 1800 m

Les Gets (1172 m)
F-74260 Les Gets
Cableways to 1850 m

Le Grand Bornand (950 m)
F-74450 Le Grand Bornand
Cableways to 1850 m

Les Houches (1008 m)
F-74310 Les Houches
Cableways to 1900 m

Megève (1113 m)
F-74120 Megève
Cableways to 2040 m

Les Menuires (1810 m)
F-73440 St-Martin-de-Belleville
Cableways to 3010 m
Skiing in summer

Méribel-les-Allues (1600 m)
F-73550 Méribel-les-Allues
Cableways to 2700 m

Morzine-Avoriaz (1000 m)
F-74110 Morzine
Cableways to 2460 m

La Plagne (1970 m)
F-73210 Aime
Cableways to 3250 m
Skiing in summer

Pralognan-la-Vanoise (1410 m)
F-73710 Pralognan-la-Vanoise
Cableways to 2265 m

St-François – Longchamp (1450 m)
F-73130 La Chambre
Cableways to 2200 m

St-Gervais – Le Bettex (900 m)
F-74170 St-Gervais-les-Bains
Cableways to 1950 m

Samoëns (720 m)
F-74340 Samoëns
Cableways to 2125 m

Tignes (2100 m)
F-73320 Tignes
Cableways to 3016 m
Skiing in summer

Val-Cenis (1450 m)
F-73480 Lanslebourg – Mont-Cenis
Cableways to 2540 m

Val-d'Isère (1850 m)
F-73150 Val d'Isère
Cableways to 3254 m
Skiing in summer

Valloire (1450 m)
F-73450 Valloire
Cableways to 2450 m
Skiing in summer

Thollon-les-Memises (1000 m)
F-74500 Evian
Cableways to 1982 m

ISÈRE

Alpe d'Huez (1860 m)
F-38750 L'Alpe d'Huez
Cableways to 3350 m
Skiing in summer

Autrans (1050 m)
F-38880 Autrans
Cableways to 1630 m

Chamrousse (1650 m)
F-38410 Uriage
Cableways to 2250 m

Les Deux-Alpes (1650 m)
F-38520 Bourg-d'Oisans
Cableways to 3166 m
Skiing in summer

St-Pierre-de-Chartreuse (900 m)
F-38380 St-Laurent-du-Pont
Cableways to 1700 m

Winter sports in the French Alps

Winter Sports Areas

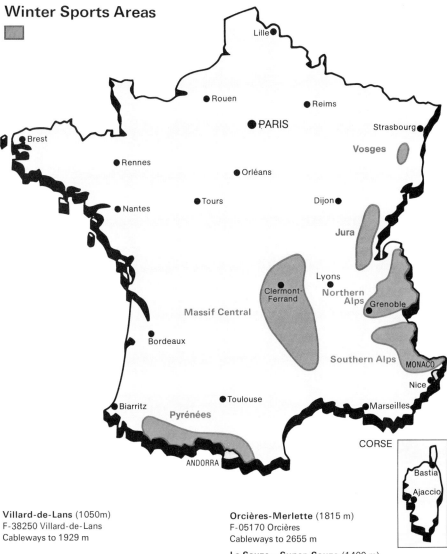

Villard-de-Lans (1050m)
F-38250 Villard-de-Lans
Cableways to 1929 m

Southern Alps

Auron (1600 m)
F-06660 St-Etienne-de-Tinée
Cableways to 2417 m

Beuil-les-Launes (1410 m)
F-06470 Guillaumes
Cableways to 2010 m

La Colmiane – Valdeblore (1500 m)
F-06420 St-Sauveur-sur-Tinée
Cableways to 1800 m

La Foux d'Allos (1800 m)
F-04260 Allos
Cableways to 2600 m

Isola 2000 (2010 m)
F-06420 St-Sauveur-sur-Tinée
Cableways to 2450 m

Montgenèvre (1860 m)
F-05100 Briançon
Cableways to 2600 m

Pra-Loup (1628 m)
F-04400 Barcelonnette
Cableways to 2502 m

Orcières-Merlette (1815 m)
F-05170 Orcières
Cableways to 2655 m

Le Sauze – Super-Sauze (1400 m)
F-04400 Barcelonnette
Cableways to 2400 m

Superdévoulu (1500 m)
F-05250 St-Etienne-en-Dévoulu
Cableways to 2500 m

Valberg (1600 m)
F-06470 Guillaumes
Cableways to 2010 m

Vars (1650 m)
F-05600 Guillestre
Cableways to 2580 m

Les Orres (1550 m)
F-05200 Embrun
Cableways to 2770 m

Pyrenees

Ax-les-Thermes (1400 m)
F-09110 Ax-les-Thermes
Cableways to 2300 m

Barèges (1230 m)
F-65120 Luz – St-Sauveur
Cableways to 2000 m

Cauterets Lys (937 m)
F-65110 Cauterets
Cableways to 2300 m
Skiing in summer

Font-Romeu (1750 m)
F-66120 Font-Romeu
Cableways to 2215 m

Gourette les Eaux-Bonnes (1400 m)
F-64440 Laruns
Cableways to 2400 m
Skiing in summer

La Mongie (1750 m)
F-65200 Bagnères-de-Bigorre
Cableways to 2360 m

St-Lary – Soulan (1700 m)
F-65170 St-Lary
Cableways to 2380 m

Les Agudes (1600 m)
F-31110 Bagnères-de-Luchon
Cableways to 2400 m

Les Angles – Formiguères (1600 m)
F-66210 Mont-Louis
Cableways to 2370 m

Folk Traditions

Scarcely any other country in Europe has preserved such a variety of regional customs, costumes and folk music as France. This reflects the mingling of many different peoples to make up the population of present-day France; for although the overwhelming majority, for all their strong local patriotism, feel themselves as French men and women, they have preserved many of the traditions of their ancestors. The list of all the various regional festivals and other events would be endless: here it is possible only to pick out a few typical traditional customs and some of the characteristic features of French folk art.

Although the population of France is largely Catholic, the *church festivals* play a much less important part in people's life than in, say, Spain or Italy. Regional differences are reflected in the various ways of celebrating **Christmas**. While the Christmas tree figures prominently in Alsace and Lorraine and in some parts of northern France, the predominant feature in Provence is the *crèche* (crib, Nativity group), often elaborately decorated, and every house has its *santons* – earthenware, wooden or metal figures from the Nativity scene. The Provençal Christmas has preserved something of an atmosphere of intimacy and mystery, with Christmas carols (Noëls de Provence) which are centuries old. Something of this atmosphere is found also in eastern France, in the areas with a population of predominantly Germanic origin. Elsewhere the French Christmas is a time of celebration, with a great festive meal (*réveillon*), wine, champagne, dancing and music. The children usually receive their presents on St Nicholas's Day (6 December) or Epiphany (6 January). In Alsace the Christ Child still appears on Christmas Eve, but elsewhere this is a time for sweets and fun for the children. New Year is also celebrated with a *réveillon* and the giving of presents (*étrennes*).

The **Carnival** was in the past looked on with disfavour by French governments and sometimes banned, since it provided an opportunity for expressing popular discontent or rebellion. The traditional Carnival is now seldom celebrated, although increasing interest has been shown in it in recent years. In Alsace there are some Shrovetide celebrations in the German tradition, though usually rather later in the

year than in Germany. The Carnival is celebrated with more abandon in some villages in Languedoc, for example at Cournonterral near Montpellier, where masked figures (*pailhasses*) cover the market square with the dregs from the wine-presses, wallow in this stinking slime and chase the "*blancs*", the "clean" members of the community, with the object of dragging them through the mire. Then there is the famous Carnival of Nice, with its battle of flowers, parades and confetti fights; but this is now mainly a commercial affair which has little connection with traditional celebrations. – *Easter* is often an occasion for a picnic, with Easter eggs of chocolate, sugar or marzipan. The German "Easter hare", which lays the Easter eggs, is found in Alsace.

The principal *secular celebrations* are 1 May (Labour Day) and **14 July** (*Quatorze juillet*), France's National Day, commemorating the capture of the Bastille in 1789, which is celebrated in most towns and villages with parades, music and dancing in the streets. The events of July 1789 are still commemorated with enthusiasm, though now rather as an occasion for jollification than from any revolutionary or political motives. On 1 May it is customary to give friends and relations a small posy of lilies of the valley.

There are also numerous *village festivals* celebrating a variety of occasions, from wine festivals to lavender festivals, from a Lemon-Blossom Festival to a Roquefort Festival, from an Oyster Festival to a Nougat Festival. All of these are basically no more than a pretext for enjoyment, with much eating, drinking and music.

In S and SW France there are bullfights and sports featuring bulls. In addition to the traditional **bullfights** (Nîmes, Arles, Bayonne, Fréjus, Béziers, Dax, Beaucaire, etc.), in which celebrated bullfighters take part, the *course à la cocarde* is also popular. In this a number of young men dressed in white, the *razeteurs*, attempt to snatch a brightly coloured cockade (*cocarde*) from between the bull's horns – a feat which calls for great skill, since the bulls are not killed and are thus battle-hardened and experienced. The best bulls are much sought after and as widely known as leading racehorses, and the local newspapers give great prominence to the successes of the *razeteurs* and of the bulls. Successful *razeteurs* and breeders win cups, money and fame. For amateur *razeteurs*, mostly adolescents and tourists, there is sometimes a modified form of the sport in which the bulls are replaced by calves or heifers with padded or blunted horns. – In the sport known as *toro piscine* a bull (or heifer), usually with padded horns, stands in a pond and the object is to walk into or through the pond unscathed. – In S and SW France there are also various rodeo-like events. In the Camargue there are the *ferrades* (branding of the bulls) and the *concours de manades*, in which the *gardians* (cattle-herds) compete in various sports and riding contests. In the *abrivado* bulls are driven through the streets by mounted *gardians*. The *bandido* is like the Spanish *encierro*: the bulls are released in the centre of the town, and anyone who wants can try his skill in avoiding their horns.

In **Saintes-Maries-de-la-Mer** the festival of Marie Jacobé is celebrated every year at the end of May and the festival of Marie Salomé in October. Gipsies gather from all over Europe to do honour to their patron saint, Sara la Noire (the servant of the three Marys), whose remains are believed to rest in the crypt of the church. This and other festivals in the Camargue give visitors a chance of seeing the local costumes. The men wear the traditional garb of the *gardians*, and women and girls, other than the gipsies, wear the costume of the Arlésienne – a long black dress, closely fitted to the waist, with three white lace kerchiefs on the bosom, a cap and a cross (usually gold) on a chain round their neck. Their long hair is wound into the traditional "bun". Another form of traditional dress is the "Mireille" costume, with brightly coloured (usually yellow) skirts.

In **Arles** and the surrounding area there is a great cult of the Arlésiennes, the women of Arles who were celebrated by Alphonse Daudet, Frédéric Mistral, Van Gogh, Georges Bizet and Francesco Cilea. At regular intervals the "Queen" of Arles is chosen; but this is by no means a kind of "Miss Arles" beauty contest. The Queen must measure up to the traditional ideal of the Arlésienne and must wear the local costume with particular grace. The local folk dancing group, "Lou Velout d'Arle", which is famous for wearing the most beautiful costumes, gives regular folk evenings in which the girls belonging to the group dance and sing. Fine examples of the local costume can be seen in the Museon Arlaten in Arles.

Traditional costumes are worn and old folk songs are sung on festive occasions in other parts of France, particularly in the country and in regions with ethnic minorities – sometimes reflecting, though perhaps only unconsciously, regional political aspirations. This is the case, for example, in Alsace, where on special occasions the girls wear a red skirt and black apron, the men white shirts, red jackets and black trousers; in Auvergne, where the girls wear full skirts in bright colours, often several on top of each other; and in Roussillon, where the main features of the local costume are *espadrilles* (brightly coloured cloth sandals with woven soles), red peaked caps and cummerbunds. The women of Brittany wear plain dark-coloured clothes with elaborately ornamented aprons and caps, often of enormous size and sometimes combined with a kind of ruff. The characteristic feature of male dress in the Basque country is the beret, which on festive occasions is usually red.

In every part of the country there are numerous traditional dances and songs, many of which are being rediscovered in our own day and, given the present interest in regional cultures and languages, not infrequently feature in the local "top ten". In Alsace a number of dialect singers, prominent among them Roger Siffer, have concerned themselves with the special position of this region lying between two different cultures. The Alsatian brass bands are very similar to their counterparts across the border in Germany. In Languedoc, a region with a language and

Breton costumes

cultural tradition differing from those of the rest of France, the traditional songs and dances are of very distinctive character. Among the folk songs, which may be of either courtly or rustic origin, the *pastourelles* are of particular importance. They usually tell the story of the love between a shepherdess and a passing knight, or – perhaps even more frequently – of the steadfastness of a girl in resisting the knightly seducer, who is sometimes an officer in the king of France's army. The most popular folk dance in Auvergne and Rouergue is the *bourrée*. In the area around Albi there is an unusual old folk song, "Lou Boule", which some authorities believe may originally have been sung by the heretical Cathars during the Albigensian wars of the Middle Ages. The five vowels are pronounced in quick succession, contrasting with a musical phrase dating from pre-Gregorian times; and it is thought that permutation of the vowels produced a kind of secret code with which the oppressed local people could communicate with one another in the presence of their enemies.

The cheerful songs of *Provence* are usually accompanied by a small flute (*galoubet*) and a long narrow drum (*tambourin*). The most popular Provençal dance is the *farandole*, a fast rhythmic round-dance. Occitanian folk music is played by the "Velout d'Arle" group already mentioned, the Escolo Mistralenco group of Arles and other well-known groups in Toulouse, Nice, Fréjus, Foix and Pau. The young "Mont Joia" group has done careful research into the origins of Provençal folk music, and their performances of folk and troubadour songs have done much to promote the popularisation of this music. Some *chansonniers*, like Marti, sing songs of political significance. For him, and others of like mind, the old Cathar stronghold of Montségur on the fringes of the Pyrenees, where the last Albigensian leaders died at the stake, is a symbol of the Occitanian struggle for independence, and one of his best known songs is devoted to this theme.

In *Roussillon*, as in Catalan Spain, the *sardana* is a popular dance. This round dance from Cerdagne (Cerdaña), which is believed to be of Greek origin, is accompanied by a band, the *cobla*, playing a number of highly unusual instruments. The invitation to the dance is played by the *fluviol*, a seven-hole flute; the *tambori*, a kind of drum, beats out the rhythm; the tenor horn plays the melody; and the rest of the ensemble, usually 11 to 15 in number, is made up of F-sharp horns (a kind of deep French horn), trumpets and double basses. Two of the best known *coblas* in the whole Catalan region (the Cobla Perpinya and the Cobla Combo Gili) are based on Perpignan, and give performances during the summer at many places in Roussillon, particularly in Perpignan itself (in front of the Loge de Mer) and in Collioure, Banyuls, Argelès and Céret. Many Catalan *chansonniers* like Joan

Manuel Serrat, Toni Montané and Lluis Llach sing both traditional and modern Catalan songs, frequently on political themes.

The *Basque country* is famous for its beautiful melancholy choral songs. The Basque dances – the most popular of which is the fandango – are among the most spectacular in Europe, notable for the acrobatic agility of the dancers and the shrill cries, rather like the crowing of a cock, in which the men give vent to their joy. Typical Basque instruments are the *ttun ttun*, a kind of drum or tabor, and the *xirula* or *txistu*, a small three-hole flute. On festive occasions the lively rhythms of *bandas* enliven the streets of the Basque towns. The song "Guernikako arbola" ("Tree of Guernica"), which celebrates the old Basque *fueros* (charter of rights), is sung in all seven Basque provinces on either side of the French-Spanish frontier as a kind of national anthem.

In *Brittany* almost every form of Celtic folk music can be found, and there are many societies dedicated to preserving this old music. Among characteristic Breton instruments are the bagpipes and the Celtic harp. Alan Stivell has made the Celtic harp known to a wide public.

The folk songs of *Corsica* have often a rather Arab sound and strike visitors from the rest of Europe as distinctly exotic. Only a few country districts still preserve the tradition of the *lamenti* which are sung after the death of a relative, and the *voceri*, the dirges which are sung by women when some member of the family meets his death by violence and are accompanied by fearful curses and calls for revenge. Quieter and more tuneful are the Corsican *nina nanne* (lullabies).

Calendar of Events

(A selection of events of particular interest)

February

Riviera, Côte d'Azur (Alpes-Maritimes)	Carnival in many places (particularly Nice).
Menton (Alpes-Maritimes)	Golden Fruit parade.

March

Ajaccio (Corsica)	Festival of Notre-Dame de la Miséricorde.
Bastia (Corsica)	St. Joseph's Day procession.
Chalon-sur-Saône (Saône-et-Loire)	Carnival.
Epinal (Vosges)	Spring Festival.
Hyères (Var)	Flower parade, horse-racing.
Lyons (Rhône)	Car race, Lyons–Charbonnières–Stuttgart.
Montagney (Haute-Saône)	Daffodil Festival.
Nancy (Meurthe-et-Moselle)	International Spring Carnival.
Paris	Scrap-Iron and Ham Fairs.
Toulon (Var)	Spring Festival.

April

Burzet (Ardèche)	Passion Play.
Caen (Calvados)	Easter Fair.
Champagné (Sarthe)	Festival of Lances.
Marseilles (Bouches-du-Rhône)	International Boating Week.
Nyons (Drôme)	Spring Festival, flower parade.
Paris	"Musical Spring" (second half of month).
St-Tropez (Var)	Water sports.
Toulon (Var)	Flower parade.

April–May

Cannes (Alpes-Maritimes)	International Film Festival.
Strasbourg (Bas-Rhin)	Spring Fair.

May

Angoulême (Charente)	Puppet plays.
Antibes (Alpes-Maritimes)	Veteran Car Rally.
Bordeaux (Gironde)	Music Weeks.
Cavaillon (Vaucluse)	Great parade.
Cerisi-Belle-Etoile (Orne)	Rhododendron Festival.
Chaville (Hauts-de-Seine)	Lily of the Valley Festival.
Clermont-Ferrand (Puy-de-Dôme)	Festival of Notre-Dame-du-Port.
Compiègne (Oise)	Lily of the Valley Festival.
Fontfroide (Aude)	Music Weeks in the abbey.
Gignac (Hérault)	"Donkey's Dance", parade.
Grande-Synthe (Nord)	Cavalcade (13 May).
Grasse (Alpes-Maritimes)	Rose Festival.
Ile d'Yeu (Vendée)	Festival of the Sea.

Fruit Festival, Menton

Magnac-Laval (Haute-Vienne)	"Nine-League Procession" (54 km).
Magny-Cours (Nièvre)	International car race.
Mazères (Ariège)	Flower Festival and veteran car parade.
Nice (Alpes-Maritimes)	May Fair.
Orcival (Puy-de-Dôme)	Pilgrimage to Notre-Dame d'Orcival (24 May).
Rambouillet (Yvelines)	Lily of the Valley Festival.
Stes-Maries-de-la-Mer (Bouches-du-Rhône)	Gipsies' pilgrimage (24–25 May).
St-Tropez (Var)	Second-Hand Fair.
Toulon (Var)	Cartoon Film Festival; veteran car rally.

May–June

Versailles (Yvelines)	Palace of Versailles Festival.

May–September

Domrémy (Vosges)	Festival of the Maid of Orléans.
Versailles (Yvelines)	"Grandes Eaux" (fountains playing) in park.

May to October

St-Germain-en-Laye, Vincennes, St-Cloud, Sèvres, Rambouillet, Fontainbleau	Promenade and other concerts in the château.

June

Ajaccio (Corsica)	Festival of St Erasmus, with procession.
Albertville (Savoie)	Festival of Military Music.
Antibes (Alpes-Maritimes)	Flower Festival.
Basque country (Pyrénées-Atlantiques)	Corpus Christi processions in many places.
Beauvais (Oise)	Summer Festival.
Bernay (Eure)	Pilgrimage of the "Charitons".
Biarritz (Pyrénées-Atlantiques)	Festival of Industrial Films.
Cavalaire (Var)	Festival of St Peter.
Chambéry (Savoie)	Cartoon Film Festival.
Coaraze (Alpes-Maritimes)	Festival of St John.
Conflans-Ste-Honorine (Yvelines)	Pilgrimage of river boatmen.
Coravillers (Haute-Saône)	Broom Festival.
Dijon (Côte-d'Or)	French Grand Prix.
Epina (Vosges)	Pictorial Illustration Festival (middle of month).
Gerberoy (Oise)	Rose Festival.
Givet (Ardennes)	Rose and Children's Festival.
Gruissan (Aude)	Fishermen's Festival.
Honfleur (Calvados)	Seamen's pilgrimage.
La Ciotat-Martigues (Bouches-du-Rhône)	Midsummer Bonfire.
La Louvesc (Ardèche)	Broom Festival.
Le Mans (Sarthe)	"24 Heures du Mans" (car race).
Le Russey (Doubs)	Gentian Festival.
Levier (Doubs)	Fir-tree Festival.
Lyons-la-Forêt (Eure)	Midsummer Bonfire.
Marcoussis-Bièvre (Essonne)	Strawberry Festival.
Menton (Alpes-Maritimes)	Festival parade.
Nîmes (Var)	Féria, bullfights, folk events.
Nice (Alpes-Maritimes)	Fishermen's Festival, St Peter's Fair.
Eastern Pyrenees (Pyrénées-Orientales)	Festival of St John in many places.
Préaux-en-Auge (Calvados)	Pilgrimage of the "Charitons".
Propriano (Corsica)	Fishermen's Festival.
St-Jean-de-Luz (Pyrénées-Atlantiques)	Festival of St John.
St-Maurice-sous-les-Côtes (Meuse)	Côtes-de-Meuse Festival.
St-Quentin (Aisne)	Rose Festival.
Sanary-sur-Mer (Var)	Fishermen's Festival.
Strasbourg (Bas-Rhin)	International Musical Festival.
Tarascon (Bouches-du-Rhône)	Festival of the Tarasque.
Toulon (Var)	Festival of the Sea.
Wissembourg (Bas-Rhin)	Costume Festival.

June–July

Angers (Maine-et-Loire)	Anjou Festival.
Le Havre (Seine-Maritime)	Festival of the Sea.

June–September

Chartres (Eure-et-Loir)	Organ recitals in Cathedral.
Corsica	Musical festivals in Ajaccio, Bastia, St-Florent and Calenzana.
Guebwiller (Haut-Rhin)	Musical festival in Dominican church (first Saturday in month).

July

Annecy (Haute-Savoie)	Festival of Old Annecy.
Antibes (Alpes-Maritimes)	"Golden Rose" Song Festival.
Besse-en-Chandesse (Puy-de-Dôme)	Pilgrimage to Notre-Dame de Vassivière.
Bourgneuf-en-Retz (Loire-Atlantique)	Costume Festival.

Bourg-St-Maurice
(Savoie)
Edelweiss Festival.

Bricquebec
(Manche)
Festival of St Anne, with cavalcade.

Buis-les Baronnies
(Drôme)
Lime-Tree, Olive and Lavender Festival.

Doué-la-Fontaine
(Maine-et-Loire)
Rose Festival.

Fécamp
(Seine-Maritime)
Festival of the Sea.

Font-Romeu
(Pyrénées-Orientales)
Sardana Festival.

Fougerolles
(Haute-Saône)
Cherry Festival.

Fumay
(Ardennes)
Boatmen's Tournament.

Granville
(Manche)
Pilgrimage of seamen's guilds.

Hersin-Coupigny
(Pas-de-Calais)
Pageant of French Revolution.

Hyères
(Var)
Festival of St Mary Magdalene, Gardeners' Festival.

Le Ménitré
(Maine-et-Loire)
Festival of Traditional Headdresses.

Les Mazures
(Ardennes)
Bilberry Festival.

Martigues
(Bouches-du-Rhône)
Folk Festival.

Menton
(Alpes-Maritimes)
Torchlight procession.

Mont-de-Marsan
(Landes)
Festival of St Mary Magdalene.

Nyons
(Drôme)
Olive Festival.

Palavas
(Hérault)
Festival of the Sea.

Réalmont
(Tarn)
International Mineral and Fossil Fair.

St-Christophe-de-Jajolet
(Orne)
Motorists' pilgrimage.

St-Jean-de-Luz
(Pyrénées-Atlantiques)
Tunny Festival.

St Mandrier
(Var)
Fishermen's Festival, Santon Fair.

St-Malo-Paramé
(Ille-et-Vilaine)
Festival of Pinks.

St-Tropez
(Var)
Fishermen's Festival.

Ste-Eulalie
(Ardèche)
Violet Fair.

Saumur
(Maine-et-Loire)
Cavalry School tournament.

Toulon
(Var)
Santon Fair.

Val d'Isère
(Savoie)
Festival.

Vézelay
(Yonne)
Pilgrimage.

July–August

Aix-en-Provence
(Bouches-du-Rhône)
International Musical Festival.

Avignon
(Vaucluse)
Festival (drama, music).

Biarritz
(Pyrénées-Atlantiques)
Summer Festival; regattas.

Cannes
(Alpes-Maritimes)
Festival (drama, music).

Cherves
(Vienne)
Village Festival.

Collioure
(Pyrénées-Orientales)
Festival in château.

Colmar
(Haut-Rhin)
Music in Dominican cloister (Thursdays).

Hagetmau
(Landes)
Traditional festival.

Nice
(Alpes-Maritimes)
Flower Festival; International Summer Academy.

Orange
(Vaucluse)
Performances in Roman theatre.

Prades
(Pyrénées-Orientales)
Casals Festival in the abbey of St-Michel-de-Cuxa.

Sénanque
(Vaucluse)
Medieval music.

Sénones
(Vosges)
Changing of the Guard and Trooping of the Colour.

July–September

Burgundy
In many places tours through the illuminated vineyards.

Dax
(Landes)
Stilt races.

Paris
Summer Festival.

St-Jean-de-Luz
(Pyrénées-Atlantiques)
Folk festivals, bullfights, pelota tournaments.

Vichy
(Allier)
Folk Festival.

August

Aix-les-Bains
(Savoie)
Flower Festival.

Ajaccio
(Corsica)
Commemoration of Napoleon's birthday (15 August).

Annecy
(Haute-Savoie)
Lake Festival.

Antibes
(Alpes-Maritimes)
Concerts in château.

Arcachon
(Gironde)
Veteran Car Parade.

Ardèche
Festivals of folk art in many places.

Auxerre
(Yonne)
Firework display.

Bandol
(Var)
Fishermen's Festival.

Basque country
(Pyrénées-Atlantiques)
Basque sports contests in many places.

Bayonne
(Pyrénées-Atlantiques)
Traditional Folk Festival.

Beaulieu
(Alpes-Maritimes)
Torchlight procession.

Beuzec – Cap-Sizun
(Finistère)
Bilberry Festival.

Béziers
(Hérault)
Féria, bullfights, folk events.

Biarritz
(Pyrénées-Atlantiques)
"Night of Magic"; firework display.

Bourdeaux
(Drôme)
Historical parade.

Chamonix
(Haute-Savoie)
Mountain Guides' Festival.

Chaon
(Doubs)
Lake Festival.

Cheverny
(Loir-et-Cher)
Illuminations of château.

Clermont-Ferrand
(Puy-de-Dôme)
Bourrée (Country Dance) Festival.

Colmar
(Haut-Rhin)
Alsatian Wine Fair.

Confolens
(Charente)
International Folk Festival.

Coulanges-sur-Yonne
(Yonne)
Fishermen's Tournament.

Dax (Landes)	Traditional Folk Festival.
Dieppe (Seine-Maritime)	Folk Festival.
Digne (Alpes-de-Haute-Provence)	Lavender Festival.
Fréjus (Var)	Féria, Vintage Festival, bullfights, encierro.
Gap (Hautes-Alpes)	Summer Festival, with flower parade.
Gençay (Vienne)	Countryside Festival.
Gérardmer (Vosges)	Festival of Light on the lake (14 August).
Grasse (Alpes-Maritimes)	Jasmine Festival.
Guingamp (Côtes-du-Nord)	Festival of St Loup (St Lupus), with Breton folk dances.
La Baule (Loire-Atlantique)	Concours d'Elégance (cars).
La Font-Sainte (Cantal)	Pilgrimage and Shepherds' Festival.
Le Havre (Seine-Maritime)	Flower parade.
Lesches-en-Diois (Drôme)	Lavender Festival.
Lorient (Morbihan)	Celtic Bagpipe Festival.
Lorraine	Mirabelle Festivals in many places.
Maiche (Doubs)	Horsemen's Festival.
Maraye-en-Othe (Aube)	Cider Festival.
Marlenheim (Bas-Rhin)	"Ami Fritz" Folk Festival.
Menton (Alpes-Maritimes)	Lantern Parade.
Metz (Moselle)	Mirabelle Festival.
Mèze (Hérault)	Traditional Folk Festival.
Moncrabeau (Lot-et-Garonne)	Election of the King of Liars.
Peisey-Nancroix (Savoie)	Costume and Mountaineering Festival.
Peyrebrune (Aveyron)	Knights' Festival.
Pont-Aven (Finistère)	Broom Festival.
Pont-d'Ouilly (Calvados)	Pilgrimage of St Roch.
Rignac (Aveyron)	Horsemen's Festival.
Roquebrune – Cap-Martin (Alpes-Maritimes)	Votive procession.
St-Jean – Cap-Ferrat (Alpes-Maritimes)	Venetian Festival.
St-Palais (Pyrénées-Atlantiques)	Basque Sports Festival.
St-Raphaël (Var)	Sea Procession.
St-Rémy-de-Provence (Bouches-du-Rhône)	Provençal Costume Festival.
Séguret (Vaucluse)	Provençal Festival.
Sélestat (Bas-Rhin)	Flower parade.
Sète (Hérault)	Fishermen's Tournament, Sea Festival.
Southern Atlantic coast (Gironde, Landes, Pyrénées-Atlantiques)	Oyster and Sea Festivals in many places.
Tende (Alpes-Maritimes)	Traditional Folk Festival.
Thiézac (Cantal)	Pilgrimage to Notre-Dame de Consolation; torchlight procession.
Wasselonne (Bas-Rhin)	Parade of drum-majorettes (middle of month).

August–September

Digne (Alpes-de-Haute-Provence)	Lavender Market.
Haguenau (Bas-Rhin)	Hop Festival.

September

Bar-sur-Aube (Aube)	Champagne Fair.
Besse-en-Chandesse (Puy-de-Dôme)	Procession from Notre-Dame de Vassivière.
Bordeaux and surrounding area (Gironde)	Vintage Festivals.
Cannes (Alpes-Maritimes)	International Amateur Film Festival.

September–October

Chartres (Eure-et-Loir)	"Musical Saturdays of Chartres".
La Ciotat (Bouches-du-Rhône)	Michelmas Fair, Fishermen's Festival.
Lyons (Rhône)	International Puppet Festival.
Mont St-Michel (Manche)	Autumn pilgrimage.
Nîmes (Gard)	Vintage Festival, bullfights.
Ribeauvillé (Haut-Rhin)	"Strolling Musicians' Day".
St-Jean-de-Luz, Ciboure, Ascain, Bayonne, Biarritz, Anglet (Pyrénées-Atlantiques)	"Musical September".

October

Espelette (Pyrénées-Atlantiques)	Spice Festival.
Montigny-en-Ostrevent (Nord)	Chrysanthemum Festival.
Nogentel (Aisne)	Flower Festival.
Paris	Scrap-Iron and Ham Markets (beginning of month); Vintage Festival, Montmartre (beginning of month).

November

Corsica	International car race.
Nuits-St-Georges, Beaune, Meursault (Côte-d'Or)	"Les Trois Glorieuses" (wine fair).
Sauzé-Vaussais (Deux-Sèvres)	Chestnut Fair.
Toulon – Solliès-Ville (Var)	Santon Fair.

November–December

Marseilles (Bouches-du-Rhône)	Santon Fair.

December

Espinal (Vosges)	Festival of St Nicholas.
Lyons (Rhône)	Pontifical high mass (25 December).
Metz-Thionville (Moselle)	St Nicholas Procession (6 December).
Nancy (Meurthe-et-Moselle)	St Nicholas Procession (3 December).
St-Bauzille-de-Putois (Hérault)	Midnight mass in Grotte des Demoiselles (24 December).
Strasbourg (Bas-Rhin)	Christmas Fair.

The *Tour de France*, the famous cycle race round France, is run in June–July. – In summer and autumn there are wine and food fairs, regattas and water sports tournaments, etc., in many places all over France.

On Easter Monday, Whit Monday, 14 July (the French National Day, commemorating the capture of the Bastille in 1789) and 15 August (Assumption) there are celebrations of various kinds all over France, with processions, flower parades, firework displays, etc. – On Christmas Eve there are midnight masses in many places, with traditional local customs.

Further information can be obtained from the French Government Tourist Office (see below under *Information*) and local Offices de Tourisme or Syndicats d'Initiative.

Public Holidays and Festivals

1 January	New Year
Easter Monday	
1 May	Labour Day
Ascension	
Whit Monday	
14 July	National Day (capture of Bastille, 1789)
15 August	Assumption
1 November	All Saints
11 November	Armistice Day 1918
25 December	Christmas Day

In Alsace *Good Friday* and *26 December* are also celebrated.

Shopping and Souvenirs

A wide range of beautiful hand-made articles are produced in France, including pottery (Normandy, Provence, etc.), articles made of wood (particularly olive wood), lace from Brittany and basket-work. Charming "bygones" and antiques are to be found in many places. – Paris is famous for its fashion shops, bookshops, record shops and antique-dealers.

Perfumes and herb essences (lavender, etc.) are a speciality of Provence and particularly of the town of Grasse – although the best known brands can of course be bought all over the country.

Many of France's culinary specialties can be had tinned or otherwise preserved, and make very acceptable gifts for gourmet friends. In buying wine or spirits to take home it is necessary to bear in mind the maximum quantities which can be taken in duty-free. If you want to take home larger quantities, paying duty, it is as well to seek the advice of a wine-producing establishment (either a *cave coopérative* or a private wine-grower).

Information

French Government Tourist Office

Head Office (Secrétariat d'Etat au Tourisme)
8 Avenue de l'Opera,
F-75041 **Paris**;
tel. (1) 7 66 51 35.

United Kingdom
178 Piccadilly,
London W1V 0AL;
tel. (01) 499 6911.

United States of America
610 Fifth Avenue,
New York, NYC 10021.

9401 Wilshire Boulevard,
Beverly Hills, CA 90112.

645 N. Michigan Avenue,
Suite 430,
Chicago, IL 60601.

323 Geary Street,
San Francisco CA 94012.

Canada
372 Bay Street,
Suite 610,
Toronto, Ont. M5H 2W9.

1940 Sherbrooke Street West,
Montreal, Que. H3H 2W9.

Within France tourist information can be obtained from regional and departmental tourism committees (*Comités régionaux de Tourisme, Comités départementaux de Tourisme*) and from the **Offices de Tourisme** and *Syndicats* *d'Initiative* to be found in almost every town.

Touring-Club de France (*TCF*)
Head Office
65 Avenue de la Grande-Armée,
F-75782 **Paris**;
tel. (1) 5 02 14 50.

The TCF has branch offices in the larger French towns.

Automobile-Club de France (*ACF*),
6–8 Place de la Concorde,
F-75008 **Paris**;
tel. (1) 2 65 34 70.

Diplomatic and Consular Offices in France

United Kingdom

Embassy
35 rue du Faubourg St-Honoré,
F-75008 **Paris**;
tel. (1) 2 66 91 42,
consular section 2 60 33 06.

Consulates-General
15 Cours de Verdun,
F-33081 **Bordeaux**;
tel. (56) 52 28 35–36,
52 89 51 and 52 48 86.

11 Square Dutilleul,
F-59800 **Lille**;
tel. (20) 52 87 90.

24 rue Childebert,
F-69288 **Lyon**;
tel. (78) 37 59 67
and 42 46 49.

24 Avenue du Prado,
F-13006 **Marseille**;
tel. (91) 53 43 32.

105–109 rue du Faubourg St-Honoré,
F-75008 **Paris**;
tel. (1) 2 66 91 42.

10 rue du Général-de-Castelnau,
F-67001 **Strasbourg**;
tel. (88) 36 64 91–93.

There are also a *consulate* at Le Havre, *vice-consulates* at Ajaccio, Bayonne, Boulogne, Calais, Cherbourg, Dunkirk, Epernay, Metz and Nantes, and an honorary consul at Perpignan.

United States of America

Embassy
2 Avenue Gabriel,
F-75008 **Paris**;
tel. (1) 2 96 12 02 and 2 61 80 75.

Consulates-General
4 rue Esprit-des-Lois,
F-33000 **Bordeaux**;
tel. (56) 65 95.

72 rue Gén.-Sarrail,
F-69006 **Lyon**;
tel. (78) 24 68 49.

9 rue Armeny,
F-13006 **Marseille**;
tel. (91) 54 92 00.

2 Avenue Gabriel,
F-75008 **Paris**;
tel. (1) 2 96 12 02 and 2 61 80 75
(consular section of Embassy).

2 rue St-Florentin,
F-75001 **Paris**;
tel. (1) 2 96 12 02 and 2 61 80 75
(visas section of Embassy).

15 Avenue d'Alsace,
F-67000 **Strasbourg**;
tel. (88) 35 31 04.

There is also a *consulate* at Nice.

Canada

Embassy
35 Avenue Montaigne,
F-75008 **Paris**;
tel. (1) 2 25 99 55.

Consular Section
4 rue Ventadour,
F-75001 **Paris**;
tel. (1) 0 73 15 83.

Consulates-General
Croix du Mail,
Rue Claude-Bonnier,
F-33080 **Bordeaux**;
tel. (56) 96 15 61.

24 Avenue du Prado,
F-13006 **Marseille**;
tel. (91) 37 19 37 and 37 19 40.

10 Place du Temple-Neuf,
F-67007 **Strasbourg**;
tel. (88) 32 65 96.

Airlines

Air France
158 New Bond Street,
London W1Y 0AY;
tel. (01) 499 9511 and 499 8611.

666 Fifth Avenue,
New York, N.Y. 10019.

1 Place Ville-Marie,
Suite 3321,
Montreal H3B 3N4, P.Q.

1 Square Max-Hymans,
F-75741 **Paris**;
tel. (1) 2 73 41 41.

Offices at all French airports.

British Airways
91 Avenue des Champs-Elysées,
F-75008 **Paris**;
tel. (1) 7 78 14 14.

Hôtel Frantel,
Rue Georges-Bonnac, **Bordeaux**;
tel. (56) 96 80 09.

c/o Air France,
8–10 rue Jean-Roisin, **Lille**;
tel. (20) 57 67 90.

3 rue Victor-Hugo, **Lyon**;
tel. (78) 37 74 61.

41 Canebière, **Marseille**;
tel. (91) 39 77 10.

Aéroport **Nice/Côte d'Azur**;
tel. (93) 83 19 61.

British Caledonian
3 rue de la Paix,
F-75002 **Paris**;
tel. (1) 2 61 50 21.

Pan Am
1 rue Scribe,
F-75009 **Paris**;
tel. (1) 2 66 45 45.

TWA
101 Avenue des Champs-Elysées,
F-75008 **Paris**;
tel. (1) 7 20 54 33.

Air Canada
39 Boulevard de Vaugirard,
F-75015 **Paris**;
tel. (1) 2 73 84 00.

French Railways (*SNCF*)

179 Piccadilly,
London W1V 0BA;
tel. (01) 493 4451–2.

610 Fifth Avenue,
New York, NY 10020;
tel. (212) 582 2110.

2121 Ponce de Leon Boulevard,
Coral Gables, Florida 33134;
tel. (305) 445 8648.

11 East Adams Street,
Chicago, Illinois 60603;
tel. (312) 427 8691.

9465 Wilshire Boulevard,
Beverly Hills, California 90212;
tel. (213) 272 7967.

323 Geary Street,
San Francisco, California 94102;
tel. (415) 982 1993.

1500 Stanley Street,
Montreal H3A 1R3, P.Q.;
tel. (514) 288 8255–6.

Information about the many British and Commonwealth **military cemeteries** of the two world wars in France can be obtained from the *Commonwealth War Graves Commission*, 2 Marlow Road, Maidenhead, Berks. SL6 7DX, tel. 0628 34221. The Commission publishes maps showing the location of cemeteries in northern France and will help to trace particular graves. Help and advice can also be obtained from the Commission's office in France – Place du Maréchal-Foch, F-62012 Arras, tel. (21) 23 03 24.

Radio Messages for tourists

In cases of great emergency the BBC (tel. 01–580 4468) will accept messages, from near relations only. These are broadcast in French on Radio France Inter (long wave, 1829 metres).

International Telephone Dialling Codes

From the United Kingdom to France
  010 33
From the United States to France
  011 33
From Canada to France   011 33

From France to the United Kingdom
  19 44
From France to the United States
  19 1
From France to Canada   19 1

When dialling from France the zero prefixed to the local dialling code should be omitted.

Emergency Calls

Emergency telephone boxes giving direct connections with the police are stationed at intervals along all motorways and some *routes nationales*.

In Paris and the larger towns the *Police de Secours* can be called by dialling 17. In country areas the local gendarmerie should be called. On the procedure to be followed in the event of an accident, see p. 267.

Road Conditions Report
(Inter Service Route), 24-hour service: Paris (1) 8 58 33 33.
Outside Paris: Paris region (1) 8 57 20 83; Bordeaux (56) 44 23 23; Lille (20) 52 22 44; Lyons (78) 54 33 33; Marseilles (91) 47 20 20; Metz (87) 75 22 24; Rennes (99) 50 73 93.

Abbeville 206
Abriès 115
Agde 234
Agen 117
Ahun 134
Aigoual 90
Aigues-Mortes 215
Aiguille à Bochard 92
Aiguille du Goûter 92
Aiguille du Midi 92
Aiguilles 115
Aiguilles Rouges 92
Aiguines 221
Ailefroide 115
Ain 128, 131
Aix, Ile d' 213
Aix-en-Provence **52**
Aix-les-Bains 238
Ajaccio **53**
Albi **54**
Alençon 165
Aleth 238
Algajola 104
Allier 254
Aloxe-Corton 85
Alpe d'Huez 113
Alpilles 215
Alsace **55**
Alsace-Lorraine 141
Alsace, Route du Vin d'
56
Altkirch 58
Alzon 205
Ambazac 134
Amboise 137
Amélie-les-Bains 223
Amiens **61**
Ammerschwihr 58
Ancenis 136
Ancy-le-France 84
Les Andelys 165
Andlau 58
Andorra **62**
Andorra la Vella 63
Anduze 90
Anet 124, 165
Angers **63**
Anglet 111
Angoulême 210
Anjou 63, **64**, 136
Anjou, Route du Vin d'
64
Annecy 239
Anthéor 106
Antibes 109
Apothicairerie, Grotte de
l' 79
Apremont 96
Aquitania 117
Arausio Secundanorum
169
Arbois 128, 129, 131
Arcachon 76, 105
Arcachon, Bassin d' 105
Arcais, 212
Arc-et-Senans 129
Ardèche 90, 171
Argelès-Gazost 223
Argelès-sur-Mer 112,
223
Argentan 165
Argentat 134
Argentière 91
Argenton 134
Argentoratum 241

Argoet 77
Argonne Forest 96
Ariège 222, 226
Aries **65**
Aries-sur-Tech 223
Armagnac 117
Armentières 206
Armor 77
Arques 101
Arras 206
Arromanches-les-Bains
165
Ars 214
Artois 206
Arve 91
Aubisque 222
Aubusson 134
Auch 117
Audincourt 129
Augustobona 249
Augustonemetum 98
Aulnay 210
Aulus-les-Bains 223
Aunis 229
Aurelianum 171
Aurignac 223
Aurillac 68
Auron 76
Autun 83, 84
Auvergne **67**, 97, 254
Auvers-sur-Oise 126
Auxerre 84
Auxerrois 82
Auxois 83
Avaricum 76
Aven Armand 118
Aven d'Orgnac 171
Avenio 69
Avignon **69**
Avoine-Chinon 137
Avranches 165
Ax-les-Thermes 223
Ax-1400 223
Ax-2300 223
Azay-le-Rideau 138

Babaou, Col de 107
Bagacum 206
Bagnères-de-Bigorre
223
Bagnères-de-Luchon
223
Bagneux 64
Bagnoles de l'Orne 165
Bains-les-Bains 142
Baixas 234
Balagne 104
Balagne Déserte 104
Balcons de la Mescia
221
Ballon d'Alsace 143,
256
Ballon, Lac du 256
Banyuls-sur-Mer 112
Barbizon 126
Bar-le-Duc 96
Barr 58
Barrage de l'Aigle 134
Barrage du Chastang
134
Barrage du Sablier 134
Bas-Armagnac 117
Basque coast 111
Bassac 211
Basses-Pyrénées 222

Bastia **71**
Baugé 64
La Baule 79
La-Baule-les-Pins 79
Baume, Cirque de
(Jura) 131
Baume-les-Dames 128,
129
Baume-les-Messieurs
129
Baumes, Cirque des
(Tarn) 118
Les Baux 67, 215
Bavay 206
Bavella, Col de 103
Bayeux 165
Bayonne 105, 111
Béarn 117
Beaucaire 215
Beauce 96
Beaugency 138
Beaulieu-lès-Loches
140
Beaulieu-sur-Dordogne
134
Beaune 84
Beauvais 122
Bélesta 101
Belfort **72**
Belgodere 104
Bellac 134
Bellegarde 131
Belle-Ile 78, 79
Bellevue (nr Paris) 202
Belvédère des Terrasses
119
Bénac 224
Bergerac 204
Bergues 206
Besançon **72**, 131
Bétharram, Grottes de
146
Betschdorf 57
Beynac-et-Cazenac 204
Béziers 234
Biarritz **73**
Bidart 111
Bienne 128
Billancourt 202
Bisanz 72
Biscay, Bay of 73
Bitche 142
Blérancourt 126
Blériot Plage 207
Blésois 136
Le Bleymard 90
Blois 138
Bloss 257
Bocage Normand 164
Bois de la Chaize 214
Bois de Meudon 202
Bois de Vincennes 126
Bois du Roi 82
Bonaguil 204
Bonhomme, Col du 257
Bonifacio 103
Bonneval 126
Bordeaux **74**
Bort-les-Orgues 69, 134
Les Bossons 91, 92
Bouchet, Lac du 222
Boulogne (nr Paris) 202
Boulogne-sur-Mer 206
La Bourboule 68
Bourganeuf 134

Bourg d'Oisans 113
Bourg-en-Bresse 84
Bourges **76**
Le Bourget 126
Bourget, Lac du 238
Bourgogne **82**
Bourne, Gorges de la
250
Bournillon, Grotte du
250
Bouxwiller 57
Brando 104
Brantôme 204
Brèche de Roland 224
Bréhat, Ile de 79
Bresse 83
La Bresse 142
Brest 79
Breteuil 124
Brévent 92
Brézé, Château de 64
Briançon 114
Brie-Comte-Robert 127
Brienne-le-Château 96
Brissac 64, 139
Brittany **77**, 228
Brive-la-Gaillarde 134
Brochon 85
Brotonne Forest 169
Brotonne Nature Park
169
Brou 84
Brouage 210
Bruyères 256
Burgundy **82**
Bussang 256
La Bussière 140

Cabourg 166
Cadillac 76
Cadouin 204
Caen **86**
Cagnes-sur-Mer 109
Cahors 145
Calacuccia 103
Calais 207
Calanche 104
Calanques 216
Calvados 86
Calvi 104
Camaret 80
Camargue 65, 66, 216
Cambo-les-Bains 223
Cambrai 207
Canadel, Col du 107
Canal du Midi 246
Canari 104
Canche 208
Canet-Plage 234
Le Canigou 222
Canillo 63
Cannes **87**
Cap Blanc-Nez 207
Capbreton 105
Cap Corse 104
Cap d'Agde 234
Cap d'Antibes 88, 109
Cap de la Chèvre 80
Cap de la Hague 166
Cap de la Parata 54
Cap Fréhel 80
Cap Gris-Nez 207
Carcassonne **89**
Carnac 78, 79
Carnon 234

Carpentras 217
Carteret 166
Cascade de la Sarennes 114
Cassis 216
Castellane 220, 221
Castellar 111
Castello della Rocca 103
Casteinaudary 90
Castrum Claremunte 98
Le Cateau 207
Caudebec-en-Caux 169
Causse Méjean 118
Causses 118
Cauterets 224
Cavalaire-sur-Mer 107
Cavalière 107
Celé 144
Centuri 104
Cerbère 112
Céret 224
Cévennes **90**
Cévennes, Corniche des 90
Ceyssat, Col de 68
Châalis 123
Chaillexon, Lac de 131
La Chaise-Dieux 69
Chalet de la Floriaz 92
Chalet Reynard 218
Chalonnes 64
Châlons-sur-Marne 96
Chalon-sur-Saône 82
Chambéry 239
Chambon reservoir 113
Chambon-sur-Voueize 134
Chambord 139
Chamet, Lac du 134
Chamonix **90**
Chamonix-Mont-Blanc 91
Champagne **92**, 249
Champagne humide 95
Champagne, Route du 95
Champagne sèche 95
Champagnole 128
Champ du Feu 256
Champlieu 126
Champs 124
Chamrousse 114
Chamrousse, Croix de 114
Chaniers 211
Channel, English 86, 157, 207
Chantilly 124
Chapeau 92
Charente **210**, 212
Charentes **210**
Charente Maritime 210
La Charité-sur-Loire 84
Charlieu 84
Les Charmettes 239
Charollais 83
Chartres **96**
Chartreuse 121
Chartreuse de la Verne 107
Château d'Alleuze 69
Château d'Arlay 130
Château de Bois-Sur-Amé 77

Château de Bonaguil 145
Château de Brézé 64
Château de Charance 114
Château de Dinan 80
Château de Labrède 211
Château de Meillant 77
Château de Plessis-Bourré 64
Château des Rochers 82
Château des Termes 101
Château de Tocqueville 165
Château d'If 152
Château d'Oléron 214
Châteaudun 124
Château du Connétable de Lesdiguières 115
Château du Pin 130
Château-Landon 126
Château de Malmaison 203
Château-Margaux 76
Châteauneuf-du-Pape 217
Châteauneuf-sur-Charente 211
Château Queyras 115
Château St-Martin 101
Château-Thierry 96, 126
Châtel-Guyon 68
Châtre 211
Chaumont-sur-Loire 139
Chauvigny 211
Chemin des Dames 96
Chenonceaux 139
Chenove 85
Cher 76, 136, 139
Cherbourg 166
Cheverny 139
Chinon 139
Choranche, Grottes de 250
Ciboure 112
Cidre, Route du 169
Cimiez 162
Circuit Bugatti 150
Cirque de Baume (Jura) 131
Cirque de Consolation 131
Cirque de Gavarnie 224
Cirque de Ladoye 131
Cirque de Vaumale 221
Cirque des Baumes (Tarn) 118
Cirque du Fer à Cheval 131
Clair-Mont 98
Clermont-Ferrand **97**
Cléron 131
Cléry-St-André 140
Clos-Lucé 137
Cluny 83, 85
Cluse-et-Mijoux 131
Cognac 211
Col d'Aubisque 222
Col de Babaou 107
Col de Bavella 103
Col de Bussang 256
Col de Ceyssat 68
Col de Finiels 90
Col de la Croix 104

Col de la Faucille 128, 129, 130, 131
Col de la Machine 250
Col de la Schlucht 142, 256, 257
Col de la Serra 104
Col de Lavezzo 104
Col de l'Iseran 114
Col de Palmarella 104
Col de Perthus 112
Col de Puymorens 222
Col de Vergio 103
Col de Vizzavona 103
Col d'Illoire 221
Col du Bonhomme 257
Col du Canadel 107
Col du Donon 256
Col du Fout 92
Col du Galibier 114
Col du Tourmalet 222, 225
Col du Géant 92
Collioure 112
Colmar **98**
Colomby de Gex 129
Col Sainte-Lucie 104
Combarelles, Grotte de 204
Combe Laval 250
Compiègne 124
Comps 221
Concarneau 80
Condom 117
Conflans-Ste-Honorine 126
Confolens 211
Conques 69, 144
Consolation, Cirque de 131
Les Corbières **101**
Cordes 55
Cordouan 211
Corniche Basque 112
Corniche d'Aleth 238
Corniche de Goumois 131
Corniche de l'Esterel 108
Corniche des Cévennes 90
Corniche des Maures 107
Corniche d'Or 108
Corniche Sublime 221
Cornouaille 80
Corps 114
Corrèze 135
Corsica **102**
Corte 103
Côte 2000 250
Côte d'Argent **105**, 117
Côte d'Azur **105**
Côte de Granit Rose 77
Côte d'Emeraude 77, 80
Côte de Jade 77
Côte d'Or 82, 84, 85, 115
Côte des Basques **111**
Côte Fleurie 166
Contentin 166
Côte Sablonneuse 233
Côte Sauvage 79, 81
Côte Vermeille **112**
Coucy-le-Château 124

Cougnac, Grottes de 204
Coulon 211, 218
Courances 124
Coutances 166
Crépy-en-Valois 126
Crêtes, Route des 257
Crêt de Chalame 129
Creuse 134
Le Creusot 82
Creux de Revigny 131
Croix, Col de la 104
Croix de Chamrousse 114
Croix de la Flégère 92
Croix-Valmer 107
Cro-Magnon 204
Crozon peninsula 80
Cuisance 131
Cunault 64, 140

Dabo 142
Dargilan, Grotte de 119
Dambach-la-Ville 58
Dauphiné **122**, 119, 238
Deauville 166
Dessoubre 131
Détroits 118
Dibio 115
Dieppe 166
Dijon **115**
Dijonnais 83
Dinan 80
Dinard 80
Dives 164
Divonne-les-Bains 129
Dole 129, 131
Doller 257
Dôme des Petites Rousses 113
Domme 204
Domrémy-la-Pucelle 142
Le Donon 256
Dordogne 134
Douai 207
Douarnenez 80
Douaumont 96
Doubs 72, 128, 131
Doubs gorges 131
Doué 64
Drei Exen 58
Dreux 126
Dunkirk 207
Durance 115, 215
Duravel 145
Durocortorum 226

Eastern Pyrenees 222
Eaux-Bonnes, Les 225
Les Eaux-Chaudes 225
Eauze 117
Eguisheim 58
Eguzon reservoir 134
Elne 112, 235
El Serrat 63
Embrun 114
Encamp 63
Enghien-les-Bains 126
Engolasters, Lac d' 63
Enserune, Oppidum d' 235
Entraygues-sur-Truyère 144

Entrèves 92
Eparges 96
Epernay 95
Epinal 142
L'Epine 96
Erbalunga 104
Erdre 160
Ermenonville 126
Los Escaldes 63
Espalion 144
Estaing 143, 144
Esterel, Massif de l' 108
Etampes 127
Etang de Vaccarès 67, 217
Etretat 166
Eure 96, 174
Euskaldunak 111
Evaux-les-Bains 134
Evian-les-Bains 239
Evreux 167
Excenevex 240
Les Eyzies-de-Tayac 204
Eze 109, 111
Eze-Bord-de-Mer 110
Eze-Village 109, 111

Falaise 167, 169
Falaises des Cavaliers 221
Faron 246
Faucille, Col de la 128, 129, 130, 131
Faux-la-Montagne, Lac de 134
Faverney 129
Fécamp 167
Felletin 135
Fenioux 211
Fer à Cheval, Cirque du 131
Ferney-Voltaire 129
Ferrette 256
La Ferté-Milton 124
Figeac 144
Finiels, Col de 90
Flanders 132, 206
Flégère 92
Flers-de-l'Orne 169
Fleurance 117
Florac 90, 118
Foix 224
Fondation Maeght 109
Fontainebleau 124
Fontaine-de-Vaucluse 217
Fontenay 85
Fontevrault 64
Fontfroide 101, 236
Font-de-Gaume, Grotte de 204
Font-Romeu 224
Forêt de l'Ospedale 103
Fougères 81
Fout, Col du 92
Francardo 103
Franche-Comté 72, 127, 128
Fréjus 108
French Alps 238
French Jura 127
French Riviera 105
Fresselines 134
Fromage, Route du 59

Galibier, Col du 114
Gallia Narbonensis 215
Gap 114
Garde-Epée 211
La Garette 212
Garonne 55, 74, 117, 246
Gartempe 212, 213
Gascony 117
Gascony, Gulf of 117
Gaube, Lac de 224
Gavarnie 224
Gavarnie, Cirque de 224
Gave d'Aspe 225
Gave de Pau 225
Gave d'Ossau 225
Geant, Col du 92
Geneva, Lake 238, 239, 240
Génissiat Dam 129
Gennes 64
Gérardmer 142
Gerbier de Jonc 136
Gevrey-Chambertin 83, 85
Gex 130
Ghisonaccia 103
Gien 140
Giens 136
Giersberg 60
Ginès 217
Gironde 210
Gisors 125
Glacier de Bionnassay 92
Glacier des Bossons 92
Glanum 67, 219
Golinhac Dam 143
Gorbio 111
Gordes 217
Gorges de la Bourne 250
Gorges de la Jonte 118, 119
Gorges de l'Ardèche 171
Gorges de la Restonica 103
Gorges de la Truyère 143
Gorges du Lot 143
Gorges du Tarn 118
Goulet, Mont 143
Gourdon 111, 204
Gourette 225
Grand Ballon 256, 258
Grand Bré (Is.) 237
Grand Colombier 130
Grande Chartreuse 121
Grande Corniche 109
Grand Canyon du Verdon 220
La Grande Motte (Roussillon) 234
Grande Motte (Savoy) 240
Grand Rhône 217
Grands Goulets 250
Grands Sables 79
Granville 168
Grasse 108
Gratianopolis 119
Le Grau-du-Roi 215
La Grave 114
Grenoble 119
Grignan 218

Grimaud 107
Grisy-Suisnes 127
Gros Rognon 92
Grotte de Combarelles 204
Grotte de Dargilan 119
Grotte de Font-de-Gaume 204
Grotte de la Mouthe 204
Grotte de l'Apothicairerie 79
Grotte de Lascaux 205
Grotte de Massabielle 146
Grotte de Médous 223
Grotte de Naours 208
Grotte de Niaux 224
Grotte des Sarrazins 146
Grotte du Bournillon 250
Grotte du Loup 146
Grotte du Portel 224
Grotte du Roy 146
Grottes de Bétharram 146
Grottes de Cougnac 204
Grottes de Choranche 250
Grottes des Eyzies 204
Gruissan 233, 234
Guebwiller 58
Guéthary 111
Guignes-Rabutin 127
Guil 115
Guillestre 115
Guimiliau 81
Guyenne 117

Haguenau 57
Hartmannswillerkopf 256, 258
Hatten 57
Hattonchâtel 96
Haut-Anjou 64
Hautecombe Abbey 239
Hautes-Pyrénées 222
Haut-Kœnigsbourg 256
Hautvillers 95
Le Havre 121
L'Haÿ-les-Roses 127
Hendaye 111, 112
Hérault 90, 247
High Pyrenees 222
Hoffen 57
Hohneck 256
Hoh-Rappoltstein 60
Le Hohwald 257
Hondschoote 206
Honfleur 168
Les Hôpiteaux-Neufs 128
Hortillonages 62
Hossegor 105
Les Houches 91
Huisne 149
Hunspach 57
Hyères 107
Hyères, Iles d' 107

Ile aux Oiseaux 105
Ile d'Aix 213
Ile de Bréhat 79
Ile de France 122
Ile de Porquerolles 107

Ile de Port-Cros 107
Ile du Levant 107
Ile Grosse 112
Ile-Rousse 104
Iles d'Hyères 107
Iles de Lérins 88
Ill 59, 241, 254
Ille 228
Illoire, Col d' 221
Indre 136, 148
Iraty Forest 226
Iseran, Col de l' 114
Isle 205
L'Isle-sur-le-Doubs 131
Isturits 226

Jade Coast 77, 210, 212
Jarnac 211
La Jonelière 160
Jonte, Gorges de la 118, 119
Josselin 81
Jouarre 123
Jougne 128
Joux 128, 130
Juan-les-Pins 88, 109
Jumièges 168
Jura 127

Kaysersberg 58
Kercado 79
Kerlescan 79
Kermario 79
Kientzheim 59
Klein-Hohneck 257

Labouiche 224
Lac d'Annecy 239
Lac de Chaillexon 131
Lac de Faux-la-Montagne 134
Lac de Gaube 224
Lac de Gérardmer 142
Lac de la Lauch 257
Lac de Montriond 240
Lac de Nantua 130
Lac d'Engolasters 63
Lac de Tignes 240
Lac de Vassivière 133, 134
Lac de Viaman 134
Lac du Ballon 256
Lac du Bouchet 222
Lac du Bourget 238
Lac du Chamet 134
Ladoye, Cirque de 131
Laffrey lakes 114
Lagrasse 101
Landes 117
Langeais 140
Langres 96
Languedoc 246
Languedoc-Roussillon 232
Laon 95, 123
Larchant 127
Larvotto 157
Lascaux, Grotte de 205
Lauch, Lac de la 257
Lautenbach 58
Lauter 57
Le Lavandou 107
Lavelanet 101
Lavezzo, Col de 104
Layon 64

Lectoure 117
Leiterswiller 57
Léoncei 250
Lérins, Iles de 88
Levant, Ile du 107
Lichères 211
Ligugé 211
Lille **131**
Limagne 97
Limoges **132**
Limonum 209
Limousin **133**
Le Lion d'Angers 64
Lisieux 168
Lison 131
Littoral du Languedoc-
    Roussillon 233
Loches 140
Locmariaquer 79
Loir 64, 136
Loire 64, 77, 82, 136,
    159, 171
Loire châteaux 136
Loire valley **136**
Longpont 123
Lons-le-Saunier 130,
    131
Lorraine **141**
Lot 143
Lot, Gorges du 143
Lot valley **143**
Loubens 224
Loudun 212
Loue 128, 131
Loup, Grotte du 146
Lourdes **145**
Lower Normandy 164
Lower Pyrenees 222
Luçon 212
Lugdunum 147
Lugdunum Convenarum
    226
Lunéville 142
Lusignan 212
Lutetia Parisiorum 176
Luz-St-Sauveur 225
Lyons **146**
Lys plateau 224

Macinaggio 104
Mâcon 82
Maillezais 212
Maine 63
Maintenon 125
Maisons-Laffitte 125
La Malène 118
Malmaison 125
Malpasset Dam 108
Le Mans **149**
Mantes-la-Jolie 127
Le Marais 125
Marais Poitevin 210,
    212
Marèges 134
Marine de Porto 104
Markstein 257, 258
Marly-le-Roy 127
Marmoutier (Alsace) 57
Marmoutier (Touraine)
    248
Marne 95, 96, 175
Marseilles **150**
Masevaux 257
Massabielle, Grotte de
    146

Massalia 150
Massif Central 55, 67,
    90, 133, 143
Massif de Chamrousse
    114
Massif de l'Esterel 108
Massif des Maures 107
Massilia 150
Matésine plateau 114
Maures, Corniche des
    107
Maures, Massif des 107
Maury 101
Mayenne 64
Mazamet 90
Médous, Grotte de 223
Megève 238, 239
Meije 114
Melie 212
Mende 118, 144
Le Ménec 79
Menton 110
Mercus 224
Mer de Glace 92
Metis 153
Metz **153**
Meudon 127, 202
Meursault 85
Meurthe 158
Meuse
Meymac 135
Meyrueis 90
Midi, Canal du 246
Mijoux 128, 131
Millau 90, 119
Les Milles 53
Millevaches Plateau 134
Mimizan 105
Mimizan-Plage 105
Mirande 118
Moine de la Vallée 131
La Molard 92
La Molaz 92
Molitg-les-Bains 225
Molsheim 59
Monaco **154**
Monaco-Ville 155
Le Moncel 123
Moneghetti 156
La Mongie 225
Mont Aigoual 90
Montagne de Roule 166
Montagne Noire 90
Montagnes Noires 81
Montagne St-Michel 79
Montanges 131
Montbéliard 128, 130,
    131
Montbenoît 130
Mont Bessou 135
Mont Blanc 92, 238
Mont Blanc Tunnel 92,
    238
Mont Charance 114
Mont Chevalier 88
Mont-de-Marsan 117
Mont-Dore 68
Monte Carlo 156
Monte Cinto 102, 103
Montélimar 218
Montenvers 92
Monte Rotondo 103
Monte Salario 54
Montesquiou 117
Monte Stello 104

Monte Viso 115
Mont Faron 246
Montferrand 98
Mont-Genèvre 114
Mont Goulet 143
Montignac 205
Mont l'Incudine 103
Mont-Louis 225
Mont Lozère 90, 118
Montmajour 67, 218
Montmorency 127
Montmorillon 212
Montpellier 235
Montpellier-le-Vieux
    119
Mont-Rond 129, 130
Montreuil-Bellay 64
Montreuil-sur-Mer 207
Mont Revard 238
Montriond, Lac de 240
Monts d'Arrée 79, 81
Mont-de-Marsan 117
Monts de Monédières
    135
Monts Dômes 97
Monts Dore 68
Monts du Beaujolais 82
Monts du Cantal 68
Monts du Morvan 85
Montségur 101
Montsoreau 65
Mont Ste-Odile 59, 257
Mont-St-Michel **157**
Mont Ventoux 218
Mont Veyrier 239
Mont Vinaigre 108
Morez 130
Morgat 80
Morienval 123
Morteau 131
Morvan 82, 85
Morzine-Avoriaz 240
Moselle 142, 153
Moselotte 142
Moselle, source 256
Moucherotte 250
Moulin de Daudet 218
Moustiers-Ste-Marie
    221
Moustoir 79
Mouthe 131
Mouthe, Grotte de la
    204
Mouthier 131
Moyenne Corniche 109
Mozac 98
Mulaz 131
Mulhouse 59
Munster 59
Munster Vallée de 59
Murat 68
Murbach 58

Nancy **158**
Nangis 127
Nantes 136, **159**
Nantua 128, 130
Napoule, Bay 87
Narbonne 235
Narbonne-Plage 236
Naours, Grotte de 208
Nebbio 104
Nemessos 98
Neuf-Brisach 59

Neufchâteau 142
Nevers 82, 85
Nez de Jobourg 166
Niaux, Grotte de 224
Nicaea 162
Nice **161**
Nid d'Aigle 92
Nideck 59
Niederbronn-les-Bains
    57
Niederhaslach 59
Nîmes **162**
Niort 212
Nivelle 112
Nivernais 82, 83
Noirmoutier 213
Noirmoutier-ne-l'Ile 214
Nonza 104
Normandie-Maine
    Nature Park 169
Normandy 164
Norman Switzerland
    169
Notre-Dame de
    Consolation 131
Notre-Dame-de-la-
    Salette 115
Notre-Dame-du-Haut
    131
Nouaillé-Maupertuis
    212
Nouailles 131
Noyon 123, 207
Nozeroy 130, 131
Nuits-St-Georges 83, 85

Obernai 59
Oberroedern 57
Oberseebach 57
Odeillo 224
Oiron 212
Oisans 114
Oléron (Is.) 214
Olmeto 103
Oloron-Ste-Marie 225
Oppidum d'Ensérune
    235
Oradour-sur-Glane 135
Orange **169**
Orbiquet 168
Ordino 63
Oréac'h 81
Orgnac 171
Orléanais 136
Orléans **171**
Ornans 130
Orne 86, 164, 169
Orthez 225
Ossau, Vallée d' 222
Ouche 144
Ouessant (Is.) 81
Ouhans 131
Ourscamp 123, 207
Ouvèze 220
Oxocelhaya 226

Le **P**alais 79
La Pallice 231
Palmarella, Col de 104
La Palud 92, 221
Paramé 80
Paray-le-Monial 85
Parc de St-Cloud 202
Paris **172**

Paris Basin 122
Parthenay 212
Parthenay-le-Vieux 212
Pas de Souci 118
Pau 225
Pavillon de Bellevue 92
Pavillon del Monte Frety 92
Pavillon des Bossons 92
Pays d'Auge 164, 168
Pech-Merle Cave 144
Peillon 111
Les Pèlerins 92
Pelvoux massif 113, 114
Pelvoux National Park 115
Périgord **203**
Périgord Blanc 204
Périgord Noir 204
Périgueux **205**
Péronne 207
Perpignan 233
Perthus, Col de 112
Pertuis d'Antioche, Bay of 231
Petit Bré (Is.) 237
Petite Corniche 109
Petit Rhône 217
Peyrepertuse 101
Phalsbourg 142
Piana 104
Picardy 61, **206**
Pic de Bugarach 101
Pic de Finiels 90
Pic de l'Ours 108
Pic de Nore 90
Pic du Cap Roux 108
Pic du Lac Blanc 113
Pierre d'Avenon 107
Pierrefonds 125, 208
Pino 104
Plan de l'Aiguille 92
Planpraz 92
Plomb du Cantal 68
Plombières-les-Bains 142, 257
Pointe de Dinan 80
Pointe de Penhir 80
Pointe des Espagnols 80
Pointe du Raz 80
Pointe Helbronner 92
Point Sublime 119, 221
Poitiers **208**
Poitou 208, **210**
Poligny 128, 130
Pommard 83, 85
Pompadour 135
Poncin 131
Pontarlier 131
Pont de Coursavy 143
Pont de l'Artuby 221
Le-Pont-de-Montvert 90
Pont-de-Poitte 131
Pont-de-Soleils 221
Pont d'Espagne 224
Pont du Gard 218, 219
Pont Napoléon 225
Pont St-Esprit 218
Les Ponts-de-Cé 64
Pornic 212
Porquerolles, Ile de 107
Port Barcarès 234
Port-Camargue 215
Port-Cros, Ile de 107

Porte des Cévennes 90
Portel, Grotte du 224
Port Grimaud 107
Port-Joinville 214
Port Leucate 234
Porto Bay 103
Porto-Vecchio 103
Port-Royal-des-Champs 123
Port-Vendres 112
Prades 225
Praz-Conduit 92
Les Praz de Chamonix 91
Prémontré 123
Propriano 103
Provence 65, **214**
Provincia 214
Provins 127
Puisaye 83
Puligny-Montrachet 85
Le Puy **221**
Puy de Dôme 67, 68
Puy de Sancy 67, 68, 69, 134
Puylaurens 101
Puymorens, Col de 222
Les Puys 68
Pyla 105
Pyrenees 62, 145, **222**
Pyrénées, Route des 222

Quercy 143, 145
Quéribus 101
Le Quesnoy 208
Queyras 115
Quiberon peninsula 81
Quilian 101
Quimper 82

Rambersvillers 142
Rambouillet 125
Rance 236, 237
Ré, Ile de 214, 231
Reculée des Planches 131
Reculées 131
Reims **226**
Remiremont 142
Rennes **228**
Restonica, Gorges de la 103
Rhine 241
Rhine-Marne Canal 158, 241
Rhine-Rhône Canal 241
Rhine valley 256
Rhône 69, 129, 146, 169, 215
Rhône delta 217
Ribeauvillé 60
Riom 98
Riquewihr 60
Rittershoffen 57
Rivesaltes 234
Rocamadour 205
La Rochecourbon 212
Rochefort-sur-Mer 212
La Rochefoucauld 212
La Rochelle **229**
La Rochepot 85
Rocher de Dabo 142
Rocher des Doms 69
Rocher d'Oëtre 169
Rogliano 104

Roland, Brèche de 224
Romanche 114
Ronchamp 131
Roquebrune 110, 111
Roquebrune-Cap-Martin 110
Roquefavour, Aqueduct of 53
Roquevignon 108
Roscanvel 80
Rosheim 60
Les Rosiers 131
Rosny-sur-Seine 125
Rotomagus 231
Roubaix 208
Rouen **231**
Rouffach 60
Rouge Gazon 143
Les Rousses 128
Roussillon **232**
Roussillon (village) 218
Route des Abbayes 169
Route des Crêtes 257
Route des Pyrénées 222
Route des Sapins 130
Route des Villages Pittoresques 57
Route des Vosges 257
Route du Champagne 95
Route du Cidre 169
Route du Fromage 59
Route du Vin d'Alsace 56
Route du Vin d'Anjou 64
Route Napoléon 108, 113, 114
Roy, Grotte du 146
Royan 213
Royat 68, 98
Royaumont 123
Le Rozier 119
Rueil-Malmaison 203

Saar 143
Les Sables d'Olonne 213
Sainte-Lucie Col 104
Saintes 213
Salers 69
Salins-les-Bains 131
Salon-de-Provence 219
Salses 234
Sancy 67
Santenay 85
Sant Juliá de Loria 63
Saône 146
Sapins, Route des 130
Sarlat 205
Sarrazins, Grotte des 146
Sarrebourg 143
Sarreguemines 143
Sartenais 103
Sartène 103
Sarthe 64, 149, 165
Sauer 57
Saumur 64, 140
Sauvette 107
Saverne 57
Savoureuse 72
Savoy **238**
Savoy Alps 238
Sceaux 125

Schirmeck 257
Schlucht, Col de la 142, 256, 257
Sedan 143
Seille 131
Seine 121, 165, 168, 169, 175, 249
Seine valley 169
Sélestat 61
Semur-en-Auxois 85
Sénanque 219
Senlis 123
Senonais 82
Sens 82, 85
Serra 104
Serrabone Priory 225
Serra, Col de la 104
Serre-Chevalier 114
Serre-Ponçon reservoir 115
Serres-sur-Arget 224
Sessenheim 58
Sète 236
Sèvres 127, 202
Signal d'Audouze 135
Silvacane 219
Simorre 117
Socoa 112
Soissons 95, 123, 124
Soldeu 65
Solenzara 103
Somme 61
Soufflenheim 57
Soultz-sous-Forêts 57
La Souterraine 135
St-Amand-sur-Fion 96
St-Amarin 257
St-Benoît-sur-Loire 140
St-Bertrand-de-Comminges 226
St-Briac 80
St-Cirq-Lapopie 144
St-Claude 128, 131
St-Cloud 125, 202
St-Cyprien 234
St-Denis 123, 203
St-Dié 143
St-Emilion 76, 213
Ste-Enimie 118
Ste-Marie-aux-Mines 257
Ste-Odile, Mont 59, 257
Stes-Maries-de-la-Mer 66, 217, 219
St-Florent 104
St-Flour 69
St-Genis-des-Fontaines 233
St-Germain-en-Laye 125, 203
St-Gervais-les-Bains 240
St-Gilles 67, 218
St-Hilaire-la-Palud 212
St-Hippolyte 131
St-Jean-de-Luz 111
St-Jean-de-Verges 224
St-Jean-du-Gard 90
St-Jean-en-Royans 250
St-Jean-Pied-de-Port 226
St-Junien 135
St-Léonard-de-Noblat 135
St-Lunaire 80

St-Malo **236**
St-Marcellin 119
St-Martin-de-Ré 214
St-Maurice-sur-Moselle 143
St-Michel (Champagne) 96
St-Michel-de-Cuxa 225
St-Morand 58
St-Nectaire 67, 68, 69
St-Nizier-du-Moucherotte 250
St-Omer 208
St-Papoul 90
St-Paul-de-Vence 109
St-Pierre-d'Oléron 214
St-Quentin 62, 208
St-Raphaël 108
St-Rémy 67
St-Rémy-de-Provence 219
St-Riquier 208
Strasbourg **240**
Strataburgum 241
Le Struthof 257
St-Savin-sur-Gartempe 213
St-Servan 237
St-Sulpice-de-Favières 123
St-Thégonnec 78
St-Trojan 214
St-Tropez 106, 107
St-Yrieix-la-Perche 135
Suèvres 141
Sully 86
Sully-sur-Loire 141
Sundgau 58
Superbagnères 223
Super-Cannes 88
Surbourg 57

Talmont 214
Tancarville 169
Tanlay 86
Tarascon 67, 220
Tarascon-sur-Ariège 226

Tarbes 226
Tarn 55
Tarn, Gorges du 118
Tas de Pois 80
Ténarèze 116
Tessé-la-Madeleine 165
Thann 61
Thillot 143
Thoiry 125
Thonon-les-Bains 240
Thouarcé 64
Thuir 234
Thury-Harcourt 169
Tiercé 64
Tignes 240
Les Tines 91, 92
Tocqueville, Château de 165
Tolosa 246
Toul 143
Toulon **245**
Toulouse **246**
Touques 164, 168
Le Touquet 208
Touraine 136, 248
Tourcoing 208
Tour de Ker Roig 112
Tourette-sur-Loup 111
Tourmalet, Col du 222, 225
Tournus 83, 86
Tours **248**
Tréboul 80
Trecae 249
Le Tréport 169
Les Trois-Epis 59, 257
Trois-Palis 211
Trouée de Belfort 72
Troyes **249**
Truyère 143
Truyère, Gorges de la 143
Tulle 135
Tullins 119
Turckheim 61

Ulrichsburg 60
Upper Normandy 164

Upper Rhine plain 55
Uriage-les-Bains 114
Ushant (Is.) 81
Ussé 141
Ussel 135
Uzerche 135
Uzès 220

Vaccarès, Etang de 67, 217
Vaison-la-Romaine 220
Valcabrère 226
Valchevrière 250
Val d'Isère 240
Valdo-Niello Forest 103
Valençay 141
Valenciennes 208
Le Val Fleury 202
Valira del Nord 63
Vallauris 88
Vallière 131
Valloire 240
Vallouise 115
Valras-Plage 234
Valserine 128, 131
Vannes 82
Vassieux-en-Vercors 250
Vassivière, Lac de 133, 134
Vaucluse Plateau 218
Vaumale, Cirque de 221
Vauvenargues 53
Vaux 96
Vaux-le-Vicomte 125
Vecchio 103
Vence 109, 111
Vendée **210**
Vercors **249**
Verdon 220
Verdon, Grand Canyon du 220
Verdun **250**
Vergio, Col de 103
Vernajoul 224
Versailles **252**
Vesontio 72, 128
Vesoul 128

Vézelay 83, 86
Vézère 133, 204
Via 224
Via Aurelia 109
Viaman, Lac de 134
Vic-Fezensac 117
Vichy **254**
Vic-sur-Cère 68
Vienne 133, 136, **255**
Les Vignes 118
Vilaine 228
Villandry 141
Villard-de-Lans 115, 121, 250
Villecresnes 127
Villefranche-de-Conflent 226
Villeneuve-lès-Avignon 71, 221
Villeneuve-sur-Lot 145
Villers-Cotterets 126
Vincennes 126
Virodunum 250
Vitré 82
Vittel 143
Vivarais 136
Vivario 103
Viviers 221
Vizille 115
Vizzavona, Col de 103
Vizzavona Forest 103
Voie Sacrée 96
Volnay 85
Vosges **255**
Vosges, Route des 257
Vosne-Romanée 85
Vougeot 85

Wissembourg 57
Woerth 57

Yeu 214
Yèvre 76
Yvoire 240

Zicavo 103
Zonza 103